THE *Illustrated* BIBLE HANDBOOK

THE
Illustrated
BIBLE
HANDBOOK

EDWARD P. BLAIR

ABINGDON PRESS
Nashville

THE ILLUSTRATED BIBLE
HANDBOOK

Copyright © 1975, 1987 by Abingdon Press

This edition is a revised and expanded version
of the ABINGDON BIBLE HANDBOOK,
ISBN 0–687–00169–2.

**Library of Congress
Cataloging in Publication Data**

BLAIR, EDWARD PAYSON, 1910–
The illustrated Bible handbook.
    Rev. ed. of:
    Abingdon Bible Handbook. 1975.
    Bibliography: p. 1–537. Includes index.
    1. Bible—Introductions.   I. Title
    BS475.2.B5 1987 220.6'1 87–11500
        ISBN 0–687–18680–3

Designed and produced by Three's Company,
12 Flitcroft Street, London WC2
Design: Peter Wyart
Editor: Tim Dowley
Charts and maps by Tony Cantale
Typeset by Creative Editors & Writers Ltd,
Watford
Worldwide co-edition organized and produced
by Angus Hudson Ltd, London

Printed & bound in Great Britain by
PURNELL BOOK PRODUCTION LIMITED
A MEMBER OF BPCC plc

To the many people
everywhere
who are eager to have
fuller knowledge
about the matters
of which they
are partly
informed

(see Luke 1:4)

FOREWORD

The translation and distribution of the Bible in our time far surpass the preparation and circulation of books and study aids that help us understand it and benefit from its rich treasures.

The question put to the Ethiopian eunuch by Philip, 'Do you understand what you are reading?' and the despairing reply of the eunuch, 'How can I understand unless someone explains it to me?' (Acts 8:30–31 TEV) reflect the condition of millions of people today who take the Bible in their hands.

It is true that much in the Bible is crystal clear and needs no explanation. The Bible societies of the world have files bulging with testimonies from people of many races, cultures, and walks of life who have found help from reading the Scriptures unaided. But it also is true that tragic misconceptions about the Bible have confused and poisoned the faith and life of multitudes. It evidently is not enough for us to read the Bible; we must know how to interpret what we read.

I have written this *Handbook* for you who find the Bible difficult or impossible to penetrate by yourself. It is my belief that if you will pay a reasonable price in time and effort and will work prayerfully and persistently with good biblical tools, you can come to a mature understanding of the Bible and its meaning for your life. Especially is this so if you will join or form a group dedicated to serious Bible study, where procedures, questions, insights, and applications to contemporary life can be shared and evaluated.

The use of this *Handbook* is no substitute for direct reading of the Bible. The *Handbook* is intended to serve as a companion on your journey of firsthand exploration. I agree with Walter Russell Bowie, who once said that the best guide in the study of the Bible is the guide who 'does not try to say too much. He tells the inquirer what lies ahead of him if he wants to look, and how he can get to the vantage point at which the wonders of the Bible will most fully make him open his own eyes' (in Walter D. Ferguson, *Journey Through the Bible* [1947], p. ix).

Part 1 ('The Bible Today') presents information you should have when you take the Bible in your hands: the meaning of the word 'Bible'; the contents of the Bible as used by Jews, Protestants, and Roman Catholics, and why the contents differ among these groups; the makeup and major characteristics of the Bible; ancient and modern translations and the best versions for use by contemporary English readers; basic principles for interpreting the Bible correctly; and practical suggestions for reading it.

Part 2 ('The Bible in History') sets the books of the Bible in the times in which they were first written and read. Basic to correct interpretation is knowledge of the circumstances and needs of the original readers, the purpose or purposes of the authors, the process by which the books came into being, their structure and central emphases, the transmission of their texts by the communities that preserved them, and the like. The books bear the marks of the ancient cultures out of which they came. You must understand these marks before you can grasp the contents of these books and relate them to your life.

Part 3 ('The Bible and Faith and Life') deals with some of the basic teachings of the Bible and shows how the beliefs behind these teachings form a structure of faith and a pattern of life. It discusses biblical perspectives on God, Satan, mankind, miracles, the way of salvation, the church, the Christian's situation in the world, and the future. A final section treats the question of the Bible's inspiration and authority for contemporary readers. You will find clues to the solution of some present-day problems of faith and life in this section.

This *Handbook* does not attempt a book-by-book and chapter-by-chapter commentary on the Bible. Commentaries in handbooks are usually so superficial as to be almost valueless. Instead, I have offered in Part 2 introductions to all the books of the Bible (including the Apocrypha). These are meant to set the course for your firsthand reading of the individual books and supply you with important background material and the scholarly judgments you need to understand them. I recommend that, in addition to this *Handbook*, you secure a good one-volume commentary on the Bible for consultation (see p. 209).

In fairness to you I should state my point of view at the outset.

I hold that the Bible is more than a relic of antiquity which one is free to consider or ignore as one's fancy directs; that it is more than a repository of information about mankind's past and a source of delightful human interest stories and salty wisdom; that it is more than great literature which educated people of our time should be acquainted with, like the works of Shakespeare; that it is more than a record of human search for God and the good life.

I believe that the Bible is the story of God's search for all people; of God's redemptive deeds in the life of the people of Israel and of 'the one-man Israel,' Jesus Christ; of the saving activity of God's Spirit in the world through the church; of God's establishment through Jesus and his disciples of the outpost of the new order called in the New Testament 'the kingdom of God.'

I believe that Jesus Christ fulfills the world's hope for peace, justice, prosperity, and stability, and that unswerving faith in him as Lord and Savior and unconditional obedience to him will bring personal and social salvation, here and hereafter.

I believe that the Bible presents the Word of God in the words of humans so that I and all people may understand and obey. I shall not have dealt seriously with this message until I have understood it as far as possible with my mind, responded to it with my will and my emotions, sought to communicate it to others, and endeavored to live out its implications in my everyday life.

I believe that I must open my mind to all truth, from whatever source it may come. I must follow no opinions about the Bible simply because they are old and long honored. If the Holy Spirit is to lead me into all truth (John 16:13), I must be willing to change my views when solid evidence points in new directions. I must live and work in the confidence that nothing that is really true can undermine my Christian knowledge and experience, for God is the God of truth and truth builds up and frees (Eph. 4:15; John 8:32). I must, however, 'test everything [and] hold fast what is good' (1 Thess. 5:21), knowing that God's Spirit will illumine and guide me.

This *Handbook* attempts, therefore, to combine sound scholarship and Christian devotion. It tries to be fair to the evidence. I have often presented more than one point of view. I have listed good Roman Catholic books, as well as conservative and liberal Protestant works, under the caption 'For Further Reading.' God's Spirit is at work today in remarkable ways in all communions where Bible study is taken seriously.

It is impossible to express my debt to others who directly or indirectly have influenced the contents of this *Handbook*. In the realm of learning, Jesus' statement to the disciples, as reported in the Gospel of John, indicates where credit usually should go: 'Others have done the hard work, and you have reaped the benefits of their labor' (4:38 NIV). Only rarely have I quoted other scholars directly, but my debt to them is great, as my fellow workers in the biblical field will know quite well.

Words of thanks are due to my wife, Vivian, for her patient and skillful assistance throughout the project.

It remains only to wish for all of you into whose hands this *Handbook* comes an exhilarating and insightful journey through the Bible.

Edward P. Blair

FOREWORD
TO THE REVISED EDITION

This revised edition of the *Abingdon Bible Handbook* introduces changes of several sorts: an updating of the chapter on translations of the Bible, with suggestions for selecting the best versions; attention to recent scholarly approaches to the study of the Bible; a completely new discussion of the problem of the Pentateuch; a revamping of the treatments of many of the biblical books; correction and expansion of the introductions to major groups of books and the inclusion of a bibliography at the end of each group; attention to the 'New Archaeology' and its relation to biblical studies; an updated survey of the Qumran manuscripts (The Dead Sea Scrolls) and other manuscripts from areas near Qumran; some alteration of perspective on the problem of Jesus' self-awareness and sense of mission; expanded attention throughout to the views of conservative, as well as liberal, scholars; and elimination, so far as feasible, of sexist or male-oriented vocabulary.

Abingdon Press has made a real effort to light up the book graphically and pictorially, so that those who travel through its sometimes dimly-lighted areas may see their way clearly and enjoy the scenery along the way.

One of my aims in the writing of the first edition of the *Handbook* was to help upgrade the category (genre) of Bible handbooks so that books of this nature will become up-to-date, reliable, comprehensive, and yet concise guides to the wonderful world of the Bible. The reception accorded the first edition (including its translation into Spanish and Chinese) has made the task of preparing the second edition tolerable and even enjoyable.

A second aim was to treat fairly both conservative and liberal scholars and their somewhat different approaches to the Bible. In this second edition I have greatly increased the space given to conservative views. These scholarly groups have been estranged too long. Both have legitimate and honored places in the quest for truth and in the household of faith. It is time that we hear them out with respect and open minds! To this end I have cited views and books from both perspectives in the discussions and in the bibliographies.

Edward P. Blair

CONTENTS

CONTENTS

Part 1
THE BIBLE TODAY

Papyrus plants growing near Hula, northern Israel. Papyrus was made into sheets which were used as a writing surface.

The Bible's Name and Contents

'The Bible' means literally 'the books.' The term rests ultimately on the Greek word *biblos* (papyrus) and comes to us by way of the Greek *biblion* (book), the Greek and Latin *biblia* (books), and the Old French word *bible*. Jews of the time of Jesus used such terms as 'the books,' 'the holy books,' and 'the book of the law' in referring to their sacred texts (Dan. 9:2; 1 Macc. 3:48; 12:9). New Testament writers referred to these texts as 'the scriptures' (Matt. 21:42), 'the holy scriptures' (Rom. 1:2), 'the law' (John 12:34), 'the law of Moses and … the prophets' (Acts 28:23), and 'the law of Moses and the prophets and the psalms' (Luke 24:44). 'Scripture' is simply the Latin rendering of the Greek word for 'writing.' From about A.D. 400 'the books,' without qualifying adjectives and meaning '*the* Books,' became the standard term of reference for the whole body of sacred writings. The exact contents of the Bible and the arrangement of its books have varied considerably in different places and periods of Jewish and Christian history.

The Hebrew Bible

Since the second century A.D. the Hebrew Bible has consisted of the thirty-nine books included in Protestant editions of the Old Testament but grouped in such a way as to number twenty-four and in a different order. 1 and 2 Samuel, 1 and 2 Kings, 1 and 2 Chronicles, Ezra and Nehemiah, and the Twelve (Minor) Prophets were each regarded as one book.

The books often used their opening words as titles, such as 'In the beginning' for our Genesis and 'And these are the names' for our Exodus. Present-day Jews use the names customary among Christians but keep the traditional Jewish arrangement.

The Greek Bible (the Septuagint or LXX)

This was the Bible used by Greek-speaking Jews of the Greco-Roman world and by early Gentile Christians. It arose largely from translations of the Hebrew Scriptures made during the third and second centuries B.C.

Besides the twenty-four books contained in the Hebrew Bible, seventeen other books or portions of books were included. Fourteen of these seventeen, plus 2 Esdras, now comprise the Apocrypha of Protestant Bibles. Roman

The Hebrew Bible

The Greek Bible
the Septuagint or LXX

THE LAW (TORAH)

Genesis   Numbers
Exodus   Deuteronomy
Leviticus

THE PROPHETS

The Former Prophets
Joshua   Samuel
Judges   Kings

The Latter Prophets
Isaiah   Jonah
Jeremiah   Micah
Ezekiel   Nahum
The Twelve: Habakkuk
Hosea   Zephaniah
Joel   Haggai
Amos   Zechariah
Obadiah   Malachi

THE WRITINGS

Psalms   Ecclesiastes
Proverbs   Esther
Job   Daniel
Song of Songs   Ezra-Nehemiah
Ruth   Chronicles
Lamentations

Song of Songs, Ruth, Lamentations, Ecclesiastes
and Esther were called 'Festival Scrolls'.

The Latin Bible

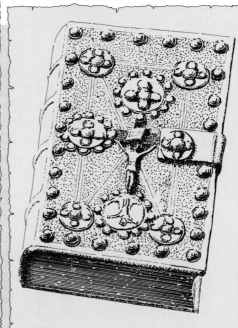

BOOKS OF LAW AND HISTORY

Genesis	Paralipomena 1–2
Exodus	(our 1–2 Chronicles)
Leviticus	Esdras 1–2
Numbers	(an apocryphal book of
Deuteronomy	Ezra and our
Joshua	Ezra-Nehemiah)
Judges	Esther (with additions
Ruth	now in our Apocrypha)
Kingdoms 1–4	Judith
(our 1–2 Samuel	Tobit
and 1–2 Kings)	Maccabees 1–4

POETIC AND PROPHETIC BOOKS

Psalms	Habakkuk
Odes (including the	Zephaniah
Prayer of Manasseh)	Haggai
Proverbs	Zechariah
Ecclesiastes	Malachi
Song of Songs	Isaiah
Job	Jeremiah
Wisdom of Solomon	Baruch
Wisdom of Jesus	Lamentations
the Son of Sirach	Letter of Jeremiah
Psalms of Solomon	Ezekiel
Hosea	Daniel (with additions,
Amos	including The Prayer of
Micah	Azariah and the Song of
Joel	the Three Young Men,
Obadiah	Susanna, and Bel and
Jonah	the Dragon)
Nahum	

OLD TESTAMENT

Genesis	Ecclesiastes	Haggai	Appendix: The Prayer of
Exodus	Song of Songs	Zechariah	Manasseh and two
Leviticus	Wisdom of Solomon	Malachi	apocryphal books of
Numbers	Ecclesiasticus (The	1–2 Maccabees	Esdras
Deuteronomy	Wisdom of Jesus the		
Joshua	Son of Sirach)		
Judges	Isaiah		
Ruth	Jeremiah		
1–4 Kingdoms (our	Lamentations		
books of Samuel and	Baruch		
Kings)	Ezekiel		
1–2 Paralipomena (our	Daniel		
books of Chronicles)	Hosea		
1–2 Esdras (our Ezra	Joel		
and Nehemiah)	Amos		
Tobit	Obadiah		
Judith	Jonah		
Esther	Micah		
Job	Nahum		
Psalms	Habakkuk		
Proverbs	Zephaniah		

NEW TESTAMENT

Matthew	1 Timothy
Mark	2 Timothy
Luke	Titus
John	Philemon
Acts	Hebrews
Romans	James
1 Corinthians	1 Peter
2 Corinthians	2 Peter
Galatians	1 John
Ephesians	2 John
Philippians	3 John
Colossians	Jude
1 Thessalonians	Revelation
2 Thessalonians	

Statue of Jerome at the Church of St Catherine, Bethlehem, where Jerome lived from AD 386.

Catholics accept twelve of these books or portions as of equal inspiration and authority with the books of the Hebrew Bible. (See below, on the Roman Catholic Old Testament.)

The order of books in the Greek Bible differs somewhat in different ancient manuscripts.

The Latin Bible

This Bible came into existence between the second and fifth centuries A.D. through the work of many Christian translators, notably Jerome (died 420). Jerome's predecessors had translated the Old Testament from the Greek Bible, whereas Jerome rendered it from the Hebrew Bible as well.

In general contents and arrangement, the Latin Bible followed the Greek Bible. The identity and number of the books included in Latin manuscripts varied somewhat before the Council of Trent (A.D. 1546). As fixed by the council, the list excluded 1 Esdras (the apocryphal Esdras) and the Prayer of Manasseh, which, with a second apocryphal book of Esdras, were placed in an appendix. 3 and 4 Maccabees apparently were never included in Latin Bibles.

Contemporary English Bibles

Roman Catholic
The New American Bible (1970) – one of the most important contemporary Roman Catholic Bibles – contains the exact list of books as noted above, except that it introduces 1 and 2 Maccabees between Esther and Job and uses the names 1 and 2 Samuel, 1 and 2 Kings, 1 and 2 Chronicles, Ezra, and Nehemiah instead of the older terminology. The books in the appendix of the Latin Bible are not included.

Jewish
These follow the content and order of the Hebrew Bible. They employ the names for the individual books traditional among Christians. The books of the New Testament, of course, are not included.

Protestant
The Old Testament in Protestant Bibles contains only the books present in the Hebrew Bible. The additional books of the Greek and the Latin Bibles are either omitted altogether or printed in a separate section under the caption 'the Apocrypha.' The books of the Apocrypha, long omitted from Protestant Bibles, are now being re-introduced, as in some editions of the RSV and the NEB. (On the history of the Apocrypha, see pp. 210–211.)

Protestant and Roman Catholic Bibles always have agreed on the content and arrangement of the New Testament.

Major Characteristics of the Bible

The Bible Is One Book and Many Books

So accustomed are we to the printed Bible published in one bound volume that we are apt to forget that its different books were written by many different people in many periods of ancient history and that the books at first circulated independently. Only gradually were they gathered together into smaller and then greater collections, until a collection of collections was formed. Certain of the writers were separated by more than a thousand years.

But the Bible is also one book. It arose out of the religious experience of one people (Israel) with their God (Yahweh). The Bible explains the origin of this people, the character of their history, the nature of their institutions, the purpose of their existence, and their ultimate destiny as the people of God. The Christian church regarded itself as the true Israel of God (Gal. 6:16; 1 Pet. 2:9–10) and the events of its founding as the fulfillment of the purpose of God as expressed in the holy writings (Luke 24:25–27, 44–46; Acts 2:16ff.; Rom. 1:1–2).

Thus the church came to see Jewish scriptures and Christian writings as complementary – as together bearing witness to the mighty deeds of God in the forming of a people of God's own out of the stock of Israel and, through the true Israel, out of the nations of the world. The Bible is therefore *one* book with a pervading theme: God's activity in the redemption of the world through a chosen, renewed, and obedient people.

The Bible Is a Collection of Approved Books

Both Israels – the old and the new – produced a large literature. Much of it is not now contained in our Bible, even in those Bibles that include the Apocrypha. In the Old Testament we find mention of books now lost: 'the Book of the Wars of the Lord' (Num. 21:14); 'the Book of Jashar' (Josh. 10:13); 'the Book of the Acts of Solomon' (1 Kings 11:41); 'the Book of the Chronicles of the Kings of Israel' (1 Kings 14:19); 'the Book of the Chronicles of the Kings of Judah' (1 Kings 14:29); and others.

Many books not mentioned in our Bible (including the Apocrypha) circulated in Judaism before, during, and after the rise of Christianity. Among them were commentaries on and paraphrases of Old Testament books; collections of Old Testament passages and of hymns; books about worship, about the end of the age, and about the beliefs and practices of religious groups (see pp. 416–27).

Christianity produced much literature not included in the New Testament as finally agreed upon by A.D. 400, such as: many Gospels and related works; many writings about the Apostles; and several books that professed to unveil the future (apocalypses).

The books that appear in our Bible are thus only a part of the large literature of the Judeo-Christian religion. Our biblical books came to the fore and maintained their prestige not only because of their assumed connection with people believed to have been God-inspired but because of their value for worship, instruction, and guidance of life in the communities for which they were written. For the most part, they became 'approved' books in their communities long before they were included by official action in a closed collection (see pp. 29–39).

The Bible, as Known in the Christian Church, Is a Two–Stage Book

The stages are: promise (the Old Testament, or more accurately, the Old Covenant) and fulfillment (the New Testament or New Covenant). Traditionally in English and Latin Bibles the Christian church has referred to the books it inherited from Judaism as 'the Old Testament' (Latin, *testamentum*).

Actually, the Hebrews spoke of a *berit* or covenant which God had made with the fathers, particularly with Moses at Mount Sinai. By this word they meant a promise, an agreement, or an arrangement involving two parties, in which at least one party was bound by an oath. The Greek Bible translated the Hebrew word *berit* (covenant) by the word *diatheke* (meaning usually 'covenant' but sometimes 'will' or 'testament' – that is, a declaration of intention concerning the disposal of an estate upon the maker's death).

It is not a 'will' that is intended in the terms Old Testament and New Testament, but an arrangement or agreement between contracting parties involving promises and sealed with oaths. Therefore, 'Old Covenant' and 'New Covenant' are to be preferred in modern translations.

The Bible represents the Old Covenant as proposed by God, accepted by Israel, and sealed in solemn ceremony at Mount Sinai. God promised to bless Israel with the divine presence and to protect and guide it to a place of pre-eminence among the peoples of the world – *if* Israel would be exclusively loyal to God, become like God in character, express this God-likeness in individual and national life, witness to the nations concerning God's saving activity in Israel's history, and invite the nations to join in the benefits and responsibilities of the covenant relationship.

But Israel was faithless to the terms of the covenant, as the great prophets unceasingly pointed out. The nation worshiped other gods, trusted for security in military alliances made with idolatrous foreign powers, aped the false way of life of the peoples around, and finally experienced national disaster as the consequence of infidelity to its covenant God. Instead of becoming

View from the Mount of Moses (Jebel Musa) in the Sinai Peninsula.

a light to the nations, it withdrew into something like a ghetto existence. God's name, rather than being honored among the nations, was blasphemed because of Israel's shameless conduct (Isa. 52:5; Rom. 2:24). The prophets Isaiah, Jeremiah, Ezekiel, and others looked forward to the day when Israel would be fully obedient to the terms of the covenant, when its national life would be renewed inwardly and outwardly and its world mission faithfully carried out. But within the pages of the Old Testament all this remains un-fulfilled promise.

The New Testament resounds with the note of fulfillment. It says that the righteous leader promised as the fulfiller of Israel's God-appointed destiny appeared with the birth, ministry, and death-resurrection of Jesus of Nazareth. It declares that he inaugurated a new and fully effective covenant between God and Israel. It claims that, as participants in the new covenant, his followers are made loyal to God, are inwardly cleansed, are indwelt by God's Spirit, are living in loving relationships with their brothers and sisters as children in a common family, and are faithfully carrying out their work of witnessing to the nations. The New Testament regards the church as the out-post of the kingdom of God and holds that the church enjoys in foretaste the life of the final kingdom.

The Bible Is Both an Ancient and a Very Modern Book

It contains old tribal traditions reaching back into the second millennium B.C. One of the supposed sources behind the Pentateuch ('J' – see pp. 100–101) may have been composed as early as the tenth or ninth century B.C.. 'The Court History of David' (2 Sam. 9 20 and 1 Kings 1, 2), unquestionably the finest piece of historical narrative in the Old Testament, was written probably in the age of King Solomon – centuries before the rise of historical writing among the Greeks.

The books of the Old Testament were created to meet the needs of the ancient communities in which they first appeared. A proper interpretation of them requires that we see them primarily as written for the circumstances of the authors' own time.

The prophets of the Old Testament were declarers of the divine will for the people of their own age. They were not primarily predictors of the future for *our* benefit.

Paul's letters were practical directives for the church of his day. He did not write, as one scholar has put it, 'with the thought that posterity [was] looking over his shoulder.' Another writer has remarked that if Paul had possessed a magic carpet, he would not have written his letters at all.

Even a book like the Revelation to John – so loudly claimed in some circles today as having been incomprehensible until now by any but ourselves, who live in the time of the final fulfillment of prophecy – was actually 'tailored' for the church in Asia Minor at the end of the first century A.D. Its first readers certainly understood it far better than we can.

Furthermore, these ancient books, addressed to ancient people and situations long gone, were transmitted through the centuries by copyists who reproduced them by hand. The original manuscripts on animal skins and papyrus soon perished. The thousands of copies showed variations due to inaccurate copying. Scholars have been at work for some two hundred years comparing the many manuscripts and recovering as far as possible the original text of the biblical books (see pp. 368–79). The Bible is an heirloom of great antiquity, bequeathed to us by countless people who produced it and passed it along to us.

Yet, when all this has been said, the Bible remains a strangely modern book, often strikingly relevant to our contemporary life. This is so in part because the human situation in every age remains fundamentally the same. We are born, grow up in families, marry, beget children, and work for a living in a natural order often hostile to our best efforts. We struggle against human enemies and cringe before the leering face of death. In every age people are tempted to worship the creature rather than the Creator and to seek self-gratification rather than the well-being of all people. Though the cultural setting of human life varies from age to age, its basic situation remains the same.

Thus Abraham, who desperately wanted what life had denied him (a son), who sought by devious means to obtain an heir, and who at length learned to trust in God in the face of human impossibility, holds up a mirror in which we see our own frustrations, lack of faith, and need of divine help. Thus Job, whose life was reduced to ashes in overpowering disasters and who found God at the end of his questioning, comforts us in our tribulations. Thus Jesus and Paul, who left father and mother, brothers and sisters, and houses and lands in obedience to the divine call and the claims of the kingdom of God, draw us after them.

The early church and Christians through the centuries have found that, under the Holy Spirit as teacher (John 14:26; 16:13–15), the sacred writings are 'profitable for teaching, for reproof, for correction, and for training in righteousness, that the man of God may be complete, equipped for every good work' (2 Tim. 3:16).

The Bible Is a Book of Rich Variety

It contains many types of literature: songs and other poetic material, historical narratives, laws, liturgies, prophetic utterances, wise sayings, short stories, Gospels, letters, sermons, apocalypses. There is reading matter for every mood. One can skip through lush meadows to the music of the birds, drink from sparkling fountains, and loll under the cedars of Lebanon (Ps. 104). One can ride the waves in a ship of Solomon's fleet in search of the gold of Ophir (1 Kings 9). One can dawdle in the pleasure gardens of kings, sipping wine from golden goblets and watching maidens from the royal harem entertain the banqueters (Esther 1–2). One can enter into the awful silence of the temple, cry out for mercy before a majestic and holy God, and depart with sins forgiven and a mission to perform (Isa. 6). One can vent his anger over the rank injustices in life, lament the day of his birth, and perhaps battle his way to faith (Job and Jeremiah) or turn to bitter pessimism (Ecclesiastes). One can spend his life in unselfish service and know the agony of vicarious suffering and death (Isa. 53 and the Gospels). One can peer into the future with prophets and seers, tremble before the great white throne, and shout 'hallelujah' with the redeemed or wail with the damned (Daniel and Revelation).

The Bible is a book that plumbs the depths of human experience on all its sides.

The Bible Is a Picture Book

Its pictures are, of course, word pictures. But so graphic are they that we see the scenes almost as if we are looking at photographs. Isaiah's description of the daughters of Zion walking with outstretched necks, glancing wantonly as they mince along with tinkling feet (Isa. 3:16) is almost as effective as a motion picture of the scene would be. Jeremiah's word picture of the drought in Judah (Jer. 14:2–6) is so realistic that our lips seem almost cracked like the parched earth and we fairly pant with the wild asses on the barren heights.

A shepherd with his flock; the shepherd is a favorite biblical metaphor.

The picture language of the Bible is technically called metaphorical language. A metaphor offers a comparison between two objects or realms of experience. When we speak of the head of a table, a leg of a chair, the foot of a bed, the face of a cliff, an arm of a sea, the hands of a watch, we characterize one object in terms of another.

In the Bible almost every page glistens with metaphors. Judah is 'a lion's whelp,' Israel 'a wild vine' and 'a wild ass ... in her heat sniffing the wind.' Jesus is said to be 'the Lamb of God' or 'our paschal lamb.' He is represented as 'the bridegroom,' and the church as his 'bride.' Christians are 'the light of the world.'

Skillful use of metaphor is characteristic of great literature.

The Bible Is an Inspired and an Inspiring Storybook

The Hebrews were a storytelling people, in some respects like their Arabic-speaking kin, who spun the delightful tales of the Arabian Nights. Some of the world's best stories are to be found in the Bible. Many literary experts regard the Joseph narrative, for example, as a supreme example of the storyteller's art.

The real power of the Bible lies in its central story – the story of redemption. The theme of this story is what God has done through the life of Israel to save all humankind from sin and folly and to bring people of every race and condition into a kingdom of love and brotherhood.

The story describes how God called the Hebrews to be his means of revelation, how God was made known to them when they were delivered from the land of Egypt, how he disclosed his will for their life in the giving of the Law at Mount Sinai, how he led them into the Promised Land, how he spoke urgent words to them through the prophets and disciplined them at the hands of foreign nations. It tells how at length God sent his Son to them; how, through the Son's life, death, and resurrection, the power of evil was broken and a new Spirit-filled community brought into being. It affirms that through Jesus Christ salvation has been made available to all people. It declares that the power of this community will increase, that the kingdoms of this world will become the kingdom of our Lord and Christ, and finally God's purpose for all people will be fully realized: God and the redeemed children will dwell together in intimate fellowship forever.

Because of the wonderful story told in the Bible and confirmed in human experience, Christians have always regarded the Bible as an inspired book. It came out of the life of an inspired people, a people granted unusual intimacy with God and special understanding of God's will. The Bible is the record written by these people about God's encounter with them. When we read it we find what God is like, what we are like, what God has done and is doing for us, and what God wants us to be and do. In the Bible we have a message from God and about God. We thus say that the Bible is the Word of God.

We do not, of course, mean that every word contained in the Bible was placed there by God. We must remember that God works in the world through people who are responsive, usable, and human. God's own Son became truly human that God might speak to us in a language we mortals could understand. To grasp this message one must view the Bible as a whole, not in piecemeal fashion, as though there were something magical about the individual words.

The Bible tells us what we need to know in order to be saved. It does not satisfy our curiosity about important questions in the fields of science, philosophy, history, psychology, and the like. Its function is to bring us to Christ, to bring us to maturity in him, and to send us out into the world to witness by our life and good deeds to his saving power. It gives us a great hope – that 'earth may be fair and all her children one' – and it assures us that 'eye hath not seen, nor ear heard, neither have entered into the heart of man, the things which God hath prepared for them that love him' (1 Cor. 2:9 KJV).

(For further discussion of the inspiration and authority of the Bible see pp. 508–17.)

For Further Reading
Alter, R., *The Art of Biblical Narrative,* 1981.
Henn, T.R., *The Bible as Literature,* 1970.
Robertson, D., *The Old Testament and the Literary Critic,* 1977.

Holy Scriptures and Sacred Canon

'Holy Scriptures' means 'writings that have been set apart.' The synagogue and the church considered them different from secular literature because they believed them to have been inspired by God. 'Sacred canon' represents a further stage at which a list of such holy writings was drawn up as a closed collection, not to be added to, subtracted from, or altered in any way.

'Canon,' from an ancient Semitic word meaning 'reed,' came to mean an authoritative standard by which other things are measured. As applied to the Bible, the word means that in this particular collection of writings – as against other writings – the Divine purpose and will for all are to be found.

The Formation of the Old Testament Canon

We have seen in the lists above (pp. 17–20) that the Old Testament canon varies in Jewish, Greek, Roman Catholic, and Protestant Bibles. Over and above the contents of the Jewish Bible there are some fifteen books or portions of books that were accepted as in some sense authoritative by Greek-reading Jews of around the time of Jesus. Protestants have sometimes included these as an appendix to the Old Testament, under the label 'Apocrypha,' or excluded them altogether. Roman Catholics accept twelve of these as 'deuterocanonical' (see p. 210) and include them in various places in the text of the Old Testament. It is important to remember that the Hebrew Bible consists of three sections: the Law or the Torah (the Pentateuch), the Prophets, and the Writings.

Recent studies of the formation of the biblical canon (by J.A. Sanders, B.S. Childs, and others) have resulted in the conclusion that the canon was not formed primarily by official decisions of authoritative persons or councils at particular moments of history. Rather the canon resulted mainly from a long process in the Hebrew and Christian communities in which people of later generations read, heard, accepted, and applied to themselves and their situation written records of God's words to and dealings with chosen people and communities of the past.

The canon, therefore, was not something imposed on others by arbitrary authority but something freely accepted by people who opened their eyes and ears to the story of the past and who sought to apply that story to the needs and circumstances of the moment. Because this story spoke with a word of clarity and power about who they were (identity) and what they should do in

the world (lifestyle), it was treasured and passed on to subsequent generations as authoritative tradition.

And only those books were passed on that had continuing meaning for the
life of the community. The rest (like the Book of Jashar [Josh. 10:13], the
Book of the Wars of Yahweh [Num. 21:14], the Pseudepigrapha [pp. 416–
20], apocryphal gospels [p. 36], etc.) simply dropped by the wayside.

While canonization was primarily a process, there were moments in which
the process was caught up and fixed by official declarations and policies.
These moments were marked by special circumstances and needs: personal
and national guidance in times of political-religious crisis (the break-up of the
Assyrian empire and Josiah's decision to go it alone in the late 7th century
B.C.); the return from the Babylonian exile and the need for guidance in the
reconstitution of national and religious life in hostile surroundings; the fall of
Jerusalem in A.D. 70 and the threat to Judaism of extinction, in part by the rise
of Christianity and its literature; the spread of Gnosticism in the church before and during the time of Marcion in the second century. These were times
when the community officially reaffirmed its effective traditions (those that
were adaptable to the continuing needs of its life) and waived aside those that
were meaningless and even a threat to its existence.

The stages of fixation are relatively well marked, but the more or less fluid
process behind them is not so easily recoverable.

Stages in the Fixing of the Old Testament Canon

1. The Recognition of the Authority of Deuteronomy
Upon discovery of this book (or part of it) in the temple in 622 B.C., King
Josiah recognized its authority as the word of Moses and of God and based a
sweeping reform on its laws (2 Ki. 22:3—23:25).

2. The Exaltation of 'the Law' (the Torah, the Pentateuch)
The Pentateuch in its present form seems to have been completed in the fifth
century B.C. and accepted officially as God's word for the nation by Ezra and
his contemporaries in the fifth or early fourth century (Neh. 8:1—10:39).

Some bodies of material (sources) of the Pentateuch certainly were drawn
together much earlier than this and undoubtedly possessed authoritative
status in the community that used them, altered and added to them, and passed them along.

Conservative scholars today believe that the Pentateuch was essentially
complete by about 1000 B.C. but was revised in minor ways until the time of
Ezra (La Sor-Hubbard-Bush). Liberals do not grant so early an essential
completion; but most of them admit the relative antiquity of traditions and
sources contained in it. Most scholars today agree that Ezra fixed the completed Pentateuch as the basis of the life of the nation around 400 B.C..

Qumran — site of Cave 1, a principal source of the Dead Sea Scrolls

3. The Fixing of the Canon of the Prophets

We have no sure knowledge here. It cannot have occurred before the time of Malachi (about 450 B.C.), since Malachi is included, and may have occurred as late as about 200 B.C. The apocryphal book Ecclesiasticus (the Wisdom of Jesus the Son of Sirach) of the second century B.C. refers in a clear-cut way to 'the law and the prophets' as well as to 'the other books of our fathers.'

What the historical circumstances of the fixing of the prophetic collection were is unknown. Was it the threat of Hellenism following upon the conquests of Alexander the Great and his successors, with its own emphasis on oracles, sibyls ('inspired' prophetesses), and Sibylline books, that made necessary a demarkation of approved literature?

Many of the books of both the Former and the Latter (Later) Prophets undoubtedly had been recognized as authoritative for a long time before the closing of the collection. Disciples of the prophets gathered together their masters' teachings, added to them, and promulgated them in their respective communities, where they were heard and applied to ongoing life.

4. The Selection of 'the Writings'

In Jewish circles of the time of Jesus much literature not in the Law and the Prophets also was read, including the eleven books now in 'the Writings,' those books and portions now in the Apocrypha of Protestant Bibles, and many sectarian books like the Dead Sea Scrolls and the Pseudepigrapha (see pp. 416–20). Apparently no attempt was made to draw up a list of approved books from this miscellaneous literature until late in the first and in the early second century A.D..

The crisis that led to the fixing of the last division of the canon undoubtedly was the destruction of Jerusalem by the Romans in A.D. 70, the threatened extinction of Judaism, whose revolutionary wing (the Zealots) had been inflamed against the Romans by questionable (apocalyptic) books (see pp. 416–20), and the rise of Christianity with a literature that was regarded by Jewish leaders as heretical. Even the Septuagint (Greek Old Testament) had fallen into disfavor with Jews because of its popularity in the Christian church.

About A.D. 90 rabbis held discussions at a town in southwestern Judah called Jamnia (Jabneel or Jabneh) about some of 'the Writings,' especially whether such books as Ecclesiastes and the Song of Solomon should be included. These discussions embraced no review of all the books in this category, as almost all of them had been in existence for several centuries and had gained status as authoritative writings. Debate about Esther and parts of Ezekiel went on after Jamnia and were resolved affirmatively by about the middle of the second century A.D. Thereafter, the canon was fixed for all time.

Standards by Which Jews Judged Their Books
Josephus (c. A.D. 37–100) gives us the best insight about how the Jews of his time looked at their sacred literature. He held that books, to be 'justly accredited,' had to be written by inspired prophets during the prophetic age, which he says ended with Artaxerxes (in the Persian period). Books written after that time have 'not been deemed worthy of equal credit with the earlier records, because of the failure of the exact succession of the prophets' (Contra Apionem I, 37–43). And the books were not discrepant and inconsistent with one another, he says.

Thus prophetic (inspired) authorship and consistency with one another were criteria for accredited books, according to Josephus. Contemporary scholars have suggested other criteria: consistency with official Jewish faith and practice; and general acceptance in the community of faith.

The Formation of the New Testament Canon

Since Christianity arose before the third section of the Old Testament canon (the Writings) was fixed in the first and second centuries A.D., Christian literature was free to circulate and gain acceptance by Jews as well as Gentiles. Christians believed that the Holy Spirit had been given to the church and that prophecy had returned to Israel (Acts 21:9; 1 Cor. 12:28; Rev. 22: 6, 9). All New Testament writings lay claim to authority, either implicitly or explicitly.

In regard to the formation of the canon of the New Testament, recent canonical study has emphasized the process that lay behind the formal listing of authoritative books in the fourth century: 'the process of the formation of authoritative religious writings long preceded the particular designation of the collection as canon in the fourth century' (B.S. Childs).

From the time of Jesus' ministry, death, and resurrection the memory of him was repeated, collected, and formulated in such a way (orally and in writing) that it became scripture through which the living Lord spoke to the community of faith. As these formulations were repeated, heard, and sung in worship and instruction, the community's self-understanding and activities were shaped and subsequent formulations were influenced. The process in the Christian church also had its stages of fixation.

Stages in the Formation of the New Testament Canon

1. The Collection of the Letters of Paul

Paul's letters were recognized by many of their first readers as divinely inspired. This is evident from the fact that these letters were preserved and that the churches addressed continued for the most part in the directions Paul pointed out.

Who first brought together Paul's letters into a collection is not known. One supposition holds that the author of Ephesians – a disciple of Paul, possibly the one-time runaway slave Onesimus – collected his master's letters

The Arcadian Way, Ephesus; the theater is in the distance.

about A.D. 90 and wrote Ephesians under his master's name as an introduction to the collection. This hypothesis cannot be verified.

Near the end of the first century Clement of Rome referred to 1 Corinthians as 'written with true inspiration.' He appealed to the authority of Paul along with that of the Old Testament. Early in the second century Ignatius wrote to the church at Ephesus that Paul 'in every letter makes mention of you in Christ Jesus' – thus indicating Ignatius' knowledge of a collection of Paul's letters.

The author of 2 Peter (first half of second century) knew the collected letters of Paul and referred to them as on a level with 'the other scriptures' (3:16), that is, probably the Old Testament and possibly some Christian writings which had gained wide acceptance in the church. The heretic Marcion published his own edition of Paul's letters about A.D. 140. This shows that the collected letters of Paul were well known in the church of Marcion's day.

2. The Emergence of Four Gospels

The church regarded both the words of the historical Jesus and those of the resurrected Christ as inspired and authoritative. (For examples of words of the resurrected Christ, see Matt. 28:18–20; Acts 1:6–8.)

The author of Luke-Acts tells us that many accounts of Christian beginnings existed when he wrote. These were based on the reports handed down by the original eyewitnesses (Luke 1:1–2). Only four accounts were included in the church's canon. Why were these four preserved?

The answer may be that each of the four became recognized as authoritative in a different important early center of the church. If this is so, these four Gospels were first circulated locally before they were circulated throughout the church.

The four Gospels were slow in gaining general acceptance. By and large the early church preferred oral reports about Jesus and the apostles. Papias (second quarter of the second century) said that 'things out of books were less useful to me than what could be learned from a living and abiding voice' – meaning, as the context shows, from some living person who had had contact with disciples of the original apostles.

Though early church writers (such as Clement of Rome, Ignatius) sometimes cited material like that in our Gospels, the first clear reference to any of our four Gospels appears in the writings of Papias. He mentions Mark's Gospel and refers to a collection of 'oracles' (sayings of Jesus) in 'the Hebrew language' (that is, in Aramaic) by Matthew. This collection of sayings of Jesus is probably not our Gospel of Matthew but rather perhaps a source used extensively by Matthew, possibly 'Q' (see pp. 230–31).

Justin Martyr (died about 165) referred to our Gospels as 'memoirs' of the apostles and of those who followed the apostles. He believed the deeds and words of Jesus were authoritatively reported in them. He indicated that on

Page from Codex Sinaiticus, which contains the only known complete Greek New Testament in uncials.

Sundays in its liturgy the church of his time read from these apostolic memoirs as well as from the Old Testament prophets. Here it is no longer the oral tradition about Jesus but the written records of him that are the center of attention and authority.

A harmony of the Gospels, known as the Diatessaron, prepared by the Syrian Tatian (around 170), appears to have used only our four Gospels. This indicates that these four Gospels had come to a place of pre-eminence by that time. In about 180 Irenaeus offered an elaborate argument for the validity of *four* Gospels: since there are four winds and four directions, so there must of necessity be four Gospels. But to him we largely owe the preservation of our *four* Gospels. He insisted on the retention of these, since they had long been in use in the churches in its various parts; and he gloried in their manifold witness to Jesus, as against others' attempt to reduce the Gospels to one harmonized version or eliminate some of them, as Marcion (about 140 A.D.) had done (see p. 38).

Many other Gospels appeared in the church during the second and following centuries, but they did not gain universal acceptance. They consist of:

An Egyptian papyrus letter from *c.* 2000 BC.

Gospels of Our Canonical Type
Their authors took traditional material about Jesus, like that in our four Gospels, and used it to advance untraditional or 'heretical' theology. (Papyrus Oxyrhynchus 840, Papyrus Edgerton 2, the Gospel of Peter, and the Gospel of the Egyptians are of this sort.)

Gospels of a Gnostic Type
These present Jesus as the revealer of secret knowledge, given to the disciples in dialogues and visions. These Gospels also stemmed from groups the church regarded as heretical. (Representative of this type are: the Gospel of Thomas, the Apocryphon of John, the Sophia Jesu Christi [The Wisdom of Jesus Christ], and the Dialogue of the Redeemer.)

Gospels Which Supplement and Embellish the Canonical Gospels
Here the desire was to satisfy curiosity by filling in gaps in the church's knowledge of Jesus. This was done from pious fancy and from legends from foreign sources. (Belonging to this type are: the Protevangelium of James, the Infancy Story of Thomas, and the Gospel of Nicodemus [Acts of Pilate and Christ's Descent into Hell].)

This Rylands papyrus is the earliest known fragment of the New Testament (see p.374).

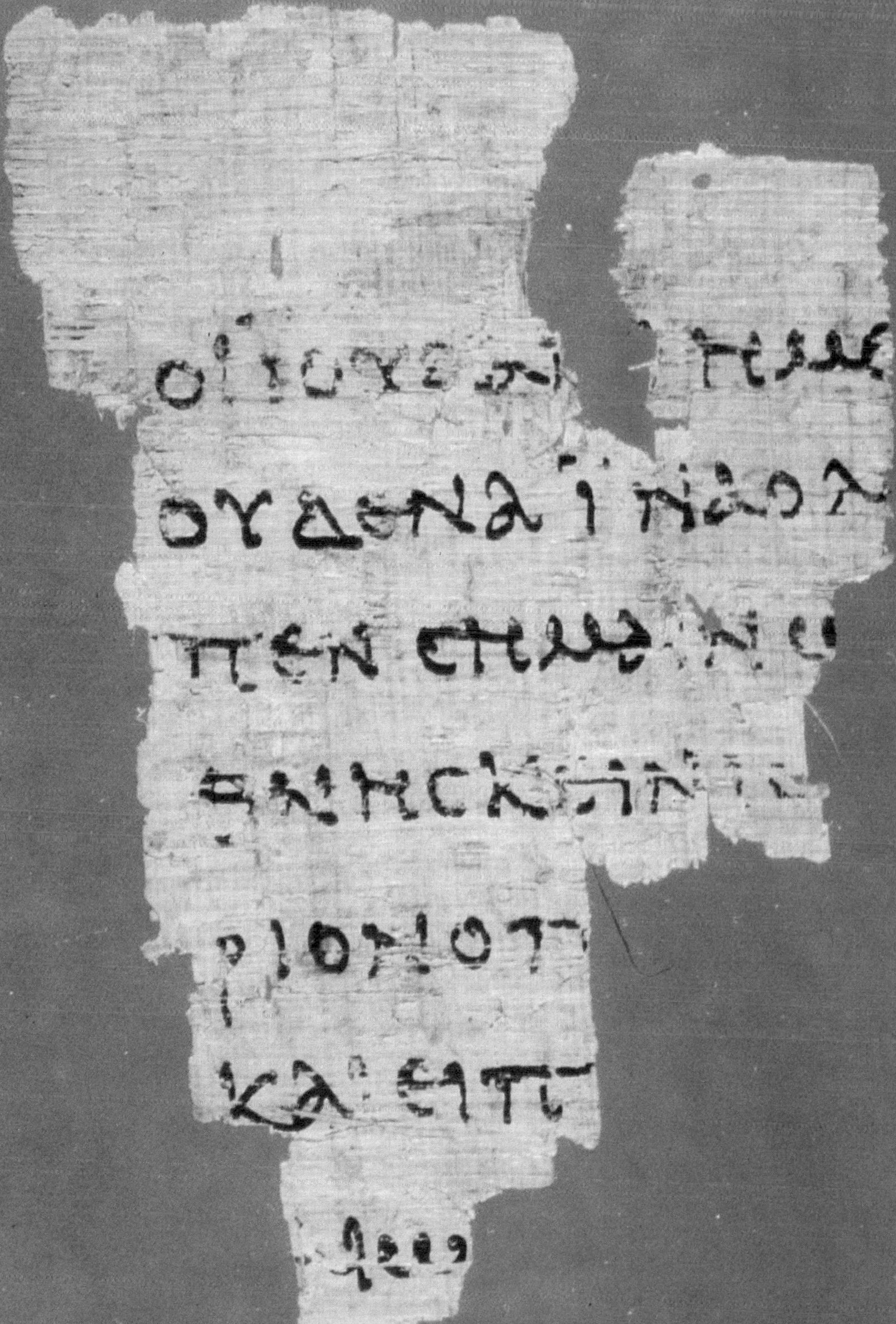

ΟΙΙΟΥΧΕ . . ΠΗΜΕ

ΟΥΔΕΝΑΙΗΔΟΛ

ΠΕΝΕΗΩΝ . .

ΘΝΗΝϹΚΩΠΗ .

ΡΙΟΡΙΟΤ

ΚΑΕΠ

Africans in Zaïre buy Bibles in their own language.

It is evident that our four Gospels made their way to the fore early, that by about 140–200 they had established themselves widely in church favor and use, and that they maintained their favored position until the New Testament canon was closed (see below).

3. The Selection of the Rest of the New Testament
In the period around 140–200 most of the remaining books of the new Testament rose to a place of wide acceptance and authority. Irenaeus, Tertullian, and Clement of Alexandria (all around the end of the second century) agreed on the authority of the following: the four Gospels, thirteen epistles of Paul, the Acts of the Apostles, 1 Peter, 1 John, and the Revelation to John. An agreement on Hebrews, James, 2 Peter, 2 and 3 John, and Jude had not yet been reached, and the authority of the Revelation to John was still contested in some quarters (particularly in the Eastern part of the church).

Some books of high quality were popular at this time but were not finally accepted into the New Testament canon: 1 Clement, the Shepherd of Hermas, the Epistle of Barnabas, the Didache, and the Apocalypse of Peter, for example.

4. The Fixing of the New Testament Canon
Marcion seems to have made the first closed collection of Christian writings. He was a Gnostic (see pp. 318–19) who rejected the Old Testament and

everything 'Jewish' and put in place of the Old Testament 'the Gospel' (an abridged edition of the Gospel of Luke) and 'the Apostle' (ten edited letters of Paul). How much influence this 'heretic' had in causing the church finally to draw up an approved list of books is not known.

It was not until Eusebius, around 325, that a careful attempt was made to distinguish approved from unapproved books. He made note of acknowledged, disputed, and rejected books. Among the disputed he named James, 2 Peter, Jude, 2 and 3 John, and the Revelation to John.

In his Easter letter of A.D. 367 Athanasius of Alexandria listed as canonical the books now contained in our New Testament. Church councils at Rome (382), at Hippo (393), at Carthage (397), and again at Carthage (419) fixed the list at those now present in our New Testament.

In some parts of the church, controversy over the inclusion of the Revelation to John and some of the General Epistles continued until the beginning of the sixth century.

Standards by Which Christian Books Were Judged
In general, three standards operated through the centuries in the church's selection of its authoritative – and, finally, canonical – literature: the extent of the acceptance and use in the church of a particular writing; the fidelity of its contents to the church's traditional teaching; and the defensibility of its claim to apostolic origin (either written or authorized by an apostle).

For Further Reading
Campenhausen, H. von, *The Formation of the Christian Bible,* 1972.
Childs, B.S., *Introduction to the Old Testament as Scripture,* 1979;
The New Testament as Canon: An Introduction, 1984.
Sanders, J.A., *Torah and Canon,* 1972; *Canon and Community,* 1984.
Sundberg, A.C. Jr., 'The Making of the New Testament Canon,' *Interpreter's One-Volume Commentary on the Bible,* 1971, pp. 1216–24.

The Translation and Distribution of the Bible

A 'version' is a translation of the Bible into a language different from those in which it was originally written (Hebrew, Aramaic, and Greek).

Ancient Versions

The Septuagint ('Seventy' or LXX): the Greek translation of the Old Testament, begun in Egypt about 250 BC with the translation of the Pentateuch and completed by various translators in about a century; alleged by ancient Jews and Christians to have been made by seventy (or seventy-two) men

Various individual Greek translations and revisions: made by Aquila, Theodotion, Symmachus, Origen, Lucian, and Hesychius in the second to fourth centuries AD

The Aramaic Targums: oral paraphrases of the Old Testament, used in Jewish synagogues for the benefit of hearers accustomed to Aramaic rather than Hebrew; eventually reduced to writing (some of them possibly in pre-Christian times)

The Latin Versions: the Old Latin translations, made from the Greek Bible; and the Latin Vulgate ('Common'), made by Jerome and one or more of his disciples (about AD 400) from both the Hebrew and the Greek texts

The Syriac Versions: the Old Syriac, the Peshitta ('Simple'), and others, from the second to the seventh century

The Coptic Versions: the Sahidic, the Boharic, and others, from the third to the sixth century

The Gothic Version: made by Bishop Ulfilas, the apostle to the Goths, in the fourth century

Ancient Versions

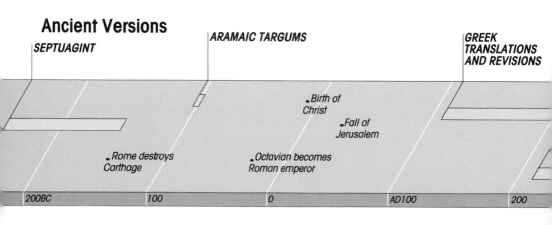

SEPTUAGINT

ARAMAIC TARGUMS

GREEK
TRANSLATIONS
AND REVISIONS

• Birth of
Christ

• Fall of
Jerusalem

• Rome destroys
Carthage

• Octavian becomes
Roman emperor

| 200BC | 100 | 0 | AD100 | 200 |

The Armenian Version: fourth or fifth century
The Georgian Version: fifth century
The Ethiopic Version: sixth century
Arabic Versions: of uncertain dates

Medieval and Modern Versions

The spread of Christianity brought with it the translation of the Bible into the major languages of the world: Dutch, English, French, German, modern Greek, Hungarian, Italian, Portuguese, Danish, Icelandic, Swedish, Spanish, Slavic (Bulgarian, Polish, Russian), etc.

By the time of the invention of printing (mid-fifteenth century) the Bible had been put, in whole or in part, into thirty-three languages: twenty-two European, seven Asiatic, four African. A spurt forward came in the nineteenth century, the century of missionary expansion, when the Bible was translated into some five hundred additional languages and dialects.

Today the Bible is unquestionably the world's most widely read book. In whole or in part it has been translated into more than seventeen hundred languages. It is estimated that more than ninety percent of the world's inhabitants have the entire Bible in their own language and more than ninety-seven percent have at least one book of the Bible. The Gospel according to Mark, the most widely translated of the Bible's books, has been put into some eight hundred languages.

There remain more than a thousand minor languages into which the Bible is yet to be translated. The work of translation and the revision of existing translations is being carried on in various parts of the world by skilled and dedicated people at an astounding rate.

For Further Reading
Cowan, G.M., *The Word That Kindles*, 1979.
Nida, E.A. and Reyburn, W.D., *Meaning Across Cultures*, 1981.
The files of the *American Bible Society Record*.

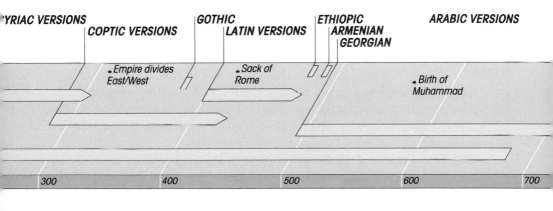

English Versions in Use Today

A bewildering number and variety of English translations of the Bible have appeared in the twentieth century. They have resulted from both the work of committees of scholars and of individual translators. Only the most widely used translations in Protestant, Roman Catholic, and Jewish circles can be discussed here. For information about the others, see 'For Further Reading' on p. 68.

1. Official Committee Translations

The King James Version (The Authorized Version)
The New King James Version

The King James Version, prepared by forty-seven scholars appointed by James I, was begun in 1604 and published in 1611. The translators were instructed to revise the Bishops' Bible, the version then officially in use, but to alter it 'as little as the truth of the original will permit.'

Much of the wording of the King James Version reflects the language of earlier English Bibles (the Geneva Bible, the Great Bible, Matthew's Bible, Coverdale's Bible, and Tyndale's translation of the New Testament and part of the Old). Approximately 60 percent of the words of the New Testament in the King James Version derive ultimately from Tyndale's work.

There were numerous editions of the King James Version in the seventeenth and eighteenth centuries, embodying hundreds of changes, until a standardized form of the translation was reached in the Oxford Standard Edition of 1769. This is essentially the form of the King James Version we read today.

The changes were designed to correct inaccurate and biased translations, infelicities of style, archaic language and spelling, and printers' errors. So hostile were many people of the time to the new version that it took more than a half century for it to displace its predecessors (the Great Bible, the Geneva Bible, and the Bishops' Bible) in the churches and homes of England.

Editions of the King James Bible usually contained the books of the Apocrypha, in a place between the Testaments, until the early nineteenth century (see pp. 210–11). In 1701 Archbishop Ussher's chronology was introduced into the margins of the biblical text of this version.

The King James translators of the New Testament worked from the Greek text of Beza of 1589. This was based on one published by Erasmus (1516–35)

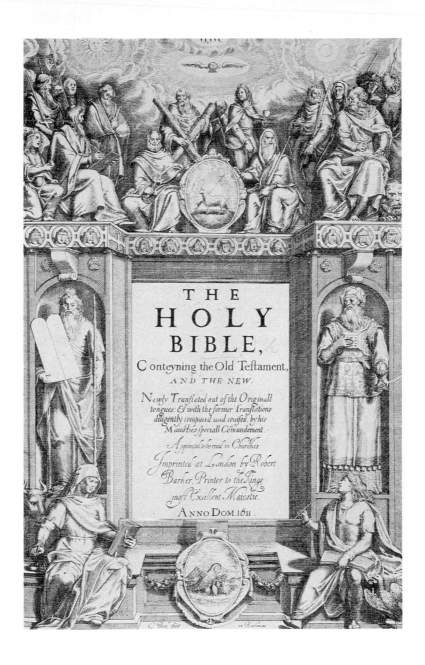

**The title page of the first edition
of the King James Version, 1611.**

from a few medieval manuscripts. Fourteen centuries of accumulated errors from manuscript copying had marred the Beza-Erasmus text. The King James scholars probably were acquainted with less than twenty-five Greek manuscripts of the New Testament.

Today scholars have access to 5,358 Greek manuscripts and fragments of the New Testament from which to eliminate copyists' errors and establish the original text. For the Old Testament the seventeenth century translators had only near-contemporary rabbinic texts, derived from a few late Hebrew manuscripts. Today about 800 Hebrew biblical manuscripts, some dating to the second century BC (Dead Sea Scrolls), are known.

All these manuscripts, critically compared, have shown that the King James Bible contains verses and passages of dubious authenticity: for example, Matthew 17:21; 18:11; 23:14; Mark 7:16; 9:44, 46; 11:26; 15:28; 16:9—20; Luke 17:36; 23:17; John 5:4; 7:53—8:11; Acts 8:37; 15:34; 24:7; 28:29; Romans 16:24. Most present-day translations, whether made by conservative or liberal scholars, agree that these passages probably were not in the original manuscripts of these New Testament books. (Look the passages up in the New International Version and the Revised Standard Version, for example.)

In addition to its textual shortcomings, today's readers find the archaic language of this version hard to understand: 'chapmen' (2 Chron. 9:14) should be rendered as 'traders'; 'ear' (1 Sam. 8:12) as 'plow'; 'leasing' (Ps. 5:6) as 'lies'; 'neesings' (Job 41:18) as 'sneezings'; 'holden' (Luke 24:16) as 'kept from'; 'let' (Rom. 1:13) as 'prevented'. The meaning of many English words has changed radically in the last four hundred years or so and many words have dropped out of usage altogether.

In spite of the above facts, apparent to us today but not to our forefathers, it must be said that the King James Version became a classic in the English-speaking world because of its dignity, power, and aptness of expression for its time. This version marked a striking advance over its predecessors and served several centuries of readers well. It is still beloved by some of our contemporaries, so much so that attempts have been made to rescue it from honorable retirement.

In 1962 a version of the King James Bible edited by Jay P. Green appeared. It substituted modern words and expressions for archaic ones but left the basic text unchanged (even where the best ancient manuscripts now known show a passage to be spurious – see above). Green started from the assumption that 'the people do not want a new Bible; they just want the old one in a form they can read and understand.'

In agreement with this assumption, in 1975 the publisher Thomas Nelson, Inc. undertook sponsorship of The New King James Version. It asked some 130 scholars, editors, and religious leaders to update the old version. The modernized New Testament appeared in 1979 and the Old Testament in

1982. In the New Testament the words of Jesus – both of the historical Jesus and the resurrected Lord – are printed in red.

All the revisers avowed that they subscribed to the plenary, verbal inspiration of the original autographs of the Bible. Their reverence for the King James Bible seemed to approach that which they held for the original Scriptures themselves.

This is to be seen in their rejection of most of the results of textual criticism of the last one hundred and more years. They argue for the accuracy of the Erasmus-Beza text (the Textus Receptus), on which the King James translation of the New Testament was based. In contrast to modern textual principles, they *counted* the number of manuscripts supporting a certain passage, phrase, or word rather than *weighing* them according to their date, line of descent, and general characteristics. They thus restored the passages listed above.

The New King James Version tries to keep the devotional and literary quality of its great predecessor, its spelling of personal and place names, its time-hallowed theological terms (propitiation, justification, sanctification, etc.), and its literal approach to translation. But it modernizes by dropping archaic pronouns (thee, thou, ye), verb endings (eth), and obsolete words (anon, eschew, trow, to wit, holden, etc.).

Unfortunately, the modern practice of paragraphing the text is not followed, although poetry is rendered in poetic form and subject headings are introduced throughout the text. Footnotes include explanatory data, alternate translations, cross references, some textual variants, and New Testament citation of Old Testament passages.

Some present-day users will like the new wine of this updated version. Others will say, 'the old is better' (Luke 5:39). It will appeal chiefly to those who believe that it is irreverent to replace the King James Version with any other translation.

The Revised Version – The American Standard Version – The New American Standard Bible

In 1870 British scholars began a revision of the King James Version to bring it abreast of the vast increase of biblical knowledge since 1611. Revision committees were formed in England and in the United States for the work, the American committees serving as advisers to the British. The revision was called the Revised Version.

At the beginning the committees hoped that the revision could be adopted on both sides of the Atlantic. However, strong differences of judgment developed between the English and American groups. This led to the publication of the American preferences in appendixes to the British edition of the New Testament (1881) and of the Old Testament (1885) and finally to an

American edition of both Testaments in 1901, under the name the American Standard Version. A British revision of the Apocrypha appeared in 1896, but no such revision was made by the Americans.

The Revised Version and the American Standard Version mark a great advance over the King James Version in accuracy of the text of the Bible (that is, in determining the original text, free from copyists' errors). But in English style both revisions are inferior. Beauty and force are sacrificed to word-for-word literalness in translation. Such literalness makes the revisions superior for study purposes but of less value for public worship and private devotion. The revisers improved on the King James Version by printing much of the Bible's poetry in poetic form and by arranging the text in paragraphs. Marginal notes suggest variant readings.

By mid-twentieth century in America many one-man translations – like Moffatt's, Knox's, Phillips' – and the authorized committee-translation known as the Revised Standard Version had begun to replace the American Standard Version. To keep this version alive the Lockman Foundation issued it in revised form as the New American Standard Bible (New Testament, 1963; both Testaments, 1971).

The Lockman revisers, some 58 conservative persons whose identity has never been revealed, made some changes in the wording and content of the biblical text of the American Standard Version on the basis of present knowledge of ancient manuscripts, altered and expanded marginal notes, and improved English style somewhat. They tightened up sentence structure, updated language, and improved the American Standard Version's rendering of tenses in the original languages. Unfortunately they abandoned paragraphing and resumed the verse-by-verse printing of the King James Bible. (However, in some recent printings paragraphing has been restored.) The revisers quite properly abandoned the divine name used in the American Standard Version (Jehovah) in favor of the designation 'the Lord' (see p. 450).

The revisers sometimes disclosed their theological position in the translation and notes. For example, there are attempts at harmonization of differing parallel accounts (2 Sam. 24:1 and 1 Chron. 21:1; Acts 9:7 and 22:9) and a reading of the New Testament into the Old through capitalization of words (including pronouns) believed to refer to the Messiah (Ps. 2:2, 6, 12; 45:1, 7; Micah 5:2, 5; Zech. 13:7).

The English style, as a whole, remains over-literal, stilted, and non-idiomatic, in spite of the revisers' announced intention to render the grammar and terminology in contemporary English.

The Revised Standard Version – The Reader's Digest Bible

From 1930 to 1957 committees of American scholars, under authorization of many major American churches which worked together in the International

Council of Religious Education and in the National Council of Churches of the U.S.A., carried out a revision of the American Standard Version and made in addition a translation of the Apocrypha.

The revisers were asked to prepare a version 'which embodies the best results of modern scholarship as to the meaning of the Scriptures, and expresses this meaning in English diction which is designed for use in public and private worship and preserves those qualities which have given to the King James Version a supreme place in English literature.'

The New Testament appeared in 1946, the Old Testament in 1952, and the Apocrypha in 1957. A standing revision committee has improved the translation in various places since those dates. The committee issued a second edition of the New Testament in 1971 and is projecting a second edition of the whole Bible for the near future (see below).

The Revised Standard Version has been widely used by Protestants, Roman Catholics, Eastern Orthodox churches, and to some extent by Jews. In 1966 Roman Catholics in England issued a special Catholic edition in which some 67 changes appeared and in which the Deuterocanonical books (twelve of the books of the Apocrypha – see p. 210) were placed throughout the Old Testament, as in the Latin Vulgate Bible. Some Catholic notes were included in this edition.

In 1973 the Revised Standard Version Common Bible (The Holy Bible – An Ecumenical Edition) was published for use by Protestant, Roman Catholic, and Orthodox readers. This 'Common Bible' contains the thirty-nine books of the Old Testament (as printed in Protestant Bibles), followed by the twelve Deuterocanonical books accepted as Scripture by Roman Catholics (see p. 210), followed by three books of the traditional Apocrypha not accepted by Roman Catholics – i.e., the First and Second Books of Esdras and the Prayer of Manasseh, and concludes with the twenty-seven books of the New Testament.

In 1977 Oxford University Press published *The New Oxford Annotated Bible, with The Apocrypha*, Expanded Edition, Revised Standard Version, which includes all the above books plus Third and Fourth Maccabees and Psalm 151, writings that long have been accepted by Eastern Orthodox churches. For the first time since the Protestant Reformation a truly ecumenical Bible came into being.

The second edition of the whole Revised Standard Bible is scheduled to appear in the late 1980s. The committee plans to eliminate the archaic forms 'thou,' 'thee,' 'thy,' and 'thine' in language addressed to God and to introduce inclusive terms, rather than masculine-oriented ones, where no violence will be done to the biblical texts (for example, 'people' for 'men' and 'any one' for 'any man'). Masculine designations for God, Jesus Christ, and the Holy Spirit will be kept.

The reception first accorded the Revised Standard Version was mixed.

Many people hailed it as a reliable, up-to-date, modern English translation which preserves the dignity of the King James Version but speaks to the average person in a language that can easily be understood. Others vilified both the version and the translators on the ground that 'modernist' and even 'communist' tendencies controlled the translation – charges that were grossly unfair and unprovable. Some scholars felt that the translators were too captive to traditional language and should have shown more originality and creativity in their renderings. It is possible that the greatest weakness of the version is its attempt to be both classical and contemporary in its style. In spite of some imperfections, it will undoubtedly stand as one of the great translations of this generation. It is the first truly ecumenical version of modern times.

The Reader's Digest Bible, published in 1982, is a condensation of the Revised Standard Version Bible. Seven Reader's Digest editors, using techniques of condensation employed for that magazine, sought to produce a shortened and clarified text for the average reader that yet retains all the sixty-six books of the Protestant canon and all its important personalities and teachings.

The Old Testament is cut by about 50 percent and the New by about 25 percent. The deletions eliminate repeated material, unnecessary rhetoric, parallel accounts (as in the Synoptic Gospels), and matter of little relevance for today's readers (genealogies, lists of nations, ritual laws, details concerning the construction of the tabernacle, etc.). Well-known passages are left untouched (such as the Ten Commandments, the twenty-third Psalm, the Lord's Prayer). In the interest of clarity, grammatical and stylistic improvements in the Revised Standard Version text appear. Each book of the Bible is preceded by a brief introduction.

The condensation is not meant to replace the full Bible. The purpose is to make Bible reading more pleasurable and 'heart-lifting' by making possible more rapid reading and quicker comprehension.

The New English Bible

The proposal for this translation arose in 1946 in the Church of Scotland. Soon the Church of England, the major free churches of England (Methodist, Baptist, Congregationalist, Presbyterian, the Society of Friends), the churches of Wales and Ireland, and the Bible societies of England and Scotland gave their support to the project.

Four panels of translators, representative of the best scholarship of the British Isles, dealt respectively with the Old Testament, the Apocrypha, the New Testament, and with English style. The New Testament appeared in 1961, and the Old Testament and the Apocrypha, together with a revised edition of the New Testament, in 1970.

The Hebrew and Aramaic text of the Old Testament translated in this version is the traditional text in the best present-day edition. However, the translators made many changes, based on the Dead Sea Scrolls, the ancient versions, variations in Hebrew manuscripts, and conjecture. Footnotes indicate alternative translations, the literal meaning of the Hebrew, the meaning of proper names, corrections of the text, changes in order of material, and the like.

The New Testament translation rests on no one Greek text. The translators carefully considered variant readings of ancient manuscripts and versions, selected the wording which appeared to be the most original, and recorded serious alternative possibilities in the footnotes.

General introductions to the Old Testament, the Apocrypha, and the New Testament are offered, so that the reader may understand the procedures and issues involved in translating each portion. The text is printed in paragraphs under sectional headings.

The New English Bible is a genuinely new translation, not a revision of the Tyndale-King James tradition, as is the Revised Standard Version. The translators were free to render the original texts in meaning-for-meaning, rather than word-for-word, language. They employed colloquial, yet dignified, forceful, direct English idiom and avoided archaic expressions and modern slang. Some Briticisms, however, do appear in spelling and vocabulary ('fortnight,' 'Whitsuntide,' 'twopence,' 'corn' for 'grain,' 'cairn,' etc.).

The translators' freedom extended to textual matters. They adopted in both Testaments some questionable readings and some conjectural ones, though in the large they followed mainline textual decisions.

This version is intended for both public and private reading. It has behind it England's and Scotland's finest biblical scholarship and authorization by the major non-Roman churches of the British Isles. A thorough revision of the entire New English Bible is now in process and should appear in print in the late 1980s.

The Jerusalem Bible

This valuable English translation (1966) – with introductory essays, extensive footnotes, tables, and maps – is in the best tradition of liberal Roman Catholic scholarship. Its editor was Alexander Jones of Christ's College, Liverpool. He was assisted by twenty-seven principal collaborators. Behind it lies a French work of 1948–54, done by a large company of scholars under the leadership of the famous Dominican scholar Roland DeVaux of Jerusalem, which appeared in a one-volume edition in 1956.

The English biblical text, while following the French translation, reflects the constant use of the Hebrew and Greek texts of the Bible by the editor and his collaborators. The Latin Vulgate, though referred to frequently in the footnotes, has dropped far into the background.

The books translated include those called 'deuterocanonical' by Roman Catholics ('apocryphal' by Protestants). These are not printed separately but are scattered in Old Testament books, as is customary in Roman Catholic Bibles.

The translation is freer than that in the Revised Standard Version. Personal names follow Protestant spelling. Use of poetic form in poetic passages is more generous than in many Bibles. Passages of doubtful authenticity (for example, Mark 16:9–20, John 5:3b–4 and 7:53—8:11) are included without differentiation through italics or separation by spacing, though footnotes indicate modern scholarly doubts concerning their originality.

The notes accompanying the text are numerous, informative, and often detailed. The scholarship is for the most part admirable. As in every translation, the theology of the translators has left its mark in some notes (for example, at Gen. 3:15; Matt. 1:25; 12:46; 16:18–19; 18:18; 19:9). The position on historical-critical problems is often quite conservative. In 1985 *The New Jerusalem Bible* (H. Wansbrough, ed.) appeared with numerous improvements.

The New American Bible

This American Roman Catholic translation of the Bible from the original languages – an American counterpart to the British-produced Jerusalem Bible – was more than a quarter-century in the making. It appeared in 1970 as the fruit of the labor of forty-six members of the Catholic Biblical Association of America and four Protestant scholars, under the sponsorship of the Episcopal Committee of the Confraternity of Christian Doctrine.

The inspiration for the new version came largely from a papal encyclical of 1943 which authorized translation from the original languages and approved 'cooperation with separated brethren' in the work. A new era in Roman Catholic biblical translation thus began.

The makers of this version declare that they have aimed at a translation, not a paraphrase, in order to retain something of the original flavor and the eccentricities of the various biblical writings. The translators worked with a large degree of individual freedom and without such strict standards and controls as governed the translation process in the production of the Revised Standard Version. A certain roughness thus characterizes the translation.

Introductions to biblical books, extensive footnotes (though not so extensive as in the Jerusalem Bible), captions in the text, an essay on biblical geography, and a glossary of biblical terms guide the reader effectively. The spelling of proper names conforms to that found in Protestant Bibles. The books of the Apocrypha (called 'deuterocanonical' by Roman Catholics) are printed in their traditional places through the Old Testament.

As a whole the translation is skillful and in the mainstream of recent ecumenical scholarship. Only rarely are distinctive Roman Catholic doctrines

Ruins of Lindisfarne Priory, on the north-east coast of England. The Lindisfarne Gospels were written and decorated ('illuminated') here *c.* 698.

evident in the introductions and footnotes – considerably less than in The Jerusalem Bible. Protestants, as well as Catholics, can use this version with great profit.

The New International Version

This version was begun in 1965 by committees from the Christian Reformed Church and the National Association of Evangelicals, carried forward by over one hundred conservative scholars of America and of English-speaking countries abroad (representing unofficially some thirty-four evangelical religious denominations and groups), and sponsored by the New York Bible Society (now the New York International Bible Society). The New Testament appeared in 1973 and the whole Bible (without the Apocrypha) in 1978.

It arose in part as a reaction to the alleged 'liberal' tendencies of the Revised Standard Version and other translations. All the translators were expected to subscribe to the 'high view of Scripture' set forth in the Westminster Confession of Faith, the Belgic Confession, and the Statement of Faith of the National Association of Evangelicals. The publisher (Zondervan) has said that the translators regard the Bible as 'inerrant in the autographs.'

This version is a fresh translation of the Hebrew, Aramaic, and Greek biblical texts, not a revision of any earlier translation. However, the translators declare that they aim to preserve some measure of continuity with the long tradition of translating the Bible into English. They avoid 'unwarranted paraphrasing' and seek to 'communicate God's revelation in the language of the people,' so that it may be 'effective for public worship (pulpit and pew), for private study and devotional reading.'

The translators employed standard textual principles in establishing the text to be translated – in contrast, one may note, to the obscurantist textual policy behind The New King James Version (see pp. 44–5). Textual information from the Dead Sea Scrolls, the Samaritan Pentateuch, ancient versions, and ancient Hebrew scribal tradition are used in establishing the Old Testament text. The best available printed Greek texts of our time are used for the New Testament. Notes explain the omission or separation off of passages of questionable authenticity (for example, Mark 16:9–20; Luke 23:17; John 5:3b–4; 7:53—8:11; Acts 8:37).

Captions divide the single column text into logical units and paragraph divisions assist the reader in comprehension. Commonly recognized poetic parts of the Bible are printed in poetic form. Speakers are sometimes identified in the margins (Job, Song of Songs). English style received careful attention, so that a flowing, dignified, and yet common vocabulary resulted.

Conservative theology has affected the translation in places: for example, in Psalms 2:2, 6, 7, 12; 16:10 and Daniel 9:25–26, where the capital letters make definite what are uncertain references to the Messiah.

As would be expected in a conservative translation, old terms are kept where new, more meaningful ones might convey more to the contemporary mind. So we find 'forgive us our debts,' 'sanctify,' 'saints,' 'righteousness,' 'justified,' 'predestined,' 'holiness.' Some renditions are questionable: 'understood' (John 1:5); 'sacrifice of atonement' and 'atoning sacrifice' (Rom. 3:25; 1 John 2:2). Some are infelicitous (for example, 'one and only' in John 3:16), and some are not fully abreast of present knowledge (as, 'our daily bread' [Matt. 6:11], where a footnote should at least suggest the translation 'our bread for tomorrow').

Many splendid renditions appear: 'keeps on sinning' (1 John 3:6, compare vs. 9); 'faith expressing itself through love' (Gal. 5:6); 'let us keep in step with the Spirit' (Gal. 5:25); 'faith is being sure of what we hope for' (Heb. 11:1); 'in all things God works for the good of those who love him' (Rom. 8:28).

This version has been enormously successful in sales and usage. Its merits far outweigh its limitations. It is likely to become the standard version of conservative, evangelical churches.

The Good News Bible (Today's English Version)

This important version of the Bible began with the appearance in 1964 of a translation of the Gospel of Mark entitled The Right Time. It was made by Robert G. Bratcher, a biblical scholar and translation expert of the American Bible Society. Assisted by an advisory committee of American and British scholars, Bratcher and this Society brought out in 1966 a translation of the entire New Testament (Good News for Modern Man: The New Testament in Today's English Version). Two subsequent editions (1967 and 1971) included improvements in the translation and increased its phenomenal sale and readership.

In translating the Old Testament a committee of six, appointed by the American Bible Society, chaired by Dr. Bratcher, and assisted by a consultant of the British and Foreign Bible Society, carried out the work (1967–75). The committee members were both biblical scholars and translation experts who were committed to the procedures in translation that led to the appearance of the Good News New Testament. In 1976 both Testaments appeared as The Good News Bible, the New Testament in a fourth edition.

The basic principle of translating used in this version (though not unique to it) is called 'dynamic equivalence.' It seeks to create in the reader in the new language the same reaction to the text the original readers had. Word-for-word translating cannot do this. The whole idea being conveyed must be put in those words of the new language that create equivalent effect. Thus this translation sometimes has the appearance of paraphrase, though it is faithful to essential meanings. And the English into which meanings have been put in this version is common English, English that can be understood by people from various walks of life, Christians and non-Christians.

Thus, ancient terms are modernized: 'Caesar' becomes 'emperor' or 'Roman emperor'; 'centurion' is 'army officer' or 'captain in the Roman army'; 'the fourth watch of the night' is 'between three and six o'clock in the morning'; 'a sabbath day's journey' is 'about half a mile'; 'ten thousand talents' is 'millions of dollars'; 'justify' is 'put right with God'; 'predestined' is 'set apart'; 'reconciled' is 'changed us from enemies into his [God's] friends.' It is evident that great care has been given to make ancient and mysterious terms meaningful to contemporary people.

The textual evidence from the biblical manuscripts is responsibly handled. In the Old Testament the translators treat the Hebrew (Masoretic – see p. 450) text in its best contemporary edition with respect but feel free to change it when evidence from ancient manuscripts or versions makes sense out of nonsense. Conjectural change is 'based on scholarly consensus' and is referred to in footnotes as 'probable text.' According to one estimate, about one-third of the some seven hundred notes to the Old Testament text concern such changes.

For the New Testament the translators follow the best critically reconstructed Greek text (the United Bible Society's Greek Text, 2nd and 3rd editions) with minor changes. Passages usually suspected as inauthentic on the basis of textual evidence are dropped to the footnotes (Matthew 17:21; 18:11; 23:14; Mark 7:16; 9:44, 46; 11:26; 15:28; Luke 17:36; 23:17; John 5:3b–4; Acts 8:37; 15:34; 24:6b–8a; 28:29; Romans 16:2). Two endings to the Gospel of Mark are printed as part of the text: 'An Old Ending to the Gospel' (16:9–20) and 'Another Old Ending' (16:9–10), both passages placed in brackets. Brackets mark off John 7:53—8:11, with a footnote explaining its variant position in the text of some Greek manuscripts.

Reader helps include: division of the text into sections with headings; cultural and historical notes; textual notes; alternative renderings; references to other passages; a word list (glossary); chronology of the Bible; and maps. Line drawings by a Swiss artist, Annie Vallotton, illustrate the translation.

Almost anyone who can read a newspaper in English can profit from this sparkling new translation of the Bible in the common English language of today.

The New Jewish Version

In 1955 a committee of distinguished Jewish scholars from the three major branches of Judaism in America, under the auspices of the Jewish Publication Society, began a new English translation of the Jewish Scriptures according to the traditional (Masoretic) text (see p. 450).

Prior to this, American Jews used widely an English translation, published in 1917, that was in reality little more than a Jewish revision of the (British and Christian) Revised Version of 1885. The New Jewish Version is a completely new translation of the Hebrew and Aramaic biblical text, by Jews and for Jews, in up-to-date, easy-to-read English.

This new version appeared in successive stages over a period of twenty years: the Torah or Pentateuch in 1962; the Megilloth or Scrolls (Song of Songs, Ruth, Lamentations, Koheleth [Ecclesiastes], Esther) and the book of Jonah in 1969; the Prophets, Former and Latter, in 1978; the Kethubim or Writings (Psalms, Proverbs, Job, Daniel, Ezra and Nehemiah, 1 and 2 Chronicles) in 1982.

The New Jewish Version follows as closely as possible the traditional Hebrew text, more closely than any other recent English translation. Footnotes frequently make reference to variant readings in ancient manuscripts and versions, but the traditional text is retained if at all possible. Conjectural changes are very few. Explanatory footnotes of various kinds justify the translation offered and assist the reader's understanding of obscure matters in the text.

The footnotes, as well as the translation, reveal the amazing scope of the translators' knowledge of the languages, literature, and culture of the ancient Near East and of the history of Jewish interpretation of the Hebrew Scriptures.

The Christian reader should be aware of the fact that this version follows the chapter and verse divisions of the Hebrew text, which are sometimes different from those in Protestant and Catholic Bibles.

The translators reject the word-for-word literalness of the King James Version and of the 1917 Jewish form of the Revised Version and strive for equivalent effect: to evoke in modern people through clear contemporary English the same effect that the ancient writers evoked in their readers through Hebrew and Aramaic. They abandon the peculiarities of Hebrew composition (for example, the coordinate sentences connected by 'and'), avoid archaic English pronouns and verb forms ('thou,' 'thee,' 'eth' endings), and employ modern equivalents of old terms ('pact' for 'covenant'; 'rule' for 'statute'; 'teaching' for 'law' (Torah); 'life' or 'whole being' for 'soul'). The English is more formal and elevated than that in the Good News Bible. Some of the poetry is rendered in exquisite English verse. The vocabulary is often rich and varied. Christians should discover and use this very fine translation alongside the version or versions favored in their particular Christian communion. It is available under the title, *Tanak – A New Translation of Holy Scripture According to the Traditional Hebrew Text*, 1985.

The Basic Bible

Using only about 1,000 different English words, a committee in England, under the leadership of S.H. Hooke of the University of London, produced

The New Testament in Basic English in 1940 and the entire Bible in 1949.

Basic English, with a vocabulary of 850 words, was devised by C.K. Ogden as an international language and as an aid to the learning of English. In translating the Bible some 150 specialized terms were necessarily added.

The translators showed great ingenuity in the rendering of difficult biblical passages in so limited a vocabulary. The result is a translation of amazing simplicity. The Basic Bible has been especially popular with people who were learning to speak and write the English language.

The New World Translation of the Holy Scriptures

The Jehovah's Witnesses published this version in 1960. Since then it has been rendered into many languages of the world. The translation is based on good recent critical Hebrew and Greek texts. It aims to be 'as literal as possible to the point of understandableness.' Paraphrase, or anything approaching it, seldom appears. No attempt is made to render in modern terms ancient language for such items as money, weights, measures, and time.

The translators make a great point of having rendered 'faithfully' in this version the divine name as 'Jehovah.' (This name, of course, is a late [sixth-seventh century AD] hybrid that resulted from the vocalization of the consonants YHWH with the vowels of the word Lord, *Adonai* – see p. 450). It is not a Hebrew word at all. The translators often insert 'Jehovah' into the New Testament where the Greek mentions 'the Lord,' sometimes meaning the Lord Jesus (as in Acts 19:20; see 19:17). The Foreword to the translation alleges a concealment of the divine name 'Jehovah' by ancient editors or copyists (for example, in Gen. 18:3) and by modern translators through the substitution of the term 'the Lord.'

The version is marred further by the attempt to justify the Jehovah's Witnesses' doctrine of Christ through the translation. This is visible in their reduction of the New Testament's view of the deity of Christ ('the Word was a God' – John 1:1; 'make yourself a God – 10:33). For the Witnesses, Christ is a created being, to be distinguished from God (note the insertion of 'of' between 'God' and 'our Savior Christ Jesus' in Titus 2:13).

The translation is often awkward and deficient on the side of English style. As a whole, it has little to commend it to members of other religious groups.

2. Private Individual Translations

Many individual scholars, great and not-so-great, have tried their hand at translating the Bible. We consider here only the more noteworthy of these translations and those which have some continuing use.

¶The Epistle off the
¶Apostle Paul / to the Ro/
maynes.

¶The fyrst Chapter.

Paul the servaunte off Jesus Christ / called vnto the office off an apostle/ putt a parte to preache the go/ spell of God / which he promy/ sed afore by his prophetts/i the holy scriptures that make mē/ sion of his sōne/ the which was beg otten of the seede of Davib/ as pertaynynge to the flesshe: and declared to be the sonne of God with power of the holy goost / that sanctifieth / sence the tyme that Jesus Christ oure lorde rose agayne from deeth / by whom we have receaved grace and a/ postleshippe / thatt all gentiles shulde obeye to the fayth which is in his name / of the which no/ umbre are ye also / which are Jesus Christes by vocacion.

To all you of Rome beloved of God / ād san/ ctes by callynge. Grace be with you and peace from God oure father / and from the lorde Je/ sus Christ.

Fyrst verely I thanke my god thorow Jesus Christ for you all / because youre fayth is publi/ sshed through out all the worlde. For god is my

Aa

The first page of Paul's letter to the Romans,
from William Tyndale's New Testament.

The New Testament in Modern Speech
by Richard F. Weymouth

An English headmaster and classical scholar translated into modern English an edition of the Greek New Testament he himself had produced. It was published in 1903, after his death, with the editorial help of E. Hampden-Cook, a Congregational minister. In 1927 James A. Robertson revised the translation.

The strength of this translation lies in its close attention to the exact force of the Greek tenses. Weymouth's 'modern speech' attempts to preserve 'a tinge of antiquity' so that there should be a 'dignity of style that befits the sacred themes.' He wanted his translation to serve as 'a succinct and compressed running commentary (not doctrinal) to be used side by side with its elder compeers' (the King James Version and the English Revised Version). He did not intend the churches to use it for public reading.

The Bible: A New Translation
by James Moffatt

Moffatt, a brilliant Scot, began his career as a translator of the Bible with The Historical New Testament (1901). This work arranged the books of the New Testament in the order of their supposed dates and literary growth.

In 1913 a second work appeared, The New Testament: A New Translation. Both Testaments were brought together in 1926 in A New Translation of the Bible. A final, revised form of this came out in 1935.

Moffatt swept aside 'Bible English' and put the original languages in strong, contemporary speech. Criticism of Moffatt's work has been directed at the Scottish idioms of his English and at the extent to which he injected into his translation particular theories about the biblical text. He rearranged the order of certain chapters and verses (for example, the position of John 14) and in places radically changed the Hebrew and Greek text (for example, 1 Sam. 14:11; 1 Pet. 3:19). Furthermore, he attempted to indicate the various sources behind the Pentateuch by varying the style of type in different passages.

His use of 'the Eternal' for the personal name of God was not altogether a happy choice. His translation of the Old Testament is generally regarded as of less value than that of the New. But he captured the imagination of Bible readers throughout the English-speaking world, including scholars, who produced an important commentary series on his text, called The Moffatt Commentary.

Moffatt put his genius for translation at the service of the committee that prepared the Revised Standard Version. He served as Executive Secretary of that committee from 1937 until his death in 1944.

The Complete Bible – An American Translation

The New Testament was translated by Edgar J. Goodspeed and the Old Testament by T.J. Meek, Leroy Waterman, A.R. Gordon, and J.M.P. Smith.

Goodspeed, a professor at the University of Chicago, was invited in 1920 by that university's Press to prepare a translation of the New Testament into the language of everyday American life. The invitation arose out of Goodspeed's criticisms before a learned society of earlier modern speech versions.

Goodspeed set out to produce a version with 'something of the force and freshness that reside in the original Greek' and that would 'make on the modern reader something of the impression the New Testament must have made on its earliest readers.' He worked from the Greek text of Westcott and Hort, rarely departing from it. The translation appeared in 1923. So successful was his American language translation that it was published in newspapers of the United States and Canada.

This success led to the Press's sponsoring of a similar translation of the Old Testament by Professor J.M.P. Smith of that institution and three of his former students. They worked from the traditional (Masoretic) text, changing it rather freely here and there on the basis of the ancient versions and what they called 'scientific emendation.' They avoided 'the level of the street' in their renderings and maintained 'a high literary plane' when the original was 'dignified, impressive, and eloquent.'

The New Testament and the Old Testament translations were joined in 1931 and published as The Bible – An American Translation. Goodspeed's translation of the Apocrypha was added in 1939 and The Complete Bible – An American Translation appeared.

Freshness and imagination mark the version in both Testaments. Since four men worked on different parts of the Old Testament, there is some variety in the style there. In the Old Testament portion one does not find the degree of passion shown by Goodspeed to translate in the plain language of the street and marketplace. However, simplicity and directness are the rule everywhere. The publisher claimed that the translation 'tries to be American in the sense that the writings of Lincoln, Roosevelt, and Wilson are American.'

Holy Bible
translated by Ronald A. Knox

This translation was made by an Oxford-trained Roman Catholic and man of letters. It marks a stage in the progress of Roman Catholic English translations of the Bible from the Rheims-Douai English Bible of the early seventeenth century (rendered from the Latin Vulgate) to the New American Bible (based on the original Hebrew, Aramaic, and Greek texts) of our period (see p. 50).

In Knox's time (the second quarter of the twentieth century) only the Latin Vulgate could be used by a Roman Catholic Bible translator. The Rheims-Douai Bible, even in the Challoner revision, was archaic and in stilted English – and largely unknown by Catholics. What was needed was a vernacular translation, something that would speak to Roman Catholics as the new Protestant versions did to Protestants.

Knox undertook the translation of the New Testament at the request of the Hierarchy of England and Wales in 1939. It appeared in 1944. His translation of the Old Testament, requested by the Cardinal Archbishop of Westminster, was published in two volumes in 1948 and 1950. A one-volume edition of the Holy Bible became available in 1955.

Knox was a master of English style. His translation is fresh, sometimes witty, and generally skillful. Footnotes explain differences between the text of the Latin Vulgate and the Hebrew and Greek originals and clarify obscure terms and customs for the reader. The notes occasionally reflect characteristic positions of Roman Catholic theology. The text includes passages now known to be spurious (those found also in the King James Version – see p. 44), retains Latinized forms of the names of biblical books, persons, and places, and presents much Old Testament poetry as prose.

In spite of its limitations – apparent to us now but unapparent to most of his contemporary British Catholics – the version was a great success and paved the way for Catholic acceptance of the New American Bible and the ecumenical editions of the Revised Standard Version (see pp. 47, 50).

The Authentic New Testament (1 ed.); **The Original New Testament** (2 ed.) by Hugh J. Schonfield

The translator, a British Jew who has written extensively on the New Testament, believes he is the first Jew to translate the New Testament into English (1955). He holds that because of his Jewish background and learning he can translate the New Testament better than any Gentile can. He has drawn heavily on Jewish sources in his translating and in his commenting on the text (in extensive footnotes).

Schonfield approaches the New Testament books 'as if they had recently been recovered from a cave in Palestine or beneath the sands of Egypt and had never previously been given to the public.' He wants to reveal the New Testament exactly as it was written, to cut away convention and tradition in the way it is translated, and to give the reader 'a New Testament authentic in accent and atmosphere.'

A lengthy introduction to first-century Christianity, to the Palestinian background of the New Testament, and to the New Testament texts themselves prepares the way for the translation. Maps, plans, and illustrations increase the usefulness of the work.

Traditional chapter and verse divisions are abandoned. The New Testament text is divided into sections under numbers and captions as the translator sees fit. Many captions are strikingly appropriate. One finds rearrangement in the order of passages within individual books and conjectural changes of wording.

The translation is often vivid and forceful. Fresh words are selected for old ones (for example, 'envoys' for 'apostles'; 'the News' for 'the gospel'). The reader who is accustomed to the more traditional translations of the New Testament will often be startled by what is found here, but the discovery will stimulate the reader to ask questions about the New Testament that would not otherwise have been considered. Second edition 1985.

The New Testament in Modern English
Four Prophets: Amos, Hosea, First Isaiah, Micah
by J.B. Phillips

Starting in 1947 with Letters to Young Churches, J.B. Phillips of England began to publish highly successful translations of the Scriptures, as follows: The Gospels in Modern English, 1952; The Young Church in Action, 1955 (the book of the Acts); The Book of Revelation, 1957; The New Testament in Modern English, 1958 (the entire New Testament); Four Prophets: Amos, Hosea, First Isaiah, Micah, 1963; a revised edition of the New Testament, 1973.

Three principles have controlled his work: the translation must not sound like a translation; the translator's personality must not obtrude; the translator must create in the reader an effect equivalent to that produced in the original readers by the author. Phillips has followed these principles with high fidelity.

There are two stages in Phillips' work: that of youthful, and somewhat careless, enthusiasm; and that of maturing, more careful scholarship. His earlier translations paraphrased freely and attempted to be startling, shocking, or even slapstick. Expressions close to slang and even what many would regard as swearing were used: 'for God's sake' (Mark 5:7); 'to hell with you' (Acts 8:19); 'may he be damned' (Gal. 1:9). The attempt to modernize led him to translate 'anoint your head' (Matt. 6:17) as 'brush your hair'; 'rob no one by violence' (Luke 3:14) became 'don't bully people'; and 'Paul had made one statement' (Acts 28:25) is rendered 'Paul added as a parting shot.' Folksy remarks, not in the Greek text, were thrown in: such as, 'as I am sure you realise', or 'you must know by now'. Such renderings appealed to the youth groups for which he first began to translate the New Testament.

His revised edition of the New Testament of 1973 shows much more accuracy in translation and restraint in language. It is based on a better Greek text (the United Bible Societies' of 1966, rather than the Greek text behind the Revised Version of 1881). He himself has written, 'I felt I must curb my youthful enthusiasms and keep as close as I possibly could to the Greek text.' He had become recognized around the world as an authoritative Bible translator and felt that his readers deserved better scholarship. In the revised edition there are more than two-thousand improvements and corrections.

His work on the prophets is generally regarded as inferior to that on the New Testament. He found that the Hebrew text did not lend itself to the sort of translating at which he was best. The lofty, dignified oracles of the prophets did not translate easily and effectively into colloquial English. No further work on the Old Testament has appeared to date.

The New Testament – A New Translation
by William Barclay

Perhaps the finest contemporary interpreter of the New Testament for the average person has been William Barclay of the University of Glasgow. His many articles, commentaries, word studies, and monographs, his years of teaching, and his unusual success in writing at a popular level superbly equipped him for translating the New Testament for today's readers.

His translation of the New Testament appears in two volumes: The Gospels and the Acts of the Apostles (1968); and The Letters and the Revelation (1969). A one-volume paperback edition came out in 1980.

Barclay's aim was to make the New Testament understandable by the average person without the use of commentaries. To do this he occasionally enlarged on what the text actually says so as to include necessary explanations. Here 'translation' became 'commentary.' In a section in Volume 2 titled 'Notes on Passages,' he justifies expanding twenty-two passages in order to bring out their meaning for contemporary readers. Fortunately, his fine scholarship gives him the right (if indeed any one can have this right!) to expand where meanings are not obvious. Some scholars and churchmen have strongly criticized him for 'arrogance' in putting his own interpretations into the biblical text.

The translation is usually accurate, clear, and often sparkling. The reader finds many helps: a section on problems and principles in translating the New Testament; brief introductions to all the New Testament books and to groups of books; definitions of and comments on many important New Testament words, alphabetically arranged; and notes on difficult passages. The books in each section of the New Testament are arranged according to Barclay's understanding of their chronological order (for example, Mark, Matthew, Luke, Acts, John).

There is a good deal of Barclay in this version of the New Testament –

something that his admirers will appreciate and others call into question. That he has helped thousands of average people all over the world to understand the New Testament can scarcely be gainsaid.

The Living Bible Paraphrased
by Kenneth N. Taylor

All accurate translation is to a considerable extent paraphrase, a restatement of an author's thought in different words. What is more than translation in paraphrase is properly 'commentary.' There is indeed a sizable slice of commentary in this paraphrased Bible, which reflects, as the Preface states, 'a rigid evangelical position.'

This paraphrase appeared in installments over some fifteen years. The complete Living Bible was published in 1971. Its phenomenal sale indicates the public's hunger for a Bible in the language of today.

Taylor did not work from the original Hebrew and Greek texts, but paraphrased the English text of the American Standard Version of 1901. (He says that his paraphrase was reviewed by Hebrew and Greek scholars, whom he does not name.)

However, he did not reproduce faithfully the text of the American Standard Version but in many places added and deleted as he thought best. Unfortunately, he followed no clear principles of textual criticism where he departed from the American Standard Version text.

He restored to the text passages that the American Standard Version had dropped to footnotes (for example, Matt. 17:21; 18:11; Mark 15:28; John 5:3b–4; Acts 8:37; 24:6b–8a; Rom. 16:24). In these cases he usually indicated in a footnote that some ancient manuscripts do not have the passage. But by putting them into the text he registered his vote for their authenticity – against the verdict of the American Standard Version and the best textual scholars of today.

He added (without footnotes), 'Let's go out into the fields' (Gen. 4:8) and 'Arabs' (Jer. 9:25) – words not contained in the American Standard Version (and the latter in no ancient text). He dropped names from the text he was paraphrasing (Num. 27:1), lumped musical instruments together as 'the band' (Dan. 3:5, 10), left out clauses ('that all might believe through him' – John 1:7), and introduced comments that bear little resemblance to the text (1 Cor. 1:15).

His footnotes to the text offer alternative translations, meanings believed implied, literal renderings, and interpretive comments. Unfortunately, the 'implied' sometimes suggests what is not implied by the text (see, for example, the notes on Matt. 15:21; Mark 1:2; Rom. 3:21; Heb. 5:7; 9:18). Sometimes the interpretive comments inject conclusions on historical matters that are highly debatable, if not erroneous. It is not true that 'all commentators believe him [the disciple sitting next to Jesus at the table] to be John, the writer of this book' (footnote on John 13:23). It is not sound interpretation to inject the first person pronoun into Psalm 132 so as to make David the author of that psalm.

Inaccuracies and inadequacies of paraphrase appear. For example, 'the Tree of Conscience' (Gen. 2:9, 17) introduces a Greek concept into a Hebrew phrase; the Hebrew people were not 'Israelis' (Ex. 9:4; 1 Sam. 14:21; Isa. 14:1) – a modern term; ancient Assyria was not 'Iraq' (Isa. 19:23); Rabbah (modern Amman) has no 'beautiful harbor' (2 Sam. 12:27); 'Sheol' to the Hebrew did not mean 'hell' (Ps. 9:17; Isa. 5:14); getting to heaven does not properly render Paul's meaning in the words 'salvation' and 'righteousness' (Rom. 1:16, 17; 3:21; 4:4); a particular (and debatable) theory of the atonement is injected into Romans 3:25 and 1 John 2:2.

On the positive side, the economy and felicity of expression often delight the reader: 'I would only be making noise' (1 Cor. 13:1); 'nothing you do for the Lord is ever wasted' (1 Cor. 15:58). There is a helpful tendency to make the general and abstract simple and concrete. Long, difficult sentences are shortened into simple ones. The language is often racy and even indelicate (John 9:34; Ruth 2:5; 1 Sam. 1:16; Acts 4:36; 23:3) – an element that may appeal to some in our culture.

The major question concerning this paraphrase probably will be, How can I know what is Bible and what is commentary? The answer must be that without a good translation (or several good translations) to lay beside this paraphrase one cannot.

It will have value for people who have little knowledge of the Bible and who wish to read it rapidly. Those who wish to 'study' the Bible and seek out in depth its historical and theological meaning should adopt one of the official committee translations described above.

The Amplified Bible

This translation stems basically from the work of Frances E. Siewert, who devoted a lifetime of research to it. It was issued under the auspices of the Lockman Foundation. It appeared first in three sections (New Testament, 1958; Job to Malachi, 1962; Genesis to Esther, 1964) and as a whole Bible in 1965.

Its purpose is 'to reveal, together with the single-word English equivalent to each key Hebrew [and Greek] word, any other clarifying shades of meaning that may have been concealed by the traditional word-for-word method of translation.' Multiple English words and phrases are inserted in brackets in the text to suggest the range of meanings in key biblical words and phrases.

The text is printed in verse-by-verse arrangement, as in the King James Version, rather than by paragraphs. Poetry is not printed as poetry. There are no sectional headings. Notes to the text justify amplifications, introduce explanatory materials, and offer comments aimed to support the veracity of biblical statements.

The loading of the Scriptural text with amplifying synonyms results in a very wordy translation. 1 Corinthians 10:13, for example, is translated in the Revised Standard Version with 44 words but here with 139 words. Precise translation results from the selection of the proper meaning of a word to express the thought the biblical writer intended. It does not help to list meanings the biblical writer did not have in mind. Many of the amplifications, instead of adding to the meaning of the text, actually confuse and detract from it.

Dubious interpretations often are inserted in the brackets. For example, Genesis 1:26 is rendered, 'God said, Let us (Father, Son, and Holy Spirit) make mankind in Our image,' whereas the 'us' may refer to God and the heavenly court (Ps. 82:1; 89:5–7) or it may be a plural of majesty, such as ancient kings used in self-glorification. In 1 Corinthians 7:38 the insertion of the words 'the father' and 'his daughter, virgin' decides categorically the meaning of a much debated passage, for which there are at least three possible interpretations – hardly a fair procedure from the standpoint of the uninformed reader.

This translation and amplification should be used with caution. It is not representative of the best biblical scholarship of our time.

Some Guidelines in Selecting a Version

The number of English versions available to people in our time is almost staggering. At no time in history has more effort, time, and money been expended in making the Bible intelligible to the world's people, including the English-speaking. Some people believe that the proliferation of versions is a hindrance to genuine knowledge of the Bible – particularly to its memorization. Church school teachers are wondering which version of the twenty-third Psalm or of the Beatitudes to inscribe on the minds of their children.

No precise answer to this problem can be given. We shall have to live with the confusing multiplicity of translations and attempt to turn what may seem a hindrance to biblical understanding into an asset. Here are some guidelines to think about in selecting a version.

1. Select a version that is suited to the needs of the person who is to use it.

The simple, direct language of The Good News Bible and its cartoon-like illustrations will appeal to children and young people more than the classical language of the New King James Version and the New International Version.

The businessman on the run, who has little knowledge of the Bible, may find the Reader's Digest Bible intriguing.

The adult church member, long immersed in Scripture, may prefer a version that maintains much of the traditional language of the King James Version, such as the Revised Standard Version and The New International Version.

The college and seminary student and the studious church member may wish a translation that reflects the idioms and structure of the underlying Hebrew and Greek text – a literal translation. They should consult the New American Standard Version.

The Roman Catholic will want the Jerusalem Bible or The New American Bible and the Jew The New Jewish Version.

The Basic Bible is invaluable for new readers of English.

Several of the individual translations (Schonfield, Phillips, Barclay) are excellent for private, at-home reading but unsuited or less suitable for Bible study groups and regular pulpit use.

For the first time in the history of the English language there are English Bibles for most kinds of readers – an inestimable asset. No one Bible translation can meet the needs of all readers.

2. Select a version that was made from the best Hebrew and Greek texts now available.

Scholars have been at work for over a hundred years comparing the texts of ancient manuscripts, investigating the ancient translations of the Scriptures and the quotations and references to them in the writings of early Jewish rabbis and church fathers – thereby discovering the mistakes, additions, and deletions of medieval and earlier copyists of biblical texts. This search for the original text (see pp. 368ff) is carried on by the major Bible societies of the world through the efforts of both conservative and liberal scholars. It is not a partisan effort. To ignore all this valuable work by using a translation based on an inferior text of the Old and New Testaments is lamentable, to say the least.

The King James Version, The New King James Version, the Ronald A. Knox translation, The Living Bible, and The Amplified Bible wholly or partly lack the benefits of modern textual study.

Today the best text of the Hebrew Old Testament is to be found in the Biblia Hebraica Stuttgartensis and of the Greek New Testament in Nestle-Aland's Novum Testamentum Graece (26th edition) or the United Bible Societies' The Greek New Testament (3rd edition). The committee translators of our time (in The Revised Standard Version, The New English Bible, The New American Bible, The Good News Bible, the New International Version, The New American Standard Version), while basing their translation largely on the printed texts listed above (or on earlier editions of them), departed in places from these texts when the evidence for a different reading seemed compelling to them. But no translators of the Bible in our time can afford to ignore these texts and return to the Received Text (the

Erasmus-Beza text) that lay behind The King James Version, as The New King James Version translators have done. Usually the Preface to a version will indicate what texts the translators have used.

3. Give preference to official committee versions, rather than to individual translations.

The reasons for this are simple. No one person can know all that one really needs to know to translate the Bible. The text of the Bible arose over a period of more than a thousand years and out of ancient, oriental languages and cultures. Information from research on those difficult languages and complex cultures is accumulating so rapidly that no one person can assimilate it all. Several specialists, pooling their information, have a better chance of arriving at a sound judgment concerning the meaning of the biblical text than any one person working alone.

Furthermore, every translator has presuppositions and prejudices. Unwittingly these presuppositions will be injected into the text if there is no one to check and correct the translator. Committees debate long (and sometimes loudly!) and in the end vote on how the text is to be translated. This process assures the exclusion of eccentric translations and results not only in accuracy but in aptness of expression.

4. Select a version whose translators (or translator) are from the same cultural background as the contemplated reader.

American readers will find British translations replete with Briticisms: 'labour' for 'labor'; 'twopence' for 'two pennies'; 'fortnight' for 'fifteen days'; 'corn' for 'grain'; 'Whitsuntide' for 'Pentecost'; etc. British readers find 'barbarisms' in American versions. The differences in American and British English explain why consultants from the opposite culture are sometimes added to a translating committee and why American and British editions of a translation are published.

5. Sample a translation before adopting it.

Read the creation story in Genesis 1, the nineteenth and twenty-third Psalms, the Beatitudes in Matthew 5, Paul's chapter on love (1 Cor. 13). Is the English simple and clear? Does the language fit the subject matter? Do you feel 'at home' in that kind of English? Is the text arranged in paragraphs with captions? Are there footnotes to assist you in understanding the text? Is the print of satisfactory size and quality?

For Further Reading

Bailey, L.R. (ed.), *The Word of God: A Guide to English Versions of the Bible,* 1982.

Kubo, S. and Specht, W.F., *So Many Versions? Twentieth Century Versions of the Bible,* 1983.

Lewis, J.P., *The English Bible from KJV to NIV: A History and Evaluation,* 1981.

The Interpretation of the Bible

The Protestant Reformation put the Bible in the hands of the common people, asked them to read and digest it, to apply its teachings to their personal and social life, and to weigh all church pronouncements in the light of its teachings.

The Roman Catholic Church long challenged the Protestant emphasis on scriptural, rather than ecclesiastical, authority and the responsibility of all people to interpret and apply the Bible for themselves. The Catholic position was that the church, under its apostles and their successors, was invested with final authority by Christ; that the church, from whose life the Bible sprang, is properly the Bible's custodian and interpreter; and that individual lay interpreters are seldom learned and skillful enough to interpret it without serious error.

Since Pope Pius XII's encyclical *Divino Afflante Spiritu* of 1943 and the famous church council known as Vatican II, a revolution has occured in Roman Catholic attitudes toward the Bible. Vatican II declared: 'It is necessary that the faithful have full access to Sacred Scripture.' This far-seeing and progressive council saw that, with respect to non-Catholics, 'Sacred Scripture makes an excellent tool in the powerful hand of God for the attainment of that unity which the Savior offers to all men.' It is a fact that common biblical interest and study have done much to unite Protestants and Catholics.

There is growing agreement today among Catholic and Protestant scholars on the nature of the Scriptures and how readers should relate to them. We now see that the Bible is not an 'it' – a *thing* to be analyzed, dissected, rearranged according to our view of historical development, set in its cultural framework, and thus 'mastered' by us. The Bible is more a 'thou' than an 'it'. Behind the written words stand people. Written words are the thoughts, feelings, and desires of people, indicated by the hand through symbols instead of by the tongue. Words, whether oral or written, are people in projection or extension.

In the Bible we are addressed by people. We are to listen carefully, ponder the message until the meaning is clear, and respond to it in some appropriate way. We are to carry on a conversation or dialogue with the people behind the words; we are not to treat the Bible as if it were a laboratory specimen.

The dialogue with the Bible thus involves two major steps: (1) we are to examine the text carefully so we understand exactly what its authors intended to say; (2) we are to let the text examine us so that its message may have its intended effect.

Both steps can be taken by individuals working independently, or they can be taken with others. Martin Luther found transformation through his own dialogue with Paul in the letter to the Romans. The synagogue at Beroea undertook group study of the Scriptures to see if Paul's message concerning the Savior Jesus was valid, with striking results for many (Acts 17:11–12).

Actually, for the fullest dialogue with the Bible both individual and group involvement are necessary. The Bible has a very personal word and a social word. By sharing in a group what has been communicated to individuals alone, everyone will grasp more adequately the full message and respond in a way that embraces both individual and group life. Furthermore, a group approach to the Scriptures will correct subjective, eccentric interpretations and applications.

Here are some guidelines within these two major steps:

Careful Examination of the Text

a. Interpret Biblical Materials in the Light of the Circumstances in Which They Were Originally Written and Read.

Biblical writers directed their message to people of their own day. Their readers had particular needs and problems due to the events and circumstances of their place and time. The message was delivered in language and forms of thought the readers could understand.

We must, therefore, project ourselves as best we can into the first readers' situation. We must investigate the social, economic, political, and religious conditions and the customs and the major events of their time. We must find out all we can about the author and the reasons for addressing *those* people at *that* particular moment.

b. Interpret Biblical Passages in the Light of Their Basic Literary Type.

All present-day writings fall into forms or types, according to their purpose and function. The business letter has its characteristic formal marks, as do the love letter and the letter home from a family member. If entertainment is the goal, there are the jingle, the short story, the skit, the novel. If the purpose is serious instruction, there are the essay, the drama, the textbook. If motivation to action is intended, there are the sermon, the religious tract, the political pamphlet.

Ancient writings also had specific relation to life situations, forms adapted to functions. In fact, ancient writers were probably more bound by conventional forms than are modern authors. Ancient customs required poetic pieces for many occasions in life: wedding songs, work songs, funeral dirges, victory songs, songs for worship, prophetic oracles (declarations) in times of national crisis, laments for occasions of national mourning, and the like.

Prose compositions filled their appointed functions in personal and national life: speeches, sermons, prayers, contracts, personal and official

The flood account on a tablet from the Assyrian version of the Epic of Gilgamesh.

letters, legal codes, genealogies, official annals, historical narratives, autobiographies, sagas (traditional stories about ancestors and national heroes), fables, riddles, visions of the future (apocalypses), gospels, and letters to churches.

Every type of literature has characteristics of its own, including a customary vocabulary and style, a certain formal structure, and a particular kind of thought content. Poetry must not be interpreted as if it were prose. Poetry makes large use of figurative language and thus suggests more than it actually says. Hebrew poetry has a distinctive characteristic called 'parallelism,' which puts ideas together in various ways (see p. 145). Alphabetic poems are poems in which each line begins with a different letter of the Hebrew alphabet in sequence.

The prose compositions present wide variations which must be taken into account in order to understand them. Sagas require treatment different from chronicles or annals. Gospels are not biographies or works of history but rather testimonials to faith in Jesus as Savior and Lord. Letters to specific churches are quite unlike essays addressed to a general public.

The approach to the Bible from the standpoint of its literary forms or types is absolutely basic to the correct understanding of it.

c. Interpret Words and Passages in the Light of Their Historical and Literary Context.

It is common knowledge that many words have changed their meaning over a considerable period of time. For example, when the King James Version was first issued, 'prevent' meant 'to go before'; today it means 'to hinder.'

It is important, therefore, to investigate the basic meaning or meanings of an important biblical word in the time when it was used in the biblical passage under consideration. These possible meanings should then be tested to see which fits the passage best.

Derivation of words (etymology) can be misleading. The English word 'nice' comes from the Latin *nescius*, meaning 'ignorant'. This is not what 'nice' means today! The meaning of a word is determined by its context, not by what root it may have come from.

There are two kinds of context: the immediate and the remote. Words constitute links in a chain. Each chain consists of an idea. Ideas put together form paragraphs, sections, and whole books. The immediate context is the sentence in which the word belongs, the sentences immediately before and after, and the paragraph as a whole in which the word is imbedded.

The remote context consists of the larger associations of the word or passage. There are degrees of remoteness, of course. The sections, the book as a whole, other books written by the same author, and the other literature of the same period belong to the remote context.

Our task in a particular passage is to discover the direction in which the author's thought is moving and to see which of several possible meanings of a difficult word or phrase best contributes to the progress of thought.

d. Respect the Individuality of the Various Biblical Writers.

If the Bible consists of a library of books written by many different authors over a period of a thousand years or more, we should expect considerable diversity in point of view among the writings. The personality and experience of writers are stamped on their creation.

We must not import Paul's theology into Matthew's account of Jesus' ministry, or Luke's theology into John's Gospel. If we do, we shall distort the distinctive witness of each writer and reduce the rich, many-sided testimony concerning Jesus to one uninspired and uninspiring version.

We can see the damage to sound biblical interpretation caused by failure to respect the individuality of the various writers in one commentator's exposition of Gen. 1:16. He declares that 'the greater light' (the sun) and 'the lesser light' (the moon) stand for 'Christ and His people' on the ground that in Mal. 4:2 'the sun of righteousness … with healing in its wings' refers to Jesus Christ and in Rev. 12:1 the moon represents Israel and the church. To

King David and musicians pictured in the medieval Ormesby Psalter.

import Jesus Christ and the church into the creation story in this manner violates all sound principles of interpretation.

We do the authors no honor if we force them all into one pattern. It is when we see clearly how different they are that we shall appreciate how similar they are.

e. Take Biblical Materials, First of All, in Their Literal Sense.

The literal sense is the meaning intended by the author or authors in a particular piece of writing. The literal sense differs from meanings the material may have taken on in the minds of others, contemporary or later in time. These other, more-than-literal meanings are sometimes called 'spiritual', 'allegorical,' 'typological,' or 'symbolic.'

The literal sense allows for the use of metaphorical devices (similies, metaphors, parables, allegories, symbols) as legitimate ways of conveying meaning. The literal sense rules out only meanings foreign to the author's original intent.

In the history of the church, secondary, alien meanings often overshadowed the literal or historical sense. Many interpreters of the biblical text put what it meant to them ahead of what it meant when it was first written. It has been the merit of modern historical study to cut through these alien interpretations to the original meanings.

f. Look at Specific Passages in the Light of the Whole Bible and the History of the Christian Church.

It is quite right to hold that biblical materials can mean more to us than they did or could to their original authors. If God was working out a purpose in the total history of Israel and the Christian church, it is not strange that early participants in that history could not understand the full meaning of their words and deeds and that it should be given to later persons to grasp that meaning in the light of subsequent events.

New Testament writers saw many Old Testament statements and events as pointing beyond themselves to a fulfillment realized in Jesus Christ and the Christian church. Isaiah 53, when read today in the light of the career of Jesus of Nazareth, takes on a meaning in harmony with, but not fully identical with, its meaning when written, some five centuries before the coming of Jesus. Likewise, Jeremiah's prophecy concerning the new covenant (31:31–34) was fulfilled by God (Heb. 8) in a way Jeremiah did not and could not conceive of.

In short, we may not exhaust the full meaning of a passage simply by determining by historical methods what was originally meant by the person who wrote it. However, we distort rather than interpret Scripture if the full meaning we see in a passage is not to some extent in harmony with the literal sense.

Examination of the Reader by the Text

A generation ago many biblical interpreters scrutinized the Bible 'objectively,' in a somewhat detached scientific manner. They assumed that different interpreters, using the same tools of interpretation, would arrive at the same results – provided they kept their personal points of view out of their work.

Today we see that a strict objectivity is impossible. We are the product of unique personal experiences and of a particular family, national, and cultural background. We cannot divest ourselves of our presuppositions and our social conditioning any more than we can shed our skin or change the color of our eyes. We can only seek to understand and allow for our background.

In regard to answering the ultimate questions of life, we are no better off than ancient people; certainly we are in no position to sit in judgment on them. In fact, what they were and what they wrote down scrutinize us quite as much as we scrutinize them.

If this is true, then statements about our attitude as we seek to understand the biblical text are in order.

a. We Should Come to the Bible with an Alert, Open Mind, and Be Ready to Accept and Obey Whatever Message the Spirit of God May Impart.

Some people come to the Bible for arguments with which to uphold their opinions and prejudices rather than to discover the will of God for their lives and find strength to obey it. Others come for an aesthetic experience. They want to sample the Bible's stories and savor its ancient wisdom. They too have no interest in God's word and its relation to their lives. They sometimes claim that no religious orientation or special piety is needed for interpreting the Bible; all one needs are the proper tools of literary interpretation.

Such people can perhaps enter part way into biblical truth, but its deeper dimensions elude them. What would a person who has never made the venture of faith in Jesus Christ make out of Galatians 2:20: 'I have been crucified with Christ; it is no longer I who live, but Christ who lives in me; and the life I now live in the flesh I live by faith in the Son of God, who loved me and gave himself for me'? It is doubtful that those with only a literary interest in the Bible can understand the radiant sense of salvation that fills the New Testament.

Readers of the Bible need eyes alert to literary phenomena, but they also need 'eyes of faith' and the willingness to act on the truth which they discover there. A spirit of quiet expectancy and receptivity is essential in one's encounter with the writers of the Bible. One scholar has said, 'The attitude of Bible-reading is rather that of a lover waiting at the trysting-place than that of a general storming a citadel' (Alan Richardson, *Preface to Bible-Study*, 1944, p. 17).

b. In Sustained, Prayerful Exposure to the Bible, Both in Individual and Group Study, We Shall See Ourselves, Our World, and God in the Mirror of the Bible.

The amazing popularity of the Bible in our world today attests to its power to affect contemporary readers. But how can people trained in modern science and with a modern world view derive any benefit from documents nineteen hundred or more years old? As someone has put it, the issue is, 'What can a bunch of camel drivers say to us who live in the jet age?'

The relevance of ancient documents was a problem faced by Hellenistic, Jewish, and Christian writers of the time of Paul and the early church and, indeed, by thinkers in every age since. What was the meaning of the old Greek myths and the writings of Homer for philosophically minded people centuries later? How were the ancient laws of Moses and the institutions of Israel, described in the books of the fathers, to be related to the thought and practices of Jews living under cultural conditions vastly different from the time of Moses? Christians of every age have had to decide what the Scriptures should mean for them. The problem will remain as long as the Scriptures and human life continue.

There is no neat formula for deciding what in ancient documents is relevant for modern readers and precisely how. We can venture only a few suggestions here.

Present-day Christian existentialists have said that what binds us to ancient people is our common humanity. In every age human beings have fundamentally the same problems, needs, and aspirations. Hunger, sickness, human and natural enemies, and death beset us. The great human ventures are alike: love and marriage, the conception and birth of children, the struggle for economic and political security, the quest for life's meaning.

Not only are the needs of people much the same, but the resources available to them are similar. One may seek to control the hostile forces of nature through the practice of magic and to overcome human enemies through military power. One may seek by individual or collective wits (including traditional 'wisdom') to work out a secure position in an insecure world. Or one may accept one's lot as inevitable, the will of God or the gods, and attempt to make the best of one's circumstances. Or again one may believe that human effort may be undergirded by divine strength and seek through prayer and action to determine the divine will and to ally oneself with it.

Human existence – in its limitations and possibilities – thus offers us common ground with people of all ages.

The Bible, the Old Testament as well as the New, is supremely the place where God reveals man and his predicament to man himself; that is why we can hold up the Old Testament ... as a mirror in which we can see our own reflected image. In the Old

Winged bull with a human face, from the entrance to the palace of Asshur-nasir-pal II (884–860 BC), Nimrud.

Testament, we might say, God shows us as in a mirror what we are; and in the New Testament he reveals to us the image of what we shall become, shining in the face of Jesus Christ. (Alan Richardson, *The Bible in the Age of Science*, 1961, p. 121.)

The Bible characterizes human existence in pictorial, symbolic, dramatic language. It represents good and evil, God and the devil, angels and demons as locked in military combat, with humanity enticed and pressured to ally itself with one side or the other. It says that the struggle will be resolved in a military-type victory, the field of battle bestrewed with the corpses of the slain (for example, Rev. 19:11–21).

When God is represented as a heavenly king, who sits on a throne with a rainbow around it (Rev. 4:1–6), or when God is said, as in Ps. 80:1, to be 'enthroned upon the cherubim' – that is, upon winged lions or bulls such as decorated the thrones of ancient kings – it is obvious that language and concepts ordinarily applied to human kings are used metaphorically of God.

We must recognize the dramatic, symbolic, pictorial language and search for the concepts underlying it. We must distinguish between *what* is said and *how* it is said. Ancient picture language, while admittedly different for modern people, is not impossible to penetrate, if modern readers are alert to its nature and function.

By looking in the biblical mirror, doors to a kind of existence beyond our imagination may open to us and our world.

For Further Reading
Caird, G. B., *The Language and Imagery of the Bible*, 1980.
Doty, W. G., *Contemporary New Testament Interpretation*, 1972.
Marshall, I. H. (ed.), *New Testament Interpretation*, 1977.
Smart, J. D., *The Interpretation of Scripture*, 1961.

Major Approaches to the Bible

The Bible has been not only the most perused book of human history but the most intensively and systematically investigated as well. Especially has this been true since the Age of the Enlightenment (seventeenth and eighteenth centuries).

Scholars have probed it from every conceivable angle, particularly from an historical perspective. Since they readily saw that its books came out of antiquity and ministered to readers at the time when they were first written, they judged it appropriate to estimate their meaning then and now in the light of the historical circumstances out of which they arose. Thus historical criticism ('criticism' meaning impartial investigation, not disparagement) came into being.

But not all modern forms of critical study have approached the Bible from the historical perspective. Some literary experts of today are viewing the Bible strictly as a literary phenomenon, quite apart from its historical rootage. In that rootage they do not have much interest (see below, under 'Literary Criticism'). And there have always been doctrinaire people (some passing as 'scholars') who have used the Bible for personal and sectarian advantage. For them the historical contexts of the biblical writings are both irrelevant and embarrassing.

The approaches to the Bible in recent centuries have been so many in number and variety that they defy cataloguing or description here. Only a few major ones can be listed.

1. Technical, Scholarly Approaches

a. Literary Criticism
In this approach the Bible is viewed as piece of world literature and studied as one would study any other literary creation. Most scholars using this technique stress the Bible's historical background as a clue to its correct interpretation, but some do not.

The historically oriented scholars have examined the Bible's books individually, in their canonical groupings, and in their relationships to the whole collection. They have assembled information about such matters as: their original texts, when freed from copyists' errors; their authorship, date, original readers, and purpose(s); the sources out of which their material came and how it was assimilated or edited; the structure of the individual books and pieces; the characteristics of vocabulary and style of writing in the various literary types; the major issues, themes, and theological concepts informing the writings and how these are presented; the similarities to and differences from known bodies of literature from other nations and cultures.

Of special interest to literary critics in recent centuries has been the process by which biblical materials came into being and whether passages and books are unified or composite. A prominent goal has been the compiling of a history of the growth of the literature of Israel and the church through correlating it with the known historical facts about those communities.

Some interpreters of the Bible, under the influence of the secularized Western culture of our present time, have turned away from both the historical and theological aspects of the Bible and are seeing it purely as a phenomenon of language and literary art. For the most part, these interpreters teach in secular universities and colleges. Their study of the Bible as literature rests on their interest in the Bible's presentation of the human situation and in the forms of language – symbols, patterns of imagery, genres (literary categories), plot structures, etc. – by which the human mind, in a kind of language code, expresses itself. The ultimate focus of their interest is the human mind. Whether there is historical and theological truth in the Bible and what that truth should mean to us is simply bypassed.

Literary criticism has been of immense value in genuine understanding of the Bible, especially when it has been carried out by scholars who are interested both in its historical background and in its religious and theological perspectives.

b. Form and Tradition Criticism

Classical literary criticism of the Bible attempted to identify, among other things, the written sources from which certain Old and New Testament materials were derived.

Early in the twentieth century scholars (Gunkel, Dibelius, Bultmann) began to probe the sources for evidence concerning the types of material they contained and for clues concerning their origin in the life of Israel and the church. They identified many forms (genres or categories) of material, such as speeches, sermons, prayers, contracts, letters, lists, laws, myths, sagas, proverbs, songs (work songs, wedding songs, dirges, victory songs), prophetic sayings, sayings of Jesus (proverbs, parables, prophetic and apocalyptic sayings, 'I' sayings, etc.), stories about Jesus (pronouncement stories, miracles stories, legends, myths). They concluded that the material in each of these forms served a practical function in the particular aspect of the life of the community out of which it arose, that it first existed orally, that it was handed down to subsequent generations in brief oral units, and that it was later recorded in written documents. They noted that in many parts of the

Bible the text seems to have been constructed out of brief, loosely joined pieces (as in the book of Genesis or in the Synoptic Gospels), pieces that can be understood better in their original life situations than in their present contexts.

They found that material handed along orally, whether for shorter or longer periods, tended to be reshaped to meet the needs of the situations in life in which it was used. It was influenced also by stories (folklore, which indeed it itself was) that were circulating in the outside cultural world of successive periods. Further reshaping occured at the literary stage, when the material was incorporated in our present texts (see under 'Redaction Criticism' below).

German scholars, in particular, believed that the tradition had become so altered through use and transmission that little confidence can now be placed in its historical reliability. On the other hand, Scandinavian scholars tended to hold that the tradition was passed along in a culture (Semitic) which stressed exact memorization and by authoritative and responsible transmitters, who sought to preserve its accuracy.

In sum, we may say that Form criticism has pointed out that Israel's and the church's historical memories, as now enshrined in many of the biblical texts, served community life on its many sides and tell us as much (or more) about the periods through which they were transmitted as about the original persons and events they describe. The texts have a long history, are in a real sense the creations of a community over a considerable period of time, and are not just products from the minds of individual authors.

c. Redaction Criticism

This is the study of the way older elements of tradition (usually written) were joined together, edited, and re-edited to form many of our present biblical texts. Redactors or editors selected, combined, and arranged existing materials to create new literary works. The redactors' purposes, mental characteristics, and theology were revealed by what was included, excluded, reshaped, and rearranged.

A good Old Testament example of redaction is to be found in 1 and 2 Chronicles, where material from 1 and 2 Samuel and 1 and 2 Kings has been utilized and re-edited to form a new work for definite purposes (see pp. 137-8). A New Testament example is afforded by the writer of the Gospel of Matthew, who utilized and re-edited the Gospel of Mark, the document Q, and other sources (see pp. 238ff). A writer of this sort is quite different from an author like Paul, who incorporates little previously existing written material in his letters. From redaction criticism scholars learn much about the history of biblical texts and about the theological outlook and purposes of the redactors (editors). Redaction criticism carries forward the process begun by literary criticism and form (tradition) criticism.

d. Canonical Criticism

In recent years some scholars have sought to bridge the gap between what biblical texts meant to their first readers, as determined by historical criticism, and what they should mean to the continuing community of faith and to the contemporary reader. Historical criticism yields little help here.

Canonical criticism starts with the final form of the canonical texts, works backward to the historical process by which they came into being in their unity and diversity, continues with an assessment of the contribution the various canonical writings make to the total canon's witness to God's redemptive activity (particularly and specifically in Jesus Christ), and ends with a call to decision by the readers concerning their response to that witness. It sees the canon as essentially kerygmatic (a proclamation of the gospel) and calling for reader involvement. It holds that the biblical writings cannot be understood if one shares little or nothing of the faith reflected by that literature. Thus the study of the Bible, if it is to be true to the Bible's essential nature, must become more than an antiquarian enterprise.

Canonical criticism holds that the other types of criticism (listed above) are indispensable in biblical interpretation, but they exist to promote an encounter with the witness of the total canon to the God who 'reveal(s) his will through this vehicle, earth-bound and fragile in its very nature' (Brevard S. Childs, whose views are chiefly summarized here).

2. An Average-Reader Approach

It probably will be obvious to you that the above approaches to the Bible exceed your competence. And it might be that, if you followed them out, they would tell you more than you want to know about the Bible anyhow. Is there an approach that will make Bible reading and study an exciting and rewarding experience with the background and level of competence you have? And how can you get access to the discoveries and insights of the biblical scholars without going through their complicated processes?

a. General Considerations

First of all, let's be clear about one thing. The mastery of the Bible, like the mastery of any discipline or skill in life, does not come without intense and constant effort. It is hardly a pursuit for dilettantes. But if you have made up your mind that the Bible is what it claims to be – the witness to Jesus Christ, who is the doorway to Life here and hereafter for yourself, your family, and the entire world – you will want to hear and ponder deeply that witness and share your exciting knowledge with others.

It is regrettable that most Bible-reading is 'catch-as-catch can' reading – a few verses before retiring at night, a paragraph between cups of coffee at the breakfast table, a sample or two to make us feel right before we go to church on Sunday morning. We somehow expect the Bible to yield up its treasures in two minutes flat. While there may be some value in such casual reading, there are dangers also. We may lift passages out of context and misinterpret and misapply them.

One Bible scholar properly reminds us that in Bible reading we need not snapshots but time exposures. We should read when our faculties are most alert, when we have time to ponder the deeper meanings for ourselves, our family, our business, our community, and our world.

We should read the Bible with the kind of excited curiosity scientists have when they are on the track of a new discovery. We should read it the way a young man in the first stages of love pores over a letter from his beloved – not once, hurriedly, but repeatedly, with attention to every detail and the exact meaning of every word.

And we should read the Bible itself, not just books about the Bible, including this *Handbook*. Too many people's knowledge of the Bible is second-hand. They evidently have a basic fear that they will get lost in the Bible's dry lists, archaic vocabulary, and curious symbols. They never experience the thrill of firsthand discovery, develop mature powers of judgment in biblical matters, and come through to a rich personal understanding of the significance of biblical perspectives for their own lives.

All in depth reading of the Bible – like all proper scientific study – proceeds through four basic steps: exact observation of data; interpretation of data; verification of results; and the application of results to life. This is a 'see-for-yourself' procedure.

Such reading requires planning and preparation: regular periods set aside for uninterrupted individual and group study; a proper physical environment; and adequate working tools.

Working equipment should include the following books:
– a modern translation of the Bible by an official committee or a competent scholar (preferably the former – see pp. 42–68)
– a second translation (or more) for sake of comparison
– a concordance to the basic translation being used
– a good one-volume commentary on the Bible
– a theological wordbook or a Bible dictionary
– an atlas to the lands of the Bible
(For suggestions on some of these see pp. 209, 367.)

b. Specific Procedures
Adequate understanding of the Bible, like the understanding of any literature, comes by reading it in logical units. These units may be whole books, sections, or paragraphs. If the material is poetry, the poem or the stanza may

comprise the unit to be grasped. The chapters of the Bible, as now marked off, may or may not be logical units.

It is not difficult to identify units smaller than a whole book. Help is given in modern translations, which divide the text into sections and paragraphs, often headed by titles. Or blank spaces in the text may indicate logical divisions.

Many books of the Bible are reasonably well constructed so that they can be approached as wholes. They are amenable to logical division and investigation by parts.

But one must not expect the kind of logical construction in ancient oriental literature that one finds in modern Western books. There are no author-composed book titles, no writers' prefaces in which they state what they are about, no logically organized tables of contents, no end-of-chapter summaries, and no smooth transitions to subsequent chapters. Loose associaton of related materials, frequent repetition of essentially the same data and of editorial comments, inept expansions and asides, lack of assimilation or rough joining of source materials, and the like, are characteristic of ancient oriental literature (especially before the Hellenistic period) and offend the modern reader's concept of logic and style. Since the books of the New Testament were written to some extent under the influence of Greek literary standards, they are better organized (from our point of view) than most of the Old Testament ones.

All of us in the Western world are heirs of Greek principles of logic and rhetoric. An approach to the Bible for you, the average present-day reader, must then proceed from the literary principles with which you are acquainted and which you consciously or subconsciously employ in general reading. Therefore, a simplified form of the traditional literary criticism described above offers the best path to biblical understanding for you. The exact literary procedures you will use on any given piece of biblical material must be determined by the nature of that material. Unified or relatively unified books must be approached differently from those that are nonunified.

Unfortunately, no clear classification of biblical books as to their degree of unity can be drawn up. Illogical elements are found in the most tightly written of them. It is often unclear whether biblical writers or compilers intended to draw up an integrated body of data or whether they were consciously passing on their material in almost the accidental and haphazard ways in which it came to them, with a minimum of editing. It appears that there is more unity in books containing historical narrative (like 1 and 2 Samuel and Luke-Acts), in letters (like Paul's), and in treatises (like Ephesians and Hebrews) than in books of poetry, wisdom, and prophecy (like Psalms, Proverbs, and Jeremiah), for example. The degree of unity must be taken into account in a study procedure.

Whether a book had one or several authors is not the decisive consideration in determining how it should be read. It is quite possible for several writers to contribute to a book in such a way that the final result holds together fairly logically.

The following outline is a rough guide. Some suggestions for systematic reading will be based on it.

Unified and Relatively Unified Books

Old Testament
Genesis, Exodus, Numbers, Deuteronomy, Joshua, Judges, Ruth, 1 and 2 Samuel, 1 and 2 Kings, 1 and 2 Chronicles, Esther, Daniel, Joel, Obadiah, Jonah, Zephaniah, Haggai, Malachi

Apocrypha
1 Esdras, Tobit, Judith, the Letter of Jeremiah, Susanna, Bel and the Dragon, the Prayer of Manasseh, 1 and 2 Maccabees

New Testament
Matthew, Mark, Luke-Acts, John, Romans, 1 Corinthians, Galatians, Ephesians, Philippians, Colossians, 1 and 2 Thessalonians, 1 and 2 Timothy, Titus, Philemon, Hebrews, 1 and 2 Peter, 1, 2 and 3 John, Jude, Revelation

Nonunified Books

Old Testament
Leviticus, Ezra, Nehemiah, Job, Psalms, Proverbs, Ecclesiastes, Song of Solomon, Isaiah, Jeremiah, Lamentations, Ezekiel, Hosea, Amos, Micah, Nahum, Habakkuk, Zechariah

Apocrypha
2 Esdras, Additions to the Book of Esther, The Wisdom of Solomon, Ecclesiasticus (The Wisdom of Jesus the Son of Sirach), Baruch, The Prayer of Azariah and the Song of the Three Young Men

New Testament
2 Corinthians, James

Reading the Unified and Relatively Unified Books

The procedure I am about to suggest is purposely detailed. It is unlikely that you will have time and patience individually to follow out all the steps. Make a selection of what you wish to do. If you work in a group, you may parcel out the steps and offer reports to the group on the results.

a. Survey the Whole Book
Individual books of the Bible have no table of contents or preface by which we can get an idea of the whole. We can accomplish this only by rapid reading or scanning. You should read books through *at one sitting*, if at all possible. Only thus can you gain a total impression. One writer has said that more than half of the sixty-six books printed in the traditional Protestant Bible can be read through in an average of about twenty minutes. The larger ones can be read selectively and scanned.

The Parthenon, Athens. The West has inherited Greek principles of logic and rhetoric.

In this first survey of the whole book you should look for answers to the following questions:

1. What type of literature is this? As noted in the previous chapter, literature must be interpreted in the light of its basic character.

2. What occasioned the writing of the book? Is the author's name given, and are there any indications concerning the author's whereabouts and circumstances? Are there any references to datable historical events that may offer a clue to the time of writing? Are there references to the condition and circumstances of the original readers and therefore to the author's reason(s) for writing?

3. What are the writer's characteristic words, phrases, concepts, and moods? What words and phrases are most repeated and most central to the writer's thought? Was the writer joyful, angry, reflective, argumentative, hopeful as the writing was done?

4. What gives the book its unity? Is the unifying factor a subject, a person, a group of people, a problem, an event of the past, present, or future? Attempt to state the unity in a sentence or a short paragraph.

5. What is the structure of the book? Has the writer anywhere stated a plan or outline? What are the major blocks of material, and where are the turning points or shifts in subject matter? Note the blank spaces (as in the RSV) or the captions in the text (as in the NEB), which modern editors placed there as an aid to understanding the book's contents. Make a brief outline of the book.

6. What impact has the reading of this book made on you? What do you like and dislike about it? What is puzzling? What message of value has come through to you?

7. How do your results from firsthand reading compare with the conclusions of others who have studied the book?

Turn now to the discussion of this book in Part 2 of this *Handbook* or to a standard introduction to the Old or New Testament or to the introductory portion of a good commentary on the book or to an article on it in a Bible dictionary. Correct and supplement your conclusions.

b. Examine the Parts of the Book.

After you have determined the general layout of a book from your initial survey, you should consider the individual parts which make up the whole.

Be selective in using the steps presented here for examining the parts. Not all parts are worthy of the same depth of scrutiny. The richer and more closely packed a book is, the more detailed the examination should be. Some books should be studied by major divisions only; others should be studied by the sections that comprise the major divisions; and still others deserve a careful analysis of paragraphs and sentences.

Books are like people. Some intrigue and some fatigue. The initial survey should indicate how much time and effort you want to spend on each. In examining a part of a book consider the following questions:

1. What type of material is contained here? The type may vary in the different parts. It is always important to be aware of the character of the material, as we noted on pp. 70–72.

2. What important variations in the wording do the footnotes offer on the basis of ancient manuscripts and versions? How do the alternate words affect the meaning of the passage?

3. Is the part composed of smaller units? A major division will usually break down into sections and paragraphs. The logical parts are not necessarily identical with the traditional chapter divisions. These divisions were made in the thirteenth century and frequently do not break the material at logical points. (In the RSV the translators frequently overrode the chapter divisions: for example, at Gen. 27:46—28:5; Exod. 5:22—6:1; 1 Sam. 3:19—4:1; Mark 8:34—9:1; 1 Cor. 10:31—11:1).

Many contemporary English translations assist the reader by printing the text in paragraphs and by indicating the larger divisions through the use of captions (headings). Rather than relying entirely on the printed captions, you should construct your own. This will help you summarize the material and see the relationship of the parts.

Give special attention to connecting words, such as *and, but, because, for, since, so, therefore, hence, however, nevertheless, finally.* These words help you dissect the thought of a passage at the joints. You must develop X-ray eyes so you can see the skeleton of a book. When you have discovered it, you should put it down in the form of a chart or outline.

4. What use, if any, is made of figures of speech (similies, metaphors, symbols)? What idea is each figure attempting to convey?

5. What are the key words around which the thought of the section or paragraph revolves? To discover the key words of a short unit of biblical material, you should strike out every word that can be eliminated without sacrificing the basic meaning, as we do when we compose a telegram. Examine the remaining important words in the light of the flow of the thought of the passage. It is often possible to determine the meaning of unfamiliar words simply by the drift of thought around them.

· It is helpful also to locate through the use of a concordance other usages of important words in the biblical book under consideration. Read them in their contexts. And finally, consult a lexicon, a Bible dictionary, or a commentary on the meaning of the words in question.

6. What in the passage is still unclear? Unfamilar customs, institutions, events, people, and world views may still remain puzzling to you after the above steps have been taken. Here you should consult a good commentary. A reader of the Bible is only cheated by sliding over things that are not understood.

7. What was the writer's purpose in this part or section? To answer this question the situation of the first readers must be brought into focus again. What did the writer want to tell them and why? What would they have missed if the part under consideration had been left out?

8. What does the passage mean in your own words? As a clinching act, write out the thought of the passage in your own words. If the passage is short, paraphrase it; if long, summarize it.

9. What is the significance of this passage for you and your contemporaries? See the section 'Examination of the Reader by the Text' (pp. 75ff).

c. Review the Whole Book.

A literary scholar has written: 'In the case of the higher literary forms the whole is a different thing from the sum of the parts. It is quite possible to have considered every detail of a literary work and yet tó be far from understanding the work as a whole' (R. G. Moulton, *The Bible at a Single View* [1919], p. 103).

The investigation by major divisions, sections, and paragraphs will lead you to more mature conclusions about the whole book than the initial survey produced. Therefore, a final survey is in order.

1. Investigate the special themes that run like threads through the book. Locate every passage dealing with one theme. It is best to find these passages by rereading the book. A concordance can help if you look up the principal words used in presenting the theme. Group the passages according to what they contain and consider them together. Consult commentaries for help on difficult passages. Draw up conclusions from studying the theme and compare them with the results of others as contained in Part 2 of this *Handbook*, in introductions to the Old and the New Testaments, and in special volumes on the biblical book under consideration.

2. *Restate the theme or message of the book and show how the major parts contribute to its presentation.* You can do this by a logical outline or a chart of the book's contents. How detailed you make it will be determined by the extent of your interest in those contents.

3. *Relate the message of the entire book to the situation of its first readers.* How did it speak to their needs?

4. *Summarize the meaning of the book for your own life and its possible significance for our times.* As pointed out before, the Bible evaluates us quite as much as we evaluate it. Here we must pray for understanding, that we neither fall into credulous acceptance of everything we read in the Bible nor proudly and self-righteously reject what does not meet our preconceptions. Perhaps three questions will help here.

How does my life look from the standpoint of this book – my personal beliefs, my emotions, my attitudes toward myself and toward others, my actions, my goals? How would contemporary life be affected if the message here were universally accepted and acted on? How does the teaching of this book check out with truth from other sources – from science, psychology, sociology, philosophy?

Reading the Nonunified Books

As explained above, nonunified books are collections of literary pieces, loosely – and often illogically – arranged. These books fall into several classes: many of the books of the prophets; the books of poetry; the books of wisdom; additions to canonical books; an apocalypse; a letter of Paul's.

How shall we treat books that are themselves little libraries of material? It is obvious that we must rearrange or group the pieces in some orderly way if we are to understand their contents. The rearrangement may follow chronological (historical) or logical lines. If the biblical material has to do with the words and deeds of people, we must reconstruct the life situations of these people with some accuracy. Hence, attention to chronological sequence is important. If the material has no biographical base, a logical grouping may yield maximum understanding. We can touch on only the major classes of the nonunified books here.

a. The Books of the Prophets
The books of the prophets deal with the words, and often the deeds, of these

prophets. The life situation of each prophet is thus the key to understanding what he said and did.

In reading the nonunified prophetic books, take the following steps:

1. If the book is short, read it through rapidly for a general idea of its contents. If it is long, sample it by scanning and reading selectively. Of particular importance are references to the times in which the prophet lived and the situation of the people to whom he spoke.

2. Read in a good secondary source a discussion of the prophet's times: in a Bible dictionary (under the name of the prophet), in an introduction to the Old Testament, in a history of Israel, in a commentary, or in Part 2 of this *Handbook*. Fix in mind the main events and situations of his period.

3. Insofar as possible, with the help of the secondary source chosen, relate the various portions of the prophetic book to their proper historical background.

4. Project yourself into each situation in which the prophet spoke. Imagine the circumstances – the place, the people addressed, the bystanders, the dress, the manner, and the temper of the speaker. Analyze his words on that occasion.

5. Try to catch the recurrent themes in the prophet's message. What is his view of God, of people and their deeds, of the proper God-human and human-human relationship? What does he have to say about the future and why?

6. Summarize the contribution of the prophet to the life of his people and his influence on later generations. What would Israel have lacked if he had not been born and called to his prophetic ministry?

7. Compare your conclusions on the above points with positions in standard reference books.

8. What of importance for us and our day is present in the words and deeds of this ancient prophet?

b. The Books of Poetry and the Books of Wisdom

In reading the books of poetry and the books of wisdom we are dealing with poetic pieces. As noted in Part 2 (pp. 144ff), Hebrew poetry falls into several major types, which must be related to the life situations out of which they arose (see also pp. 70–72).

Before reading books of this kind, it is best to consult brief introductions, such as in Part 2 of this *Handbook*, in a Bible dictionary, or in a standard introduction to the Old Testament. They will indicate the basic nature and structure of each book so that it may be read piece by piece in some logical and understandable way.

For example, it is best to read the Psalms by types (see pp. 149ff), and a book like Job requires some knowledge of its dramatic structure for intelligent reading. Do not try to go it alone on complicated collections of material such as the poetic and wisdom books contain.

c. Prose Books
In reading nonunified prose material you need to be aware of the loose arrangement of the book, so that you will not try to discover a unity which is not there. Here too the help of other reference books will point the way to intelligent reading. Finally, keep firmly in mind that the focus of attention should always be the biblical material itself, never some secondary discussion of it.

For Further Reading
Adler, M. J., *How to Read a Book*, 1940.
Barton, J. *Reading the Old Testament*, 1984.
Blair, E. P., *The Bible and You*, 1953.
Hayes, J. H. and Holladay, C. R., *Biblical Exegesis: A Beginner's Handbook*, 1982.
Wink, W., *Transforming Bible Study*, 1980.

Programs of Reading the Bible

We come now to the question concerning the order in which we should read the books of the Bible.

People read the Bible from many different points of view. Literary people read it because of its superb literary qualities. Historians pore over its pages for information about ancient cultures, personages, and events. Scientists test its assertions concerning the origins of the earth and humankind. Philosophers and religious educators trace in it the development of moral standards.

The Bible itself, so far as it speaks of its purpose, leads us to believe that we should read it from quite different motives. According to John 5:39–40 Jesus said to the Jews, 'You search the scriptures, because you think that in them you have eternal life; and it is they that bear witness to me; yet you refuse to come to me that you may have life.' From this passage we learn that the Scriptures point to Jesus Christ, the source of eternal life, and that they lead people to him. In 2 Tim. 3:14–17 we read that the Scriptures lead to salvation through faith in Christ, train believers in righteousness, and equip them for Christian service. The Bible nowhere suggests that we should view it as a book of history, philosophy, morality, science, or as a masterpiece of literature.

Around the middle of the twentieth century biblical scholars began to see more clearly than before the basic nature and purpose of the Bible. They believed they discovered amid all its diversity of subject matter and points of view an underlying unity. This unity consists in the story of what God has done, is doing, and will do for the redemption of humankind. The center of his activity is Jesus Christ and the church. Jesus is the long-promised deliverer of Israel, and the church is the faithful remnant through which God will save both Israel and the nations. All God's deeds lead to Jesus Christ, and all subsequent events are shaped by the fact that he came.

If Jesus Christ is the point of brightest illumination concerning the purpose and activity of God, it is clear that we should see all the rest of the Bible in relation to him. This means that we should start with those materials which most fully present him to view – the four Gospels. Then we should trace the impact Jesus had on his first followers, as portrayed in the Acts of the Apostles, in the letters of Paul to specific churches, and in the general letters of the early church. We then read on to Jesus' final triumph over the powers of evil, to his inauguration of the heavenly kingdom of God, and to the glories of the church's life in that kingdom, as pictured in the book of Revelation.

Now we should search to discover how God set the stage for the coming of Jesus: how humankind came to be in need of redemption; how God found redemptive agents and sought to educate them for their role in the world; how unresponsive people thwarted him and how God yet persisted; and how God ultimately raised up a deliverer and a remnant people who fulfilled his purpose for the world.

The books of the Apocrypha also celebrate the deeds of God in the life of the nation and of its righteous individuals. In those writings we see God as a mighty protector in national and personal crises, as the giver of spiritual and material blessings, as the revealer of truth to the chosen servants, and as the guarantor of people's future when they fully obey God's law. The longing of the nation for full redemption shines through this literature.

You will now have a choice between two reading programs which follow this line of approach: a longer and a shorter program. The first covers the entire contents of the Bible, including the Apocrypha. The second includes the major books and portions of books – enough to offer an adequate view of the sweep of the biblical materials.

The order of the books follows no one principle. I have tried to join theological, chronological, and historical-critical considerations with a commonsense approach, in the attempt to find a sequence that will lead to maximum understanding when supplemented by the help on the individual books offered in Part 2 of this *Handbook*.

Additional Note

In addition to reading the Bible by books, you may wish to follow themes that run through the Bible or considerable parts of it and also to approach it by way of its principal characters. Both methods are valid, if used by skillful interpreters. In following a theme, if you simply join passage to passage, without regard to the specific context of each, you will distort meanings and arrive at erroneous conclusions.

The meaning of words and the content of ideas changed through the centuries. What is said in Genesis does not necessarily agree with what is said in Isaiah or in Romans. You should undertake the tracing of themes only after you have a careful grounding in the literature of the Bible in its historical setting. This method is thus for advanced students of the Bible.

The same remarks apply to the study of the Bible by its principal characters. By considering verses, chapters, and portions of books without regard to the literary and historical contexts, an inexperienced reader can understand neither the characteristics of nor the reasons for particular portraits in various passages. It is best for such a reader to view biblical characters in the context of the entire biblical books in which they appear.

The Longer Program

The New Testament

1. Mark
2. Matthew
3. John
4–5. Luke-Acts
6. 1 Thessalonians
7. 2 Thessalonians
8. 1 Corinthians
9. 2 Corinthians (chief attention to chaps. 1–9)
10. Galatians
11. Romans
12. Philemon
13. Colossians
14. Philippians
15. Ephesians
16. 2 Timothy
17. Titus
18. 1 Timothy
19. 1 Peter
20. Hebrews
21. James
22. 1 John
23. 2 John
24. 3 John
25. Jude
26. 2 Peter
27. Revelation (chaps. 1–5 and 19:6—22:21; sample 6:1—19:5)

The Old Testament

28. Genesis
29. Exodus (chief attention to chaps. 1–24)
30. Leviticus (scan and sample)
31. Numbers (chief attention to 10:11—21:35)
32. Deuteronomy (chief attention to chaps. 1–11 and 27–34)
33. Joshua (chief attention to chaps. 1–12 and 22–24)
34. Judges (chief attention to chaps. 1–16)
35–36. 1–2 Samuel
37–38. 1–2 Kings (scan and sample)
39–40. 1–2 Chronicles (scan and sample)
41–42. Ezra-Nehemiah (chief attention to Nehemiah)
43. Amos
44. Hosea
45. Micah
46. Isaiah (chaps. 1–39; chief attention to chaps. 1–12)
47. Zephaniah
48. Jeremiah (chief attention to chaps. 1–25 and 30–33)
49. Nahum
50. Habakkuk
51. Ezekiel (chief attention to chaps. 1–24 and 33–39)
52. Obadiah
53. Lamentations
54. Isaiah (chaps. 40–66)
55. Haggai
56. Zechariah (chief attention to chaps 1–8)
57. Malachi
58. Joel
59. Ruth
60. Jonah
61. Psalms (read some representatives of each major type)
62. Job (less attention to chaps. 32–37)
63. Proverbs (chief attention to chaps. 1–9)
64. Song of Solomon
65. Ecclesiastes
66. Esther
67. Daniel

The Apocrypha

68. 1 Esdras (special attention to 3:1—5:6)
69. The Prayer of Manasseh
70. The Letter of Jeremiah
71. Baruch
72. Additions to the Book of Esther (scan and sample)
73. Tobit
74. Ecclesiasticus (The Wisdom of Jesus the Son of Sirach) (sample either Book 1 [chaps. 1–23] or Book 2 [chaps. 24–50])
75. 1 Maccabees (special attention to 1:1—9:22)
76. 2 Maccabees
77. Judith
78. The Prayer of Azariah and the Song of the Three Young Men
79. Susanna
80. Bel and the Dragon
81. The Wisdom of Solomon (chief attention to chaps. 1–9)
82. 2 Esdras (chief attention to chaps. 3–14)

The Shorter Program

The New Testament

1. Mark
2. John
3. Luke-Acts
4. 1 Thessalonians
5. 1 Corinthians
6. Romans
7. Philemon
8. Philippians
9. Ephesians
10. 2 Timothy
11. 1 Peter
12. 1 John
13. Revelation (chaps. 1–5 and 19:6—22:21; sample 6:1–19:5)

The Old Testament

14. Genesis
15. Exodus (chaps. 1-24)
16. Numbers (10:11—21:35)
17. Deuteronomy (chaps. 1–11)
18. Joshua (chaps. 1–12 and 22–24)
19. Judges (sample)
20. 1–2 Samuel (sample)
21. 1–2 Kings (sample)
22. Nehemiah
23. Amos
24. Isaiah (chaps. 1–12)
25. Jeremiah (chaps. 1–25, 30–33)
26. Isaiah (chaps. 40–55)
27. Ruth
28. Jonah
29. Psalms (some examples of the major types)
30. Job (chaps. 1–14 and 38–42)
31. Proverbs (chaps. 1–9)
32. Daniel (chaps. 1–6; sample chaps. 7–12)

The Apocrypha

33. Tobit
34. Ecclesiasticus (The Wisdom of Jesus the Son of Sirach) (sample chaps. 1–23)
35. 1 Maccabees (1:1—9·22) or 2 Maccabees
36. Judith.
37. The Wisdom of Solomon (chaps. 1–9)
38. 2 Esdras (chaps. 3–14)

Part 2
THE BIBLE IN HISTORY

The Pentateuch

Name
The term 'Pentateuch' (Greek for 'five
scrolls') apparently arose during the first
century AD among Alexandrian Jews as a
name for the first five books of the Old
Testament. The early church fathers
Tertullian and Origen used the term in
the second and third centuries.

Hebrew-speaking Jews normally called
the five books 'The Law' (Torah), 'The
Law of Moses,' 'The Book of the Law of
Moses,' or 'The Book of Moses.'

General Contents
The Pentateuch seeks to explain how
Israel became the chosen and covenanted
people of God and what this relationship
to God involved for the life and destiny of
Israel and all humankind.

Genesis tells how God chose the
covenant family from among the peoples
of the earth; Exodus, how God redeemed
this chosen family – greatly enlarged –
from bondage in Egypt and how God
entered into a covenant with it at Mount
Sinai; Leviticus, how God consecrated
the new nation for service and educated it
in worship; Numbers, how God purged
and disciplined it according to the
provisions of the covenant during its
wandering in the wilderness; and
Deuteronomy, how Moses exhorted it to
perpetual fidelity to God and to the terms
of the covenant it had accepted.

Place in the Hebrew Canon
The Pentateuch comprises the first
division of the threefold Hebrew canon:
the Law (Torah), the Prophets, and the
Writings.

That these five books occupied the
leading place in the Hebrew Canon long
prior to New Testament times is clear
from their position and separation from

the other canonical books in the
Septuagint (Greek translation of the Old
Testament, 3rd–2nd centuries BC) and
from evidence in the second century BC
book, Ecclesiasticus (The Wisdom of
Jesus the Son of Sirach). The Prologue of
this book speaks of 'the law and the
prophets and the other books of our
fathers.' In the New Testament 'the law
and the prophets' (Matt. 5:17) and 'the
law of Moses and the prophets and the
psalms' (Luke 24:44) are referred to.

Apparently the books of the
Pentateuch were the first writings
regarded by the Jews as authoritative (see
p. 30). From early times – how early we
do not know – Moses was regarded as the
author or compiler of these books, a view
taken over by the Christian church.

Authorship and Formation
There is no scholarly consensus today
concerning the process by which the
books of the Pentateuch came into being,
even though the problem has been under
investigation for over two hundred years.

The major hypotheses are as follows.

a. *One Author and Later Editors*
In Graeco-Roman times Jews (Philo,
Josephus) and Christians (John 5:46–47;
7:19; Acts 3:22; Romans 10:5) believed
that Moses wrote these books. This belief
persisted, with occasional challenges,
until the time of the Enlightenment
(seventeenth–eighteenth centuries). In
that period of rationalism and deism,
several influential philosophers and
biblical scholars (including Spinoza)
denied Moses' authorship. Some, as had
others earlier, attributed the Pentateuch
to Ezra.

In the centuries after the Enlightenment, liberal scholars uniformly repudiated the Mosaic authorship, preferring a view that held to a multiplicity of authors and documents behind the Pentateuch. Against them were arrayed conservative church people and scholars, who staunchly sought to maintain the traditional view.

The grounds for the liberals' challenge of the Mosaic authorship lay in part in phenomena in the text of the Pentateuch itself.

How could Moses have composed the account of his own death (Deut. 34:1–8)? What does one do with the anachronistic references to the Israelite kings (Gen. 36:31), to later place names like 'Dan' (Gen. 14:14; see Judges 18:29), and to the 'Philistines' as in the land during Abraham's and Isaac's time (Gen. 21:34; 26:14–18), when in reality they entered several hundred years after these patriarchs? What of the later perspective indicated by the phrase 'to this day' (Gen. 32:32; Deut. 3:14; 34:6) and by the references to the Canaanites and Perizzites as formerly in the land (Gen. 12:6; 13:7)? Why do different versions of the same material appear: two stories of creation (Gen. 1:1—2:4a; 2:4b–25); three accounts of a patriarch representing his wife as a sister (Gen. 12:10–20; ch. 20; 26:1–11); two accounts of the naming of Beersheba (Gen. 21:31; 26:33) and of Bethel (Gen. 28:19; 35:15); two renamings of Jacob (Gen. 32:28; 35:10)? Why is there disagreement concerning the kind and number of animals Noah took into the ark (Gen. 6:19–20; 7:2, 8–9) and the time at which worship of Yahweh began (Gen. 4:26; Ex. 6:2–3)?

Conservatives have explained these phenomena in various ways: by postulating Moses' use of different documentary sources; by emphasizing ancient writers' love of duplication, repetition, and multiple naming of persons and deities; and by stressing the role of later scribes in updating ancient place names, in supplementing stories from parallel accounts, and in correcting and clarifying puzzling data in the texts they were editing.

Conservatives do not argue that Moses wrote the story of his own death; and some are willing to grant that blocks of material (for example, Deuteronomy 1–11 and 32–33) 'were added at a somewhat later time' (R. K. Harrison). This scholar contends that Moses and the scribes after him used the standard literary procedures of their age, as illustrated in the compositions we possess from Mesopotamia.

In general, conservatives hold that scribal editing was completed early, probably by the death of Samuel (late eleventh century BC) or at least by the time of David (about 1000 BC). Some allow for 'modest amounts of revision' until about the time of Ezra (c. 400 BC) (La Sor-Hubbard-Bush).

One scholar stated his position as follows: 'Who in Israel's history was better prepared than Moses to write the Pentateuch? He had the time and also the training and learning to do so. Also, as human founder of the theocracy, he had the information that was requisite. The Pentateuch exhibits an inner plan and structure that betray a great mind. Who, better than Moses, could have produced such a work?' (E. J. Young, *An Introduction to the Old Testament*, 3rd. ed. 1964).

b. *Several Authors and Later Editors*
In 1753 Jean Astruc, a French physician, published a book in which he contended that Moses used two main parallel sources in compiling the book of Genesis: one referred to God by the name *Elohim* (Deity) and the other by YHWH (Yahweh). He postulated in addition ten fragmentary sources. This began a long search on the part of scholars for major documents that might lie behind the Pentateuch.

The most careful and influential analysis of the sources of the Pentateuch was made by the German scholar Julius Wellhausen (1876–77), who built on the views of Graf, Kuenen, and others. Wellhausen and his followers believed that the earliest parts of the Pentateuch came from two originally independent, extensive, and largely parallel sources.

One, written by a Judean author about 850 BC, uses the divine name YHWH, is cast in epic style, revels in the deeds of the Patriarchs whom God chose to bring into being a glorious new, redemptive kingdom in the earth, and presents the Deity (YHWH) in humanlike terms. These scholars gave to this document the symbol J (standing for 'Jahweh,' the German spelling of the divine name).

The other document, written in the northern kingdom in the eighth century BC, uses the name *Elohim* (thus the symbol E), exalts Jacob and Joseph, gives prominence to the northern sanctuaries of Bethel and Shechem, especially praises Moses, and sees and evaluates Israel's history from the standpoint of prophets like Amos and Hosea.

The two documents were joined by an unknown editor (thus JE) in the seventh century.

Wellhausen and his followers saw two other major documents behind the Pentateuch: Deuteronomy (called D), which they identified in whole or in part with the law book found in the temple in the time of Josiah (622 BC; 2 Kings 22–23) and which they held to be a product of the period immediately preceding this; and a priestly document (P), containing material of a ritualistic and statistical character (as in the book of Leviticus and in the Pentateuch's genealogies, tribal lists, chronological notations, etc.). They dated P to the period after the Babylonian Exile (500–450 BC) and suggested that this document afforded the framework into which some unknown editor fitted the three other documents, perhaps in Babylonia in the late fifth century BC.

According to this hypothesis, the Pentateuch was in process of formation for some four hundred years. While Wellhausen did not regard Moses as the author of the Pentateuch, he did accord him a high place as 'the founder of the nation out of which the Torah and prophecy came as later growths' and as 'the people's leader, judge, and center of union.'

Refinements of Wellhausen's views went forward in liberal scholarly circles in the first half of the twentieth century. Some of the supposed basic documents (JEDP) were divided into yet other documents (J into J1 and J2, E into E1 and E2, and P into P1 and P2). J has been most divided, one scholar separating out from it a 'lay' source (L), another scholar a 'nomadic' source (N), another a 'Seir' or 'Southern' source (S), and yet another a 'Kenite' source (K).

The critical knife has been very busy since the time of Wellhausen. The lack of agreement among the subdividers became a factor in a growing, widespread loss of confidence in this whole way of attacking the problem of the origin of the Pentateuch and caused researchers to turn to yet other approaches.

c. *Oral Traditions, Multiple Authors, and Late Editors*

The attention of important scholars (Gunkel, Noth, von Rad, Engnell) began to focus on the growing evidence that oral transmission of Israel's memories of the past lay behind and alongside the writing down of the Pentateuchal material. They observed that oral transmission of historical memories and folklore was strongly operative in other cultures around the ancient Hebrews and indeed exists in some modern societies.

They studied the forms in which oral traditions circulate and are handed down, the practical uses these forms have in the life of the people who create and use them, the changes in the traditions (expansions, alterations, reinterpretations) that occur in transmission, their clustering into cycles of traditions, and their reduction to writing.

They concluded that oral traditions were circulating in Israel long before the writing of J and the other Pentateuchal sources. Indeed, the documents were simply crystalizations of cycles of oral tradition. They asserted that the really creative process in the formation of Israel's record of the past was the oral process.

Each generation received the stories of the past, affirmed them, altered them in the light of their own circumstances and needs, created some new traditions, and passed them all on to the next generation. Cult centers, such as Shechem and Gilgal, particularly after the formation of the twelve-tribe confederacy (amphictyony) in the time of Joshua, utilized the traditions in worship and instruction in connection with sacred festivals. The traditions set forth God's promises to the Fathers, God's deliverance of the oppressed Israelites from Egypt, God's guidance through the wildnerness, God's revelation of the Law and God's formation of a covenanted nation at Mount Sinai, and God's provision of a home for the new nation in the Promised Land. It has been suggested that in connection with the annual recital of these traditions at Shechem the covenant was renewed and the worshipers repledged to obedience to its terms. The J writer may have been the first to give traditions literary form and others (the writers of E, D, P) and later editors assembled and shaped yet other cycles.

This general view of the formation of the Pentateuch was widely accepted for about a quarter of a century (from about 1940 to 1965). Today it is being seriously challenged. Some scholars doubt that a long stage of oral transmission can be argued from the Pentateuchal materials, that changes in orally transmitted material can really be identified, that an amphictyony ever existed to bring the traditions together, that the concept of a covenanted nation existed prior to the seventh century BC, and so on.

d. *Late Editors of Traditional Materials*
Some scholars (for example Van Seters) recently have contended that there were

no long, somewhat parallel, and comprehensive written sources (JEDP) to be woven together, as Wellhausen and his successors assumed. Rather, editors during the Babylonian Exile and after it put together collections of folktales of the time (some of them may have been in written form) to serve the pressing community need: the reconstitution of the shattered nation by an interpretation and application of its manifold traditions about its forefathers, its ancestral laws, and its reason for existing. As thus conceived, the Pentateuch is through and through a late composition, both as to its time of writing and the kind of material it enshrines.

Our brief survey here of the major hypotheses concerning the authorship and formation of the Pentateuch has shown that the documentary hypothesis, as advocated by Wellhausen and his followers for a century, has well nigh come apart. And the study of the oral traditions assumed to lie behind and within the documents, as carried out by Noth, von Rad, and others, has done less than enough to save the documentary hypothesis and convince the scholarly world of the adequacy of the tradition-document approach. The conceiving of the Pentateuch as comprised of non-historical (folktale) matter, put together by Exilic and post-Exilic editors, for religious and national purposes imposes an unproved hypothesis on the Pentateuch and smacks of rationalistic skepticism. The chaos in liberal scholarship today has led one astute observer to say, 'Pentateuchal studies is hardly in a favorable position at the present point' (D.A. Knight in Knight and Tucker (eds.), *The Hebrew Bible and its Modern Interpreters*, 1985).

Conservatives continue to support the traditional belief in Mosaic authorship – with generous allowance for the work of editors after Moses' time – but they fail to convert many liberals. The question of the origin of the Pentateuch is more open today than it has been in a hundred years.

Historical Reliability

The advocates of Mosaic authorship of the Pentateuch believe that authentic early documents and traditions were available to Moses and that he added his own recollections to form a trustworthy narrative of the beginnings of the world, human society, and the people of Israel. Conservatives tend to defend the verbal inerrancy of this material, while allowing for textual corruptions in the process of transmission.

Some liberal scholars, who have accepted the documentary hypothesis along the lines laid down by Wellhausen (W. F. Albright and his students), have refused to accept Wellhausen's skepticism about the historical value of the Pentateuchal materials. Wellhausen put his position frankly:

'We attain to no historical knowledge of the patriarchs, but only of the time when the stories about them arose in the Israelite people; this later age is here unconsciously projected, in its inner and outward features, into hoar antiquity, and is reflected there like a glorified image.'

In the middle third of the present century, the Albrightians argued that Wellhausen was wrong in this judgment, that archaeology has established the historical accuracy of innumerable data of the Pentateuch, that the oral and written transmission of Israel's traditions was on the whole faithful, and that we can believe that the fountainhead of Hebrew faith and life was Abraham and Moses – both historical persons – who fit well in the cultural contexts in which the Pentateuch places them. However late the basic Pentateuchal documents may be and however much they were edited, they present a reasonably accurate picture of the distant past.

Today the Albrightians are being attacked with vigor by somewhat secular Syro-Palestinian archaeologists and students of ancient Near Eastern religions

(Dever, Van Seters, T. L. Thompson). They accuse the Albrightians of theological bias and unsound archaeological methodology. They see in archaeological data no supporting evidence for the historicity of the Pentateuchal materials. Since the Pentateuch was put together during and after the Babylonian Exile, more than a thousand years after the supposed time of the Patriarchs, when probably little authentic memory of ancient events existed, these scholars believe that even the historicity of the Patriarchs is open to question and the stories about them and Moses are in all likelihood pious fiction. It is easy to detect a strong rationalistic skepticism in the attitudes of these scholars, who are guilty of conditioning presuppositions quite as much as the Albrightian scholars they oppose.

Not all liberal scholars hold that the sort of oral-literary process that seems to lie behind the Pentateuch necessarily empties it of usable data for historical reconstruction. These 'moderate' liberals join with the conservatives in holding that Abraham and Moses constitute the fountainhead of Hebrew belief and life, that they were central actors under God in the raising up of Israel as a redemptive people, and that the stories about them, however shaped they may be by transmissional processes, are vastly more than 'pious fiction.'

Conclusion

It is agreed by most conservative and liberal scholars that the Pentateuch in its present form is the product of more than one mind and of several centuries, at least, and is a vast treasure chest of Israel's historical memories. Both groups agree that long copying of the Pentateuch and the translating of it into other languages resulted in many changes to the text and that it is the common responsibility of all scholars to discover the changes and restore the text as nearly as possible to its earliest form. This work is known as textual criticism (see pp. 377–8).

The view at sunrise from the Mount of Moses (Jebel Musa).

There is considerable agreement between both groups that 'neither Testament ascribes the entire work to Moses, although both attribute substantial parts to him' (D. A. Hubbard, a conservative scholar). Passages that refer to Moses' writing down 'all the words of the Lord,' 'this law,' and the like (Ex. 17:14; 24:4; 34:27; Num. 33:1–2; Deut. 31:9, 22) refer to certain parts like the great legal codes (Ex. 20:2—23:33; 34:11–26; Deut. 5—26) and the Israelites' itinerary (Num. 33:2), says Hubbard. This conservative scholar can even write, 'As far as the Gn. [Genesis] stories are concerned, Moses may or may not have been the one who compiled them from their written and oral forms.' He allows as 'credible' the final editing of the Pentateuch during the time of Saul and David, with some 'modernizing of vocabulary and style' even later (all quotations from the article 'Pentateuch' in *The Illustrated Bible Dictionary*, 1980).

Though Moses apparently did not write the whole Pentateuch in its present form, he clearly stands behind its laws, institutions, religious concepts, and ceremonies described there. He was the central actor under God in the liberation of Israel from Egypt and in the organization of Israel's life on its many sides. Adaptations of Moses' laws and institutions to meet changed conditions undoubtedly were made in his spirit in later times and are now included in the Pentateuch. These too witness to the towering greatness of Moses.

In sum, if Moses was not the 'author' of the Pentateuch, in the modern understanding of that term, he was its fountainhead. And the book of which he is the veritable center and heart is thus not inappropriately called 'the book of Moses' (Mark 12:26).

Genesis

Woman at a window; Nimrud ivory, 8th century B.C.

For Further Reading

Hayes, J. H., *An Introduction to Old Testament Study*, 1979.
Knight, D. A., 'The Pentateuch,' in Knight, D. A. and Tucker, G. M. (eds.), *The Hebrew Bible and Its Modern Interpreters*, 1985.
La Sor, W. S., Hubbard, D. A., and Bush, F. W., *Old Testament Survey*, 1982.
Miller, J. M. and Hayes, J. H., *A History of Ancient Israel and Judah*, 1986.
Soggin, J. A., *Introduction to the Old Testament*, 1976.
Wiseman, P. J. (Wiseman, D. J., ed.), *Ancient Records and the Structure of Genesis: A Case for Literary Unity*, 1985.

Title

The word 'Genesis' means 'beginning.' This title comes from the Greek translation of the Old Testament (the Septuagint). The Hebrews, like other peoples of the ancient East, often titled literary works after their opening word or words. For example, Genesis was called originally 'In the beginning,' and Leviticus 'And he called.' The Septuagint and the Vulgate tended to name books after their contents, not their opening words, and from these titles the English names are derived.

Contents

The subject of Genesis is: Why and how God chose Israel to be his redemptive people. The *why* is explained in chaps. 1–11 and the *how* in chaps. 12–50.

a. Gen. 1–11: The Corrupted Creation

Chaps. 1–11 show humankind's need for redemption. Genesis opens with two accounts of creation (1:1—2:4*a* and 2:4*b*–25). The first account, in magnificent, formal cadences and in balanced, seven-part

> ## Outline
>
> **The corrupted creation** (chaps. 1–11)
> **The redemptive family** (chaps. 12–50)
> The Abraham saga (12:1—25:18)
> The Jacob (and Isaac) saga (25:19—36:43)
> The Joseph story (chaps. 37–50)

Marshlands near biblical Ur, Mesopotamia.

structure, celebrates the creation of the heavens and the earth and all things therein. It shows that the created order re sulted from the purposive act of one transcendent God. All that God created was good. God made people, the highest of all creatures, in his moral image and appointed them to have dominion over the created order. God intended people to worship and live in perpetual fellowship with him.

The second creation story deals, in much simpler language and style, not so much with the origin of the universe as with the beginnings of life on the earth. In this story God creates man before vegetation, animal life, and woman. He shapes man out of earth, animates him by his breath, and places him in a beautiful Garden 'to till it and keep it.' To supply man a companion, God creates animals, which prove inadequate, and then woman.

Instead of recognizing their creaturely dependence and rendering obedience to God, Adam (meaning 'earthling') and Eve (interpreted in 3:20 as 'the mother of all living') attempt to break out of their status as human beings. They wish to possess the powers that belong to God alone: unlimited knowledge and immortality. Their rebellion against God and alienation from him end quite other than they had planned: in God's curse and their expulsion from the Garden.

The story of Cain's murder of Abel shows how the break between humankind and God becomes also a breach in human relationships. Sin is now a fact of earthly existence. It crouches as a demon at the door of the evildoer (4:7). It must be mastered. Blood feuds between agriculturalists (Cain) and herdsmen (Abel), with their rival forms of worship, mar the earth. People begin to build cities and forge a civilization without God (4:17–22). Revenge, violence, and death become awful realities of human experience (4:23–24). Even heavenly beings – so an ancient story said – formed unions with the daughters of men, and giants came into being (6:1–4).

So wicked did humankind as a whole become that God was sorry human beings had been made (6:5–6). God's judgment on them came in the form of a great flood which all but destroyed humankind from the earth. Even after the flood evil people in their arrogant desire to make a name for themselves, to ensure their security and self-sufficiency, built a great city and a great tower. God met their arrogance by confusing their languages and by scattering them over the face of the earth. Thus God decisively broke up the challenge to his sovereignty. The story shows that the tragic divisions in the human family are not the will of God but the result of human pride, arrogance, self-trust, and self-worship.

While Genesis records the judgment of God on rebellious people, it also depicts his unfailing mercy toward them. God seeks to deliver them from the condition into which their folly has brought them. Though their struggle with evil will be long and acute (3:15), we learn that God will make a way of escape. A remnant – a righteous line obedient to God – will become his saving instrument in the world.

Adam's son Seth is shown as the father of the faithful. In his days (or those of his son Enosh) 'men began to call on the name of the Lord [Hebrew, *Yahweh*]' (4:26). (Other traditions connect the beginning of Yahweh worship with Moses – Exod. 3:13 ff.; 6:2–3). The righteous line of Seth at length produced Enoch and Noah who 'walked with God' (Gen. 5:22, 24; 6:9); that is, they lived in intimate moral fellowship with him. Noah became God's instrument in the preservation of humankind from the judgment of the flood and a participant with God in a special covenant relationship (9:1–17). From him came Shem, who was especially blessed above his brothers (9:26–27); and from Shem descended the line leading to Abraham, the origin of the redemptive people Israel.

b. Gen. 12–50: The Redemptive Family

The stories of the Patriarchs (Abraham, Isaac, Jacob, Joseph) occupy most of the book of Genesis. Technically most of these stories should be called sagas (material dealing with the exploits of tribal heroes and their clans, transmitted in oral form from generation to generation).

Several groups of material may be identified in chaps. 12–50: (1) the Abraham saga (12:1—25:18); (2) the Jacob (and Isaac) saga (25:19—36:43); (3) the Joseph story (chaps. 37–50).

The Abraham Saga (12:1—25:18)

This material deals with God's call of Abraham, his journeys to and in the land of Canaan, his descent into Egypt, his relations with his nephew Lot, his experiences in securing a true son and heir, his dispute with Abimelech, his test of faith in the ordeal concerning Isaac, his purchase of a family burial cave, his obtaining a wife for Isaac, and the death of Abraham.

Several emphases appear here. First, there is God's call and constant guidance of Abraham. Abraham's departure for a new land is spiritually motivated: God thrusts him out from his kindred and his father's house into a new existence. The life in a new land is designed to lead to a great destiny – the forming of a new nation which will be a blessing to the whole earth.

Some scholars see in Abraham's response to God's call the beginnings of the rejection of polytheism (the worship of many gods) and the planting of the seed of monotheism (the worship of one God), a crucial turning point in the life of humankind. It appears that for Abraham no other God had existence or meaning. He entered into a covenant with the God who called him (chap. 17) and rendered this God exclusive attention and obedience.

Second, Abraham's wholehearted response to this God is stressed. He departed from Haran 'as the Lord had told him' (12:4). He built in the new land a string of altars where he had heard the voice of God and worshiped (12:7, 8; 13:4, 18). He believed God's promise that he would have a son (15:6). His absolute obedience to God in relation to the covenant of circumcision (chap. 17) and the offering up of Isaac (chap. 22) stand out.

Third, his humane and righteous

attitudes are frequently highlighted. He allowed Lot first choice of land (chap. 13) and then rescued him from the consequences of that choice by defeating four foreign kings at great personal cost (chap. 14). He interceded for righteous Lot and his family in the wicked city of Sodom (chap. 18). He was unselfish in his refusal to receive spoils of war from the king of Sodom (14:21–24).

Fourth, God's purpose to redeem all humankind is repeatedly emphasized (12:2–3; 17:3–7; 18:18; 22:17–18; 26:3–5; 28:14). To reverse the effects of Adam's fall is apparently what God intends. God will work out this purpose in spite of delays, lack of faith on the part of chosen instruments (18:11–15; chap. 16), and interference by foreign rulers (12:9–20; chap. 20).

The Jacob (and Isaac) Saga (25:19—36:43)
Isaac is not a main character in Genesis. The amount of material dealing with him is small (chiefly chap. 26), and when he does appear he is a pale reflection of Abraham or background for the schemes and triumphs of Jacob. He is a connecting link in the chain of descent of the righteous line, the official bearer of the covenant and its promises (26:24), but he is basically only stage setting for the more significant Jacob and his sons.

The Jacob saga revolves around two poles: Jacob's deceit, treachery, self-centredness, and general perversity, on the one hand; and the divine grace operating in an undeserving life, on the other.

The first is illustrated in such stories as those about the unscrupulous way he obtained the birthright from Esau (25:29–34), the theft of Isaac's blessing (chap. 27), the sharp-witted fleecing of Laban (30:25–43), and the insincere promise to Esau at the time of reconciliation (33:12–17).

The second is seen in the dream at Bethel (28:10–22), where the divine assurance and promise come to a fearful,

Herodian walls surround the Cave of Machpelah (Haram el-Khalil) Hebron.

fleeing youth, and in the crisis at Peniel, where Jacob prevailed in his struggle with the divine visitor (32:24–32). The latter experience seems to say that Jacob, after an encounter with God and with himself as he really was, emerged a changed man, ready for the tasks to be assigned him in the redemptive purpose of God. The change of his name from Jacob (explained as meaning 'he takes by the heel' or 'he supplants') to Israel (interpreted as 'he who strives with God' or 'God strives') is symbolic of a new self, a new status before God, and a divine destiny.

Jacob in Genesis is clearly a symbol for the nation Israel. Both were unsuited for the role God had cast for them, but God made them useful through his transforming and empowering grace.

The Joseph Story (Chaps. 37–50)

The story of Joseph is widely regarded as one of the literary masterpieces of the world. Unlike the Abraham-Isaac-Jacob material, which consists of individual episodes drawn together into a loose narrative, the Joseph story is tightly written and moves carefully, and almost without interruption, to its climax and resolution. The closely knit character of the story argues against a background in oral tradition.

Its purpose is to join the varied traditions concerning Abraham, Isaac, and Jacob with those about Moses, the Exodus, and the conquest of Canaan. It shows how Israel got to Egypt and how God prepared the way for the work of Moses and the birth of the nation.

The story moves through well-marked stages: how Joseph became a slave in Egypt (chap. 37); his rise to power (39:1—41:57); the coming of his brothers to Egypt (42:1—45:28); Jacob in Egypt, his burial in Canaan, and the death of Joseph (46:1—50:26).

A seeming digression is the story of Judah and Tamar (chap. 38), which actually has a justifiable place in the narrative. Judah is one of the sons of Jacob, whose descendants are being discussed in this section. Through Judah the promises made to the fathers are to be realized (49:10). But again the fulfilment is threatened, this time through the conduct both of Judah and his sons. The threat is overcome in God's mysterious way and posterity for Judah came about (see also Ruth 4:12; 1 Chron. 2:4; Matt. 1:3). This whole section continues the message previously set forth: God cares for chosen people and carries out his divine purpose through them in spite of obstacles.

The central message of the Joseph story is that God cares for his chosen people. He turns foul deeds against them into a source of ultimate blessing. The story shows that people are free to do what they choose, but they cannot control the consequences of their choices. These are in the hands of God. This teaching comes to focus in 50:20, where the magnanimous Joseph says to his brothers, 'As for you, you meant evil against me, but God meant it for good, to bring it about that many people should be kept alive, as they are today.'

Sources and Historical Value

For a discussion of the problem of the sources of Genesis, see the comments on the Pentateuch (pp. 98–103). Here we shall consider only the cultural sources and attempt an estimate of the historical value of the book.

Except for the Joseph story, archaeological discoveries show that much of the content of Genesis reflects traditions, customs, and conceptions of Mesopotamia. (See pp. 404–10.) This agrees with the clear claim in the book that Mesopotamia was the ancestral home of the patriarchs. Abraham and Lot must have brought with them at least some of their cultural heritage. Furthermore, Canaan was heavily influenced by Mesopotamian culture long before their arrival and long after.

Both stories of creation in Genesis show marks of Mesopotamian thought, literary forms, and language. The Babylonian creation epic *Enuma Elish* ('When above'), discovered among the ruins of the library of King Asshurbanapal (c. 668–627 BC) in Nineveh, offers an account of creation both strikingly similar to and different from that in Gen. 1:1—2:4a. The order of the events of creation is the same, and many details are alike. However, the differences, growing out of the belief in many gods in the one case and in one all-powerful God in the other, are equally striking. (See pp. 406–7.)

The story of the Fall contains similarities to the Gilgamesh Epic and the Myth of Adapa. The list of long-lived, pre-flood patriarchs in Gen. 5 seems to rest on a Mesopotamian tradition of similar kings. The flood story strikingly parallels that in the Gilgamesh Epic (see pp. 408–9). The Tower of Babel narrative (11:1–9) unmistakably reflects knowledge of Mesopotamian ziggurats (pyramidal temples).

The Abraham-Isaac-Jacob stories contain reflections of Mesopotamian customs and beliefs. For example, many scholars have pointed out that at Haran in upper Mesopotamia a husband could adopt his wife as a sister, regardless of actual blood ties, and thereby secure for her special standing and protection in society. This may explain why Abraham and Isaac represented Sarah and Rebekah as their sisters (12:9–20; 20:1–18; 26:6–11) – an attempt to show that they were especially important before the law and to their husbands and thus legally untouchable.

The adoption of a slave as a son and heir, with the stipulation that the subsequent birth of an actual son would require the adopted son to give way as principal heir to the real son, was standard practice in upper Mesopotamia and may explain the Eliezer-Isaac situation (Gen. 15:2 ff.).

The theft of Laban's household gods by Rachel may have been her way of securing leadership in the family and perhaps title to Laban's estate for herself and Jacob, as seems possible from tablets discovered from this region. (See also p. 404.)

Genesis consists of stories of various types from hoary antiquity, many like Mesopotamian ones (especially those in Gen. 1–11), some with marks from Egypt (the Joseph narrative), and the rest from traditions about the patriarchs handed down in Canaan. All were assimilated into the theological perspective of Israel by deeply religious Hebrew writers and made instruments of the revelation of God's redemptive purpose. The stories must be looked on not as histories in a narrow sense, but as vehicles for the communication of profound religious truth. (See pp. 403–10.)

Structure and Theology

In its present form Genesis could well be called 'the Book of Generations.' It is structured as a whole in the framework of ten occurrences of a genealogical formula: 'these are the generations of...' (with slight variations; see 2:4; 5:1; 6:9; 10:1; 11:10, 27; 25:12, 19; 36:1 (9); 37:2). 'Generations' clearly means 'offspring' or 'descendants.'

The formulas are followed either by genealogies or narrative accounts. The formulas hook the lines of descent together, show the place of the chosen line among the peoples of the world, and offer an opportunity for introducing traditions about key persons and events in that line of descent. The over-arching purpose is to show that the created world and its inhabitants are the arena of God's saving purpose and activity through a special people.

Central in Genesis are God's promises to the patriarchs. The promises appear in many different forms and are made to both individuals and groups. They concern progeny and the land. It is shown emphatically that the promises will be fulfilled in spite of all impediments to that fulfillment (12:10–20; 15:1–6, 12–16; 22:1–19; 37:2–36; etc.). God cannot be defeated in carrying out his purpose. He actualizes it in unexpected ways, even through the deeds of evil persons (50:19–20).

The Ancient Near East

Aral
Sea

Caucasus Mts.

Caspian Sea

Kara Kum

ARMENIA

MITANNI
aran

• Nineveh

ASSYRIA

Asshur   R. Tigris

• Ecbatana

R. Euphrates

Mari   Zagros Mts.

BASYLONIA   PERSIA

Babylon •

                • Susa
        • Nippur

        • Ur   • Persepolis

Dumah

Arabian
Desert
                                    Persian
                                    Gulf   Gulf
                                                            of Oman

Exodus

Title

In Hebrew the title consists of the opening words, 'And these are the names.' In the Septuagint 'Exodos' means 'a going out,' with reference, of course, to the going out from Egypt in the time of Moses.

Contents and Theology

Genesis tells why and how God chose, led, and preserved (in Egypt) the redemptive family. Exodus records how this family became a free nation under God – how he redeemed it from bondage, sealed it in a covenant relationship, and prepared it, through the construction of the tabernacle, for his perpetual presence.

The dominant personality of Exodus, as in Genesis, is God (El Shaddai, Yahweh). In these books Abraham, Isaac, Jacob, Joseph, and Moses are the human instruments through whom God works.

The theological heart of Exodus is God's self-revelation. It is God's purpose that all shall 'know' who he is, what he is

doing or has done, and what he will do for his people. First of all, he knows the people's suffering in Egypt (3:7) and he knows Moses' name (33:12, 17). To *know*, according to these passages, means to care about and to seek to help the one known. Then Moses is to know God's name, nature, and purposes (3:13–17; 6:2–8) – that 'Yahweh' cares about Israel and about Moses himself (33:17). Israel is to know what Moses knows, not only by Moses' words (6:6–8) but also by God's mighty acts in its behalf (16:6–12; 29:46). The children in succeeding generations are to know what God has done for Israel (10:2). Pharaoh and the Egyptians are to know who the true God is (7:5, 17; 14:4), that there is no god like him in all the earth (8:10; 9:14), and that all the earth is God's (9:29).

The whole book deals in one way or another with God's self-revelation, not only of his identity, nature, sovereignty, and purposes, but of his will for Israel's life. The latter is spelled out in the terms of the covenant sealed at Mount Sinai: in the unqualified stipulations of the Ten Commandments, covering relations with God and with other people (20:3–17); in the provisions of civil law (21:1—23:9); in laws governing worship (20:22–26; 23:10–19); and the like.

The lengthy sections concerning the making of the tabernacle (chaps. 25–31; 35–40) suggest: (1) God's loftiness (transcendence), holiness (separation from all that is common and unclean), and desire to be present with his people (immanence); and (2) the conditions on which sinful people can approach God. These sections thus play their part in the self-revelation of God, as presented in the book of Exodus.

The book reveals also the depth of human resistance to God, not only on the part of the Egyptians (chaps. 1–15) but also of the chosen people. God's mighty deed of liberation from the bondage of Egypt, his magnificent self-revelation (theophany) at Mount Sinai, and his gracious covenant extended to Israel have

Outline

The redemption from Egyptian bondage (chaps. 1–18)

The sealing of the covenant between God and Israel at Mount Sinai (chaps. 19–24)

Israel's preparation for God's abiding presence (chaps. 25–40)

barely been experienced and accepted when the people repudiate all that has happened and turn to idolatrous bull worship and fertility rites (chap. 32).

But the God of mercy is also the God of judgment, as manifested in the slaying of three thousand persons and a plague upon the people (32:28, 35). Yet God does not make a full end. In response to Moses' intercession, he renews the covenant, reaffirms promises, and moves forward toward their fulfillment (chap. 34).

Historical Background

Precisely when the family of Jacob descended into Egypt cannot be determined. Many scholars think the career of Joseph fits best into Egyptian history in the time of the Hyksos (meaning 'rulers of foreign countries'). They were invaders of mixed ethnic origin who ruled Egypt around 1650 to 1542 BC. These foreign kings (among whom there appear to have been Semitic elements) might well have looked with favor on a brilliant foreign youth and have promoted him to a position of responsibility in the government. Egyptian records indicate that it was customary to admit Bedouins and Asiatics in time of famine.

Whether all the Israelite tribes or only part of them went down into Egypt – and thus whether all participated in the Exodus – is not clear. Various pieces of evidence, such as the cordial relations of the invading Israelites under Joshua with the inhabitants of Shechem (Josh. 24), indicate that groups related to Israel had remained in Canaan. It is unlikely that the seventy persons who are said to have descended into Egypt (Gen. 46:27; Exod. 1:5) comprised all the Israelites born during a period of some 200 years' settlement in Canaan prior to the descent into Egypt.

The date of the Exodus is likewise uncertain. A widely held view today is that it occurred about 1280 BC under Ramesses II (c. 1290–1224 BC). This pharaoh and his predecessor, Sethos I (c. 1305–1290) may have been oppressors of Israel (Exod. 1:8–11) who forced the Israelites to work at fortifying Pithom and Ramesses (the latter city called at various times Zoan, Avaris, or Tanis) in the delta.

Other dates suggested for the Exodus fall in the fifteenth and the twelfth centuries. It is now disputed whether there is archaeological evidence for Joshua's conquests in Palestine in the thirteenth century, as was widely claimed a generation ago by Albright and his students (see pp. 124–26). The memorial stone of the Egyptian king Marniptah, set up about 1220 BC, may indicate that Israel was established in parts of Canaan by that date, but the evidence is inconclusive. That there was an oppression in Egypt and an Exodus of some sort seems clear to almost all scholars, but its exact nature and its date are elusive.

According to the book of Exodus, Israel responded to Yahweh at Mount Sinai by entering into a covenant with him to be his chosen people and to obey his commandments. There has been much debate about the nature of this covenant.

It is possible that Israel's covenant was patterned after the suzerain-vassal treaties drawn up by ancient kings of the Middle East and known to us from Hittite texts. These agreements had several elements: a preamble, naming the author of the covenant, with his titles, attributes, and genealogy; a historical statement concerning the benevolent acts performed by the king in behalf of the vassal state; a list of the obligations imposed on and accepted by the vassal; a statement requiring the deposit of the covenant document in the temple and its periodic public reading; a list of deities who stood as witnesses to the covenant; blessings and curses which would ensue if the covenant was kept or broken.

Most of these elements appear in the Pentateuch (see especially Exod. 20:1–17; Deut. 5:6–21; 31:9–13, 26; and chaps. 27–28), which seem to show that Israel thought of its relationship to God in the same general fashion as vassals who were subjects of great kings. The parallel is

The Exodus

(Traditional route)

BONDAGE IN EGYPT
The Hebrews built store cities for Pharaoh at Pithom and Raamses (Ex. 1:11)

CROSSING THE RED (REED) SEA
The Hebrews went by the desert road towards the Red Sea (Ex. 13:18)

WATER FROM THE ROCK
At Rephidim and/or Kadesh the Israelites obtained water after Moses struck the rock (Ex. 17:1–7; Num. 20:2–13)

SPIES SENT INTO CANAAN
After leaving Sinai, Moses sent twelve spies to Canaan (Num. 13:1–24)

TEN COMMAND-MENTS GIVEN
At Mount Sinai Israel entered into a covenant with God to obey his command-ments (Ex. 19—24)

SOME FORTY YEARS IN DESERT
The Israelites spent about forty years in the desert before entering Canaan (Num. 14: 11–38).

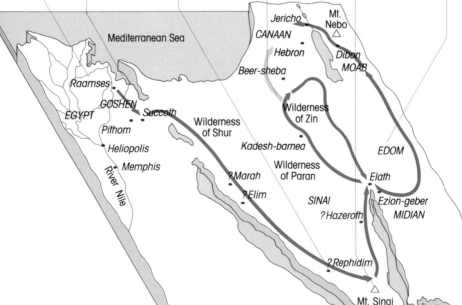

impressive and may disclose to us the background of the covenant at Mount Sinai.

However, some scholars recently have argued that the covenant form entered the theology and worship of Israel much later than Moses' time (perhaps in the seventh century BC) and that it probably came from the Arameans or Assyrians, who used the form with their subjects.

But it seems that the biblical covenant is closest in form and spirit to the earlier Hittite treaties. And that there was some kind of a formal agreement between Israel and Yahweh as the foundation of the new nation, for obedience to the terms of which the great prophets later appealed, seems incontrovertible.

Meaning of the Exodus

The miracle of the deliverance from Egypt made an indelible impression on the memory of Israel. In later centuries poets, prophets, wise people, and priests celebrated it as a mighty demonstration of the mercy of God expressed toward the chosen people.

The Exodus was to Jews and the Old Testament what the life, death and resurrection of Jesus were for the first Christians and the New Testament – a merciful act by which unworthy, helpless people were delivered from bondage into glorious liberty as the people of God.

Old Testament writers saw the giving of the Law at Mount Sinai as God's gracious instruction of the chosen children concerning what he expected of those whom he had redeemed. (For a discussion of authorship, sources, and dates, see pp. 98–103.)

Leviticus

Title

The Hebrew title is 'And he called.' Our title is derived from the Septuagint and the Latin Vulgate and suggests that this book pertains to the work of the Levitical priests who guided the worship of the people of God. Ancient rabbis called it 'The Priests' Manual.'

Contents and Sources

Leviticus, in contrast to Genesis and Exodus, contains very little narrative (only chaps. 8–9; 10:1–7, 16–20; 24:10–14, 23). It consists almost wholly of regulations for governing the relationship between Israel and God.

God is 'holy' (i.e., high above all that is profane and unclean). This book tells how a secular and unclean people can relate themselves to a God of indescribable glory and absolute purity – how they can meet the divine command, 'You shall be holy; for I the Lord your God am holy' (11:44–45; 19:2; 20:26; 21:8).

Outline:

Laws concerning sacrifices (chaps. 1–7)

The ceremony of consecration of the priesthood (chaps. 8–10)

Laws concerning ritual purity (clean and unclean) (chaps. 11–16)

The Law of Holiness (chaps. 17–26)

Laws concerning vows and tithes (chap. 27)

That Leviticus is a great compendium of rites and laws stemming from and regulating the cultic life of Israel is obvious. It declares that God gave all of Israel's ritual law to Moses at Mount Sinai (1:1; 27:34). Chapters 8 and 9 form the literary continuation of Exodus 29. Both sections have to do with God's instructions for the inauguration of the priestly service of Aaron and his sons. Scholars long have recognized that the book contains earlier and later materials, but how early and how late is disputed.

Conservatives ascribe the heart of the material (the various offerings, the procedure for consecrating the priesthood, the prescriptions for the Day of Atonement, and the hygienic regulations, for example) to Moses himself and allow for the possibility of later minor revisions.

Liberals have assigned the book's origin to Jerusalem priests of the rebuilt temple (about 500 BC or later), who, along with their own formulations, incorporated previously existing materials (laws of sacrifice and a 'Holiness Code' [Lev. 17—26]). Some of these, they believe, may go back to practices in various Israelite sanctuaries of the monarchical period (about 1020–587 BC) and even earlier.

Theology and Significance

Leviticus expresses the ancient Jews' conviction that God – the only God – is supremely pure and that people are unclean sinners, whose ways are an abomination to God. However, God wants to make people into his image so he and they can dwell together in fellowship (26:11–12).

Sin and pollution can be purged away from sanctuary and people by God-appointed means: repentance and fasting, burnt offerings, sin offerings, guilt offerings, and Day of Atonement rites. And good relations with God can be maintained by cereal offerings and peace offerings.

Since blood is life (Gen. 9:4; Lev. 17:14; Deut. 12:23) and thus akin to the life that is characteristic of God (Hos. 1:10), blood is sacred and is efficacious in purifying that to which it is applied: in Leviticus, to altar and sanctuary. People's individual sins defile the altar and sanctuary and threaten to drive God from his dwelling place. So the sanctuary must be cleansed by the priests on the sinners' behalf by periodic individual sacrifices; and both sanctuary and people must be purged on the annual Day of Atonement.

On that Day the cleansing of the people results from repentance and fasting (16:29; 23:27–32) and the transference of their sins to the scapegoat (16:22). Here atonement is in the form of substitution: the goat bears away the sins so that God's favor, rather than judgment, may come on the sinners.

It is important to note that in the theology of Leviticus 'blood is not given to God as atonement. Indeed God is never the direct object of the verb "atone" as though the sacrificial offering must somehow affect him' (D. J. McCarthy, *Interpreter's Dictionary of the Bible, Supplement,* 115). And furthermore, atonement by sacrifice does not automatically redress wrongs done to one's fellows. One must make restitution prior to the making of his guilt offering (6:1–7).

In Leviticus it is pointed out that the priests are to teach the nation the difference between 'the holy and the common … the unclean and the clean' (10:10) and to help it to become holy as God is holy. As for the treatment of the neighbor, 'you shall love your neighbor as yourself' (19:18).

New Testament writers saw God's true sanctuary as the human heart and the body of believers, not as a temple of wood and stone (2 Cor. 6:16; Eph. 2:19–22, 1 Pet. 2:4–5). Cleansing of the conscience to be the dwelling place of God becomes possible through the perfect sacrifice – 'the blood of Christ,' not 'the blood of goats and bulls' (Heb. 9:12–14). They saw the old sacrificial system as pointing beyond itself to him who 'gave himself up for us, a fragrant offering and sacrifice to God' (Eph. 5:2).

Numbers

rebellious, impetuous, licentious Israel, that he might prepare an unworthy but chosen nation to inherit the Promised Land.

Title

The Hebrew title 'In the Wilderness' is a more adequate designation than the Septuagint and Latin Vulgate title 'Numbers.' The numbering of the tribes (chaps. 1–4, 26) is only a small portion of the book, and it is only one aspect of Israel's many-sided life 'in the wilderness'.

Contents

In general, the book describes miscellaneous experiences of Israel from the final days of sojourning at Mount Sinai until the encampment on the plains of Moab before entering the Promised Land. The material is loosely organized, laws and narratives being combined in a not altogether logical way. (For a discussion of the problem of the sources of the book of Numbers, see the comments on the Pentateuch on pp. 98–103.)

According to the book's own chronology, only twenty days are covered in Part 1 (see 1:1 and 10:11). Part 2 involves about thirty-eight years (10:11; 33:38, the latter passage dating Aaron's death as recorded in 20:23–29). Part 3 spans about six months (33:38; Deut. 1:3). The tradition that Israel spent forty years in the wilderness (Exod. 16:35; Num. 14:33–34; 32:13) has shaped the whole book. (For a historical evaluation of this, see below.)

Perhaps the dominant note of Numbers is God's patient discipline of faithless,

Historical and Religious Significance

We must sift carefully the traditions in Numbers about Israel's life in the wilderness in any fair estimate of their historical value. It is hardly believable that Israel in the wilderness should have been able to count 603,550 fighting men (1:46). This number would make the total company of Israelites about two million, an impossible multitude in view of the shortage of water and food in this desolate area.

Many scholars believe that the census lists of chaps. 1 and 26 originally related to a later period (the times of the Judges or of David) and are out of place chronologically here. It has been suggested also that the Hebrew word now translated 'thousand' (e.g., in 1:21) may mean a unit or subsection of a tribe. Thus the tribe of Reuben (1:21) would have had 46 subsections totaling 500 persons, rather than 46,500. Clearly the numbers as they now stand are impossible for the wilderness period. Conservative scholars agree that the numbers are not to be taken literally (R. K. Harrison; La Sor-Hubbard-Bush).

Since ancient peoples often reckoned a generation by the round number forty years (as did the Phoenicians and the Carthaginians), we apparently have a traditional number here signifying a generation. Actually a generation (from father's birth to son's birth) was about twenty to twenty-five years. The chronology of Numbers is thus traditional and not strictly historical in its numbering.

It is altogether probable that Israel, after the escape from Egypt, wandered from oasis to oasis in the wilderness south of Canaan for about a generation, unable to penetrate the well-fortified land (chaps. 13–14). Their principal base was Kadesh-Barnea, an important oasis about fifty miles south of Beersheba. Finally they skirted the edges of settled, fortified areas (Edom and Moab) and attacked the land of Canaan from the east.

The legal sections of Numbers (*e.g.,* chaps. 5–6; 8:1—9:14; chaps. 28—29) obviously have been inserted into the narrative setting with little regard for suitability of context. The purpose seems to be to connect the various laws with the Mosaic period to give them Mosaic authority.

The stories in Numbers offer a vivid picture of the frustrations, petulance, rivalry, rebellion against authority, rashness, licentiousness, and occasional heroism and nobility that characterized Israel's life in the wilderness. The stories emphasize the importance of wholehearted trust in God and unflinching obedience to the divine will, and portray God's unending patience in the disciplining of stubborn children.

Paul and the author of the book of Hebrews found 'instruction' for the church in these experiences of Israel in the wilderness. The instruction in essence was: Do not fall into the attitudes and sins of the wilderness generation or, like them, you'll die there and not get into the Promised Land (the kingdom of God) (1 Cor. 10:4–11; Heb. 3:7–19).

Deuteronomy

Title and Importance

Our name 'Deuteronomy' came from the Septuagint by way of the Latin Vulgate. The Septuagint mistranslated the Hebrew phrase 'a copy of this law' in Deut. 17:18 by rendering it 'second (or repeated) law' (*deuteronomion*).

This word apparently became the name of the book because it indicates a prominent aspect of the material: a repetition by Moses of the deeds of Yahweh and the content of his Law for the benefit of the generation about to enter the Promised Land.

Deuteronomy is one of the four Old Testament books most quoted in the New Testament (the others are Isaiah, Psalms, and Genesis). Jesus used its words in resisting the tempter in the wilderness (Matt. 4:4, 7, 10). Like the Jewish teachers of his time, he summarized the primary demand of God by quoting Deut. 6:5: 'You shall love the Lord your God with all your heart, and with all your soul, and with all your might' (Matt. 22:37; Mark 12:30; Luke 10:27–28).

Deuteronomy was early regarded as canonical, that is, as containing an authoritative standard for the life of the covenant people (see p. 30).

Contents

Deuteronomy is not a book of law in a narrow sense. It is a book of sermons about the gracious deeds of God in Israel's behalf and *how* Israel should respond to

Outline

First address of Moses: what God has done
(1:1—4:43)
The mighty acts of God, which call for
exclusive loyalty, are recited.

Second address of Moses: what God
requires (4:44—28:68)
The meaning and obligation of the covenant
relationship, its specific terms, and the
enforcement by God of those terms are set
forth.

Third address of Moses: what God proposes
(29:1—30:20)
A renewal of the covenant by the new
generation is contemplated.

Narrative about the change in leadership
from Moses to Joshua (31:1—34:12)

God's gracious deeds and *why*.

The theme of the preaching is: In view
of God's love for the chosen people, his
gracious deliverance of them from the
bondage of Egypt, and the gift of the covenant at Horeb (Sinai), they should respond by loving God, remaining staunchly loyal to him, and wholeheartedly obeying his will as expressed in the terms of the
covenant. If they obey God's laws, he will
bless them with rich life in the new land; if
they do not, they will be blighted with a
horrible curse and perish in that land.

The central notes of Deuteronomy are
'remember,' 'obey,' 'behold': *remember*
God's gracious attitudes and deeds; *obey*
God's words in unswerving loyalty and
fidelity; *behold* what God has in store for
the chosen people!

Circumstances of Writing

Most scholars believe that Deuteronomy,
in whole or in part, was the book found in
the temple by Hilkiah the priest, in the
time of King Josiah.

This book became the basis of a sweeping religious reformation (2 Kings 22—
23). The reforms instituted by Josiah –
the rooting out of polytheism; the reestablishment of exclusive worship of the

ancestral God of Israel and the centraliza-
tion of worship in one sanctuary at
Jerusalem; the abolition of child sacrifice,
sacred prostitution, and the practice of di-
vination and magic – are in line with the
teaching of Deuteronomy. The threats
and promises of the book (chaps. 27—28)
seem to have had an electric effect on this
king (2 Kings 22:11–13; 23:1–3).

We do not know how long the book had
been in existence before its discovery in
the temple. Many liberal scholars of today
believe that Deuteronomy is part of a
great theological interpretation of Israel's
history that reaches from the book of
Deuteronomy itself to the end of our 2
Kings (*i.e.*, Deuteronomy and the Former Prophets – see p. 121). Long ago the
Graf-Wellhausen school of critics (see pp.
99–100) identified a layer of material in
the Pentateuch and in the books of Joshua
through Kings which has definite stylistic
and theological characteristics and which
they labelled D. It is now proposed that as
many as three editors (or editorial circles)
contributed to the Deuteronomistic History: the first in the late eighth or early
seventh century (during the reign of
Hezekiah or Manasseh); the second at the
time of Josiah (about 622 BC); and the
third during the Babylonian Exile (about
550 BC).

Conservatives argue for 'substantial
Mosaic authorship' of Deuteronomy and
allow only for minor additions in the immediate post-Moses period. They reject
the hypothesis of a long Deuteronomistic
History now imbedded in Deuteronomy
through Kings.

There is a growing consensus that much
of the material in our book of
Deuteronomy is older than the time of
Hezekiah or Josiah. According to one
hypothesis, reminiscences of the words of
Moses may have been carried down in oral
or written form, preserved by Levitical
preachers of the covenant in northern Israel, and enshrined in our Deuteronomy
(or part of it) in the time of Hezekiah or
Josiah. Thus the book may be both early
and late in origin.

Theological Emphases

a. Yahweh is the Lord of the nations and of history. Yahweh has assigned all people their lands and their forms of worship (2:5, 9; 4:19; 32:8).

b. Out of Yahweh's love Israel was chosen as God's special possession (7:6–8). God gave Israel a goodly land, a law to govern its life, a form of worship, and the promise of a magnificent future (28:1–14).

c. Israel must give exclusive loyalty to Yahweh (4:1–40). It must eliminate idolatrous peoples and the worship of other gods from its land by 'holy war' (7:1–5), centralize its worship at the one sanctuary in Jerusalem (12:2–28), and faithfully perform the ceremonies prescribed by God (14:22—16:17).

d. God's love should be reciprocated with love, and this love should bring about obedience to God's righteous will in all areas of personal and national life.

Members of the covenant community must be loving and faithful both to God and to one another. Lost property is to be restored speedily to its owner (22:1–4). Money is to be lent to a neighbor without interest charges (23:19–20). The cloak of a poor man, offered as security, must be returned before nightfall (24:12–13). A widow's garment is not to be taken as security (24:17). Generosity toward the poor will dictate leaving some of the harvest for them to gather (24:19–21). Fellow Israelites are not to be forced into slavery or sold (24:7). The withholding of wages from servants is strictly forbidden (24:14–15). Honest weights and measures must be used in all transactions (25:13–15). The God of love and mercy requries love and mercy of those who live in fellowship with him.

Abiding Significance

On the historical side, we may suggest that Deuteronomy is to the teaching of Moses what the Gospel of John is to the teaching of Jesus. Authentic notes of each teacher are undoubtedly preserved in each writing, but both bodies of teaching have been transposed into a different key and made to apply to new situations. Moses stands behind Deuteronomy, even as Jesus stands behind the Fourth Gospel.

Deuteronomy stands at the center of Judeo-Christian theology. The heart of the gospel in both Testaments is that we should love and serve God because God first loved and redeemed us. Deuteronomy presents God's deeds as the basis of his requirements, a point made strongly by both Jesus and Paul. And that true ethical behavior springs out of a loving, dedicated heart is a profound and important insight.

The Historical Books

The historical books of the Old Testament are Joshua, Judges, Ruth, 1–2 Samuel, 1–2 Kings, 1–2 Chronicles, Ezra-Nehemiah, Esther. The word 'historical' may be misleading here. These books do not contain history in the modern sense of that term. Although they possess materials of great value to the historian, they are shaped so strongly by theological interests that often they are more like preaching than straightforward historical narrative.

That this is so is suggested by the fact that in the Hebrew Bible the books of Joshua through Kings are called 'The Former (or Early) Prophets,' while Isaiah, Jeremiah, Ezekiel and the Twelve (Minor) Prophets are called 'The Latter (or Later) Prophets.' This terminology recognizes the truth that the books of Joshua through Kings record Israel's obedience or disobedience to the word of God as spoken through special agents; and the books point out the blessed or dire consequences in personal and national life of that obedience or disobedience.

While these books are related to the writings of the Latter (or Later) Prophets on the one hand, they are related to the Pentateuch on the other. In content they continue the story of God's redemptive activity in the life of Israel.

Deuteronomy ends with the appointment of Joshua as a successor to Moses and with the story of the latter's death. The book of Joshua picks up the story there and records the conquest and division of the land and the farewell addresses and death of Joshua. The books that follow record God's activity in the period of the Judges of Israel, in the formation of the monarchy under Saul, David, and Solomon and in its disruption

after Solomon's death; and they trace the progressive degradation of the two kingdoms (Northern and Southern) until the destruction of each at the hands of Israel's enemies.

1–2 Chronicles and Ezra-Nehemiah point out strongly the wisdom of personal and national obedience to God and the folly of disobedience. So close is the book of Joshua to the content, style, and assumed sources of the Pentateuch that many scholars prefer to include it with the five books before it and speak of the 'Hexateuch' (six scrolls or books). They say that J, E, D, P (see pp. 100–101) underlie the book of Joshua, P terminating with this book. Some scholars have argued that J, E, and D run through 2 Kings and that the books Joshua through 2 Kings have a common literary history with the books of the Pentateuch.

Yet other scholars prefer to split Deuteronomy off from Genesis to Numbers and to speak only of a 'Tetrateuch' (four scrolls or books). They believe that Deuteronomy is the first book of a long Deuteronomistic history of Israel extending through 2 Kings, written in the sixth century BC. They deny the existence of the main Pentateuchal sources J and E in Joshua to Kings and argue that a writer or writers with the Deuteronomic point of view put the narrative in these books together out of many fragments. They hold that Deuteronomy was separated from Joshua to Kings when Moses' authorship of the opening books of the Bible became a fixed dogma in Judaism. Thus whether Deuteronomy belonged originally with the books before it or after it is a debated point.

Since conservatives cling to the concept of a Pentateuch written by Moses (with minor later additions), they reject the concept of a Tetrateuch or Hexateuch created out of late documents (JEDP – see pp. 100–101). They argue for an earlier dating for the writing of Joshua, Judges and 1 and 2 Samuel than the Deuteronomistic History view allows.

Joshua

Canaanite deity from Hazor, c. 14th century B.C.

For Further Reading
Ackroyd, P. R., 'The Historical Literature,' in Knight, D. A. and Tucker, G. M. (eds.), *The Hebrew Bible and Its Modern Interpreters*, 1985.
Hayes, J. H., *An Introduction to Old Testament Study*, 1979.
La Sor, W. S., Hubbard, D. A., Bush, F. W., *Old Testament Survey*, 1982.

Title

The English title is from the Septuagint and the Latin Vulgate, which named books by their contents rather than their opening words. The name Joshua (Hebrew, *Yehoshua* or *Yeshua*) means 'Yahweh is salvation.' The Greek form of the name is *Iesous* (English, Jesus). There are two great Joshuas in Judeo-Christian literature, the second being Joshua of Nazareth.

Contents and Theology

The book of Joshua is both a climax and a new beginning. It records the fulfillment of the promise made to Abraham concerning the gift of the Land of Canaan (Gen. 12, 15) and the beginning of a long life for the people of Israel in that land. The exodus from Egypt and the covenant in the wilderness have meaning in Israel's history only because a homeland was won in which a redeemed people could work out their destiny under God.

The point of view throughout is identical with that in Deuteronomy. God is regarded as a holy and jealous God, who

---

Outline

The conquest of Canaan (1:1—12:24)

The division of the land (13:1—21:45)

Final acts and instructions of Joshua (22:1—24:33)

The mound at Tell es-Sultan, Jericho, marks many successive settlements.

tolerates no worship of other gods by the chosen people. God is the Lord of history, who works out the pattern of events in such a way as to fulfill his purposes. (Note the sovereign 'I' in 24:2–13.) He has called Israel into being and guided its destiny at every stage. He has given the people a homeland. This land has been won not by Israel's bow or sword but by the terror or panic sent by the Lord on the land's inhabitants (24:12). Although much territory remains to be taken, the whole land is included in God's promise, and it will be possessed if Israel will be loyal and obedient to God.

In view of the gracious purpose and deeds of the Lord, Israel should love and serve God faithfully (23:11; 24:14–15). This means abhorrence of other gods, no intermarriage with foreign peoples (23:12–13), and complete destruction of forbidden possessions (chap. 7). The only path to national security and prosperity is exclusive loyalty to God with the whole heart and soul (22:5).

Author, Sources, and Date

Many interpreters believe that the book of Joshua was put together from a variety of sources – some of them of early date – by a compiler who lived not earlier than the late seventh century BC and probably in the sixth.

This writer may have been the author of the book of Deuteronomy in its present form. The stylistic and theological characteristics of Deuteronomy and Joshua are strikingly similar. It is possible that Joshua is the second part of a great Deuteronomistic history of Israel reaching from Moses to the fall of Jerusalem (see p. 121). It may be that some portions of Joshua were added after the great history was completed (possibly Josh. 13—21 and 24).

We cannot say precisely what sources were used in compiling the book of Joshua. It has been suggested that an old JE narrative furnished the basic material of chaps. 1—12. The JE narrative must have contained an account of the fulfill-ment of the promise made to Abraham (Gen. 12, 15) in the gift of the land. Hence, these interpreters hold that this fulfillment in altered form appears in the narrative of Josh. 1—12.

The material contained in Josh. 13—21 may have come from lists of tribal borders and towns, of cities of refuge, and of Levitical cities, dating perhaps from the eleventh to the seventh centuries. Some who deny that JE materials underlie the story of the conquest of the land in Joshua find the source of this material in sanctuary and tribal traditions freely re-worked by the Deuteronomistic author.

Conservative scholars, who reject the documentary hypothesis concerning the formation of the Pentateuch (see p. 102), have either ascribed the bulk of the book to Joshua himself (with minor later addi-tions) or assigned its writing to an un-known person of the time of Samuel (mid-dle of the eleventh century), with the suggestion that Samuel may have contri-buted in some way to its composition.

No certainty on authorship, sources, or date is possible. Whatever the sources and whoever the author, the narrative he put together about the conquest and its after-math offers informative and absorbing reading.

Historical Significance

Opinions differ sharply on the historical value of the book of Joshua. Liberal schol-ars have long noted that the massive, sweeping, and almost uniformly success-ful character of Joshua's campaigns, as presented in this book, differs from the painful, piecemeal, tribe-by-tribe efforts at conquest described in the first chapter of Judges. They have accepted the Judges account and discredited that in Joshua as consisting of fanciful hero tales told through the romanticizing haze of the years and as popular stories which arose in explanation of various customs and land-marks. Similarly, they have seen little of value for understanding the settlement of

the tribes in the conquered land in the lists offered in Josh. 13—21, so late and con-fused have these materials seemed to be.

Conservative scholars, however, have defended the accuracy of the book of Joshua and sought to validate it by appeal-ing to the results of archaeology. Several views among contemporary scholars of both categories have emerged concerning the nature of Israel's conquest of Palestine (and concerning the historical character of the book of Joshua).

1. Joshua and his followers, from a base east of the Jordan River, conquered the land to the west of it in a sweeping, three-pronged military invasion. They de-stroyed many cities and their populations and divided the conquered land among the Israelite tribes – exactly as the book of Joshua claims. Since Joshua himself wrote the book, or most of it (G. Archer), or since it was written not long after Joshua's time in the lifetime of Samuel (about 1045 BC) and possibly by his assistance (R. K. Harrison), we ought to accept the record at face value.

Moreover, archaeologists have con-firmed this view of the conquest. They have uncovered the charred remains of several Canaanite cities (Bethel, Debir, Lachish, Hazor) Joshua is said to have de-stroyed and have found strikingly differ-ent Israelite houses and pottery above the destroyed level. The evidence shows that the land was *occupied* through a God-or-dained, God-led, sweeping military cam-paign but not completely *subjugated* by it, as Judges 1 shows. Subjugation continued until the time of David. Hence, both Joshua and Judges are historically accurate.

2. The land was won not by military action but by gradual occupation and, for the most part, peaceful settlement by semi-nomadic (or pastoralist) Israelite tribes from east of the Jordan and perhaps else-where (Alt, Noth, J.M. Miller).

These tribes moved at different times into the largely open hill country to the west of the river in search of pasturage, many of them settling down there to till

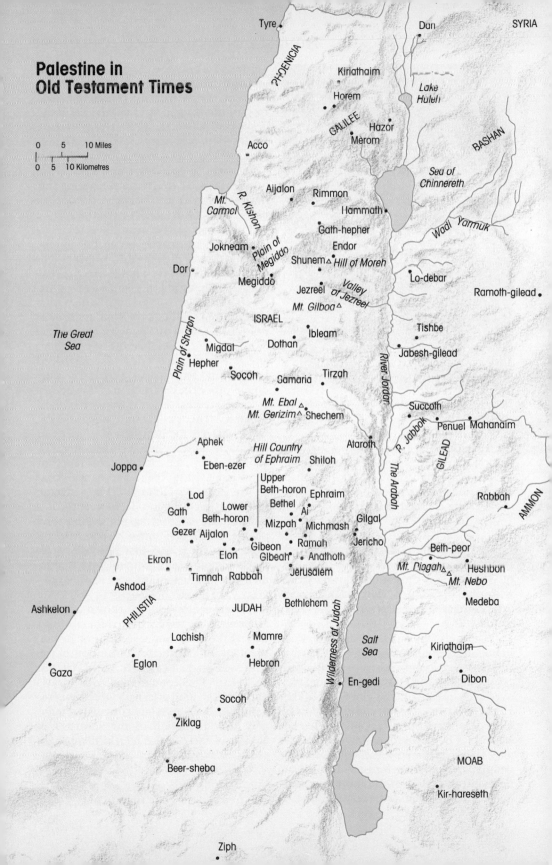

Palestine in
Old Testament Times

0   5   10 Miles

0   5   10 Kilometres

SYRIA

Tyre

Dan

PHOENICIA

Kiriathaim

Lake
Huleh

Horem

GALILEE

Hazor
Merom

BASHAN

Sea of
Chinnereth

Acco

Aijalon

Rimmon

Hammath

Wadi Yarmuk

Mt.
Carmel

R. Kishon

Gath-hepher

Jokneam

Plain of
Megiddo

Endor

Lo-debar

Shunem △ Hill of Moreh

Ramoth-gilead

Dor

Megiddo

Jezreel

Valley
of Jezreel

Mt. Gilboa △

ISRAEL

Tishbe

The Great
Sea

Ibleam

Jabesh-gilead

Migdal

Dothan

Plain of Sharon

Hepher

Socoh

Samaria

Tirzah

River Jordan

Succoth

Mt. Ebal △

Mt. Gerizim △ Shechem

Penuel Mahanaim

Aphek

Hill Country
of Ephraim

Ataroth

R. Jabbok

GILEAD

Eben-ezer

Shiloh

The Arabah

Joppa

Upper
Beth-horon

Ephraim

Lod

Bethel

Rabbah

AMMON

Gath

Lower
Beth-horon

Ai

Gezer

Aijalon

Mizpah

Michmash

Gilgal

Elon

Gibeon

Ramah

Jericho

Ekron

Gibeah

Anathoth

Beth-peor

Timnah

Rabbah

Jerusalem

Mt. Pisgah △

△ Heshbon

Ashdod

Mt. Nebo

Ashkelon

PHILISTIA

Bethlehem

Medeba

JUDAH

Salt
Sea

Kiriathaim

Lachish

Mamre

Gaza

Eglon

Hebron

Dibon

Socoh

Wilderness of Judah

En-gedi

Ziklag

Beer-sheba

MOAB

Kir-hareseth

Ziph

The great stone tower dating from 7000 BC at Tell es-Sultan, Jericho.

The exodus of Hebrews from Egypt and the subsequent conquests in Transjordan served as a catalyst for an upheaval west of the Jordan. Without the aid of the oppressed people there, who were striking for freedom and better economic circumstances, the Canaanite rulers could not have been ousted and a new egalitarian order set up. Through the motivating and unifying power of Yahweh worship, a covenantal confederacy was formed.

This view is a 'between-the-lines' construction and makes little use of the specific data of the book of Joshua.

4. A combination view holds that the conquest was both military and social-political, both sudden and gradual (Bright).

It is inherently likely that there was military action in the conquest of the land, considering the militaristic atmosphere and activities of the period. The destroyed levels found by archaeologists, while they do not prove the destruction of those cities by the Israelites, do agree with the biblical account. The swift capitulation of the land, without the destruction of many of its towns in the hill country, may be explained by the presence in them of people related by blood and background to the invading Hebrews. These people had not been in Egypt. They were the impoverished, landless, exploited pastoral people mentioned above. Anxious to escape from their serf-like bondage, they made common cause with the invading Israelites. 'The conquest was to some degree … an inside job!' (Bright).

Several centuries of effort by individual Hebrew tribes were required for subjugation of the land. Some sections of Joshua seem aware that the total conquest of the land was gradual (13:2–6; 15:13–19, 63; 23:7–13). The combination view draws the biblical and archaeological data together in a coherent and convincing manner. For discussion of the accounts in Joshua of the capture of Jericho and Ai, see pp.401–402.

the soil along with their pastoral activities. At first they were accepted by the Canaanites, to whom some of them may have had ethnic and historical ties; but at a later stage (from the end of the period of the Judges to the time of David) there was military conflict. The tribes grew closer together in the hill country through the effects of shared sanctuaries in the worship of Yahweh and through mounting strife with the Canaanites. This view makes little contact with the account in the book of Joshua.

3. The land west of the Jordan was won not so much by military conquest but by internal revolt of native, subjugated people against their Canaanite, feudalistic overlords (Mendenhall, Gottwald). The ruling class in city-states of Canaan was locked together in an oppressive feudal system. The revolutionaries were serfs and landless, impoverished, pastoral people, many of them long resident in Canaan and ancestrally and culturally related to the Hebrews who came out of Egypt.

Judges

mean not legal experts who rendered decisions in a court of law, but heroes who, by divine call and empowerment, delivered Israel from the oppression of surrounding enemies. However, these heroes evidently had judicial functions during the period of their leadership (4:5). They were virtually dictators in all matters pertaining to the life of their followers.

Some scholars hold that two types of leaders are combined in the book: tribal military heroes and city or district rulers. According to this hypothesis, the great Judges (Othniel, Ehud, Deborah, Gideon, Jephthah, and Samson) were military heroes, and the minor ones (Shamgar, Tola, Jair, Ibzan, Elon, Abdon) were city or district rulers. Both types may be included under the Hebrew word 'judges' because God's Spirit was believed to guide both the warriors and the magistrates of Israel.

Title

'Judges' was the title given to the book in the Hebrew Old Testament as well as in the Septuagint and the Latin Vulgate.

The title came from the text of the book (*e.g.*, 2:16–18), where the term seems to

Mount Tabor rises some 1,938 feet (588 metres) above the Plain of Jezreel.

General Contents and Theology

Part 1 offers an account of the conquest of Canaan roughly parallel to that in the book of Joshua, though with a sharply different emphasis. Here the conquest proceeds by tribes, there by a united attack on the whole land.

The material in Part 1 lays a good foundation for the rest of the book, since it explains the source of many of Israel's troubles in this period: the presence of Canaanite inhabitants in many of the chief cities and the influence of their religion (Baalism) on the life of Israel.

Part 2 contains the courageous and often bloody exploits of the 'judges.' Twelve – six major and six minor (Abimelech, a thirteenth, seems a supplemental figure in the story of Gideon) – are placed before the reader, the minor ones with little more than brief mention.

The stories about the six major judges illustrate a theology of history characteristic of the book of Deuteronomy, especially of chap. 28. This is that exclusive loyalty to God and faithful obedience to *all* God's laws bring national prosperity and security, but disobedience results in complete disaster.

This point of view is illustrated from the experience of Israel in the time of the judges. The experience runs in a repeated cycle: the people of Israel are faithful to Yahweh during the days of the God-sent leader; after his death, they turn away and worship the baals; an enemy conquers and oppresses them; they repent and cry to Yahweh for deliverance; God shows mercy and sends a deliverer; they are faithful to Yahweh during the lifetime of the deliverer; then, again, they worship the baals; again, an enemy overcomes them; etc.

Part 3 is only loosely connected with the preceding material. It apparently seeks to illustrate the statement: 'In those days there was no king in Israel; every man did what was right in his own eyes' (17:6; 21:25; *cf.* 18:1; 19:1). The writer, by showing the relative anarchy of the period of the judges because Israel had no central authority, prepares for the narrative yet to come about the rise of the monarchy. The two stories offered here (chaps. 17–21) exalt the importance of the Levites and may well have come from pre-monarchical Levitical traditions.

Sources and Historical Value

Basic to the book are old hero stories which were told in the individual tribes at various local centers and sanctuaries. The Song of Deborah (chap. 5) may have been composed and sung soon after the event described in it (twelfth century BC). Various short pieces seem to be of early date (Jotham's fable, 9:7–15; Samson's riddles, 14:14, 18; 15:16, for example.)

Liberal scholars believe that these and other old materials were put together in some hero narrative (possibly as part of JE) between the tenth and the seventh centuries BC. A version of this narrative was issued in the late seventh or sixth century by a Deuteronomistic editor (or editors) who cast the whole in the cyclic theology of history described above. A final edition, including some additions and changes, seems to have been made in the postexilic period, perhaps in the fifth century BC.

Conservative scholars give a different view of the book's origin. They believe that its true sources have no relationship to the hypothetical Pentateuchal sources (JEDP) but are oral and written traditions about tribal and national heroes preserved at various early sanctuaries, possibly collected in part by Samuel, and put together

Shiloh, permanent resting place of the Ark of the Covenant in the period of the Judges.

into our present book by an unknown person in the early days of the monarchy (tenth century BC), possibly by Nathan or Gad (1 Chron. 29:29). Some (La Sor-Hubbard-Bush) suggest a tenth-ninth century date for the writing and allow that editing continued until about the sixth century.

The book offers a graphic picture of Israelite life in the first years of the settlement in Canaan. The tribes, loosely federated, maintained a precarious hold on part of the land, while they attempted to beat off attacks of local Canaanite groups and parry the thrusts of enemies from neighboring countries. Wars among Israelite tribes (chaps. 19—21) weakened their resources and their resistance to common enemies. Without a central government, Israel of necessity had to rely on voluntary cooperation of the tribes, tribes too often interested in their own local affairs to help their brethren at a distance. Baal religion, which along with an agricul-

tural way of life Israelites picked up from the Canaanites, weakened loyalty to Yahweh, the God of the desert of Sinai, and contributed to the disunity of the tribes. The book of Judges accurately mirrors all these conditions.

That the judges did not rule over all Israel in succession, as the book claims, but rather to some degree at the same time in the various tribes is evident from the fact that altogether 410 years are assigned to the period of the judges in the chronological notations of the book. 1 Kings 6:1 puts only 480 years between the Exodus and the building of the temple under Solomon. It seems certain that many of the judges were tribal, rather than national, figures, whose careers overlapped and who together occupied a period of not more than about 200 years.

Religious Significance

The basic conviction expressed in the book is like that in Deuteronomy and Joshua: God requires loyalty of covenant people and demands complete rejection of false religion. God's blessings depend on unswerving obedience. To follow any other god is to forfeit personal and national destiny. For a wandering people to return to God is the highest wisdom, the way to forgiveness, success, peace.

This is the teaching of the prophets written boldly in this book. Christianity largely transferred the rewards and the punishments to the spiritual realm, but it did not abandon the concept of recompense for loyalty and disloyalty to the true God.

Ruth

Basic Nature and Contents

The book of Ruth, named after one of its three principal characters, appears in the Septuagint and the Latin Vulgate after the book of Judges because of the opening words: 'In the days when the judges ruled' (Ruth 1:1).

In the Hebrew Bible Ruth falls among the Writings – that is, after the Former (Early) and Latter (Later) Prophets. It originally had no connection with the book of Judges, the statement in the Talmud that 'Samuel wrote his own book and Judges and Ruth' to the contrary notwithstanding.

In form it is an entertaining and instructive short story, based on an old narrative or possibly a poem long told in Israel. The writer of the story in its present form has shaped it into what Goethe called 'the liveliest little epic and idyllic whole that tradition has given us.'

The story of the loyalty of Ruth, the widowed Moabitess, to her mother-in-law, Naomi; of the journey of both to Bethlehem (Naomi's ancestral home); of Ruth's marriage to Boaz; and of the birth to them of Obed, the grandfather of David, is so well known as to need no outlining in detail here.

Purpose and Date

Several purposes of the book have been suggested:
a. To revive or reinforce the obligation of a male relative to take a dead man's sonless widow as a wife in order to raise up an heir for the deceased;
b. To protest against the policy of exclusion of foreigners carried out by Ezra and Nehemiah (Neh. 13:1–3, 23–27; cf. Ezra 10) by showing that God blessed the union of a Jew and a Moabitess with the gift of Obed, the grandfather of David;
c. To show how God guides and helps those who are faithful to their obligations to him and who are merciful toward one another, even to foreigners; and how in hidden and mysterious ways God directs people and the course of history to the fulfillment of the divine purpose – the coming of King David.

In recent years some liberal and most conservative scholars have come together in their assessment of the date of the book of Ruth. The former once held that Ruth's position in the Hebrew canon among the (late) Writings, its supposed late words (Aramaisms), and the nature of its teaching (tolerance of foreigners) argue for an origin in the post-Exilic period (about 400 BC), especially if the story was intended to counter Ezra's and Nehemiah's hostility toward foreign wives.

Conservatives long have dated the book to the time of David or thereabouts. Today there is considerable agreement that the story arose in the early monarchic period (10th – 8th centuries). There is debate about the date of the genealogy at the end of the book (4:18–22). It may be post-Exilic.

There are no clear reasons why the story should be regarded as entirely fictional, as some scholars do. Historical data and religious truth (as in point c above – probably the book's main purpose) are often clothed in artistic dress by master storytellers, poets, and dramatists.

We do not know the identity of the author. It is evident that he was a man of culture, deep piety, and largeness of heart.

1–2 Samuel

Title

1 and 2 Samuel were originally one book and were so presented in Hebrew manuscripts before the fifteenth century AD.

The separation into two books dates to the Septuagint, which, moreover, put Samuel and Kings under the title 'Kingdoms' and numbered them from one to four. Greek, unlike Hebrew, is written with vowels as well as consonants and requires about one and three quarters more space than Hebrew. Therefore, two rolls became necessary for the translation of each Hebrew book. The division into four books passed into the Latin Vulgate and into English editions.

The Hebrew Bible called the original book 'Samuel' either because Samuel was regarded in Jewish tradition (based on 1 Chron. 29:29–30) as its author or because he was a main character in the book.

The name is not altogether appropriate. Samuel could not have written it, since his death is reported in 1 Sam. 25:1 and all the events of 1 Sam. 25–31 and 2 Samuel occurred thereafter. Furthermore, Saul and David surely had equal right to be considered in the naming, since they figure so largely in the narrative.

Contents and Theology

In general, 1–2 Samuel covers the story of the founding of the Israelite monarchy by Samuel and the careers of its first two kings, Saul and David.

In its present form 1–2 Samuel elaborates the theme that obedience to God by personal righteousness in attitudes and deeds is the basic requirement for leadership of God's chosen people. It draws a contrast between disobedient, evil leaders, and God-fearing, good leaders.

God rejected the priest Eli and his sons because they violated the standards of priestly conduct. They were weak, licentious, and greedy (1 Sam. 2:12–17, 22–25, 27–36). Samuel, on the other hand, was 'a man of God,' fully obedient to God's voice (1 Sam. 3). The people declared that he was righteous all his days (1 Sam. 12:1–5).

Saul was a promising young man upon whom the Spirit of God came in mighty power (1 Sam. 11:6). He did not realize his promise because he did not obey the word of Yahweh (1 Sam. 13:13–14; chap. 15; 28:17–18). He finally confessed that God had rejected him because of his unrighteous attitudes and deeds (1 Sam. 24:17–20).

David, by contrast, also was chosen by God for leadership and filled with his Spirit (1 Sam. 16:1–13). He showed himself zealous for God's cause (1 Sam. 17:36), continually 'strengthened himself in the Lord his God' (1 Sam. 30:6), and lived in humility among his fellows (1 Sam. 18:18, 23). He showed consideration and respect for his personal enemy Saul (1 Sam. 24:6; 26:9; 2 Sam. 1), manifested zeal for the worship of God by bringing the ark to Jerusalem and planning the building of a temple (2 Sam. 6–7), and achieved victory in all his foreign conquests by the power of the Lord (2 Sam. 8:6). He 'administered justice and equity to all his people' (2 Sam. 8:15). He was 'a

David fled from King Saul to En-Gedi

man after his [God's] own heart' (1 Sam. 13:14).

And yet even David was judged by God when he sinned by coveting his neighbor's wife and arranging that neighbor's death (2 Sam. 11). Even his repentance (2 Sam. 12:13) could not avert the tragic consequences that sin brought in its wake. David's house was shaken to its very foundations (2 Sam. 11–20).

The whole narrative in 1–2 Samuel makes abundantly clear that God has a standard by which rulers are judged. When they violate God's will and refuse to cooperate with God's purposes, he removes them from leadership or severely punishes them.

Sources, Authorship, and Date

Many students of the book have claimed that written sources lie behind it. They point to duplicate accounts of the same events and to contradictory perspectives in them. In regard to the establishment of the monarchy, one account (1 Sam. 9:1—

10:16; 11:1–11, 15) represents the monarchy as God's intention and gracious gift to save the people from their enemies (9:16). Another (1 Sam. 8; 10:17–27; chap. 12) holds that its establishment was due to the people's wish and was an act of rebellion against God. Twice God rejects Saul (1 Sam. 13:8–14; 15:10–31); twice David is introduced to Saul (1 Sam. 16–17); twice David flees to the King of Gath (1 Sam. 21:10–15; chap. 27); twice he has mercy on Saul (1 Sam. 24 and 26); etc. It seems that different sources had different versions of these events.

Much of 1–2 Samuel is loosely written, with episodes hooked together. 2 Sam. 9–20 and 1 Kings 1–2, however, contain a fairly tightly constructed narrative, done by an accomplished writer. An eyewitness of the events described may have written this narrative in the age of Solomon (tenth century BC). Ahimaaz, the son of the high priest Zadok, or Abiathar, the high priest under David, have been suggested as its author.

Underlying the remainder of 1–2 Samuel may be some of the same sources imbedded in the Pentateuch (J, E), though this view has now largely died out (see p. 121).

In its place is the hypothesis of a Deuteronomistic History (Deuteronomy through 2 Kings), compiled in the 7th–6th century BC from many and various sources and touched up editorially in the postexilic period. It is said that behind 1 and 2 Samuel are individual narratives, groups of stories, a succession narrative (2 Sam. 9—1 Ki. 2), a few lists and poems, and possibly a prophetic history of some kind. It must be quickly added that the whole concept of a Deuteronomistic History has been challenged by some liberals as well as by conservatives.

Conservative scholars deny that there are any duplicate and contradictory narratives which can form the basis of source analysis of 1 and 2 Samuel. They are willing to grant the prior existence of the succession narrative, certain stories concerning the ark, and pieces of tradition about

Saul and David. They place the unknown writer of 1 and 2 Samuel somewhere in the tenth century BC, probably near its end.

Historical and Religious Value

Scholars agree that the most valuable section of 1–2 Samuel for the historian is 2 Sam. 9–20 (and its conclusion in 1 Kings 1–2). This narrative has been called 'the History of the Throne Succession.' Its realistic, true-to-life presentation of people and events, its factual and psychological accuracy, and its artful structure make it the finest specimen of historical writing in the Old Testament. Neighboring civilizations produced nothing like this until the time of the Greek historians centuries later.

The Samuel and Saul stories are less complete, seem less consistent with one another, and less historically accurate than those about David. They are sagas rather than eyewitness narratives. But they convey to us a substantially accurate picture of the times when the monarchy was formed in the face of Philistine pressure on Israel.

The lively stories of 1–2 Samuel drive home powerfully the view that priests and kings are subject to divine law and that the will of God is absolute righteousness in attitudes and deeds.

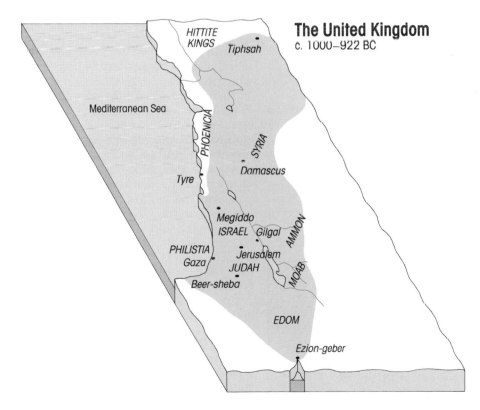

The United Kingdom
c. 1000–922 BC

1–2 Kings

Title

The Hebrew Bible's 'Samuel' and 'Kings' were divided by the translators of the Septuagint into four books called 'Kingdoms' and designated individually by the first four letters of the Greek alphabet. The Vulgate continued the division into four books and called them at first 'Kingdoms' but later 'Kings.' English Bibles use the fourfold division but keep the Hebrew designations 'Samuel' and 'Kings.'

Contents, Literary Method, and Point of View

The history of the kings of the united and the divided kingdoms presented in 1–2 Kings runs from Solomon (c. 961–922 BC) to Jehoichin's release from prison in Babylonia (c. 561 BC), a period of some 400 years.

1–2 Kings opens with events which follow those in 2 Samuel 20. (We noted above that 2 Sam. 9–20 and 1 Kings 1–2 comprise a 'History of the Throne Succes-

> ## Outline
>
> **The accession and the reign of Solomon**
> (1 Kings 1–11)
>
> **The kings of the divided monarchy**
> (1 Kings 12—2 Kings 17)
>
> **The kings of the surviving Southern Kingdom** (2 Kings 18–25)

sion,' 2 Sam. 21—24 forming appendixes.)

The record of the reigns of the various kings is set in a more or less stereotyped pattern, consisting of an introduction, some important facts about each reign, and a conclusion. The introduction includes: (1) the year of the king's accession, dated by reference to the year of reign of the king in the opposite kingdom (Israel or Judah); (2) his age at his accession (for kings of Judah only); (3) the length of his reign; (4) his capital city; (5) his mother's name (for kings of Judah only); (6) a judgment concerning his loyalty to Yahweh, as determined by his attitude toward religious cults other than that of the temple of Yahweh at Jerusalem. The facts offered vary from the briefest notices to rather full accounts of the king's reign.

The conclusion contains: (1) a reference to a source where additional information about the king can be found; (2) a mention of his death and place of burial; (3) the name and relationship of his successor.

The kings of Israel (the Northern Kingdom) are almost without exception condemned for infidelity to Yahweh in that they followed in the 'way of Jeroboam' who made Israel sin by setting up shrines at Bethel and Dan (1 Kings 12:28 ff.). Even Jehu, who launched a great attack on the worship of Baal in Israel but did not eliminate the worship at Bethel and Dan, is censured (2 Kings 10:28–31).

As for the kings of Judah, only Hezekiah and Josiah are unconditionally approved; some (Asa, Jehoshaphat, Jehoash, Amaziah, Uzziah, and Jotham) receive limited approval; and the rest are condemned for doing wrong in the eyes of Yahweh. David is regarded as the ideal king. His successors are measured by comparison with him.

Emphasis in the book falls on people and events of religious importance. Much attention is given to the work of Elijah and Elisha, because they championed the cause of Yahweh in the struggle with Baal worship. Kings considered unimportant religiously, however great they were politically and commercially, are passed over quickly. Omri, the founder of the city of Samaria, the conquerer of Moab, and certainly one of the greatest figures in the history of the Northern Kingdom is given only six verses (1 Kings 16:23–28). The religious reformers Hezekiah (2 Kings 18–20) and Josiah (2 Kings 22:1—23:30) are treated in great detail. Solomon's building of the temple and its dedication are given top attention (1 Kings 6–8). While there is political, economic, and sociological information in the book, it is everywhere evident that the major concern is religious. The authors wanted to show how loyal the leaders were to the covenant made with Yahweh at Mount Sinai – to the worship of *one* God at *one* sanctuary and to God's will as expressed in the Law.

Sources and Purpose

The chief sources used seem to be: (1) the History of the Throne Succession (1 Kings 1–2); (2) the Book of the Acts of Solomon (1 Kings 11:41); (3) records of the Jerusalem temple (perhaps drawn on for the account of the temple's description and furnishings – 1 Kings 6–7); (4) the Book of the Chronicles of the Kings of Israel and the Book of the Chronicles of the Kings of Judah (1 Kings 14:19, 29, and many other references), apparently annals or official chronicles or records based on them; (5) a collection of Elijah and Elisha stories; (6) an Isaiah source (2 Kings 18:13—20:19); and (7) an Ahab source (1 Kings 20; 22:1–38). The two books of 'Chronicles' above are not our 1–2 Chronicles but much earlier and very different works.

The dominant view today among liberal scholars is that 1 and 2 Kings are part of the great Deuteronomistic History (Deuteronomy through 2 Kings) described above (p. 121). Whether it was first written in the pre-exilic period (perhaps in the time of Josiah, about 620 BC) and supplemented and reworked somewhat during the Babylonian Exile (about 550 BC), or entirely written at the latter period is still debated.

Conservatives emphasize the writer's familiarity with the ('Mosaic') book of Deuteronomy, accept authorship in either the time of Josiah or the Exile or both, but reject the hypothesis of the Deuteronomistic History.

It is clear to all that the writer(s) held to the theology expressed in the book of Deuteronomy. He (they) stressed the importance of absolute loyalty to one God (Yahweh), who was to be worshiped in one temple (Jerusalem); bitterly opposed worship at Bethel and Dan and at local shrines; emphasized rewards and punishments by God according to one's loyalty and disloyalty; and illustrated this by showing what happened to the kings of Israel and Judah. Indeed, the whole work may have been written to explain why the nation was destroyed (disloyalty to the Mosaic covenant) and to hold up the promise of renewal through repentance and obedience. God's promise to the line of David will be fulfilled (1 Kings 11:36; 15:4; 2 Kings 8:19; 25:27–30 [in the release of Jehoiachin, David's heir]).

Historical and Religious Value

The historical value lies primarily in the basic information, derived from reliable contemporary sources, with which the record is so lavishly furnished.

Without the record contained in 1–2 Kings the outside sources (Assyrian monuments and annals, Egyptian records, the Moabite Stone, and the like) would have much less meaning for Bible students.

The zeal for pure worship, for hearing and obeying the word of God as spoken through faithful prophets, and for learning the lessons of history as a guide to the present and future mark these writers as faithful members of the people of God.

1–2 Chronicles

Title and Position in the Old Testament

1 and 2 Chronicles, like 1 and 2 Kings, were originally one book. It became two when translated into Greek, because of the greater space required when vowelless Hebrew is translated into voweled Greek.

Its Hebrew name was 'The Words (or Matters) of the Days,' that is, the events of the times. In the Septuagint it is called 'The Things Omitted' (*i.e.*, omitted from the books of Samuel and Kings). Jerome, the translator of the Vulgate, suggested that the work be called 'a chronicle of the whole divine history.' It is from this that the English title 'Chronicles' comes.

It is clear from the language, style, method of writing, interests, and general point of view that 1–2 Chronicles and Ezra-Nehemiah were composed as one continuous work by the same author. The proclamation of Cyrus in 2 Chron. 36:22–23, presented in fuller form in Ezra 1:1–3, ties the two portions of the work together.

In the Hebrew Bible, Ezra-Nehemiah precedes, rather than follows, 1–2 Chronicles, in defiance of the sequence of events the books record. Apparently Ezra-Nehemiah became part of the canon earlier than 1–2 Chronicles, because Ezra-Nehemiah contains information available in no other work, whereas 1–2 Chronicles largely duplicates (with additions and alterations) material already present in other canonical books. When admitted to canonical status, 1–2 Chronicles was simply added on as the last work of the total collection, without regard to its proper chronological and logical place.

For Jesus, the Hebrew Scriptures consisted of Genesis to Chronicles.

Contents, Purpose and Theology

Though 1–2 Chronicles appears to offer a history of the Jews from Adam to the Babylonian exile, the author's real concern is not with history as such but with exalting Jewish worship, Jewish institutions, and Jewish national life in a time when the struggling Jewish community of the postexilic period was overshadowed by great foreign powers (Persia, Greece) and faced with a rival temple and worship in Samaria (see p. 431).

The author wishes to demonstrate the supremacy of the Jews and their religion over all rival peoples and cults. He accomplishes this by showing how God, dwelling in the temple in Jerusalem and worshiped by a holy people, fulfilled the divine purpose, long ago announced to the forefathers of the Jews, of establishing an imperishable kingdom on earth. Though the Judean kingdom may appear insignificant in the eyes of the 'great' peoples of the world, it is a kingdom with a noble past and a glowing future. For the only true God dwells in Jerusalem, and is worshiped there in proper forms and ceremonies by accredited priests and a holy people. Let no one despise the Jews, but let them consider the authenticity, the antiquity, and the authority of their religion,

The Israelites submit to Shalmaneser III of Assyria (841 BC); Nimrud, c. 825 BC.

and let them recognize the great destiny of this people under the only true God!

It is also clear in these books that God rewarded those kings who worshiped him exclusively and obeyed his laws and that he punished those who did not. The author explains that the exception to this divine principle of retribution – the unusually long reign of the wicked Manasseh – was due to his repentance and conversion while he was a captive in Babylon and his subsequent restoration by God to his throne in Jerusalem (2 Chron. 33:11–13). 2 Kings 21:1–18 knows nothing of Manasseh's captivity, repentance, and restoration.

Sources, Date, and Authorship

The sources of 1–2 Chronicles are, first of all, the books of Genesis to Joshua (for the genealogies of 1 Chron. 1–9) and the books of Samuel and Kings (for much of the remaining material). The Chronicler uses these canonical sources with consid-

erable freedom, selecting, omitting, modifying, and adding to create the impression he wishes to give.

For example, he omits almost all material from the book of Kings having to do with the Northern Kingdom, so that he may show how the Judean kings carried out God's purpose in the founding and continuance of the Jerusalem temple worship. He passes over the abundant material in Samuel and Kings about the personal life and deeds of Saul and David, since this material has no bearing on the life and worship of the sacred community in Jerusalem. He modifies when necessary, as in his story of Manasseh's repentance and restoration and in the attributing of David's census to Satan instead of to Yahweh (1 Chron. 21:1; 2 Sam. 24:1). He adds much material about the ceremony of transporting the ark to Jerusalem (2 Sam. 6:12–23; 1 Chron. 15–16) and about David's preparations for building the temple in Jerusalem and establishing its ritual (1 Chron. 22–29). He skillfully shifts the credit for planning and building the temple from Solomon (1 Kings 5–7) to David. He is anxious to connect David prominently with the Jerusalem temple worship.

The Chronicler refers to several uncertain sources: 'The Book of the Kings of Israel and Judah' (2 Chron. 27:7; 35:27); 'The Chronicles of the Kings of Israel' (2 Chron. 33:18); 'The Commentary on the Book of the Kings' (2 Chron. 24:27); the chronicles, prophecies, visions, and stories of various prophets (1 Chron. 29:29; 2 Chron. 9:29; 20:34; 26:22; 32:32; 33:19). Those titles which contain reference to 'kings' may all refer to a lengthy commentary on the kings of Israel and Judah (2 Chron. 24:27) no longer in existence. The prophetic writings mentioned, in part at least, may also have belonged to the same commentary (2 Chron. 20:34; 32:32). This commentary may, in fact, have been a commentary on our books of Samuel and Kings. The main sources seem thus to be our books of Samuel and Kings and a commentary based on them.

Since the Chronicler's record in 1–2 Chronicles and Ezra-Nehemiah runs down through the career of Ezra, who came to Jerusalem in 458, 428, or 398 BC (see p. 141), and since the genealogies may run to a somewhat later time still, the author may have lived in the late fifth, fourth, or even the third century BC. Conservatives hold to a date in the latter part of the fifth century, close to about 400 BC. Albright's suggestion that the Chronicler was Ezra has not gained general acceptance. The Chronicler's strong interest in the temple – its origin, its personnel (priests, Levites, musicians, custodians, etc.), its liturgy, and its authority and significance for the Jews and the world – makes it likely that he was a religious functionary there, perhaps a Levite and a singer.

Historical and Religious Significance

The Chronicler's use of his sources, so far as this can be checked, and the emphases of his writing show that he was a religious teacher rather than a historian. In rewriting the history of his people from Adam to Ezra (from David to Ezra in detail) he sought to demonstrate the divine origin, great antiquity, and permanent validity of the Jews' religious institutions and practices – so that all the world would know that God, the only God, was with them, protecting them, and helping them toward a divine destiny. He also wished to encourage his fellow Jews to believe in God's promises to David and Solomon and in their own future as the people of God. Above all, he wanted them to be wholeheartedly obedient to the covenant law and to God's great prophets; for only thereby could they realize their glorious destiny.

He wrote *interpreted* history, *apologetic* history, more so than any other Old Testament writer. Every piece of his work must be sifted critically if one's objective is the recovery of historical *facts*. Sometimes he offers supplementary material of historical value. The work is, of course, of great significance for a knowledge of the times in which he lived.

The writer's belief that true worship of God and absolute loyalty to God are the indispensable bases of national existence as the people of God is in line with the best emphases of the Old Testament. Some of the sermons and prayers of the book give expression to noble faith, and have influenced life and worship through the centuries. (See, *e.g.,* 1 Chron. 29:10–19, esp. vs. 14.)

Ezra-Nehemiah

theological interpretation of the history of the Jews. 1–2 Chronicles is the first.

The Hebrew Bible has Chronicles last in the Old Testament canon, immediately preceded by Ezra-Nehemiah. This order is probably due to the prior acceptance of Ezra-Nehemiah into the canon. The Septuagint, the Latin Vulgate, and our English Bibles preserve the true order.

After the separation of Ezra-Nehemiah from 1–2 Chronicles and its division into two books, the two were variously designated. In the Septuagint our Ezra and Nehemiah are books two and three (designated by the second and third letters of the Greek alphabet) of the books called 'Esdras.' The first is now in the Apocrypha (see p. 212). In the Vulgate, Ezra and Nehemiah are numbers one and two of four books called 'Esdras' (see pp.19–20). In Hebrew texts since the fifteenth century the names 'Ezra' and 'Nehemiah' have been used, as in English Bibles.

Relation to 1–2 Chronicles, Place in Canon, and Name

The Hebrew Ezra-Nehemiah constituted one book. Like the books of Samuel, Kings, and Chronicles it was divided into two in the Septuagint. Ezra-Nehemiah is the second volume of the Chronicler's

Part of the 'broad wall' built by Hezekiah to protect Jerusalem from the Assyrians.

Contents and Order of Material

Ezra-Nehemiah covers a relatively brief period: from the Edict of Cyrus (538 BC), providing for the return of the Jews to their land and the rebuilding of their temple in Jerusalem (Ezra 1:2–4; 6:3–5), through the work of Ezra and Nehemiah (sometime between 458 and 398 BC; see below), around one hundred years.

The Chronicler tells us nothing directly about the life of the Jews in exile in Babylon. The center of his interest is the worship of God in the temple at Jerusalem and the holy community there. Ezra-Nehemiah shows how this worship and communal life, interrupted by God's punishment of his people through foreign captivity, was restored by God's providence through the work of Sheshbazzar, Zerubbabel, Ezra, and Nehemiah. All these men are portrayed as zealous for the worship and service of God. Their efforts centered in two endeavors: the rebuilding of the temple and the holy city; and the bringing of the life of the Jews into complete conformity with the Law of God as given to them through Moses.

We may divide Ezra-Nehemiah into two unequal parts: (1) events leading to the rebuilding of the temple in Jerusalem (Ezra 1–6); (2) the work of Ezra and Nehemiah in restoring the holy community in Judah (Ezra 7—Neh. 13).

The order of materials in Ezra-Nehemiah is considerably confused. Two illustrations must suffice.

Those who returned from exile, listed in Ezra, chap. 2, presumably accompanied Sheshbazzar, prince of Judah, on the first return from Babylon, shortly after the edict of Cyrus (538 BC). Ezra 2:2 and Neh. 7:7 (at which point the entire list is reproduced again), however, associate this group with 'Zerubbabel, Jeshua, Nehemiah.' Zerubbabel appears to have been Sheshbazzar's nephew and successor as governor of Judah, who led a second return at some time between 538 and 522 BC. Jeshua was the high priest associated with him (Ezra 5:2; Hag. 1:1). Nehemiah does not come to Judah until 445 BC. The list in Ezra 2 telescopes periods and persons; the nearly 50,000 persons embraced by it

The Cyrus Cylinder tells how Cyrus captured Babylon without a battle.

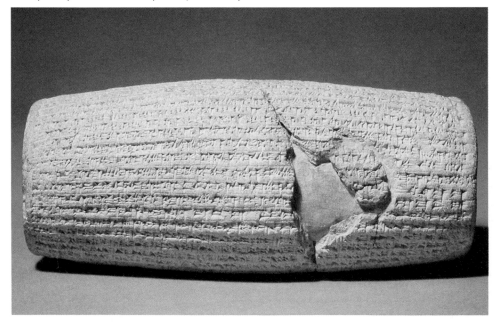

(2:64–65) thus seem to include the total number of several returns. Or it may be that the whole list is a census list of the time of Nehemiah. And events in the time of Artaxerxes (465–424 BC), discussed in Ezra 4:7–23, are placed before the time of Darius (522–486 BC), as we clearly see in Ezra 4:23–24.

For proper understanding we must rearrange the text about as follows: Ezra 1:1—4:6; 4:24—6:22; 4:7–23; Neh. 1:1—7:5; chaps. 11—13; 9:38—10:39; Ezra 7—10; Neh. 8:1—9:37. (Neh. 7:6–73 duplicates Ezra 2:1–70.)

Sources

The sources of Ezra-Nehemiah are more identifiable than those of 1–2 Chronicles. They appear to have been about as follows:

a. Ezra memoirs (in the first person) – Ezra 7:27—9:5 (or possibly 7:11—9:15);
b. Nehemiah memoirs (in the first person) – Neh. 1:1—7:5; 11:1–2; 12:27—13:31;
c. Aramaic sources – Ezra 4:8—6:18; 7:12–26, consisting of official documents and narrative material;
d. Lists – Ezra 2; Neh. 7:6–73a; Ezra 8:1–14.

Historical and Religious Value

We have seen that Ezra-Nehemiah is somewhat disorganized in contents. When the text is carefully rearranged, the contents are of the highest value, since they offer us our major source of knowledge of the period of restoration in Judah after the Exile in Babylonia.

Problems remain, however. How is the work of Sheshbazzar and of Zerubbabel related? When did Ezra come to Jerusalem, and how did his work relate to that of Nehemiah? The following reconstruction of the history of the period has gained favor with many scholars:

a. a return under the edict of Cyrus (about 538 BC), led by Sheshbazzar, who made some ineffective attempts to begin rebuilding the temple;

b. another return under Cyrus or Cambyses (sometime between 538 and 522 BC), led by Zerubbabel and Jeshua, who, under the stimulus of the prophets Haggai and Zechariah, succeeded in rebuilding the temple and reinstituting its worship;

c. two visits of Nehemiah and his companions in the time of Artaxerxes I (465–424 BC), resulting in the building of the walls of Jerusalem and in certain social and religious reforms;

d. the coming of Ezra, the scribe, in 458 or 428 BC, in the time of Artaxerxes I (465–424 BC), or in 398 BC, in the time of Artaxerxes II (404–358 BC), to exalt the Law of Moses over the life of the people in Judah.

Most scholars regard the memoirs of Nehemiah as the most valuable part of the book. These memoirs recount the story of a great, unselfish man, beset by staggering problems, who by constant prayer, incessant work, and indomitable will power built the walls of Jerusalem and revived the national life of the Jews.

Esther

The Septuagint text of Esther contains many passages not in the Hebrew text. We now call these passages the Additions to Esther. They seek to deepen the religious content of the originally quite secular book (see below) and to bolster its reliability. Jerome gathered these additions together at the end of the Hebrew book, as chaps. 11–16. Luther placed them among the Apocrypha, where they stand today in Protestant Bibles (see p. 210).

Jews of the first and second centuries AD questioned the right of this book to a place in the Canon, probably because of its secular character. Luther heartily disliked the book. He regarded it as too Judaistic and full of 'heathen perverseness.'

Title and Place in the Old Testament

The book takes its title from its heroine's non-Jewish name, Esther (perhaps from a Persian word meaning 'star' or from the name of the Akkadian goddess Ishtar). Her Hebrew name is given in 2:7 as Hadassah (meaning 'myrtle').

In the Hebrew Old Testament the book falls in the third division (the Writings), but in the Septuagint it stands after the historical and before the prophetic books, as in the English Bible today.

Contents and Literary Form

The story centers in a deliverance of the Jewish people brought about by a Jewish maiden who became the queen of the Persian king Ahasuerus (Xerxes I [486–465 BC]; less probably, Artaxerxes II [404–358 BC]). In cooperation with her cousin, Mordecai, she cleverly turned an intended

The Great King of Persia in a chariot, on a coin of Sidon.

extermination of Jews all over the Persian world into the liquidation of the perpetrators of the plot. In joy over the deliverance, the Jews inaugurated an annual festival called Purim.

It is evident that the story reflects some historical information about Persian palaces, manners, and customs in the time of the great Persian kings. However, various details make it difficult to regard it as historical in a narrow sense. Xerxes' queen, according to Herodotus, was Amestris, not Vashti or Esther. Mordecai, carried off from Jerusalem in 597 BC (2:6), can hardly have become grand vizier of Persia in the twelfth year of Xerxes (3:7; 8:2). At that time he would have been more than 124 years old! The extermination by the Jews, by permission of the Persian king, of more than 75,000 of his non-Jewish subjects (9:1–16) and a gallows 83 feet high (5:14) are strange, to say the least.

There have been attempts to explain these historical difficulties. Esther may have supplanted Amestris, even though Herodotus does not record this. The person carried into captivity in 597 may have been Kish, the great-grandfather of Mordecai. Exaggerated numbers are frequent in the Old Testament and do not argue against the basic historical truth of the events.

If the story is not fully historical, it is a historical romance based on some actual (but otherwise unknown) deliverance of the Jewish people in Persia. It wishes to show that the Jews are altogether invincible (4:14; 6:13) – that evil planned against them returns on the head of the planners.

A further aim is to explain the origin of the Feast of Purim as it had come to be observed in the time of the writer and to urge its faithful observance.

Point of View, Author, and Date of Writing

The book as a whole has a somewhat secular point of view when compared with Jewish literature in general. God, prayer, and corporate worship are nowhere mentioned. Yet the writer appears to believe in an overruling providence (4:14) and in fasting (4:16; 9:31). He is conscious of the uniqueness of Jewish law and the separateness of the Jewish people (3:8). His spirit as a whole may be said to be nationalistic rather than truly religious.

The writer's date is unknown. He has been placed late in the Persian period (550–331 BC) or in the Greek period (331–63 BC). The secular viewpoint would fit well the religious situation about 200–175 BC, before the revival of religious zeal under the Maccabees, though an earlier date (c. 350 BC) by a Jew living in Persia is not impossible.

The Feast of Purim is not mentioned again until 2 Maccabees (15:36–37), about 50 BC. Esther is the only book of the Old Testament not represented in the manuscript finds at Qumran (see p. 423).

The Poetic and Wisdom Literature

Poetic compositions originated very early (third millennium BC) among the people of the ancient Near East, particularly in Mesopotamia. The Canaanites, by about the middle of the second millennium BC, had an extensive written literature, much of which was in poetic form. Archaeologists have recovered myths, epics, legends, religious rituals, hymns, prayers, laments, oracles and prophecies, proverbs and precepts, work songs, and love poems as illustrative of the poetry of the ancient Near East.

The Hebrews, like their neighbors, made extensive use of poetic form. Approximately one third of the Old Testament is in poetry. In ancient cultures poetry was regarded as vigorous and virile, appropriate for national victory celebrations, national festivals, and important declarations on national policy by the prophets. It also gave expression to deep inner feelings and personal experiences: at family gatherings, at social occasions of families, clans, and neighbors, at weddings and funerals, at individual and family ceremonies in the temple, and the like.

Hebrew poetry may be classified roughly into lyric poetry (hymns, laments, prayers, songs of thanksgiving, battle songs, victory songs, harvest songs, love songs, etc.), oracular poetry (pronouncements of Yahweh through priests and prophets), and didactic poetry (proverbs, riddles, fables, dialogues, wisdom psalms).

The Wisdom literature (Proverbs, Job, Ecclesiastes, some of the Psalms, the Wisdom of Jesus the Son of Sirach, and the Wisdom of Solomon) belongs to the didactic (instructional) poetry of Israel. This poetry was created and passed along by sages who, since ancient times in the Near East, sought to instruct people how to live effective lives through observing fundamentally right principles of conduct. Right conduct consisted of those actions which caused a person to fit well into the existing order of the universe, to achieve some mastery of life, and to surmount successfully its problems. It is likely that right conduct was always conceived as life that is pleasing to God (the gods) and suited to the nature of things, so that there never was a purely 'secular' wisdom.

Wisdom's 'seat in life' was the clan, the royal court, and the scribal school. The nature of clan wisdom is little known, though some of it must be preserved in Proverbs 10–31. Part of the function of court wisdom was the training of young men who were seeking government service. After the return from Exile scribal schools were conducted, in part at least, in the homes of wise men (Sirach 51:23), who brought into a synthesis for their students wisdom and covenant law (Sirach 24:1–12, 23).

Wisdom was widespread in the world outside Israel, as 1 Kings 4:30–31 shows. Considerable amounts of Mesopotamian and Egyptian wisdom have come to light. Proverbs 22:17—23:11 so closely parallels the Instruction of Amenemopet from Egypt that dependence on that source can scarcely be denied.

Solomon was a sage of wide repute (1 Kings 4:29–34). He apparently had great knowledge and understanding of the world of nature (vs. 33). In the book of Proverbs, reflections on people and human relationships are ascribed to him also (Prov. 10:1; 25:1). It is probable that there gathered around him at his court many sages who created, gathered, and classified knowledge of both nature and humankind. In Jeremiah's time 'the wise' were a recognized class along with priests and prophets (Jer. 18:18). In the postexilic period law and wisdom fused in the heat of nationalistic glorification of the Mosaic covenant.

Yahweh became the source of all wisdom and the Jews its privileged custodians. The highest form of wisdom – indeed, all wisdom – was found in the Law of Moses, and the 'fear of Yahweh' became 'the beginning of wisdom.' Priestly scribes (men learned in the Law, in the Prophets, and in the Wisdom tradition) became the teachers of the nation.

Hebrew poetry has recognizable features. One is 'parallelism,' which has to do with the way lines are put together. The second line of a couplet may repeat in different words the thought of the first line (e.g., Ps. 51:3; 103:10); or the second line may offer a contrast to the first line (e.g., Ps. 1:6; Prov. 3:5); or the second line may complete the thought begun in the first (e.g., Ps. 2:6; Isa. 40:1); or one line may employ a simile or a metaphor to illustrate the thought present in the other (e.g., Ps. 42:1; 103:11); or the successive lines may mount up by repetition and extension (e.g., Ps. 3:1–2; 29:1–2); or four lines may be arranged so that the first is parallel to the fourth and the second to the third (e.g., Ps. 51:1).

Stanzas or strophes may be formed out of groups of lines. Sometimes alphabetic poems appear, in which each line begins with a different letter of the Hebrew alphabet in sequence.

Hebrew poetry also has rhythm. A common pattern is a three-beat first line, followed by a two-beat second line (the dirge meter, as in the book of Lamentations). Couplets with three stresses in each line (as often in Isa. 40–55 and Proverbs) are frequent. Other patterns appear: two-beat lines and four-beat lines. Often the metric patterns are mixed in one poem. Metrical fluidity, rather than exactness, is characteristic of Hebrew and other Near Eastern poetry. Rhyme, except where accidental, is not a feature of Hebrew poetry.

For Further Reading

Anderson, B. W., *Out of the Depths: The Psalms Speak for Us Today*, 1983.
Blenkinsopp, J., *Wisdom and Law in the Old Testament*, 1983.
Crenshaw, J. L., 'The Wisdom Literature,' and Gerstenberger, E. S., 'The Lyrical Literature,' in Knight, D. A. and Tucker, G. M. (eds.), *The Hebrew Bible and Its Modern Interpreters*, 1985.
La Sor, W. S., Hubbard, D. A., Bush, F. W., *Old Testament Survey*, 1982.

Job

The book of Job is one of the recognized literary masterpieces of the Bible. Its haunting question about the meaning of human suffering and its suggestions concerning how sufferers should conduct themselves when misfortune descends mercilessly upon them are superbly treated.

The book takes its place alongside the great ancient Sumerian and Akkadian theodicies (works dealing with the problem of divine justice) and Greek tragedies and stands in an honored place in the line of similar literature reaching all the way to Dostoevski, Thomas Hardy, Eugene O'Neill, and Archibald MacLeish.

Contents and Structure

The book divides naturally into three parts:
1. The Prologue (chaps. 1—2)
2. The Discourses (3:1—42:6)
3. The Epilogue (42:7–17)

The Prologue portrays Job as a God-fearing, righteous, and prosperous man, whom God allowed Satan to test to see whether his piety was motivated by selfish interests. The testing included the loss of all his possessions, his children, and his health, and misunderstanding by his wife. The Prologue pictures Job as enduring the test – as holding fast to faith in God as the giver of both good and evil (2:9) and as not blaming God for the treatment he had received. It ends with an account of the visit of three friends.

The Epilogue deals with God's rebuke of Job's friends, with provisions for their deliverance from punishment, and with the full restoration of Job to health, family, prosperity, and a long life.

Literary Forms

The Prologue and Epilogue are in prose (for the most part), and the Discourses are in poetry. The prose parts may preserve an ancient, popular folktale, probably pre-Israelite, similar to other old Near-Eastern stories (chiefly Egyptian and Mesopotamian) dealing with the problem of bitter suffering in relation to divine justice. Whether the folktale came to the author(s) of the Discourses in written or oral form is not known.

The poetic Discourses center in a dispute between Job and his friends over the cause and the cure of suffering. Here the style and thought reach a lofty level, in fact, as exalted and effective as any writing in the Old Testament. The writer(s) of these poems (see below) are clearly educated men, acquainted with the traditions of Israel and of surrounding peoples and with the myths and science of their day.

Asshurbanapal and his queen feasting; Nineveh c. 645 BC.

The poems show points of contact with several literary forms – laments, lawsuits, epics, tragic dramas, dialogue-debates – but actually they fall into no one classification. It is generally agreed that they are unique in the literature of the ancient Near East.

Authorship, Place of Writing, and Date

Many liberal scholars believe that several people contributed to the book as it now lies before us. The Prologue-Epilogue, as noted above, may have existed before the poetic parts were written and possibly may represent an Israelite writer's adaptation of an ancient Canaanite or Edomite epic poem.

More than one person may have written the Discourses. The principal poet probably contributed at least chaps. 3—31 (except for some alterations in chaps. 24—27 and the whole of chap. 28). The poem on Wisdom in chap. 28, though a masterpiece of writing, does not fit its context

and may thus come from another hand.

The Speeches of Elihu (chaps. 32—37) may be insertions by a later writer, to judge from their somewhat different style, repetitious theology, and argumentative tone. Elihu is not mentioned along with Job's friends in the Epilogue.

The Discourses of God (chaps. 38–41) and Job's brief responses (40:3–5; 42:1–6) may or may not have come from the writer of chaps. 3—31. Job's demand that the Almighty answer him (31:35) requires some word from God. Strangely, two speeches of God are offered (38:1—40:2 and 40:6 ff.) and two responses of Job (40:3–5; 42:1–6). Whether both of the speeches and responses are original, or only one of each, or none, remains a question. But the double responses of both God and Job have considerable effectiveness, whether resulting from the work of one author or more.

Though materials of foreign origin may appear in the book, in its present form it was almost certainly composed in Palestine. Some of the vocabulary appears to be relatively late, and the maturity of the theology argues for a late, rather than an early, period in Israel's history. The fifth or fourth century BC (with some additions and alterations in the third century) seems an appropriate time.

Conscrvative scholars take Job as an historical person, Israelite or non-Israelite, who lived in the late second millennium BC. The author, surely an Israelite, may have lived at any time from the age of Solomon to the Exile. La Sor-Hubbard-Bush opt for the period 700–600 BC. They believe that the book is the product of one author, in spite of the somewhat different theology and style of some of the parts. Some explain the presence of poetical material in a prose framework as in harmony with the ancient Mesopotamian practice of enclosing the main part of a literary work in language of contrasting style.

Teaching and Purpose

The central question with which the book deals is: What should righteous people expect to receive from the hand of God? Should they expect only good fortune or should they also expect bad fortune?

The Prologue-Epilogue affirms clearly that both come to the righteous from God. Job first had great prosperity, but then everything was swept away from him except his life. At last prosperity returned to him. God had brought it *all* on him. Foolish, undiscerning people expect only good to come to the righteous, but the wise know that evil also comes to them from God (2:10) as a test of their loyalty. Job passed the test and was approved by God.

The Dialogue in the three speech-cycles exhibits the wrong views of Job's friends. They hold that the righteous should expect only good fortune from God. If bad fortune comes, it is clear evidence that they are not really righteous. They should confess their secret sins, repent, and be restored to God's favor. Job bitterly repudiates such a view. He insists that his

suffering is not due to unconfessed sin in his life, and he cries out for a fair hearing before God. He expects ultimate vindication by God.

The speeches of Elihu add little to the discussion of the problem. They reaffirm the view that God sends suffering to turn the wicked from their sins.

The Discourses of God and Job's final response indicate that the righteous should humbly and silently trust in God's goodness and justice in bad fortune as well as good, believing that even bitter suffering issues from God's mysterious but purposeful activity. Whatever their condition, the righteous can rest in the knowledge that God is, that they stand in right relationship with God, and that they can look forward in their suffering to eventual liberation by God.

The book of Job clearly is a protest against the long-standing view that in this life righteousness always results in prosperity, and wickedness in misfortune. This viewpoint is present, for example, in 1–2 Kings, 1–2 Chronicles, and some of the Psalms.

The idea that both good and evil come to the righteous from the hand of God for some ultimate purpose, which the righteous may not understand, laid the foundation for the New Testament interpretation of the cross and the suffering of Christians.

The Psalms

ler collections of psalms without logical arrangement. Some psalms appear twice (14 = 53; 40:13–17 = 70; 57:7–11 + 60:5–12 = 108). The comment 'The prayers of David, the son of Jesse, are ended' in 72:20 is contradicted by later notes (see the titles of Psalms 86, 101, 103). Psalms of 'the Sons of Korah' (42–49; 84–85; 87–88) and of 'Asaph' (50, 73–83) point to different origins, as does the variation in the divine name (chiefly 'Yahweh' in Books I, IV, V, and 'Elohim' in Books II, III).

Jesus and the early Christians loved the Psalms. So also did the covenanters at Qumran, to judge from the many manuscripts of the Psalms found in the caves there. (On the Dead Sea Scrolls, see pp. 420–427).

Through the centuries since, Christians and Jews alike, in their agonies and in their victories, have found spiritual strength and the language of praise in the words of the Psalms.

Martin Luther called the Psalter 'a Bible in miniature' and affirmed that in it 'all things which are set forth more at length in the rest of the Scriptures are collected into a beautiful manual of wonderful and attractive brevity.'

Title and General Contents

'Psalms' comes from the title of the book in the Septuagint (psalmoi) and means 'songs'. Ancient Jews called the book tehillim – praises. 'Psalter,' meaning 'stringed instrument,' derives from the title psalterion found in some manuscripts of the book in the Septuagint.

The Psalter now contains 150 psalms, arranged in five books: I, 1–41; II, 42–72; III, 73–89; IV, 90–106; V, 107–150, each concluding with a doxology. The Septuagint has an additional psalm at the end, number 151, and divides and numbers some of the psalms differently. The division into five books was probably made in imitation of the Pentateuch.

The Psalter is a great collection of smal-

The Superscriptions and Notations

These contain a variety of items, such as: musical directions ('with stringed instruments'); names of tunes ('according to the Hind of the Dawn'); indications of authorship and circumstances of composition ('A Psalm of David, when he fled from Absalom his son'); designations of earlier collections ('Asaph,' 'Korah' – see above); names of types of compositions ('Mizmor' or 'Shir,' a song; 'Maskil,' a didactic poem; 'Tehillah,' a hymn or song of praise; 'Tepillah,' a prayer; 'Mikhtam' and 'Shiggayon' are of uncertain meaning). 'Selah' may mean 'musical interlude.'

Types and Use

The prevailing view now is that the psalms were composed largely for use in worship – in the public and private ceremonies of the temple – and that they may be classified according to their basic nature and function in worship. The principal types are:

a. *Hymns* – songs of praise to Yahweh for his greatness as revealed in the creation of the world. They celebrate Yahweh as King of the universe and praise Zion, with its sanctuary. The hymns were chanted by temple singers, congregation, and individuals, often accompanied by musical instruments, at the great annual festivals, at processions, sacrifices, and private ceremonies in the temple. Representatives of this class are: 8; 15; 19:1–6; 24; 29; 46; 47; 48; 93; 96–99; 122.

b. *Laments* (or Entreaties) – by individuals and by the nation, invoking God's help in time of personal and national disaster and expressing hope of God's deliverance. Individuals came to the temple for healing when sick and for justice when accused by enemies. There they poured out their complaints before God. The nation in times of calamity cried out, 'Why?' and 'How long?' and implored God's merciful deliverance. Representatives of this class are: 3; 4; 6; 10; 22; 26; 36; 39; 51; 80; 90; 102; 137.

c. *Songs of Thanksgiving* – offered by individuals and the nation in the temple, after receiving some benefit from the hands of God. Belonging to this group are: 30; 32; 40:1–11; 63; 65; 67; 107; 111; 116; 136.

Some scholars list other types – Royal Psalms (2; 18; 20; 45; 72; 110; 144), Wisdom Psalms (1, 37; 49; 73; 112; 128), Liturgies (15; 24; 50; 85; 118), Pilgrim Psalms (84; 122), and still others.

Authorship and Date

Seventy-three of the psalms are ascribed to David and some to other individuals (Moses, Solomon, Ethan the Ezrahite, Heman the Ezrahite, Asaph, and the sons of Korah). Thus the Psalter does not claim that David is the author of all the psalms, as many people believe today. Some psalms clearly reflect the destruction of Jerusalem and the experience of Israel in exile in Babylonia (sixth century BC), for example, 74, 126, 137.

Some psalms appear to be adaptations of earlier texts: 19:1–6 may represent a rewriting of an ancient Canaanite hymn to the sun; Ps. 29 may have come from a reworking of a Canaanite hymn to the storm god Baal; and Ps. 104 seems to borrow from a Canaanite version of the Egyptian sun hymn of Amenhotep IV. Canaanite terms and ideas influenced quite deeply the worship materials of Israel.

The writing of the Psalms reached from about the tenth century BC (the time of David) to the postexilic period. David, who had poetic gifts and musical talent (1 Sam. 16:16–18; 2 Sam. 1:17–27; 6:5), took the first step toward a hymnody for Israel's worship. Many people over a half dozen centuries or more added their creations to the collection, which was put into final form, probably by temple personnel, as late as the third century BC. The men of Qumran, who gave us the Dead Sea Scrolls, were experts in the composition of psalms.

Religious Teachings and Significance

The Psalms are songs of praise to the creator, sustainer, and redeemer God and prayers that God will deliver, protect, and sustain his people. They glorify the place where God is revealed (Jerusalem, the city of the great king, and the holy temple) and exalt the instrument of God's revelation (the Law).

They emphasize the importance of living by the standards of the Law and point out the blessed consequences of obedience and the dire results of disobedience. Righteous kings, people, and individuals, worshiping aright in God's city and temple, will declare his praise among the nations.

The Psalms celebrate God's wonderful works in the past and invoke similar mercies for the future. 'Great is the Lord, and greatly to be praised' (96:4). 'Hallelujah!'

Jesus nourished his life on the Psalms (Matt. 26:30; Mark 15:34; Luke 23:46), and Paul urged the Christians at Colossae to 'sing psalms and hymns and spiritual songs with thankfulness in your hearts to God' (Col. 3:16). Both Judaism and Christianity have been singing religions.

Wadi Qilt, between Jerusalem and Jericho; a 'valley of the shadow of death' (Ps. 23).

The Proverbs

In addition to the priests and the prophets of Israel, there existed a class of the wise to whom we owe the material of the book of Proverbs.

These sages, probably attached to the court, assembled the wisdom of their time, both Israelite and foreign, for the benefit of court workers, including trainees. The aim of these teachers was to produce wise and good people who would know how to live well and work effectively.

Though some parts of the book have a pronounced religious cast, much of the teaching is grounded in human experience rather than in divine revelation. Formal, institutional religion and even Israel's unique historical experiences play little part in the book. The practical moral philosophy has had a strong appeal through the centuries to religious and secular people alike.

Name, Superscriptions, and Collections

'The Proverbs' comes from the title that heads the book in the Hebrew text: 'The proverbs of Solomon, son of David, king of Israel' (1:1).

The Hebrew word behind 'proverbs' (*mashal*) means basically 'a comparison' or 'a likeness' and properly designates a statement which shows the real nature of something by a comparison with something else. It can also mean a standard of behavior and an utterance of hidden truth. The statement so designated can vary in form from a single line to a complex, lengthy poem. The meaning of the word is thus broader than the English word 'proverb.'

Several superscriptions in the book assign the various parts to different authors or collectors: Solomon (1:1; 10:1; 25:1); the Wise (22:17; 24:23); Agur (30:1); Lemuel (31:1). In 25:1 we are told that some of the proverbs of Solomon were transmitted by 'men of Hezekiah,' probably professional scribes at Hezekiah's court.

Several collections of proverbs are contained in our present book, as follows:
a. chaps. 1–9 (ascribed to Solomon)
b. 10:1—22:16 (ascribed to Solomon)
c. 22:17—24:22 (ascribed to the Wise)
d. 24:23–34 (also ascribed to the Wise)
e. chaps. 25–29 (ascribed to Solomon; transmitted by Hezekiah's scribes)
f. chap. 30 (ascribed to Agur of Massa)
g. chap. 31 (ascribed to Lemuel, king of Massa)

Authorship and Date

The superscriptions do not claim that all the proverbs of the book came from Solomon. Like the Psalms, Proverbs is a great collection of collections, probably put in its present form after the Exile (fifth or fourth century BC). Conservative scholars tend to attribute most of the contents of Proverbs to Solomon himself (10th century), while allowing for some later additions to the Solomonic collection (the sayings of the Wise and those ascribed to Agur and Lemuel) and assign final compilation to the time of Hezekiah (715–686 BC) or shortly thereafter.

1 Kings 4:29–34 asserts that Solomon uttered 3,000 proverbs concerning nature (trees, hyssop, beasts, birds, reptiles, fish). However, those ascribed to him in the book of Proverbs concern people and human relationships. Both types, of course, may have come from him, 1 Kings and the book of Proverbs each reflecting a different type.

Solomon was clearly a patron of learning. At his court and under subsequent kings (*e.g.,* Hezekiah, Prov. 25:1) wisdom materials from many sources were accumulated. After the Exile most of these materials, whatever their actual origin, were ascribed to Solomon, under whose patronage this type of learning and literature received emphasis in Israel.

Agur and Lemuel of Massa (30:1, 31:1) are unknown persons. They may have belonged to an Ishmaelite tribe of north Arabia (Gen. 25:14). Sages similar to Solomon lived in many countries of the Middle East (1 Kings 4:30–31). Extensive bodies of Wisdom material have been recovered from Egypt and Mesopotamia, one piece from Egypt ('The Instruction of Amenemopet') being closely parallel to Prov. 22:17—23:11. The Edomites were especially renowned for their wise men (Jer. 49:7). All these people were the 'scholars' of antiquity.

The earliest materials of the book of Proverbs appear in chaps. 10–29. These have the greatest claim to Solomonic origin. Chaps. 30–31, forming an appendix to the book, are of uncertain date (likely postexilic). Chaps. 1–9 contain some of the later materials, whether late preexilic or postexilic is disputed.

Nature and Value of the Teaching in the Proverbs

Since the book of Proverbs consists of a collection of collections from several periods of Israel's history, the teaching of the book will hardly be of one kind. There is, furthermore, no systematic arrangement of the proverbs in the book; hence, conclusions concerning the teaching as a whole are difficult.

In general, formal emphases of Israel's religion are less evident in chaps. 10–31 than in chaps. 1–9. Belief in God as creator and ruler of the world undergirds chaps. 10–31, but it is held that people must achieve their goals largely through their own efforts. The wise person will shun every attitude and practice that works against his best interests (laziness, drunkenness, licentiousness, bad company, etc.) and devote his intelligence and honest efforts to his highest goals. Wisdom here is practical common sense, which will enable people to lead a prosperous and happy life. The Lord takes account of what one does and rewards or punishes accordingly.

Chaps. 1–9 are more explicitly 'religious'. All wisdom comes from God. Wisdom, which was active at the creation, has come to earth and persistently seeks admission to the minds of people. They are free to accept or reject God's gift. If they accept, they will know how to live well in this world; if they reject, they will feel the full consequences of their folly. The wise (the righteous) are always rewarded; fools (the unrighteous) are invariably punished – in *this* life!

The theology of Israel's sages appears to be both too self-centered and too limited in scope. While beneficial results usually or often follow righteous living, it is not invariably so, as the book of Job and the experience of righteous martyrs show.

Ecclesiastes

This is the strangest book in the Bible. Many readers have regarded it as an illegitimate child in the family of inspiration, so radically different from traditional biblical teachings are the views expressed in it.

Some Jews of the late first century AD disputed its right to a place in their sacred scriptures. The book was apparently little valued by early Christians, for it is not cited in the New Testament. Christian interpreters through the centuries have strained to find justification for its place in the Bible. Today, however, discerning readers agree that it makes its own unique contribution to the literature concerning people's quest for meaningful faith.

Title

'Ecclesiastes' comes from the Septuagint, where it is a translation of the Hebrew *Qoheleth*, the title given to the author in 1:1: 'The words of Qoheleth, the son of David, king in Jerusalem.' *Qoheleth* may mean 'speaker or teacher of the assembly' or even 'assemblyman.' Some scholars connect it with a Hebrew word meaning 'harangue,' or 'argumentative speech,' thus 'haranguer' here. What the author's real name and position were is unknown. (See below under 'The Author and Date.')

'Better is a poor and wise youth than an old and foolish king...' (Eccl. 4:13).

Arrangement of Material

The book consists of a loosely organized series of reflections on God, the world, and the meaning of life. They are spoken in the first person (1:12–18; 2:1 ff.), in the second person (5:1–8; 11:1–6), and in the third person (1:2–11; 3:1–8; 7:1–8; 10:1–3). They state what 'I' have seen, known, and done; what you – 'young man' – should know, be, and do; and what is generally true.

No clear outline of the contents is possible. The sages paid little attention to logical arrangement of materials. The only general statement we can make is that the author set forth his basic philosophy in the first part of the book and the ethic deriving from it in the second. 'All is vanity,' established at the beginning, becomes the basis for 'Rejoice, O young man, in your youth' at the end. Some sections (e.g., 10:1–20) would fit in as well almost anywhere in the book as in their present position.

Philosophical and Religious Outlook

The book contains a curious mixture of doubt and faith – of rationalism, skepticism, pessimism, and fatalism, on the one hand, and traditional or orthodox confessions, on the other. How to relate these two strands of thought is a difficult problem.

Some thirty times this or that or 'all' is said to be 'vanity' or 'vain' (i.e., a vapor, a breath, something unsubstantial or fleeting). Meaningless change and endless repetition are the law of life, with no permanent gain, result, or new achievement. 'There is nothing new under the sun' (1:9). Since all is meaningless flux – in nature and in human life – all human strivings are worthless. Wisdom, wealth, women, and even righteousness bring sorrow and disappointment. The fate of the righteous and the wicked is the same: death – a fate which comes to humans and animals alike (3:19–21). Wise and righteous people fare no better in life than do

fools and the unrighteous (2:14–16; 7:15–16; 8:14; 9.2–3, 11).

There is deep skepticism about the possibility of knowing and understanding God. God is impenetrable mystery, whose purposes and work no one, not even the wise person, can fathom (8.16–17). This mysterious God has consigned all people to one fate: 'one fate comes to all' (9:3); 'time and chance happen to them all' (9:11). Every person should 'accept his lot' in life (5:19). There is no knowledge available concerning 'what is good for man while he lives the few days of his vain life' (6:12). And there is no blessed future life (3:19–21; 9:10). It would be better not to have been born at all (4:3; 6:3).

Over against this dreary pessimism and cynicism, one finds optimistic, orthodox statements. Wisdom and the wise are sometimes praised and valued (2:13–14; 7:19; 8:1; 9:17–18). God's judgment of the righteous and the wicked is affirmed (3:17; 11:9; 12:14), together with the promise that 'it will be well with those who fear God, ... but it will not be well with the wicked' (8:12–13). The fear of God is commanded (5:7; 7:18; 8:13; 12:13). The enjoyment of life and work is repeatedly affirmed as a person's duty and privilege, as gifts from the hand of God (2:24; 3:12, 22; 5:18–19; 8:15).

Some interpreters of the book have suggested that an orthodox editor or editors attempted to soften the pessimism by adding orthodox statements. Many scholars, however, believe that the two points of view are not wholly irreconcilable in one mind.

It is clear that the author believed in God, but in a different kind of God from that revealed in the Law and the Prophets. For him God was unrevealed mystery, who decreed unalterably what the world should be like ('crooked' rather than 'straight' – 7:13). Human beings cannot alter the nature of their existence in this world. They simply accept it and find what enjoyment they can from living in it. They cannot be sure that a righteous life will yield any better results than an evil one. Death will end everything for everyone. Resignation to what is, is the advice offered to youth in this book. Such resignation will bring a certain pleasure in living. The fear of God is reverence and acceptance of the unalterable.

The Author and Date

The 'teacher' was a wise man who devoted himself to 'weighing and studying and arranging proverbs with great care' (12:9). He probably lived in Jerusalem in the fifth or fourth century BC, although it is not impossible that his home was Alexandria or Phoenicia.

He seems to have been acquainted with Egyptian, Mesopotamian, and Greek thought, which differs from orthodox Hebrew beliefs. Like the author of the book of Job, he challenged traditional beliefs – particularly the doctrine of retribution in this life.

Several facts show that the book was not written by Solomon but was attributed to him by a postexilic Hebrew sage: the late Hebrew language of the book, the inappropriateness of several statements for the lips of Solomon (1:16; 4:13; 10:16–17), the generally pessimistic and fatalistic character of its thought, and its position in the latest section of the Hebrew Canon (see pp. 18, 32).

It has been suggested that the author may have been of the line of David (and Jehoiachin), an appointee by Persia as governor of Palestine in the postexilic period, who could with some right refer to himself as 'the son of David, king in Jerusalem.'

Significance

The book gives expression to the ancient and modern struggle to find faith and meaning in a world that often seems meaningless and full of contradictions. It joins its voice to the book of Job in questioning simple answers to the difficult problems of human existence. It acts, as one writer has put it, 'as a counterweight

to smug assurance and unreflective belief' (R.B.Y. Scott, *Proverbs, Ecclesiastes* [*The Anchor Bible*], 1965, p. 207). As such, it meets the disillusioned of our time where they are and offers them a point of beginning for exploring other biblical books which reveal the purpose of God in our 'mysterious' existence.

Additional Note

Conservative scholarship is divided on the question of the authorship and date of Ecclesiastes. One position argues for direct authorship by King Solomon (tenth century BC). It explains the peculiarities of language in the book as due to Canaanite (Phoenician) influences on the mind of Solomon and as characteristic of the style of wisdom writers of that period. It defends the theology as possible for Solomon. It holds that the book's purpose is to present Solomon's final conclusion: that life has no meaning apart from God and his holy will.

The other position is that the book was written about the fifth century BC by a wise man, accustomed to the use of Aramaic as well as Hebrew, who undertook to represent the mind of Solomon on the meaning of human existence. This subject may well have occupied the attention of the historical Solomon toward the end of his life.

Advocates of this view point out that the book makes no direct claim to authorship by Solomon and that some passages seem to contradict such authorship. They agree with the first position that the author intended to show that life is devoid of meaning without God and the wisdom that comes from God.

The Song of Solomon

Some conservative scholars cling to Solomon's authorship. They deny that the language contains late (postexilic) forms and words, and they point out characteristics in the songs typical of Solomon (interest in flora and fauna, cavalry, and imported cosmetics). They claim also that the geographical situation reflected in the book argues for a tenth century date. Other conservatives think Solomon probably was not the author, though the Song reflects some of the aspects of his age. In its present form it comes from about the time of the Exile (La Sor-Hubbard-Bush).

Title

In the Hebrew text the title is 'The Song of Songs, which pertains to Solomon' (1:1). 'The Song of Songs,' after the pattern of such expressions as 'the holy of holies' or 'vanity of vanities,' is a superlative and means 'the finest song.'

Authorship, Date, and Place of Origin

It is not certain that the title attributes the authorship to Solomon. 'Which pertains to Solomon' can mean 'belonging to,' 'in honor of,' 'in the fashion of,' 'concerning,' or 'by' (in the sense of authorship).

The title evidently was placed at the head of the book by an ancient editor who wished to connect it in some way with Solomon, the reputed author of 1,005 songs (1 Kings 4:32).

Solomon is mentioned several times in the songs (1:5; 3:7, 9, 11; 8:11–12) but not in such a way as to imply that he wrote them. It is likely that a collection of songs of various dates (some of them possibly quite old) was drawn together by an unknown editor of the postexilic period (fifth or fourth century BC). Certain words and constructions fit the postexilic period best.

The rural scenes, as well as some of the language, suggest to some interpreters the northern part of the country, rather than Judea, as the place of origin; but this is uncertain.

Form and Contents

In form, interpreters view the book in different ways: as a poem, as a drama, or as a collection of originally separate love songs.

It is difficult to find any clear theme in the book, such as a unified poem possesses. And marks of dramatic structure, in which various actors play various parts (or one actor assumes several roles), are indistinct or non-existent. It is probably best to regard the book as a collection of originally disconnected songs, about twenty-five in number, which were joined together into a continuous text by a wise man of the postexilic period.

Interpretation

How to understand the Song of Songs has given rise to wide differences of opinion. The poems obviously celebrate the glories of courtship and marriage, often describing in frankest terms the charms of the female beloved, the strength and beauty of her lover, and the pleasures of loving relationships. Even nature is included in the pleasure-loving sensuousness that characterizes this poetry. Nowhere is the name of God mentioned, and any attempt at religious instruction is veiled, if present at all.

What is the meaning of this poetry? Various positions are possible:

a. The poetry is allegorical or parabolic.

Spring flowers in a garden near Samaria.

The lover is really God or Christ, and the beloved is Israel or the church. Advocates of this view point out that both Testaments speak of the relation of God and Christ to Israel and the church and use the symbol of marriage. Many Jews and Christians, ancient and modern, have so viewed the book. Others have argued that the relation between God and the individual human soul is described here.

b. The poems had their origin in the worship of non-Israelite fertility deities. In those religions the lover was the dying and rising fertility god whose beloved was his sister or mother. Their relationships were celebrated in songs at agricultural festivals. Israel adapted these songs for use at its own agricultural festivals, and thus they passed in a modified form into Israel's liturgy.

c. The Song of Songs is a dramatic portrayal of the relationships between King Solomon and the (female) Shulammite (6:13), who has been identified by some as Abishag of 1 Kings 1:1–4, 15; 2:17–22. The poems celebrate their conjugal love. (A variation holds that Abishag rejected Solomon and remained faithful to her shepherd lover.)

d. The poems are oriental love poetry, some of them perhaps composed for and sung at wedding festivities. Poetry of this sort is common in the modern Near East. It hails the bridegroom and bride as 'king' and 'queen' and celebrates the physical attributes of the pair.

Value

The last view, the dominant one today, justifies the inclusion of the Song of Songs in the Bible by pointing out the Hebrews' simple delight in sexuality as a gift of the Creator.

Jewish scholars near the end of the first century AD debated the propriety of the book's inclusion in the Canon. Individual Christian scholars of modern times have questioned it also. However, many interpreters today praise its frank acceptance and celebration of the gentleness, the strength, and the delights of human love – as God's ordained purpose for humankind.

The Prophets

additional material not preserved in the Hebrew Bible). We thus get the sequence: the Pentateuch, the historical books, the poetic and Wisdom books, and the prophetic books.

Meaning of 'Prophet' and the Prophet's Role and Message

The meaning of *nabi*, the Hebrew word for prophet, is uncertain. It may come from a root meaning 'to call' and thus may designate 'one who is called' or possibly 'one who calls out', *i.e.*, a spokesman or announcer.

Prophets in some respects like Israel's existed in ancient Mesopotamian, Assyrian, and Canaanite religion. Eighteenth-century BC tablets from Mari on the Euphrates mention male and female messengers of God, attached to a temple, who received messages through omens, dreams, and ecstatic experiences and delivered these messages as oracles. Some Assyrian texts from the seventh century BC contain collections of oracles from 'ecstatics,' 'revealers,' and 'votaries.' An Egyptian papyrus of the eleventh century BC relates the experiences of Wen-Amon in Phoenicia, where a young attendant of the prince of Byblos was seized with a prophetic ecstasy and delivered to that prince a divine oracle. The Old Testament frequently speaks of prophets of the Canaanite god Baal (1 Kings 18:19–20; 2 Kings 10:19) and, indeed, of prophets in many surrounding lands (Jer. 27:9).

There is no evidence that Israel borrowed prophecy from one or more surrounding nations. It is a phenomenon more or less common to many nations, ancient and modern, which can appear when religious and social conditions come to a certain point. And its characteristics can be markedly different in the varying cultural and religious situations.

Israel's prophets were different from those in neighboring countries by so much as their concept and experience of God differed from others'. All of Israel's

The prophets, often scorned in their own day, came to be venerated in later centuries as men of clear vision, matchless faith and experience, and heroic courage. Jesus and the primitive church drank deeply from the springs of prophetic teaching and experience, as the many references to the prophets in the Gospels and the Epistles show. Even many secular people of our time regard the prophets as authentic human beings, unshackled by tradition and free from oppressive attitudes and practices – thus prototypes of the kind of humanity that must come into being.

Place in the Canon

The Hebrew Bible has two groups of prophetic books: the Earlier Prophets (Joshua, Judges, Samuel, Kings) and the Later Prophets (Isaiah, Jeremiah, Ezekiel, and the Twelve). As indicated earlier (p. 121), theological interests so dominate Joshua to Kings that these books are often more like preaching than straightforward historical narrative. It is thus appropriate to call them 'the Earlier (or Former) Prophets.'

The Greek Bible, followed by the Latin and the English Bibles, puts the prophetic books after the poetic and Wisdom books (*i.e.*, after Job, Psalms, Proverbs, Ecclesiastes, Song of Solomon) and adds to the prophetic books Lamentations and Daniel (and some prophets agreed that Yahweh had elected Israel as the chosen people and that they enjoyed a special relationship with God. They believed that God was the Lord of nature and history. As many scholarly studies have shown, they all seem to have known Israel's traditions: the call of the fathers, the redemption from Egypt, the Mosaic covenant with its personal and national obligations, the conquest saga. They knew themselves to be Yahweh's representatives and spokesmen: to keep alive the memory of the redemptive events and Israel's obligations within the covenant; to declare God's will in the crises the nation faced; and to point out the consequences of obedience and disobedience. Israel's prophets saw themselves as proclaimers of the divine will in the circumstances of the moment, not as clairvoyant predicters of the long-range future, though they did foresee what kind of future would emerge out of the present when their hearers obeyed or disobeyed God's will.

There were, of course, differences among the prophets. They were heirs of different lines of tradition that reached back to David and the exodus-conquest period and beyond. They interpreted their particular tradition with some freedom; and they applied it in their own way to the times and circumstances in which they lived, in the light of a new word of Yahweh that had come to them.

Some concentrated on the exodus-covenant-conquest traditions (Amos, Hosea, Jeremiah); some on the David's-line (2 Sam. 7) and Zion-as-Yahweh's-royal-city traditions (Ps. 48:1–2; 76:1–2; Isaiah, to some extent Micah, Joel, Zechariah); and some on both (Second Isaiah, Ezekiel). This made for different emphases among them.

Furthermore, they came from different social backgrounds and were related in different ways to Israel's cult and royal establishment. There were guilds of prophets, attached to royal courts and sanctuaries (Bethel, Jerusalem). These prophets evidently served alongside the

priests, delivering to the people the word of God on this matter and that and interceding with God for them. They advised the rulers on policies, particularly in times of crisis. They often were strongly nationalistic in outlook. On the basis of the David-Zion traditions (and probably of considerations of self-interest) they held that the king and Yahweh's people were invincible so long as they kept up the religious practices through which atonement for sins could be achieved. With some exceptions (Micaiah, 1 Kings 22:1–38) they said that Israel's relation to Yahweh as the chosen people guaranteed victory over every enemy.

Connection with the cult and the royal house did not in itself make prophets 'false.' Habakkuk and Joel, at least, seem to have been cultic prophets.

Israel's major (canonical) prophets explain 'false' prophecy as due to many things: drunkenness (Isa. 28:7), mercenary attitude (Micah 3:5; Jer. 6:13; 8:10); personal immorality (lying and adultery) and the support of evil doers (Jer. 23:14; 29:23); hypocrisy by hatching up words of the Lord from their own minds (Jer. 14:14; 23:16) or stealing them from others (Jer. 23:30) and representing them as words of the Lord; idolatrous attachment to Baal (Jer. 2:8, 26–27; 23:13); and disloyalty to prophetic tradition (Jer. 28:8). They are condemned for personal and group failures that violate the morality inherent in Israel's covenant with God and for departing from the path marked out by his authentic historical representatives, not for membership in a prophetic cult-guild and attachment to the temple and royal house.

Along with the professional prophets stood the great individual, non-professional prophets. They had no claim to the prophetic office other than God's call. Amos, for example, said, 'I am no prophet, nor a prophet's son; but I am a herdsman, and a dresser of sycamore trees, and the Lord took me from

Israelite porters bring tribute to Assyria (841 BC); Nimrud c. 825 BC.

following the flock, and the Lord said to me, "Go, prophesy to my people Israel'" (Amos 7:14–15).

These God-appointed prophets did not assure Israel of an irrevocable claim on God. They saw God as righteous judge of both Israel and the nations, who would punish Israel for its sins by defeat at the hands of foreign powers, unless there was radical repentance and amendment of life. The continuance of religious ceremonies without personal and social righteousness was offensive to God, they said, and would lead to disaster. Religious practices, backed by personal and social righteousness, would lead to individual and national security and to all the blessings God had promised for the coming age.

These prophets did not oppose on principle the ceremonies carried on at the temple, even though their words appear radical (Amos 5:21–24; Isa. 1:11–15; Jer. 7:21–22). They held that such practices, *divorced from righteous living*, are of no avail before God.

Disasters at the hands of Assyria (721 BC) and of Babylon (598 BC and 587 BC) proved the professional prophets wrong. After the Exile in Babylonia they ceased to function as a class and were absorbed into the guilds of temple singers. The great nonprofessional prophets were increasingly venerated, and their words and deeds were remembered and collected.

Formation of the Prophetic Books

The prophets ordinarily delivered their message in oral form. In exceptional circumstances they put it in writing (Isa. 8:1–4; 30:8; Jer. 36; Ezek. 43:11). They also taught by their lives, as evidenced by Hosea's marriage (Hos. 1–3), Isaiah's nakedness (Isa. 20:2–3), Jeremiah's celibacy (Jer. 16), Ezekiel's strange actions (Ezek. 4:3; 12:6, 11; 24:24).

They used many forms of expression: the oracle (the pronouncement of a divine message, usually introduced by 'Thus says Yahweh,' in which the immediate

A nation reaps what it sows; God will restore prosperity to the land if his people return to him.

future is shown to be favorable or unfavorable according to the course of action taken); the threat (an announcement of judgment because of sin); the covenant lawsuit (the arraignment of guilty Israel before the Divine Judge for breaking covenant law); the promise (the offer of salvation as a consequence of repentance and amendment of life); exhortations; the report of a vision or a symbolic action; the use of standard rhetorical forms such as hymns, laments, dirges, love songs, proverbs, prose narratives, etc. Their preaching and teaching contained great variety of form and style.

The compilation of the prophetic books probably went through the following stages:

a. The writing down of some of the prophetic utterances by disciples, with or without the express command of the prophet, for the sake of extending the effectiveness of the message;

b. The gathering of written materials into small collections;

c. The joining of small collections into larger ones;

d. The assembling of larger collections into prophetic books, with additional matter supplied by the editor or editors.

Some prophetic books are fairly logically arranged; others are quite unsystematic. Some have relatively little editorial matter, but others have large blocks of it. (For details, see the comments on the individual books below.)

The 'Major' and 'Minor' Prophets

Popularly and traditionally, the prophets have been classified as 'major' and 'minor' on the basis of the size of the books that bear their names. The 'major' prophets are thus Isaiah, Jeremiah, and Ezekiel; the 'minor' are twelve in number (Hosea, Joel, Amos, Obadiah, Jonah, Micah, Nahum, Habakkuk, Zephaniah, Haggai, Zechariah, Malachi). No estimate of the relative importance of the prophets in the life of Israel or in the fulfillment of the purposes of God is intended by the distinction – a distinction made at least from the time of Augustine (354–430 AD).

For Further Reading
Blenkinsopp, J., A History of Prophecy in Israel, 1983.
Efird, J.M., The Old Testament Prophets – Then and Now, 1982.
Rad, G. von, The Message of the Prophets, 1967.
Lindblom, J., Prophecy in Ancient Israel, 1962.
Wolff, H.W., Confrontation with Prophets, 1983.

Isaiah

Place in the Canon

In the Hebrew Bible Isaiah heads the sec
tion known as the Later Prophets. In the
Septuagint the Twelve (Minor) Prophets
come first. The Latin Vulgate and modern
versions follow the Hebrew order.

Isaiah's first place in the Hebrew Bible
is probably due to its size and thus apparent importance, not strictly to chronological considerations. Amos and Hosea of the
Twelve Prophets were written earlier than
Isaiah.

Isaiah – so full of glowing promises concerning Israel's future – was one of the
favorite books of the Jews of Jesus' time,
to judge by the number of copies of it discovered at Qumran by the Dead Sea (see
p. 423). Early Christians also loved this
book, because they believed the promises
in it were fulfilled in the coming of Jesus
and the formation of the church.

Unity and Authorship

There are three major positions:

a. The whole book comes from Isaiah,
the son of Amoz, who lived in Jerusalem
in the eighth to seventh centuries BC.
Apart from a couple of Jewish scholars,
one in the second and the other in the
twelfth century AD, no one seems to have
doubted the unity of the book until the

Assyrian Empire
Eighth Century BC

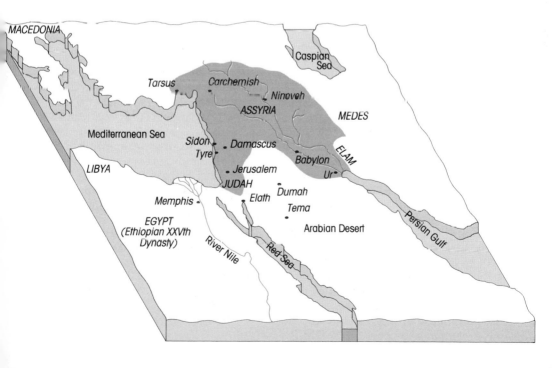

eighteenth century. In our time, some Old Testament scholars support the traditional view. (See Additional Note, below.)

b. The book contains the prophecies of two men: chaps. 1–39, of Isaiah of Jerusalem; and chaps. 40–66, of an unknown prophet of the Babylonian exile (sixth century BC). The mention of Cyrus as liberator of the Jews (44:28; 45:1), the contemplated fall of Babylon (not Assyria) in 47:1 and 48:14, and the difference between the two sections in literary style and theological emphases have led many to assume a dual origin for the book.

It is claimed by a contemporary Israeli scholar (Y.T. Radday) that a computer analysis of the language of the two parts confirms the hypothesis of two authors from different historical periods.

c. The book contains the utterances of three prophets, at least: chaps. 1–39, largely from Isaiah of Jerusalem; chaps. 40–55, from a sixth century prophet of the Babylonian exile (so-called Second Isaiah); chaps. 56–66, from a third prophet (Third Isaiah), who lived in Palestine in the late sixth or early fifth century. Contributions from still other prophets may have been made to the material in chaps. 56–66.

It seems clear to most scholars that we must assume several authors for the book. Isa. 36–39 corresponds closely to 2 Kings 18:13—20:19 and appears to be taken from that historical work. Pieces in Isa. 1–35 (*e.g.*, chaps. 24–27) bear the marks of postexilic authorship. The book as we now have it appears to be a collection of prophetic sayings reaching from Isaiah of Jerusalem (eighth century BC) to postexilic writers who assembled and edited the whole. We may think of the various contributors as standing in an 'Isaiah tradition,' as disciples in some sense of the original Isaiah.

Such discipleship would explain the striking term for God that appears throughout the book – 'The Holy One of Israel' (twelve times in chapters 1–39, fourteen times in chapters 40–66, but only seven times elsewhere in the Old Tes-

tament) – as a term beloved by the teacher and adopted by his followers. Quite the reverse of this, this way of referring to God has been cited by some conservatives as 'the strongest argument for the unity of Isaiah' (see additional arguments for unity in the Additional Note below).

If the book as we have it is composite, how did the parts get together? We can only guess: space considerations (the unused end of a scroll?), the practice of attributing to the master the work of disciples (as perhaps in the Pastoral Epistles of the New Testament – see p. 320). The joining of the parts together was done fairly early, as Ben Sira (the author of Ecclesiasticus about 180 BC), the great Dead Sea Scroll of Isaiah (about 100 BC), and the New Testament show.

Isaiah, Son of Amoz (Chaps. 1-39)

Isaiah was a Jerusalemite, probably from an aristocratic family and possibly educated as a priest or a scribe (wise man). He was married to a prophetess and seems to have had two sons (7:3; 8:1–4).

He was called to be a prophet 'in the year that King Uzziah [Azariah] died' (6:1), about 742 BC. He prophesied during the reigns of Jotham, Ahaz, and Hezekiah, when Judah was seeking desperately to adjust to the pressure of Assyrian power under the great kings Tiglath-Pileser III (745–727), Shalmaneser V (726–722), Sargon II (721–705), and Sennacherib (704–681). His latest prophecies, so far as we know, date to the year 701. Tradition says he died a martyr under King Manasseh (687–642).

His vision of God in the temple at the time of his call impressed him with the holiness of God and his own and his nation's sin. He learned also the possibility and reality of cleansing. He sought to turn

The ram's horn (shophar) was the national trumpet of the Israelites.

> ## Outline of chaps. 1–39
>
> **Prophecies** (chaps. 1–35)
>
> **1.** Concerning Judah and Jerusalem (chaps. 1–12)
>
> **2.** Concerning foreign nations (chaps. 13–23)
>
> **3.** Concerning God's final universal judgments and the salvation of Israel (chaps. 24–27)
>
> **4.** Concerning the Assyrian crisis of the time of King Hezekiah (chaps. 28–33)
>
> **5.** Concerning the fall of Edom and the restoration of Israel (chaps. 34–35)
>
> **Historical appendix** (chaps. 36–39)
>
> Concerning the Assyrian threat to Jerusalem and that city's miraculous deliverance in the time of King Hezekiah; and concerning the sickness and recovery of Hezekiah and the coming of messengers from Babylonia.

his people away from trust in false gods and foreign alliances for national security to absolute trust in Yahweh; from greed on the part of the wealthy to concern for the poor and oppressed; from lavish ritual, relied on as a guarantee of Yahweh's favor and protection, to righteous living and good deeds.

He kept on preaching fearlessly even though he was convinced that the nation would not repent but would experience God's judgments at the hand of Assyria. He believed that God would preserve a remnant and through it, under a righteous king of the line of David, Israel's destiny would be realized.

The 'Isaiah' of the Exile (Second Isaiah) (Chaps. 40–55)

The name of this prophet is unknown (hence, 'Second Isaiah' or 'Deutero-Isaiah'). His ministry probably fell between the beginning of the Persian king Cyrus' victorious career (c. 550 BC) and his capture of Babylon (539 BC), which resulted in the liberation of the Jews from Babylonia in 538.

The contents of Isa. 40–55 are difficult to analyze. There seem to be about fifty poems in the section, grouped according to similarity of content. We may distinguish two general stages in the thought development:

a. The deliverance of Israel from Babylonian captivity, by the power of the only true God, Yahweh, is to come about through Cyrus (chaps. 40–48).

b. Israel, having suffered God's judgment in the punishment by exile and having been restored to and exalted in its homeland by Yahweh, will see in its sufferings and exaltation God's redemptive activity for itself and for the nations (chaps. 49–55).

Second Isaiah declared the non-existence of the gods of Babylon and of the nations (44:9–20). He emphasized the omnipotence of the only God, Yahweh, and Yahweh's beneficence toward Israel and all peoples (chap. 40; 55:5). He urged his fellow Jews to have absolute confidence in their God, who would lead them tenderly back to their homeland and establish them eternally as a purged, renewed, holy people under God's sovereign, universal rule (49:8–23).

Second Isaiah spoke of a servant of Yahweh through whom redemption would come to all people (42:1–4; 52:13—53:12). Whether this servant is the nation of Israel as a whole (44:1–2, 21), or a righteous remnant within it (49:3–6), or a single righteous individual (a prophet? the Messiah?), or all three, has been much debated.

Whoever the servant is, the teaching is unmistakable here that unmerited suffering, gladly accepted by the righteous in the course of their work for God, moves the unrighteous who behold it to repentance and renewal of life (see 2 Macc. 7:37–38).

Jesus, 'the one-man Israel,' seems to have accepted this calling and work for himself (Mark 9:12; 10:45; 14:24; Luke 22:37), thereby drawing both Jews and Gentiles to the God of Israel and to membership in his family.

The 'Isaiah' after the Exile (Third Isaiah) (Chaps 56–66)

Chaps. 56–66 seem to reflect religious conditions in Judea after the return from Babylonian exile. The temple appears to be standing and foreigners (proselytes) to be participating in the worship of Yahweh (56:1–8). Bad conditions exist: false worship under corrupt religious leaders (56:9—57:13), many wicked people (59:1–15), and insincere performance or nonobservance of religious duties (58:3–5, 13). The walls of the city are not yet rebuilt (58:12). These conditions suggest the period between the rebuilding of the temple in 520–515 BC and the reforms of Nehemiah and Ezra about the second half of the fifth century BC.

This prophet emphasized strongly the importance of repentance, pure worship, and exact obedience to the Law, together with consideration for the poor, the oppressed, and even the foreigner. He clearly tried to keep his people from sinking to the level of corrupt peoples living in and around his land and to lift the worship of Yahweh by righteous Jews and sincere proselytes to its proper level. He made glowing promises for the future – on condition of Israel's obedience to God.

Some fourteen different pieces of material are included in these chapters, some of the pieces possibly from still other hands.

Additional Note

There are scholarly defenders of the unity of Isaiah. They point out the lack of agreement among those who dissect the book and assign its parts to various authors, editors, and historical situations, that is, to two or three Isaiahs and multiple editors, all but one of them unknown in name, place, and time.

They believe it strange that the identity of so great a prophet as the Second Isaiah is alleged to have been should have been altogether forgotten.

They hold that the historical situation reflected in the various parts of our present book is substantially identical. In all

A watchtower from which the owner would guard his ripening crops (Isa. 5:2).

Relief of Tiglath Pileser III of Assyria.

parts the Hebrews and the writer are assumed to be in Palestine. The idolatry opposed by the writer (44:9–20; 57:5, 7; 65:2–4) is almost everywhere plainly of the Canaanite variety, such as existed in Israel in the time of the eighth-century Isaiah (1:29; 2:8 ff.; 8:19). They claim that idolatry was not a real threat to Israel during the Exile or after, inasmuch as God's judgment in the destruction of Judah at the hands of Nebuchadnezzar had cured the nation of idolatrous ways.

They point out many agreements in language and style between the latter and former parts of the book and find close correspondence between the theology of the latter part and the theology of Micah, a contemporary of Isaiah. They argue that there is even a correspondence in the order of the materials in the two parts of the book.

They affirm that the eighth-century Isaiah was capable of predicting the Exile, and even the coming of Cyrus as future deliverer (44:28; 45:1); for prediction was an authentic function of Old Testament prophets (1 Kings 13:1 ff.; Mic. 5:2; Ezek. 26:2 ff.).

One such scholar (R.K. Harrison, whose views are summarized above) holds that the book is an anthology of Isaiah's utterances, containing examples of his thought and style in the various periods of his life, which was put together as a manual of instruction in two parts (chaps. 1–33 and 34–66) by his disciples within a half-century of his death (i.e., c. 630 BC).

Other conservatives (La Sor-Hubbard-Bush) do not attempt to defend the whole book as Isaiah of Jerusalem's direct or indirect production in the eighth century BC but view it as containing Isaiah's long-remembered prophecies which were put into their present form by his partisans after the return from the Babylonian exile. These scholars see a parallel with the Pentateuch, where 'the Torah is essentially Mosaic, although how much of it actually was written down by Moses is not at all clear.' They thus conclude that Isaiah was 'responsible for the entire prophecy,' though some one else some two hundred years later put it into its present form.

Jeremiah

The book of Jeremiah is particularly rich in information about the life, the personality, the times, and the message of the prophet who stands behind it. We know more about Jeremiah than about any other Old Testament prophet.

The Man and His Times

Jeremiah's ministry, like Isaiah's, extended over some four decades. He was born at Anathoth, a village of Benjamin, about two and one-half miles northeast of Jerusalem, apparently into a family of exiled priests (1 Kings 2:26–27). The date of his birth is unknown, but most scholars believe it was about 645 BC, during the closing years of the long reign of King Manasseh (687–642).

His call to the prophetic office then occurred during the reign of Josiah (640–609), about the year 627 (Jer. 1:2). His ministry was carried out under kings Josiah, Jehoahaz (609), Jehoiakim (609–598), Jehoiachin (598/597), and Zedekiah (597–587). After the deportation of Judean captives to Babylon in 587 Jeremiah was taken forcibly into Egypt, where he continued to prophesy for an unknown length of time until his death there.

Some scholars have proposed an alternative chronology for the beginning of Jeremiah's career: birth about 627 BC; and beginning of his ministry in 609 or 605. Some advantages of this chronology are: the foe from the north in the early chapters of the book would be the well-known

Babylonians, rather than the shadowy Scythians; Jeremiah's silence (or relative silence) about the reforms of Josiah (628–622) would be explained, since his ministry had not yet begun; and the supposed inactive period of Jeremiah's career (621–609) – on the other chronology – would be eliminated. The suggestion is attractive but flatly contradicts Jeremiah 1:2 and lacks enough supporting evidence to be convincing.

Jeremiah sought to supply direction for his nation at a time when it was striving to adjust to the pressure of foreign military powers. King Manasseh had found it impossible to resist Assyria. He had paid tribute and had recognized officially in Jerusalem the overlord's gods, with the inevitable contamination of Judah's religion and national life.

In the closing years of the reign of King Asshurbanapal of Assyria (668–627) Assyrian power over the west weakened, and King Josiah struck for freedom (c. 628). He launched sweeping reforms aimed at achieving full independence from Assyria politically and religiously. These reforms came to their climax in 622, after the discovery of the book of the Law (some form of our book of Deuteronomy) in the temple (2 Kings 22). Jeremiah had a high estimate of Josiah and his work (Jer. 22:15–16), though he soon came to see the superficiality and inadequacy of the reformation.

After Josiah's death, in 609, at the hands of the Egyptian king Neco II, Jeremiah found himself in bitter conflict with evil Jehoiakim, who had been made king by Neco against the wishes of the Judean people. They had crowned Jehoahaz three months before, only to have him deposed by Neco. Jehoiakim remained a vassal of Egypt until 605, when Nebuchadnezzar of Babylon defeated the Egyptians at Carchemish and took over control of the west.

Within a short time Jehoiakim transferred his allegiance to Nebuchadnezzar. However, relying on the help of Egypt, he rebelled against Nebuchadnezzar. This

brought the Babylonian army into Judah in 598. The sudden death of Jehoiakim (perhaps by assassination) resulted in the crowning of the eighteen-year-old Jehoiachin, who, after a three-month reign (598/597), was carried to Babylonia by Nebuchadnezzar, together with high officials, prominent citizens, and much booty. The Babylonians put Mattaniah (Zedekiah) on the throne as a sworn vassal (597).

Zedekiah (597–587), a vacillating king, began plotting rebellion with other western kings (594/593). Encouraged by fanatical nationalists and some surrounding peoples, especially the Egyptians, by 589 he had broken his covenant with Nebuchadnezzar and launched on a course of open rebellion. The army of Nebuchadnezzar soon appeared and systematically destroyed the fortified cities of Judah. After a long and terrible siege, Jerusalem was captured and destroyed (587). Zedekiah was blinded and carried in chains to Babylon. Other prominent persons and a sizable group of the population were deported. The kingdom of Judah came to its final end.

Jeremiah favored the policies of only Josiah. He found Jehoiakim greedy, disloyal to traditional Yahwism, paganizing, opportunistic, oppressive, unjust. He rebuked Zedekiah for repudiating his covenant with Nebuchadnezzar. He saw Nebuchadnezzar's rule over Judah as God's punishment for the people's sins, a punishment from which they should not seek to escape. He predicted destruction of the nation as the consequence of rebellion, the promises of false prophets to the contrary notwithstanding.

Jeremiah was considered a traitor by most of his compatriots and subjected to untold suffering and perhaps a martyr's death in Egypt.

The Assyrians assault Lachish (701 BC) with a siege engine; from Sennacherib's palace at Nineveh c. 695 BC.

Outline

Jeremiah's prophecies concerning Judah and Jerusalem (chaps. 1–25)

Biographical narratives about Jeremiah (chaps. 26–45)

Prophecies concerning foreign nations (chaps. 46–51)

A historical appendix (chap. 52)

The Book and Its Making

The process by which the book came to its present form is fairly evident. According to chap. 36, Jeremiah dictated two scrolls to Baruch, his scribe. Jehoiakim disdainfully burned the first one shortly after the battle of Carchemish (605). Jeremiah dictated the second not long afterward and somewhat expanded its contents over the first (36:28–32). It appears that this second scroll forms the basis for our present chaps. 1–25. These chapters seem also to include some later utterances of Jeremiah.

Chaps. 1–25 contain pronouncements of Jeremiah probably from the beginning of his ministry to the fall of Jerusalem in 587 and some autobiographical pieces (e.g., 1:4–19; 3:6–13; 11:18–23; 12:1–6; 13:1–14; 16:1–13).

Chaps. 26–45 are almost entirely in prose. It appears that Baruch wrote them about the experiences of Jeremiah. The order of events is not chronological. The 'Book of Consolation' (chaps. 30–31) is an independent collection of expanded sayings of Jeremiah introduced here by Baruch or a later editor in connection with the story of Jeremiah's act of faith in the nation's future (chap. 32).

The prophecies concerning foreign nations (chaps. 46–51) contain genuine sayings of Jeremiah but show signs of later expansion. Jeremiah considered himself 'a prophet to the nations' (1:5).

The historical appendix (chap. 52) agrees quite closely with 2 Kings 24:18—25:30 and probably came from that source. It means to suggest that Jeremiah's threats against Judah and

Jerusalem were historically fulfilled.

Several editors had a hand in the composition of the book, and its text was not fixed for a long time. The Septuagint shows this, for its text of Jeremiah is about one-eighth shorter than the Hebrew text.

A recent scholar (Robert P. Carroll) holds that the book of Jeremiah is largely the product of exilic and postexilic Deuteronomistic editors (see p. 119), who reshaped such material about Jeremiah as they had (chiefly Jeremiah's poetic oracles) so as to make Jeremiah 'a spokesman for their school.' So completely did they interpose their own material into the tradition about Jeremiah that we can know little about his life and deeds, even less than we can know about the historical Jesus. This view runs counter to the dominant position today that Jeremiah is the best known person in the Old Testament; and it appears to many scholars to be unjustified skepticism.

The Message of Jeremiah

Assyrian workmen's tools; Nineveh *c.* 695 BC.

Jeremiah's roots lie deep in the religion of Moses and of the prophets before him, particularly Hosea. Like Hosea he saw Israel as Yahweh's beloved bride who deserted her Divine Lover for false lovers. But the Divine Lover never gave up. Yahweh pursued the unfaithful one in unfailing compassion and sought to restore the broken relationship. Jeremiah pled long and intensely with his nation in the attempt to bring it to repentance.

Jeremiah saw that Yahweh was not satisfied with formal obedience to his laws. He believed that Josiah's reformation, which had centralized worship in the Jerusalem temple and cleansed it of foreign elements, had been unsuccessful in reaching the hearts of the worshipers and bringing mercy and justice in everyday relationships. He looked forward to the day when God's law would be written in the heart and would find expression in a new kind of human relationship (31:31–34).

Jeremiah opposed the pursuit of national security by alliance with foreign powers and recognition of their idolatrous religion. He resisted the many influential false prophets who claimed that Israel's covenant relation with Yahweh would guarantee its security, if the provisions of that covenant (such as pure temple worship) were maintained. He contended that only personal and national heart-loyalty and life-loyalty would avail. Without these, temple worship was irrelevant. God would allow even the destruction of the temple. Without these, Yahweh would abandon the people to the terrors of the covenant-judgments (Deut. 28).

Jeremiah saw no hope for his nation in the course it was taking. He regarded Nebuchadnezzar's punishment of Zedekiah's rebellion as an act of God to purge the nation and prepare it for a new and righteous future beyond the Exile. In that future a righteous king (23:5–6) would lead his people and the nations into perfect knowledge of God and obedience to God's will.

Lamentations

Jeremiah and Jesus

What we learn about Jeremiah reminds us strangely of Jesus, a similarity noted by some in New Testament times (Matt. 16:13–14). Both grew up and served as God's messengers to the nation in a time of fanatical nationalistic rebellion against foreign powers (Assyria and Babylon for Jeremiah; Rome for Jesus). Both sought unsuccessfully to avoid catastrophe for their country by counseling repentance and absolute loyalty to God, who alone could assure Israel's future. Both challenged the hollow ceremonialism, divorced from practical morality, that characterized temple worship in their time and predicted the destruction of the temple. Both reacted against the legalism of book religion and advocated a religion of the heart. Both loved their people deeply, preached in virile, poetic language, often dramatically acted out the message, and wept over the people's hardness of heart. Both suffered deeply at the hands of those they loved; and it seems that both were martyred for their efforts. Jesus brought into being the new covenant envisioned by Jeremiah (Heb. 8:8–13). Both looked beyond the tragedy of national destruction to a New Age in which the purposes of God for Israel and the world would be fulfilled.

Name and Place in Canon

The Hebrew title comes from the opening word of chaps. 1, 2, and 4, which means 'Ah, how!' Funeral dirges began with this word. The English title comes from the Latin Vulgate's *lamentationes*. In some ancient translations, 'of Jeremiah' or 'of Jeremiah the prophet' was added to the title, and the book was placed after the book of Jeremiah. In the Hebrew Bible its position is in the third division of the canon (The Writings).

Literary Style and Type

The five poems of this book, corresponding to the five chapters, present a mixture of literary types: funeral dirges in which dead Jerusalem is mourned (1, 2, 4), individual laments (3 and some parts of the others), and community laments (5 and parts of others). Most of the poems are in the meter of the elegy or dirge.

The poems are carefully constructed and patterned in various ways after the order of the Hebrew alphabet. For example, in poems 1 and 2 the first line of each three-line stanza (strophe) begins with a different letter of the Hebrew alphabet in sequence, while in poem 3 each letter of the alphabet is used to begin three successive lines before the next letter is introduced. Poem 5 has as many lines as there are letters in the Hebrew alphabet (22), though the letters are not in sequence.

Contents

Poem 1 (chap. 1): Desolate, devastated Jerusalem weeps over its condition, confesses its sins, acclaims God's punishment as just, and prays for vengeance on its enemies.

Poem 2 (chap. 2): The destruction of Jerusalem is Yahweh's doing alone, in fulfillment of his word of judgment.

Poem 3 (chap. 3): The awful consequences of God's judgments lead to a consideration of his great mercy – for God is a God of both judgment and mercy.

Poem 4 (chap. 4): The horrors of the siege and the devastation of Jerusalem, brought on by the sins of prophets and priests, were unrelieved by the nation's ally (Egypt); gloating Edom will be punished.

Poem 5 (chap. 5): The miseries resulting from the capture of Jerusalem lead to a prayer for restoration by the eternal King Yahweh.

This neat structuring of the material interferes somewhat with free, logical flowing of ideas. It may be that the alphabetic form was a memory device to help the leader and congregation through the laments (see below). It may also suggest completeness, as we would say, 'from A to Z.'

Date, Authorship, and Purpose

The poems reflect at close range the events and conditions of the fall of Jerusalem in 587 BC. They were probably written by one or more eyewitnesses of those tragic events, perhaps for use at an annual ceremony of mourning for the ruined temple and city. Such lamentation began soon after the destruction (Jer. 41:5) and continued in the postexilic period (Zech. 7:3; 8:19). A date between 587 and 540 is likely.

The Latin Vulgate's ascription of the book of Lamentations to Jeremiah has little to support it. Jeremiah would hardly have said that Jerusalem's prophets 'obtain no vision from the Lord' while he was still present (2:9), or that he had looked for help from an alliance with an outside nation (4:17), or spoken in high terms of vacillating King Zedekiah (4:20), or expressed perplexity over the severe judgments of God (3:43–44; 5:1–18). And the artificial style of construction of the poems is unlike anything in Jeremiah's prophecies as we know them from the book of Jeremiah. Who wrote the poems is unknown.

While conservatives point out that the book is anonymous and its authorship is uncertain, they leave open the possibility of Jeremiah's authorship on the basis of such data as the following : 2 Chronicles 35:25, where a lament by Jeremiah over King Josiah is mentioned, and passages in the book of Jeremiah which mention lamentation (7:29; 8:21; 9:1, 10, 20); some similarities of vocabulary and style with the book of Jeremiah; and Jeremiah's known presence at the time of the fall of Jerusalem (which is so graphically portrayed here by some eyewitness).

Value

In these poems we have moving penitential liturgy. It contemplates the stark consequences of human sin and misery, sees God's hand in them for ultimate good (3:37–39), and hopes fervently in the midst of tragedy for deliverance and a bright future by the mercy of God.

The book has long been chanted by Jews on the fast day recalling the fall of Jerusalem in 587 (the ninth of Ab [July–Aug.]) and is used today by Christians during Holy Week in calling to mind the sufferings of Jesus.

For centuries Jews have come to the western Temple wall in Jerusalem to mourn the destruction of the Temple.

Ezekiel

To most people today Ezekiel is a curious and puzzling prophet. His strange otherworldly visions, his 'abnormal' personality, his obscure imagery, his monotonous and harsh language and style, his interest in correct religious forms and ceremonies, his high regard for meticulous fulfillment of the Law – all remove him from the areas of interest of most contemporary Western people.

To the courageous and imaginative, however, who are willing to enter sympathetically into Ezekiel's world and situation, the rewards are considerable. His emphasis on individual responsibility before God and on inner conversion (God's gift of a new heart and a new spirit) alone entitles him to an honored place among Israel's teachers and among the forerunners of Christianity.

The Man

Information in the book does not allow certainty concerning the outline of his life and career. Scholars have made many conflicting constructions of it. According to the most probable view, at the beginning of his career Ezekiel was a priest attached to the temple in Jerusalem. He was carried as a captive to Babylonia along with King Jehoiachin and others in 597 BC. He lived in a house of his own in the community of Telabib by the river Chebar (3:15; 8:1). There in 593 BC he received his call to be-

come a prophet (1:2). His beloved wife died at Telabib at the time of the siege of Jerusalem by Nebuchadnezzar (588 BC). He used her death as a symbol of the inevitable destruction of beloved Jerusalem and the temple, and his numb unexpressed grief as a symbol of the people's appropriate reaction to God's righteous judgment on that city (24:15–24). His ministry in Babylonia continued until around 571 BC (29:17). He often delivered the word of the Lord to elders of the exiles who came to his house (8:1; 14:1).

There is evidence that the book was added to and altered by Ezekiel's disciples and successors. The additions seem to fall in line with Ezekiel's own point of view. Duplicate passages (3:17–19=33:7–9; 18:25–29=33:17–20; etc.) and chronological displacements (26:1; 29:1; etc.) offer proof of a complicated literary history. Ezekiel's authorship may be justly claimed for the bulk of the material, however. When the book reached its present form is not known. Responsible estimates range from the sixth to the fourth centuries BC.

Ezekiel's Message

Ezekiel's prophecies before the fall of Jerusalem in 587 BC apparently were intended both for the exiles and the inhabitants of Judah and Jerusalem. He wished all to understand that Jerusalem was doomed on account of its sins, to prepare them for its fall by separating them from dependence on it, and to declare God's will concerning its future. After the fall he sought to bring about a renewal of the life of the exiles so that they could enter into that future as God's chastened and redeemed people.

Ezekiel also pronounced God's judgments on the nations which gloated over Jerusalem's destruction and lived in defiance of the will of God (chaps. 25–32).

His hope embraced many elements: the resurrection of the nation (the dry bones will come alive); the return to Zion; the uniting of Israel and Judah into one kingdom; the reign of God's servant, a descendant of David, over it; marvelous fertility of the land; the rebuilding and glorification of the temple and careful observance of its holy rites; and the worship of a holy God by a people indwelt by his Spirit. This renewed people will obey God's will from the heart. A new covenant will be established, which will stand forever. God and the chosen people will live togther in mutual possession ('You shall be my people, and I will be your God').

The dominant theological notes in Ezekiel's message are: the loftiness and absolute holiness of God; his activity and nearness in his Spirit; human sinfulness; the certainty of divine judgment on sinners; individual, as well as collective, responsibility before God; inner conversion and renewal of the repentant; the certainty of a glorious future for God's renewed people.

Forms of Thought and Literary Style

Ezekiel was a many-sided prophet, perhaps the most versatile in Israel's entire history. He was a priest, a prophet, a pastor ('watchman'), an apocalyptist, a theologian, a religious and political planner, a poet, an artist.

As priest he had a deep concern for ritual and personal purity, for correct corporate worship, and for exact obedience to the law of God. The holiness of God overshadowed all his life and thought.

As prophet he exposed Israel's and the nations' sins and announced the coming judgment of God. He called his hearers to repentance and promised God's mercy on all who sincerely turned to God.

As pastor he was called to warn, protect, and comfort his people.

As apocalyptist he was caught up into visionary trances and described God's truth in dramatic symbols.

As theologian he interpreted the meaning of the catastrophe of Jerusalem's fall and the conditions of national restoration and renewal.

As religious and political planner he laid the foundation for the postexilic community, with its life centered in the new temple.

As poet and artist he was strikingly imaginative, his creations often bordering on the bizarre. He communicated through powerful allegories, metaphors, symbols, and symbolic actions. He spoke and wrote in both prose and poetry. His laments are particularly powerful (e.g.,19:2–14).

Influence

Ezekiel left his mark on the postexilic community. He contributed to its passion for separation from the unclean, its strong legalism, and its growing apocalypticism (see Daniel below). On most of the New Testament Ezekiel has left little impression, but the visions of the Revelation to John owe much to him, as does the figure of the good shepherd in the Gospel of John (Ezek. 34; John 10:1–30).

Daniel

The stories of the book of Daniel are beloved wherever the Bible is known. They are great stories, full of adventure, suspense, pageantry, and emotion.

Few, however, understand their purpose and meaning in the book to which they belong. This is because they are lifted out of their context. Actually, they bear the same relation to the book as illustrations to sermons. The author meant them to be seen in relation to great truths which the book as a whole expounds.

The stories comprise chaps. 1–6. Chaps. 7–12 report the visions of Daniel. Though perplexing in some ways, the stories are on the whole fairly easy to grasp. But to understand their purpose requires penetrating the mysteries of the visions. This is difficult for many people.

Literary Type

Daniel and the Revelation to John belong to a type of literature called 'apocalyptic.' This literature became fashionable among Jews between about 200 BC and AD 100. Christians adopted and developed it. (For its characteristics see pp. 356–7.)

The word 'apocalypse' means 'unveiling,' 'disclosure,' 'revelation.' The claim is made in the apocalypses that God has revealed to a particular prophet the divine purpose to overthrow the enemies of the chosen people and give freedom, prosperity, world sovereignty, and religious leadership to them. God's secret plan for

accomplishing this result is revealed as well. The enemies are referred to only through symbols (the oppressor Antiochus IV is 'a little horn' – Dan. 8:9).

The message of apocalypses is: Wait patiently and in faith for God's plan to be accomplished; do not worship the oppressors' gods or accept their pagan way of life; obey God's law as revealed to the fathers; do acts of righteousness; at the last you will be on the winning side; God's program for the future is being accomplished and is on schedule.

Contents

In Part 1 the author portrays Daniel as a true Jew, loyal to God under the pressures of life in a foreign land (Babylon). His God-given ability in the interpretation of dreams brings him to a high position at court.

In Part 2 there are four visions. They reveal to Daniel what will come to pass before the enemies of Israel are defeated and the kingdom of God, with Israel ruling the nations, comes. Here Daniel, the interpreter of the visions of others (chaps 1–6), has trouble understanding his own, so confusing is their content and so remote their fulfillment. The angel Gabriel helps him discern in part their meaning concerning God's plan for the consummation of history (8:15–19), but their full import still lies beyond his grasp (8:27).

Part 2 outlines the succession of four empires which will dominate the world until the coming of God's kingdom. They seem to be the Babylonian, Median, Persian, and Greek empires (but see p. 183). The amount of detail offered about the last of these is impressive (chap. 11). The history of this empire (apparently presented here as unfulfilled prophecy) is

Mythical beast on glazed tiles from the Ishtar gate of Babylon.

traced down to the time of Antiochus IV (175–163 BC), who defiled the temple in Jerusalem and whose paganizing activities brought on the Maccabean rebellion and the suffering and death of Jews loyal to God (11:21–39). Antiochus' death is predicted (11:45) and the kingdom of God is promised soon, after the resurrection of many of the dead (12:2). Daniel is directed to seal up the prophecy until the time of its fulfillment draws near (12:4, 9).

For some reason, parts of the book are in Hebrew (1:1—2:4a and chaps. 8–12), and a considerable portion is in Aramaic (2:4b—7:28). One explanation suggests that the materials of the book were first composed in Aramaic and that the first part (1:1—2:4a) and the last part (chaps. 8–12) were rendered into Hebrew in order to assure canonical acceptance of the book.

Author and Date

Chaps. 8–12, written in the first person, seem clearly to attribute the writing of the book to Daniel. The author places him in Babylon during the reigns of Nebuchadnezzar, Belshazzar, Darius, and Cyrus. According to 1:1, Nebuchadnezzar took him from Jerusalem to Babylon in 606 (or 605) BC.

Modern liberal scholarship as a whole questions the authorship of the book by a sixth-century person and concludes that it was written around 165 BC by an unknown author (or authors, see below) about, rather than by, an ancient Daniel. Some of the reasons for this conclusion are:

a. The writer's knowledge of the third and second centuries BC seems considerably fuller and more accurate than of the sixth century.

The stories about events in the sixth century (chaps. 1–6) may belong to a literary type known as *midrash* or *haggadah* (popular stories told to set forth religious or moral truths). Such stories were not meant as exact history, though they sometimes were based on historical facts.

A story of this kind may be that of the three young men who refused to worship Nebuchadnezzar's image and came out of the super-heated fiery furnace without even their hair singed (chap. 3). The historical fact is that Jews in Babylon and in Palestine repeatedly underwent pressure to conform to pagan religious practices and social customs. The teaching is that no real harm can come to those who refuse, because God is on their side. God will support them, refine them by their suffering and death, and ultimately give them life in the coming age (11:33–35; 12:1–3).

The narratives of chaps. 1–6, if midrashic, were written not by someone contemporary with the events described but by an author who looked back through the centuries with the eyes of a preacher and teacher. The stories he used may have had a long period of popular use and retelling. Scholars have pointed out various historical inaccuracies in them (such as the attributing to Nebuchadnezzar of a mental illness actually experienced by Nabonidus [chap. 4] and the wrong sequence of foreign kings given in 6:28 and 9:1).

Dan. 11:2–39, on the contrary, contains an astonishingly detailed and accurate chronicle of events during the Greek period down to the Seleucid king Antiochus IV (175–163 BC). The last events mentioned seem to be the profanation of the Jerusalem temple by this impious ruler and the rebellion it evoked (11:31–35), events of 167–164 BC.

b. The Hebrew and Aramaic of the book are of late, rather than of sixth century, type; and some Persian and Greek words point to a late date.

c. The book appears in the latest section of the Hebrew canon (the Writings), not in the earlier division called the Prophets.

It apparently was unknown to the writer of Ecclesiasticus (The Wisdom of Jesus the Son of Sirach), about 200–180 BC.

d. The religious concepts (angelology, resurrection of the dead, etc.) and the literary form (apocalypse) fit better in the second than in the sixth century BC.

e. The figure of Daniel in the book appears to be drawn in part against the backdrop of traditions about a very ancient Daniel (or Dan'el), referred to in Ezek. 14:14, 20, along with Noah and Job. This Dan'el appears as a just and merciful king in the Canaanite Ras Shamra tablets of the fourteenth century BC. Daniel stories had long been told in the Middle East. Our author apparently gathered together some of these in the second century BC and added to them visions of his own.

In the light of the above data, the date of the writing of the book would be between 167 and 165 BC.

Liberal scholarly opinion is divided between the hypothesis of one author, who used earlier traditions now included in chaps. 1–6, and several like-minded authors who composed different parts of the book from the third century to the middle of the second century BC. According to the multiple-author hypothesis, we should speak of 'compilers' and 'editors,' rather than 'authors.'

A recent view (John C. Trever) holds to one author and identifies him as the 'Right Teacher' (or 'Teacher of Righteousness') known to us from the Dead Sea Scrolls, who may have been the founder of the Qumran community in the Wilderness of Judea and author of some of the scrolls (see p. 420). This view highlights the many similarities between the theology and language of the book of Daniel and those texts, even if it falls short of proof of that Teacher's authorship of the book of Daniel. (For the conservative view of the authorship see Additional Note on pp. 182–3.)

Modern reconstruction of the Ishtar Gate, Babylon.

Historical Situation and Message

Antiochus IV ('Epiphanes,' *i.e.*, 'the god manifest'), king of Syria-Palestine, aided by Greek-influenced Palestinian Jews, sought to unite his territories with the cohesive force of Greek religion and culture, including the worship of himself as the visible manifestation of Zeus. He built an altar to Zeus on the altar of burnt offering in the Jerusalem temple. He forbade the offering of sacrifices to Yahweh, the circumcision of children, and the observance of the Sabbath and dietary laws; and he ordered all copies of the Jewish scriptures destroyed. He raided the temple treasury to get money for his administrative and military operations. (See the discussion of 1 and 2 Maccabees, pp. 223–4.)

His policies brought on bitter opposition by Jews loyal to their ancestral religion, including the writer of the book of Daniel. This writer undertook in this crisis to encourage his fellow Jews to resist Antiochus' demands and to remain faithful to the laws of God. He showed how Daniel and his three friends were exposed to similar pressure during the Exile but refused to give in, and how God protected them and made them prosper. He predicted the speedy overthrow of Antiochus and the coming of the kingdom of God about three and one-half years after the defiling of the temple (7:25; 8:14; 12:7, 11, 12). In this kingdom the faithful would be rewarded for their loyalty.

The central truths of the book, both in the stories and in the visions, are the following:

a. There is one God in the universe, to whom all people owe allegiance. Though they are asked to bow down to false gods, the truly wise will stoutly refuse.

b. God's holy and righteous will is revealed in divine laws. Loyalty to these laws will pay in the end.

c. Rulers govern by divine sufferance and are held reponsible for the way they rule. When they flout God's laws, God removes them from their thrones.

d. This God is the Lord of history, whose will for human society is being carried out, in spite of indications to the contrary. God makes even the deeds of dictators advance his holy purposes.

e. It is God's plan to sweep evil and evildoers aside and to give his faithful servants a kingdom of righteousness.

f. This kingdom is God's gift, not human achievement. The stone was cut out without hands (2:31–45). But the saints have their part to play. They are to be loyal in life, outspoken in witness, and heroic in active deed.

g. Suffering, patiently and loyally borne, can result in purification of life.

h. The righteous dead have not died in vain. They will participate in God's ultimate triumph over the forces of evil.

Contemporary Significance

As we have seen, the book of Daniel was written to give hope to Jews in a bitter crisis of the second century BC by holding out to them the promise of God's deliverance and the gift of God's kingdom. The writer apparently believed this kingdom would come in about three and one-half years (7:25; 12:7). In this prediction events proved him wrong, as events always do to those who set dates. Jesus refused to set dates for the coming of the kingdom (Mark 13:32; *cf.* Acts 1:7). He preferred to leave this matter in the Father's hands.

Those who make Daniel into a divinely revealed blueprint of events in *our* time and seek to determine from it where we stand on God's time clock ignore the original purpose of this book and make God's business their business. But to share the faith of the writer as stated in the central truths above is the highest wisdom.

Additional Note

Most conservative scholars argue that the book of Daniel is a literary unit and that it was written in its entirety in the sixth century BC by the Jewish statesman whose name it bears. A recent conservative work (G.L. Archer Jr. and R. Youngblood in *The NIV Study Bible*, 1985) puts the time of writing by Daniel himself at *c.* 530 BC, shortly after the capture of Babylon in 539 by Cyrus.

Conservatives claim that chaps. 1–6 are fully accurate historically. They believe also that the predictions of the future contained in the visions are authentic, divinely inspired predictions, not history disguised as prophecy.

They interpret the four kingdoms of the book as the Babylonian, the Medo-Persian, the Greek, and the Roman (rather than the Babylonian, Median, Persian, and Greek), on the ground that Darius the Mede (5:31; 6:1 ff.) was thought of by the author not as an independent monarch but as the Median governor of Babylon under appointment of King Cyrus, the Persian.

Such a construction of the succession of kingdoms avoids the conclusion that the author's prediction concerning the nearness of the end of the age and the coming of the kingdom of God (three and one-half years from the defiling of the temple by Antiochus IV) failed to come to pass. This construction allows for the contention that we are still in the Roman period and that the prophecies concerning the end will yet be literally fulfilled.

By interpreting the fourth kingdom as Rome it is possible, by a certain way of reading Dan. 9:25–26, to find a reference to the coming of Jesus, his crucifixion, and the destruction of Jerusalem by the Romans. Those who take the fourth kingdom to be Greece identify the 'anointed one, a prince' (vs. 25) with Cyrus, Zerubbabel, or the priest Joshua (Hag. 1:1) and the 'anointed one' who is 'cut off' (vs. 26) with the high priest Onias III, who was deposed about 175 BC and subsequently murdered.

Conservative interpreters see Antiochus IV of the third (Greek) empire as typifying the Antichrist, who is to come after the fourth (Roman) empire, and find the Antichrist's work sketched in 11:40–45.

A somewhat more liberal position in conservative scholarship leaves open the possiblity of the compilation of Daniel's experiences and visions (as handed down orally or in writing) by someone later than Daniel: 'not later than the middle of the fifth century BC' (R.K. Harrison); or the fourth or third century BC (La Sor-Hubbard-Bush). The latter scholars say that Daniel is a book of apocalyptic prophecy about the End and does not intend to give exact historical data about the past or predictions to be literally fulfilled in the future. It has a timeless message, applicable to any age.

It is evident that strong differences in the interpretation of the book of Daniel and in the understanding of its meaning for us today exist among scholars of different theological positions.

Hosea

In the Hebrew Bible Hosea stands first in the collection of shorter prophetic books known as 'The Twelve.' This collection is now generally called 'The Minor Prophets' (see p. 162).

The order of these Twelve is not strictly chronological. Amos, for example, was earlier than Hosea. But those who put the Hebrew Bible together apparently attempted a rough chronological grouping. Hosea, Joel, Amos, Obadiah, Jonah, and Micah were believed to belong to the period of the height of Assyrian power over Israel and Judah (second half of the eighth century BC). Nahum, Habakkuk, and Zephaniah were thought to belong to the period of the end of Assyrian power (the last third of the seventh century). Haggai, Zechariah, and Malachi were recognized as belonging to the Persian period (sixth through fifth centuries). It is possible that Hosea was put first in the first group because it is the longest book of that group.

Life and Times of Hosea

Hosea carried out his ministry in the Northern Kingdom during the closing days of the reign of Jeroboam II (786–746) and for some time after that king's death, possibly as late as 725. Though some of his words reflect knowledge of conditions in the Southern Kingdom (5:8—6:6), he directed his message toward the situation in the north.

He lived in a turbulent age. Jeroboam II expanded the borders of Israel and brought great prosperity to his kingdom, at least to the upper classes. The rich, however, oppressed the poor. The poor, robbed and dispossessed, could get no justice in the courts. Religious decay had set in. Though king and people worshiped Yahweh in great shrines, pagan fertility rites glorifying Baal had a place in these shrines and also flourished independently (Hos. 1–3; 4:6–14). Professional prophets fell in with the spirit of the times and offered no rebuke in the name of Yahweh and the Mosaic tradition.

The death of Jeroboam brought the Northern Kingdom to a virtual state of anarchy. Five kings reigned in a period of ten years. Several of them died at the hands of illegitimate pretenders. Assyria, under the powerful Tiglath-Pileser III (745–727), took advantage of the anarchic situation, extended its authority over the Northern Kingdom, and exacted heavy tribute. Soon an anti-Assyrian coalition, involving usurper Pekah of the Northern Kingdom and King Rezin of Damascus, sought to force King Ahaz of Judah into the coalition. Tiglath-Pileser forthwith destroyed the coalition and brought the west to its knees.

A final attempt at rebellion against Assyria was made by King Hoshea (732–724) of the Northern Kingdom, who hoped in vain for help from Egypt. Tiglath-Pileser's successors, Shalmaneser V and Sargon II, after a two-year siege of the capital city of Samaria, brought an end to the Northern Kingdom and deported 27,290 of its citizens to upper Mesopotamia and Media (721 BC).

Hosea apparently died shortly before the fall of the Northern Kingdom.

Little is known of Hosea's personal life. We learn only that his father's name was Beeri (1:1) and that his relationship with his wife, Gomer, was to him a symbol of Yahweh's relationship with Israel. It is evident from the high quality of his prophetic utterances that he was an educated man.

> **Outline**
>
> Hosea's marital experience and its meaning (chaps. 1–3)
>
> Hosea's prophetic utterances (chaps. 4–14)

The Book

The second division contains threats against corrupt priests, idolatrous and immoral people, and the royal family, together with some promises of restoration when God's judgments are over.

The content of chaps. 4–14 consists of small collections of material arranged according to catchwords (*i.e.,* material drawn together by the presence of identical words in disconnected pieces) and according to similarity of subject matter.

The autobiographical material of chapter 3 ('I', 'me') clearly goes back to Hosea himself; and the biographical matter in chapter 1 ('he', 'him') may come from the hand of one of his disciples. The sayings of the book may have been assembled by Hosea or his disciples. A Judean editor (1:1) probably put the book together in its present form from separate pieces carried to Judah sometime after the fall of the Northern Kingdom (721).

Conservative scholars, however, hold that the book was substantially completed within the lifetime of the prophet himself.

Hosea's Marriage

The book seems to present the prophet's personal marital experience as a parable of God's relationship with Israel.

Unfortunately, the details of Hosea's domestic life, as alluded to in chaps. 1 and 3, are far from clear. Different reconstructions are possible.

a. Hosea married *one* woman, Gomer, who either was a prostitute (probably attached to a Baal temple) when he married her or became a prostitute after he married her. He had children by her to whom he gave symbolic names as a means of conveying his message about the coming judgment of the nation by God (1:4–8). She later left his home, perhaps through divorce, became the property of another, and was finally bought back by Hosea and restored to his home.

b. Hosea married *two* women: the first was the bride of his youth, Gomer, who either was at that time, or later became, a prostitute. Hosea divorced her as a symbol of Yahweh's coming repudiation of Israel. He later bought an unnamed prostitute, married her, and took her into his home, as a symbol of God's coming mercy on unworthy Israel.

Some interpreters have taken chaps. 1 and 3 allegorically – not as reports of a real marriage but only as a literary device by which to convey the message of God's judgment and love. Others have held that a dream or vision lies behind the stories.

It is best to understand the chapters realistically, as actual events of the prophet's life. The real problem is whether Hosea's message of God's judgment and love arose from his personal tragic marital experience or whether his message was prior to and led to his marriage (or marriages) as a way of dramatizing that message for his hearers. The prophets often engaged in deeds that symbolized their teaching (Isa. 20; Jer. 19).

We may conclude this much, at least: that Hosea had an unfortunate marriage, whatever its exact nature; that he saw a parallel between it and God's relation with Israel; and that by his actions in the marital relationship he sought to declare both God's judgment and mercy on the nation.

Hosea's Message

Hosea describes the connection between God and Israel as a marriage relation (1:2; 2:16) or as a father-son relationship (11:1). The bond between God and the people began with the exodus from Egypt (12:9; 13:4) and issued from God's love (11:1). God delighted in the people at first (9:10), but shortly they turned to other gods (11:2; 13:5–6). Their history was

In turning to Baal worship, the people had come to believe that Baal was responsible for the fertility of the fields.

a history of rebellion (9:9; 10:9).

Baal worship had perverted their national and personal life. They had come to believe that the Baals, not Yahweh, were responsible for the fertility of flocks and fields and must therefore be worshiped (2:5–8; 4:13). They engaged in sacred prostitution as practiced in the Baal cult (4:13–14).

The political and religious leaders were an affront to God. The priests and prophets were corrupt and blind (4:4–9). Political leaders grabbed for the throne through assassination (4:2), law and order collapsed (7:1), security was sought through foreign alliances instead of through trust in God (5:13; 7:11). The nation was heading toward destruction at the hands of Assyria. Yahweh will turn the nation over to the disaster of exile and new bondage (8:13; 9:3). Hosea did not offer repentance to the nation as a way of forestalling disaster. Israel's doom was just and absolutely certain.

But God's love will reach beyond punishment to a new beginning. Cast off, repentant Israel will be restored to its bountiful home (14:4–8) and to the pro-

tection and perpetual fellowship of its merciful God (2:14–23). While Hosea does not describe the new order beyond the disaster, his strictures against cultic worship (2:8, 11, 13; 4:13; 6:6; 8:13; 9:4) imply that the new worship will be from the heart and from the lips (prayer and praise), without animal sacrifice (6:6; 14:2, 'the bulls of our lips').

Influence

Hosea's influence on Jeremiah, Jesus, and the early church was profound. Jeremiah also represented Yahweh as a spurned lover who persistently pursued his beloved with a view to restoring her to exclusive relationship (Jer. 2:1—4:4).

Jesus' compassion for the outcasts (the irreligious, the harlots, and the tax collectors) reflects the attitude of Hosea that God desires steadfast love and not sacrifices (Hos. 6:6; Matt. 9:13; 12:7).

The early church saw God's magnificent love manifested in the adoption of an unworthy people (the Gentiles) as his own (1 Pet. 2:10; Hos. 2:23).

Joel

Joel (probably meaning, 'Yahweh is God') is a short but powerful book. The man behind it apparently was a priest-prophet, about whom we are told nothing other than that he was 'the son of Pethuel' (1:1). He was the bearer of 'the word of Yahweh' (1:1) in a national crisis in his generation, a word that has echoes in the New Testament and meaning for our time.

The Occasion and Date of the Prophecy

Joel 1:2—2:27 describes in vivid symbolic language a horrible plague of locusts and a severe drought that have impoverished the land and reduced its inhabitants to despair and mourning. So severe is the famine that the offerings of food and drink for temple worship are no longer possible (1:9, 13). It is the prophet's role to interpret for the sufferers the meaning of this tragic experience.

We cannot be certain when it took place. Plagues of locusts, droughts, and resulting famines have occurred regularly in Palestine. There is no nonbiblical or other biblical evidence for a great disaster such as the book of Joel describes.

But some general indications are at hand. The language and religious ideas, especially concerning the future, belong to a late date, almost certainly postexilic. Joel seems to be acquainted with several prophetic writings – Isaiah, Jeremiah, Ezekiel, Obadiah, Zephaniah, Malachi –

whose ideas and words he echoes. The political and religious situation in Jerusalem fits the postexilic period: no king, but elders and priests as leaders; religious life centering in the temple, especially in the daily offerings; the dispersal of the inhabitants of Judah and Jerusalem among the nations; and Jews having been sold as slaves to Greeks. The best date is perhaps the fifth or fourth century BC.

A few scholars have argued for a preexilic date, in the time of Jeremiah (late seventh century) or even in the late ninth century, but on grounds generally regarded as inadequate.

Some have claimed that the book does not describe an actual plague and drought but predicts these for the future in connection with the coming day of the Lord (i.e., the day of judgment). However, the graphic, realistic description, plus the call for a day of repentance by the whole nation (1:14; 2:12–17), and the prophet's interpretation of the meaning of the catastrophe (the locusts are the Lord's army for the judgment of his people – 2:11, 25) all convince the reader that a real event is being described.

Unity

In English Bibles Joel is divided into three chapters. The Hebrew Bible has four chapters, the third chapter beginning at our 2:28 and the fourth at our 3:1.

Some students of the book have argued that the two parts come from two authors. They see stylistic and thought differences between the parts, especially the apocalyptic character (see pp. 356–7) of the second part. However, the view is gaining ground

---

Outline

The disaster (locusts and drought) **and the national religious response** (lamentation, repentance, prayer, hearing of God's promise) (1:2—2:27)

God's gift of the Spirit, God's final judgment of the nations, and the triumph and glorification of Jerusalem (2:28—3:21)

that the whole book stems from the mind of one prophet, each of the parts and perhaps even sections of them having originated at different times in his life.

Message

Joel's horror that temple sacrifice has ceased, his high regard for the priests as 'the ministers of the Lord' (1:9, 13; 2:17) and 'ministers of the altar' (1:13), his veneration of the temple as 'the house of the Lord' and place of 'solemn assembly' (1:4), and his passion for Jerusalem, the holy city and dwelling-place of God (3:17–18) make it probable that he was a priest whom God's word turned into a prophet.

This word came to him at the time of a great locust plague and drought. Joel saw them as a judgment of God on his sinful people. The locusts are the army of the Lord, he said (2:11, 25). Deliverance can come only by true repentance (returning to the Lord and trusting in God's gracious forgiveness and goodness – 2:12–14), carried out in solemn national assembly in the temple.

It seems that Joel saw the locust plague as the beginning of the woes that were to introduce God's final age. By punishment Israel would return to God. God would pour out the Spirit on renewed people (2:28–29), make them mighty warriors able to conquer the nations (3:9–12), and exalt Judah and Jerusalem to world leadership (3:16–21). The 'day of the Lord' (1:15; 2:11, 31; 3:14), as the time of judgment and salvation, is the keynote of Joel's prophecy.

Significance

Joel was a man of his times and of all times. His view that natural disasters are God's punishments for people's sins must be qualified. That they are opportunities for repentance and renewal cannot be denied.

His concept of the people of God as mighty warriors who 'beat [their] plow-shares into swords, and [their] pruning

A bedouin woman bakes bread in the traditional manner.

hooks into spears' (3:10) – a strange reversal of Isa. 2:4 and Mic. 4:3 – and slay the nations round about reminds us of the Zealot movement during and after Jesus' time (see pp. 439–41).

His vision of the New Age as the time of pouring out of God's Spirit on all flesh and of the worship of God by a renewed people in Jerusalem had its impact on the New Testament. Peter quoted the passage about the Spirit on the day of Pentecost (Acts 2:16–21), and the idea of the New Jerusalem underlies the Revelation to John.

For Joel, salvation seems to be limited to Jews ('all flesh' for him is not 'all nations' but all classes or groups of Jews), whereas in some Old Testament passages and in the New Testament salvation is open to all nations (see pp. 192–4, 299–300).

Amos

One of the mightiest preachers of Israel was the shepherd-herdsman and caretaker of sycamore trees, Amos of Tekoa in the Southern Kingdom.

He was not a prophet or a prophet's son (7:14); that is, he was not a professional prophet attached to the court and temple at Jerusalem. He was a skilled, middle-class laborer, whom God called to be a prophet (7:15).

His prophetic ministry, so far as we know, was short and apparently limited to the Northern Kingdom. This was not his home country. He regarded Israel as one people and felt himself called to deliver God's message in the especially needy north.

The Historical Situation

The superscription of the book (1:1) dates Amos' prophetic activity to the reigns of Uzziah (Azariah) of Judah (783–742) and Jeroboam (II) of Israel (786–746). The mention of the earthquake here does not help in precise dating, for it is undatable. The general prosperity of the times, as indicated in the book, points to a late period in these reigns, perhaps to 760–750.

Both kings defeated their enemies, expanded their borders, achieved internal stability, and engaged in extensive commerce. (On the times see p. 184.) We learn from Amos that the upper class 'built houses of hewn stone' and 'planted pleasant vineyards' (5:11). They lolled on 'beds of ivory' (6:4), feasted, drank wine, and anointed themselves with costly oils (6:4–6). Base women of Samaria debauched themselves and their husbands (4:1). Merchants could scarcely wait for the Sabbath and the days of the new moon to end, so eager were they to be on with their moneymaking (8:4–5). But in the midst of prosperity there was poverty. The wealthy grew richer by exploiting the poor through sharp lending practices (2:8a), fines (2:8b), and bribing judges in court (2:6–7a; 5:7, 12; 6:12).

We learn that there was a royal sanctuary at Bethel, presided over by a priest named Amaziah, who considered it his duty to protect Jeroboam's interests (7:10–13). There were also sanctuaries at Gilgal (4:4; 5:5) and Dan (8:14). We do not know whether Amos visited these as well as Bethel.

The worship of Yahweh at the sanctuaries consisted of daily ceremonies in which various types of sacrifices and offerings were presented (4:4–5) and of occasional great festal gatherings. At the latter, 'fatted beasts' were offered (5:22), and singing, eating, drinking, and even sexual intercourse were indulged in (5:23; 2:7–8). There was also out-and-out idolatry in the worship of Assyrian gods (5:26).

Around opulent, decadent Israel were corrupt neighbors who had little regard for basic human rights: Damascus, Gaza, Tyre, Edom, Ammon, Moab (1:3—2:3). And farther away were predatory Assyria and Egypt, waiting to plunder the palaces of Israel (3:9–11).

Outline

Title and theme (1:1–2)

The coming doom of surrounding nations and of Judah and Israel (1:3—2:16)

The sins of Israel and the coming destruction (3:1—6:14)

The prophet's visions and the messages derived from them (7:1—9:15)

189

Contents and Growth of the Book

In the fourth section a piece concerning Amos' encounter with Amaziah appears (7:10–17), apparently because of the mention of Jeroboam in 7:9.

It is likely that Amos himself wrote much of the present book, probably by dictation to a scribe. The first-person account of his message and visions (5:1; 7:1–9; 8:1 ff.; 9:1 ff.) supports this conclusion.

Others seem to have contributed some of the material. For example, 7:10–17 is in the third person and interrupts the first-person reporting. Some scholars have assigned the oracles against Tyre (1:9–10), Edom (1:11–12), and Judah (2:4–5) to a period later than Amos, as well as some hymnic pieces (4:13; 5:8–9; 9:5–6) and the conclusion of the book (9:8–15 or 9:11–15). It is probable that Amos' written materials were edited and added to by later hands, possibly as late as the early postexilic period.

Plowing near Samaria (cf. Amos 6:12).

Conservative scholars hold that Amos himself was responsible for the contents of the book (possibly with scribal help) and find the hypothesis of later editorial changes and additions unprovable.

Amos' Career and Message

How long Amos preached is unknown. After his call (7:14–15) he went to the Northern Kingdom, perhaps to the capital city, Samaria (3:9; 4:1; 6:1), possibly to the sanctuary at Gilgal (4:4; 5:5), and certainly to the state sanctuary at Bethel (7:10–17). At the latter place, perhaps at the time of an important festival, his pronouncement of doom on the Northern Kingdom and its king, Jeroboam, led to an accusation of treason by the high priest, Amaziah. This priest banished Amos, apparently by command of Jeroboam. Amos then seems to have returned to Tekoa. Whether he had a further prophetic ministry in Judah is unknown, but it is unlikely. His career as a prophet may have lasted only two or three months.

That short ministry left a lasting impression on the nation and on the centuries since, so potent were the words of Amos.

His message may be summarized as follows:

a. The God of Israel is the Lord of the whole earth. Though God stands in a special relationship to Israel (3:2), his interest and activity are directed also toward the Ethiopians, Philistines, and Syrians. God gave homelands to them as well as to Israel (9:7). He holds not only the people of Israel accountable for their actions but also their enemies, for his jurisdiction extends over all nations (1:3—2:3).

b. God is a God of righteousness. There is nothing fickle, cruel, or unethical about him. God and the good are closely identified (5:4, 14). God is forever against nations and individuals who do wrong. His chief complaint against the people of Israel is that 'they do not know how to do right' (3:10).

c. God's requirements are moral. Elaborate sacrificial rites at the sanctuaries do not bring his favor (5:21–24). What God wants of people is unfailing justice in their relationships with one another (5:24; 2:6–7; 4:1; 8:4–6). Sin is not a failure to worship in the right way; it is a failure to do what is right in daily living.

d. God supports those who do right and punishes those who do evil. Those who seek the good (God) will live (5:4, 6, 14). The unrighteous will be destroyed (1:3—2:16; 5:16; 6:4–14; etc.). God has no favorites and makes no exceptions. Israel has no special claim on God and will fare no better than other nations that have violated fundamental principles of morality. The 'day of the Lord' (the day when God judges), instead of bringing victory and vindication to Israel, will result in destruction and humiliation (5:18–20).

Amos' Significance

Amos marks the beginning of a new era in the history of religion. No prophet before him saw so clearly the universal sovereignty of Israel's God and God's unwavering requirement of right conduct by all people, especially those standing in closest relationship to him (3:2). Special privilege involves special responsibility, said Amos.

The call to repent and do the will of God or perish was reaffirmed by the prophets after him and formed the cornerstone of the preaching of Jesus (Luke 13:3–9; Mark 1:15).

The view that 'God shows no partiality, but in every nation any one who fears him and does what is right is acceptable to him' (Acts 10:34–35) could hardly have arisen without the work of Amos.

Obadiah

This is the shortest book in the Old Testament. Nothing is known of Obadiah, whose name means simply 'Servant of Yahweh,' a name borne by nearly a dozen other Old Testament persons.

From the character of his prophecies it appears that he lived at the time of the fall of Jerusalem in 587 BC. Some precise details (vss. 11–14) and the heat of his wrath against the country of Edom for their part in that event indicate that he was an eyewitness of the fall and composed his oracles soon after it.

However, evidence for the time of his ministry is inconclusive. Scholars have suggested dates ranging from the ninth century to the fifth century or later.

Edom's basic sin was unbrotherliness in a time of misfortune. It failed to help Judah against its enemies, gloated over a brother nation's misfortune, looted at the time of the destruction, and captured and delivered to the enemy fugitives from the stricken country. Obadiah regarded this as strange and reprehensible conduct from blood relatives (Esau, the father of the Edomites, was Jacob's [Israel's] twin – Gen. 25:30; 36:1).

Obadiah called down the wrath of God on such perfidy. Edom, which inhabited the high, rugged mountains to the southeast, would be brought down and annihilated (vss. 3–4, 10). As the Edomites had done, so would it be done to them (vs. 15). The coming 'day of the Lord' (vs. 15) would redress the injustice. Edom and

Jonah

The port of Jaffa (biblical Joppa) today.

One of the best known, but least understood, stories of the Old Testament is that of Jonah and the great fish (commonly called a whale).

The sheer magnitude of the miracle described here unfortunately has drawn attention away from the book as a whole. One is left with a wonder tale which one may feel forced to reject as impossible or which one may try to swallow after the example of the fish's alleged treatment of Jonah! What is needed is an approach to the Jonah narrative that will put the episode about the fish into proper perspective.

Name and Place in the Canon

Jonah means 'dove.' The dove seems to have been a traditional symbol for Israel (Ps. 74:19; Hos. 11:11).

This fact leads immediately to some questions. Did the author intend the man Jonah to symbolize the Jewish nation as a whole in its disobedience to God, in its prejudice against Gentile nations, and in its misunderstanding of God's purpose and methods? And did the Jews misunderstand when they should have known better because of their highly privileged position as God's representatives – God's prophet-people?

Though occupying a place among the Twelve Prophets, the book differs from the other eleven in that it is a narrative about a prophet rather than a record of his

other wicked nations would pass away, Israel would be saved (vss. 16–18), and Israel's God would be sovereign over all the earth (vs. 21).

Obadiah sounds like a nationalistic prophet of narrow and vengeful spirit. There is no forgiveness of enemies in what he said. He had, however, a lively sense of justice and called on God to correct injustice in the great day of judgment.

It is possible that verses 19–21, which contemplate a return of dispersed Israelites and their conquest of Edom and other territories, were added to Obadiah's prophecies at some later time.

prophetic utterances together with some
biographical material. It is nearer to the
stories about prophets in 1 and 2 Kings
than to the prophetic books proper.

It found a place among the Twelve
Prophets because of the identification in
1:1 of its central character with 'Jonah the
son of Amittai,' an obscure eighth-century prophet mentioned in 2 Kings 14:25.

Contents

Jonah's 'No' to God brings him speedily
to disaster. He finds he cannot run away
from God without dire consequences for
himself and others. His 'Yes' to God,
however reluctant, brings him to new
knowledge of God and his purpose for the
world.

Historical and Literary Character

Controversy has long raged about whether
or not the incidents described in the book
actually happened. Did the author intend
to write a sober piece of history about the
eighth-century prophet mentioned in 2
Kings, concerning whom he had special
information, or did he wish to create an
allegory or a parable meant to convey
religious truth without regard to historical
fact?

Those who argue for the historicity of
the story do so on several grounds:

a. A Jonah, the son of Amittai, actually
existed during the period when the Assyrians ruled from the capital city of
Ninevah (2 Kings 14:25). Further biographical information about his ministry
might well have been preserved.

b. Jesus accepted as fact the experience
of Jonah in the belly of the fish and the

conversion of the Ninevites (Matt.
12:40–41).

c. Other prophets (Elijah and Elisha)
were concerned with foreign peoples, and
the lives of these prophets were characterized by miraculous experiences.

d. Rejection of the historicity of the
Jonah narrative rests on skepticism and
unbelief in the power of the living God.

Those who believe that the author intended the narrative to be an allegory or a
parable and that it belongs to the category
of instructional, not biographical, literature argue as follows:

a. The problem in the narrative is not
miracle in general but these particular
'miracles': the storm as God's judgment
on Jonah for his flight to Tarshish; the
identification of Jonah as the culprit by
the casting of lots; the miraculous cessation of the storm after Jonah is tossed into
the sea; the fish's swallowing Jonah and,
after seventy-two hours, depositing him
safely on shore; the repentance of the
King of Nineveh and all the inhabitants of
that city; a plant growing tall enough in a
night to offer shade to Jonah, and its with-
ering in the same length of time. God is indeed the God of nature, they say, but this
particular collection of wonders is strange,
to say the least.

b. Nineveh is represented as so large
that it required three days to cross it (3:3).
Excavations there have shown the city to
be about three miles long and somewhat
less than one and one-half miles wide.

c. Jesus, if he was truly God become
human, was limited in knowledge as all
human beings are (Mark 13:32). Omnis-
cience is no more possible for one who is
truly human than is omnipresence. He
used the story of Jonah in his preaching,
but this does not necessarily validate its
historicity.

d. Israel's teachers were skilled in the
use of stories, with or without historical
foundation, to drive home religious truth.
Such stories are Jotham's fable (Judges
9:7–15), Nathan's parable of the ewe lamb
(2 Sam. 12:1–4), and Jesus' parables of
the good Samaritan (Luke 10:30–37) and

the rich man and Lazarus (Luke 16:19–31).

e. Jonah seems to be a symbol of Israel as a whole: in being called by God for a mission to all peoples; in disobediently fleeing from God's presence and from that mission; in reluctant obedience after chastening; in prejudice against foreign nations and unwillingness to believe in the magnificent graciousness of God toward all peoples.

Authorship, Date, and Literary Unity

Those who hold that the story is historically true believe it was written by the eighth-century prophet Jonah, mentioned in 2 Kings 14:25, probably soon after his return from Nineveh (about 750 BC).

Those who take the story as a parable regard it as having been composed by a postexilic writer (perhaps in the fifth or fourth century) out of traditional story material, some of which may have gathered about the figure of the eighth-century prophet Jonah. They hold that the identity of the writer is unknown and that the psalm in 2:2–9, a song of thanksgiving for rescue, is inappropriate to its context. Jonah should have been praying for deliverance from the fish! The psalm may have been added to the story after it was first written.

Those believing in a postexilic date also point to 3:3 as evidence that Nineveh no longer existed at the time of writing (it fell in 612 BC), that much of the language of the book fits the fifth and fourth centuries rather than the eighth, and that the story as a whole is directed to the postexilic situation.

Historical Situation, Message, and Significance

The main teaching of the book is that God loves the Assyrians, all people, and even the animals. God's attitude is quite different from the Jewish desire for the destruction of foreign nations. God earnestly seeks their repentance and continued life.

God's love and mercy are not for Israel alone.

Together with this is the teaching that although God's chosen instruments often try to run from their assigned mission, they cannot ultimately escape God and their appointed work. 'The hound of heaven' follows them, disciplines them, educates them, until they are fit instruments for service. The fish story is a symbolic illustration of God's sustaining, disciplining activity.

This message fits best the postexilic time in Judah, when strong nationalistic, exclusivist emphases were dominant, particularly under Ezra and Nehemiah. Jewish men were forced to divorce foreign wives, Jewish worship was closed to participation by foreigners, and blood purity was highly regarded. (See p. 431.) Some large-hearted writer, through a story about the past, sought to broaden the outlook of his narrow-minded contemporaries by portraying God as God actually is and Jews as they ought to be.

Jesus' compassionate attitude toward despised peoples probably owed much to Jonah. The book has been a pillar in the structure of the modern missionary movement.

Micah

Presumably Micah preached mostly in Jerusalem.

The book contains threats and promises in alternating blocks of material.

Outline

The coming destruction of Israel and Judah because of their sins (chaps. 1–3)

The ultimate triumph of the reassembled and renewed people of God under a ruler born in Bethlehem (chaps. 4–5)

God's controversy with Israel because of its ingratitude, ceremonialism, and unbrotherly attitudes and acts (6:1—7:7)

The eventual exaltation of Israel by its loving, forgiving God (7:8–20)

Name, Place, Date, and Contents

Micah is an abbreviated form of Micaiah and means 'Who is like Yah(weh)?'

A number of Old Testament people bore this name. The best known today is the eighth-century prophet from Moresheth-gath (1:1, 14) in the low hill country, some twenty miles south-west of Jerusalem.

This Micah, like Amos, was a man of the country who was appalled at the sins of the big cities – in Micah's case, Samaria and Jerusalem. He was sympathetic to the needs of the poor, oppressed farmers and shepherds among whom he grew up. His home in the low hills above the Philistine plain, across which the armies of antiquity marched, helped him become an observer of international affairs.

Mic. 1:1 places the prophet's ministry during the reigns of Jotham (742–735), Ahaz (735–715), and Hezekiah (715–687). In Jeremiah's time the elders of the land remembered vividly Micah's prophecy of the destruction of Jerusalem and the temple and dated it to the reign of Hezekiah (Jer. 26:18). Some utterances of Micah are clearly prior to the fall of Samaria in 721 (1:2–9), and some may reflect the Assyrian campaigns in Judah of 711 and 701. Most of his sayings are undatable.

Micah was a younger contemporary of Isaiah and seems to have been influenced by the older prophet (compare Mic. 1:10–15 with Isa. 10:27b–32, and Mic. 2:1–3 with Isa. 5:8–10).

As the above outline shows, the disaster-deliverance motif is present twice in the book.

Authenticity of the Materials

Most students of the book agree that 1:2—3:12 contains authentic words of Micah. There is substantial support for 6:1—7:7 as his also. These sections contain threat of disaster, for the most part.

Some scholars have assigned all the prophecies of hope to disciples of Micah and later editors. However, there is a growing tendency today among liberals to accept some, at least, of the prophecies of hope as authentic. Conservative scholars, of course, defend them.

Some sections appear to be later than the prophet's time: 2:12–13; 4:8–14; 7:7–20, for example. They reflect later circumstances: Zion's going to Babylon (4:10); and the rebuilding of the walls, apparently of Jerusalem (7:11).

The famous passage 4:1–4 is present in Isa. 2:2–4. Whether Isaiah or Micah or some unknown prophet composed it cannot be determined. The prophecy of the ruler to be born in Bethlehem (5:2–4) is also of uncertain origin. The value of these passages does not depend on the identity of their author.

Some conservatives hold that, while Micah wrote almost all of the book, a post-exilic editor may have added some passages (for example, 4:6–8 and 7:8–20) and in some minor respects reshaped the material.

Historical Circumstances and Message

For a description of Micah's times, see the discussion of the books of Isaiah and Hosea (pp. 163–8; 184–6). Micah was disturbed by the oppression of brother by brother: of the poor by the rich (2:1–2, 8–9), of subjects by their rulers (3:1–3), of citizens by unjust judges (3:11), of customers by merchants (6:10–12). 'Each hunts his brother with a net' (7:2), says Micah, and 'a man's enemies are the men of his own house' (7:6). Injustice and social disruption reached even into families.

He was disturbed also by corrupt religious leaders and empty ceremonialism. Both priests and prophets were greedy for gain. They often aided and abetted the rich against the poor, while assuring the nation of God's presence and protection (3:11). Micah repudiated the claim that God's protection and help are assured to Israel regardless of its obedience to the laws of God. Rather, the city of Jerusalem and the holy temple will be destroyed because of Israel's sins (3:12). Multitudinous offerings – and even child sacrifice – will not win the favor of God (6:6–7). What God really wants is the practice of justice in human dealings, gracious loyalty to one another in the bonds of the covenant relationship, and an obedient life in relation to God (6:8).

Whether Micah looked beyond God's judgment of the nation to a new day when the dispersed peoples would be reassembled in a renewed Zion under a ruler from Bethlehem is disputed. It is likely that he did, for elements of this hope can be found in the thought of Amos, Hosea, and Isaiah before him. At least, those who followed Micah cherished this hope, for in the present book judgment is tempered by mercy

and disaster turns into deliverance under the hand of God.

Significance

Micah's powerful preaching of God's coming judgment left its mark on later generations, even providing support for Jeremiah's unpalatable prediction concerning the destruction of the temple (Jer. 26:16–19).

According to Matt. 10:35–36, Micah's words concerning family divisions (7:6) were quoted by Jesus.

The great declaration concerning God's true requirements (Mic. 6:8), which link ethical responsibility toward other people with genuine piety before God, anticipated the summary of the Law by Jesus (Mark 12:29–31).

The early church saw in Mic. 5:2 a prophecy of the birth of Jesus (Matt. 2:6).

Nahum

The book of Nahum, like the book of Obadiah, is a collection of prophecies directed against a foreign nation. Like Obadiah's verbal assault on Edom for its hostility toward Judah, Nahum's clipped, pregnant words pour venom on Assyria and rejoice in the prospect of its obliteration. Both books exude nationalistic fervor and are weak in the religious insights characteristic of the great Hebrew prophets.

Nahum and His Times

The superscription (1:1) tells us that Nahum came from Elkosh, a place of unknown location.

From references in the book, his career may be dated at some time between the capture of Thebes in Egypt by the Assyrians in 663 BC (referred to in 3:8–10) and the fall of Nineveh in 612. The destruction of Nineveh is clearly still future in the prophecies themselves.

With the death in 627 of Asshurbanapal, the last great Assyrian king, the Assyrian empire began to disintegrate. In 626 the Babylonians decisively defeated the Assyrians and gained their independence. From this time on, it would be apparent to perceptive observers that Assyria's days were numbered. Nahum's utterance thus probably derives from the period 626–612 BC.

Some conservatives date Nahum's prophecies somewhat earlier: shortly before 626 BC or not long after the fall of Thebes (663 BC).

Assyrians carry booty from the captured city of Lachish (701 BC); Sennacherib's palace, Nineveh c. 695 BC.

Contents and Authenticity

The disconnected character of the contents up to 2:1 is obvious to any thoughtful reader. Many scholars believe that a later editor added the alphabetic hymn at the beginning and interspersed utterances of Nahum (1:11, 14) with comments and additions of his own or adapted from traditional liturgy (1:12, 13, 15). He also may have added 2:2. Conservatives defend Nahum's authorship of the alphabetic hymn in 1:2–8.

The heart of Nahum's work appears to be 2:1—3:19 (except perhaps for 2:2).

Literary and Religious Value

We have in this book a magnificent ode over the coming downfall of a cruel oppressor of Israel. It contains some of the finest poetry of the Old Testament.

Many students of the book have seen in it marks of temple liturgy – perhaps a liturgy for a thanksgiving celebration at the New Year festival following the destruction of Nineveh. The congregation may have recited the alphabetical hymn. Prophets attached to the temple may have taken a prominent role in this liturgy. If this view is correct, Nahum's utterances were put to use in the worship of Judah and thus preserved. It is possible that Nahum himself was attached to the temple as a cult prophet.

Nahum was overpowered by a sense of Yahweh's rule over the nations and history. He saw Yahweh as a God who measures even the mighty Assyria, finds it wanting, and decrees its doom. He viewed Nineveh as 'a bloody city, all full of lies and booty' (3:1), a great harlot who had betrayed the nations through deceitful and treacherous dealings (3:4–15). Those who used the sword would perish by the sword (2:11–12; 3:15) was Nahum's prediction.

There is no call to repentance and to amendment of life in the book – themes characteristic of Israel's great prophets. The passages seemingly later than Nahum strike tender notes that supply a needed balance in the picture of God (1:7, 12, 15; 2:2).

Nahum was a great poet, if not a great religious thinker. In his attitude toward Assyria his views are a far cry from the large-heartedness of the author of the book of Jonah!

Habakkuk

Habakkuk was the first prophet to raise in sharp form the problem of the suffering of righteous Israel at the hands of unrighteous foreigners. The problem arose from Israel's belief that God rewards the righteous and punishes the unrighteous. Habakkuk has been called 'the skeptic among the prophets.'

While the book begins in doubt, it ends in faith, showing that the prophet in his personal struggle at last found grounds for believing in the justice and goodness of God.

The Title and the Name of the Prophet

The title (1:1) calls the contents of the book 'the oracle of God which Habakkuk the prophet saw.' The Hebrew word translated 'oracle' is literally 'burden' and came to be a technical term for a message from God given to a prophet for delivery. 'Which Habakkuk ... saw,' rather than 'heard,' suggests that the message came in a vision (2:2).

Habakkuk is not a Hebrew name. It probably comes from an Akkadian word meaning 'a garden plant.' We know nothing about him except what we find in this book.

Contents and Literary Form

The book contains mainly a dialogue between the prophet and God. In this respect Habakkuk was like his contemporary Jeremiah, who often gave himself to entreaties and arguments before God.

It is clear that chap. 3 was used in the worship of the temple, for it contains liturgical notations (*Shigionoth* – meaning unknown; *Selah* – perhaps a pause for a musical interlude; and the note to the choirmaster at the end). Scholars disagree on the question of Habakkuk's authorship of this psalm.

Whether chaps. 1 and 2 were used in temple worship has not been settled. Some experts regard the contents of the book as a whole as a prophetical liturgy. They believe that Habakkuk was a temple prophet who had a vision in the temple and who communicated this vision in liturgical form. Others think the material of these chapters is hardly suited for liturgical use.

Some scholars think Habakkuk simply imitated liturgical style without expecting actual use of the material in formal worship.

Date and Historical Situation

There is fairly wide agreement today that Habakkuk was a preexilic prophet, a contemporary of Jeremiah, though some scholars put him during the Babylonian Exile or in the postexilic period.

Crucial is the identification of the wicked one (or ones) in 1:4. Since the Chaldeans (1:6) seem to be deliverers from the oppressions of the wicked one (or ones), it is possible that the latter are the Assyrians or perhaps the wicked Judean king, Jehoiakim.

If the Assyrians are meant, the date of the prophecy would fall between 626 BC (the rise of the Chaldeans under Nabopolassar) and the reforms of Josiah in 622, which officially threw off Assyrian control. If Jehoiakim (and perhaps his evil associates) is meant, the prophecy would fall about the time when Nebuchadnezzar extended Babylonian authority over Judah, over Jehoiakim its king, and over the west as a whole (605 BC).

Faith must have been sorely tried at the close of the seventh century BC. The righteous Josiah's reign (640–609), which had seen the end of Assyrian rule and had reformed national life after the pattern set down in Deuteronomy (2 Kings 22–23), was followed by a dark period under Jehoiakim, in which old idolatrous practices revived and injustice flourished (Jer. 22:13–17). Assyrian rule was exchanged for Babylonian; both were cruel and financially demanding.

Where was Israel's God in all this? Why did God allow people to suffer bitterly at the hands of unrighteous tyrants, both within and outside the nation? Was God too weak to help, or too indifferent to care, or was God in some mysterious way ordering events according to his good purpose? If the latter, what was this purpose?

Message

Habakkuk said that his answer came out of a vision after much agony of soul (1:2–4, 13; 2:1). The vision revealed to him was that God is not too weak or too indifferent to set the situation right. God was in fact using the Chaldeans as agents of justice to punish the oppressors of God's righteous people. But the Chaldeans themselves, violent, rapacious, tyrannical, would fall under the same judgment of God. They did not see themselves as agents of God, but they trusted arrogantly in their own god and their own strength (1:7–11).

When their work of chastisement was done, the peoples they oppressed would rise up and plunder them (2:7–8). National destruction, as the end of a course of bloody iniquity, is the result of the working of God's will (2:13). The whole world will see God's glory in the judgment of evil Chaldeans (2:14).

What do oppressed righteous people do in the meantime? They wait patiently for God's appointed time of vindication (2:3). The righteous will survive through their fidelity to God (2:4).

The oppressed righteous, then, may rejoice in Yahweh's mighty vindication, which is sure to come. Yahweh is reigning in his holy temple; let all the earth stand in awe of him (2:20). God's mighty acts in Israel's past are a guarantee of his mighty and merciful acts in the future (3:3–15). So in the midst of disaster the righteous person can say, 'I will rejoice in the Lord, I will joy in the God of my salvation' (3:17–18).

Abiding Significance

Habakkuk was avidly studied by the community living by the Dead Sea in the time of Jesus (the community that gave us the Dead Sea Scrolls [see pp. 420–27]). One of those scrolls is a commentary on Habakkuk, which points out that Habakkuk was prophesying events of the commentator's own time.

Paul found in Habakkuk a pillar passage for his message of salvation by faith. For Paul, 'faith' was trust in and obedience to Jesus, the Messiah, as the way to righteousness before God, whereas for Habakkuk it was trust in and fidelity to God as the deliverer of the already righteous.

Habakkuk's trust in God, who vindicates the righteous and defeats the purposes of evil people, offers a word of comfort to all who suffer injustice and the even greater agony of its seeming meaninglessness.

Zephaniah

The theme of Zephaniah's prophecies – the coming of the day of the Lord, the time of God's judgment of the nations and his salvation of a remnant in Israel – echoes in part the preaching of Amos and Isaiah.

Zephaniah (meaning 'Yahweh protects'), according to the title of the book was a descendant of Hezekiah, possibly King Hezekiah (715–687 BC). If the king was not meant, it seems there would have been little reason to carry the genealogy back four generations (1:1).

The Man and His Message

If Zephaniah was of royal blood, he was a relative of King Josiah (640–609 BC). His prophecies, unlike Amos', show no particular concern for the socially depressed classes, but criticize the national life from the top: the court officials (1:8), the judges, the cult prophets, the priests (3:3–4), the idolatrous practices officially tolerated (1:4–6), the foreign customs and dress adopted by wealthy persons (1:8), the prosperous and religiously indifferent Jerusalemite householders (1:12–13), the proud boasters of the holy city (3:11).

He apparently belonged to the same devout religious circle that nourished Josiah in his youth and that repudiated, under the leadership of Josiah, the evil political and religious policies of Manasseh (687–642) and Amon (642–640).

We can fairly well determine the date of Zephaniah's prophetic activity. He prophesied before Josiah's reformation began in 622 BC (2 Kings 22–23), for he rebuked the practices Josiah eliminated (Zeph. 1:4–6). Zephaniah may have meant the Scythians when he referred to an enemy from the north as the coming destroyer of Jerusalem (1:10–13). According to the Greek historian Herodotus, the Scythians swept through Palestine around 625 BC. Whether or not the Scythian invasion was in Zephaniah's mind, he fits nicely into the early years of the reign of Josiah, that is, about 635–625 BC.

The Book

Some sections of the book may come from writers later than Zephaniah, particularly parts of chaps. 2 and 3. Conservative scholars hold to Zephaniah's authorship of the whole.

Theology and Influence

No prophet depicted more awesomely the terrors of God's coming 'day of wrath' (e.g., 1:15, 18) for the wicked in Judah and outside. On the other hand, he stressed God's magnificent mercy on the righteous remnant. The thought moves between doom on the entire world and its human and animal inhabitants, and the delights of salvation in a renewed world for those who escape the doom.

The righteous remnant is promised one language for the common worship of Yahweh (3:9). Thus the curse of Babel (Gen. 11:1–9) will be removed. The remnant will be humble, morally pure, and

Haggai

Winged genius of Babylonia, 8–7th century B.C.

secure (3:12–13). Yahweh will reign over them in a community characterized by joy and singing (3:14–18).

The doctrines of the day of Yahweh and of the righteous remnant to whom God would give his kingdom, taught by several of the great prophets, appear to have influenced the mind of Jesus. No prophet said more potently than Zephaniah that God expects to deal decisively with evil people in this world and that the righteous are on the winning side.

Haggai and Zechariah opened the third period in Hebrew prophecy. Before the Exile the prophets warned about the coming punishment of Israel and the nations. During the Exile they sought to comfort God's people and prepare them for a new future in their homeland. After the Exile they attempted to stimulate the rebuilding of the religious and political life of the restored community according to the Law of God. The prophetic word was always shaped by the historical situation; it was therefore never static or stereotyped.

Name, Date, and Historical Situation

Haggai means 'festal' or perhaps 'born on the feast day.' His ancestry is given neither in the book that bears his name nor in two references to him in Ezra (5:1; 6:14).

He may have seen the temple of Solomon before its destruction in 587 BC (Hag. 2:3). He may have served as a prophet to the Judean exiles in Babylonia and returned with Zerubbabel (Ezra 2:2). If so, he was an old man when he began the prophetic work reported in the book of Haggai. But there is no certainty here.

His prophecies fall within a four-month period (August to December) of the second year of Darius I (520 BC).

Some of the exiles had been back in Palestine since soon after Cyrus' edict of 538. Under the terms of this edict Sheshbazzar, a prince of Judah, and a small company of enthusiastic Jews had attempted to rebuild community life there (Ezra 1:5 ff.).

Whether Sheshbazzar began the work of rebuilding the temple (Ezra 5:16) or whether this was first undertaken in 520 under Zerubbabel (Ezra 3:6–11; Zech. 4:9) is not clear. If Sheshbazzar made a beginning, the work did not proceed far.

Haggai, in 520, rebuked his hearers for preoccupation with building their own houses and neglect of a house for Yahweh (1:4, 9). Dismal economic conditions due to the devastated condition of the country, drought, the hostility of neighbors, and the like made sheer survival the central concern and prevented work on the temple.

Haggai's prophetic mission was to stimulate the beginning (or resumption) of temple reconstruction and to keep enthusiasm and activity alive until it was completed. He was assisted in this by Zechariah.

Contents and Compilation

The book consists of four dated utterances of Haggai:

Outline

Yahweh's command to the governor, the high priest, and the people to begin rebuilding the temple, and their response (1:1 15) (August, 520 BC).

Yahweh's word of encouragement to the builders concerning the future glory of the temple (2:1–9) (September, 520)

Yahweh's clarification about certain 'unclean' matters affecting the life and future of the people (2:10–19) (December, 520)

Yahweh's promise concerning Zerubbabel's coming role as messianic king (2:20–23) (December, 520)

Some scholars think the text is out of proper order in a few places. The most important suggested rearrangement is to place 2:15–19 after 1:15a and change 'ninth' to 'sixth' in 2:18.

The book obviously was put together by someone other than Haggai, who collected his utterances, prefaced them with introductions containing dates, and added a narrative portion (1:12–14). The editor may have lived quite close in time to Haggai.

Message and Abiding Value

Haggai's message was centered in the importance of the temple and its liturgy for the life of the community. He lamented the materialistic, self-centered attitude of the returned exiles, who put 'paneled houses' above the house of God in their scale of values. He attributed the misfortunes that had befallen the people since their return to their neglect of the proper worship of God in a proper temple.

He said that if they would put God first by rebuilding the temple, their condition would change. In fact the glories of the Messianic Age would be theirs. God would judge the nations and bring their treasures into the temple, making it more splendid than the temple of Solomon (2:6–9). Zerubbabel, the governor (who was of Davidic descent), would be installed by God as messianic king to rule the nations (2:21–23).

When the people lost their enthusiasm because the new structure was not as splendid as the temple of Solomon, Haggai encouraged them with promises concerning its future glorification by God. When the deep and pervasive uncleanness of the people became apparent, and it seemed that this might frustrate their future under God, Haggai reaffirmed the certainty of that future. The past cannot defeat God's future, he said: 'From this day on I will bless you' (2:19). Put God first, and things will come out beyond your fondest dreams, in spite of the failures of the past!

Haggai's criticisms of materialism and self-centeredness and his emphasis on God-centeredness are applicable to people of every age. However, his promise of material prosperity for those who put God

Zechariah

Bedouin traders at the Beer-sheba market.

first helped to raise questions about the undeserved suffering of the righteous, such as are dealt with in the book of Job. Israel by Haggai's time had not thought its way very deeply into this problem (see pp. 148, 200).

Name, Identity, Date

Zechariah means 'Yahweh has remembered.' Zech. 1:1 identifies the prophet as the son of Berechiah and grandson of Iddo. In Ezra 5:1 and 6:14 Zechariah is called 'the son of Iddo.' The explanation may be that 'son' often means any descendant, or that some ancient editor inserted Berechiah into Zech. 1:1 because of the mistaken belief that this Zechariah was the same as the one mentioned in Isa. 8:2.

Neh. 12:16 makes Zechariah head of the priestly house of Iddo. In Neh. 12:4 we learn that Iddo came back from the Babylonian exile with Zerubbabel and Jeshua. From these facts it is clear that Zechariah belonged to a priestly family and that probably he had been in Babylonia.

Zechariah was a younger contemporary and associate of Haggai. Both directed their energies toward rebuilding the temple in 520–515 BC. Zechariah's ministry began only about two months later than Haggai's (Zech. 1:1; Hag. 1:1). It continued longer than Haggai's four-month ministry, that is, to 518 BC (Zech. 7:1) and possibly to 515, when the temple was finished and dedicated. Zech. 3:8–9 probably was spoken on that occasion.

On the historical situation in which both men worked, see the discussion of Haggai (pp. 202–204).

Outline

The visions of Zechariah and additional prophecies about the future of the land (chaps. 1–8)
a. Introduction: A call to repentance, referring to the experience of the fathers (1:1–6)
b. The visions of the night regarding the coming of the New Age for the Jews (1:7—6:8)
c. The crowning of Joshua (and Zerubbabel) (6:9–15)
d. God's requirement for the time of restoration: not fasting but righteousness and love (chap. 7)
e. The future glory of Jerusalem and Judah (chap. 8)

Yahweh's judgment of the nations and the establishment of a universal kingdom (chaps. 9–14)
a. First prophecy: The coming humbling of the nations, the reassembling of the exiles, and Israel's need for a true shepherd (chaps. 9–11)
b. Second prophecy: The coming of the day of Yahweh when Jerusalem's enemies will be repulsed, its inhabitants will mourn over one who has been martyred, prophecy will cease, and Yahweh will appear in glorified Jerusalem to reign over and be worshiped by all the earth (chaps. 12–14)

Carving of a seven-branched lamp (menorah); from Tiberias.

The Literary Problem

All serious students of the book admit that the two parts identified above are quite different in character.

Chaps. 1–8 clearly reflect a definite historical occasion: the time of the rebuilding of the temple under Zerubbabel and Joshua (520–515). Chaps. 9–14 lack specific grounding in historical events and could be assigned, as far as historical references are concerned, to many points in the life of the nation from the eighth to the second centuries BC.

The style, thought, and to some extent the language of the two parts differ. Chaps. 1–8 contain mostly visions with interpretations related to a specific occasion. They are in prose. Chaps. 9–14 contain many poetic pieces called oracles (9:1; 12:1), unrelated to any identifiable historical situation, and presenting in highly symbolic language the author's views concerning the day of the Lord and the final coming of the kingdom of God. So mysterious is some of this material (e.g., 11:4–17) that scholars despair of discovering its meaning.

The most widely held view today as signs the materials of chaps. 1–8 to Zechariah, the prophet of 520 BC, and attributes chaps. 9–14 to later minds, usually to a Second (chaps. 9–11) and to a Third (chaps. 12–14) 'Zechariah.'

These later writers may have lived in the fourth and third centuries BC. The reference to the triumph of the Jews over the sons of Greece (9:13) seems to point to the Greek period following Alexander the Great (after 331 BC), rather than to the Persian period of the prophet Zechariah.

Conservative scholarship once attributed chaps. 9–14 (or at least chap. 11) to Jeremiah because in Matt. 27:9 a passage now present in Zech. 11:12–13 is credited to Jeremiah. Today conservatives argue that Zechariah, the son of Berechiah, probably wrote both halves of the present book. Against the differences in style and theology of the two parts, they identify similarities. It is suggested that Zechariah may have written the second half late in his life (perhaps 480–470 BC).

A computer study of the language of the book of Zechariah (sentence length, word length, vocabulary, parts of speech, connectives, etc.) by Israeli scholars (Radday and Wickmann) led to the conclusion that there is not enough evidence to declare a sharp break between chapters 8 and 9. However, the chances of the same authorship for chapters 1–11 and 12–14 turned out to be only 2:1,000.

Message and Significance

The Zechariah who worked with Haggai believed profoundly that the building of the new temple was God's first act in the drama of the end, and the end would involve the coming of the Messianic Age for God's people and the world.

Zechariah went so far as to have crowns made for Joshua and Zerubbabel. Though Zerubbabel's name no longer appears in the text of 6:9–14, the mention of 'crowns,' 'the Branch' (which is appropriate to Zerubbabel as Messianic King – Hag. 2:20–23), 'a priest by his throne' (Zech. 6:13), and 'both' (6:13) show that Zerubbabel too, not just Joshua (6:11), was in the prophet's mind. For some reason the text has been altered by a later editor to exclude Zerubbabel. Possibly his reason was that Zerubbabel did not become the Messiah; the civil and religious life of the nation came under the leadership of the high priest alone. Thus the prophecy was brought into harmony with the course of history, and Joshua only is mentioned here.

Zechariah's concept of the New Age involved not only Jewish political supremacy over the nations but religious and moral leadership also. Idolatry, stealing, and perjury would be done away. Ceremonialism (fasting) would give way to justice, kindness, mercy for the oppressed, and good-heartedness (7:8–10; 8:16–17). God's presence among the chosen people would arouse the desire of foreigners to share in God's worship and experience the blessings of the New Age (8:20–23).

The person (or persons) responsible for chaps. 9–14 brings before us the certainty of the ultimate establishment of the kingdom of God over all peoples. The allusion to the mourning over 'him whom they have pierced' (12:10) appears in the New Testament as a reference to Jesus (John 19:37; Rev. 1:7). The passage may echo Isa. 53. Whether the original reference was to Jesus or to another (unknown) prophet, Jesus fulfilled the prophecy in the way he fulfilled other Old Testament expectations: by incorporating in his life and death all that is valid in them, as he understood the will of God for himself and his people.

Malachi

Place in the Canon

The last book of the Hebrew Bible is not Malachi but Chronicles. In the Latin Vulgate the last Old Testament books are 1 and 2 Maccabees, immediately preceded by Malachi.

When Luther removed all the books and portions of books not found in the Hebrew Bible to an appendix at the end of the Old Testament, Malachi fell in last place, where it remains in English Bibles to this day.

Malachi has a peculiar relationship to Zechariah. After Zech. 1–8 there are three segments of material which carry the same superscription: 'An oracle, the Word of Yahweh' (Zech. 9:1; 12:1; Mal. 1:1). Since Malachi means 'my messenger' and is probably not a proper name (see next section), it seems likely that three anonymous prophetic oracles were attached to Zech. 1–8. Later, perhaps to form a collection of *twelve* lesser prophets, Malachi was separated off to form the twelfth book. Then or later Malachi was regarded as a proper name.

Name, Date, Historical Circumstances

As noted above, Malachi means 'my messenger.' In 3:1 it is certainly not a proper name, though the editor who added the superscription in 1:1 may have so taken it.

The Septuagint has in 1:1 'by the hand of his messenger,' and later Jewish tradition sometimes ascribed the book to Ezra. It is hardly likely that Malachi was the prophet's name. What it was we do not know.

His approximate date is fairly easy to determine. A governor rules over Judah (1:8). The temple and its ritual are in full operation (1:6–14; 3:1, 10), but its services have become boring to both priests and worshipers (1:6–14; 3:8). The people are questioning the love of God for Israel and the justice of God, arguing that there is no profit in serving God (1:2–5; 2:17; 3:13–15). Divorce and marriage to heathen women are prevalent (2:11–16).

Such conditions suit the time just before Nehemiah and Ezra. The failure of Haggai's and Zechariah's glowing hopes for the future brought the struggling community to a state of despondency and cynicism. It was Nehemiah's and Ezra's task to restore the nation's faith, purity of life, and enthusiasm for the future. A date about 460 BC for Malachi seems correct.

Statue of Elijah, Carmel.

Outline

Superscription (1:1)

God's love for Israel (proved by the punishment of Edom) (1:2–5)

The priests' contempt for Yahweh (their polluted offerings in the temple and their false teaching), **Gentile respect for God, and the coming judgment of the priests** (1:6—2:9)

The lack of faithfulness of Jewish males to the ancestral covenant (divorce of wives and marriage with foreign women) (2:10–16)

The people's disbelief in the justice of God (cynical complaints about the successes of evildoers and their participation in evil practices) **and God's coming refining judgment** (2:17—3:5)

Israel's departure from Yahweh's requirements (nonpayment of tithes and offerings) **and the need for repentance** (3:6–12)

The arrogant unbelief of the ungodly (their claim that they get along in life quite as well as the godly) **and Yahweh's eventual punishment of the wicked and reward of the righteous** (3:13—4:3)

Conclusion to the Book of the Twelve Prophets: A command to obey the Law of Moses and to await the coming of Elijah, the restorer of Israel before the day of judgment (4:4–6)

(The sections follow a basic pattern: first a declaration, then an objection, and finally a substantiation or proof. It is a kind of dialogue or debate form.)

Message and Abiding Significance

Malachi addressed a people who believed God had let them down. The reestablishment of pure worship in a rebuilt temple had not brought the blessings predicted by Haggai and Zechariah. Instead, Judah was under the heel of a foreign government (Persia), crop failures and famine were frequent, the hostility of non-Jewish peoples in and around the nation was intense, and general hopelessness infected the national spirit. Of what use was the elaborate worship of God and personal fidelity to the Mosaic covenant? Those who ignored God and the Law seemed to succeed as well as those who piously attended to traditional duties.

Malachi championed the reverent worship of God when it was unpopular to do so. His argumentative style indicates that he was often locked in controversy with skeptics.

His main convictions may be summarized as follows:

a. God loves Israel in spite of all indications to the contrary. This love will be manifested at the coming day of Yahweh, if the people are faithful to God and to one another, as the Mosaic covenant directed.

b. Respect for God involves the giving of the best we have to God. Tossing God a few unwanted scraps will not do.

c. Earnest and reverent Gentile worship is more acceptable to God than insincere and indifferent Jewish worship ('my name is great among the nations' – 1:11, 14).

d. Marriage is sacred and indissoluble. To cast off a faithful wife and to marry another (particularly a foreigner) is a violation of the covenant bond (3:5).

e. The coming kingdom is for the righteous. God intends to refine the chosen people through an appointed messenger, so that the day of judgment will find them prepared for their future life in that kingdom.

Malachi was more legalistic and ritualistic than the great preexilic prophets. He was also oversimple in his stress on suffering as a direct consequence of sin, and prosperity as the fruit of righteousness (see the contrary view in Job). But his firm belief in God and in God's future for the righteous, when outward facts do not seem to justify it and when unbelievers are loudly cynical, entitles him to an honored place among the prophets and forerunners of Christianity.

The hope for the coming of Elijah and the return of the Lord to the temple reappears in the New Testament (Mark 6:15; 9:11–13; Matt. 11:10; and the primitive church's preoccupation with the temple, according to Acts 2:46; 3:1 ff.).

Remains of Solomon's North Palace, Megiddo.

For Further Reading Concerning the Books of the Old Testament
Achtemeier, P.J. (ed.), *Harper's Bible Dictionary*, 1985.
Anderson, B.W., *Understanding the Old Testament*, 4th ed., 1986.
Childs, B.S., *Introduction to the Old Testament as Scripture*, 1979.
Harrison, R.K., *Introduction to the Old Testament*, 1969.
Hayes, J.H., *An Introduction to Old Testament Study*, 1979.
La Sor, W.S.; Hubbard, D.A.; Bush, F.W., *Old Testament Survey*, 1982.
Soggin, J.A., *Introduction to the Old Testament*, 1976.

One-Volume Study Bibles
Barker, K. (ed.), *The NIV Study Bible*, 1985.
May, H.G.; Metzger, B.M. (eds.), *The New Oxford Annotated Bible with the Apocrypha, RSV*, 1977.

One-Volume Commentaries on the Bible
Brown, R.E.; Fitzmyer, J.A.; Murphy, R.E. (eds.), *The Jerome Biblical Commentary*, 2 Vols., 1968.
Laymon, C.M. (ed.), *The Interpreter's One-Volume Commentary on the Bible*, 1971.
Rowley, H.H. and Black, M. (eds.), *Peake's Commentary on the Bible*, rev. ed. 1962.

The Apocryphal Books

The Apocrypha of the Old Testament, as presented in the Revised Standard Version and the New English Bible, consists of fifteen books or portions of books. None of these writings appears in the Hebrew Bible; but, with the exception of 2 Esdras, all are present in copies of the Septuagint (Greek Old Testament) and all, including 2 Esdras, appear in Latin manuscripts of the Bible.

'Apocrypha' means 'hidden things.' As applied to writings it means 'hidden books,' withdrawn from common use and suited only for the initiated, or books improper for use because they contain heretical teachings, or simply books outside the Hebrew canon.

Protestants use the term in the last sense and apply it to all fifteen books or portions. Roman Catholics use it in a somewhat different way. They speak of 'protocanonical books' (those books recognized from the earliest times of the Christian church as authoritative), 'deuterocanonical books' (those books and portions which came later to be recognized as authoritative in the church), and 'apocryphal' (those books never recognized by the church as authoritative).

Of the fifteen that Protestants call 'apocryphal,' Roman Catholics apply the term only to three – the Prayer of Manasseh and 1 and 2 Esdras. The other twelve are regarded as deuterocanonical; they were declared 'sacred' and 'canonical' at the Council of Trent in 1546. The many other Jewish books not in the Hebrew Bible or the Latin Vulgate, which Protestants label 'Pseudepigrapha' ('false books,' because so many are attributed to persons who did not write them), are included by Roman Catholics, along with the three mentioned above, under the term 'Apocrypha.' Protestants have three categories: canonical, apocryphal, pseudepigraphic. Roman Catholics also have three: protocanonical, deuterocanonical, and apocryphal. But the books are distributed somewhat differently in the two systems.

The fifteen apocryphal books came under attack by the Protestants during the Reformation. Luther gathered them together as an appendix to the Old Testament under a caption which said that they 'are not held to be equal to holy scripture and yet are profitable and good to read.' The Reformed Church similarly segregated and appended them to the books of the Hebrew Bible.

As early as 1599 some English copies of the Bible omitted the apocryphal books altogether. The King James Version of 1611, however, contained them. The hostility of the Puritans toward the Apocrypha led increasingly to their omission from English Bibles. The important non-Roman Catholic English

The Apocryphal Books

1 and 2 Esdras
Tobit
Judith
The Additions to the Book of Esther
The Wisdom of Solomon
Ecclesiasticus (the Wisdom of Jesus the Son of Sirach)
Baruch
The Letter of Jeremiah
The Prayer of Azariah and the Song of the Three Young Men
Susanna
Bel and the Dragon
The Prayer of Manasseh
1 and 2 Maccabees

Entrance to catacomb at Bet Shearim, which rose to importance after the Bar Kochba revolt.

translations, commissioned by official religious organizations during the last 100 years, have included them: the English Revised Version; the Revised Standard Version; and the New English Bible.

The canon of the Orthodox churches (Greek, etc.) is the broadest of all. It includes all of the books accepted by Protestants and Roman Catholics plus 1 Esdras, the Prayer of Manasseh, 3 and 4 Maccabees, and Psalm 151. In 1977 a Revised Standard Version Bible appeared with this comprehensive content – a truly ecumenical edition – aimed to meet the needs of all three major divisions of Christian readers. (See p. 47.)

The apocryphal books are of uneven value. Some of them contain material of high religious and ethical significance. Others are fairly trivial. Their influence on literature, music, and art through the centuries has been profound. Some Roman Catholic doctrines (such as purgatory and masses for the dead) find in the Apocrypha their chief biblical support.

The Apocrypha and Pseudepigrapha (or the deuterocanonical and apocryphal books) help us understand Judaism at the time of Jesus. They also throw considerable light on the New Testament. Intelligent students of both Judaism and Christianity should know these books. And one will frequently find light by which to live breaking forth from them.

For Further Reading
Metzger, B.M., *An Introduction to the Apocrypha*, 1957.
Nickelsburg, G.W.E., *Jewish Literature Between the Bible and the Mishnah*, 1981.
Stone, M.E. (ed.), *Jewish Writings of the Second Temple Period*, 1984.

1 Esdras

2 Esdras

This book is called 3 Esdras in the Latin Vulgate, where, since the Council of Trent in 1546, it has appeared in an appendix after the New Testament. The books called Ezra and Nehemiah in Protestant Bibles are 1 and 2 Esdras in the Vulgate.

A Jewish author, probably toward the end of the second century BC, excerpted and partially rewrote the end of 2 Chronicles, the book of Ezra, and part of Nehemiah. He supplemented his biblical sources with a charming, lengthy tale, probably of Persian origin. It tells about a contest among three pages or bodyguards of King Darius which, won by Zerubbabel, a Jew, resulted in Darius' helping to rebuild the Jerusalem temple.

The book covers Jewish history from King Josiah (640–609 BC) to the reforms of Ezra (458 or 428 or 398 BC). The writer's interest centers in the temple and its ceremonies. He has nothing of historical significance to contribute over and above his biblical sources.

Josephus used this book in the writing of his *Antiquities of the Jewish People* (c. AD 93).

This book appears in the Latin Vulgate as 4 Esdras.

Like Daniel and the Revelation to John, it is an apocalypse (see pp. 356–7). It unveils the plan of God for the end of the world and the coming of the final age. The secrets of God are revealed to Ezra through seven visions which the angel Uriel interprets.

The main part of the book, the seven visions (chaps. 3–14), was written by a Jewish author about AD 100, that is, about 30 years after the destruction of Jerusalem by the Romans. Later, Christian writers added chaps. 1–2 and 15–16 (probably in the second and third centuries), with the double intent of showing that Christians, not Jews, are the heirs of the coming age and of pronouncing God's doom on the Roman empire.

Chaps. 3–14 represent Ezra as having experienced his seven visions in Babylon in the thirtieth year after the fall of Jerusalem (*i.e.,* in 557 BC). (Ezra, of course, actually lived during the fifth century BC.)

These chapters describe Ezra as greatly troubled over God's treatment of the Jews and his governing of the world in general. Why has he allowed people more unrighteous than the Jews to overrun and oppress them? Why has God made human life in the world so difficult, particularly the attainment of righteousness? Since sin has so deeply affected people's hearts and lives, and they are to be judged by the

Tobit

hard demands of the Law, perhaps it would be better if they had never been born. Why will so few be saved? The author pours out all the hard questions that Israel's traditional faith and historical experiences (recently the fall of Jerusalem in AD 70) had aroused in thoughtful minds.

Ezra is told in his visions that the coming age, near at hand, will provide the solution to all present inequities and distresses. The righteous will be vindicated, the wicked punished. The Son of man (Messiah) will inaugurate that age. It will come when the predestined number of the righteous has been made up. Ezra must wait in faith. He cannot now expect to understand all the mysteries of God.

The book was widely read in the early Christian church, which preserved it. After the futile rebellion of Bar Kochba against Rome (AD 132–35), the Jews rejected it along with apocalyptic literature and apocalyptic theology in general.

Tobit has long been one of the most popular of those books now called apocryphal or deuterocanonical. Luther wrote of it, 'Is it history? Then it is a holy history. Is it fiction? Then it is a truly beautiful, wholesome and profitable fiction, the performance of a gifted poet.'

It is not hard to prove that the book is

Ruins of Herod the Great's northern palace-villa, Masada.

fictitious. In 1:4 Tobit is described as a young man when the tribe of Naphtali (and the other northern tribes) split off from Jerusalem (922 BC). 1:2 says that he was deported to Nineveh by the Assyrians in the time of Shalmaneser (726–722 BC), and 14:15 says that his son Tobias lived until after the destruction of Nineveh (612 BC). Sennacherib, rather than Sargon, is made the successor of Shalmaneser (1:15). Nebuchadnezzar and Ahasuerus (Xerxes), rather than Nabopolassar and Cyaxeres, are made the conquerors of Nineveh (14:15). Inaccuracies are to be found also in the geography of the book.

The value of the story lies not in its historical contribution but in what it teaches about religious and domestic fidelity. The main characters are all models of piety and morality. They observe the Law faithfully and win out by God's help, given through the angel Raphael, over many serious troubles. Marriage and the home are glorified. Good deeds are exalted, and almsgiving is declared to atone for sins (4:6, 10; 12:9). The golden rule in negative form is to be found here (4:15). The characters are models of what true Jews ought to be. The story teaches that those who obey God faithfully experience his help in ways beyond their imagining.

The original language of the book was probably Aramaic. It could have been written in Palestine, Egypt, or Mesopotamia, most likely around 200 BC. Some Hebrew and Aramaic fragments have been found at Qumran by the Dead Sea.

Several older folktales which circulated widely in the ancient world (the Grateful Dead, the Dangerous Bride, the Story of Ahikar) have been used in the narrative. The author combined and rewrote them from the standpoint of the devout Judaism of his time.

Judith

This superb example of the Jewish storyteller's art revolves around the exploits of a beautiful and daring woman who single-handedly delivered her nation from extermination at the hands of a powerful and arrogant enemy.

The story should be classified as historical romance and not history because of the many inaccuracies it contains. Nebuchadnezzar, actually king of the Chaldeans in Babylon, is called king of the

Two soldiers from the Assyrian imperial guard; Nineveh c. 695 BC.

The Additions to the Book of Esther

Assyrians, with his capital at Nineveh (1:1). The book's events are supposed to have occurred during his reign (605–562 BC), but we read that the crisis described took place when the Jews 'had only recently returned from the captivity' (4:3), after the rebuilding of the temple (520–515 BC). The three-day march from Nineveh to southeastern Asia Minor (2:21) – a distance of some 300 miles – was, of course, impossible. It may be that the writer intentionally introduced inaccuracies to indicate subtly that the story was not to be taken literally.

'Judith' means 'Jewess.' The heroine of the story is devout and scrupulous in the observance of Jewish law. She implicitly trusts in the providence of God. She is prosperous, intelligent, and eminently desirable. She is the symbol of what the nation should be. Because she did not sin, God made her invincible. The author conceives of sin largely in legal and ceremonial terms. Lying to Nebuchadnezzar's general, Holofernes, and decapitating him was not sin, but eating his food would have been!

The story reflects the Maccabean struggle against the attempts of the Seleucid king Antiochus IV (Epiphanes) to destroy Judaism and to replace it with worship of himself as Zeus Olympus (167–164 BC). The clash between Nebuchadnezzar as God and the true God of the Jews is a prominent theme (3:8; 6:2, 4). Faithfulness to God and to the Law, even in peril of death, brings invincibility. Such is the teaching of the book.

Its date is probably about 150 BC, its original language Hebrew, and the place of writing Palestine. Some scholars believe that certain Persian elements in the story indicate that it originated in Persian times (c. the middle of the fourth century BC) and that it was rewritten in the Maccabean period.

The Greek and the Old Latin texts of the book of Esther include 107 verses not present in the Hebrew text. These verses belong to six sections which are distributed through the narrative. Jerome, when making the Latin Vulgate (c. AD 400), assembled them and placed them at the end of the book of Esther.

The printing of these sections together in the King James Version, as if they constituted 10:4—16:24 of the book of Esther, ignored their basic character as fragments and rendered them incomprehensible. Present-day Roman Catholic Bibles print them in their proper place in the book of Esther, with a clear indication that they are additions to the Hebrew text.

The additions are of three types: prayers, which supply religious content to the book (see p. 143 about the secular character of the book of Esther); texts of edicts only mentioned in the narrative, to increase the reader's sense of its trustworthiness; and details to strengthen the story. The added portions stress God's deliverance of the people when they call upon him and highlight his control of history. Victory was not simply the result of Esther's beauty, courage, and sagacity but of her complete reliance on God.

The additions are perhaps from the late second century BC. Some of them probably were introduced by a Jew named Lysimachus, who translated the Hebrew Esther into Greek. There is general agreement that the additions have little or no historical value. Their purpose was to make the Esther narrative more palatable to pious Jews.

The Wisdom of Solomon

This book is probably the high-water mark of the Apocrypha. Its lofty wrestling with the big problems of human existence, its artistic style, and its daring synthesis of Greek and Hebrew ideas endeared it to some of the best minds of the early church.

Some scholars believe that Paul knew the book and echoed its thought and language in various passages, particularly in Romans. But it may be that the background and training of the two writers was somewhat similar and that they drew from the same well of language and thought.

The book claims to have come from King Solomon (7:1-6; 9:7, 8, 12). This claim places it in the Wisdom tradition, behind which stood the figure of Solomon (see p. 144).

Many characteristics indicate that it came from a period centuries later than Solomon: the peculiar fusion of Hebrew and Greek thought; the technical Greek terms ('self-control,' 'prudence,' 'justice,' and 'courage' [8:7], which are the four cardinal virtues of Stoicism); the philosophical concepts (the preexistence and immortality of the soul); and the bombastic style of much of it.

The author was probably a Hellenistic Jew of Alexandria, who wrote the book in Greek. A recent attempt to date it (M. Gilbert) assigns its writing to the reign of Augustus at the earliest (after 30 BC) or possibly in the first decades of the first century AD.

Chaps. 1-6 show that, in spite of appearances to the contrary, the suffering righteous (the Wise) will be rewarded by God with a blessed existence beyond death, while their wicked persecutors (the Fools) will vanish without a trace. The suffering of the righteous is the discipline a loving Father gives his sons.

Chaps. 7-9 contain praise of the attributes and works of Wisdom and show how Wisdom came to Solomon and will come to others.

Chaps. 10-19 deal with Wisdom's works in history, especially how Wisdom helped and saved Israel's forefathers. A discourse on the folly of idolatry (13:1—15:17) interrupts the historical account of Wisdom's activity.

A notable concept of the book is the associating of Wisdom, Logos (Word), and Holy Spirit as agents of God's activity in the world. In Paul (1 Cor. 1:24; 12:8) and in the Gospel of John (1:1-18; 7:37-39; 20:22) a similar association occurs.

In the New Testament, suffering as a mark of sonship to the Father and as a learning experience is applied both to Jesus (Heb. 5:8-9) and to his followers (Rom. 8:14-25; Heb. 12:3-11).

Ecclesiasticus
(the Wisdom of Jesus the Son of Sirach)

This is the longest book of the Apocrypha and one of the most important as well. It was known in the early Christian church as Ecclesiasticus, meaning probably 'the church book' or 'to be read in church.'

Its contents consist of the teaching of a wise man and scribe (teacher of the Law) named Yeshua ben Sira (in Hebrew), who had a school in Jerusalem (50:27; 51:23). Since he had traveled widely (34:11; 51:13), it is possible that he was in the diplomatic service.

This is the only book of the Apocrypha whose author's name is known. We are fortunate to learn from the prologue that the translator of the book into Greek was the author's grandson, who accomplished this task sometime after the thirty-eighth year of Euergetes (Ptolemy VII, whose thirty-eighth year was 132 BC). This means that the grandfather must have written down his teachings about 190 BC.

About two-thirds of the Hebrew text of the book was found in 1896–1900 in a repository for worn-out manuscripts of a synagogue in Old Cairo. Fragments were discovered in a cave at Qumran by the Dead Sea (1956) and at Masada (1964). In general, they all show that the grandson's translation of the Hebrew text into Greek was faithfully and skillfully done.

The point of view pervading the whole book is that life in accordance with the Law is the highest wisdom (19:20). The author tells how Wisdom came to Israel. Wisdom came forth from the mouth of God and sought a dwelling place among the nations of humankind. In response to the commandment of the Creator she took her dwelling in Israel as 'the book of the covenant of the Most High God,' as 'the law which Moses commanded us' (24:3–23). Whoever learns and keeps the commandments (both the written Law and the tradition of the fathers – 8:9) will be abundantly blessed by God with a prosperous and long life (1:12) and their memory will long endure (39:9, 41:13). For this author God's demands are both moral and ceremonial. He was the heir of both prophetic and priestly religion.

Like Proverbs, the book is loosely put together. There are small groups of sayings according to subjects, but there is no overall logical organization. It is possible that we have two volumes in our present book: Book 1, chaps. 1–23; Book 2, chaps. 24–50; with chap. 51 as an appendix. Divided thus, each book begins with the praise of Wisdom (chaps. 1 and 24).

The whole book is a treasure house of practical advice, set in the culture of second-century BC orthodox Judaism, concerning how young men, in particular, should deport themselves: their table etiquette, their family relationships, their friendships, the care of their health, their self-discipline. There is a strong emphasis on the importance of prayer and good deeds. One of the best-known portions is the praise of famous men (Enoch to Nehemiah). Here the author yearns that there may be successors to them in his time (46:12; 49:10).

Yeshua ben Sira's pupils were soon to be tested in the fires of the persecution instigated by Antiochus IV (Epiphanes) in 167–164 BC. Undoubtedly, some of the wise who remained loyal to the covenant (Dan. 11:35; 12:3) drew their inspiration from this great teacher.

Baruch

Baruch was the disciple and secretary of Jeremiah, who, according to Jeremiah 36, wrote two scrolls at the prophet's dictation. The second of these is included in our present book of Jeremiah (see p. 171). It was to this trusted companion that Jeremiah gave the deed for property he bought at Anathoth as an act of faith in the future of the country (Jer. 32:12–16).

Because of Baruch's prominence in the book of Jeremiah in connection with writ-

An Israelite tower dating from seventh century BC Jerusalem.

ing and with Jeremiah's predictions concerning the future, his name was attached to various books in later periods, especially those dealing with Israel's future as the people of God. In this class belong the present book and the second-century AD Syriac Apocalypse of Baruch.

The book of Baruch in the Apocrypha claims to have been written by Baruch in Babylon after the destruction of Jerusalem by the Chaldeans, read to the captives there, and sent to Jerusalem for reading in the temple on feast days as a confession of sins (1:14).

The contents fall into two main parts, after a brief introduction explaining the book's origin (1:1–14).

Part 1 (1:15—3:8) is a confession of Israel's sins from the time of the Exodus from Egypt 'to this day' (1:20) and an appeal for forgiveness and return from exile. It is in the style of a national song of lamentation.

Part 2 (3:9—5:9) consists of two poems. The first praises Wisdom as God's gift to Israel in the Law, blames Israel's misfortunes on the forsaking of Wisdom, and pleads for a return to Wisdom's ways. The second contains Jerusalem's lament over its pitiable condition and promises deliverance for its scattered children and its ultimate glorification. The two parts are loosely related and may come from different writers. But the common theme of Exile and Return in the two parts may point to authorship by one person.

The book, probably written in Hebrew, is difficult to date, since it makes reference to no historical events after the sixth century BC. The confession (Part 1) seems to show dependence on Daniel's prayer (Dan. 9) or the two may have drawn on a traditional prayer and be independent of one another. If Daniel's prayer was used, the date would be after c. 165 BC; and if not, then a date early in the second century is possible.

The Letter of Jeremiah

The Latin Vulgate and the King James Version of the Apocrypha have the Letter of Jeremiah at the end of the book of Baruch.

Actually, this letter originally had nothing to do with the book of Baruch but was an independent composition. It stands in various places in ancient manuscripts and versions. The Septuagint (The Greek Old Testament), for example, places it in the sequence: Jeremiah, Baruch, Lamentations, the Letter of Jeremiah. The Revised Standard Version, therefore, prints the letter as a separate book, although it keeps the chapter and verse numbers of the King James Version.

The letter obviously was inspired by Jer. 29:1–23, where the prophet's letter to the Babylonian exiles is quoted, and by Jer. 10:1–16, where idols are ridiculed as made by people and powerless. The apocryphal letter contains a bitter and lengthy attack on idols. It expands Jeremiah 10 and echoes the language there.

It claims to have been written by Jeremiah for Jewish captives about to go into Babylonian exile (597 or 587 BC), in order to warn them of the length of their captivity and of the danger of idolatry in the land to which they were going. In fact, it is part of a fairly large body of Jewish literature in which exilic and postexilic writers ridiculed Gentile gods (Isa. 44:9–20; Pss. 115, 135; Wisd. of Sol. 13:1—15:17).

The original language was probably Hebrew, though we have it only in Greek.

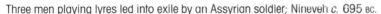

Three men playing lyres led into exile by an Assyrian soldier; Nineveh c. 695 BC.

A tiny fragment in Greek on papyrus was found at Qumran by the Dead Sea, dating to about 100 BC.

The time and place of writing are uncertain. In view of the author's familiarity with some aspects of Babylonian religious practices, it is possible that he wrote the letter in that country, perhaps in the fourth century BC. However, he could have used his knowledge of that religion anywhere where idolatry was a threat, for example, in Palestine near the beginning of the second century when the Seleucids were enticing the Jews toward apostasy (see pp. 412–13).

To Jews who were succumbing to false worship, the writer said eleven times (in various words), after scathing exposés of the idols' utter worthlessness, 'We have no evidence whatever that they are gods; therefore do not fear them.'

The Prayer of Azariah and the Song of the Three Young Men

The stories of the book of Daniel became so popular that they were soon embellished and expanded. Three additions to the book of Daniel appear in the Greek and Latin versions: the Prayer of Azariah and the Song of the Three Young Men, Susanna, and Bel and the Dragon.

Following the account of the throwing

Part of the monastery-like Essene settlement at Qumran.

of Shadrach, Meshach, and Abednego into the fiery furnace (Dan. 3:19–23), the Greek and Latin versions insert the Prayer of Azariah (Abednego) and the Song of the Three Young Men.

Altogether the insertion consists of sixty-eight verses and falls into three parts.

1. The prayer of Azariah (vss. 3–22) contains a confession of national guilt and a plea for pardon of the nation, for its deliverance, and for vengeance on its oppressors. It is in the style of a national song of lamentation, not altogether suitable here. It probably was adapted from an existing liturgical prayer.

2. Verses 23–27 offer information about the furnace: its intense heat; the burning of those who threw the three young men in; and the angel of the Lord who transformed the interior of the furnace to 'a moist whistling wind' (vs. 27).

3. A song of praise to God by the three youths concludes the insert (vss. 28–68). This imitates Pss. 136 and 148. It seems to have been adapted from an earlier composition, as the closing reference to the three youths (vs. 66) and the stereotyped refrain – suggesting use in worship – indicate. This addition to the text of Daniel makes the faith of the young men and the mighty deeds of the God of Israel yet more awesome.

When the addition was made is unknown, perhaps in the late second century BC. The original language was probably Hebrew.

Susanna

A second addition to Daniel (see the first, p. 220) is the suspenseful tale about the beautiful and virtuous Susanna and her rescue from the lustful elders by the wise young Daniel. It is a masterpiece of the storyteller's art.

In the Greek and Latin versions the story comes at the end of the book of Daniel as chap. 13. In other ancient texts and versions it appears as an introduction to the book of Daniel, perhaps because Daniel is described in Susanna as 'a young lad' (vs. 45).

Daniel means 'God has judged' or 'God is my judge.' In the Canaanite literature of the fourteenth century BC, King Dan'el (Daniel) was a dispenser of justice to widows and orphans. In Ezek. 14:14 Daniel is associated with Noah and Job, and in Ezek. 28:3 his great wisdom is mentioned. Evidently there was a long tradition in Canaan-Israel about Daniel, the wise judge. The Susanna story, in which the young Daniel trips up the crafty and lecherous elders, is a further development of this tradition.

The story teaches that God supports the virtuous and punishes the wicked and that he who accuses his brother falsely shall have done to him what he intended against his brother (Deut. 19:18–21). In the book of Susanna the vicious elders, whose false testimony brought about the sentence of death for the innocent Susanna, were themselves put to death.

The book seems to have been written in Hebrew. The date is uncertain, but a good guess is the late second century BC.

Bel and the Dragon

Boundary stone of Marduk from Babylonia.

This third addition to Daniel (see pp. 220–221) consists of two fanciful tales in which Daniel demonstrates the unreality of foreign gods and the dishonesty of their priests. Judaism's contest with idolatry offered opportunity for sport as well as for serious theologizing.

The first tale shows how the wise Daniel exposed the trickery of the priests of Bel (Marduk), who made the statue of their god appear to consume large quantities of food and drink daily. Daniel proved that the statue was nothing but clay and brass and 'never ate or drank anything' (vs. 7), and that the eating and drinking were done secretly by the priests and their families.

The second tale concerns Daniel's killing of a great dragon, which was worshiped as a god, by feeding it cakes made from pitch, fat, and hair. The worshipers, furious at Daniel, threw him into a lions' den for six days. While there Daniel was fed by the prophet Habakkuk, whom an angel transported from Judea to Babylon by the hair of his head and returned the same way to his home. The tale ends with the conversion of the king of Babylon and with Daniel's opponents thrown into the lions' den and devoured.

The theme of the stories is put on the lips of Daniel: 'I do not revere man-made idols, but the living God, who created heaven and earth and has dominion over all flesh' (vs. 5; cf. vs. 25).

In Greek manuscripts Bel and the Dragon appears at the end of the book of Daniel (after chap. 12). In the Latin Vulgate the story of Susanna forms chap. 13 of the book of Daniel, and Bel and the Dragon is chap. 14.

The original language was probably Hebrew and the date the late second century BC.

The Prayer of Manasseh

1 Maccabees

This prayer of fifteen verses undoubtedly arose from the references in 2 Chron. 33:12–13, 18–19 to King Manasseh's prayer of repentance in exile through which God forgave him, restored him to his throne, and brought about the religious reformation of his kingdom.

2 Chron. 33:18 states that Manasseh's prayer was available in a source known to the Chronicler. It is very clear that the prayer attributed to Manasseh in the Apocrypha cannot be the prayer referred to in 2 Chronicles.

First, the apocryphal prayer appears only in Greek form and has no firm anchorage in the Septuagint. In those Septuagint manuscripts where it does appear, it is introduced not in connection with Chronicles but in a collection of hymns and odes attached to the Psalter.

Second, it is not present in the Old Latin translation, and Jerome seems not to have known it. The earliest surviving text of it is in the Syriac Didascalia, a church manual of the third century AD.

Third, its form, contents, and language mark it as late in date, perhaps first century BC or AD.

A late Jewish author, then, sought to supply the words of Manasseh's prayer. His composition, probably written first in Hebrew (though perhaps in Greek), is a noble one. It is infused with deep piety and mature theology. It stresses the mercy of God in forgiving even the blackest of sinners, as Manasseh was, according to Jewish tradition.

> **Outline**
>
> **Introduction:** Alexander the Great and his successors (1:1–9)
>
> **The causes and the beginning of the Maccabean revolt** (1:10—2:70)
>
> **Judas Maccabeus** (3:1—9:22)
>
> **Jonathan Maccabeus** (9:23—12:53)
>
> **Simon Maccabeus** (with brief reference to John Hyrcanus) (chaps. 13–16)

1 Maccabees is a book of high historical and literary worth. The religious faith which shines through it is of a quiet, strong type. In this respect it stands in contrast to 2 Maccabees, the pages of which are full of dramatic wonders and stupendous miracles (see p. 224).

The book contains a detailed account of political and military affairs in Judea from the accession of Antiochus IV (Epiphanes) to the throne of Syria-Palestine (175 BC) to the death of Simon Maccabeus, ethnarch (ruler) and high priest, in 134 BC. A brief reference to the reign of John Hyrcanus (134–104 BC) ends the book.

An introduction tells of the career of Alexander the Great and the division of his kingdom among his generals after his death (1:1–9). This leads to a discussion of the attempts of Antiochus IV, in cooperation with renegade Palestinian Jews, to impose Greek ideas and customs upon the Jewish nation. These attempts provoked loyal Jews, under the leadership of a

2 Maccabees

family of priests, to organized resistance. Their remarkable military victories led not only to religious freedom but also eventually to complete political independence. The stories in the book center in the careers of Judas, Jonathan, and Simon of the family now known as the Maccabees (from a word probably meaning 'the hammer,' originally applied to Judas).

1 Maccabees undoubtedly was written originally in Hebrew. What its Hebrew title was is unknown. 'Maccabees' as a title for this and three other books (1–4 Maccabees) arose in the Christian church, probably with Clement of Alexandria in the second century.

The author, apparently living in Jerusalem, was almost certainly an eyewitness of some of the events he records. He used reliable sources – oral tradition, letters and official documents (probably from the Jerusalem archives), a Syrian (Seleucid) chronicle, a biography of Judas, chronicles of the high priests Jonathan and Simon, and the like. He must have written shortly after the end of the reign of John Hyrcanus (134–104 BC), probably about 100 BC, although a date a few years later is possible.

His point of view is that if the Jews are faithful to God's Law and do their part in the struggle against God's enemies, an undergirding providence will guide and sustain them in their efforts. He does not claim that God intervenes in miraculous ways.

Outline

Introduction: Two letters from the Jews of Jerusalem and Judea to the Jews of Egypt, urging observance of the Feast of Dedication in Egypt (1:1—2:18)

Prologue: The abridger's explanation of the purpose and nature of his work (2:19–32)

The summary of Jewish history from Seleucus IV and Onias III to the defeat of Nicanor and the achieving of religious freedom (3:1—15:36)
a. The miraculous punishment of Heliodorus, who attempted to rob the temple (chap. 3)
b. The attempted conversion of Jerusalem to Greek ways by corrupt Jewish high priests and by the Syrian king Antiochus IV, including the murder of Onias III, the profanation of the temple by Antiochus, and the persecution of Jews who resisted (chaps. 4–7)
c. The resistance of Judas Maccabeus and his followers, resulting in the recapture and rededication of the temple (8:1—10:9)
d. Judas' victories during the reigns of Antiochus V and Demetrius I, especially his victory over Nicanor (10:10—15:36)

Epilogue: A plea for the reader's indulgence (15:37–39)

(See also the discussion above of 1 Maccabees.) 2 Maccabees is an amusing and informative combination of history and legend.

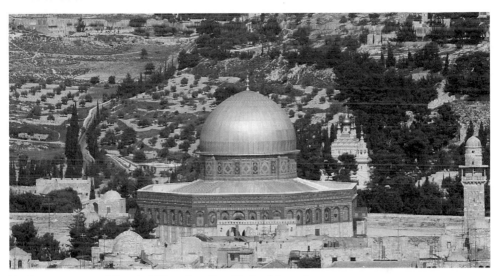

The Temple area and Mount of Olives from the old city of Jerusalem.

The writer's goal was to please and to profit readers, while requiring little effort on their part (2:24–31; 15:38–39). The verdict of the centuries since has been that he succeeded notably.

The book, for the most part, is an abridgment of a five-volume history, no longer in existence, written by a certain Jason of Cyrene. The abridger tells his readers how diligently he worked to compress his source (2:23–32).

The abridgment, now 2 Maccabees, covers Jewish history from about 180 to 161 BC – from the time of Seleucus IV of Syria and of the high priest Onias III of Jerusalem to the defeat of the army of Nicanor, the Syrian governor of Judea, in the time of the Syrian king Demetrius I.

1 Maccabees, as we have seen, spans the period 175–134 BC (apart from brief references to earlier and later events). By beginning at an earlier point, 2 Maccabees offers a much better understanding of what provoked the Maccabean rebellion and of the complex events associated with the recapture and rededication of the temple by Judas Maccabeus, with whose career the book ends.

On the religious side, the book is full of interesting emphases: God's miraculous interventions (through angelic warriors, for example) by which God's mighty power is revealed; the sanctity of the temple; the justice of God as operating inflexibly in punishment and reward according to one's deeds; the suffering of the Jews as God's discipline; the atonement made by martyrs for the nation as a whole; the resurrection of the martyrs; prayers and sacrifices for the dead; emphasis on exact obedience to the Law. The general point of view is that of the Pharisees (see p. 434).

The book, like its five-volume source, was almost certainly composed in Greek. The source probably was written toward the end of the second century BC and the abridgment made in the first half of the first century BC. Some scholars have argued that the letters at the beginning were added by an editor after the abridgment was made. Alexandria may have been the place where all the literary work was done.

The teaching about the suffering of the righteous martyrs as an atonement for the nation (7:38; 8:3) offers an important perspective for understanding the New Testament view of the meaning of Christ's sufferings (Mark 10:45, for example). The teaching concerning the resurrection (chap. 7) also offers valuable background material for understanding parts of the New Testament.

The Four Gospels

Christians must know what sort of man he was and what God was purposing and saying in him. The Gospels offer us precisely this information: important facts about Jesus and what these facts mean or should mean to us.

Literary Form

Until recent years most scholars claimed that with the appearance of the Gospels a new and distinctive form of literature came into existence. They contrasted the Gospels with examples of Hellenistic biography and concluded that in literary category (genre) the Gospels are closer to sermons (kerygma) than to biography.

The Term 'Gospel'

'Gospel' comes from 'godspell,' an Anglo-Saxon word meaning 'good story' or 'good news.' It derives from the Latin *evangelium* and that word in turn from the Greek *euangelion*.

The Greek *euangelion* had several meanings: originally the reward given to one who brought good news; then the good news itself; then the good news proclaimed by Jesus; then the good news proclaimed about Jesus; then the books containing the church's memories of Jesus.

The last two meanings are seen in the opening verse and in the title of Mark's Gospel: 'The beginning of the gospel of Jesus Christ,' that is, the good news about Jesus Christ; and 'The Gospel according to Mark,' meaning the account of that good news about Jesus Christ written by Mark.

Recent studies have largely reversed this position and have tended to see the Gospels as a form of Hellenistic biography. Biographical literature arose in the Hellenistic period out of a growing interest in the achievements of great individual persons (poets, philosophers, rulers), many of whom were seen as embodying and manifesting divine powers. Stories about the deeds of gods and people (aretalogies) circulated freely in the Hellenistic world and were drawn into the biographies. Readers of that time would understand biographical accounts of a great person (Jesus), whose acts testified to the divinity within him. Thus in literary type a Gospel was suited to the literary tastes of its time.

The truth seems to be that the Gospels are not simply Hellenistic-type biographies or expanded sermons (kerygma) but both in a unique combination. The Gospels proclaim the meaning of the cross and the resurrection of Jesus and show how the events of his life lead up to this climax. They invite the reader to a decision concerning Jesus. It is the peculiar combination of biographical material and proclamation that constitutes 'a Gospel.'

Importance

The four Gospels may well be the four most important books in human history. They present history's most influential man – Jesus of Nazareth. So influential was he that we divide all time by the date of his birth.

For Christians the Gospels are the apex of New Testament literature. If the Christian faith that God became incarnate in the human Jesus is true, then

The Church of the Annunciation dominates the modern town of Nazareth.

In the Gospels historical facts and interpretative proclamation are put together in differing proportions. Of the Gospels, Luke is the most historical and John the most theological and sermonic. Scholars once regarded Mark as the least theological and therefore as closer to the plain facts of Jesus' life. We now know Mark to be deeply shaped by theology, though more subtly than Matthew or John. All the Gospels, to some degree, share the purpose expressed by the author of the Gospel according to John when he said that he was writing 'that you may believe that Jesus is the Christ, the Son of God, and that believing you may have life in his name' (20:31).

Why Four Gospels?

Irenaeus (c. AD 180) naïvely explained the fact of four Gospels by appealing to the pattern of fours in the universe and in Scripture: four principal regions of the world, four winds, four covenants, four living creatures around God's throne, etc. As noted earlier in this Handbook (p. 34), it was in large part the church's usage of the four Gospels as official, authoritative documents in different areas of primitive Christianity that led Irenaeus and others to insist on precisely these four. Had not the Gospel of Mark been the favorite Gospel of some early church (probably Rome), it might have been eliminated, since almost the whole of it is contained in Matthew and Luke and not much attention was paid to it abroad in the church in early Christian centuries.

Stages in the Creation of the Gospels

a. Jesus' Deeds and Teachings (c. AD 28–30)

As far as we know, Jesus committed none of his teachings or experiences to writing. He did, however, cast some of his sayings in a form that could be remembered easily. For example, various scholars have shown that Luke 12:24–28 is poetic

in structure, as are many scattered sayings throughout the Synoptic Gospels.

His striking use of language devices – metaphors, parables, pithy (wisdom-like) proverbs, antithetic parallelism (two elements in a saying, the second in contrast to the first), rhythm, alliteration, etc. – made his sayings easy to remember.

It was customary for disciples of a revered teacher to preserve their master's instruction by memorization, by oral transmission, and eventually by collection in written form (as in the prophetic books of the Old Testament and the Mishnah of third-century Judaism). Fidelity to a rabbi's teaching was important to Jews.

b. The Oral Transmission of Jesus' Words and Deeds (c. AD 30–50)

For the following reasons the disciples were slow to record their memory of Jesus in writing:

1. Like other Jews, they preferred oral, eyewitness testimony about happenings of importance, rather than written accounts of them. Written accounts were valuable to them when eyewitness testimony was no longer available.

2. The first disciples were not literary persons, though undoubtedly – as expected of all Jewish males – they could read and write.

3. Writing materials were expensive, and the reproduction of manuscripts was slow and costly.

4. The first Christians believed that the end of the age was near (1 Cor. 7:29–31; Rom. 13:11–13; 1 Pet. 4:7; James 5:8; Rev. 1:1–3; 22:6–7, 10, 12). Writing a record of the past and building up libraries of written material had less meaning for them than for those who expected an ongoing future in this world.

It was the spread of Christianity into the more literary Gentile world, the death of the eyewitnesses of Jesus' ministry, and the continuance of life in this age, with its accompanying problems within and without the church, that led to the

Fishing is still an important activity on the Sea of Galilee.

creation of records of the church's past as an aid to its present and future.

Since 1919 New Testament scholars have probed the period of oral transmission (*c.* AD 30–50) in the attempt to determine how oral transmission affected the form and content of our surviving Gospel material. They have concluded that the church preserved those materials which were useful in preaching the good news, in instructing converts, in disciplining its members, in conducting its services of worship, and in refuting its opponents.

They have found also that the material circulated in the church in small, independent units in fixed forms. These forms can now be identified in our Gospels. The two main groups of them are: sayings of Jesus (some introduced by a brief story, others without narrative setting, still others in the form of parables); and narratives about Jesus (his miracles, his controversies, his individual experiences – baptism, temptation, transfiguration – the events of his passion).

Unknown persons assembled many of these units into small collections of similar material (see next section). As far as we know, the author of the Gospel of Mark was the first to join some of the collections together according to a traditional recollection of the general outline of Jesus' ministry.

The uses to which the traditional material was put in the church led to some alterations – to contraction, to expansion, to loss or change of original context, to redirection of meaning. The tradition was fairly flexible during the oral period. This fact makes it difficult to reconstruct with certainty the original teachings and happenings of Jesus' career. (See p. 467).

The scholarly study of the oral period is known as *Formgeschichte* (form history or form criticism).

c. Early Oral and Written Collections (c. 50–65)
Included in the Gospel of Mark are collections of material which presumably

are older than that Gospel, such as conflict stories (2:1—3:6), parables (4:1–32), miracles (4:35—5:43), prophecies concerning the end (13:5–37), the Passion story (14:1—16:8) It is understandable that the church needed to sort the material into categories that could be easily used.

About 250 verses containing sayings of Jesus appear in Matthew and Luke in virtually identical wording but are not present at all in Mark. These sayings seem to come from an early written collection which was used independently by Matthew and Luke. Modern scholars call the supposed document 'Q' (from the German *Quelle*, source). It apparently had no Passion story and almost no narrative material. It probably was a handbook of Jesus' sayings for the instruction of converts. The order of its material has been reconstructed from the passages used by Luke, who quoted material in blocks in the order in which they were in his sources. Palestine or Antioch in Syria may be the place of its origin, and the date about AD 50–60. Its author is unknown.

Contained only in Matthew are some 400 verses of material which scholars call 'Special Matthew.' This consists mainly of about a dozen quotations from the Old Testament (introduced by a formula noting fulfillment of prophecy), some twelve narratives (such as the nativity story, Peter's walking on the water, the coin in the fish's mouth, and stories connected with the Passion and Resurrection), and a large body of sayings and parables in chaps. 5–25, notably about three fifths of the Sermon on the Mount.

This large body of sayings and parables may have come from a Jerusalem source, either written or oral. It is anti-Gentile in point of view, its scholarly symbol is 'M,' and its date is about AD 65. It is possible that Matthew drew on two or three sources besides 'M' for his special material.

Similarly, more than one third of the Gospel of Luke has been labeled 'Special Luke.' 'Special Luke' consists of both narratives and teaching matter and constitutes one of the most valuable parts of Luke's Gospel. Luke's nativity stories (chaps. 1–2) probably came from a different source than the rest of 'Special Luke.' We do not know whether most of 'Special Luke' came from one written document ('L') or from several written records or from oral sources. There is a Palestinian flavor about 'Special Luke,' as well as a universal outlook. Caesarea may have been the place of the collection of this material, and the date about AD 60.

Some scholars have argued that 'Q' and 'L' were joined by the author of Luke before he came across Mark's Gospel, and that Luke then inserted sections of Mark into Q + L. These scholars give to Q + L the name 'Proto-Luke.' But there are weighty arguments against Proto-Luke, and most scholars deny that it ever existed. It is evident that various collections of material, written and oral, lie behind our Synoptic Gospels as sources.

Our Four Gospels

a. The Gospel According to Mark
Mark was almost certainly the first of our four Gospels and the first book to be written in the literary form we now know as 'Gospel.' Mark, probably John Mark of Jerusalem (see p. 245), joined together early traditional sayings and stories and supplied connecting links. He meant his book to explain the puzzling question, Why did the Messiah die at the hands of Jewish and Roman leaders? He aimed also to encourage Christians to bear their sufferings in imitation of Jesus. He probably wrote in Rome about AD 65–70. (See p. 245)

b. The Gospel According to Matthew
Matthew is an expanded version of Mark, supplemented by a collection of the sayings of Jesus (Q) and by material from a source or sources accessible only to its

its author (M).

This Gospel was shaped to meet the needs of the church in its struggle with Judaism (c. AD 85). It attempted to show that the church, not the synagogue, is the true people of God and the heir of the coming kingdom of Heaven. It urged the church to exhibit before the Jews and the world the moral standards expected of the people of God. It tried also to help the inner life of the church: by reassuring it of the validity of its faith in Jesus; by guiding its discipline of members; by stimulating worship, evangelism, and brotherly service; and by encouraging patient endurance of suffering.

It seems to have been written in Syria, perhaps Antioch, by a learned Jewish Christian of a cosmopolitan turn of mind, who may have been heir to a tradition about Jesus associated with the Apostle Matthew. (See pp. 239, 240.)

c. The Gospel According to Luke

Luke is volume one of a two-volume work, called today 'Luke-Acts.' Luke-Acts constitutes more than one fourth of the total bulk of the New Testament.

As sources for his Gospel, Luke used the Gospel of Mark, Q, and Special Luke (L). He wished to defend and reinforce the church's position in the world of his time by showing that Christianity is *true* Judaism. It is a divinely initiated and guided movement, not a subversive political plot to overthrow either duly constituted Jewish institutions or Roman sovereignty. Therefore, neither Jews nor Romans have any valid grounds of complaint against the church. In fact, all who hear the true facts about Jesus and about the miraculous growth of the church, which issued from his ministry, should join the new faith. Christians, through knowledge of their venerable history, should take courage and fulfill their God-appointed evangelistic mission in the world until the eventual coming of the kingdom of God.

From Jesus to the Four Gospels

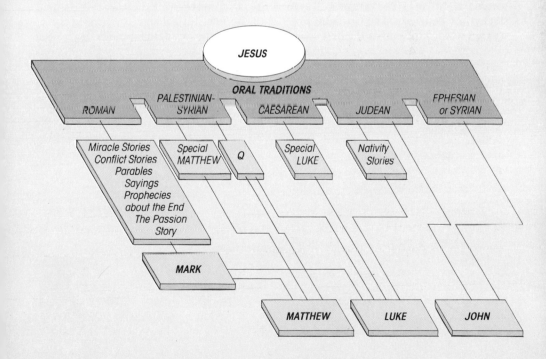

Its author probably was Luke, 'the beloved physician' and missionary companion of Paul, who wrote somewhere in the Hellenistic world (Greece? Rome?) between AD 70 and 90. (See p. 253.)

d. The Gospel According to John
This Gospel now appears to have been based on a tradition of Jesus' ministry, death, and resurrection which was independent of the tradition lying behind the Synoptic Gospels. This tradition may have stemmed from the Apostle John, who taught it to his disciples in Ephesus.

One of these disciples, a man of rare theological and literary gifts, shaped it into our present Gospel in the name and in the spirit of his teacher. He meant to strengthen Christians in the face of attacks by opponents outside and inside the church – by hostile Jews, possibly by the disciples of John the Baptist, and by false teachers within the church. By presenting Jesus as the incarnation of the Word and the Wisdom of God, whose glory was disclosed and attested by signs to the believing, he undoubtedly wished to make converts to the faith, as well as to strengthen believers. The Gospel was written toward the end of the first century, probably in Ephesus. (See p. 260).

The careful study of the way the writers of the Gospels used the written sources and the oral traditions available to them is known today as redaction criticism (or composition criticism). From the contractions, expansions, omissions, substitutions, ways of connecting pieces of material, interjected comments, and alterations of fact or theological meaning, we can learn much about the writers' characteristics, historical situation, purpose, and theology – as the following discussion of the individual Gospels will show.

Additional Note
Not all scholars today agree that the four Gospels originated in the way described above. Many alternative hypotheses have been suggested. Only one (by Pierson Parker) can be cited here.

The first Gospel to be written was an earlier form (in Aramaic) of our present (Greek) Gospel of Matthew. We may call it 'Proto-Matthew.' A Jewish Christian of Palestine wrote it about AD 55. He insisted on strict obedience of Christians to the Jewish Law and he opposed the Gentile mission. Someone soon translated

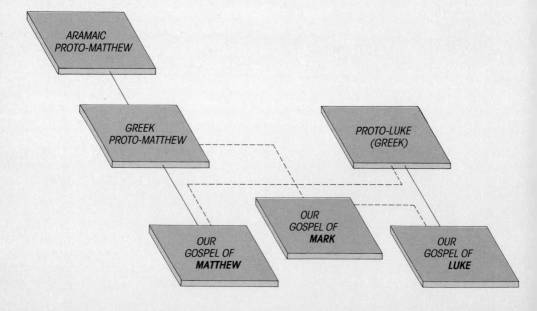

the 'Proto-Matthew' into Greek.

Mark used this Greek Proto-Matthew as his chief source. He abridged it sharply, omitted its Judaistic sections, and introduced a Gentile perspective. Through many inaccuracies in his geography, chronology, representation of Jewish institutions and customs, etc., he shows his distance from the first Christian circles. He was a Gentile – not John Mark of Jerusalem – of a later, rather than an earlier, period of Christianity.

Our Gospel of Matthew is Greek Proto-Matthew in expanded form. An editor added to Proto-Matthew materials from another early source which we may call 'Proto-Luke.' Proto-Luke had a universalistic cast and contained many sayings of Jesus of this nature. Thus we have both Judaistic and universalistic elements in our Gospel of Matthew. The materials unique to Matthew (usually called 'M') were in Proto-Matthew from the beginning and do not come from a separate source.

Luke used 'Proto-Luke'. Into this document he inserted some 60% of our Mark and thus created our present Gospel of Luke. A chart of the interrelationships, according to this hypothesis, would look something like the chart opposite.

The distinctive element in this hypothesis is that our Gospel of Mark is not the earliest Gospel of the Synoptics and the one on which our Matthew and our Luke are based. It is rather a late abridgment and considerably altered form of a document behind our Matthew.

Variations of this hypothesis by a few contemporary scholars continue to appear. Most experts, even conservative ones, hold to the priority of our Mark, as shown in the chart on p. 231.

For Further Reading

Kee, H.C., *Understanding the New Testament*, 4th ed. 1983.
Martin, R.P., *New Testament Foundations*, Vol. 1 'The Four Gospels', 1975.
Nickle, K.F., *The Synoptic Gospels*, 1980.

Matthew

five great blocks of sayings and a formula of transition (in 7:28; 11:1; 13:53; 19:1; 26:1) leading from one section to another. The blocks of sayings concern discipleship: the nature of the goodness expected by Jesus, the call to suffering service involved in apostleship, the character of the knowledge revealed by Jesus to his followers, the relationship of members within the church, the future to be expected by disciples in the present world and at the coming of the kingdom.

The position of Matthew's Gospel at the head of the New Testament canon reflects the regard in which the early church held it. Research has shown that in the second century it was the most read, quoted, and valued book of our present New Testament. Especially prized, then as today, was the Sermon on the Mount. In the words of Jesus early Christians found guidance for the conduct of their lives and an explanation of the relationship between the new that came in Jesus and the old in Judaism.

Noteworthy in the outline below are

View of Jesus

We may summarize Matthew's portrait of Jesus as follows: In the coming of Jesus of Nazareth God fulfilled his announced purpose of sending a Savior to humankind. This Savior (Messiah, Son of God, Son of man, Servant, and second Moses) was recognized as such by only some of the Jewish people, to whom the Father revealed his true identity. Those who accepted the revelation, believed in him, and became his disciples and apostles

---

Outline

Theme: Jesus, the divine-human Messiah, gathers together the people of the kingdom of heaven.

The lineage, birth, and childhood of Jesus, the divine-human Messiah (chaps. 1–2)

The preparation for his public work as the divine-human Messiah (3:1—4:11)

The gathering and teaching of his disciples (4:12—7:29)
First block of sayings – 'Concerning Discipleship' (5:3—7:27)

The redemptive deeds and words of the Messiah and his apostles (chaps. 8–10)
Second block of sayings – 'Concerning Apostleship' (10:5–42)

Reactions to the Messiah (11:1—13:52)
Third block of sayings – 'Concerning the Mystery of the Kingdom of Heaven' (13:3–52)

The formation and organization of the Messiah's church (13:53—18:35)
Fourth block of sayings – 'Concerning Relationships within the Church' (18:3–35)

The Messiah's preparation for death and his prediction concerning the establishment of his kingdom (chaps. 19–25)
Fifth block of sayings – 'Concerning the Coming Judgment' (chaps. 23–25)

The death of the Messiah for the forgiveness of sins, his resurrection, and his exaltation to universal authority (chaps. 26–28)

The Mount of Beatitudes, traditionally the site of Jesus' Sermon on the Mount.

This synagogue at Capernaum probably dates from the third or fourth century AD.

received forgiveness of sins, became his righteous people (the 'church'), and were appointed heirs to the kingdom of heaven, which he promised to inaugurate soon. As disciples they were to trust implicitly in him, be inwardly good rather than outwardly correct, and imitate him in acts of loving service. As apostles they were to spread the good news to all concerning the salvation available in him. By being and doing what he asked, they would be granted admission to his kingdom.

A few comments on this summary may make it more meaningful:

a. The Father's revelation to receptive people of Jesus' true identity comes to the fore in such passages as 3:17; 11:25–27; 13:11, 16–17, 51; 16:13–17; 17:5–6.

The multitudes, who did not understand who Jesus really was, regarded him as a 'prophet' (21:10–11, 46), and the religious leaders saw him as a false 'teacher' (9:11; 22:16, 24; 27:63). But the disciples, to whom God had revealed his true identity, knew that he was the unique Son of the Father, 'God with us' for the salvation of all people (1:21–23).

His supernatural birth (1:18–25), his miracles (14:28–33), and the Father's direct declaration (3:17; 17:5–6) prove that Jesus belonged to the realm of deity, though he lived on earth as a human being. The many Old Testament prophecies he is said to have fulfilled (1:22–23; 2:15, 17–18, 23; 8:17; etc.) show that he is the Deliverer long promised to the Jews.

The Father raised him from the dead, exalted him to authority over the universe, and appointed him judge of all people and ruler of the coming kingdom of heaven (25:31–46; 28:18).

b. Jesus' work as redeemer from sin, not merely as teacher of the divine will, appears in 1:21; 18:18; 26:28 (only Matthew has 'for the forgiveness of sins'). Jesus is the servant of the Lord, 'an offering for sin' (Isa. 53:10; Matt. 12:18), and the second Moses (Matt. 2:15; 5:1 ff., where Jesus gives teaching [Torah] from a mountain). Both the first Moses and the

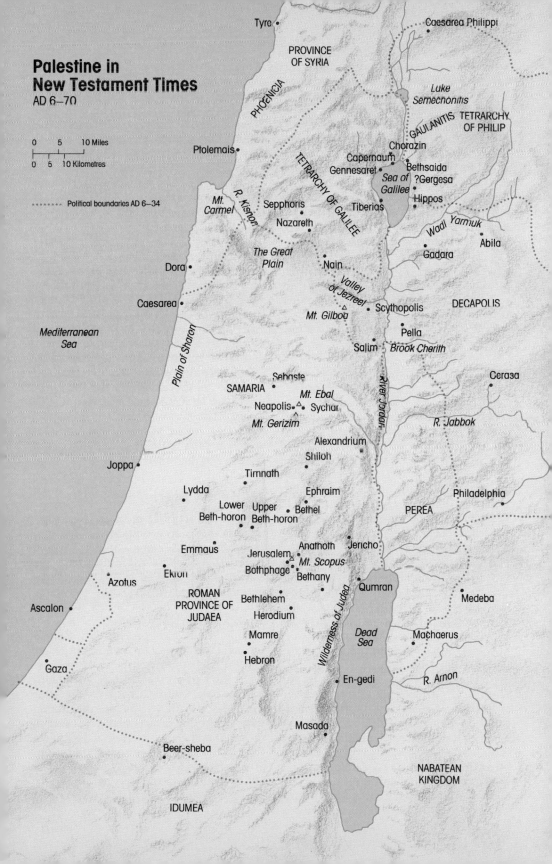

Palestine in New Testament Times

AD 6–70

0   5   10 Miles
0   5   10 Kilometres

········· Political boundaries AD 6–34

Tyre

PROVINCE
OF SYRIA

PHOENICIA

Luke
Semechonitis

Caesarea Philippi

GAULANITIS   TETRARCHY
OF PHILIP

Ptolemais

Chorazin
Capernaum
Gennesaret   Bethsaida
Sea of   ?Gergesa
Galilee
Hippos

TETRARCHY OF GALILEE

Sepphoris
Nazareth
Tiberias

Mt.
Carmel

R. Kishon

Waal *Yarmuk*

Abila

Gadara

Dora

The Great
Plain

Nain

Valley
of Jezreel

Scythopolis

Mt. Gilboa

DECAPOLIS

Caesarea

Mediterranean
Sea

Plain of Sharon

Pella

Salim   *Brook Cherith*

Sebaste

SAMARIA

Mt. Ebal

Neapolis   Sychar

Mt. Gerizim

Gerasa

R. Jabbok

River Jordan

Alexandrium

Shiloh

Joppa

Timnath

Lydda

Ephraim

Philadelphia

Lower
Beth-horon

Upper
Beth-horon

Bethel

PEREA

Emmaus

Anathoth

Jericho

Jerusalem

Ekron

Bethphage   *Mt. Scopus*

Azotus

ROMAN
PROVINCE OF
JUDAEA

Bethany

Bethlehem

Qumran

Medeba

Ascalon

Herodium

Mamre

Wilderness of Judaea

Dead
Sea

Machaerus

Gaza

Hebron

En-gedi

R. Arnon

Masada

NABATEAN
KINGDOM

Beer-sheba

IDUMEA

second Moses were deliverers from bondage, as well as givers of Torah (teaching).

Jesus' work is to gather out from the world 'the sons of the kingdom' (13:37–43), to call together the true Israel (16:18; 21:43), which he will admit to the kingdom at the last day (25:31–46). The terms of admission are: implicit faith in him (8:26; 14:31; 16:8), inner goodness rather than external correctness (5:17–48; 6:1–18; 23:23), imitation of his acts of loving service (9:13; 10:42; 12:7; 25:31–46), and fidelity in the evangelistic mission (10:16–42; 28:19–20).

c. The Gospel of Matthew is deeply interested in the church as the true and truly righteous people of God. Among the Gospels, only Matthew uses the term 'church' (*ekklesia*) as a designation for Jesus' followers (16:18; 18:17).

Purpose

The Gospel of Matthew reflects the church's conflict with Judaism, which became acute in the last quarter of the first century. The fall of Jerusalem (AD 70) led to the triumph of the Pharisees over all rival Jewish sects. The Pharisees insisted on obedience to the Law, as they interpreted it. They expelled Christians from the synagogues because they claimed to be the true Israel but did not obey the Law as the Pharisees understood it.

The writer of Matthew insists that the true people of God is the Christian church and the true interpretation of the Law is that offered by Jesus and practiced by his followers. The Law, says he, is properly observed when one becomes inwardly good (loving) and when one practices in daily life what love requires (7:12; 22:37–40). The book is thus an apology for the church in its struggle with the synagogue.

But this Gospel was written also to build up the church within: to teach new converts the requirements of their adopted faith; to reassure Christians of the validity of their trust in Jesus as the world's Savior; to urge them to imitate him in personal goodness, in suffering service, and

in spreading the gospel of the kingdom; to offer them materials from the church's memories of Jesus for the purposes of worship, evangelism, and inner discipline. Libertine, lawless teachers were threatening the moral life of the church (7:15–23; 13:36 ff.; 22:11–13) and compromising its witness to both Jews and Gentiles. The book warns the church that only those who are morally like Jesus and do his work in the world will enter the kingdom of heaven.

This Gospel also interprets Jesus and the Church in ways Gentiles, as well as Jews, could appreciate. The presentation of Jesus as the Son of God would be congenial to Gentiles of the author's time. They would be well disposed toward a divine-human being who had been born of a virgin, who had confirmed his supernatural origin by his miraculous powers, whose true identity and function God had revealed to special people so that they might understand and be saved. They were accustomed to divine saviors (kings, emperors, roving prophets) who were revealed as such to the elect in many of the religions of their day.

Sources

Two views of the sources of Matthew's material have been dominant. The first, the traditional Roman Catholic view, has held with Augustine that Matthew was the earliest of the Gospels, that it was written in Hebrew and subsequently translated into Greek, and that the Gospel of Mark is an abridgement of Matthew.

This view has present-day Roman Catholic and Protestant supporters. They argue that behind Matthew, Mark, and Luke lies a primitive Aramaic document, written by a Jewish Christian of Palestine (probably Matthew, the apostle) sometime before the destruction of Jerusalem in AD 70 and the scattering of Jerusalem Christians. The first apostles and missionaries may have used this document as an aid to memory in their preaching, teaching, and evangelizing. In Greek translation this document ('Proto-Matthew') became the basic source of our Synoptic Gospels. Materials from other sources were added to Proto-Matthew during the last quarter of the first century to form our present Gospel of Matthew. (See Additional Note, pp. 232–3.)

The second view resulted from careful investigation of the literary similarities among the first three Gospels in the nineteenth century and the first quarter of the twentieth. The investigators concluded that Mark, rather than being an abridgment of Matthew, was one of Matthew's principal sources of information. The author of Matthew, who used over 90 percent of Mark, followed Mark's order of events, shortened many of Mark's narratives, improved Mark's style, and in places altered Mark's theology (compare Mark 6:5 with Matt. 13:58, and Mark 10:18 with Matt. 19:17).

This view holds also that the author of Matthew used, besides Mark, a sayings source (now called 'Q,' from the German word *Quelle*, meaning 'source') for some 250 verses containing mostly words of Jesus. He had in addition a third source of information (Special Matthew) for many stories and sayings (such as the nativity narrative, Peter's walking on the water, the coin in the fish's mouth, Pilate's wife's dream, many sayings of the Sermon on the Mount, and many parables) not available

The Herods

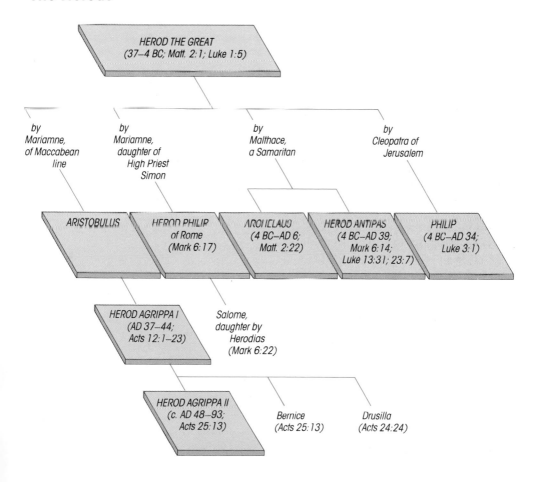

HEROD THE GREAT
(37–4 BC; Matt. 2:1; Luke 1:5)

by Mariamne, of Maccabean line

by Mariamne, daughter of High Priest Simon

by Malthace, a Samaritan

by Cleopatra of Jerusalem

ARISTOBULUS

HEROD PHILIP of Rome (Mark 6:17)

ARCHELAUS (4 BC–AD 6; Matt. 2:22)

HEROD ANTIPAS (4 BC–AD 39; Mark 6:14; Luke 13:31; 23:7)

PHILIP (4 BC–AD 34; Luke 3:1)

HEROD AGRIPPA I (AD 37–44; Acts 12:1–23)

Salome, daughter by Herodias (Mark 6:22)

HEROD AGRIPPA II (c. AD 48–93; Acts 25:13)

Bernice (Acts 25:13)

Drusilla (Acts 24:24)

to the other Gospel writers. The sayings and parables may have come from a written Jerusalem document (now called 'M' by some), and the stories from a special line of oral tradition. The second view is the dominant one today. (See pp. 230–31.)

Date, Place of Origin, Authorship

The reasons for dating Matthew to the last quarter of the first century are: (1) the apparent reference to the fall of Jerusalem in Matt. 22:7; (2) Matthew's use of Mark (written AD 65–70); (3) the strong defense of the Christian church against the attacks of the synagogue, from which the church seems to have been completely separated by the author's time; (4) the nature of the teaching opposed in Matthew, known from the Pastoral Epistles, the letters of John, the book of Revelation, Jude, 2 Peter, and elsewhere as a strong threat in the late first and early second centuries; (5) the advanced theology contained in this Gospel (the church with a universal mission, the image of the apostles defended and enhanced, the rich and highly complex view of Christ).

We do not know the exact place of origin of this Gospel, but it probably came from the eastern end of the Mediterranean. Early church tradition places it 'among the Hebrews in their own language,' that is, Palestine (Irenaeus, c. AD 180); but the strong evidence that the Gospel of Matthew used the Gospel of Mark in Greek as a principal source and was probably written in Greek speaks against Palestine. The most likely place is Syria, and probably Antioch.

The early church ascribed this Gospel to the Apostle Matthew. Why it did so is not known. The title 'According to Matthew' was added to manuscripts of the book in the second century.

Objections to Matthew's authorship of the book are weighty. Why would Matthew, an eyewitness, use over 90 percent of Mark, the work of someone not an eyewitness? Why do the changes of Mark made in Matthew look so little like the changes an eyewitness would have made?

It may be that the Apostle Matthew was the author or compiler of some source used in this Gospel (Q or M) and that his name thus passed over to the final book. It is also possible that the Apostle Matthew had gathered around himself followers who handed on his memories of Jesus. One of these toward the end of the first century may have put the present Gospel together in his name and, as it were, under his authority.

The final author was apparently a Jewish Christian who had been influenced by Greek culture, perhaps spiritually akin to Stephen's group at Jerusalem (Acts 6–7; 11:19–20). He wrote for Christians of this type in the emerging universal church of the late first century.

Conservatives tend to cling to the early tradition of authorship by the Apostle Matthew. Those conservatives who hold to the priority of Mark and its use by Matthew explain his use of it in some such way as the following: 'he agreed with it [Mark] and wanted to show that the apostolic testimony to Christ was not divided' (*The NIV Study Bible*, 1985).

Ruins of the black basalt synagogue at Chorazin, in the hills above Capernaum 3–6 cents. AD.

Mark

The Gospel of Mark is both a simple and a profound book. It contains a fast-moving story, told in plain language in dramatic episodes. These lead step by step to a bittersweet climax. When read at one sitting in a contemporary translation, it has the power to arouse the enthusiasm even of jaded teen-agers and adults, much as the rock opera *Jesus Christ, Superstar* did.

It is at the same time a sophisticated book, full of profound theology. Scholars who are still probing its subtleties confess that its depths elude them. In some ways it is the most difficult of the four Gospels to comprehend.

Mark is regarded by most scholars of our time as the earliest of our Gospels and probably as the first 'Gospel' ever written. With it something new came into being – a combination of biographical narrative with aretalogy (accounts of mighty deeds of gods and god-like persons) and with preaching (kerygma). (See p. 226.)

Mark does not divide easily into sections, as the variety of outlines offered in commentaries and handbooks shows. It appears to be organized geographically, however.

View of Jesus

Mark's Jesus is a divine being in human form, whose true identity and work are known to the demons (1:23–27, 34) but are hidden from people as a whole (4:11–12) and are only dimly and inaccurately perceived by his disciples (6:45–52; 8:14–21, 31–33; 9:10, 30–32).

The hidden Deity, the Son of God incarnate, has come to destroy the powers of evil and to inaugurate the kingdom of God. He is the Messiah (anointed King) of Jewish expectation and the heavenly Son of man (the coming judge of the world and inaugurator of the kingdom).

He achieves his redemptive work in a way surprising and mystifying to all: by unselfishly ministering to those bound by the demons' power, by suffering at the hands of his enemies, by dying on a cross, and by rising again. In his suffering and dying he pours out his life as a means of freeing 'many' from their bondage, for they cannot free themselves (10:45). By his death he seals a covenant bond between God and believing people, offering them a new relationship based upon forgiveness and reconciliation (14:24).

As risen Lord, he will come soon in glory (13:24–31), perhaps appearing in Galilee to inaugurate his kingdom (14:28; 16:7).

Purposes

We must infer Mark's purposes in writing, since they are nowhere stated.

a. He tells the stories about Jesus' mighty deeds, about his work of teaching, and about his death and resurrection not so much to present a history or biography of Jesus but to give evidence that God has acted in Jesus for the redemption of all people. He wants to promote faith in Jesus. In short, Mark preaches 'the gospel,' the good news about Jesus, by means of episodes from the earthly life of Jesus.

b. Mark offers a defense of Christianity because of the official Jewish rejection of it and because of its offensiveness to many Gentiles. 'Christ [Messiah] crucified' was 'a stumbling block to Jews and folly to Gentiles' (1 Cor. 1:23). Mark shows that God's way of salvation in the suffering, dying Jesus is indeed mysterious and mystifying – even the first disciples could not grasp it – but it is nonetheless the true and effective way of salvation for all people. The book thus grapples with the difficult problem of the scandal of the cross.

c. Mark's preoccupation with Jesus' ministry in Galilee (rather than in Jerusalem, as in the Gospel of John) and in the surrounding Gentile regions (Tyre, Sidon, Caesarea Philippi, the Decapolis, etc.) may suggest that he seeks to include the Gentile church in Jesus' intention. Mark sees the good news as destined for the whole world (13:10; 14:9).

Palestine in Jesus' Day

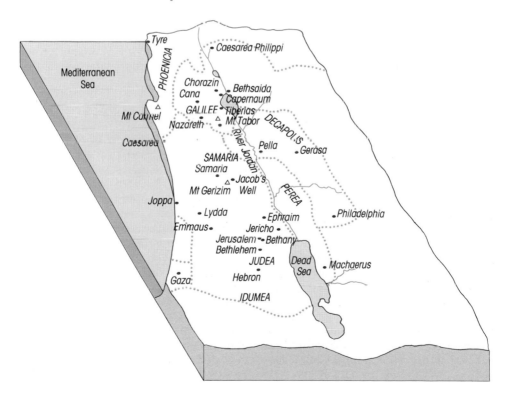

d. The emphasis in this Gospel on sacrificial suffering as the true mark of Christian discipleship (8:34–38; 10:35–45), together with the picture of Jesus as the Messiah who had to suffer to fulfill his God-given mission (8:31; 9:12, 31; 10:33–34, 38, 45), may indicate that Mark wrote the Gospel for Christians everywhere who needed strengthening as they drank the bitter cup of suffering.

But he may have meant this emphasis especially for Christians in Rome. Early church tradition connects the writing of this Gospel with Rome during the last days of Peter there, or after the martyrdom of Peter and Paul (see below). Nero's vicious slaughter of Roman Christians in AD 64 and the consequent hostility of the Roman populace would make an explanation such as Mark gives helpfully reassuring. This was: Christians have to suffer because Jesus had to suffer.

e. It is possible also that Mark wrote his Gospel to prepare Christians for the coming of Jesus as Son of man. If it was written just before or soon after the destruction of Jerusalem by the Romans (see below on 'Authorship, Place, Date'), in a time of excited anticipation by Christians of the End, the sufferings Mark believed they faced were the Endtime ones. They would need to know how to cope with them so that they might share in the glory of the coming Lord's kingdom. Indeed, the sufferings under Nero may have been seen by Mark and Christians as part of the appointed Endtime tribulations.

Sources

We know nothing certain about Mark's sources of information. Early church tradition (Papias, Irenaeus, Clement of Alexandria, and others) held that this Gospel was based on Mark's memory of the preaching of Peter, whose companion and interpreter Mark was.

Many scholars strongly challenge this tradition today, since form criticism (see p. 229) has made it likely that Mark's Gospel was put together from many independent, or loosely associated, pieces of early Christian tradition. Furthermore, they claim that no details or points of view characteristic of Peter are clearly present in the Gospel.

In their view, the only closely knit piece of material in Mark is the Passion story (Mark 14:1—16:8). It is widely agreed today that the events leading immediately to the cross and the Resurrection were the first to be drawn together into a continuous narrative. These events explain why Jesus, the Messiah, died – a problem for faith, as we have seen. By drawing on individual stories and groups of stories circulating in the church, Mark extended the explanation backward from the final events to the beginning of Jesus' ministry in Galilee. Thus he offers a full story on the subject: Why did Jesus, the Messiah, die?

According to this view, in addition to the Passion story Mark used such earlier collections of material as conflict stories (2:1—3:6), parables (4:1–32), miracle stories (4:35—5:43), and prophecies concerning the End (13:5–37). There is, to be sure, the hypothesis that Mark is an abridgment of the Gospel of Matthew (see p. 232–33). To most scholars the case for this is not convincing.

Authorship, Place, Date

The writer of the Gospel of Mark was a collector and arranger of early church tradition concerning Jesus. He did this so skillfully from his own theological perspective that he must be considered an 'author,' not just a compiler.

Who he was has been much debated. Ancient tradition does not claim that he was an eyewitness of the ministry of Jesus. The conjecture that he was the young man mentioned in 14:51–52 has little merit, since he is not named or othewise identified in the text.

The early Christian writers mentioned above (Papias, Irenaeus, Clement of Alexandria) and the superscription in early manuscripts of the Gospel ('According to

Solomon's Pools – built in Hasmonean times to supply water to Jerusalem.

Mark') tell us that his name was Mark. Clearly John Mark of Jerusalem, the companion of Barnabas, Paul, and Peter (Acts 13:5, 13; 15:37–40; 1 Peter 5:13) was meant. And two of the above early writers locate the place of writing as Rome, one dating it after the death of Peter and Paul and the other before the death of Peter.

Opinion is divided today about the accuracy of this early Christian tradition. Some scholars consider it 'worthless' (Willi Marxsen). They hold that Mark was a very common name in the Roman world, that the Mark that wrote this Gospel knew little about Palestine (its geography and Jewish customs and institutions), that the Gospel shows no direct influence of Peter, and that Syria or Galilee, rather than Rome, accords best with the Gospel's contents as the place of writing. The Latinisms in the Gospel 'could occur at any place where a Roman garrison was stationed and Roman law was practiced' (Helmut Koester) and do not necessarily point to Rome.

Others, including many liberal scholars, have long contended for authorship by John Mark of Jerusalem and for its Roman origin. They point to: evidence of Mark's association with Peter in Rome (the ancient tradition and 1 Pet. 5:13, where 'Babylon' apparently is a pseudonym for Rome); the apparent use of the Gospel of Mark in Roman Christian works (1 Clement, the Shepherd of Hermas); some slight evidence of Petrine perspectives in the Gospel (for example, the Gospel as an expansion of Peter's sermon in Acts 10:34–43); and the appropriateness for Roman Christians who had suffered under Nero of the strong emphasis in the Gospel on suffering as the normal expectation for Christians. They admit some inexactitude in geographic and other details but think it not serious enough to overturn the tradition about the authorship.

The date of writing seems to be in the late sixties or shortly after the destruction of Jerusalem by the Romans in AD 70. The early traditions put the writing during the ministry or after the death of Peter in Rome; and the destruction of Jerusalem may be anticipated or reflected in Mark 13, probably the former.

Historical Reliability

Since Mark is a 'Gospel' and not a chronicle of the events of Jesus' career, to what extent does it supply reliable information about Jesus of Nazareth?

Some scholars have said that Mark's outline of the ministry of Jesus is unreliable on the ground that it is his own construction, that it is a device to hold together the various bits of tradition that came to him, and that it serves his own theological interests.

However, the fact that Mark's story was adopted by Matthew and Luke as the backbone of their narratives and that this Gospel was accepted, cherished, and preserved in some important early Christian church (Rome? Antioch?) argues that it was recognized early as an essentially reliable portrait of Jesus.

While Mark's story of Jesus is far from complete, as the other Gospels show, the general sequence of events is historically probable. This sequence makes sense: Jesus began his ministry in Galilee after the imprisonment of John the Baptist; called disciples; carried out a healing and teaching ministry first in the synagogues; aroused opposition from straitlaced religious leaders; sent out the Twelve in an attempt speedily to reach the nation; withdrew from Galilee when Herod Antipas desired to arrest him as a dangerous troublemaker; faced, in a period of retreat, the question of the future course of his ministry; decided to go to Jerusalem for an appeal to the nation in its capital city; journeyed there with his disciples; attacked abuses in the temple and ran afoul of the religious and political leaders there; was consequently executed for treason. This outline is surely not something Mark created and imposed on traditional stories. It is true, of course, that there is no strict, detailed chronological order of events (3:1–6, for example, must come from relatively late in Jesus' career).

That Jesus, as Mark says, tried to stop people from proclaiming him openly as Messiah and that the disciples should have failed to grasp during his ministry what sort of a deliverer he regarded himself to be likewise make sense; it is not a theory imposed by Mark, as some have claimed. Messiahship to Jesus was a matter not of status but of redemptive action. The Messiah was suffering Servant – a concept hard to grasp, then as now!

The Ending of Mark's Gospel

Among ancient Greek manuscripts and versions there are differences in the way Mark's Gospel ends. Most of these documents contain what is now Mark 16:9–20, but in important early ones (e.g., Codex Sinaiticus and Codex Vaticanus – see pp. 374–6) vss. 9–20 are missing. Eusebius and Jerome (fourth century) indicate that the passage was absent from almost all manuscripts known to them.

Scholars agree today that 16:9–20 differs considerably from Mark's vocabulary, style, and concepts and contains elements drawn from the other Gospels and the Acts. It is probably a second-century addition to the Gospel of Mark.

A brief (two-sentence) ending is found after 16:8 in a few manuscripts; and one important manuscript (Codex Washingtonensis – see p. 376) inserts between 16:14 and 16:15 a long passage containing a defense of the twelve apostles and an otherwise unrecorded saying of Jesus.

These various early endings suggest that for some reason the conclusion of Mark was thought unsatisfactory. Was the end accidentally or deliberately torn off at an early date? Or did Mark himself end the Gospel at 16:8, in a way that later seemed to others to be abrupt and deficient in the light of the other Gospels?

Scholars today increasingly believe that the Gospel of Mark as originally written ended at 16:8. Matthew and Luke seem to have known Mark as far as 16:8. And the fear (awe) on the part of the women confronted with the Resurrection is not an inappropriate way for Mark to have concluded his book.

Luke

The French writer Ernest Renan called this Gospel 'the most beautiful book in the world.' Of the four Gospels, many Christians regard Luke as their favorite.

Its charm arises from many characteristics: its appealing picture of Jesus as the God-given, righteous humanitarian who sealed his redemptive love of outcasts, foreigners, the poor, and women with his death on the cross; its sheer literary artistry (in content, structure, phrasing); its emotional heights (suspense, pathos); its comprehensiveness (much rich material, including parables, not found in the other Gospels); its cosmopolitan outlook; its devotional quality (emphasis on the importance of prayer and life in the Holy Spirit); its domestic scenes and tone; its charming birth and infancy stories; and much else. We would be a great deal poorer in our knowledge of Jesus without this Gospel.

Theme and Outline

The Gospel according to Luke is volume one of a two-volume work which we now call 'Luke-Acts.' The preface to the Acts of the Apostles (1:1–5) mentions and describes 'the first book,' our Gospel of Luke (though some think it 'Proto-Luke' – see p. 230) and mentions again the recipient of the two-book work, Theophilus (*cf.* Luke 1:3). The theme, contents, and style of the Acts show that the two volumes belong together. The following outline therefore will present the whole work.

Bethlehem.

Outline

The theme of Luke-Acts is: The Christian church is the true people of God, called into being by God through the ministry, death and resurrection of Jesus of Nazareth and empowered by God for a redemptive mission to all the earth; it is not a perversion of Judaism or a subversive society promoting rebellion against the Roman government.

Vol. 1 (The Gospel according to Luke): The Christian church originated in the ministry, death, and resurrection of Jesus of Nazareth, the Spirit-filled Savior, whom God sent to the Jewish people and to all nations.

The preface — the author's sources of information and purpose in writing (1:1–4)

The introduction — the birth and childhood of John the Baptist and Jesus (1:5—2:52)

The preparation for Jesus' public ministry through the ministry of John the Baptist and through Jesus' baptism and temptation (3:1—4:13)

Jesus' ministry in Galilee (4:14—9:50)

Jesus' ministry on the way to Jerusalem (9:51—19:27)

Jesus' ministry, death, and resurrection in Jerusalem (19:28—24:53)

Vol. 2 (The Acts of the Apostles): The universal Christian church came into being through the heroic, Spirit-filled witnessing of Jesus' disciples to Jews and Gentiles concerning the power of God which is redemptively active in the world through the crucified and resurrected Jesus. (For a detailed outline see p. 262.)

View of Jesus

This Gospel represents Jesus as a God-begotten, God-appointed, God-empowered, God-guided person, whose task was to free all people, without distinction as to race, sex, class, religion, from whatever bondage had victimized them. He brought them to experience in this life in foretaste the blessings of the New Age over which he would reign as king.

According to the author of this Gospel, Jesus announced the purpose of his mission at the very beginning of his public activity by quoting Isa. 61:1–2:

The Spirit of the Lord is upon me,
because he has anointed me to preach good news to the poor.
He has sent me to proclaim release to the captives
and recovering of sight to the blind,
to set at liberty those who are oppressed,
to proclaim the acceptable year of the Lord. (Luke 4:18–19)

Luke shows that the Holy Spirit was not only the begetter of Jesus (1:35) but came upon him 'in bodily form' at his baptism by John (3:22), guided him during his temptation in the wilderness (4:1–2), empowered him in his ministry in Galilee (4:14), and worked through him in healing diseases and casting out evil spirits (6:17–19). A life of constant prayer lay behind his possession of the Holy Spirit (3:21–22; 5:16–17; 6:12; 9:18; 10:21; 11:1).

Though he was a Jew sent to Jews ('the son of Abraham' – 3:34), he was also sent to all people ('the son of Adam' – 3:38). He was 'a light for revelation to the Gentiles' (2:32). The hated Samaritans received his benefits (17:11–19). He ministered to women, even the harlots and the demon-possessed, and received them into his company of followers (7:36–50; 8:1–3; 10:38–42). He had special concern for the poor (4:18; 6:20; 7:22; 16:19–31), for tax collectors (5:27–32; 15:1–2; 19:1–10), and even for Pharisees (7:36 ff.; 11:37; 14:1).

Luke takes pains to show that Jesus, God's Spirit-filled Son (1:32, 35; 3:22; 4:41; etc.), the friend of all humanity, came to his death on the cross through no fault of his own. Pilate three times declared him innocent of any wrongdoing (23:4, 14–15, 22), as did Herod Antipas (23:6–12, 15) and the Roman centurion at the cross (23:47). The rejection of Jesus began among Jews in Galilee (4:16–30),

The River Jordan near Tiberias.

Herod the Great's family tomb has a great round stone at its entrance.

was furthered by Jewish religious teachers (5:17—6:11); 11:53–54; 13:14–17; 15:2), and came to its climax among the Jewish religious authorities in Jerusalem (22:66 —23:25; 24:20). He was a threat not to Roman authority but only to corrupt Jewish traditions and institutions.

Luke affirms that Jesus' death carried out the purpose of God for the redemption of all people (9:22, 30–31; 17:25; 24:25–27, 44–47). The long travel narrative, depicting Jesus on the way to Jerusalem (9:51—19:27), shows Jesus and the disciples treading the way of suffering marked out by the Father (13:33; 22:22, 37). Luke makes much of the concept of the *way* of Jesus and the *way* of the church as the *way* marked out by God. This way leads to 'glory' (24:26), to the life of the kingdom of God.

The ascension, twice recorded (Luke 24:51; Acts 1:9), was for Luke the occasion of Jesus' divine enthronement. While as King he awaits the consummation of all things (Acts 3:21), he is active in the world through the Holy Spirit, which he has sent to the church (Acts 2:33) to enable it to proclaim the gospel to the nations (Acts 1:8).

Luke sees the purpose of God in the salvation of the world as embracing three historical stages: (1) the period of Israel (of the Law and the prophets, including John the Baptist); (2) the period of Jesus (his preaching of the coming kingdom and manifestation in his ministry of the power of that kingdom); (3) the period of the church (when the Spirit enables Jesus' disciples to carry the good news throughout the world and to draw together the universal people of God). (See Luke 16:16; 19:11; Acts 1:6–8; 3:21.)

The period of Jesus is thought of by Luke as 'the center of history' (Hans Conzelmann). In Jesus, God has fulfilled the promises contained in the law and the prophets (Luke 4:18–21; 24:25–27, 44–47). In Jesus, God has drawn together the people of the coming kingdom (the church). It is their task to continue in the work entrusted to them until the kingdom of God finally appears (19:11–27). Luke seems to play down expectancy of the immediate coming of the Lord and the final kingdom and to emphasize patient, faithful Christian activity in the meantime (19:11–27; 21:7–9).

Luke's favorite titles for Jesus are Lord, Christ, and Son. In Luke-Acts these are applied to him both before and after his death and resurrection

Sources

Luke says that he was not an eyewitness of the events of Jesus' ministry but that he had investigated carefully the information contained in the eyewitness traditions and the written accounts available to him (1:1–4).

Most scholars agree that Mark was one of Luke's principal sources. More than 60 percent of Mark appears in Luke, and Mark's sequence of events is largely followed. Luke abbreviated some of Mark's stories, often improved his language, and avoided expressions and stories that would be misleading or offensive to Gentile readers (*e.g.,* Mark 7:24–30; 11: 12–14, 20–25).

The Church of the Holy Sepulchre, Jerusalem, probable site of Jesus' death.

A second source appears to have been the document we call Q (see p. 230), which he employed as a source for the words of Jesus. He used materials from Mark and Q in blocks, following first one and then the other. He seems to have reproduced Q's order rather faithfully.

More than one third of Luke has no parallel in the other Gospels. Whether this material came from a written source or from miscellaneous oral traditions is not known. Its point of view is Palestinian. There is a strong interest in 'the poor' and a close association of poverty with piety. Jesus' compassion toward women and the Samaritans is prominent in it. It may be that this material came into Luke's possession from his contact with the church at Caesarea when he was with Paul there (Acts 23:33—26:32).

It has been held that Q and Luke's special material had been joined into an earlier form of our Luke (Proto-Luke) before the sections from Mark were added. But this hypothesis is yet to be proved.

Luke's birth and infancy stories (chaps.

1–2) seem to have come from yet another source (or sources), because of their peculiarities of style and language. Luke welded his sources together skillfully.

Purposes

a. A Historical Purpose

The author realized that he lived a number of years after the events of Jesus' life, that many traditions and records of that life existed, and that considerable controversy and uncertainty about Jesus prevailed in his time. He wished to set the facts straight by his record.

He makes a solid attempt to relate Jesus to world history by mentioning the census of Augustus under Quirinius (2:1–2), by the chronological context of the appearance of John the Baptist (3:1–2), and by naming Roman emperors and officials (Acts 11:28; 18:2, 12).

He wishes also to explain how the church of his time arose. He regards it as important in the life of the empire and believes it will continue in the world for some time yet (19:11; 21:7–9). Thus he connects Jesus not only with world history but with church history.

b. An Apologetic Purpose

He wishes by the historical facts to clear up misunderstandings about the Christian movement. He refutes the charge that Jesus and the apostles and Christian missionaries were political revolutionists by showing that Pilate three times declared Jesus innocent (chap. 23), that Herod found no grounds for accusing him (23:6–12, 15), that the centurion at the cross attested his innocence (23:47), that the Jewish authorities in Jerusalem (particularly Gamaliel) had reservations about the early Christians' guilt (Acts 5:33–40), and that Paul was repeatedly cleared or left uncharged by Roman authorities (Acts 18:12–17; chaps. 24–26). Ungodly Jews were the ones who instigated the opposition to Jesus and early Christian leaders. These leaders were true, God-pleasing Jews. Therefore, Christianity is entitled to the sufferance and protection that the Romans traditionally allowed Judaism.

He wishes also to show Jews and those Gentiles who were favorable to Judaism ('God-fearers' – see p. 406) that Christianity is not a perverted, but rather an authentic, Judaism. God (the Holy Spirit) was behind the Christian movement from the beginning. The apostles were loyal to the Old Testament rightly interpreted and to the temple (Luke 24:52; Acts 2:46). Paul received his call to Gentile missions in the temple (Acts 22:17–21). The church's true home was the holy city Jerusalem (Luke 24:52; Acts 1:4). The author was convinced that Old Testament hopes had found their fulfillment in the coming of Jesus, in the gift of the Holy Spirit to the church, and in the Christian world mission. Therefore the Jews have no real grounds of complaint against the Christian church.

c. An Evangelistic Purpose

It is evident that the author was a devout Christian, fully convinced of the truth of the Christian gospel, proud of the remarkable accomplishments of Jesus and the Christian church, and zealous to spread the new faith. Paul, the great missionary to the Gentiles, was obviously one of the author's heroes (Acts chaps. 13–28).

It may be that the author hoped to convert Theophilus and other readers to whom the book might come by clearing away objections commonly raised to Christianity. And he apparently wants the church of his time to concentrate on its Christ-appointed task of evangelism, rather than to dissipate its energy in speculation about the End.

Original Readers and Author

Theophilus, meaning 'friend (or beloved) of God,' was a proper name borne by both Greeks and Jews of the period. It is probably not to be understood here as meaning any reader beloved of God into whose hands the two-volume work might come.

The Citadel, Jerusalem; probable site of Jesus' judgment before Pilate.

The term 'most excellent,' used in Acts 23:26; 24:2; 26:25 in address to high government officials, seems to indicate that Theophilus was a man of importance. Whether he was a Christian or a "God-fearer' (a Gentile who had become a half-convert to Judaism – Acts 10:2; 13:16) or a high Gentile official suspicious of or opposed to Christianity has been much debated. Luke's eagerness to defend Christianity makes it unlikely that Theophilus was a Christian.

Apparently Luke, according to the custom of the time, expected Theophilus, as the addressee, to see to the distribution of the book. In this sense he was a patron of the author.

The author's identity is not beyond dispute. Early church tradition (Irenaeus, the Muratorian Canon) assigns the work to Luke, the physician and companion of Paul (Col. 4:14). An attempt has been made to prove from the language of Luke-Acts that its author was a physician, but this has been refuted by the fact that there is no more medical language in this work than in works known to be by non-medical authors of the period. The 'we' passages of Acts (16:10–17; 20:5–15; 21:1–18; 27:1—28:16) may indicate that the author was an eyewitness of the events narrated in these passages, but it is also possible that these sections are based on an itinerary or diary compiled by someone other than the author of Luke-Acts and do not, therefore, indicate our author's personal participation.

The strongest arguments against authorship by a companion of Paul have been raised on the ground of the author's apparent lack of accurate knowledge about Paul's career and his theology (see p. 269).

The strongest arguments in favor are: (1) since Luke was not an apostle, the church of the second century would hardly have assigned the authorship to him without sufficient reason; and (2) the author's cultural characteristics (excellent Greek style, historical interests, cosmopolitan outlook, etc.) imply a person such as Luke the physician must have been.

Whoever he was, he was the one great historian between Polybius, the last of the great Greek historians, and Eusebius, the first important church historian.

Date and Place of Composition

The use of the Gospel according to Mark (written about AD 70) in Luke-Acts, the author's seeming knowledge of the destruction of Jerusalem by the Romans in AD 70 (Luke 19:41–44; 21:20–24), and the appropriateness of a learned defense of Christianity in the face of strong Jewish attacks and persistent Gentile suspicions suggest a date between AD 70 and 90 (with 80–85 the most likely). Some scholars have argued for a date before the end of Paul's trial in Rome, shortly after the last event described in the Acts; but this puts the writing of Mark too early. Some few have dated Luke as late as about AD 125 and the book of Acts a decade or so later.

Antioch, Caesarea, Achaea (Greece), and Rome have been suggested as the place of writing, but these are only conjectures. A location outside Palestine is likely in view of the cultured, Greek-speaking readers for whom the work was intended.

John

Christian readers, ancient and modern, have reacted differently to the Gospel of John. In the second century some Christians known as 'Alogoi' judged its teaching, particularly about the Holy Spirit, unorthodox, denied its apostolic origin, and assigned its authorship to Cerinthus, a Gnostic heretic (see p. 348). Clement of Alexandria, on the other hand, thought this Gospel 'inspired by the Spirit.' He called it 'a spiritual gospel.'

In the nineteenth and twentieth centuries many scholars have denied its apostolic origin and its historical and religious value. Others, like William Temple, Archbishop of York, have confessed their deep love of the book. Today, the pendulum has swung toward a positive appreciation of both its historical value and its religious significance.

View of Jesus

The author's thought about Jesus revolves around three main centers.

a. Jesus Is the Son of God.
The phrases 'Son of God' and 'the Son' are found about twenty-eight times in this Gospel. Two emphases occur in them.

First, the Son has a unique intimacy with God, his Father. He is God's *only* Son (1:14; 3:16, 18), 'only' meaning 'unique' or 'only one of its kind.' This unique relationship involves essential identity with God, both in the Son's preexistent state (17:5, 24) and in his incarnate existence (5:17–18; 14:9). The Father's love for the Son is stressed (3:35; 5:20; 15:9; 17:23, 24, 26). Some scholars argue that the union between Father and Son claimed in this book is a love union, rather than a union of substance or essence (15:9; 17:23–26), since believers can share in it (14:20, 23; 17:21–23).

Second, the Son is subordinate to and dependent on the Father: 'the Father is greater than I' (14:28); 'I can do nothing on my own authority' (5:30). The Son is *sent* by the Father (8:42; 10:36; 11:42; 13:20; 17:3; etc.) to accomplish the Father's work in the world (5:30, 36; 14:10, 31). Here the Hebrew practice of appointing an official legal representative, who is invested with all the authority of the sender, is evident (13:20). For instance the Son is completely obedient to the Father (4:34; 6:38; 15:10).

The work of the Son, like that of the Father, is to give life to people (5:21; 6:35, 48–51; 11:25) and to pass judgment on them (5:22, 27, 30; 9:39–41).

Jesus' sonship in this Gospel involves identity with and moral likeness to God.

Both Jews and Gentiles would find meaning in the characterization of Jesus as the Son of God. Jews referred to Israel, Israel's king, the righteous in Israel, the angels, and perhaps to the Messiah as the son or sons of God, while Gentiles used the term to suggest the divinity of their emperors and kings. In Judaism it signified close religious relationship with and obedient service to God, and in Greek usage it meant divine origin and essential divinity. In the Gospel of John both usages flow together.

b. Jesus Is the Son of Man.
Thirteen times Jesus is said to be 'the Son of man.' His true home is heaven (3:13; 6:62). He has come down to earth to be the Savior of the world through exaltation on

Jerusalem in Jesus' Day

HEROD'S PALACE
Pilate used this palace as his Jerusalem residence and judged Jesus here. (John 18:28— 19:16)

GOLGOTHA
In Jesus' time a disused quarry outside the city walls; probable site of Jesus' crucifixion. (John 19:17–42)

ANTONIA FORTRESS
Built by Herod the Great to overlook the Temple.

HEROD'S TEMPLE
Jesus threw the money-changers out of the Temple courts. (Mark 11:15–18)

GETHSEMANE
Jesus went here to pray after the Last Supper and was betrayed and arrested here. (Mark 14:32–52)

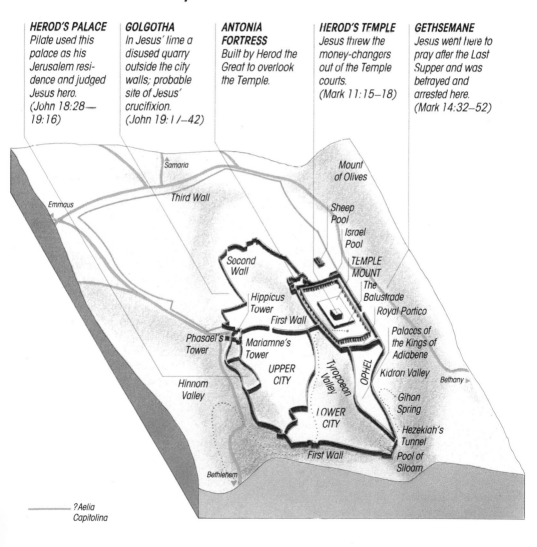

the cross (3:14–15; 8:28; 12:23). After gathering together the scattered children of God (11:52), he will ascend again into heaven (6:62). He is the judge of all humanity (5:27–29). This judgment is both a present and a future action (9:39–41; 5:27–29). As Son of man he is the point of contact between earth and heaven (1:51).

Jewish thought in the first century had been deeply influenced by Greek and oriental concepts. Widespread was the belief in a heavenly, ideal man, a glorious Adam, who was the pattern after which humankind was fashioned and who would descend at last to fallen earth and restore people to the blessedness they had lost. Paul speaks of Christ as 'the last Adam,' 'the man of heaven,' who will give believers spiritual bodies for the life of the age to come (1 Cor. 15:45–49). Such a heavenly redeemer is described in Jewish apocalyptic books (1 Enoch, 2 Esdras) and lies behind the theology of the Gospel of John.

c. Jesus Is the Word and the Wisdom of God.

The Prologue (1:1–18) interprets Jesus by use of the widespread concept of the Word (*Logos*) of God. Greek philosophers spoke of inward thought and the outward expression of thought in speech as Word (*Logos*). They also spoke of God as *Logos*, as a fiery vapor capable of thinking, permeating all things, holding the universe together, and rationally governing all change. For them *Logos* was rational creative power and rational expression (revelation).

Judaism had a counterpart in the concept of Wisdom. Wisdom was with God before the creation (Prov. 8:22 ff.) and served as an active agent in creation (Wisd. of Sol. 7:22). Wisdom is the binding force linking the world to its Creator (Wisd. of Sol. 1:7). Wisdom came to earth and invited people to receive instruction (Prov. 8:1–11), but foolish ones refused (Prov. 1:24–25). Wisdom is the reflection of God's eternal light (Wisd. of Sol 7:26). It is God's truth, meant to lead people to life (Prov. 8:35) and immortality (Wisd.

Coin of the procurator Pontius Pilate, AD 30.

of Sol. 6:18–19). Wisdom seeks disciples (Prov. 1:20–23) and makes them friends of God (Wisd. of Sol. 7:14, 27). But Wisdom's coming divides hearers into receivers and rejecters, with the consequences of life or death.

The Gospel of John represents Jesus as having preexisted with God (1:1; 17:5). He served as agent in creation (1:3). He descended to earth to dwell among the Jewish people (1:10–11, 14; 3:13; 6:38). He revealed the mind and purposes of God (1:18; 7:16, 29). He sought out disciples, who were then united into one family of God (1:12–13; 11:52; 17:6–23). He experienced both acceptance and rejection (1:11–13; 3:20–21; 9:35–41). He brought light and life to believers (1:4; 8:12; 11:25–26) and death and judgment to unbelievers (3:18–20; 5:28–29; 12:48).

Though much in this picture of Jesus comes from concepts current in the author's age, he is unique at one central point. He alone declares that the Word (or Wisdom) 'became flesh' (1:14). To say that eternal creative Reason appeared as a man among human beings for the purpose of revelation and redemption was possible only by those who had seen God's glory in the man Jesus (1:14; 2:11; 17:22).

John and the Synoptic Gospels

Even the casual reader is aware of the striking differences between the Fourth Gospel and the first three. See p. 257.

The differences call for explanation.

The Fourth Gospel	The Synoptics
Jesus' ministry is chiefly in Judea and Jerusalem.	Jesus' ministry is chiefly in Galilee.
Jesus talks about himself and the significance of his ministry.	Jesus preaches and teaches about the kingdom of God.
Jesus teaches in long discourses, often of a controversial nature.	Jesus teaches in short, pithy sayings, in parables, in conversations in normal life situations as well as in controversy.
Jesus' enemies are 'the Jews.'	Jesus' enemies are the Pharisees.
The reason for the hostility to Jesus is his claims regarding himself.	The reason for the hostility is Jesus' revolutionary (liberal) attitude toward the Law of Moses.
Jesus' miracles are 'signs' which point to his true identity.	Jesus' miracles are works of compassion for the needy.

Can both pictures of Jesus be correct? Which better describes the historical Jesus? Or are both needed for a true understanding of him?

The Sources of the Gospel of John

In the first third of the twentieth century many scholars believed that the author of John had used the Synoptic Gospels (at least Mark and Luke) in writing his Gospel, that he was dissatisfied with their picture of Jesus, and that he wished to replace it with his own. They held that there was little, if any, historical tradition in his Gospel where he was not dependent on the Synoptics.

Today the dominant view among liberal scholars is that the author of the Gospel of John did not use the Synoptics, that he drew on a line of tradition unknown to the Synoptic writers, and that this tradition contained several elements.

1. Some historical information about Jesus not contained in the Synoptic Gospels: such as, his enlistment of John the Baptist's disciples (1:19–51); an early Judean ministry of Jesus (3:22–24); several appearances of Jesus at Jerusalem feasts (chaps. 5–10); an earlier date for the Last Supper (18:28; 19:14).

2. Some collections of materials, written and oral, about Jesus' self-disclosure and the resultant controversies with 'the Jews,' about the 'Signs' (miracles) he performed, and about the Passion-Resurrection events.

3. A theological interpretation of Jesus by a Christian community (probably in Syria) that had been forged out of and was in continuing contact with many cultural and religious perspectives: rabbinic Judaism; sectarian (Essene) Judaism; Hellenistic Judaism; prophetic Judaism (of the John the Baptist variety); Samaritan Judaism; and perhaps Gnostic Judaism.

These scholars believe that the Gospel of John is in part the product of one (or two) individual minds but it is also the creation of a particular community in which the tradition that was used was shaped.

Conservative scholars assume only one source for the Gospel – the recollections of the beloved disciple (13:23; 19:26; 20:2; 21:7, 20, 24). That the Gospel was written by an eyewitness is supported, they say, by the following data: the use of 'we' in 1:14; the possible reference to himself as eyewitness of the blood and water from the Lord's side (19:35); and the personal affirmation of eyewitness authorship in 21:24. They point out many small touches in the narrative that only an eyewitness would include.

Purposes

The Gospel itself suggests its purpose: 'that you may believe that Jesus is the Christ, the Son of God, and that believing you may have life in his name' (20:31).

Unfortunately, all Greek manuscripts do not read the same in this verse. Some have a verbal form which must be translated 'that you may continue to believe,' and others have 'that you may come to believe.' The first would imply that the readers were Christians who needed support for their faith in Jesus, and the second that the readers had not yet come to faith in him. In 19:35 the same problem appears, but the best manuscripts have 'continue to believe.' This is probably the meaning in 20:31.

The author's purposes seem to have been:

a. To strengthen the Faith of Christians in the Face of Attacks of Opponents
The Jews denied the messiahship of Jesus; John affirms it strongly (1:41; 4:25–26). The Jews insisted on the validity of their religious institutions and worship; John claims that in Jesus and the church these are superseded (2:13–22; 3:1–14; 4:20–24; 6:31–32). Since Christianity is the fulfillment of Judaism (5:39–47; 8:56; 12:41), Judaism has lost its preeminence. 'The Jews' in the Gospel are evil men who, by rejecting Jesus, showed that they belonged to 'the world,' to darkness and the devil (8:44).

This Gospel may have been addressed to Christians still in Jewish synagogues of the Greco-Roman world who, in the last quarter of the first century, were being pressured to renounce faith in Jesus on pain of excommunication. The book would encourage them to persist in their trust in Jesus.

It is possible that it was meant also to counter the claims of the disciples of John the Baptist that their master, not Jesus, was the Messiah (1:6–8, 15, 19–36; 3:28–30).

Enemies of the faith were inside, as well as outside, the church. Some Christians claimed that Jesus was not really human, that God could not be clothed in evil flesh.

The Dome of the Rock stands over the site of the Jerusalem temple.

John's insistence on the real humanity of Jesus (1:14; 19:34) may be aimed to counteract this false teaching.

And doubt, aggravated by the church's opponents, may have been plaguing the readers. Their knowledge of Jesus and the formative events was fragmentary and at second or third hand. This Gospel seems meant to reassure them that there is one who has full and intimate knowledge – the Beloved Disciple – and that his witness is certified by the community (or at least those who published the Gospel) as true (21:24 note the 'we'). Thus the Gospel speaks to the problem raised by the passing years and the emerging of new generations with the answer, 'Blessed are those who have not seen and yet believe' (20:29).

b. To Convert Non-Christians

Some scholars hold that this Gospel had as one of its aims the conversion of Hellenistic Jews and of intelligent pagans who were concerned about the true way of salvation. Such a purpose would be in harmony with one way of reading 20:31 (see above) and may have been included in the author's objective.

Author, Place of Writing, and Original Readers

About AD 180 Irenaeus ascribed authorship of this Gospel to the Apostle John in these words: 'John, the disciple of the Lord, who also reclined on his bosom, published his gospel, while staying at Ephesus in Asia.' Debate has raged over the accuracy of this statement by Irenaeus. Did John the Apostle publish (surely meaning write and publish) our Fourth Gospel while living at Ephesus? Several answers have been given.

1. *Irenaeus was confused and inaccurate.* Its author was neither John the Apostle nor did this Gospel originate in Ephesus. In fact, who the author was is no longer recoverable and it is more likely that it originated in Syria (or possibly Alexandria) than at Ephesus.

Liberal scholars who hold this view argue that the Gospel's internal evidence makes John the son of Zebedee's authorship impossible. Note: the striking differences between the Fourth Gospel and the first three (see p. 257); the speculative and sophisticated theology of the Gospel of John (see pp. 254–6), which would do credit to a Hellenistic philosopher and is inexplicable as coming from an 'uneducated Galilean' (Acts 4:13); the uncertainty whether the Gospel actually means to identify the Beloved Disciple with John the son of Zebedee and to attribute the writing of the Gospel to him; the evidence that this Gospel was little recognized in the early part of the second century and may, in fact, have arisen from traditions preserved by early Gnostic Christians, probably in Syria, rather than from so illustrious a person as the Apostle John; and the tradition in the church, dating to the fifth to ninth centuries, that both James and John were killed early by Jews (as may be suggested in Mark 10:39 and certainly happened to James in AD 44 – Acts 12:2).

Against Irenaeus' claim of the Apostle's residence in Ephesus is the fact that Papias (about AD 140) mentions an Elder John who lived there, whom Irenaeus probably confused with the Apostle John.

2. *The author of the Gospel was not John the Apostle but a disciple of the Apostle,* who put the witness and teaching of the Apostle into his own cultivated idiom and literary form and credited his teacher as the authority for what he recorded. This may have been done at Ephesus. Irenaeus thus was not wholly wrong in his ascription of the Gospel to the Apostle John at Ephesus.

These scholars point out that ancient teachers gathered around them disciples to whom they committed their recollections and teachings and who carried on their thought and influence after their death. In this case, it would be natural for this disciple to refer lovingly to his great teacher as 'the disciple whom Jesus loved' and to issue the book in his name and under the teacher's authority (see p. 320).

If the recollections of the Apostle lie behind this book but were transposed into a higher key by a disciple, this process would account for certain Hebrew and Palestinian elements in the book (knowledge of Jewish customs and Palestinian geography), some similarities in language and thought to the Dead Sea Scrolls, its apparent independence from the Synoptic tradition, its preservation of some authentic data not in the Synoptic Gospels (such as the date of the Last Supper – 18:28; 19:14) and allow at the same time for its unique elements (speculative and sophisticated theology, etc.). This disciple may have lived at Ephesus and published the book there.

One scholar (C.K. Barrett) suggests that the Apostle John had several disciples: one wrote the book of Revelation; another (possibly two) wrote the Johannine epistles; and yet another ('a bolder thinker and one more widely read both in Judaism and Hellenism') wrote the Fourth Gospel – except for chap. 21.

3. *Conservative scholars put weight on Irenaeus' and other early writers' testimony affirming authorship by John the Apostle at Ephesus.* They contest the accuracy of the late tradition regarding the early death of John and reject the possibility of a different John at Ephesus (the Apostle and Elder are the same person). They believe that the Gospel clearly identifies John the Apostle as the Beloved Disciple and as the author of the book. They stress the suitability of the Hebraic and Palestinian elements for John's authorship, point out certain 'eyewitness' details in the narratives, refute the claim that John was 'uneducated,' and reconcile the differences between John's Gospel and the Synoptics by suggesting that Jesus' approach in his Galilean proclamation (as reflected in the Synoptics) was different from that in controversies with religious leaders in Jerusalem. In general, they follow B.F. Westcott's view that the author was a Jew, a Palestinian, an eyewitness, a disciple of Jesus, and the Apostle John.

Other views have been advanced, such as that John Mark was the authority behind the Fourth Gospel and the Beloved Disciple was Lazarus; but they have not been widely accepted. On the whole, the second position above seems to do justice to the tradition of authorship by the Apostle John and to the striking differences between this Gospel and the Synoptic Gospels that cry out for explanation. It also takes account of the kind of relationship that seems to have existed between teachers and disciples at that time.

Date of Writing

The discovery of an early papyrus fragment of the Gospel of John (Papyrus Rylands Gk. 457 [known as Papyrus 52], containing John 18:31–33, 37–38, dating to about AD 135–50, and of Egyptian origin) seems to require a date around the end of the first century for this Gospel. (See p. 374.) If the papyrus was written in Ephesus, one would assume about a generation for its wide dissemination in Egypt.

If the author of the Gospel of John meant to encourage faith in Christians who were threatened with excommunication from synagogues in the Gentile world, the date may be as early as AD 80–90, or slightly later (90–100), a time when such pressure was acute.

The Acts of the Apostles

We pointed out in the discussion of the Gospel according to Luke that the Acts of the Apostles is volume 2 of a two-volume work, commonly known as Luke-Acts. The summary of the contents of volume 1 and the mention of Theophilus in Acts 1:1, plus the style, thought, and obvious purposes of the two volumes, make this clear.

In the second century, volume 2 was separated from volume 1 (the Gospel according to Luke). The latter was classed with the three other books of its type, and the four Gospels came as a group into early canonical lists. The Acts obviously belonged to a different category of literature and contained different subject matter. It was associated in early New Testament manuscripts with the Catholic (General) Epistles or with the Pauline Epistles.

Its present position is most fitting, for it shows how the work of Jesus continued after his death and resurrection in the spread of the church 'to the end of the earth.' And it makes understandable the letters of Paul and the other New Testament letters to the scattered churches.

Importance

The Acts has been called Christianity's 'Hall of Fame.' Here is the absorbing story of history-making events, centered in heroes of the faith who established the church in both the Jewish and Gentile worlds. Without this narrative we would have only scattered information, chiefly from the letters of Paul, about one of the most dynamic and creative movements of human history. It is the only bridge we possess between Jesus and Paul, between the gospel *of* Jesus and the gospel *about* Jesus, between the informal fellowship of disciples who gathered around Jesus and the sturdy organization called the church that sank deep roots in the soil of the first-century world.

Theme and Outline

Theme: The universal Christian church came into being through the heroic, Spirit-filled witnessing of Jesus' disciples to Jews and Gentiles concerning the power of God which is redemptively active in the world through the crucified and resurrected Jesus.

The Egnatian Way, famous Roman road traveled by Paul.

Outline

The Preface (1:1–2)

The establishment of the church in Jerusalem through the disciples' witnessing (1:3—8:3)
The preparation for witnessing (1:3—2:13)
The witnessing of Peter, John, and all the apostles and the establishment of the church through persecution (2:14—5:42)
The witnessing and the persecution of the Hellenist (Greek-speaking) Christians (6:1—8:3)

The establishment of the church in Samaria and Judea through the disciples' witnessing (8:4—11:18)
The witnessing of Philip in Samaria and the coastland (chap. 8)
The preparation of Saul for Christian witnessing (9:1–31)
The witnessing of Peter in Lydda, Joppa, and Caesarea and its sequel in Jerusalem (9:32—11:18)

The establishment of the church in Gentile lands through the witness of the Jerusalem Greek-speaking Christians and of Paul and his associates (11:19—28:31)
The founding of the church in Antioch (11:19–30)
The persecution of the church in Jerusalem and the death of Herod, the persecutor (12:1–25)
The first witnessing mission of Paul (in Cyprus and southern Galatia) and its sequel at the Jerusalem Council (13:1—15:35)
The second witnessing mission of Paul (in lands around the Aegean Sea) (15:36—18:22)
The third witnessing mission of Paul (in Asia, Macedonia, Achaea) and his journey to Jerusalem (18:23—21:16)
Paul's arrest in Jerusalem, the hearings in Caesarea, and his journey to and activity in Rome (21:17—28:31)

This outline is one of several ways of analyzing the contents of the Acts. Some interpreters divide the book into two parts: 'The Acts of Peter' (chaps. 1–12) and 'the Acts of Paul' (chaps. 13–28) or 'From Jerusalem to Antioch' (chaps 1–12) and 'From Antioch to Rome' (chaps. 13–28). Others find five or more divisions and

some none at all. The outline above takes as its clue Acts 1:8.

Theology

The word 'witness,' both as a noun and as a verb, is very prominent in this book. The theme of the Acts appears first in Luke 24:46–49, where it says that the disciples are witnesses of the fact and of the redemptive significance of the death and resurrection of Jesus. 'Clothed with power from on high,' they are to preach 'repentance and forgiveness of sins ... in his name to all nations.'

According to Acts 5:29–32, this is precisely the role Peter and his associates fulfilled as 'witnesses' to Israel. Throughout the Acts, testimony to the fact and the meaning of the Resurrection is (or is to be) offered by witnesses (1:22; 2:32, 40; 3:15; 4:33; 5:30–32; 10:39–42; etc.). Included also is witnessing to the God-anointed ministry of Jesus (10:38–39; *cf.* 1:21–22).

From these references we may conclude that a witness is one who has *seen* certain events. But he is also one who *explains* the meaning of the events he has seen. He speaks of both happenings and meanings. He is thus a kind of prophet (10:41–43).

In the Acts the term 'witness' is used also for Paul, who had seen and heard the heavenly, not the earthly, Jesus (22:15; 26:16). Sometimes the prophets (10:43), God (14:3; 15:8), the Holy Spirit (20:23), the Council (the Sanhedrin – 22:5), the Jews (26:5), and even the enemies of the faith (6:13; 7:58) are said to be witnesses. Basically the term is a legal one, meaning one who testifies (usually at a trial), on the basis of personal knowledge and experience, to the truth of something. In another usage in the church (Heb. 12:1; 1 Tim. 2:6) the term came to mean one who testified to the truth of the faith by sacrificing his life, that is, a martyr.

Many sermons in the Acts set forth the early testimony about Jesus, especially about his resurrection. These follow a somewhat common pattern, similar to Old Testament creedal recitals (such as

Part of the impressive Roman aqueduct at Caesarea. The city was founded by Herod the Great, and after AD 6 became the Roman capital.

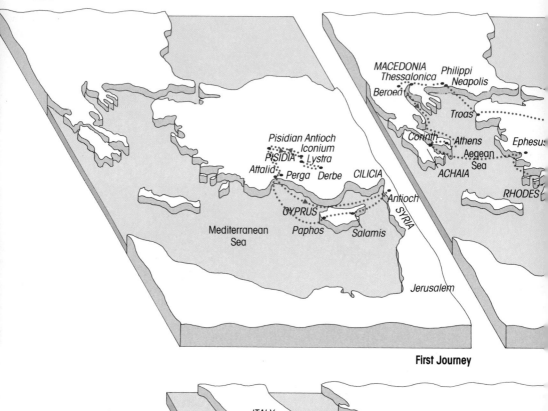

First Journey

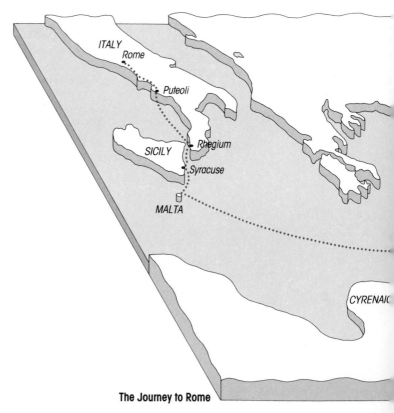

The Journey to Rome

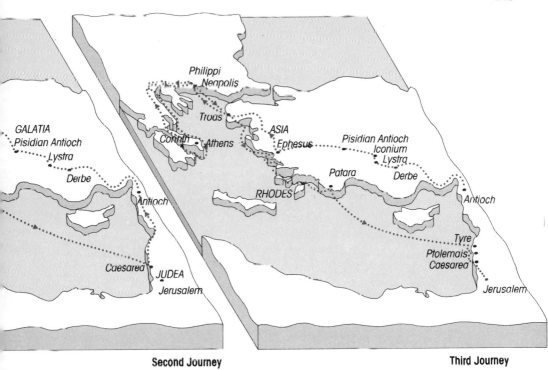

Second Journey

Third Journey

Paul's Missionary Journeys

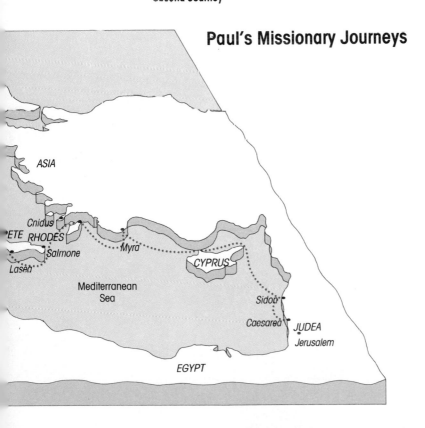

The Forum, Rome.

Deut. 26:5–9; Josh. 24:2–13) which recount God's acts in the redemption of his people. Early Christian preaching stressed God's redemptive activity and showed how it culminated in Jesus (Acts 13:16–41).

At least three major emphases occur in these sermons:

a. Jesus' death, resurrection, and exaltation are the deeds of God, who worked through the deeds of wicked people, in fulfillment of Old Testament prophecy concerning the redemption of Israel and the nations.

b. The resurrected, exalted Jesus is both Lord (Sovereign Master) and Christ (God's anointed King of the New Age and judge of all nations).

c. In view of the rejection and crucifixion of Jesus, people should repent, accept Jesus as Savior in baptism, receive the gift of the Holy Spirit, and inherit God's promise of the New Age.

Sometimes, perhaps particularly for Gentile audiences, the witnesses included facts of Jesus' career (10:36–39).

The Acts tells us that the witnessing was carried out in the power and under the direction of the Holy Spirit. The book's title might properly be 'The Acts of the Holy Spirit Through the Apostles.' The Holy Spirit was God's gift poured out on the disciples by the exalted Jesus (2:33), usually in an experience of prayer (Luke 3:21–22; Acts 1:14; 2:1 ff; 4:31; 8:15) but sometimes through baptism (2:38), often through the laying on of hands (8:12–17; 9:17–18; 19:2–6) or simply during the proclamation of the gospel (10:44–48). Receiving the Holy Spirit was an event which occurred more than once (2:1 ff.; 4:31). The Spirit was God's gift to every Christian.

The Holy Spirit's presence in believers resulted in miraculous achievements, such as speaking in tongues (2:1 ff.; 10:46) and healings (5:12–16; cf. 10:38); courage and wisdom for witnessing (1:8; 4:8 ff., 31; 13:9); knowledge of future events (11:28; 20:23); guidance in decision-making (8:29; 10:19–20; 15:28; 16:6–8); moral and spiritual fruits in personal life (6:5; 9:31; 11:24; 13:52; 15:8–9); and brotherly sharing in the church (2:44–46; 4:32–35).

Prayer was the means by which God's guidance and power came to the church. The first Christians prayed in many circumstances: while awaiting the fulfillment of Jesus' promise concerning the coming of the Holy Spirit and of the New Age (1:14), when threatened by enemies or suffering at their hands (4:23–31; 12:12; 16:25), when confronted by the sickness and death of others (9:40; 28:8), when concerned about the spiritual needs of others (8:15), when parting from fellow Christians (20:36; 21:5), when selecting or commissioning persons for special service (1:24; 6:6; 13:3; 14:23), when facing martyrdom at the hands of persecutors (7:59–60). They prayed also at the set time and places of prayer (3:1; 6:4; 10:9). They prayed in homes (1:13–14; 12:12), in the temple (2:46; 3:1; 22:17–21), in jail (16:25), on the seashore (21:5), on shipboard (27:35). They prayed for the Holy Spirit for themselves and others, for guidance in choices, for courage in the face of opposition, for deliverance from danger, for the welfare of friends, for power to do the humanly impossibly, for God's help for people given special responsibility in the church, for forgiveness of enemies.

Purposes

On the historical, apologetic, and evangelistic purposes of Luke-Acts, see the discussion on pp. 251–2.

Sources

The question of the sources of the Acts is particularly difficult. Investigators have sought a solution in two directions:

a. Written Sources

Some have regarded Acts 1:1b—15:35 as a translation into Greek of an Aramaic document, done by the author of 15:36—28:31. They hold that he wrote this latter part from personal knowledge. Others

Model of Jerusalem in New Testament times; Herod's Temple is in the foreground.

have thought that three or more written sources lie behind chaps. 1–15, these sources having come from Jerusalem, Antioch, and Caesarea.

The unexplained appearance of 'we' in sections of the latter half of the Acts (16:10–17; 20:5–15; 21:1–18; 27:1—28:16) and the similarity of this material to a diary or intinerary have led some to conclude that a travel narrative, written by the author of Luke-Acts or by someone else, was the source of this portion of the book.

b. Oral Sources

Form criticism (see p. 229) has led some scholars to conclude that underlying the Acts are no written sources but only pieces of oral tradition. The author of the Acts put these pieces together. He formed a framework of narrative for them and put his own stamp of thought and style on them. He may have used his own written notes for such events as he had personal knowledge of. But he had no lengthy,

written documents from which to write.

It is likely that the many speeches of the Acts are summaries in the author's own language – not stenographic reports – of what he had been told or believed was said on the various occasions.

Authorship, Original Readers, Date, Place of Composition

See the discussion of the Gospel according to Luke, pp. 252–3.

Historical Accuracy

We shall forever be in debt to the author of Luke-Acts for gathering together information from many sources about the founding and spread of early Christianity. During those feverish and uncertain first days, few persons, if any, could have had much interest in, or even thoughts about, the preservation of exact records.

What we have in the Acts, particularly in chaps. 1–15, is more or less isolated,

Roman tombs line part of the Appian Way, outside Rome.

fragmentary, and disconnected pieces. But they are of great historical worth. The author's purposes and his language and style shaped their present form, to be sure, as they did the material he used in the writing of his Gospel.

It is plain that there are differences in fact and point of view between the material in the Acts and in the letters of Paul. For example, the Acts has Paul in Jerusalem twice before the Jerusalem Council (9:26–30; 11:27–30), whereas Paul himself states flatly he was there only once (Gal. 1:18—2:10). It is possible that Acts 11:27–30 and Acts 15 refer to the same journey and should not have been separated by the author of the Acts. And the picture of the nature of Paul's contacts with the Jerusalem Christian leaders on his first return to that city presents differences (in Gal. 1:18–24 private talks with Peter and James only; in Acts 9:26–30 contact with 'the apostles' and a public ministry there). There are some important differences in the theology of Paul as represented in the Acts and in his letters.

But the Acts is certainly not 'historical fiction rather than history,' as some have claimed. The author is more than 'a fascinating narrator' who wove together an entertaining story of Christian beginnings. His interest in dates, places, official terminology, customs, local color, and the like gives substance to his claim that he wished to write both accurately and in an orderly fashion and that he had a deep regard for the truth (Luke 1:3–4).

The Letters of Paul

Twenty-one books of the New Testament are in the form of letters. Of these, thirteen are expressly ascribed to Paul in their opening greeting:
Romans
1 and 2 Corinthians
Galatians
Ephesians
Philippians
Colossians
1 and 2 Thessalonians
1 and 2 Timothy
Titus
Philemon

Almost all manuscripts of Paul's letters from the fourth century on include another biblical book – Hebrews. Its text does not claim authorship by Paul or by anyone else. Though in some respects it resembles Paul's letters, in others it differs widely from them and almost surely came from some other writer (see p. 332).

The letters ascribed to Paul in most Greek manuscripts of the fourth century and later, as in our modern translations, are arranged according to their recipients and their length. Letters to churches come first, from the longest (Romans) to the shortest (2 Thessalonians). Next are the letters to individuals, again from the longest (1 Timothy) to the shortest (Philemon). The anonymous Hebrews comes as an appendix.

Since the early nineteenth century many scholars have challenged Paul's authorship of the Pastoral Epistles (1 and 2 Timothy and Titus) on the ground that the historical facts, the style, the language, and the theology in them make Paul's authorship impossible and point rather to a disciple of Paul. Some argue that genuine fragments by Paul may be included in them. The question about authorship and sources is still open (see pp. 320–22).

Some influential present-day scholars assign other letters to a disciple or disciples of Paul: Ephesians, Colossians, 2 Thessalonians. Here the variation from Paul's quite certainly authentic letters – 1 Thessalonians, 1 and 2 Corinthians, Galatians, Philippians, Philemon, and Romans – is considerably smaller than from the Pastoral Epistles. Consequently, other investigators staunchly defend Paul's authorship of Ephesians, Colossians, and 2 Thessalonians.

Computer research on the text of the letters traditionally assigned to Paul has led some to believe that even 1 Thessalonians, Philippians, and Philemon were not written by Paul. This would leave as authentic only Romans, Galatians, and 1 and 2 Corinthians. However, the computer method of studying the text has built-in limitations, and the results may not be accurate.

We may say by way of summary that Paul quite certainly wrote the following: Romans, 1 and 2 Corinthians, Galatians, Philippians, 1 Thessalonians, Philemon. To these we may add, with less certainty, Ephesians, Colossians, 2 Thessalonians. More question exists about the Pastoral Epistles. They may contain authentic fragments from Paul. Or it may be a disciple wrote all of them in the name of his admired teacher.

Conservative scholars accept without much question Paul's authorship of all the letters except the Pastorals. Here they admit the difference in style and content from Paul's other letters but explain them as due to several factors: the different addressees (individual persons rather than churches); a different subject matter (the duties of church officers, a subject not addressed in the other letters); a different period in Paul's life; a different amanuensis (secretary), who may have modified sentence structure, vocabulary, and grammar. But since the letter would have been read back to the author for approval, it would carry his sanction and authority. 'Nonsense is thus made of computerized methods of determining authorship' (E.M. Blaiklock).

Paul's letters follow in general the form of the letters of his day, as known to us from thousands of papyrus letters found in Egypt since the end of the nineteenth century. Paul's form consists of an opening greeting, a thanksgiving/blessing and a prayer for the readers, the message itself (including moral exhortation), closing greetings, and benediction. He often inscribed the greetings and benediction in his own handwriting (1 Cor. 16:21–24; Gal. 6:11–18; Col. 4:18; 2 Thess. 3:17–18). His handwriting served to authenticate the letter.

Paul's letters are neither personal letters nor literary epistles. Even Philemon and the Pastorals (if regarded as Paul's) were meant to be read and used by the churches (Philem. 2; cf. the plurals in 1 Tim. 6:21; 2 Tim. 4:22; Titus 3:15). Literary epistles were addressed to the general public. Paul had specific readers in mind – individual churches or groups of churches – with specific problems and needs. He intended his letters to be read aloud in the public worship of the churches addressed, and sometimes they were to be exchanged with other churches (1 Thess. 5:27; Col. 4:16).

His letters contain authoritative preaching, teaching, and exhortation. They come close to being sermons or addresses. Paul's purpose was to convey to the church the divine will for the edification of believers.

Several Pauline letters – Ephesians, Philippians, Colossians, and Philemon – form a group known as 'The Prison (or Captivity) Epistles.' This name arose because the letters themselves place their author in prison at the time of writing (Eph. 3:1; 4:1; 6:20; Phil. 1:7, 13; Col. 4:3, 10, 18; Philem. 1, 9, 23). If the Pastoral Epistles were written by Paul, 2 Timothy also belongs in this category (1:8, 17; 2:9).

From evidence in the letters many scholars have concluded that Ephesians, Colossians, and Philemon were written at the same time and sent with Tychicus (Eph. 6:21; Col. 4:7) and Onesimus (Col. 4:9; Philem. 10). Philippians was written at another time – and also 2 Timothy, if Paul's.

There is disagreement concerning the place of the writing of the Prison Epistles. Paul was in prison many times (2 Cor. 6:5; 11:23; seven times, according to 1 Clement 5:6). The most likely places are Rome (Acts 28:16, 20); Caesarea (Acts 23:35; 24:23, 27), and Ephesus (1 Cor. 15:30–32, 2 Cor. 1:8–10). Many arguments are possible in support of each place for all or some of the four (or five) letters, but no firm conclusion is possible now. Fortunately, the exact place of writing of these letters is not particularly important for interpreting them.

For Further Reading

Doty, W. G., *Letters in Primitive Christianity*, 1973.
Keck, L. E. and Furnish, V. P., *The Pauline Letters*, 1984.
Martin, R. P., *New Testament Foundations*, Vol. II, 1978.
Meeks, W. A., *The Writings of St. Paul*, 1972.

Romans

suggested that it would be well worth memorizing, so that it could be recited word for word.

The impact of Romans on the church through the centuries has been profound. Its effect on Augustine, Luther, Calvin, Wesley, and Karl Barth, and on the history-changing theological movements stemming from them, has led to its recognition as undoubtedly the most important theological book ever written.

Martin Luther wrote in his preface to Romans that this book is 'rightly the chief part of the New Testament' and that it contains 'the clearest gospel of all.' He

The Message

The letter to the Romans contains a carefully formulated statement of Paul's total message, a message that appears in pieces,

Outline

Theme:
The gospel – the power of God for salvation of everyone who has faith

Introduction (1:1–17)
Greeting (a brief summary of the gospel) (1:1–7)
Thanksgiving and explanations (1:8–15)
Theme (1:16–17)

Body (1:18—15:13)
The world's need of salvation (1:18—3:20)
1. The need of the Gentiles (1:18–32)
2. The need of the Jews (2:1—3:20)

The way of salvation and its validity (3:21—4:25)
1. Faith in Jesus Christ, whom God sent to take away human sin (3:21–31)
2. Old Testament proof that salvation is by faith alone (4:1–25)

The consequences of salvation through faith in Jesus Christ (5:1—8:39)
1. From wrath and death to reconciliation and life (5:1–21)
2. From the old life of sin and bondage to the new life of righteousness and service of God (6:1–23)
3. From the Law and the sin it incites to freedom in Christ (7:1–25)
4. From fleshly existence to life in the Spirit and final salvation (8:1–39)

Jews and Gentiles in God's purpose of salvation (chaps. 9–11)
1. Jewish rejection of the gospel in the light of God's sovereignty (9:1–29)
2. Jewish rejection in the light of human freedom (9:30–10:21)
3. The fulfillment of God's saving purpose for both Jews and Gentiles through the Remnant (chap. 11)

The ethical responsibilities of those who are being saved (12:1–15:13)
1. Total dedication to God in the life of love inside and outside the church (chap. 12)
2. Loyal citizenship in the state while awaiting the time of final salvation (chap. 13)
3. Mutual helpfulness, not censorious conflict, in acting out one's convictions (14:1–15:13)

Conclusion (15:14—16:23)
Paul's right to counsel the Romans (15:14–21)
His plans for the immediate future (15:22–29)
His request for their prayers (15:30–33)
Personal commendation, greetings, and warnings (16:1–23)

Doxology (16:25–27)

Coin of the Roman emperor Nero.

often illogically arranged, in his other letters.

The key to the contents of the letter is Rom. 1:16–17. The subject of the letter is 'the gospel,' the good news concerning God's Son (1:3), which has power to bring salvation to everyone (Jew and Gentile) who responds in faith.

'Salvation' means one's becoming righteous (that is, being put into right relationship with God) through God's righteousness (that is, God's faithful, loving, redeeming activity in Jesus Christ). The gospel reveals to people this redemptive activity and the salvation offered to them, if they respond in faith (acceptance, trust, obedience).

Paul's starting point is that people are not in right relationship with God (1:18—3:20). The gospel reveals, first of all, the tragic plight of the human race: human-kind's guilt before God and the present and future doom.

The Gentiles (1:18–32) cannot plead ig-norance of God, for they have seen, in the wonders of creation, God's everlasting power and Godness (that is, that God is God and not creature). But they did not receive this knowledge in gratitude and act on it; they refused to recognize and worship God as God and worshiped what was created rather than the Creator. Their idolatry has led to a revolting sensuality

and to antisocial attitudes and acts. At the lowest stage of depravity, they actually applaud the doing of evil. They stand under God's wrath (punishment, shown in the progressive spiritual and moral de-gradation of humankind) and under his sentence of death (present and future sep aration from God).

The Jews (2:1—3:20) also have know-ledge of God. In addition to the revelation offered in nature, they have the Law of Moses and the Holy Scriptures ('the ora-cles of God' – 3:2). Of these they are jus-tifiably proud, and on the basis of them they claim the right to be teachers of humankind. They condemn the Gentiles for their idolatry and immorality. But per-versely and hypocritically, many Jews in-dulge in the very things they condemn in the Gentiles: stealing, adultery, sacrilege (or temple-robbing – 2:22). Their hearts are proud and stubborn; they are self-cen-tered and committed to wrongdoing. The covenant-mark on their bodies (circumci-sion) gives them no special standing be-fore God, who requires inner dedication and inner goodness, rather than outer cor-rectness. They too stand under God's judgment, for God treats all people alike.

In short, all people are sinners. They have rebelled against the God who is re-vealed in various ways: in the created order, in the inner light (2:15), and in the Scriptures. All live under the power of sin (3:9), and all are guilty before God.

But God has provided in Jesus Christ a way for guilty, alienated people to come into right relationship with himself (3:21–31). This way is not by earning acceptance through obedience to the Law, which no one can keep and which serves to reveal one's sin rather than to break its power (3:20). It is the way of faith (trust) in God's gracious, saving work in Jesus Christ. God does for people what they cannot do for themselves and asks only for their grateful response. Their freedom and new relationship flow from Christ Jesus' sacrificial death, which God made a means of taking away their sin and guilt. Since the new relationship comes from

Detail from the Arch of Titus, Rome, commemorating the capture of Jerusalem.

God's act, gratitude, not boasting in human achievement, is the appropriate attitude of the believer.

The consequences of trust in God's saving act in Jesus Christ are far-reaching (5:1—8:39). Believers have a new status before God. They enjoy the divine favor, have peace, are reconciled. They have a new spirit. They exult in their hope and in their sufferings. They have a new knowledge: that suffering has blessed results. They have a new self: the Holy Spirit and God's love within. They are participants in a new humanity. They are freed from the realm of sin and death, introduced by Adam, to a new order of right relations with God and new life, introduced by Jesus Christ.

They have a new kind of life under a new master. They no longer serve sin and the Law and earn wretchedness and death as their pay, but they experience a new quality of existence, serve God and righteousness, and receive the gift of eternal life. They at last escape the power of sin, which has the Law as its agent and the flesh as its host, and are introduced to life in the Spirit, a life pleasing to God, as befits the children of God. As children of God they are heirs of a glorious future, which no hostile power in the universe can prevent them from obtaining.

Who is going to participate in this glorious future? Will it include both Jews and Gentiles (chaps. 9–11)? The hard fact is that most Jews have rejected the good news that right relation with God comes through faith in Jesus Christ. Does this mean that God is going to fail to bring about the salvation of the chosen people? Emphatically, no! The rejection by the majority of the Jews is to be seen in the light of the divine selectivity that has always been at work in Israel, by which God preserved a faithful remnant, a remnant useful for God's purpose of salvation for all (9:1–29). But Jewish rejection can also be attributed to the Jews' free choice: having heard the gospel of salvation by faith in Jesus Christ, they preferred salvation by works (9:32; 10:3). Their zeal for God was misguided (10:2). They stand condemned (10:21).

Yet God brings good results out of people's evil decisions. Jewish rejection led to the preaching of the gospel to the Gentiles, and that in turn will lead to the ultimate salvation of the Jews. When the Jews see the Gentiles becoming heirs of the promises made to Abraham, they will desire to be included too and will turn to Christ in faith. Thus God's merciful plan for both Jews and Gentiles will be accomplished (11:11–32).

The new life in Christ determines the character of one's existence in the church and in the world (12:1—15:13). Right relations with God and others require total surrender of one's self to God and learning and doing God's will.

God's will is that we love one another in the church (12:3–13), and even our enemies (12:14–21), and live as responsible citizens of the state (13:1–10). Love, furthermore, requires consideration of those whose convictions differ from our own (14:1—15:13). The Christian is not to be pleased but to please God and neighbor (14:3; 15:1–2). 'Walking in love' (14:15) glorifies God and builds up the church. By such conduct children of the day await the coming of the Day (13:11–14).

Original Contents

The precise contents of the original letter are in some doubt, because of the following facts:

a. Some ancient manuscripts omit the words 'in Rome' in 1:7, 15.

b. In some manuscripts the Grace ("The grace of our Lord Jesus Christ be with you") occurs twice (16:20, 24), as in the King James Version; but in others it is found only once (either in 16:20 or 16:24),

The Church at the Close of Paul's Ministry
c. 65 AD

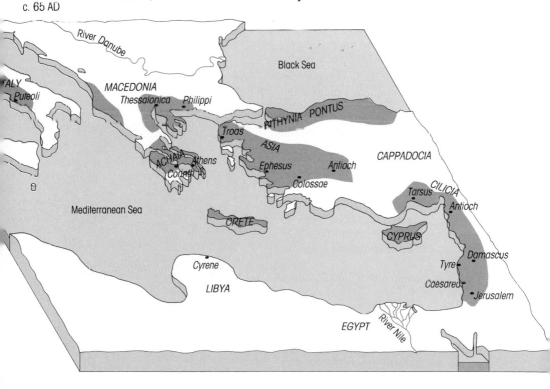

as in the Revised Standard Version (at 16:20).

c. The doxology (16:25–27) appears in different places in ancient manuscripts: at the end of chap. 16; after 14:23 (and sometimes also at the end of chap. 16); after 15:33; and once is omitted altogether.

d. The many personal greetings in 16:1–23, in a letter to a church (Rome) where Paul had never been, call for an explanation. Prisca and Aquila were in Ephesus shortly before the writing of this letter (1 Cor. 16:19). Epaenetus' original home was Asia, probably Ephesus, not Rome (Rom. 16:5).

e. The doxology (16:25–27) seems to contain un-Pauline words and ideas.

It is difficult to account for these facts. Two major hypotheses have appeared, but neither has yet won general acceptance:

1. *Paul's original letter to the Romans was 1:1—16:23.*

Prisca and Aquila could have returned to Rome, where they formerly had lived (Acts 18:2); and Epaenetus and the other friends and acquaintances of Paul, mentioned in Rom. 16, may have moved to the capital city over a period of several years. Col. 4:10ff., written to a church where Paul had never been, shows that he made use of personal contacts for his advantage.

The doxology in 16:25–27 is a second-century addition, composed to fit after 14:23. From Origen's writings, in the third century, it appears that the heretic Marcion (middle of the second century) abbreviated Romans at 14:23 for doctrinal reasons. A doxology was thus needed to conclude the letter. In some manuscripts this doxology became attached also to 16:23. Marcion's mutilation of the letter may have included the deleting of 'in Rome' in 1:7, 15.

2. *Paul's original letter to the Romans consisted of chaps. 1–15.* This, of course, contained the words 'in Rome' in 1:7, 15.

Because of the suitability of this letter for other churches as well (see below), Paul sent a copy to the church at Ephesus without the words 'in Rome.' He added to

this the material in 16:1–23. Phoebe of Cenchreae (near Corinth) may have carried this letter to Ephesus (16:1–2). The friends of Paul mentioned were thus residents of Ephesus, where Paul had spent nearly three years.

Marcion cut off chaps. 15 and 16. The doxology of 16:25–27 was first added to Marcion's shortened text (after 14:23) and later placed after 16:23.

The earliest manuscript of the letters of Paul now known (Papyrus 46, about A.D. 200), in placing the doxology after 15:33, lends support to this second view.

Other hypotheses exist, such as that chap. 16 came from (or comprises) an altogether separate letter of Paul's and was added to Rom. 1—15 by the first editor of Paul's letters. This is less likely than the two hypotheses above.

Occasion and Purpose

Paul apparently was at Corinth when he wrote Romans. He was about to leave for Jerusalem with the collection for the

Roman lamp showing a ship leaving harbor.

Jerusalem church (15:25–27). He was apprehensive about the trouble he might face there (15:31) and wished he could go west to Rome and Spain rather than east to Jerusalem (15:23–24, 28, 32). Acts 20:2–4 gives the general setting and lists his companions for the eastward journey.

Why he wanted to go to Rome and why he wrote this letter have been much debated. Several suggestions can be offered from the text itself. As God's priest for all the Gentile churches (15:16a), he felt special responsibility for the Roman church (11:13; 15:16b), even though he had not founded it. He wanted to impart to it some spiritual gift for its strengthening (1:11), to encourage it through faith-sharing (1:12), and to improve the acceptability before God of its life and service (15:16). He also may have desired to help it settle the problem of Gentile-Jew relationships in the church (chaps. 9—11; 14—15). Then, he needed to let the members know of his plans: to go to Jerusalem with the offering (15:25–27, 31), to come to Rome (15:24), and then to go on to Spain (15:24, 28).

In return, he hoped from this renowned church (1:8) personal acquaintance and fellowship (1:11; 15:24, 32), encouragement from faith-sharing (1:12), and an opportunity to discharge his mission of preaching the gospel and making converts among Roman Gentiles (1:13–15). He wished prayer support for the success of his Jerusalem trip and the journey to Rome (15:30–32) and also some sort of support (moral? personnel? financial?) in his mission to Spain (15:24).

Were there other reasons not evident on the surface? It is possible he wished by this letter to counteract before his arrival any misunderstanding of his objectives and of the nature of his gospel, in view of the widespread slander directed at him by some fellow Christians and many Jews. Without such clearing of issues, his arrival would be unpleasant, his work in Rome inhibited, and his mission to Spain jeopardized. One scholar (Guenther Bornkamm) has suggested that Romans is

Paul's last will and testament – a summation of his entire teaching at the end of his career – for the church as he faces his departure for Jerusalem and the possibility of death there.

Paul may have felt that the whole church, including the Romans, needed a clearer understanding of the theology of salvation: the relation of the new Christian movement to Judaism and the Old Testament; the proper terms of admission to the church; the status of Jew and Gentile outside and inside the church; God's future for Jew and Gentile; the moral and missionary demands of the new faith; Paul's own place in the purpose of God; and the like. He and others had fiercely debated these matters in the years before the writing of Romans, and he now wished the entire church to understand his hard-won positions. Thus he may have sent copies of this letter to both Rome and Ephesus.

Authorship and Date

Paul's authorship of Romans is undisputed. The date of writing falls somewhere between A.D. 55 and 58, with 56 the most likely year.

1 Corinthians

The letter to the Romans and the first letter to the Corinthians, while they come from the same general period of Paul's life and contain the same mature, masterful theology, are very different in character.

Romans is theology-centered; 1 Corinthians is life-centered or problem-centered. Romans offers us little information about the situation of the Christians in Rome, but 1 Corinthians opens doors and windows through which we may view Corinthian Christians at home, in the marketplace, and in the church.

We find that the Corinthian Christians were living in a culture in many respects like our own, with many of the same temptations and problems. Nowhere else in the New Testament is the tension between the church and the world more apparent. 1 Corinthians is thus uniquely a book for our time.

Contents

1 Corinthians is a string of varied gems, rather than one massive stone with several facets. But whether there is a string at all is debated.

Several unifying themes have been suggested: the Resurrection, the nature of Christian freedom, the place of love in building the church, and, negatively, the refutation of the Gnostic heresy (see below) that infected the Corinthian church. All are important in the letter, but none serves very well as a theme for the whole. To use Paul's own figure of speech (3:1; 14:20), we might formulate the subject as: How to grow from babyhood to maturity in Christ.

Background of the Letter

The author of Luke-Acts places the evangelization of Corinth by Paul, Silvanus, and Timothy on Paul's second missionary journey. His stay in Corinth for about eighteen months (Acts 18:11) probably occurred in A.D. 50–51.

Paul first preached in the synagogue at Corinth, then in a house adjacent to the synagogue. The latter ministry, directed toward Gentile 'God-fearers' (half-proselytes to Judaism), resulted in both conversions and fierce Jewish hostility. A court hearing before the proconsul Gallio, resulting from this hostility, led to a dismissal of the charges (Acts 18:12–17) and some protection for the infant church.

The Christians there were largely Gentiles (1 Cor. 12:2) and mostly from the lower classes (1:26ff.). A few were of higher status (Acts 18:8; 1 Cor. 11:21–22; Rom. 16:23), and some were Jews (Acts

Steps to the *bema* (platform), Corinth, where Paul may have been brought before the pro-consul.

18:4, 8; 1 Cor. 7.18).

Corinth, the capital city of the province of Achaea, strategically situated between two seas, was a bustling commercial city, notorious for sensuality, according to ancient Greek (mostly Athenian) writers. The Roman geographer and traveler Strabo said that the temple of Aphrodite there had one thousand prostitutes who sold themselves in service to the goddess. Recent scholarship has concluded, however, that the picture of Corinth's sensuality was probably overdrawn by ancient writers, due to commercial rivalry between Athens and Corinth, and that Corinth was not a center of sacred prostitution and probably was no more wicked than any other large port city of the first century A.D. But that Paul found the moral atmosphere of Corinth depressing, to say the least, may be reflected in his characterization of human sinfulness in Romans 1:18–32, written while he was in Corinth.

The inhabitants – Romans, Greeks, Orientals – brought with them almost every religion of the Mediterranean world. They worshiped such gods as Jupiter, Aphrodite, Isis, Osiris, Cybele, Attis, Atargatis, and Yahweh of the Jews. The biennial games brought thousands of visitors to Isthmia, an adjacent town.

The church there was subject to many of the pressures of paganism: idolatry and idolatrous feasts, gluttony, lax sexual behaviour, superstition, magic, demonism, religious frenzy, philosophical skepticism, materialism, and social strife.

After Paul left the city and before the composition of our 1 Corinthians, he wrote what is now called 'The Previous Letter,' mentioned in 1 Cor. 5:9. It dealt with the relations of moral and immoral church members at Corinth but was understood – or deliberately misunderstood – by them as having to do with Christians' relations to immoral people outside the church. The poison of paganism was at work in the life of the church. Some scholars have claimed that part of the Previous Letter is now present in 2 Cor. 6:14—7:1 (see pp. 292–3).

When Paul was at Ephesus (on the third missionary journey, according to the Acts), disturbing reports about the condition at Corinth came to him, perhaps from Chloe's household (1 Cor. 1:11). Paul sent Timothy to Corinth by way of Macedonia to deal with the problems there (1 Cor. 4:17; 16:10; Acts 19:22). Whether he arrived, or when, we do not know.

Later the Corinthians Stephanus, Fortunatus, and Achaicus came to Paul (1 Cor. 16:17) with a letter containing specific inquiries (1 Cor. 7:1; 8:1; 12:1 16:1). They described the situation at Corinth in detail and sought help from Paul. They probably carried our 1 Corinthians home with them.

The Problems in the Church at Corinth

Apparently the most serious problem in Paul's eyes – for he treats it first and devotes most space to it – was the disunity of the church. Paul speaks of 'divisions' and 'quarrels' (1:10–11). The Corinthians claimed superiority over one another by virtue of their attachment to different Christian leaders – Paul, Apollos, Peter ('Cephas' is Aramaic for 'rock'), and Christ (1:12). We do not know whether there were four distinct groups, each with a theology supposedly patterned after the views of its leader, or whether individuals were simply being loyal to the person who had baptized them into the faith.

If the groups were clearly defined, what may they have stood for? Perhaps the Paul group stood for salvation by faith alone (*i.e.*, apart from merit through obedience to the Law). Its members believed that faith resulted from the preaching of Jesus, the Messiah, crucified for our sins and raised to put us right with God (Rom. 4:25; 1 Cor. 2:2–5).

The Apollos group may have gloried in that preacher's Greek intellectualism and rhetoric (Acts 18:24–28).

The Peter group may have stressed, to the disadvantage of Paul, Peter's superior rights as an apostle and valued Peter's approval of the observance of the Law by Jewish Christians.

The Christ group may have rejected the exaltation of human leaders and favored life under the direct control of Christ and of the Spirit (*cf.* 2 Cor. 10:7). This group probably wished to have no external controls on conduct.

Those scholars who believe that the squabble over leaders did not really divide the church into separate groups with differing theologies think there was one basic theological error underlying the individual preference for leaders. It consisted in a Gnostic (from a Greek word meaning 'knowledge') interpretation of the gospel. The Gnostics, as we know them in the second century and later, stressed salvation by supernaturally revealed knowledge. This knowledge helped the soul, which had fallen from heaven into the evil world of matter, escape the prison of the flesh. The Gnostics believed that the resurrection, proclaimed as future in Judaism and Christianity, had already occurred in the liberation of a person's spirit through faith in Jesus Christ and that they were already enjoying in its fullness the salvation of the kingdom of God (1 Cor. 4:8). In their 'freedom' many of them fell into immorality. (For further information about the Gnostics see pp. 318–9.) It is true that most, if not all, of the problems treated in 1 Corinthians are more or less explainable in the light of Gnostic-type thinking.

Paul's downgrading of human wisdom (1:17–25; 2:1–5; 3:18–20) implies its glorification by some Corinthians. Their pride in their achievements (4:7–8) forces Paul to humble them (4:9–13, 18–20). Their arrogance over the case of incest in the church (5:1–8) illustrates their imagined freedom from all human regulations, as does their indifference to property rights, their consorting with harlots, and their general hell-raising (chap. 6).

Head of Dionysus, from the mosaic floor of a Roman villa, Corinth.

When spirit and flesh are sharply distinguished and the latter is regarded as an impediment to the former, the problem of marriage becomes acute (chap. 7). Is marriage evil or good?

The 'knowledge' that allowed Christians to eat meat sacrificed to idols and even to participate in feasts in heathen temples (chap. 8), regardless of the effect on less 'enlightened' fellow Christians, fits the Gnostic perspective.

The 'freedom' movement – exhibited by the women in flouting church regulation regarding the covering of their heads (11:2–16), by gluttony at the Lord's table (11:21), by unbridled Spirit-ecstasy in services of worship (chap. 14), and by disbelief in the future resurrection of the body (15:12) – points to this type of thinking.

If we assume that there were four theological groups, we may identify the Christ group as the Gnostic group. It was this group that offered the real danger to the church at Corinth.

Paul's Treatment of the Problems

Disunity (1:1—4:21)
Paul points out that excessive attachment to human leaders arises from a misunderstanding both of the basic nature of Christianity and of the proper function of Christian ministers (1:13—4:13).

The Christian's attachment is to Christ, not to human leaders. Baptism is in Christ's name. In Christianity salvation is obtained neither by ceremonies conducted by special mediators nor through the imparting, however eloquent, of human knowledge or wisdom. Salvation comes by hearing and responding in faith to the story of God's deed for all people in the cross of Jesus Christ, proclaimed in simple language (1:18—2:5). In this message, however, God discloses the true and secret purpose (wisdom) for the redemption and enrichment of humankind in the age to come (2:6–16).

Christian leaders are fellow laborers for God, not rivals (3:1–9). They are builders, accountable to God, whose materials and methods differ and whose work may not be of equal value (3:10–15). They are all cooperating in the plan of God for the good of those to whom they minister; they are not to be gloried in for what they may be individually (3:18–23). They are responsible to God, not to people, for their conduct (4:1–5). Their spirit of humility, suffering, and sacrifice is to be imitated by those whom they serve (4:6–13).

The Case of Incest (5:1–13)
A male member of the Corinthian church had married or was living with his stepmother, a relationship forbidden by both Jews and Gentiles. The church saw nothing wrong with this relationship and may even have gloated over it as an example of the new freedom over the flesh and over rules and regulations that their rebirth to the life of the New Age had brought (4:8).

Paul was horrified both by the relationship and by their attitude. They are to repent, not gloat, and officially remove the man from church membership as a means of his ultimate salvation. By being put outside the church into the world (the realm of Satan), the offender would experience physical suffering and perhaps death at Satan's hands and through this refining experience find salvation at the day of judgment (*cf.* 1 Pet. 4:1).

All evil must be purged from the church because of its corrupting power. Christianity is a way of moral righteousness (right relations). Without morality church members are offensive to God (5:9–13).

Lawsuits Between Church Members (6:1–11)
The church should handle disputes among its members and not air them in Gentile courts. Members wise enough to judge disputes can be found. How inconsistent it is for Christians to be judged by pagans, when Christians are destined to participate with Christ in judging both the world (*cf.* Matt. 19:28; Rev. 20:4) and angels (*cf.* Jude 6; 2 Pet. 2:4)! It would be better to bear the wrong than to go to

court about it. (Nonretaliation to evil-doers is the Christian way of life – cf. Matt. 5:39ff.; 1 Pet. 2:23.) But why should Christians be doing wrong at all? The Christian is called to a righteous life and to membership in the coming kingdom of God.

Union with Prostitutes (6:12–20)

Do not act on the principle 'all things are lawful' in such a way that it leads you into immorality. You must consider the effects of what you do. Is what you do beneficial? Will doing it enslave you? And you must distinguish the areas in which the principle rightly applies. It properly applies to food but not to sexual relations. Sexual union with a harlot will separate you from union with Christ, to whom you properly belong and with whom you will be united in the resurrection life. What Christians do with themselves is important: they are the temple of the Holy Spirit; they are the property of God.

Marriage (chap. 7)

Paul's answer here was specifically requested in the Corinthians' letter (7:1). His counsel falls into two main categories.

1. Counsel for the Unmarried

Celibacy is the best state (vss. 1, 7, 8, 26–27), because the celibate are free to serve the Lord without the distraction of marriage (vss. 34–35) and because of the closeness of the end of the age and its accompanying troubles (vss. 28–31).

But there is no evil in marriage. Marriage is advisable for most people. One should marry if it is necessary for the maintenance of virtue (vss. 2, 9, 36). This applies to the unmarried in general (vss. 1, 8), to widows (vs. 8), and to the engaged (vss. 36–38). Remarriage after the death of a spouse is legitimate if it is to a Christian (vs. 39). God has no set will for all people. Christian persons are free to decide for themselves what they should do (vs. 7).

The reconstructed Stoa of Attalos, Athens.

2. Counsel for the Married
The sexual needs of each partner should be fulfilled within the marriage relationship (vss. 3–5).

Divorce is forbidden on the authority of Christ (vss. 10–11). If the wife separates from her husband, she must remain single or be reconciled to her husband (vs. 11).

In mixed marriages (one partner Christian and the other not), the partners should remain together, if possible, in the hope that the non-Christian may be won to the Christian faith and life (vs. 16). The participation of a non-Christian partner does not make the marriage unclean; in fact, the Christian partner makes the marriage sacred and the children holy (vs. 14). In a mixed marriage, remaining together must be voluntary by both partners (vs. 15).

In the time remaining before the end of the age, let all persons (the unmarried, the married, the uncircumcised, the circumcised, the slave, the free) remain in the status they had at the time of their conversion (vss. 17–24).

Food Offered to Idols (8:1—11:1)
Meat dedicated to gods in sacred rites at temples and then sold in the market for public consumption offered a serious problem for Jews and Christians. It was offensive to Jews because it was associated with the worship of false gods. It had not been slaughtered in the proper way, and the tithe had not been paid on it.

Gentile Christians, though free from these considerations, were likewise bothered by its idolatrous associations. The bold – that is, the 'enlightened' among them – such as the Corinthian Gnostics, who professed knowledge that 'an idol has no real existence' (8:4), ate the food with relish, unconcerned about the feelings of other Christians.

Paul treats the problem at length. Chap. 8 lays down the principle that knowledge, which leads to rights and freedoms, must be controlled by love for others. The unrestricted use of knowledge and the freedoms it offers will inflate the self-esteem of the enlightened, wreck the

The Greek god Apollo.

more conscientious, and ultimately destroy the church.

Chap. 9 illustrates the principle from Paul's own conduct. He has knowledge of his special relation to Christ as an apostle and the rights stemming from it, notably, the right to economic support from his converts for himself and a wife. This right is proved by the precedent of other apostles, by comparison to other fields of labor, by Scripture, and by command of Jesus. But love for others, shown in his desire to share with them the blessings of the gospel, has led Paul to forgo this right and thus to evangelize free of charge. All rights give way before the compelling power of love. Love requires any sacrifice for the sake of the salvation of others. Paul does not insist on exercising his rights, furthermore, because such exercise without discipline might harm his own prospect of final salvation.

Chap. 10 reinforces the principle by an appeal to history (vss. 1–13) and to logic (vs. 14–22). Knowledge, privilege, and the rights they bring may lead to spiritual disaster, as the experience of Israel after the Exodus shows. Though people of great privilege, they fell into immorality and did not inherit the promised land. Furthermore, common sense shows that the kind of boldness that leads to dabbling in idolatrous practices is inconsistent with one's unity with Christ. One cannot be united to Christ and to demons at the same time!

What is sold in the marketplace may be eaten, unless eating it will harm others. Christians should seek the good of their neighbors, not exercise their rights for their own selfish benefit (10:23—11:1).

Disorders in Worship (11:2—14:40)

Some Corinthian women were taking part in church worship (praying and speaking) with unveiled heads (11:2–16). In the culture of Paul's day women of good reputation did not appear in public without a head-covering. This rebellion against custom may have arisen partly out of Paul's teaching about the equality of men and women in Christ (Gal. 3:28) and partly out of Gnostic ways of thinking. Probably these women believed that their experience of the life of the New Age had lifted them above the limitations of the old 'fleshly' order.

Paul uses several arguments to counter this overemphasis on 'freedom,' some of them rather curious to us: that there is a God-ordained order of relationships (in which women are subordinate to men) which must be honored; that the holy angels, present at the worship service as guardians of order, will be offended; that nature, by giving women long hair, favors head-covering; that veiling by women is the universal practice in Christian churches. Paul believed that as long as the present age lasts, the *status quo* in outward human relationships should be maintained (7:17–24), though he did hold that such relationships should be Christianized (see the discussion of the letter to Philemon, pp. 326–8).

The selfishness, gluttony, drunkenness, and divisiveness at the church's sacred meals (11:17–34) were shocking to Paul. Though the Supper was supposed to be in honor of the Lord Jesus, it did not honor him. It was an occasion for self-indulgence rather than an experience of sharing with others.

Paul deals with the situation by recalling the solemn meaning of Jesus' Last Supper with the disciples. At that Supper Jesus indicated that his death would accomplish for them a new relationship with God. He instructed them to observe the Supper in remembrance of his sacrificial act for others. His disciples should seriously examine their attitudes and their behavior in the knowledge that God's judgment falls on those who eat the Supper unworthily.

The Corinthians' confusion about the Holy Spirit's gifts and the use of them in the church is the subject of a long section (12:1—14:40). Paul had said that the Corinthians were well endowed with spiritual gifts (1:5–7), and now we learn that there was bitter controversy over their relative value. Members who possessed the more dramatic gifts (especially speaking in tongues) received high honor, and those with less spectacular gifts were belittled. Exhibitionists in speech were creating bedlam in church meetings, so that outsiders were being repelled by the confusion.

The discussion on gifts runs through several phases:

1. How to test whether people are being moved by the Holy Spirit or some other spirit (12:2–3): do they exalt Jesus as Lord?

2. The character and purpose of the Holy Spirit's gifts (12:4–11): they originated from one source; they are bestowed for the benefit of all; and they are of many types.

3. The relation of members with different gifts to one another (12:12–31): church members, variously endowed, complement one another for the good of the whole body.

4. The general spirit underlying and directing the use of the gifts (chap. 13): love,

God's gift to all Christians, makes all other gifts meaningful and useful.

5. The comparative worth and proper use of the gifts (chap. 14): prophecy ('speaking God's message' – TEV) is of more value than tongues ('the language of ecstasy' – NEB). Since prophecy can be understood by everyone, it builds up the church and converts unbelievers. Christian worship should consist in an orderly use of the gifts for the good of all present.

Disbelief in the Resurrection (Chap. 15)
Disbelief in a final resurrection of the dead apparently had two roots: a high valuation of the human spirit (a piece of divinity which had fallen from a higher realm), and a low valuation of the body (a prison from which the spirit would one day escape). The spirit-flesh dualism rendered the doctrine of the resurrection of the body unnecessary and ludicrous. Furthermore, the belief that in conversion the resurrection of the spirit had already occurred (*cf.* 2 Tim. 2:18) and that the life of the kingdom of God was already being experienced in fullness (1 Cor. 4:8) left no place for a future resurrection.

Paul refutes the disbelief by showing that Jesus' resurrection is supported by Scripture, by the testimony of many witnesses to his post-resurrection appearances, and by the belief and preaching of the church. He affirms that Jesus' resurrection is the ground of the believers' coming resurrection. Jesus is 'the firstfruits of the harvest of the dead' (NEB).

Finally, he clears away some wrong conceptions of resurrection by characterizing the nature of the resurrection body. Since God has an appropriate form of body for all created beings in their particular habitats, he will give us the sort of body appropriate to our new and glorious stage of existence. That existence will not be physical (earthly) but spiritual (heavenly) in character, fashioned after 'the man of heaven' (Jesus Christ). At his coming there will be a transformation of both the living and the dead for life in the final kingdom. Then will be ac-

complished God's final victory over death, sin, and the Law. There is more yet ahead, he says. Life in the kingdom of God has not been experienced in its totality here, as the Gnostics think!

The Collection (16:1–3)
The individual Corinthians are to set aside a sum each week to be paid into a central fund when Paul arrives. Delegates will carry the money to the church in Jerusalem.

Is the Letter a Unity?

Several scholars, because of supposed contradictions between certain sections of 1 Corinthians and seeming roughness in its subject and thought sequence, have supposed that two or more letters of Paul were joined by someone later on to form our 1 Corinthians. It has been thought, for example, that the Previous Letter of 1 Cor. 5:9 is not wholly lost but is to be found preserved in 2 Cor. 6:14—7:1; 1 Cor. 6:12–20; 9:24—10:22; 11:2–34; 15:1–58; 16:13–24. This would make the rest of our 1 Corinthians (1:1—6:11; 7:1—9:23; 10:23—11:1; 12:1—14:40; 16:1–12) the second letter.

Theories that dissect 1 Corinthians into different letters have not convinced most scholars. Our 1 Corinthians is a long letter. Its roughness probably is due to its dictation over a considerable time and to changes in Paul's and the Corinthians' circumstances.

Place of Writing and Date

The letter was written in Ephesus (16:8). It was probably carried to Corinth by Stephanus, Fortunatus, and Achaicus (16:17). The date was mostly likely AD 54.

2 Corinthians

We have in 2 Corinthians the finest statement anywhere in the New Testament about the nature of the Christian ministry. Paul's enemies at Corinth and elsewhere forced him to defend his character and his ministry.

The Situation in the Corinthian Church and Paul's Purpose in Writing

Our 1 Corinthians, for all its helpful content, did not cure the spiritual sickness at Corinth. Neither did Timothy's visit, if he actually arrived there (1 Cor. 4:17; 16:10).

From references in 2 Corinthians we know that Paul journeyed to Corinth from Ephesus to deal with the situation himself, but he failed (1:23—2:1; 13:1–2). On that visit some member of the Corinthian church personally wronged Paul (2:5; 7:12); how we are not told. Not only Paul but the whole church was injured by the act (2:5–8). We may guess that this member – possibly encouraged by some group within the church or by intruders from the outside (see below) – viciously attacked Paul's authority as an apostle.

Paul then returned to Ephesus and wrote a stinging letter to the church in deep anguish of spirit (2:3–4, 9; 7:8, 12). It apparently contained, among other things, demands that the church demonstrate its loyalty to him by disciplining the person who had insulted him (2:5–11; 7:12). Who carried the letter to Corinth we do not know, but it may have been Titus. Some scholars have contended that

Cenchreae, the port for ancient Corinth, was in the middle of this bay.

this letter in large part is contained in 2 Corinthians 10–13, but others think it is entirely lost (see below). After dispatching it, Paul regretted for a time that he had sent it (7:8). But it turned out to be effective (7:8).

If Titus did not take the Severe Letter to Corinth, at some point before Paul left Ephesus he sent Titus to check on the situation there and perhaps to begin the process of collecting the offering for the church in Jerusalem (1 Cor. 16:1–4). Since Paul expected to conduct a mission in Troas on his way to Macedonia, he instructed Titus to meet him at Troas with a report on the Corinthian situation and perhaps with money from the Corinthian collection. Titus did not arrive at Troas as scheduled and Paul, undoubtedly concerned about his safety, as well as about the condition of the church in Corinth, in anxiety of spirit pressed on to Macedonia (2:12–13).

There, probably at Philippi, the two met and Titus reported that the Corinthians had repented of their treatment of Paul, had disciplined the offending person, as Paul had demanded in the Severe Letter, and had reaffirmed their loyalty to him (7:6–16). The letter and Titus' visit had achieved the desired result; the crisis was over. In great relief and thanksgiving Paul wrote our 2 Corinthians (in whole or in part, see below).

Paul then sent Titus back to Corinth with this letter and along with him two unnamed companions who were to attend, before Paul's arrival, to the collecting of the Corinthians' contribution to the offering for the Jerusalem church (8:16–22; 9:3–5).

In addition to expressing his joy over the Corinthians' renewed regard for him (2:6), their reacceptance of his apostolic authority, and the disciplining of the offender by a 'majority' of the church members (2:6), he sought in this letter to clear up remaining causes of misunderstanding among the minority: his seeming insincerity and deceitfulness in his failure to visit Corinth on his way to Macedonia as he had

promised (1:12—2:4); and remaining questions about his credentials as an apostle of Jesus Christ and about the character and conduct of his ministry (2:14—7:3). He wanted also to caution against excessive punishment of the offending brother and to urge complete forgiveness of him and his restoration to the fellowship of the church (2:6–11). Finally, he wished to motivate the Corinthians to speedy and generous giving to the offering for the Jerusalem church.

After dispatching Titus, the two companions, and the letter, Paul remained in the churches of Macedonia for some months. It may be that new and disturbing reports from Corinth prompted him to write another letter (our 2 Corinthians 10–13? see below) to clear the way for his arrival in Corinth (his third visit there). It is evident that he eventually got to Corinth and remained there for some time before going to Jerusalem with the delegation that carried the offering (Acts 20:1–6).

Who Paul's enemies at Corinth were is far from clear. Their pupose, however, is unmistakable: they wanted to discredit Paul as an apostle of Jesus Christ and to advance their own 'superior' claim to authority over the Corinthians. Among their charges against him were: insincerity and inconstancy in regard to promises (1:12, 15–17); deceptiveness and arrogance in his letters (1:13; 10:9–11); lack of proper credentials (3:1); crafty twisting of the truth and thus the preaching of a false gospel (4:2; 12:16); emotional instability (insanity?) (5:13); cupidity and dishonesty in regard to the collection for the Jerusalem church (7:2; 8:20–21; 12:16); ineffective personal presence (in appearance and speech) (10:1, 10; 11:6); boastfulness about his achievements, and possessiveness of missionary territory (10:13–15); deficiency in knowledge (experience) of Christ and in Christian service (11:6, 23); inferiority to other apostles in the church (11:5); lack of love for the Corinthians, as shown by his refusal to accept support from them and his inconsistent acceptance of gifts from other

The Areopagus, Athens, seat of the ancient supreme court.

churches (11:7–11; 12:13); and false claim to apostolic authority (12:12; 13:3).

Paul's criticism of them is no less sharp. They 'trade on the word of God' (2:17 NAB) by accepting financial support (11:12, 20). They commend themselves (10:12, 18) and bolster their pretensions with letters of recommendation (3:1). They apparently boast of knowledge gained through visions and revelations (12:1, 11), of their special relationship to Christ (10:7, 11:23), and of the signs and wonders they perform (12:12). They are proud of their Hebrew origin (11:22). They preach a different Jesus and a different gospel from Paul's (11:4). They operate in missionary territory belonging to other people and take credit for work done by others (10:15–16). They are immoral and do not repent (12:21; 13:2). They are false apostles and servants of Satan (11:13–15), seducers of the church (11:2–4).

These opponents have been variously identified. Some think Paul speaks of two groups here: (1) 'superlative apostles' (11:5; 12:11), perhaps Peter, James and John of the Jerusalem church, and (2) 'false apostles' (11:13), who were sent out as representatives of the 'superlative apostles' into the churches Paul had raised up. Others rightly contend that Paul has in mind here only one group, designated in two ways, as the contexts in which the two terms appear show. Who may they have been? There are three suggestions.

1. They were Jewish Christians who were sent out from Jerusalem with letters of recommendation (3:1) to Judaize the Gentile church and bring it under the authority of the Jerusalem church.

2. They were Jewish-Christian Gnostics, like – if not identical with – those Paul opposed in 1 Corinthians (see p. 280).

3. They were itinerating Jewish-Christian missionaries of a charismatic type, probably with no direct connection with

Jerusalem. They had letters of recommendation from churches where they had served. They emphasized their visions and revelations, performed miraculous deeds, dazzled with their rhetoric, and stressed their conformance to traditional missionary practice (living off the gospel – see p. 284). They tried to discredit Paul and take over his churches. They certainly were Jews (11:22) and proud of it; and, like Paul, they were Hellenized. But they were more philosophical and rhetorical in orientation and training and were self-centered and mercenary in motivation. The weight of evidence favors number 3.

When they entered the church at Corinth is not known, but probably at some time after Paul's second letter to the Corinthians (our 1 Corinthians). They may have provoked the challenge to Paul's authority by some individual on the occasion of Paul's hurried visit to Corinth from Ephesus (2:1, 5–11; 7:12); and they continued to control the thinking of the minority even after the disciplining of the offending member (2:6). The reconciliation Titus reported to Paul was thus not representative of the attitude of the whole church.

When Titus and the two companions returned to Corinth to take up the collection, they apparently found the church in open rebellion against Paul. On hearing the news – from whom we do not know – Paul may have dispatched another severe letter from Macedonia. On the hypothesis that this is in large part contained in 2 Corinthians chapters 10–13, see below.

Paul's Authority and Ministry

2 Corinthians is the most personal of all Paul's letters. Paul did not like to talk about himself, but his enemies forced him to defend his motives and his work. The charges made against him were vicious slander. In his defense he bared his soul in a most intimate way. We learn what it cost Paul to be a faithful minister of Jesus Christ and how he viewed Christian ministry in general.

Theme and Outline

Theme: Paul, a true minister of the New Covenant.

Introduction (1:1–11)
Greeting (1:1–2)
Thanksgiving for God's comfort in affliction (1:3–11)

Body (1:12—13:10)
The recent crisis at Corinth (1:12—7:16)
1. Explanation of his change of travel plans (1:12—2:13)
2. His true ministry as an apostle (2:14—7:3)
3. His joy over reconciliation with the Corinthians (7:4–16)

The collection for the Jerusalem church (chaps. 8–9)
1. The generosity of the Macedonian churches; and the collectors he is sending (chap. 8)
2. Reasons why the Corinthians should give generously to this project (chap. 9)

The defense of his apostolic authority and ministry (10:1—13:10)
1. The charge of face-to-face weakness, and boldness at a distance (10:1–11)
2. The charge that he is overreaching the area of his authority (10:12–18)
3. His 'boasting' versus the boasting of the 'super' (but false) apostles (11:1—12:13)
4. His paternal care for his Corinthian children and their proper preparation for his coming to Corinth (12:14—13:10)

Conclusion (13:11–14)

Paul discusses the Christian ministry in this letter from several standpoints.

a. *Its Authority*
The basis of the Christian ministry is a call from God to live under the new covenant and to serve it. 'It is God who establishes us with you in Christ, and has commissioned us' (1:21). 'The qualification we have comes from God; it is he who has qualified us to dispense his new covenant' (3:5–6 NEB).

The new covenant differs sharply from the old. The old consisted of a written law which condemned people and brought them death (*cf.* Rom. 7:7–11). The new covenant is God's law written in the heart through the life-giving activity of the Holy Spirit (2 Cor. 3:6; *cf.* Rom. 2:28–29).

b. *The Character of a Christian Minister*
Sincerity (pure motives) is a necessary quality (1:12; 2:17). Unacceptable is the double-dealing involved in a hidden No when a Yes is uttered (1:17–18). Shameful, cunning, underhanded ways on the part of those who proclaim the gospel (4:2) do not represent the ever trustworthy God, who faithfully fulfills promises. As there is no duplicity in him or in his Son, Jesus Christ, there can be none in a true minister (1:18–20).

Humility, not boasting, should mark the spirit of the Christian minister. The false apostles boast of their knowledge (11:6), their heredity (11:22), their credentials (3:1), their special relation to Christ (10:7), their achievements (11:23). Self-commendation and boasting are incompatible with the spirit of the gospel (10:12, 17–18). Paul does not like to boast of 'worldly things' but his enemies, by their bragging, have forced him to justify himself (12:11). But if he must, he will boast of his sufferings and weaknesses, for in these God's mighty power is seen (11:30—12:10).

Consideration for the welfare of others is characteristic of the true Christian minister. All of Paul's activities in relation to the Corinthians – his change of plans for his proposed visit to Corinth (1:23—2:3), his severe letter (2:3–4; 7:12), his self-support when evangelizing at Corinth (11:7–11), his bitter sufferings as an apostle (6:4–10; 11:23–29) – were meant to help them, not to enrich himself: 'it is you I want, not your possessions' (12:14 JB).

Forgiveness is the hallmark of Christian ministry. Paul freely forgave the Corinthian man who had wronged him and urged the church there to do likewise (2:5–11).

Unflagging courage and indomitable hope in difficult circumstances reveal the true minister: 'we never lose heart' (4:1 NEB); 'we are often troubled, but not crushed; sometimes in doubt, but never in despair' (4:8 TEV). The servant of God, while suffering temporary afflictions and the daily wasting away of physical life and vitality, knows that his inner life is being renewed constantly (4:16). He knows that the resurrection life of the risen Jesus, at work in him now (4:7–12), points forward to the glory of the final life with God (4:14; 5:1–5). The Holy Spirit within is the guarantee of final victory (5:5).

c. *The Christian Minister's Message*
Paul summarizes it this way: 'For what we preach is not ourselves, but Jesus Christ as Lord, with ourselves as your servants for Jesus' sake' (4:5). Jesus Christ (the Messiah), the risen Lord (Master), who is the likeness of God (4:4), brings to the believer at the new birth a wondrous inner light, dispelling the darkness of unbelief and sin. It is God's light, as real as the light of creation, brought by Christ into the very center of the believer's being, that banishes the prince of darkness and with him the blindness he causes (4:4).

Jesus Christ, the God-given Redeemer, who died for all that he might reconcile them to God, has called his servants to a ministry of reconciliation (5:14–21). The minister's work is the abolition of hostility: one's hostility to God and to one's fellows. Thus the Corinthians and Paul, as God's reconciled children, must open their hearts to each other (6:11–13; 7:2), and the proclamation of God's reconciling activity must go on into unreached lands (10:15–16).

d. *The Glory and Terror of the Christian Ministry*
In spite of all opposition, God leads his apostles in a triumphal procession through the world, and knowledge of God is spread everywhere. The message of Christ's saving work, proclaimed by the apostles, has a double effect: those who reject it are sent farther on the way to death, but those who welcome it are sent

progressively on the way to life. What a staggering responsibility it is to bring people to a decision with such far-reaching and irrevocable consequences! Who is adequate for such a task? Only a divine commission could make one assume this awesome role (2:14–17).

The Question of Unity

The letter has a certain disjointedness, which calls for explanation. The three main parts (chaps. 1–7; 8–9; 10–13) are loosely connected, and the first and second parts have sections that do not fit together well. In part 1, 2:13 is followed naturally by 7:5 (making 2:14—7:4 something of a digression). And within this digression, 6:14—7:1 seems to be a further digression (or an erratic block of material in the train of thought). Part 2 (chaps. 8–9) is not related closely to part 1 (chaps. 1–7). Furthermore, chap. 8 and chap. 9 seem to present two accounts of the collection for the Jerusalem church, the second beginning in 9:1 as if chap. 8 did not exist.

But the most startling break in the flow of thought occurs between chaps. 9 and 10. At the end of chap. 9 Paul is serenely confident of the support of the Corinthians for the collection and full of gratitude for his restored, happy relationship with them. Then suddenly (in chaps. 10–13) he launches into a bitter attack on his enemies, as if no reconciliation had occurred. One wonders whether chaps. 10–13 would not have reopened the wound which Titus said had begun to heal.

Three major explanations of these facts have been offered.

a. Someone after Paul formed 2 Corinthians out of several letters written by Paul and possibly one fragment not from Paul. In order of writing these might be:

6:14—7:1 – a part of Paul's letter to the Corinthians mentioned in 1 Cor. 5:9 (or it might be a piece of non-Christian writing, possibly Essene [see pp. 436–9], that had come into Christian hands);

2:14—6:13 and 7:2–4 – a defense of Paul's ministry under the new covenant, written possibly from Ephesus after our 1 Corinthians and near the beginning of the trouble at Corinth;

chaps. 10–13 – from Paul's severe letter to the Corinthians, mentioned in 2 Cor. 2:3–4; 7:8, 12, written from Ephesus after his unsuccessful visit to Corinth;

1:1—2:13 and 7:5–16 – Paul's letter of thanksgiving for his reconciliation with the Corinthians, written from Macedonia;

chaps. 8 and 9 – two brief letters to Corinth about the collection, both from Macedonia, with only a short interval between them.

If we assume that 2 Corinthians contains parts or most of several letters of Paul, this would mean that someone after Paul joined these letters together into our 2 Corinthians, possibly at the beginning of the second century and perhaps at Corinth. Chaps. 10–13 (from the severe letter) may have been put last because it was the fashion in Christian writings of that period to warn readers at the end of documents concerning errors they would face in the time before the end of the age.

b. A more probable solution is to assume that our present 2 Corinthians now contains the major parts of two letters: the earlier one, our chapters 1–9; and the later one, our chapters 10–13; and possibly one intrusive piece in 6:14—7:1. Under this hypothesis Paul wrote five letters to the Corinthians:

Letter A – Concerning Non-association with Immoral Christians (mentioned in 1 Cor. 5:9 and now lost)

Letter B – Our 1 Corinthians

Letter C – A Severe Letter (mentioned in 2 Cor. 2:3–4, 9; 7:8, 12 and also now lost)

Letter D – Our 2 Corinthians 1–9 (a thankful letter, written soon after his arrival in Macedonia, to rejoice over the reconciliation with the 'majority' as reported by Titus, to refute remaining criticisms of the minority group, and to appeal for speed and liberality in connection with the offering for the Jerusalem church)

Letter E – Our 2 Corinthians 10–13

(an attack on the 'false apostles' who have overturned the reconciliation between Paul and the 'majority' and who threaten the success of the offering; a valiant attempt to right the Corinthian situation before Paul's departure from Macedonia for his third visit to Corinth)

An editor about the end of the first century joined Letter E to Letter D by dropping the ending of D and the opening of E. He may also have inserted the intrusive piece (6:14—7:1) from some source, if indeed Paul did not place it there himself (see below).

c. Though the letter is loosely constructed, Paul put it together himself in its present form.

Advocates of this position speak of Paul's tendency to digress (one of many examples of which is 6:14—7:1) and of the probability of his having composed the letter at several sittings, thus accounting for the roughness of style and content. They argue that the difference between chaps. 1–9 and 10–13 is not as great as claimed: that Paul is defending himself in chaps. 1–9 (see, e.g., 1.17 ff., 2.17; 4:2–3; 5:12, 13), as well as in chaps. 10–13, for there was still a rebellious minority at Corinth (2:6). In this view chaps. 10–13 would be addressed to this rebellious minority, with the hope that their opposition might be overcome before his arrival there (12:14, 20; 13:1–2, 10). Or Paul may have received additional disturbing news that evoked the sharp tone of chaps. 10–13, or his 'moods' may have caused him at a later dictating session to take a dimmer view of the Corinthian situation, or he may have followed the practice of reserving his strong words of warning for the end of his letters. Scholars now are sharply divided on the problem of the letter's unity.

Authorship, Place, Date

Only 6:14—7:1 has been assigned to some author other than Paul, and this on the basis of some variance in vocabulary and theology from Paul's normal usage. But the grounds are inconclusive.

If 2 Corinthians was put together from several letters (as in 'a' above), the different parts probably came from Ephesus and Macedonia and were joined by an editor, possibly at the beginning of the second century. If 2 Corinthians consists of the major parts of two letters (as in 'b' above), chaps. 1–9 were written soon after Paul's arrival in Macedonia, probably in Philippi, and likely in the fall of AD 55; and chaps. 10–13 were sent from Macedonia (from Thessalonica or Beroea?) in the spring or summer of 56 (Victor Paul Furnish's dates).

If we have 2 Corinthians in its original form, the place of writing was Macedonia and the date about AD 55.

Galatians

Martin Luther said, 'The epistle to the Galatians is my epistle; I have betrothed myself to it: it is my wife.' Someone has remarked that Luther put this epistle to his lips as a trumpet to blow the reveille of the Reformation. It is the Magna Carta of Christian freedom and the charter of evangelical faith. Through it and through the letter to the Romans, Paul has powerfully affected Christian theology.

The first two chapters of Galatians supply us with the earliest primary source of information about the primitive Christian church; and the book as a whole offers an eyewitness glimpse of the church's struggle to free itself from the matrix of Judaism and a summary of the theology by which the separation was effected.

The Literary Form

When Paul wrote the letter to the Galatians he was following a literary form well known in his time: the apologetic letter (letter of personal defense). This kind of letter arose in the fourth century BC among the disciples of Socrates and was frequently used in the Hellenistic-Roman period. One contemporary scholar (H.D. Betz) has shown that the book of Galatians follows this form rather closely. According to this scholar, its elements, as it appears in Galatians, are as follows: (1) Prescript (1:1–5); (2) Introduction (1:6–11); (3) Narrative Statement of Facts (1:12—2:14); (4) Proposition to be Discussed

(2:15–21); (5) Proofs of the Proposition (3:1—4:31); (6) Exhortation (5:1—6:10); (7) Postscript (6:11–18).

By being structured in conventional apologetic form, the letter would be readily understood by the Galatians and its argument convincing to a degree beyond our grasp. The outline that follows, while it does not reproduce the apologetic form as set forth by Betz above, does exhibit the progress of the argument in Galatians in some detail.

Theme: My gospel of justification (*i.e.*, right relationship with God) by faith in Jesus Christ – and not by obedience to the requirements of the Law – is the one and only Divine gospel.

The Basic Issue

Paul maintains in this letter that both Jews and Gentiles come into a right relationship with God and with one another through trust in Jesus Christ, God's incarnate Son (4:4), who by his death on the cross rescued believers from their bondage to sin and demonic powers and opened to them the life of the New Age (1:4).

He insists that people cannot win acceptance by God and a right relationship with him by conformity, however complete, to God's Law: 'a man is not justified by works of the law but through faith in Jesus Christ ... by works of the law shall no one be justified' (2:16).

Two ways of salvation are contrasted throughout this letter: salvation by divine rescue, provided in Jesus Christ and accepted gratefully and trustingly by those who know themselves to be sinners and in need of salvation; and salvation by human effort directed toward making oneself acceptable to God according to standards contained in what is regarded as a God-given moral code. Actually, all religions of the world today may be divided into religions of rescue and religions of achievement, though strains of both tend to appear in some of them.

Hebrew religion, as expressed by Israel's

Outline

great prophets and psalmists, emphasized God's saving activity in behalf of rebellious, idolatrous Israel and humankind. It stressed the transformation by God's grace of one's inner life and the expression of that inner renewal in outward acts of justice and mercy. The priests, the wise men, and the rabbis tended rather to accent obedience to God's commands, as revealed in the Law of Moses, in order for the individual and the nation to enjoy the approval of God and prove worthy of inheriting the promises he made to Israel. Many Jews came to think righteous and merciful acts were of so great merit that they could atone for sin (see Tobit 4:10–11; 12:9; Sirach 3:30). Some rabbis said that the patriarchs had laid up great stores of merit before God, and that others of lesser merit could draw on these stores.

Marble street, Ephesus.

This doctrine appeared in medieval Roman Catholicism as the merits of the saints, which could be transferred through prayer to those of lesser achievements. In modern Judaism the doctrine of merit continues. One Jewish scholar has written, 'Rabbinic Jews and modern Jews believe that each person, through repentance and good deeds, works out his own personal atonement' (Samuel Sandmel, *A Jewish Understanding of the New Testament*, 1956, p. 38).

The doctrine appears also in those forms of contemporary Protestantism that stress salvation through education and becoming through doing. One theologian has written: 'We know in the last analysis that our characters are the one thing we can and must create for ourselves. What is our character? It is our will to live by our ideals, "sacrificing" whatever is needed to realize them ever more completely. And we know that our character is the fortress that we must build by our own efforts' (Peter Bertocci, *Religion as Creative Insecurity*, p. 61).

Paul held that people are gripped by forces too strong for them to conquer. Sin is an invading, corrupting power, making the will incapable of moral action and bringing the whole of humankind into bondage and ultimate death (Rom. 7:13–24; 5:12–14). Only God's identification with sinners through Jesus Christ and sinners' trusting identification with Jesus can bring deliverance for individual persons and for humanity as a whole. This faith-identification brings the gift of the Holy Spirit and inner renewal (Gal. 2:20; 4:6), and out of this renewal flow acts of Christian love and moral change (Gal. 5:13—6:10). (See the summary of the message of Romans, pp. 272–5).

Paul, therefore, resisted violently those who taught the Galatians that right relationship with God must be won by obedience to the Law, in addition to faith in Jesus Christ.

Location of the Galatian Churches

Two views are held today, with opinion about equally divided.

a. They were in upper central Asia Minor (modern Turkey), in the territory occupied by the Gauls (Celts) in the third century BC, including the cities of Ancyra, Pessinus, and Tavium. Advocates of this view (commonly called the North Galatian theory) believe Paul founded these churches on his second missionary journey (Acts 16:23).

b. They were located in south central Asia Minor, in territory which had become part of the Roman province of Galatia in 25 BC, including the cities of Antioch, Iconium, Lystra, and Derbe. Proponents of this view (the South Galatian theory) hold that the churches were founded on Paul's first journey, as recorded in Acts 13:13—14:23, and visited by him on the second (16:6) and the third (18:23).

Opponents of Paul's Gospel

The facts concerning the exact identity of Paul's opponents are inconclusive. Some scholars have held that Paul may have had incomplete or inaccurate information about them. Several views are possible:

a. They were Jewish Christians from Jerusalem, who belonged to the legalistic wing of the church (Gal. 2:4; Acts 15:5). They insisted on conformity to the Law of Moses, as well as on faith in Jesus Christ, for the salvation of both Jews and Gentiles. They hotly opposed Paul's law-free gospel by journeying to his churches and attempting to set his converts right. Scholars have long called them 'Judaizers.'

b. They were Gentile Christians, living in Galatia, who had become Judaized (accepted circumcision and other requirements of the Law of Moses) and wished other Gentile Christians to do likewise.

c. They were Jewish-Christian Gnostics, somewhat like those at Corinth (see p. 280), who were leading the Galatian Christians into the worship of world powers and certain ritual observances (including circumcision and the keeping of sacred days and feasts – Gal. 4:9–10), as well as into immoral conduct. Those who hold this view believe Paul did not really understand these opponents and described them as if they were Jewish Christian legalists.

It is doubtful that we know more about these opponents than Paul did. Since he indicated clearly that they demanded acceptance of the Law as essential to salvation (4:21; 5:4; cf. 2:16; 3:21), it is perhaps best to identify them with the legalistic Jewish-Christian minority in the Jerusalem church (2:4; Acts 15:5), which seems to have strongly opposed Paul's law-free mission to the Gentiles.

The opponents' zeal for the Law could have had political, as well as religious, roots. Jewish nationalism of the time, under the mounting influence of the Zealots, was seeking to rid Jewry of Gentile defilement. It was emphasizing separation from Gentiles and strict loyalty to everything Jewish, not only in Palestine but in the Roman world as well. The Zealots were aware that the Christian church as a whole included many Gentiles who were not required to keep the Law and who fraternized freely with Jewish Christians who also were not strictly law-abiding. If the church (and especially the Palestinian church) was to escape persecution in this nationalistic upsurge, it would have to demonstrate its complete loyalty to the Law (see Acts 21:17–26). Thus pressure on Gentile Christians in Galatia and elsewhere to judaize may have been mounted from the Jerusalem church.

Time and Place of Writing

Here again there is no agreement. The crucial questions are: (1) What does Paul mean in Gal. 4:13, where the Greek can mean either 'at first' (or 'originally') or 'on the first of my two visits'? (2) Is Paul's journey to Jerusalem, described in Gal. 2:1–10, to be identified with that in Acts 15:1–21 or with the one in Acts 11:27–30; 12:25?

If Paul had been in Galatia only once before the writing of this letter, and the Jerusalem council described in Acts 15:1–21 had not yet occurred but the famine relief visit of Paul had, the letter to the Galatians could have been the first of all Paul's letters (about AD 48 or 49, possibly from

Ephesians

Head of Zeus from the northern Peloponnese, 2nd century B.C.

Antioch). If two visits to Galatia had taken place and Gal. 2:1–10 is Paul's account of the Jerusalem council, then the letter was written about AD 54 or 55, probably from Ephesus. The strong similarities in subject matter, language, and thought between Galatians and Romans make a date near the writing of Romans likely, though by no means certain. (See on Romans, p. 277).

Samuel Taylor Coleridge called the epistle to the Ephesians 'one of the divinest compositions of man.' Theologians have long regarded it as the most profound of the writings ascribed to Paul, and some have held it to be the crown and climax of the entire New Testament.

Ephesians has been described as 'doctrine set to music.' Much of the book sings about God, Christ, human redemption, the church, God's victory over the demonic powers that tear life apart, the unification of the world by the power of love, and the final inheritance planned for God's children. Praise, prayer, and exhortation are strikingly intermingled in a composition that is more like a tape of an inspiring worship service than of a theological lecture.

Scholars have discovered that the writer of Ephesians caught up portions of the hymnody and the confessions in use in the church of his time and wove them, together with his own words of praise, into a doxology to 'the God and Father of our Lord Jesus Christ' (1:3).

And wherever Christians have worshiped, the majestic liturgical passages of Ephesians have seemed appropriate to express their gratitude for the miracle of their redemption and for their unity – in spite of all human and demonic barriers – in Christ. Ecumenical Christians of every age have found much inspiration in Ephesians.

Theme and Outline

Theme: It is God's purpose to unite the universe in Christ and the church.

Greeting (1:1–2).

Body (1:3—6:20).
The Divine plan for the unification of all things in Christ and the church (1:3—3:21).
1. Praise of 'the Trinity' for projecting the plan (1:3–14).
2. Prayer for the readers' understanding of the plan (1:15–23).
3. The plan at work in the unification of Jews and Gentiles (2:1–22).
4. Paul: God's instrument in the revelation of the plan (3:1–13).
5. Prayer (resumed) for the readers' understanding of and full participation in the plan (3:14–19).
6. Doxology (3:20–21).

The Christians' role in the fulfillment of the plan (4:1—6:20).
1. They must build the church up by mutual service and love (4:1–16).
2. They must abandon completely the old pattern of life and espouse wholeheartedly the new (4:17—5:20).
3. Family members must live together in mutual submission (5:21—6:9).
4. Christians must be fully equipped for the spiritual warfare in which they are engaged (6:10–20).

Conclusion (6:21–24).

Message

Ephesians begins with the purpose of God 'before the foundation of the world' to bring into being a family of loving and morally blameless children from all peoples of the earth. It shows that God realized this purpose through Jesus Christ and through the ministry of 'holy apostles and prophets' and of Paul himself (3:1–13).

Ephesians describes the kind of life appropriate for God's 'beloved children' who await the time when they will inherit the New Age (1:14, 21; 2:7; 4:30), that is, 'the kingdom of Christ and of God' (5:5).

And it sweeps on to brief and suggestive intimations of the character of that 'fulness of time' when God will accomplish the Divine purpose for the unification of all things – in heaven and on earth.

The opening thanksgiving hymn (1:3–14), marked by a refrain ('to the praise of his glory' – 1:6, 12, 14), contemplates the God and Father who blessed, chose, and destined 'us' (*i.e.*, the church) to be God's family of morally blameless children (vss. 3–6). The hymn considers 'the Beloved' Jesus Christ, who through his sacrificial death brought forgiveness of sins and began the unification of the universe (vss. 7–12). It celebrates the gift of the Holy Spirit to the church as the guarantee of the promised heritage of the coming age (vss. 13–14).

Chap. 2 shows that God is uniting Jews and Gentiles. Both formerly were under the power of sin and the devil, hostile to one another, spiritually dead, and subject to God's judgment. Through God's great mercy, love, and graciousness they have shared together in the benefits of Christ's resurrection (victory over sin, death, and evil powers). This glorious result came about not through anything they themselves had done, but only through God's graciousness, met by their faith (trusting acceptance).

Jesus Christ is the bridge between Jews and Gentiles. A new humanity, a new international family of redeemed children, at peace with God and with one another, has come into being. All members of the family have equal access to the Father through the Holy Spirit. Together they constitute the new temple in which God's Spirit dwells.

Paul's peculiar mission to preach to the Gentiles 'the good news of the unfathomable riches of Christ' (3:8 NEB) and to make known to them the Divine plan for the unification of all things leads on to what the members of the new family of God must be and do to further God's purpose.

They must have the qualities of spirit that promote unity (4:2–3); emphasize the things that unite them, not the things that divide them (4:4–6); use Christ's gifts for building up the church by mutual service and love (4:7–16); abandon completely the old pattern of life and wholeheartedly accept the new (4:17—5:20); 'defer to one another' in family relationships 'out of reverence for Christ' (5:21 NAB); become fully equipped for the spiritual warfare in which they are engaged (6:10–20).

The inheritance God will give the children at 'the day of redemption' (4:30), as this phrase implies, is freedom. It will be final freedom from sin, death, and evil powers – whose doom is already sealed (1:21–22; 3:10; 6:10–20) – and membership in 'the kingdom of Christ and of God' (5:5). The New Age will be marked by God's immeasurable riches of grace (2:7). Universal harmony will come about (1:10), and God's children will experience the wonder of all that God is and imparts to them (3:19).

Authorship

Authorities divide about equally on the question of whether Paul wrote Ephesians. Those who favor Paul's authorship cite:

a. *The clear claim of the epistle itself* (1:1; 3:1; 4:1; 6:20)
b. *The second-century church's ascription of the epistle to Paul*
c. *Its Pauline literary structure* (opening greeting, thanksgiving, doctrinal section, ethical section, conclusion and benediction)
d. *Its Pauline language and theology* (the language is 90 or 95 percent in accord with Paul's style; the thought in every important respect is Paul's)

Those who favor authorship by a disciple of Paul, who wrote from Paul's general point of view and in his name, cite:

a. *The language of the epistle* as being significantly different from the genuine Pauline letters (about 90 words in

The temple of Artemis (Diana), Ephesus, depicted on a Roman coin.

Site of the Roman harbor, Caesarea.

Ephesians not used elsewhere in Paul's letters; several non-Pauline expressions; long sentences and imposing liturgical style)

b. *The literary relationships* between Ephesians and other New Testament material (its curious overlapping with Colossians in such a way as to suggest an imitation and, to some degree, an alteration of ideas in Colossians; its similarity in vocabulary and thought to late New Testament literature such as 1 Peter, Luke-Acts, the books of John, and to the Apostolic Fathers of the second century)

c. *The period and perspective* of the writer as reflected in the letter (the Jewish-Gentile controversy is regarded as settled, a condition achieved only after Paul's time; the veneration of the apostles and prophets [2:20; 3:5] expresses a deference unlike Paul [Gal. 2])

d. *The striking differences* between the theology of Ephesians and that of the genuine letters of Paul (the high doctrine of the church in Ephesians, the description of Christ's person and work in Gnostic concepts and language, and the absence of the expectation of the return of Christ)

e. *The known custom* in New Testament times of ascribing a disciple's work to his master as a means of honoring him and perpetuating his teaching and influence (see p. 320)

At present no final decision on authorship seems possible.

Original Readers and Purpose

The words 'in Ephesus' are omitted in important early manuscripts (Vaticanus, Sinaiticus, Papyrus 46). Marcion, of the second century, regarded the letter as Paul's epistle to the Laodiceans (Col. 4:16); hence, 'in Ephesus' could not have stood in Marcion's text.

The impersonal character of the epistle (no personal greetings, no practical problems) would be strange in a writing addressed to the church in Ephesus, where Paul had spent over two years (Acts 19:10). Furthermore, the writer has only 'heard of your faith' (1:15) and assumes that the readers have heard of his special commission to a Gentile ministry (3:2).

If Paul was the author, and he was a

prisoner at the time of writing (3:1; 6:20), we must assume that his long reflection on his mission to the Gentiles and on the church in many lands led to his writing a general statement to all the churches about the significance of the church in the universal purpose of God. He may have directed that several copies of the document be made and sent, perhaps by personal representatives, for reading in the churches (6:21). The copy we have may have come from the church in Ephesus, and hence the words 'in Ephesus' were added by the collector of Paul's letters. Other copies, existing without those words, gave rise to uncertainty about the original destination.

If a disciple of Paul wrote the letter in Paul's name and spirit, we probably must assume that he was thoroughly familiar with Colossians and with Paul's letters as a whole. He wished to keep Gentile Christianity (by his time considerably influenced by Greek and Gnostic thought) aware of its roots in Jewish Christianity and in the eternal purpose of God as seen in the sending of Christ to the Jews (1:12; 2:12–13). If this hypothesis is correct, the author was a Jewish-Christian (1:12; 2:3, 11, 17) familiar with Greek and Gnostic thought. (On Gnosticism see pp. 318–9.)

One scholar has proposed that Ephesians was written by the collector of Paul's letters (Onesimus) to serve as an introduction to the whole collection.

Place and Date of Writing

If Paul was the author, the work must be assigned to one of several places where Paul was in prison: perhaps to Rome, Ephesus, or Caesarea. The date would fall somewhere between AD 54 and 62. If a disciple was the writer, the date would seem to be about AD 80–95, the place indeterminable.

On the question of the place of origin of Paul's prison epistles, see p. 271.

Philippians

Theme and Outline

Theme: The progress of the gospel

Introduction (1:1–11)
Greeting (1:1–2)
Thanksgiving for the Philippians' part in advancing the gospel and prayer for them (1:3–11)

Body (1:12—4:20)
The progress of the gospel through the events and circumstances of Paul's life (1:12–26)
1. His imprisonment (1:12–14)
2. His Christian opponents (1:15–18)
3. The coming verdict in his trial (1:19–26)

The advancing of the gospel within the church at Philippi (1:27—4:9)
1. By the achievement of unity through cooperative effort in behalf of the faith and through imitating the self-denying, brotherly spirit of Jesus Christ (1:27—2:11)
2. By cooperating with God in the effort to reach the goal of final salvation (2:12–18)
3. By accepting the help of deeply committed Christian leaders (2:19–30)
4. By rejecting false teaching and pressing on in the true way of salvation (3:1–21)
5. By mutual helpfulness, prayer, absolute trust in God, concentration on what is good, and imitation of Paul (4:1–9)

The Philippians' gift as evidence of their partnership in the advancing of the gospel (4:10–20)

Conclusion (4:21–23)

Remains of a dungeon, Philippi, possibly Paul's jail.

Philippians is Paul's most joyful letter. It was not his circumstances that made him happy, for he was a prisoner (1:7, 13, 14, 17) facing the possibility of death (1:20–24; 2:23–24), misunderstood and opposed by fellow Christians (1:15–18), and threatened by the possible subversion of his converts by enemies outside and inside the church (3:2–21). From every human point of view life had fallen in on him.

The secret of his joy finds expression in his own words: 'How great is the joy I have in my life in the Lord! ... I have learned to be satisfied with what I have. ... I have the strength to face all conditions by the power that Christ gives me' (4:10–13 TEV). He found that by divine transformation, suffering becomes a source of strength.

The Question of Unity

As the letter is now organized, there is considerable roughness in the sequence of materials. One would expect the personal matter concerning Timothy and Epaphroditus in 2:19–30 to come at the end of the letter, rather than in the middle. The sudden outburst in 3:2ff. is surprising. The farewell and benediction of 4:4–9 seem appropriate for the end of the letter. However, the end does not come until after a long section on Epaphroditus and the Philippian gift (4:10–20). Furthermore, one would expect the thanks for the gift to appear at the beginning of the letter, rather than at the end. Paul's letters usually are more logical than this.

This roughness and a reference by Polycarp (a Christian martyr of the second century) to Paul's 'letters' to the Philippians lead some scholars to conclude that our Philippians contains two or three letters joined together by someone after Paul, perhaps by the first collector of Paul's letters.

The hypothesis of two letters involves the following arrangement of material:

Letter 1 (3:2—4:23), written after the arrival of Epaphroditus with the

Philippians' gift, to warn the Philippians against false teachers, whose activities Epaphroditus reported to Paul, and to express thanks for the gift. The one who joined the letters omitted the salutation.

Letter 2 (1:1—3:1), written about a year later to accompany Epaphroditus on his return to Philippi. Its purpose was to bring the Philippians up to date on Paul's situation, to inform them of the coming of Timothy, and to prevent any criticism of Epaphroditus. The ending of this letter was dropped (or may now be found in 4:21–23).

The hypothesis of three letters goes as follows:

Letter 1 (4:10–20), Paul's note of thanks after the arrival of Epaphroditus with the gift;

Letter 2 (1:1—2:30 [or 3:1] and 4:21–23; possibly also 4:2–9), written to accompany Epaphroditus on his return to Philippi;

Letter 3 (3:1 or 3:2 through 4:1 or 4:9), written just before Paul's death, as his last will and testament, warning against Jewish enemies, whom Paul blames for cutting short his life and ministry.

These hypotheses are interesting but unprovable. We do not know the precise circumstances and conditions under which Paul dictated the letter. Furthermore, it is an informal letter and may have been dictated over a period of some days. Abrupt changes of subject and style are not unknown in Paul (Rom. 16:17ff.; 2 Cor. 2:14ff.). Those who hold that the letter is a unity find that the loss of the beginnings and endings of the supposed letters, as well as the curious way the hypothetical editor put them together, is as hard to explain as the roughness of thought and style.

Purpose

a. To thank the Philippians for their gift (1:5; 4:10–20)
b. To ensure a good reception for Epaphroditus, who was returning with the letter (2:25–30)

c. To inform the Philippians of Paul's present situation and his prospects for the future (1:12–26; 2:24)
d. To prepare the way for the coming of Timothy (2:19–23)
e. To assist in settling certain problems in the church of Philippi:
(1) Persecution by unknown opponents, possibly Gentiles stirred up by Jews (1:28–30; cf. Acts 16:11–40)
(2) False teaching by Jews or Jewish-Christian legalists or Jewish-Christian Gnostics (see p. 280) (3:2–19)
(3) Dissension among members (1:27; 2:2–3; 4:2–3)

Teaching

Philippians bubbles over with religious feeling sublimely expressed. It shows how one who is gripped by the power of God in Jesus Christ reacts to the hard realities of life and death. We are told that when the going is toughest, the footing is surest, the strength most abundant, and the joy most radiant.

Christian Joy
For the length of the letter, 'joy' and 'rejoice' occur a surprising number of times (sixteen times in the various forms of the Greek word).

What occasioned Paul's joy? He found joy in prayer (1:4); in the proclamation of Christ, even by his enemies (1:18); in the knowledge that his prison experience and trial would honor Christ and aid in his ultimate salvation (1:19–20); in the thought that his death might have a sacrificial significance for the Philippians (2:17); in the hoped-for steadfastness and unity of his converts (4:1; 2:2); and in the Philippians' gift (4:10). And he wanted the Philippians to have joy in the progress of their faith (1:25); in the possibility of his sacrificial death for their sake (2:18); in their renewed fellowship with Epaphroditus (2:28–30); in the fact of their incorporation in Christ and the church ('rejoice in the Lord' – 3:1; 4:4); and in the hope of Christ's coming (4:5).

Ruins of Roman agora, Philippi; an early Christian basilica stands behind.

Even if in some of these passages 're-joice' should be translated 'farewell' – the other meaning of the word – as is possible in 3:1 and 4:4 (see NEB), the intensity of joy loses little; for 'farewell' carried somewhat the meaning of 'cheerio' – that is, 'be happy,' 'be joyful.'

The confident mood of the Christian life shines in the words, 'I can do all things in him who strengthens me' (4:13).

Self-Denying Concern for Others

The greatest passage in the letter is undoubtedly 2:5–11, a hymn composed by Paul or possibly by some other Christian poet-theologian and used here by Paul. Its theme is Christ's self-denying concern for others and his exaltation by God. Paul introduced it here to counteract the selfish, grasping spirit of some of the Philippians who were bent on personal privilege and glory (2:3; 4:2–3) and were about to wreck the church.

Church members should have the attitude of Christ, says Paul. Christ, who bore the image (or the divine nature) of God, did not (like Adam) grasp greedily at equality with God, but, on the contrary, 'made himself nothing' (NEB) by taking the nature of a slave. The heavenly Son of man became a person like us; and in obedience to God, whose slave he was, he accepted the most abject of humiliations: death on a cross. Because of his self-renunciation, God rewarded him with the sovereignty he did not grasp at: God made him King over the universe, to be worshiped by every creature, equal with God the Father in the exercise of Divine sovereignty.

A disciple should imitate his Lord in radical self-renunciation. If he does so, divisions stemming from self-seeking will vanish from the church. God will set his seal on such self-renunciation.

The Path to the Glory of the Resurrection

False teachers were about to lure the Philippians from the path leading to the prize God had in store for them: life with Christ in the glory of the coming age.

Paul, therefore, marks out this path in the clearest terms. It involves the following:

1. Renunciation of merit – all human assets from heredity, from personal choice, and from personal accomplishment (3:4–8)

2. Identification with Christ through faith – sharing in his sufferings, his death, and the power of his resurrection (3:9–11)

3. Relentless concentration on reaching the goal of life eternal (or the resurrection from the dead), never being satisfied with one's degree of progress (3:12–16)

4. Imitation of those Christian leaders who have set their minds on heavenly, rather than on earthly, realities and thus are destined for life in the New Age (3:17–21; *cf.* 4:9)

Place of Writing and Date

The probable location was Rome, Ephesus, or Caesarea, some time between about AD 54 and 62. On the whole question of the place of writing of Paul's prison epistles, see p. 271.

Colossians

John Calvin called the epistle to the Colossians 'an inestimable treasure.' He based this judgment on its presentation of Christ: 'What is of greater importance in the whole system of heavenly doctrine than to have Christ drawn to the life, so that we may clearly contemplate his excellence, his office, and all the fruits that accrue to us therefrom?'

Colossians' importance clearly lies in its view of Christ – in the way it relates Christ to God, to the church, and to the universe. The author drew his portrait of Christ against the back-drop of some heresy we do not fully understand. But our lack of knowledge here, while exasperating, is not particularly tragic. Whatever the heresy was, it stimulated the writer to a characterization of Christ which stretches the mind of the most competent theologian and mature Christian. The profundities of Colossians almost defy comprehension. Who indeed can grasp the full significance of the one 'in whom are hid all the treasures of wisdom and knowledge' (2:3)?

The Writer's Purposes

a. To counteract the Colossian heresy and to urge the Colossians to continue growing in the faith they had learned from Epaphras, Paul's convert and fellow worker (1:7).

It is clear from 1:4 and 2:1 that Paul did not know the Colossians personally.

The Colossian church was mostly, if not completely, Gentile. The heresy, taught by unknown persons, involved the worship of angelic, cosmic powers (2:8, 18, 20) in addition to Christ. These were celestial spirits, who apparently were regarded as God's agents in governing the movements of the heavenly bodies. Thus these spirits in some respects controlled human destiny, as astrological thought holds. Their worshipers observed feast days, special seasons, and certain practices to honor and perhaps appease them (2:16–23).

Apparently all these powers, along with Christ, constituted God's 'fullness,' that is, the full range of God's attributes and manifestations. Allegiance to Christ was not enough to guarantee salvation; the ruling powers also had to be recognized and pacified.

This 'philosophy' (2:8) stressed special visions offering secret knowledge of ultimate reality and the way of salvation. The writer of Colossians thought such knowledge led to lofty pretensions and self-congratulation (2:18).

The heresy seems to have been an amalgam of elements from several sources: Judaism (perhaps like that in the [Essene] Dead Sea Scrolls – see pp. 420–27); early Gnosticism (like that at Corinth – see p. 280); and Hellenistic astrology and pagan mystery cults. The author held that glorification and pacification of astral powers debased Christ and introduced practices that were a threat to Christian freedom.

b. To introduce Tychicus, the carrier of the letter and envoy of the writer, who was to encourage the Colossians in the true way and inform them about Paul's circumstances (4:7–8); and to ensure a good reception for Onesimus, the converted runaway slave, who was returning in company with Tychicus to his master at Colossae (4:9).

c. To enhance Epaphras' standing with the Colossians (4:12–13). The founder of the church in Colossae was apparently under attack by the heretics and needed

Epaphras, his fellow prisoner (Philem. 23), told him about the situation in Colossae. Because of his sense of responsibility for the Gentile church as a whole (1:23–29), Paul undertook to deal with the Colossians' problems. Epaphras, a native of Colossae (4:12), also had founded churches at the neighboring cities of Laodicea and Hierapolis (2:1; 4:13).

Paul's support against them.

d. To prepare the way for the possible visit of Mark (4:10).

e. To urge Archippus to carry out faithfully some responsibility in the Lord's service entrusted to him (4:17).

What this responsibility was is unknown. Perhaps he was requested to carry on Epaphras' pastoral responsibilities, since the latter, like Paul, was a prisoner (Philem. 23); to continue the collection for the Jerusalem church which was so important to Paul (1 Cor. 16:1–4; 2 Cor. 8–9); to receive Onesimus in a brotherly way and perhaps free him for evangelistic service (an interpretation possible only if Archippus, not Philemon, was Onesimus' master [see p. 327]).

f. To establish Paul's authority and teaching firmly in the Gentile churches, both those founded directly by him and those raised up by his followers. The instruction concerning the exchange of letters between churches (4:16) is evidence of this purpose. (It has been suggested that 'the letter from Laodicea' is our Ephesians or our Philemon; or the letter may be lost.) The strong emphasis on Paul's unique mission to the Gentiles (1:23–29) and his authorization of Epaphras as a conveyor of the true faith also clearly support this purpose.

Teaching

The Supremacy and All-Sufficiency of Christ

The Colossian heretics taught that faith in Christ must be supplemented by recognition of the heavenly spirits which control human destiny. The author of Colossians did not deny the existence of these spirits, but he did deny that they have any power over believers in Christ and that worship and ceremonies of appeasement need be directed to them. Christ broke their hold over people by his triumph on the cross (2:15).

A great hymn of praise to Christ (1:15–20), which the writer may have created or adapted from an already existing composition, celebrates the absolute supremacy of Christ over all ruling spirits ('thrones,' 'dominions,' 'principalities,' 'authorities' – 1:16). It affirms Christ's all-sufficiency for the salvation of mankind and for the final unification of the universe.

The writer applies to Christ language and concepts usually applied to Wisdom and to the Word of God in the Old Testament and the Wisdom of Solomon (see p. 216). Here these words and ideas are: 'the image of the invisible God' ('the visible likeness of the invisible God' – TEV); 'the first-born of all creation' ('the primacy over all created things' – NEB); the agent of God in creation; and the cohesive force which binds the whole universe together.

In Christ the divided and discordant universe is destined to be reunited. He himself, the resurrected one, is the beginning of the new creation, the head of the church (his Body). His death on the cross was the means of the final reconciliation of all powers in the universe.

In sum, God was in Christ, not partially but fully. Christ contains and represents all that God is, and he makes Christians participants in his magnificent completeness. Why, then, should any Christian pay deference to the discredited, defeated powers?

Christian Existence

The readers were at one time enemies of God (1:21), captives of the cosmic powers in the realm of darkness (1:13; 2:8, 20; *cf.* Eph. 6:12), and subject to the rules and regulations of these powers (2:16, 20–23). They lived as fleshly persons (2:11) and practiced evil deeds (1:21). They were spiritually dead by reason of their sins (2:13) and guilty before God's law (2:14). Their sins were 'fornication, indecency, lust, foul cravings ... ruthless greed ... anger, passion, malice, cursing, filthy talk ... lying' (3:5–9 NEB). Those who lived thus belonged to the world (2:20).

But God rescued them from the realm of darkness and bondage to its cosmic powers and made them members of the kingdom of the beloved Son (1:13). Their sins are forgiven (1:14). They are now alive together with Christ (2:13), 'rooted and built up in him' (2:7). They have come to 'full life in union with him' (2:10 TEV). They have been reconciled to God (1:22). They are now 'saints', that is, set apart as God's people (1:2; 3:12). They have a new self, the old self having been destroyed (3:9–10). They are becoming like God in character (3:10). Love is the central quality of their life (3:14), thankfulness and singing its dominant mood (3:15–17), and faithful service of Christ in a life of good deeds its objective (1:10; 3:23–24). Since they have been raised with Christ, they live already in a new heavenly world, while they await the final victory of Christ in the establishment of his glorious kingdom (3:1–4). Union with God through Christ is not a wistful hope but a glorious accomplishment (3:3).

God's power at work in Christ's death on the cross and in his resurrection from the dead brought about their transformation. Preaching evoked trust in that power (1:23, 28), and baptism accomplished union with Christ in his death and resurrection (2:12). Baptism brought spiritual circumcision, that is, circumcision of the heart, and marked them as members of God's purified people (2:11–12).

Authorship

Two positions are widely held today:

a. Paul, as the letter clearly claims (1:1, 23; 4:18), was the author. As was customary with him (1 Cor. 16:21; Gal. 6:11; 2 Thess. 3:17), he added an authentication in his own handwriting (4:18). There is some variation in language, style, and theology from Paul's other letters, due to the special circumstances under which Colossians was written. But the similarity to these letters is greater than the dissimilarity. No one in the early church, so far as we know, doubted Paul's authorship.

Moreover, strong ties to Philemon, undoubtedly written by Paul, argue for Paul's authorship of Colossians. One notes in both letters the same senders (Paul and Timothy); greetings from many of the same persons (Aristarchus, Mark, Epaphras, Luke, Demas), who were with Paul when the letters were written; the special mention of Archippus ('fellow soldier' with a special ministry to perform); and the reference to the return of the runaway slave Onesimus.

b. A disciple of Paul wrote the letter in Paul's name. Many facts argue that Paul was not the author of the letter. A few are: the use of many words not found elsewhere in Paul's certainly genuine letters; the absence of Paul's characteristic ideas (righteousness, justification by faith alone, the purpose and function of the Law); the highly speculative view of Christ, especially in 1:15–20; and the strong emphasis on apostolic tradition as a way of counteracting heresy. It is possible that a disciple of Paul, who was thoroughly familiar with Paul's language and thoughts, used his master's authority as a way of meeting heresy sometime soon after Paul's death. The strong similarities between Ephesians and Colossians may imply that a disciple of Paul wrote Colossians first and then himself (or another disciple) reproduced much of its language and theology in the later Ephesians.

The defenders of Paul's authorship reply that most of the new and different features of Colossians are due to the peculiar nature of the heresy Paul opposed and to his subtle and flexible mind. Among the defenders are both liberal and conservative scholars.

Place and Time of Writing

If the letter was written by Paul himself, the place probably was Rome, Ephesus, or Caesarea. (See on the prison letters, p. 271.) The date was about AD 54–62. If a disciple wrote it, the time was about AD 70–90, the place unknown.

1 Thessalonians

1 Thessalonians is Paul's most solicitous, affectionate letter. Here the great apostle appears not as a warrior doing battle for the truth (as in Galatians), or as a lawyer arguing a case (as in Romans), or as a fireman rushing to extinguish a devastating blaze (as in 1 and 2 Corinthians). Here he is a tender shepherd of newborn lambs – a pastor – who lovingly feeds, protects, and encourages the young. To use the letter's own figures of speech, Paul is a nurse caring for children (2:7), a father gently encouraging his little ones (2:11).

The letter conveys a tender tone by the many times the readers are addressed as 'brothers' (1:4; 2:1, 9, 14, 17; 3:7; 4:1, 9–10, 13; 5:1, 4, 12, 14). Paul expresses his delight in the Thessalonians in the words, 'You are our pride and our joy' (2:20 TEV), and the depth of his emotional attachment to them in the exclamation, 'Now we really live if you stand firm in your life in the Lord' (3:8 TEV).

Occasion and Purpose

According to the Acts, Paul founded the church at Thessalonica on his second missionary journey (Acts 17:1–9). For three sabbaths he argued in the synagogue that the Old Testament predicts the coming of a suffering Messiah and that Jesus of Nazareth fulfills this expectation.

His converts were mostly 'godfearing Gentiles,' 'influential women' (Acts 17:4 NEB), and some Jews. The Gentiles were half-converts to Judaism (see p. 431).

Opposition by unbelieving Jews led to mob action against Paul's converts and to a charge of treason against the missionaries. A night journey to Beroea by Paul and his companions left the infant church alone, exposed to the fury of its enemies, and uncertain of its future.

Paul's ministry in Thessalonica was longer than a period of three sabbaths. This is apparent from the fact that the missionaries worked in the city to support themselves (1 Thess. 2:9) and that they remained there long enough to receive two offerings from the church at Philippi

Theme and Outline

Theme: Your new Christian faith and experience are valid; go on to maturity of life in Christ.

Introduction (1:1–3).
Greeting (1:1).
Thanksgiving (1:2–3).
Note: Structurally the Thanksgiving concludes at 3:13. But from the standpoint of content, much of chaps. 2 and 3 is argument (defense of Paul's conduct) rather than thanksgiving.

Body (1:4—5:24).
The remarkable conversion of the Thessalonians as evidence of the validity of their new faith and experience (1:4–10).

Paul's and his associates' blameless conduct at Thessalonica and afterward as proof of the integrity of the missionaries and the validity of the Thessalonians' new faith and experience (2:1—3:13).
1. At Thessalonica (2:1—16).
2. After leaving (2:17—3:13).

The Thessalonians' need for maturity of life in Christ (4:1—5:24).
1. The call to maturity (4:1–2).
2. Sexual purity (4:3–8).
3. Mutual love and personal industry (4:9–12).
4. Growth in theological understanding (4:13—5:11).
   a. Concerning the fate of the Christian dead (4:13–18).
   b. Concerning the coming of the day of the Lord (5:1–11).
5. General instructions concerning Christian life and experience (5:12–24).

Conclusion (5:25–28).

(Phil. 4:16). A stay of two or three months is likely, including the three sabbaths at the synagogue.

When Paul arrived at Athens he sent Timothy back to Thessalonica to assist the infant congregation and to bring him word of its condition (1 Thess. 3:1–5). Meanwhile, Paul crossed over to Corinth and began a mission there. Timothy brought a good report to Paul at Corinth (Acts 18:5; 1 Thess. 3:6). It is possible that he also brought a letter to him from the Thessalonians, inquiring about some matters to which Paul responded in 1 Thess. 4–5.

1 Thessalonians is Paul's joyful reaction to the news of the fidelity of the Thessalonians in spite of their sufferings and also his attempt to guide them to a fuller Christian life through a solution to their problems.

Their problems were:

a. Persecution by fellow townspeople, probably spearheaded by the unbelieving Jews who had forced Paul from the city (Acts 17:5; 1 Thess. 2:14–16; 3:3–4)

b. Doubts about the integrity of the missionaries, spread probably by hostile Jews (1 Thess. 2)

c. Confusion about the validity of their new faith and experience in the light of Jewish attacks (1:4–10); about the Christian view of the future (the fate of Christians who have died before the coming of Christ, the time of Christ's coming, and Christian activity meanwhile – 4:13—5:11); and about the place of suffering in the life of Christians (3:3–4)

d. Sexual irregularities (4:3–8), idleness and troublemaking (4:11–12), carelessness (5:1–11), and quarreling (5:13)

Message

The central message of 1 Thessalonians is: Stand fast in your newly found faith in spite of opposition and press on to Christian maturity!

The letter begins with a thanksgiving for the clear evidence Paul sees that the

Roman theater and forum, Thessalonica.

Thessalonians have a secure place in God's great redemptive purpose. This evidence consists of the striking nature of their conversion experience and the character of its fruits.

Both the missionaries and the Thessalonians were moved by the Holy Spirit, the former to mighty, persuasive preaching of the gospel and the latter to joyful reception of the message, even though they were persecuted for it.

The Thessalonians became imitators of the missionaries and of Christ and an example for Christians in other places. Their faith showed itself in action, their love resulted in labor, and their hope produced great fortitude (see NEB 1:3). They turned from idolatry to the worship of the living and true God and to the hope of the coming of Christ with final salvation.

This dramatic conversion, with its fruits of love and service, shows beyond a doubt, says Paul, that their new faith and life are from God and that the missionaries are his true and faithful servants.

Paul next defends his conduct both at Thessalonica and after leaving there against the malicious charges of enemies. His ministry at Thessalonica was courageous (2:2), sound doctrinally (2:3–4), uncompromising (2:4–5), selfless and self-giving (2:6–8), self-supporting (2:9), blameless (2:10), and patient (2:11).

To the charge that he cares little about the Thessalonians, since he 'ran out' on them and has not returned to help them with their problems, he replies that it was impossible for him to return because of factors beyond his control (illness? hostile magistrates or Jews at Thessalonica? problems at Corinth?), interpreted by Paul as the activity of Satan. His sending of Timothy to aid them and his joy over the good news brought by him are evidence that he cares deeply about them. Paul hopes yet to visit them; they are very dear to him.

Meanwhile, they must face their problems and come to spiritual maturity in Christ. Paul calls this maturity 'holiness' or 'sanctification' (3:13; 4:3, 7; 5:23).

These English words come from Hebrew and Greek terms which signify the condition of persons or things which have been separated from the common or profane by God and infused with his power. By association with God they become like God. Holiness (sanctification) is God's gift (5:23–24). For Paul holiness (sanctification) is both an accomplished fact (1 Cor. 6:11) and something yet to be completed (2 Cor. 7:1; 1 Thess. 4:3). Christians are to go on becoming, by God's gracious help, what they already are in principle. One does not progress *to* holiness but *in* holiness, according to Paul.

The life separated from the common and the unclean by God's activity in Christ (1 Cor. 1:30; 6:11) and filled by God's Spirit (1 Thess. 1:6; 4:8) has certain characteristics: sexual purity (4:3–8), mutual love (4:9–10), attention to one's own business (4:11), industriousness (4:11–12), mature understanding of Christian truth and emotional stability (4:13–18), spiritual alertness (5:1–11), respect for leaders (5:12–13), patient helpfulness of others (5:14–15), thankfulness and prayerfulness (5:16–18), and moral discrimination (5:19–22).

Their lack of mature understanding of Christian truth and the harmful emotional and moral effects of this misunderstanding were associated with their wrong ideas about the future. Paul obviously had taught them about the second coming of Christ to judge the world and to gather believers into the final kingdom of God. He had stressed the nearness of these events. He apparently left them with the impression either that Christians, with the divine life in them, would not die, or that the end of this age was so close that all who had believed at Thessalonica would be alive and participate in these glorious happenings. But the passage of time brought death to some Christians and with it the fear that the dead would not be included in Christ's triumphant inauguration of the New Age. Some may have begun to doubt Paul's teaching about the second coming of Christ because of the delay (5:3), and they, thus, began to live carelessly (5:4–8).

Paul's answer is, first, that death before Christ comes will not prevent Christians from fully participating in the blessings of the New Age. Through resurrection, based on the resurrection of Jesus to whom they are united, they will share with living Christians in perpetual life with their Lord. The coming Lord will summon both dead and living to himself at the time of his heavenly appearance. Therefore, there is no cause for grief over the fate of departed Christians. Second, he reaffirms the reality and the suddenness of the second coming and warns that they must prepare for the strict judgment of that day.

Authorship, Date, Place of writing

A few scholars have argued that the letter comes from someone later than Paul, since certain Pauline notes are absent (e.g., justification by faith alone) and some portions are unlike Paul (e.g., the details about the coming of Christ in 4:13–18). But the vocabulary, style, and overall theology seem to be genuinely Paul's. Furthermore, it is unlikely that a later writer would have attributed to Paul the unfulfilled expectation that he would live until the second coming (4:15, 17).

1 Thessalonians, dating to about AD 50 and written from Corinth, is probably the earliest of the preserved letters of Paul. This honor has been claimed for Galatians, but without adequate proof (see pp. 297–8).

2 Thessalonians

1 Thessalonians is intensely personal, warmly affectionate, and gently persuasive. 2 Thessalonians is more formal, authoritarian, and theological.

In the first letter Paul encouraged the Thessalonians to continue in their faltering steps as little children in the faith. In the second he both encouraged them and scolded them for departures from Christian belief and practice. He mixed encouragement and discipline in differing proportions in his letters as the situation required.

2 Thessalonians is noteworthy chiefly for its teaching about the second coming of Christ. Nowhere else in the letters of Paul is the teaching so explicit concerning the succession of events leading to it and its meaning for both sinners and saints.

Occasion and Purpose

The letter indicates that reports had come to Paul about problems in the church at Thessalonica (3:11). The first problem concerned the persecution the church was experiencing, probably from both Jews and Gentiles (see p. 310–11).

The second problem centered in wrong ideas about the second coming of Christ. Someone claimed Paul as the authority for the false view that 'the day of the Lord has come' (2:2). The practical result of this mistaken view was that some people quit

Theme and Outline

Theme: The truth about the second coming of Christ.

Introduction (1:1–4).
Greeting (1:1–2).
Thanksgiving (1:3–4).
Note: Technically, thanksgiving and prayer continue to 2:17, but theological argument appears in 1:5–10 and 2:1–12. This makes structural and logical analysis difficult.

Body (1:5—3:15).
The coming will bring the day of recompense for unbelieving persecutors and for faithful believers (1:5–10).
The coming has not yet occurred; it will be preceded by events still to take place (2:1–12).
To be prepared for the coming, Christians must obey the pattern of Christian doctrine and living taught by Paul and his associates (3:1–15).

Benediction and authentication (3:16–18).

their daily work; there was a great deal of idleness and meddling in other people's affairs (3:6, 11). Paul had faced the problem of lazy spongers when he was at Thessalonica (3:10), but his instructions went unheeded. Indeed, the situation had gotten much worse.

We can only guess who was teaching church members at Thessalonica that the day of the Lord had actually arrived. Gnostic Christians at Corinth (see p. 280) seem to have believed that they were enjoying the kingdom of God already (1 Cor. 4:8), and a clear statement in 2 Tim. 2:18 attributes to two false teachers in the church the view that 'the resurrection is past already.' Such people taught that Christians have been enlightened by secret knowledge; they have risen in spirit from the bondage of the flesh. Since redemption is already accomplished, nothing more is to be expected. The idle and disorderly way of life was the natural outgrowth of a view that claimed perfection of spirit and showed indifference and contempt for the flesh and the concerns of life in this 'evil' world.

Paul denies that he is in any way responsible for this heresy. He has taught them nothing or written them nothing to this effect, whatever the false teachers claim (2:2). The sample of his handwriting Paul appended (3:17), possibly as a sign of genuineness, may suggest that a forged letter under his name was circulating at Thessalonica.

The purpose of 2 Thessalonians is thus to stop the false teaching and its devastating consequences for Christian living.

Teaching

The discussion of the coming of Christ begins from the situation of the Christians at Thessalonica. They were experiencing bitter persecution. Paul praises them for their steadfastness and continued growth in faith and love. He insists on doing so, in spite of their objection that they are unworthy of such praise (1:3).

He sees the patient endurance of persecution as proof of God's righteous (right, just) judgment. This judgment is seen now in God's support of the suffering Christians while they are prepared through their suffering for membership in the coming kingdom; it will be fully seen at the glorious coming of the Lord Jesus (1:5 ff.), when recompense will be meted out to the afflicted and their tormentors.

The reward for the persecuted Christians will be 'rest' (relief from trouble and suffering) and eternal fellowship with the Lord in his kingdom, while the recompense of the wicked will be trouble and eternal ruin, that is, separation from the presence of the glorious and mighty Lord (1:7, 9).

Following the discussion of the coming of Christ at the day of recompense, Paul turns to the time of the coming (2:1–12). Here he deals with the error that the day of the Lord has already come by showing that the preliminary events on the divine timetable have not yet run their course.

Christ will not come until the self-deifying 'man of lawlessness' appears. This one will come as the human incarnation of all evil. He will deceive people by Satanic power and induce them to false worship. Christ will appear to destroy this devil's messiah and to render judgment on his unrighteous worshipers. Paul says that the mysterious force of lawlessness is now at work in the world, but the coming of the 'man of lawlessness' is being held back by something or someone – what or who the Thessalonians are said to know and are not told again here (2:5–6).

Who 'the man of lawlessness' is and what or who the restrainer is elude us. Was some Gentile or Jewish leader, someone like Antiochus Epiphanes (see p. 182) or the mad emperor Caligula (AD 37–41), expected to appear as the embodiment of all evil and as the devil's instrument in the final great struggle between the forces of good and evil at the end of time? It is unlikely that Paul had some specific historical person in mind. Certainly he was not predicting the coming of a wicked pope, or of Mussolini, Hitler, Hirohito, Stalin, or Mao, as has been claimed! The passing of time has shown identifications of this sort to be illusions.

Some guesses about the identity of the restrainer are: the Roman empire (and the emperor), which held back the surge of lawlessness; an angel, perhaps Michael; the Holy Spirit; Paul and the proclamation of the gospel to the Gentiles. Speculation is useless. The main point is that God's calendar of historical events has not yet been fulfilled and, until it is, the end of the age and the coming of the kingdom of God – to be introduced by the return of Christ – cannot take place. The Gnostics, who claim that salvation has been *fully* realized in the resurrection and liberation of the self from the bondage of matter, are wrong. Salvation, whatever its present aspects (and these are not treated in this letter), is emphatically God's *future* gift (2:10, 13–14).

While Christians await the second coming of Christ and the salvation to be bestowed in the gift of life in God's kingdom, they must be obedient to the pattern

Arch of Galerius, Thessalonica.

of doctrine and living taught them by Paul and his associates (2:15; 3:4, 6–12). This means a life of good works and words (2:17) – not idleness and gossip and trouble-making, but the Christian activity of prayer (3:1), personal industriousness (3:6–12), and tireless well-doing (3:13).

Authorship, Date, Place of Writing

Several views on the problem of authorship and date are possible.

a. The letter was not written by Paul but at a later date by one of his disciples and without the knowledge or approval of Paul. The letter would thus be a pseudepigraph (a document under an assumed name). The disciple used Paul's name to claim his support for a message to the church of a later time (perhaps when the Jewish-Roman war and the fall of Jerusalem did not culminate in the coming of the Lord) that the delay in the coming was due to the fact that the timetable of events had not yet run its full course. (A few scholars have held that the disciple wanted to degrade and replace 1 Thessalonians, with its emphasis on the soon coming of the Lord, and did so by the trick of Paul's alleged signature in 3:17. Not many have accepted this 'trick' explanation.) There are, however, serious arguments against authorship by Paul.

(1) The view of the future in 2 Thessalonians is not consistent with that in 1 Thessalonians. In the latter, the second coming of Christ is to occur soon and without warning signs; but in the former, the coming is not immediate and is to be preceded by specific signs. Both positions could hardly come from Paul. Furthermore, the 'man of lawlessness' and the detailed preliminary signs have no parallel in the genuine letters of Paul.

(2) The many striking similarities in subject matter and wording between the two letters to the Thessalonians, can be more easily explained as the result of a disciple's imitation of his master's thought and language than as the repetitiousness of the master himself, especially since

there are theological differences as well.

(3) The historical situation behind 2 Thessalonians seems not to be a natural outgrowth of the situation we see in 1 Thessalonians. The church's concern about the delay in the second coming of Christ would hardly have turned so quickly into the belief that he had already come. If a disciple of Paul wrote 2 Thessalonians, there would have been adequate time for such a shift in perspective.

b. The letter was not written directly by Paul but by one of his associates with Paul's full knowledge and endorsement. Timothy (or some other close associate) has been suggested as the writer, who used 1 Thessalonians as his model and wrote under Paul's general direction. Paul subsequently signed the letter to authenticate it as his own message and will (3:17). Thus the similarities to and differences from 1 Thessalonians would be explained.

c. Paul is the author, as the letter claims (1:1; 3:17). Arguments are:

1. Fluctuation between belief that the end was near and unpredictable and the view that certain events must occur first was common in visions concerning the future at the time of Jesus and Paul. Both emphases appear in the teaching of Jesus about the end (Matt. 24:36; Luke 21:34–36 and Matt. 24:32–33; Luke 21:29–30). They were therefore theologically possible for Paul.

2. Similarities in thought and language between the two letters do not necessarily indicate imitation by a disciple. Two letters written to the same church within a few weeks would naturally involve some repetition, and desirably so, for the sake of emphasis. The letters are different as well as similar, the differences being due to new factors in the situation at Thessalonica.

3. Gnostic teaching about redemption as a completely accomplished fact could arise quickly in a church in the Greek world, as indeed it did relatively soon at Corinth. We need not assume a long

1 Timothy

Detail from the Arch of Galerius, Thessalonica.

period for its development and change.

Some scholars have suggested that the two letters were written in the reverse order or that 2 Thessalonians was addressed to a Jewish-Christian minority at Thessalonica and sent along with 1 Thessalonians, which was meant for the Gentile-Christian majority. Others have held that 2 Thessalonians was originally addressed to the church at Philippi or Beroea. None of these theories has convinced the majority of scholars.

Today the pendulum is swinging toward non-Pauline authorship of 2 Thessalonians in some form of 'a' above. But the possibility of 'b' or 'c' cannot be ruled out. If Paul wrote or authorized it, the date would be about AD 51, a short time after the writing of 1 Thessalonians, and the place probably Corinth. If a later disciple wrote it without Paul's knowledge, the date would be sometime after AD 70.

1 Timothy belongs to a subgroup of the letters ascribed to Paul which has been known since the eighteenth century as the Pastoral Epistles. The other letters in this group are 2 Timothy and Titus. These writings contain instructions and admonitions concerning the work of pastors in Christian churches.

In many respects these books are more like church manuals than personal letters. This is especially true of 1 Timothy, where personal information is almost entirely lacking. Since most of the material in these manuals would surely have been known already by Paul's long-time associates Timothy and Titus, it is likely that the books were written more for the benefit of church members than for the leaders mentioned though the latter, of course, were included.

A hint that church members as well as the leaders were addressed appears in the benedictions of the three writings, where the 'you' is plural in the Greek (in the best manuscripts). Furthermore, the center of interest in all three is the problems of faith and conduct of church members and how to meet these problems with the help of accredited leaders.

These books contain many crisp, salty sayings and instructions for the church. They do not probe the depths and scale the heights of life in Christ and the church as the other letters ascribed to Paul do, but their practical morality and wise counsel

---

Theme and Outline

Theme: Timothy's role in preserving the true faith and life of the church from the false instruction and way of life of heretical teachers

Greeting (1:1–2)

Body (1:3—6:19)
Paul, the model of sound teaching and living, and Timothy, his true disciple, versus the false teachers and their message (1:3–20)
Regulations concerning public worship and church leaders (2:1—3:13)
Timothy's responsibility for teaching the Christian mystery (truth) and way of life (3:14—4:16)
Timothy's role in preserving the family-like nature of the church (5:1—6:2)
The false teachers' love for money; Timothy's and the true Christian's love for God and good deeds (6:3–19)

Concluding charge to Timothy and benediction (6:20–21)

---

offer help to churches tempted to stray from the straight path of historic Christianity. Their keynote is: At all costs keep the faith delivered to you by the great apostle Paul!

False Teaching and Its Refutation

It is difficult to pin down the exact nature of the false teaching opposed in the Pastoral Epistles, so vague and general are the references to it. Several characteristics seem evident, however:

a. An Emphasis on Myths and Genealogies (1 Tim. 1:4; 4:7; 2 Tim. 4:4; Titus 1:14; 3:9)
According to Titus 1:14, these are 'Jewish' and are propagated by those of 'the circumcision party' (Titus 1:10), meaning apparently Jewish Christians. 'Quarrels over the law' (Titus 3:9), 'speculations' (1 Tim. 1:4), 'vain discussion' (1 Tim. 1:6), and 'stupid controversies' (Titus 3:9) by those who desire to be 'teachers of the law' (1 Tim. 1:6–7) make it appear that fanciful Jewish interpretation of the Old Testament was being advocated in the church.

b. Salvation by Knowledge or Mystical Illumination
Some Christians had been stressing knowledge at the expense of faith (trust) and moral obedience, as the comments about 'speculations,' 'vain discussions,' 'stupid controversies,' and 'what is falsely called knowledge' (1 Tim. 6:20) show. The emphasis on traditional belief and good works in the Pastorals (see below) seems aimed to counterbalance this speculative emphasis.

It is likely that the knowledge these teachers offered included more than 'proper' interpretation of the Old Testament. In the first and second centuries AD the philosophical-religious movement we call Gnosticism was spreading through the Mediterranean world. It offered people secret, saving knowledge of the universe: of the supreme, pure-spirit God, untouched by 'evil' matter; of the many divine beings (aeons) thought to connect him with the evil world, which had been created by the lowest aeon; of human nature as spirit enmeshed in an evil body; of the releasing of one's spirit from evil flesh for its ascent to its proper heavenly abode through enlightenment brought by a divine savior and through secret, sacramental rites and mystical experiences; of practices permitted and forbidden those who have achieved freedom of spirit; of the coming liberation of the soul from the body at death, as the seal and consummation of a resurrection already achieved in mystical experience.

The following emphases in the Pastorals indicate that some such teaching was threatening the church: the oneness (not the plurality) of Deity; the single mediatorial position and role of 'the man Christ Jesus' (1 Tim. 2:5); the goodness of the created order and its free use by humans (1 Tim. 4:4); sin (disobedience to God's law) as the root of the human predicament, not entanglement in evil matter (1 Tim. 1:8–11; 4:7–8; 6:18; Titus 2:11–14; 3:3); a salvation involving true reverence for God ('godliness'), obedience to God's will, faith in Christ as Savior, and the doing of good deeds (1 Tim. 1:8–11; 4:7–8; 6:18; Titus 2:11–14); the certainty of the future coming of the Lord Jesus 'to judge the living and the dead' (2 Tim. 4:1; cf. 1 Tim. 6:14–15) and thus the certainty of a future resurrection.

c. The Practice of Magic Through Demonic Power

Like Pharaoh's legendary magicians Jannes and Jambres, these heretics sought to demonstrate their superior powers and capture allegiance to their heresy (2 Tim. 3:6–9, 13). Behind them, we read, lay satanic, demonic power (1 Tim. 4:1; 2 Tim. 2:26).

Gnosticism combined Jewish and Greek-oriental concepts into a system of impressive proportions. Its central error from the standpoint of Christian truth was its cleavage between God and the world (matter), the latter being regarded as evil and the place of imprisonment of unenlightened human souls. Salvation as escape from evil matter was a perversion of the historic belief in salvation from sin. Perverted also was the view that God's good provisions for humankind (marriage, food, drink) were forbidden (1 Tim. 4:3; 5:23). And to teach that the only resurrection the Christian would have was the resurrection experienced in his own rebirth was to empty the faith of its hope of the final resurrection of the whole person to communal life in the kingdom of God (1 Cor. 15:35–57; Rev. 21:2–4).

The church resisted the heresy by insisting on the correctness of Paul's divinely given teaching. It claimed that Paul had delivered this teaching to his personal followers, and that they had passed it on to responsible teachers in the church (1 Tim. 1:12–16; 2 Tim. 1:11–14; 2:2).

The Temple of Antoninus and Faustina, Rome, now occupied by a church.

Authorship and Date of the Pastoral Epistles

No firm conclusion has been reached on these subjects. There are three main positions in regard to the authorship.

a. As the books themselves clearly claim, Paul was their author, either directly or indirectly. From the late second century, at least, until the nineteenth, the church believed Paul wrote them. Advocates of this view admit that the personal facts about Paul, Timothy, and Titus contained in the Pastorals do not fit into the outline of Paul's career as pictured in the Acts. The Acts has no mission by Paul and Titus on Crete (Titus 1:5), no evidence that Paul spent a winter at Nicopolis (Titus 3:12), or that shortly before his Roman imprisonment (2 Tim. 1:16–17) he had been in Asia Minor, where he had left Trophimus ill at Miletus (2 Tim. 4:20).

Defenders of Paul's authorship argue that Paul was released from the Roman captivity mentioned in Acts 28:16; that he evangelized on Crete and elsewhere in the Mediterranean area, even possibly in Spain; that the events and circumstances described in the Pastorals occurred during this period of release; and that he was arrested and imprisoned in Rome a second time. During the second imprisonment he wrote the Pastorals.

Supporters of this view explain that the many new words and ideas in the Pastorals are due to Paul's advancing age, his broadening contacts and experience, and the new situation addressed (the need for strengthening the church against rising heresy). They see the heresy Paul opposed in the Pastorals as somewhat like that attacked in Colossians and less formal and organized than the Gnostic systems of the second century AD.

Some admit the possibility that Paul may have allowed a secretary (perhaps Tychicus or Luke) considerable freedom in the composition of the Pastorals. They suggest that this may account for some of the new features of these writings. In any case they were written at Paul's direction and under his authority.

b. The Pastorals were written by a disciple of Paul, considerably after Paul's death, perhaps in the first quarter of the second century. He used Paul's name and influence to check the Gnostic heresy and to keep the church on the path marked out by the great apostle.

Scholars favoring this position point out that it was a recognized practice in antiquity for a disciple to write in the name of his teacher and to ascribe his insights to his honored master. This involved no dishonesty. Schools of learning gathered around great teachers and the traditions left by them. These traditions were handed down through successive generations.

Those holding this view offer several major objections to Paul's authorship (either direct or mediated through a secretary).

1. The personal facts do not fit the career of Paul as we know it from the definitely genuine Pauline epistles and from the Acts. Since there is no solid evidence for a ministry between two Roman imprisonments, these facts can hardly be historical. In fact, some passages in the Acts (20:25, 38) rather clearly indicate that the author believed that Paul did not return again to his churches in the East.

2. The situation in the church, reflected in the Pastorals, is not that of Paul's time but of a later period. The organization of the church, as seen in the Pastorals, is too advanced for Paul's time. Timothy and Titus appear here as ruling bishops who appoint elders, discipline them, guard the church doctrinally and morally, and serve as a pattern for the church members to imitate. Such an episcopal role did not come into being until the second century.

The Colosseum, Rome, built by the Emperors Vespasian and Titus.

Furthermore, the role of elders as ordained tradition-bearers (2 Tim. 2:2) and the order of widows dedicated to continual prayer and sexual abstinence (1 Tim. 5:3–16) seem to reflect a time considerably later than Paul.

3. Some emphases in the theology of the Pastorals seem not to be Paul's. Many themes do accord with Paul's preaching and teaching, but others depart from his thought to some degree.

Paul's 'faith' (trust) becomes in the Pastorals 'the faith' (a body of truth handed down from an authoritative source). Christians become those who have a 'sound' or 'healthy' faith to which they are loyal and which they pass on to others.

The Holy Spirit is not prominent in the Pastorals, as in the letters of Paul, and the Holy Spirit of the Pastorals is communicated not spontaneously and unpredictably but by the church rite of laying on of hands (1 Tim. 4:14; 2 Tim. 1:6–7).

The emphasis in the Pastorals is on good works, on proper conduct, rather than on one's total response to God's grace as the way to a new relationship with God ('in Christ' or 'in the Spirit').

4. The glorification of Paul as the great achiever and martyr who passed on the torch to those who came after him (1 Tim. 1:16; 2 Tim. 1:11–14; 3:10–13; 4:6–8) and the exaltation of the Pauline tradition (1 Tim. 1:18; 4:6; 6:20; 2 Tim. 1:13–14; 2:1–2; Titus 1:3) seems strange coming from the apostle himself, who was reluctant to 'boast' and gloried rather in his weaknesses (2 Cor. 11:16—12:10). It is easier to understand from the pen of an admiring disciple, who felt that his great master had the answer to later problems.

5. The vocabulary and the style of the Pastorals vary markedly from those in Paul's unquestionably genuine letters. About 175 words that appear in the Pastorals are found nowhere else in the New Testament. More than one third of the words used in the Pastorals are not found in Paul's certainly genuine letters, and many of Paul's words are used in a different sense. The language and style as a whole are akin to those in late New Testament books and in writings of the second century.

On the assumption that the author was not Paul but a follower or admirer of Paul, the period of writing might have been at any time from around the end of the first century to about the middle of the second century. Those who place the Pastorals at the late date believe their author meant them to counteract the teachings of the famous Gnostic heretic Marcion, whose views were refuted also by Irenaeus and other church leaders.

c. The third position mediates between the other two. It holds that both Paul and a disciple were involved in the making of the Pastorals. Paul wrote several short notes to his trusted helpers Timothy and Titus. A later admirer of Paul wove them into the present Pastorals in order to preserve them and to give his writings Pauline impact and authority.

Three such notes have been identified: (1) Titus 3:12–15; (2) 2 Tim. 4:9–15, 20, 21a, 22b; (3) 2 Tim. 1:16–18; 3:10, 11; 4:1, 2a, 5b–8, 11–19, 21b–22a. It is possible to fit the information in them into Paul's known career. The first note may have been written to Titus from Macedonia just after Paul's severe letter to Corinth (see p. 287). The second may have gone to Timothy from Nicopolis a little later. The third, Paul's last letter, may have been written from Rome at the close of his imprisonment there (as mentioned in Acts 28:30, 31).

In conclusion we may say that the problem of the authorship of the Pastorals is one of the most vexing in the field of New Testament studies. The many striking differences in language, style, and theology between the Pastorals and Paul's certainly genuine letters make Paul's direct authorship of the Pastorals difficult to defend. It appears that either he gave a secretary large freedom in their composition or that a disciple put them together in his name and in his spirit (possibly using some of Paul's notes) to serve the needs of the church after the apostle's death. Who

Who the disciple was and where he lived are quite unknown. Asia Minor has been suggested.

The Value of 1 Timothy

1 Timothy, a handbook of church administration and discipline, is not filled with sublime and inspiring passages. The author did not blaze new trails in Christian thought, but rather sought to consolidate, conserve, and protect the conquests already made by the church. This is no small achievement, even if it is less dramatic than pioneering work.

Of lasting value are the following:

Loyalty to the truth and the preservation of a good conscience (1:5, 19; 3:9) – instead of succumbing to attractive, erroneous novelties which gratify the senses – belong to the essence of Christianity, as Christian martyrs later demonstrated.

The spiritual and moral requirements for church officials, set forth here, offer generally valid guidelines for every age (c.g., 'if a man does not know how to manage his own household, how can he care for God's church?' – 3:5).

The Christian teacher, as an example to those who are taught (1:16; 4:12–16), exhibits Christianity as truth incarnate.

The emphasis on the goodness of the created order and human right enjoy it (4:3–5) opposes recurring asceticism in Christian thought and life.

2 Timothy

1 Timothy and Titus are manuals of church administration. 2 Timothy is much more personal and is something of a last will and testament. Literary testaments (the instructions of a dying patriarch to his children) were common in Judaism at that time. So here Paul, facing the hour of his death (4:6–8), instructs his beloved son Timothy (1:2; 2:1) how to carry on after his departure. If Timothy follows these instructions, he will escape the dangers that threaten him and the people under his care.

Theme and Outline

Theme: Be loyal to me and my gospel, and you will be rewarded with eternal life.

Greeting (1:1–2)

Body (1:3—4:21)
An appeal for personal loyalty on the basis of past experience (1:3–18)
An appeal for doctrinal loyalty on the basis of the gospel as preached, lived, and suffered for by Paul (2:1—4:8)
Timothy's final ministrations to Paul (4:9–21)

Benediction (4:22)

The Roman Emperor Nero, A.D. 54—68

High Points in 2 Timothy

The intimate personal bond between Paul and Timothy is everywhere evident in the letter. Timothy is called 'my beloved child' (1:2; cf. 2:1); Paul has knowledge about his family (1:5); Paul had participated in his ordination to the work of ministry (1:6; cf. 1 Tim. 4:14); Paul had been his teacher (1:13; 3:14); and Paul prays constantly for him (1:3). Paul wants to strengthen the bond of personal loyalty which his imprisonment might conceivably weaken (1:8). The close relationship between Paul and Timothy is evident also in Phil. 2:19–24.

The purpose of strengthening the bond is that Timothy may be fully loyal to Paul's gospel in the face of the destructive heresy that is threatening the church. (On the nature of this heresy see the discussion of 1 Timothy.) Timothy's opposition to the false teachers will cost him much suffering. He must be willing, as his teacher has been (1:8, 16; 2:9), to take his 'share of

suffering for the gospel in the power of God' (1:8; cf. 2:3).

The nature of Paul's gospel comes to clear focus in 2:8. It centers in Jesus as the fulfillment of Israel's history and hopes (the Messiah from the line of David, a real human person), who died and rose from the dead, as the mighty Son of God and inaugurator of the salvation of the New Age. (See also Rom. 1:3–4; 15:12.) His resurrection is the promise of the resurrection of all believers, contrary to the teaching of the heretics (2 Tim. 2:17–18).

How Timothy is to deal with false teaching is treated in considerable detail:

a. He and his people should avoid senseless controversy and the false teachers who engage in it (2:14, 16, 23; 3:5). They should be kind, forbearing, and gentle (2:24–25).

b. He must be a good interpreter of Christian truth himself (an unashamed workman, 'rightly handling the word of truth' – 2:15).

c. He and his people must live righteously and associate with those others who live in the same manner (2:22).

d. They must realize that God's church is basically unshakable, for God knows and cares for those who belong to him (2:19).

e. They must realize that the church is a mixed community, with good and bad members, and that individual and group discipline is constantly needed (2:20–21).

f. They must keep in mind what hour it is on God's time clock – the time of great evil and suffering before the End, when God's people must defend the truth and persevere in righteousness, according to the teachings of the Holy Scriptures. On the day of judgment God will richly reward them (3:1—4:8).

Authorship, Date, Original Readers, Circumstances of Writing

See the discussion of 1 Timothy.

Titus

> ## Theme and Outline
>
> **Theme**: Teach Christians in Crete to think straight and live right, for this is what God expects of those who have experienced his boundless generosity in Jesus Christ and are heirs of the eternal life which he has promised.
>
> **Greeting** (1:1–4).
>
> **Body** (1:5—3:14).
> **Appoint suitable elders (bishops) for leadership in the church** (1:5–16).
> 1. Their qualifications (1:5–9*a*).
> 2. Their duties (1:9*b*–16).
>
> **Teach and exemplify sound doctrine and right living in the church** (2:1—3:11).
> 1. Instruct the various church groups how to think and act – and why (2:2–15).
> 2. Teach all church members their responsiblities toward the state, their fellow citizens, and the life of good deeds – and why (3:1–8).
> 3. Avoid senseless controversy and those who promote it (3:9–11).
>
> **Perform acts of personal service and urge others to do the same** (3:12–14).
> 1. Return to Paul after duty on Crete (3:12).
> 2. Assist traveling fellow Christians (3:13).
> 3. Urge all Christians to do deeds of helpfulness (3:14).
>
> **Final Greetings and Benediction** (3:15).

The letter to Titus is more similar in its contents to 1 Timothy than to 2 Timothy. The latter, as we have seen (pp. 323–4), contains the last will and testament of a father in the faith to his son in the gospel, while the others, on the whole, deal with church order and discipline. 1 Timothy offers fuller instructions on these matters than does the letter to Titus.

Titus, like Timothy, was a trusted companion of Paul and emissary to his churches. He was the spearhead of Paul's movement to free Christians from the Law of Moses. Paul made a test case before the mother church in Jerusalem and won acceptance of Titus as an uncircumcized Gentile Christian (Gal. 2:1–5). He was a gifted and skillful person, to judge from his part in the successful reconciliation of the rebellious Corinthian church to Paul (2 Cor. 7:6–16) and his effective service in collecting the offering for the church in Jerusalem (2 Cor. 8:6, 16, 23).

The letter to Titus represents this Christian leader as head of the church in Crete by Paul's appointment (1:5). His task was to organize and discipline the church there – in an admittedly disorderly place (1:12). We hear of him last as on a mission to Dalmatia (2 Tim. 4:10), a territory now in Yugoslavia.

Words in the greeting show that Titus was one of Paul's converts: 'my true child in a common faith' (1:4).

High Points

This brief letter is full of charm and help for effective Christian living. Its setting is interesting. An old apostle is writing to a son in the gospel (1:4) to assist him in carrying out his mission in a tough spot (Crete). The son was living and working among people who were notorious as 'liars, evil beasts, lazy gluttons' (1:12). The nature of the counsel offered him indicates that the church members there were undisciplined in personal habits, quarrelsome, insubordinate, and indolent in their Christian service. Their way of life was not markedly different from that of their heathen neighbors. And false teachers were destroying whatever foundations of Christian understanding and living had been laid down when they had first been evangelized.

Titus' task is to improve the understanding of Christian truth and the level of Christian living and service in the Cretan church. To do this, he must teach 'sound' (*i.e.,* healthy) doctrine (1:9; 2:1), as opposed to the sick teachings of the heretics (see pp. 318–9). Sound doctrine teaches that:

a. God wills the salvation of all people from their 'ungodly living and worldly passions' (2:12 TEV) and from their unloving attitudes (malice, envy, hatred – 3:3).

b. This salvation is both present ('he saved us' – 3:5) and future ('heirs in hope of eternal life' – 3:7) and consists in rebirth and renewal in the Holy Spirit, effected in baptism, through Jesus Christ's act of redemption (2:14; 3:5–6).

c. One who has been saved and awaits final salvation lives a self-controlled, upright, and godly (*i.e.,* truly devout) life in this world (2:12). Specifically, this means these qualities: temperance, self-control, chastity, honesty, hospitality, kindness ('perfect courtesy toward all men' – 3:2), submission to authority, mutual helpfulness. Those who live thus 'will add lustre to the doctrine of God our Saviour' (2:10 NEB).

d. Christians live in hope of the coming triumph of Christ (2:13) and of the life eternal (1:2; 3:7).

(On the problems of authorship, date, nature of the heresy opposed, and original readers see the discussion of 1 Timothy.)

Philemon

On the surface, this little letter looks like a private communication. Many readers have wondered why it was preserved among the church letters of Paul.

While it clearly is much like an ancient private letter, the fact that it is addressed not only to individuals but also to a house church (vss. 1, 2) shows that it was more than that.

From the Christian perspective the return of the runaway slave Onesimus, now a Christian brother (vs. 16), was as much a concern of the church as of his legal master. The church needed to understand what had happened to the returning slave, to be prepared to receive him warmly into its fellowship, and to use its influence with his master to ensure an appropriate reception.

The letter is important historically and theologically, because it shows how, in practical terms, the new Christian movement began to work and must work in effecting both personal and social change.

Circumstances of Writing

Paul was a prisoner when he led Onesimus to new life in Christ (vss. 9, 10). (On the location of Paul's imprisonment see p. 271.)

How Onesimus came to Paul is not known. Did one of Paul's helpers, perhaps Epaphras of Colossae (Onesimus' home town – Col. 4:9), come upon the slave accidentally and bring him to Paul?

Did the runaway seek Paul out because of previous friendly contacts with him and because he was now homesick, lonely, out of money, and in need of a place of asylum? Or was Onesimus, by strange providence, housed in the same prison with Paul?

It is evident from the letter that Onesimus had fled with some of his master's money or property (vss. 18, 19). The stealing and the flight put the slave in a difficult legal position before his master, who had absolute power of life and death over him.

Paul wanted to keep Onesimus with him as an aide, for he found him useful (Onesimus means 'useful' – vs. 11). But his service belonged to his master, and the Christian faith demanded repentance and restitution. Therefore, Onesimus had to return to his master, cast himself on his mercy, and seek forgiveness. With Onesimus went Tychicus (Col. 4:7–9) and this letter. Both were meant to intercede with the master for forgiveness and restoration.

Some students of the letter have contended that Paul indirectly asked for Onesimus' release from slavery and his return to Paul for subsequent service (vss. 13, 14, 21). But this is not stated, and vs. 15 ('that you might have him back for ever') argues against it.

Who was the slave owner, and where did he live? There are two views.

a. He was Philemon of Colossae, one of Paul's converts, perhaps in the city of Ephesus (since Paul had not been to Colossae – Col. 1:4; 2:1). Philemon's house in Colossae was the meeting place of the church in that city. Apphia may have been his wife, and Archippus his son (vs. 2).

b. The owner was Archippus of Colossae, host of the house church there. Philemon was the overseer of the churches of the Lycus Valley, where Colossae, Laodicea, and Hierapolis were located. Philemon lived at Laodicea. Apphia was his wife. The letter was sent first to him so that he might add his influence to that of Paul when the letter was sent on to Archippus at Colossae. The ministry to be

---

Theme and Outline

Theme: Paul's appeal to Philemon for Christian forgiveness

Introduction (vss. 1–7)
Greeting (vss. 1–3)
Thanksgiving (vss. 4–7)

Body: The Entreaty Concerning Onesimus (vss. 8–21)

Conclusion (vss. 22–25)

---

fulfilled by Archippus (Col. 4:17) was to free Onesimus for the work of evangelizing. Advocates of this view hold that the letter Paul sent to Laodicea (Col. 4:16) is our letter to Philemon.

The first view is to be preferred. Philemon is first mentioned, not Archippus. The ministry Archippus is to perform 'in the Lord' was 'received' (that is, 'handed on,' as by tradition) and must refer to some service in the church, not simply to the freeing of Onesimus.

The 'letter from Laodicea,' to be read by the Colossians, was more likely addressed primarily to that church, not primarily to an individual, as is the case with Philemon. The Laodicean letter seems to have perished. (An apocryphal epistle to the Laodiceans in Latin circulated widely in the early and medieval church. It consists of a number of passages by Paul, chiefly from Philippians, patched together to close this gap in the collected letters of Paul. It is obviously a forgery. Marcion in the second century, without adequate justification, regarded our Epistle to the Ephesians as the letter to the Laodiceans.)

The Nature of Paul's Appeal

The letter is a model of tactful persuasion. Paul's appeal to Philemon has many sides.

By addressing the letter to Philemon, his family, and the whole church Paul makes the problem of Onesimus' return more than a private matter between a master and a slave. The tactic practically ensures a Christian solution, not merely a legal consideration of the problem.

Neapolis, the seaport for Philippi in Paul's day.

The mention of Philemon's reputation for loving attitudes and actions (vss. 4–7) would stimulate him to yet another act of generosity.

Paul's loving appeal, rather than an authoritative command based on status and rank, would tend to evoke a loving response (vss. 8, 9).

Paul's high regard for Onesimus (he is 'useful to you and me,' he is 'my very heart,' 'my child') would motivate Philemon to a like regard (vss. 10–13).

Paul's consideration for Philemon's rights as slave owner is deftly aimed at leaving the initiative toward generosity with Philemon (vs. 14).

Paul's suggestion that the hand of Providence is to be seen in the whole affair (vss. 15, 16) would move Philemon to gratitude to God, instead of personal vengeance.

The appeal to the common membership of Paul, Philemon, and Onesimus in the Christian church (vss. 16, 17) offers a theological ground for Paul's entreaty for mercy.

The reminder of what Philemon owes Paul, as well as Paul's willingness to assume financial responsibility for Onesimus' irresponsibility (vss. 18, 19), would have strong effect.

The request for a personal favor and the joyous anticipation that it would be abundantly granted (vss. 20, 21) would be hard to resist.

The suggestion that Philemon will soon meet Paul face to face in a proposed visit (vs. 22) would hasten speedy and favorable action.

By adding the names of his companions (vss. 23, 24) Paul suggests that they join him in the appeal for Onesimus.

Paul and Slavery

Neither Jesus, nor any of the first Christians, including Paul, had as a goal the abolition of slavery. Slavery was provided for in the Law of Moses and in contemporary Jewish and Greco-Roman law.

But the teachings of Jesus and the church ultimately undermined slavery. They set forth the infinite value of every person before God (Matt. 6:26; 10:29–31; Mark 10:13–16; Luke 15; etc.) and the equality and essential oneness of all believers in Jesus Christ (Gal. 3:28: 'there is neither slave nor free'; cf. Eph. 6:5–9; Col. 3:11). They emphasized love and deeds of mercy toward the unfortunate and the needy as the central demand of Christian discipleship (Matt. 22:37–40; 25:31–46; John 13:35; 1 John 3:17; James 2:1–17). Since a Christian slave master was 'a slave of Christ' and since a Christian slave was 'a freedman of the Lord' (1 Cor. 7:22), they occupied common ground in Christ.

Such a view and such a position could not but radically affect, and in time eliminate, the institution of slavery.

Hebrews

The Letter to the Hebrews contains the most eloquent writing in the New Testament. Its author was a brilliant early Christian thinker who scaled theological and literary heights equaled by few, if any, Christians of the first century.

Unfortunately, the text contains little information about its author, its original readers and their circumstances, its date, its purpose, and its theological background. Even its literary form is somewhat mysterious. It is like Melchizedek, 'without father or mother or genealogy' (7:13), for we know so little about its antecedents and its family relationships.

Literary Character

Hebrews calls itself a 'word of exhortation' (13:22). It is more like a sermon than a letter. It has no greeting at its opening, as letters almost always did (1 John is like Hebrews here). However, its ending follows the normal pattern of letters, with personal matter, greetings, and benediction (13:18–25).

The references to the author's *speaking* (2:5; 5:11; 6:9; 8:1; 9:5), while possible in a letter, fit better an oral address, especially the remark that 'time would fail me to tell of' (11:32). The oratorical tone of the whole book would seem to indicate that it is a sermon.

If such was its original form, its author adapted it to serve as a message to be carried and read to some group of Christians. At that time he may have added 13:18–25 as an epistolary ending to his sermon.

The message requires about fifty minutes for reading aloud, not too long for an early Christian worship service.

The question of whether it is a sermon or a letter is not of much significance, however, since the New Testament letters were all addressed to churches and intended for reading at worship services (see p. 271).

Original Readers and Purpose

The title 'To the Hebrews' represents the opinion of the church from the latter part of the second century concerning the first readers.

'Hebrews' apparently meant Jewish Christians, for the work plainly was intended for Christians, not Jews (3:1; 6:1–12; 12:22–24). The heavy use of the Old Testament, the constant reference to the ritual institutions and practices of Israel, the contrast of the old and the new covenants, and the like, might have led the early church to conclude that it was written to Hebrew (Jewish) Christians, quite apart from any tradition to that effect. Whether the title correctly defines the first readers is questionable.

The major positions on the identity of the readers are:
a. They were Jewish Christians. The elaborate argument in Hebrews to show the superiority of Christianity over Judaism, together with the many indications that the readers were drawing back from full allegiance to Christ and the church (2:1–3a; 5:11–14; 6:1–12; 10:23, 35–39), may suggest that the recipients were about to give up Christianity and return to Judaism. They may have wanted

to go back to Judaism because of disappointment over the failure of Christ to return as expected, or because of the appeal or pressure of Zealot nationalism in the period before AD 70, or even the attraction of the ceremonies of the old Jewish cult, which they missed as Christians.

They may have lived in Jerusalem or in some other part of Palestine. When the Qumran texts (the Dead Sea Scrolls) came to light (see pp. 420–27), the many similarities in language and theological concepts with the book of Hebrews led some scholars to think that the readers were converted members of the Essene sect (see pp. 436–9), who still held to some of their old beliefs. Another scholar has proposed that the readers were a monastic community of Jews from abroad who had come to live near Mt. Zion (Jerusalem) to wait for the inheritance God had promised to Abraham.

Still others have argued that the readers were a Jewish Christian minority (perhaps

Cistern and tower, Qumran.

The Arch of Titus, Rome, commemorates the capture of Jerusalem.

a house church) in some city like Rome, Corinth, Ephesus, or Antioch.

b. They were Gentile Christians. Gentile Christians used the Septuagint, were saturated in it, and regarded themselves as the true Israel (Gal. 6:16; 1 Peter 2:9–10).

Hebrews nowhere indicates that the readers were considering returning to Judaism. What threatened them was a general let-down due to the delay in the second coming of Christ (9:28; 10:23–25) and the bitter sufferings Christians were enduring at the hands of both Jews and Gentiles (12:3–13). The author wished to show these Gentile Christians that in Christ God had fulfilled his purpose for the redemption of *humankind*. To turn away from God was to turn away from God's future for *all* people.

On this second view, the readers could have been Gentiles living anywhere in the Gentile world.

c. They were both Jewish and Gentile Christians – simply Christians as Christians, irrespective of background. They had become discouraged (for the reasons suggested in *b*) and needed a ringing challenge to press on.

It is possible that the letter was intended for the mixed church at Rome or for some other such church in Italy. Arguing for a location in Italy is the acquaintance of Clement of Rome with Hebrews (*c.* AD 95; 1 Clement 17:1; 36:2–5). In addition, the most natural interpretation of 'those who come from Italy send you greetings' (Heb. 13:24) is that Italians present with the author outside Italy send greetings home to their fellow countrymen. That the readers were both Jewish and Gentile Christians, probably residing in Italy, is the most likely hypothesis, but a Jewish-Christian house church (*i.e.,* a minority group) in Rome is a strong contender.

Authorship

Many authors have been suggested.

Paul

The Eastern church, from the end of the second century, regarded Paul as the author and placed the book among the letters of Paul, after the Letter to the Romans or after 2 Thessalonians. The Western church accepted Paul's authorship only from the second half of the fourth century, as a result of Eastern influence.

Almost all scholars agree today that the form, style, and theology are unlike Paul. Paul did not write anonymous letters. He did not alternate sections of argument and exhortation but usually reserved his major appeal for the end of his letters. The style is highly polished, whereas Paul's was frequently rough, marked by digression, and sometimes by unfinished sentences. Paul's distinctive themes are missing, or practically so: justification by faith, not by works of the Law; the equality of Jew and Gentile in God's purpose; the mystical union of the believer with Christ. The figure of Christ as high priest is absent from Paul's letters. Paul made little of the Law as a foundation for Israel's sin-removing sacrificial system, but rather stressed the Law as a sin-revealing and sin-stimulating instrument. Paul says nothing about the impossibility of a second repentance (6:4–8; 10:26–27; 12:17). Hebrews 2:3 seems to put the author later than the eyewitness generation, which would exclude Paul.

Apollos

Martin Luther's suggestion that Apollos of Alexandria was the author has won many advocates. Apollos was 'an eloquent man, well versed in the scriptures' (Acts 18:24). His presumed training in Greek rhetoric and Greek philosophy might account for the style and thought of Hebrews (see below on 'Formative Influences'). His contacts with Paul and Timothy (1 Cor. 16:12) were close. This would explain both the Pauline characteristics of the book and his interest in Timothy (Heb. 13:23).

Luke

Clement of Alexandria (late second century) thought that Luke had translated Paul's original Hebrew text of this book into Greek. Some modern scholars have found similarities between Hebrews and the Acts of the Apostles, particularly in the speech of Stephen (Acts 7). However, the differences from Luke's theology as a whole are so striking that his authorship of Hebrews is extremely unlikely; and Hebrews shows no evidence of translation from a Hebrew text.

Coin of the Second Jewish Revolt, showing the Temple as it was remembered.

Barnabas

Tertullian (died *c.* AD 220) attributed Hebrews to Barnabas, a Levite from Cyprus (Acts 4:36). A Levite (a member of an ancient priestly group which attributed its origin to Levi, a son of Jacob) would have knowledge of temple ritual. Barnabas means 'Son of encouragement' (*cf.* 'word of encouragement,' or 'exhortation,' mentioned in Heb. 13:22). He may have been an educated man capable of so profound a writing, but there is little to support the conjecture.

Others

Other suggestions are: Clement of Rome, Silvanus (Silas), Philip (one of the seven deacons), and Priscilla (wife of Aquila). Origen (third century) concluded, 'Who wrote the epistle God alone knows certainly.' Origen's judgment still stands.

Date of Writing

Clement of Rome's knowledge of Hebrews around AD 95 places it before that date, but how much before is uncertain.

There is no reference to the destruction of the temple in Jerusalem (AD 70). Timothy has been released (from some imprisonment?), but the time and circumstances are not given (13:23). The mention of 'former days,' when the readers were persecuted (10:32–34), could refer to the time (*c.* AD 49 or 41?) when Claudius expelled the Jews from Rome (Acts 18:2) or to persecutions by Nero in AD 64. But the latter, which involved martyrdoms, seems unlikely from the statement in 12:4 that 'you have not yet resisted to the point of shedding your blood.' If the epistle was directed to the church at Rome, this statement would date it before AD 64 – probably not long before, since the author and readers seem to be second-generation Christians (2:3).

If the epistle was not for the Roman church, where Nero's persecutions occurred, 12:4 would have no direct bearing on the date. It could then have been written as late as about AD 81–90, in the time of the erratic emperor Domitian, when the Christian's lot was becoming difficult. The early 60s and the period 81–90 are the alternatives.

Theology

Hebrews is a Jesus-centered book. Its keynote is, 'Let us keep our eyes fixed on Jesus, on whom our faith depends from beginning to end' (12:2 TEV; *cf.* 2:9).

The author's portrayal of Jesus and his meaning for the life of humankind is unique in the writings of the New Testament. Only Hebrews declares Jesus to be 'a great high priest' and summarizes his achievement as the offering up of himself as a perfect sacrifice for the sins of all people. The daring of this concept is readily apparent. A high priest did not offer up himself but 'the blood of goats and calves' (9:12). He was sacrificer but not also the one sacrificed.

In Hebrews Jesus is the perfect sacrifice for sins and the perfect sacrificer because he is the eternal Son of God. The highest language is used to characterize his relation to God: 'he reflects the glory of God and bears the very stamp of his nature' (1:3). He was the agent of God in creation and is the upholder of the universe (1:2–3). This glorious Son became a true human being (2:14), 'made like his brethren in every respect' (2:17). He suffered, prayed, and implored God's help (5:7). 'He learned obedience through what he suffered; and being made perfect he became the source of eternal salvation to all who obey him' (5:8–9). The complete humanity of Jesus as incarnate Son of God is more prominent here than anywhere else in the New Testament. Because he became one of us (short of sinning), he was able to sympathize with us and our weaknesses (4:15) and thus to serve as our high priest before God.

His priestly ministry was perfectly effective. The ministry of the Jewish priesthood was not. The blood of animals could not take away sins (10:4, 11) and purge the conscience (9:9, 14). His ministry, while in some respects like that of the Jewish high priest, was in reality of a higher order. He belonged to the priestly order of Melchizedek, not to that of Aaron and Levi (5:10; 6:20—7:22).

Our author sees two priestly lines in the Old Testament. The superior one began with Melchizedek, the priest-king of Jerusalem at the time of Abraham. Abraham recognized his superiority by accepting his blessing and by paying him tithes (Gen. 14:18–20). It was to this priestly line that King David belonged (Ps. 110:4). From this line the priest-king Messiah was to come.

The other line came from Levi, Jacob's son (Gen. 49:5–7; Exod. 32:26–29). It included Aaron, Moses' brother, and Aaron's sons, who became Israel's priestly family (Lev. 8:5–30).

The author of Hebrews sees the priests descended from Levi and Aaron as inferior to the line of Melchizedek and to the Messiah and High Priest, Jesus, whom Melchizedek foreshadowed (Heb. 7).

Not only is Jesus' priestly line superior to the Levi-Aaron line, but his ministry is based on God's new covenant with the people, not the old, obsolete Mosaic covenant (8:8–13).

Jesus' place of ministry is also superior. He officiates not in an earthly sanctuary but in heaven (8:1–5). There he offered up before God the perfect sacrifice of his own life (9:11–12), and there he now intercedes before God in behalf of humankind (9:24; 7:25).

He accomplished what the Mosaic law and worship could not: the removal of the worshipers' sins, their sanctification, holiness, perfection (i.e., their separation from all defilement and their becoming like God in character – 10:10, 14; 12:14). Thus they became fit to stand in the very presence of God (10:19–22; 12:22–23).

He awaits the arrival of the Father's time for his return 'to save those who are eagerly waiting for him' (9:28), to receive from God sovereignty over his enemies (10:13, 25, 37), and to enable people to enter with him into the promised sovereignty over all creation in the kingdom (or city) of God (2:5–13; 12:22–28; 13:14).

Those who have the Holy Spirit have already experienced in foretaste the life of that kingdom (6:4–5). Those who have had this high privilege must beware of becoming indifferent and unbelieving, of being carried away by 'the deceitfulness of sin' (2:1; 3:12–13) in their pilgrimage toward the final city. Else they may fall in the wilderness, as unbelieving Israel did (3:7–19). They must press on in faith, like the heroes of faith before them (chap. 11). They must devote themselves to righteous living and loving deeds (chap. 13), for the day of judgment and promise is drawing near (10:25).

Formative Influences

Jesus' high priesthood is echoed or assumed in other New Testament writings (e.g., the high priestly prayer of John 17; the priestly garb worn by the Son of man of Rev. 1:13). The concept is based on the interpretation of Ps. 110 as referring to a future Messiah, and possibly on the belief within Judaism of the coming of both a priestly Messiah and a kingly Messiah. Its unique development in Hebrews arises from the profound reflection of a creative and subtle Christian mind at work on traditional materials.

The concept of the Law of Moses as 'a shadow of the good things to come instead of the true form of these realities' (10:1) and the earthly tabernacle as 'a copy of the true one' in heaven (9:23–24) seems to reflect Greek (Platonic) views of the relation between the things of heaven and the things of earth and may point to the author's Hellenistic training. This is confirmed in part by his use of the Greek Old Testament (the Septuagint) for his quotations.

Some scholars have seen at various points in Hebrews a marked similarity to the thought of the Greek-influenced Jewish philosopher Philo of Alexandria (c. 10 BC to AD 45). Others have identified

James

Representation of the Jerusalem Temple on a coin of the Bar Kochba revolt, A.D. 132–135.

Gnostic elements in the theology of Hebrews (on Gnosticism see p. 280). And yet others argue for the impact on the author of sectarian Judaism, such as appears in the Dead Sea Scrolls.

The extent of Paul's influence on the author is not clear. There are both similarities to and striking differences from Paul. On the whole, the approach in Hebrews to the Law and Israel's sacrificial system is fundamentally different from Paul's. It is evident that Judaism, Greek culture, and primitive Christianity all contributed to the portrait of Jesus in Hebrews.

One of the most controversial books in the history of the church has been the Letter of James. It first appeared in a time of hot controversy over the relative importance of faith and works in Christian belief and practice, and it entered the lists on the side of works.

The book was slow in gaining general acceptance in the church. The writings of important early church fathers such as Irenaeus, Tertullian, Cyprian, and Hippolytus do not quote from or mention it. Origen (third century) is the first church leader we know of to quote from it and to regard it as authoritative. Athanasius, in his Easter letter of AD 367, put it among the twenty-seven books (those now in our New Testament) which were to be regarded as canonical and 'divine.' Its place was finally made secure by Jerome's inclusion of it in the Latin Vulgate at the end of the fourth century. But some portions of the church, particularly in Syria, continued to contest its right to a place among the New Testament books.

Martin Luther called the book 'an epistle of straw,' in contrast to the pure gold of the gospel contained in Romans and Galatians. He felt that it did not properly teach Christ and the true way of salvation as set forth by Paul.

Today the Letter of James is looked on more sympathetically, as a valid protest against a form of heresy which exalted 'faith' to the neglect of 'deeds.' Most interpreters now believe that Paul would have agreed with James that a faith which is not expressed in moral conduct is not *Christian* faith. The book argues powerfully and correctly that faith needs hands and feet – a point Paul also stressed.

Literary Character and Contents

At a first look, the book appears to be an epistle or letter. But, apart from the greeting of the first verse, it bears no marks of a letter. It has no conclusion and farewell; it offers no information about the readers to whom it might be addressed.

Its contents are like the book of Proverbs, Ecclesiasticus (the Wisdom of Jesus the Son of Sirach) of the Apocrypha, and various sections of New Testament books dealing with ethics. Some of its sayings echo the Sermon on the Mount. It presents crisp, salty wisdom about the true way of life after the manner of Israel's Wisdom teachers (including Jesus).

Like the Jewish Wisdom books, the Letter of James has no clear pattern or

organization. The sections are somewhat loosely strung together.

The book deals with themes dear to the heart of Israel's wise men (true versus false wisdom, the power of the tongue, the lot and destiny of rich and poor, the meaning of suffering, the importance of God's law and obedience to it, the example of Old Testament figures). In form and content James is a book of wisdom, rather than an epistle or letter. It undoubtedly served in some portion of the early Christian church as a book of instruction in the meaning and way of Christian discipleship.

Purpose and Message

The book seems to have both a specific and a general purpose. The author attacks vigorously a heresy which exalts faith and ignores works. He insists that 'faith apart from works is dead' (2:26) and argues for the importance of works by an appeal to Old Testament examples (2:21–25). One might think he is attacking Paul directly (Rom. 3:28), even using Abraham to prove exactly the opposite conclusion from that drawn by Paul (Rom. 4).

Probably, he is attacking not Paul but a distortion of Paul's teaching by people who lacked Paul's balance. Paul believed that good works are the result of a trusting, loyal relationship to God. One's faith becomes active in deeds of love (Gal. 5:6). Paul and James emphasize different sides of the faith-works debate, but neither regards the other side as unimportant. Paul's teaching was seized on by people who turned it into an excuse for immorality (Rom. 6:1 ff.; 1 Cor. 5:1—6:20; Phil. 3:17–19). It is against such persons that the book of James argues.

More generally, the book speaks to Christians everywhere who find their cup of suffering full to overflowing. In addition to the sufferings that are the common lot of humankind, there are those which arise from Christian living in a pagan world. The writer wants the readers to see their sufferings as an opportunity for

---

Outline

The Greeting: James to God's pilgrim people (the church) in many lands of the world (1:1)

The Teaching (1:2—5:20)
The joy of trials (1:2–4)
The double-minded person (1:5–8)
The perishing rich (1:9–11)
The enduring righteous (1:12–15)
God, the source of all good (1:16–18)
Hearing and doing (1:19–27)
Impartiality (2:1–13)
Faith and works (2:14–26)
Requirements for teachers in the church (3:1–18)
Submission to God (4:1–10)
The evil of evil-speaking (4:11–12)
The sin of presumption (4:13–17)
The doomed rich (5:1–6)
The coming of the Lord (5:7–11)
Absolute truthfulness (5:12)
Prayer and the power of God (5:13–18)
Restoration of the erring fellow Christian (5:19–20)

spiritual growth. He wants them to have confidence in God's good purpose for them and to remain loyal to him in every distressing circumstance. He holds out for the righeous the prospect of a blessed reward at the day of judgment, which he sees immediately ahead. Meanwhile they are to live in peace with one another, to avoid various dangers to their faith, to seek physical and spiritual health, and to act out their faith by deeds of love in daily life.

The Letter of James is a book of practical morality, a healthy corrective to a deviant form of Christianity. It contends that the kind of religion approved by God consists not simply in correct belief, inner feelings, and pious confessions but also in righteous conduct and deeds of mercy.

Authorship and Date

In the sixteenth century Erasmus, recognizing the excellent Greek in which the letter was written, denied that its author could have been James, the brother of Jesus.

In our time many scholars have argued that the book was written by some later James. Some have held that it was originally a Jewish work which was edited and reissued as a Christian book, chiefly by the insertion of the name 'Jesus Christ' in two places (1:1; 2:1).

There are still influential defenders of the traditional authorship. They claim that James, Jesus' brother, could indeed have come to a first-class knowledge of Greek and that the thought of the book agrees with what we know about this Jerusalem Christian leader from the Acts and Paul's letters.

The Greeting (1:1), they say, is to be taken literally: the letter was sent to dispersed Jewish Christians, who were scattered after the death of Stephen (Acts 8:1). They point to the author's lack of knowledge of Paul's letters and to the appearance in the book of an early form of future hope and of the primitive tradition

The Damascus Gate, Jerusalem.

The Temple Mount area and Mount of Olives from the wall of the old city, Jerusalem.

about the teaching of Jesus (5:12).

But doubts persist about the traditional authorship and purpose of the book. It is quite possible that it contains actual memories of the teaching of James, the brother of the Lord, put together by a disciple of James under his teacher's name. Such issuance of a famous teacher's material by a disciple under the teacher's name seems to have been common in that day. (See p. 320.)

If the letter was indeed written by James, the Lord's brother, the date falls before AD 62, when, according to Josephus, James was martyred. If a follower of James issued the book under his teacher's name, the date would be around the end of the first century.

Original Readers

The epistle is addressed to 'the twelve tribes in the Dispersion' (1:1). Does this mean Jews of the Diaspora (Dispersion), thus Jews living outside Palestine? The contents of the book lead to a negative answer. The problems of Diaspora Jews are not discussed, and there is no evangelistic appeal.

Does it mean Jewish Christians, as distinguished from Gentile Christians, in various parts of the Greco-Roman world? Probably not, for the teaching seems to apply to all Christians, not just to those of one ethnic background.

It is likely that 'the twelve tribes' means to suggest that the whole Christian church is the true Israel, which lives on earth as a pilgrim or sojourner and whose home is heaven (Gal. 6:16; Phil. 3:20; 1 Pet. 2:11; Heb. 11:13–16).

Many Christian marks show that the book was not originally a Jewish work: for example, the name 'Lord Jesus Christ' (1:1; 2:1); the reference to the readers as 'first fruits' (1:18; cf. 1 Cor. 15:20; Rom. 8:29; Rev. 14:4); the characterization of God's law as 'the perfect law, the law of liberty' (1:25), a phrase not used in Judaism; the many echoes of the teaching of Jesus (1:5, 17=Matt. 7:7 ff.; 1:22= Matt. 7:24 ff.; 4:12=Matt. 7:1; 5:12= Matt. 5:34–37). The author was a Christian, undoubtedly of Jewish background, who wrote for Christians everywhere.

1 Peter

1 Peter is one of the most attractive books in the New Testament. It joins together several important strains in the Judeo-Christian religion: the priestly (*e.g.*, 1:14–19; 2:5), the prophetic (*e.g.*, 1:22–25; 2:9–12), the devotional (*e.g.*, 1:6–8;

4:13–14), and the theological (*e.g.*, the meaning of baptism and of undeserved suffering, and the Christian hope for the future).

The whole book glows with the warmth of personal and communal devotion to Jesus Christ. It looks forward in joyous anticipation to the great homecoming of all the children of God at the appearance of Jesus Christ and shows how one should spend time in the pagan world meanwhile.

First Readers and Purpose

The letter is addressed to 'the exiles of the Dispersion in Pontus, Galatia, Cappadocia, Asia, and Bithynia' (1:1). These are places in Asia Minor, comprising most of the country we now know as Turkey.

The readers were Gentile Christians, some of them possibly former God-fearers

---

Theme and Outline

Theme: You are heirs of salvation through suffering.

Greeting (1:1–2).
The apostle Peter to God's scattered people, who lodge for awhile in Pontus, Galatia, Cappadocia, Asia, and Bithynia: Grace and peace.

Body (1:3—5:11).

God's purpose of salvation for you (1:3—2:10).
1. You are its appointed heirs (1:3–5).
2. You are its joyful, though disciplined, heirs (1:6–9).
3. You are its fortunate heirs (1:10–12).
4. You are to be its holy heirs (1:13–25).
5. You are to be its full-grown and fully-equipped heirs (2:1–10).

God's standard of conduct for you (2:11—4:11).
1. Maintain good conduct among the Gentiles, so that they may be converted by your good behavior (2:11–12).
2. Be subject to God, to the emperor, to governors, and to every human authority so that you may silence ignorant and stupid criticism (2:13–17).

3. Let servants obey and respect their masters, both the considerate and the harsh ones, for in bearing patiently unjust suffering they are following the example of Christ (2:18–25).
4. Let wives be submissive to their husbands, reverent, chaste, and modest; and let husbands be considerate of their wives – for they share together God's gracious gift of life (3:1–7).
5. Be zealous for what is right, caring nothing about any suffering that may result (3:8—4:6).
6. In the time before the end, pray, love one another, and use the gifts God gave you to serve one another (4:7–11).

God's discipline of suffering for you (4:12—5:11).
1. Suffering is for your benefit (4:12–19).
2. Suffering sheep must be tended by sympathetic shepherds (5:1–5).
3. Suffering is according to the will of God – to perfect, establish, and strengthen (5:6–11).

Conclusion (5:12–14).

(see Acts 10:2, 13:16, 26; 16:14; 17:17; 18:7). These uncircumcized Gentile auditors in the synagogues of the Greek world were prime prospects for conversion by the first Christian missionaries.

The pagan background of the readers is several times mentioned (1:14, 18; 2:9–10; 3:6; 4:3). The phrase 'exiles of the Dispersion' in the address (1:1) indicates not that they were Jews living in the Gentile world but that they, as Christians, were children of God scattered abroad in the world, away from their true home in heaven (see Phil. 3:20; Heb. 13:14; James 1:1; 1 Pet. 2:11).

Grievous troubles had befallen these Christians. The exact nature of their situation is difficult to determine. Two views are possible.

First, the persecution may have consisted of vicious assaults by pagan neighbors who resented the Christians' new and exclusive manner of life (4:3–4; cf. 2:12, 15; 3:9, 14–16; 4:14) and possibly haled them before local police and magistrates. However, no references to imprisonments, confiscation of property, trials before judges, or bloody martyrdom appear in the book. And the counsel to be obedient to the emperor and to governors (2:13–14) seems to imply satisfactory relationships with the state.

Second, official governmental persecution is a possibility. 'The fiery ordeal' (4:12) may refer to the drastic experience of trial by an imperial court for bearing the name of Christ (4:14, 16) and a subsequent death sentence. Such persecution took place in the time of the emperor Trajan and of Pliny, the imperial legate of Bithynia-Pontus (c. AD 110).

On the whole, the first view is preferable. The phrases 'for the name of Christ' (4:14) and 'as a Christian' (4:16) do not necessarily mean that being a Christian was an offense punishable by the government (as in the time of Trajan and Pliny). Since there was no organized, worldwide governmental persecution of the church until the third century, the suffering of the church mentioned in 5:9 cannot have been of this sort. It must rather have consisted of widespread local harassment, arising from the ill will of the pagan populace. The positive attitude toward the state in 2:13–14 supports this conclusion.

The purpose of the letter, then, was to encourage the Christians of the territories mentioned to bear patiently the undeserved suffering they were experiencing; they were to understand that such suffering is used by God to test, purify, and strengthen the sufferers and to prepare them for the day of judgment and the reward God will give to the faithful.

Composition

One theory is that the letter came into existence in two stages. Since 1:3—4:11 seems to be more of a sermon than a letter, since it appears to deal with suffering as possible rather than actual, and since it ends with a doxology (4:11), it may originally have been a baptismal sermon. Later, when there was an outbreak of severe persecution, this sermon was transformed into a letter by the addition of a greeting (1:1–2), specific comments about the readers' proper response to the present crisis (4:12—5:11), and a conclusion (5:12–14).

It is quite apparent that 1:3—4:11 has baptism and the new life into which it leads as a prominent theme (1:3, 23; 2:2, 9–10, 25; 3:21). However, the argument that this section was originally a baptismal sermon falls short of proof.

That the suffering mentioned in 1:3—4:11 is possible rather than actual is contradicted by 1:6, where the Greek is best translated, 'In this you exult, even though now you have been distressed for a short while (since it has to be) by various trials' (J.N.D. Kelly). In 4:4 the suffering is plainly indicated as present.

Barren landscape in Cappadocia, central Turkey.

The doxology in 4:11 is probably not the sign of the conclusion of an earlier piece of writing but simply an outburst of awe and devotion in contemplation of the marvelous grace of God and the fulfillment of humankind's true end in the glorifying of God (*cf.* Rom. 11:33–36; Gal. 1:5; Phil. 4:20; Eph. 3:21).

It is best to hold that the author composed the whole of 1 Peter as a general letter to Christians spread over a wide area of Asia Minor. He meant it to be circulated among the churches for reading in services of worship. He called their baptismal experience to mind to bring into focus their status as children of God and to remind them of the implications of their new life in God's family for their existence in the world.

Authorship and Date

There are differing views on the authorship and date.

a. Peter the apostle was the author, either in a direct or an indirect sense. From at least the time of Irenaeus (end of second century) the church regarded Peter as the writer. Certain facts in the letter may support Peter's authorship: references to the sufferings of Jesus (2:21–24; 3:18; 4:1; 5:1); echoes of Jesus' teaching, of a sort one would expect from Peter (*cf.* 1 Pet. 1:22 with John 13:34–35; 1 Pet. 2:12 with Matt. 5:16; 1 Pet 2:13–17 with Matt. 17:24–27); and parallels with Peter's speeches in the Acts of the Apostles (*cf.* 1 Pet. 1:10–12 with Acts 2:14–36). However, these facts hardly prove Peter's authorship, since most of them would be known to any church teacher from the gospel tradition and from the church tradition in the Acts.

Some scholars have argued that Silvanus, a scribe or secretary (5:12), composed the letter at Peter's direction, perhaps using Peter's outline of contents and his basic ideas. Peter may have added personally the note about Silvanus and the rest of the text (5:12–14). If Peter was the author, directly or indirectly, the date

would fall during Peter's residence in Rome ('Babylon' – 5:13), about AD 62–64.

b. The letter was written in Peter's name by an unknown author who lived at the time of Domitian's persecution of the church (*c.* AD 90–95) or in the time of Trajan and Pliny (*c.* AD 110). The Roman government carried out the persecution mentioned in the letter.

Some object to Peter's direct authorship on several grounds: that the Greek of 1 Peter is too flawless and sophisticated for a Galilean fisherman; that it is unlikely he would have quoted from the Greek (rather than the Hebrew) Old Testament; that his theology shows dependence on Paul's; and that the letter contains no special knowledge of Jesus of the sort an eyewitness would have possessed. And, as noted, they believe the persecution was the kind not experienced by the church until three decades after Peter's death.

Peter's direct authorship is unlikely. Silvanus or some other skilled writer seems to have played a major role in the creation of the letter, either in the sixties or around the end of the first century.

Teaching

The author regards the readers as newly begotten children of God who, according to the Father's will, are for a time scattered abroad in Asia Minor. They await the great homecoming in the Father's house, soon to be brought about by the return of Jesus Christ (1:5, 7, 13; 4:7, 17; 5:4).

As newborn babes, they are in need of spiritual food and spiritual growth (1:22 —2:3). They must understand and value the high destiny their Father has in store for them and not be turned aside from the goal by unbelief (2:4–8), by 'the passions of the flesh' (2:11; *cf.* 4:2–4), by love of earthly things (3:3–4; 5:2), by self-seeking and bickering (2:1; 3:8; 4:8; 5:5), and by the hostility they are experiencing from their fellow countrymen.

This hostility and the suffering it causes can be turned to good account. Christ's

2 Peter

sufferings had blessed results, both for himself and for others. Through 'being put to death in the flesh,' he was 'made alive in the spirit' (3:18 – *i.e.*, through suffering he came from mortal life to resurrection life); and through his death he brought us to God. He achieved a complete triumph over the disobedient evil spirits (3:19, 22), which opposed him and afflict his followers.

Since Christ's sufferings had such blessed consequences, the readers ought to imitate him in patient endurance of suffering (2:21–25). They must realize that suffering 'for the name of Christ' brings refinement of character (1:7), ethical fruit for one's own life (4:1), possession of the Holy Spirit (4:14), approval and reward at Christ's day of judgment (1:7; 4:13; 5:4), and ultimate participation in the glory of the coming age (1:7; 5:1, 4, 10).

'So even those whom God allows to suffer must trust themselves to the constancy of the creator and go on doing good' (4:19 JB).

2 Peter has long been a controversial book. The church of the first four or five centuries accepted it as canonical only slowly (see below); Erasmus, Calvin, and Luther had questions about its authenticity and authority; and many modern scholars have held it to be mediocre in quality alongside most of the books of the New Testament, including 1 Peter. One scholar of our time has called it 'the most dubious writing in the New Testament' (Ernst Käsemann).

Recently the pendulum has begun to swing toward a more positive evaluation, particularly by liberal scholars. Several see it not simply as an ancient document addressed to a long dead heresy but as a writing whose 'primary function from the outset was to execute the canonical role of instructing future generations of believers in the faith' (Brevard Childs). Through the figure of Peter, glorified to be sure in this book, memories of Jesus and the teaching of the first apostles (the apostolic tradition) are extended into the future, even to our time, to assist the church in its theology and life.

Purpose and Circumstances of Writing

This letter is 'an apology for primitive Christian eschatology.' This means a justification, in the face of attack, of the Christian hope of the second coming of

Theme and Outline

Theme: The certainty of the second coming of Christ and the relation of that coming to Christian living.

Greeting (1:1–2)

Body (1:3—3:18a).

The promise of the coming of Christ and his kingdom (1:3–21).
1. Entrance to that kingdom depends on moral renewal and moral living (1:3–11).
2. Fulfillment of the promise is assured by the experience on the Mount of Transfiguration and by divine revelation in Scripture (1:12–21).

Those who deny the promise and their coming doom (2:1–22)
1. In the past false prophets and disobedient angels were judged by God, and the righteous were preserved by him (2:1–10a).
2. The present false prophets will be destroyed (2:10b–22).

A refutation of the deniers and a reaffirmation of the promise and its moral requirements (3:1–18a).
1. The sure word of God, through the holy prophets and through the Lord Jesus and his apostles, announced both the appearance of these deniers and the certainty of the end of the world by fire (3:1–7).
2. The delay in Christ's coming and the end of the world must not be interpreted as a failure of the promise to be realized but as a brief opportunity for all to repent (3:8–10).
3. The hope for 'the day of God' and the coming of the New Age should stimulate believers to holy living (as Paul also urged) and to spiritual growth (3:11–18a).

Doxology (3:18b).

Christ, the end of this world, and the establishment of the New Age.

Disbelievers ('scoffers') had arisen in the church. They questioned Christ's coming (3:3–4); they led self-indulgent lives; and they led others into disbelief and sensual living (2:1–3a, 10b–22), in-

cluding those newly converted from paganism (2:18). They threatened to pervert the whole church by returning to the mire from which they had once been delivered and encouraging others to wallow there (1:9; 2:22).

The 'scoffers' were a group within the church. They may have had their own dissolute love feasts (2:13 RSV margin). They stressed their freedom in Christ from all restraints (2:19). They seem to have resembled the Gnostics at Corinth who believed they were above temptation and any earthly controls because they already were living in the New Age (see p. 280). Since salvation for these Gnostics was fully present, the traditional teaching about the second coming of Christ and the arrival of the New Age thereafter made no sense. Furthermore, they pointed out scornfully that much time had elapsed since the promise was first made to 'the fathers' (3:4, *i.e.*, the first Christians) and that the hope was therefore empty and meaningless.

2 Peter was written to counteract this anti-apocalyptic and anti-moral teaching in the church at large (1:1) by presenting to full view the figure of Peter as authoritative guarantor of the truth of the church's traditional theology and pattern of life. Its purpose was much the same as that of the Pastoral Letters, where Paul stands in heroic splendor as the God-ordained witness to the truth for subsequent generations. (On apocalyptic literature see pp. 356–7.)

Author, Date, and Place of Writing

The letter claims repeatedly that Peter the apostle was its author. Besides the direct mention of 'Simon Peter' (1:1), facts about Peter are mentioned: a direct word from Jesus about Peter's imminent death (1:14); his presence at the transfiguration of Jesus (1:16–18); a reference to another letter written to the readers (3:1 – probably our 1 Peter); and Peter's relation to Paul as that of a 'beloved brother' (3:15).

Most scholars today believe that Peter

Mount Hermon is snow-capped for much of the year.

could not have been the author but that the letter was written in his name by a disciple and admirer. The reasons for this belief are:

a. In the early church, up to the fourth century, some prominent leaders (Origen, Eusebius, and Jerome, for example) expressed or reported serious doubts that Peter the apostle wrote this letter. The letter was slow in gaining wide acceptance in the church as attested by the fact that it is nowhere mentioned by important second and third century writers (Irenaeus, Tertullian, Cyprian, Clement of Alexandria), and the somewhat later Muratorian Canon.

b. The letter has a strong Greek character. Words and phrases like God's 'excellence' (1:3), 'virtue' (1:5), 'partakers of the divine nature' (1:4), 'eyewitnesses' (1:16 – a term designating those initiated into the highest grade of the mystery religions) seem unlikely from the mind of an unhellenized Jew. The letter's wordy, pompous Greek style ill fits Peter.

c. The author of 2 Peter borrowed extensively from the letter of Jude (cf., for example, 2:1–18 with Jude 4–16, and 3:1–3 with Jude 17–18). This seems strange for the eminent Peter but not so strange for a lesser figure. And the late date of Jude (about the end of the first century) puts the later 2 Peter long after Peter's death, which occurred between AD 64 and 67.

d. The nature of the heresy attacked, and particularly the heretics' scoffing at the church's unfulfilled hope for the future, points to a time considerably later than the death of Peter. We learn from 1 Clement (c. AD 95) that doubting and questioning of Christ's return was expressed in the church of that time.

e. The collection of Paul's letters, their acceptance as 'scripture' (3:15b–16), and the implied authority of the church in the interpretation of scripture (1:20–21) point to a time later than Peter.

f. There grew up in the early church a considerable body of literature which claimed Peter as author but which clearly was not written by him (a Gospel of Peter, an Acts of Peter, and an Apocalypse of Peter). It was not uncommon for disciples of a great teacher to write works in his name.

Conservative scholars in the main attempt to refute these data. They hold to the following points among others: the letter clearly claims to be from Peter (1:1, 12–18; 3:1); though late in being recognized as his, its claim was eventually sustained by the church; the language and style is not impossible for Peter, as there are marked similarities to 1 Peter (which they regard as unquestionably Peter's); the differences are due to variation in subject matter, differing circumstances of writing, different scribes used, etc.; Paul's letters were collected earlier than liberal scholars assume.

But even conservatives have bent under the weight of the arguments against Peter's authorship. One (R.J. Bauckham) has recently surrendered Petrine authorship and proposed that the readers would know immediately that the letter was 'intended to be an entirely transparent fiction,' since this type of fictional letter was well known in Judaism.

Precisely who our author was is unknown. He probably was a Gentile Christian who wrote sometime between AD 100 and 150, probably nearer the later date. Many regard the letter as the latest writing in the New Testament.

The place of writing may have been Egypt, Rome, or Asia Minor.

Literary Form and Message

In literary type 2 Peter is a last will and testament to the church, offered by its author before his imminent death (1:12–14). He wishes to leave a legacy from his vast knowledge and experience to guide others after his departure. Farewell addresses and testaments of this sort were employed in both Judaism and Christianity (Gen. 49; The Testaments of the Twelve Patriarchs; Acts 20:17–35; 2 Timothy). In this type of literature there is a rehearsal of significant events in the testator's life, an ethical exhortation based on what has been said, and a foretelling of what will happen in the last days.

Here the great stature and authority of Peter are emphasized: his divine call, his empowerment, his specially accorded revelations of God's promises, of the way to participate in the divine nature (1:3–4), and of his coming death (1:14). Strongly stressed is his eyewitness privilege at the Transfiguration (1:16–18), which was granted to him as a foreshadowing of the Lord's coming in glory, future judgment of the wicked, and the establishing of 'new heavens and a new earth' (3:13). Therefore these promises are sure to be fulfilled (1:16, 19). In view of all of this the testator then tells them what sort of persons they ought to be (3:11, 14, 17–18).

The message is that the church's historic faith is precious. The readers should value it and perpetuate it. Perverted people seek to undermine and destroy it.

Especially precious is the promise of the second coming of Christ and the inauguration of the 'new heavens and a new earth in which righteousness dwells' (3:13). Contrary to the teaching of the heretics, we cannot fully obtain salvation in this life; we are called and elected to 'entrance into the eternal kingdom of our Lord and Savior Jesus Christ' (1:11). Of the coming of this kingdom prophets and apostles – the latter at the command of Jesus – spoke (3:2).

The present world is a place where moral corruption dwells (1:4). The world will be destroyed (3:7). We do not have a stable eternal order here, as maintained by the heretics. (Here the author shares the early Christian view that Christians are pilgrims and strangers in the earth, who have here 'no lasting city, but ... seek the city which is to come' (Heb. 13:14; cf. Phil. 3:20; 1 Pet. 1:1; 2:11; Rev. 21:1).

There are moral requirements for entrance to the coming kingdom. From the beginning of God's dealings with humankind, he has judged sinful people – and

1 John

Statues lining the Via Sacra in the Forum, Rome.

even sinful angels! – and has preserved the righteous. Thus the lewd, greedy, lawless heretics will be condemned to 'the nether gloom of darkness' (2:17). The kingdom *now* or *then* is not theirs!

The delay in the coming of the kingdom is an expression of God's mercy. He wants everyone to repent and enter it (3:9). While the righteous await that day, they should dedicate themselves to holy and godly living (1:5–11; 3:11, 14, 18).

Here are authentic teachings of early Christianity, warmheartedly urged on Christians of all ages. (On the second coming of Christ see pp. 502–7.)

1 John is one of the New Testament's most loved books. It shares this distinction with the Gospel of John, to which it is in many respects strikingly similar.

Its appeal is due to many features: its tender tone – an old man speaking to his 'little children'; its clarity on what it means to be a disciple of Jesus; its balance between doctrine and behavior; its gems of wisdom; its simplicity and yet its profundity; its personal nature – 'that which we have seen and heard we proclaim ... to *you*' (1:3); its joyful, victorious spirit; and much more. It stands near or at the height of New Testament literature.

While the book has an identifiable central emphasis, its contents are somewhat disorganized. Subjects do not follow one another in strict logical relationship but recur frequently in new combinations, like themes in a musical composition. A logical outline, therefore, can only approximately represent the contents.

Literary Form and Destination

In form the document is more like a tract or a sermon than a letter. It has no opening and ending characteristic of a letter and no reference to individuals. It is evident, however, that author and readers were well known to each other. The intimate forms of address show this: 'my little children,' 'children,' and 'beloved.' There is a pastoral tone to the book, such as would be normal if a trusted leader were giving

Outline

Theme: The message of the apostles is the standard of Christian truth and experience.

Prologue: The apostolic testimony to the word of life (1:1–4).

Body (1:5—5:12)
The apostolic message concerning God's holiness, human sin, and the way of salvation (1:5—2:17).
The betrayers of the apostolic message and their deceptions (2:18–27).
The apostolic message and life in the family of God (2:28—3:24).
Tests of fidelity to the apostolic message and experience (4:1—5:12).

Epilogue: Summary of Christian certainties (5:13–21).

counsel to followers who loved and respected him.

It is possible that the author or someone commissioned by him reproduced copies of this document and sent or carried them to churches in a certain geographic area, perhaps Asia Minor or Syria, to help them with a problem common to all.

Since the earliest evidence for the existence of 1 John comes from Polycarp and Papias (second quarter of second century), both of whom lived in Asia Minor, it is reasonable to conclude that the book originated there. Some scholars, however, advocate a Syrian origin.

Circumstances of Writing

False teachers were unsettling the church by denying its long-standing faith in Jesus as the Messiah, the Son of God (2:22–23; 5:5), and as the Messiah–Son of God come in the flesh (4:2).

Apparently these teachers were not simply taking the Jewish position, which denied flatly that Jesus was the Messiah promised to God's people, for these heretics had been members of the church. Rather they denied that the heavenly Christ–Son of God was fully and inseparably to be identified with the man Jesus of Nazareth. This heavenly Christ–Son of

God could not have become flesh, they reasoned, for flesh was essentially evil. The view of flesh as essentially evil was characteristic of the Gnostics (see below).

The false teachers boasted about their superior knowledge and love of God (2:4; 4:20) and their fellowship with him (1:6; 2:9), but they did not follow Jesus' way of life (2:6). They lived in sin (2:4; 3:8, 10), even though they claimed to be above all sin (1:8, 10). They loved the world of sense and sensuality and apparently justified their indulging in its pleasures (2:15–17; 4:5).

They seem to have had little concern about preserving peaceful relations with their fellow Christians; in fact, they stirred up discord (2:9–11; 3:10–16). They were schismatics who withdrew from the fellowship and formed a rival group (2:19). They sought to entice others into their circle (2:26; 3:7).

Our author calls them 'antichrists' (2:18; 4:1–3). According to Jewish and early Christian belief, many antichrists were to come before the end of the age (Mark 13:6, 22; Matt. 24:4–5; 2 Thess. 2:3–12). He sees these false teachers as agents of the devil to lead people astray. At his coming the Messiah (Christ) will destroy them and rescue the righteous for life in his kingdom. Their appearance is thus for our author a sign that it is 'the last hour' (2:18). The appearance of Christ (2:28; 3:2) and the day of judgment (4:17) will expose the heretics for what they really are.

Their denial that the Savior came 'in the flesh,' their assertion that knowledge of God lifted people above all commandments and restraints, and their fleshly involvement with 'the world' point clearly to the Gnostic heresy that arose in the church in the second half of the first century and came to a head in the second century. (See pp. 318–9.)

The heresy that 1 John seeks to counteract bears some resemblance to the teaching of a certain Cerinthus, who appeared in Asia Minor toward the end of the first century. He held that the world

The Asclepium and theater, Pergamum.

was made by a lower power, not the supreme God, that Jesus was conceived and born like all other people, that he became more righteous and wiser than others, and that after his baptism the Christ descended upon him in the form of a dove. Before his crucifixion the Christ withdrew from him, because the heavenly, spiritual Christ could not suffer.

The heretics' denial, described in 1 John, that the Christ–Son of God had come 'in the flesh,' fits this general outlook. Their claim that they were above sin accords with the Gnostic view that they had entered through baptism the life of the Resurrection and were therefore exempt from all earthly restraints (see p. 344). Their fleshly involvement with the world arose from their doctrine of creation, which held that the material world was created by a lower power and is essentially evil, while spirit is the creature of the Supreme Power. Since a person is not a unity, what goes on in the flesh cannot affect what goes on in the spirit. To let worldly desire have free reign is to act in accordance with what one is by creation. Therefore, the flesh may legitimately be indulged.

Thus, the heresy struck at the very vitals of the Christian faith. Christians who clung to the traditional beliefs were being upset in doctrine, morals, and emotional certainty.

Some scholars have suggested that the heretics withdrew from the church as the result of a controversy over the proper interpretation of the tradition in the Gospel of John. The secessionists read the Gospel through Gnostic eyes and downplayed the importance of Jesus' earthly life and death in the effecting of salvation. The other group, to which the author of 1 John belonged, insisted that the Gospel emphasized the reality and necessity of the incarnation and Jesus' death as expiation for sin. 1 John is this author's commentary on the Gospel of John (even a sort of imitation of it) to show how it should be interpreted – as teaching that the Word really became flesh and that the apostles actually heard, saw, and touched 'the word of life' (1 John 1:1–3) and that his death (blood) was totally efficacious (1:7; 2:2). While the church of later centuries did use 1 John to interpret the Gospel of John, it must be said that evidence is lacking that the author meant his treatise as a commentary on that Gospel.

Message

The author says that he is writing to believers that they may know that they have eternal life (5:13). The message, then, is one of reassurance.

First, the author reassures them doctrinally. The faith handed down to the church from the beginning was based on the moral nature of God: 'God is light and in him is no darkness at all' (1:5). Fellowship with God is possible only on the basis of people's moral renewal and obedience to God.

This renewal is gained through confession of one's sin and through divine forgiveness made effective for us through the death of Christ and his intercession for us (1:6—2:2). Moral obedience is the result of the imitation of Christ (2:3–6). So the church has always taught and must continue to teach!

The agent of our moral redemption is Jesus Christ. He was the incarnate Son of God by whom the life of eternity was manifested in time. The church, through its first apostles, had indisputable experience of this God-in-flesh revelation. The humanity of Christ was real, not an appearance; it could be experienced by the senses (1:1–3).

Jesus' power to redeem rests not only on his receiving the Holy Spirit at his baptism (so that he could reveal divine mysteries to human beings) but also on his death as the incarnate Son of God (so that he might be 'the remedy for the defilement of our sins' – 2:2 NEB). Through the God-man, both in his baptism and death (5:6), our lives are enlightened and our sins are taken away. Furthermore, he

is our present helper ('one to plead our cause with the Father' – 2:1 NEB). So the church has always taught and must continue to teach!

Those who by faith in Christ find their sins canceled and their lives united to God are united also in the fellowship of the family of God. The bond of union is love, 'for God is love' (4:8). To live in love is to fulfill Christ's 'new commandment' (2:8). To live in love means to serve one another in practical ways (3:16–18).

And life in union with God, Christ and fellow Christians means a life of victory over sin. The believer is perpetually cleansed from his sins (1:8–10). 'The man who lives "in Christ" does not habitually sin' and 'the man who is really God's son does not practice sin' (3:6, 9 Phillips). Thus, the heretics' fleshly indulgence is contrary to the gospel's demand as preached from the beginning.

How may one know for sure that he has eternal life and that the heretics are wrong? There are tests: (1) the test of love (do we love fellow Christians? – 3:14; 4:7–8, 16); (2) the test of belief and confession (do we believe and confess Jesus as the Son of God incarnate? – 4:2, 15; 5:1, 5); (3) the test of conduct (do we imitate Christ and do what is right? – 2:5b–6, 29; 3:7, 10); (4) the test of conscience (does our heart condemn us? – 3:21); (5) the test of the Spirit (does God's Spirit abide in us? – 2:20, 27; 3:24; 4:13). Christians can know that they have eternal life (5:13).

Author and Date

Several views of the authorship of 1 John have been advocated.

a. The writer was the Apostle John, the son of Zebedee. Some suggested proofs are: the testimonies of Irenaeus, Clement of Alexandria, and Tertullian (second-third centuries); the writer's claim to personal contact with Jesus (1:1–4); the air of authority in the epistle (a 'father' writing to 'little children'); striking similarities to the Gospel of John (believed to be by John the Apostle).

2 and 3 John

b. The writer was John the Elder, who also wrote 2 and 3 John (2 John 1; 3 John 1). The three epistles are strongly similar and 2 and 3 came from the hand of one who does not claim apostolic status.

c. The writer was an unknown disciple of John the Apostle. After the Apostle's death several of his followers gathered his teachings and perspectives into written form: one authored the Gospel of John, another the three epistles (unless 1 John came from one disciple and 2 and 3 John from another), and yet another the book of Revelation (C.K. Barrett's suggestion). Thus there was a Johannine circle. The group of disciples understood themselves as the continuing voice of their great teacher.

Conservative scholars advocate 'a' and liberal scholars divide into some form of 'b' and 'c'. Both groups put the date of writing around the end of the first century, on the basis of the knowledge of 1 John by such early church writers as Polycarp and Papias (both second quarter of second century), the nature of the heresy attacked, and the use of or similarity to the Gospel of John.

These letters, probably each originally written on one sheet of papyrus, offer good examples of the informal letters of the Greco-Roman world. They are not literary productions. They owe their survival to the fact that their author was an important person in the church. Their contents alone would hardly justify their inclusion in the New Testament. In vocabulary, style, and general ideas they are strikingly similar to 1 John and the Gospel of John.

Situation and Purpose

All three letters of John reflect the same general situation: the spread of Gnostic teaching in the church, particularly the denial of the complete and indissoluble union of the eternal Son of God with the man Jesus (see pp. 348–50).

2 John addresses a specific local church ('the elect lady' – 1:1) to commend those in that church who have been faithful to the truth; to warn the members of the danger of the heresy for the life and future of the church; and to direct the readers to deny the heretics all hospitality and even friendly greeting. The heresy must be stopped through excommunication.

3 John speaks to an individual, Gaius, apparently an important and somewhat affluent person. He was a beloved friend, and perhaps a convert, of the elder (vs. 4). He had been loyal to the true faith and had shown this by receiving and assisting

Themes and Outlines

2 John

Theme: A warning against receiving and entertaining traveling false teachers

Greeting: The elder to 'the elect lady' (some local church) (vss. 1–3)

Body (vss. 4–11)
A commendation of some church members for fidelity to truth (vs. 4)
A reminder of the commandment to love one another (vss. 5–6)
A warning concerning traveling teachers of false doctrine about Jesus Christ and a command not to receive and entertain them (vss. 7–11)

Conclusion: The writer's plans and final greeting (vss. 12–13)

3 John

Theme: Hospitality and financial assistance for traveling missionaries who teach true Christian doctrine

Introduction (vss. 1–4)
Greeting: The elder to Gaius (vs. 1)
Prayer and thanksgiving: Prayer for Gaius' wellbeing and thanksgiving for his loyalty to the truth (vss. 2–4)

Body (vss. 5–12)
Commendation of Gaius' past help for traveling missionaries and encouragement to continue it (vss. 5–8)
Criticism of the arrogant Diotrephes for his opposition to the writer, his inhospitality to the traveling misisonaries, and his excommunication of hospitable members (vss. 9–10); encouragement of Gaius to imitate good, rather than evil, persons (vs. 11)
Commendation of Demetrius (vs. 12)

Conclusion: The writer's hope for a personal visit and his final greeting (vss. 13–15)

financially certain traveling preachers of true doctrine. The author commends him for this and urges him to continue his good work.

Quite a contrary attitude characterized a certain Diotrephes, apparently in some local church known to Gaius but of which Gaius was not a member. (If Gaius and Diotrephes had lived in the same community and belonged to the same local church, the elder would hardly have needed to inform Gaius of Diotrephes' evil attitudes and deeds.) Diotrephes turned away the missionary representatives approved by the elder, forbade others to welcome them, and excommunicated – or attempted to excommunicate – those who had received them.

What authority for his actions Diotrephes claimed is not known. Was he a member of the board of elders of a local congregation? Had he assumed authority not rightfully his? Or was he (more probably) a bishop over a local church or possibly an area? Was he a Gnostic? He certainly stood opposed to the work the elder was trying to do, namely, to counteract Gnostic heresy. (See the discussion of 1 John.) The doctrinal clash had resulted in a clash of authority.

Author and Date

The writer calls himself 'the elder.' This can mean an old man or a member of the directing body of a local church. But more probably the title had a special meaning in Asia Minor. Irenaeus, from Smyrna in the second century, referred to elders as disciples of the Apostles. The term thus designated one who, because of personal contact with the apostles, was honored as an authoritative teacher of the historic faith.

If this is the meaning of 'the elder,' he was a disciple of an apostle. This apostle may have been John, the Son of Zebedee (see p. 259), whose historical memories and interpretation of the faith the elder, as disciple, passed on. Conservative scholars believe that this 'Elder' was John the Apostle himself.

The date was around the end of the first century, perhaps 90–115.

Jude

We know Jude best today for the doxology with which it concludes (vss. 24–25). Not many read the whole book, for its content is largely negative and its references to little-known persons and obscure apocryphal books seem to give it a dated character.

It goes without saying that the book served a purpose in the life of the church at the time when it was written. Its urgent appeal to Christians to 'contend for the faith which was once for all delivered to the saints' (vs. 3) was evidently a rallying cry in orthodox circles in its day.

This cry may well remind Christians that the backward look must be joined to the present and future look if authentic Christianity is to continue in the world. Tradition, while it must not hinder progress, must guide it and test it.

Form, Circumstances, and Purpose

Jude is more of a tract than a letter. It has no specific addressees and no personal ending, but rather a liturgical one (a doxology). It must have been addressed to the church in general. The tract seems to oppose a form of Gnosticism that was threatening the life and future of the church (see the discussions of 1 Corinthians, Colossians, 1 Timothy, 2 Peter, 1 John). Jude tells us little about its doctrine but a great deal about its moral consequences. Doctrine and practice are clearly

---

Theme and Outline

Theme: God's judgment will fall on those in the church who undermine the faith and way of life once for all delivered to the saints.

Introduction (vss. 1–4)
Greeting: Jude to called, beloved, and kept Christians (vss. 1–2)
Occasion of writing: The appearance in the church of persons who are undermining the historic faith by perverting God's grace into an opportunity for immorality and by rejecting Jesus Christ (vss. 3–4)

Body (vss. 5–23)
Reminders from the past of God's judgment on the unbelieving, rebellious, and immoral (vss. 5–7)
The sins of the godless people and others like them in the Old Testament (vss. 8–13)
The prophecies of Enoch and the apostles concerning the coming of these evil persons and their judgment by God (vss. 14–19)
What the faithful must do to protect themselves and counteract these godless ones (vss. 20–23)

Doxology (vss. 24–25)

---

tied together in the statement that these heretics 'pervert the grace of our God into licentiousness and deny our only Master and Lord, Jesus Christ' (vs. 4).

Their evil practices evidently were based on the belief that God's grace allowed them freedom to indulge the flesh, in fact, commanded them to do so. Their reasoning seems to have been that by the resurrection experienced in baptism they became truly spiritual people, no longer subject to the laws of their pre-resurrection life. They were free children of God. Furthermore, since by creation the flesh is essentially evil and the spirit good, and since only the spirit is eternal, what one does in the flesh cannot affect what one is in the spirit. They thus plunged into licentiousness and its associated evils with abandon and relish.

The statement that they 'deny our only Master and Lord, Jesus Christ' may mean only that their immoral behavior denies the moral requirements laid down by

Model of Jerusalem in AD 66.

Jesus (*e.g.*, Matt. 5:27–28). But it probably means more, as the author's interest in true doctrine indicates (vss. 3, 20–23, 25). In 1 John 2:22 the heretics deny 'that Jesus is the Christ,' that is, that the heavenly Christ, the Son of God, became flesh in the man Jesus. The suggestions that the immoral people attacked in Jude receive secret revelations (vs. 8) and regard themselves as Spirit-filled, but are not (vs. 19), point to Gnostic views.

It appears that they did not withdraw from the church. They were present at the love feasts (vs. 12), that is, at church suppers in connection with which the Eucharist was often observed (1 Cor. 11:17–34). They turned these into orgies.

Their disrespect for authority and the angels, appointed by God to enforce the natural and moral orders, was shocking to the author (vs. 8), as was their harsh, unloving spirit and their greed (vs. 11).

The author's purpose may have been to unmask these heretics and build up the faithful by encouraging them to continue in the traditional way. He exhorts them to pray in the Holy Spirit, to abide in God's love, to look forward in hope to eternal life, and to rescue as many fellow Christians as possible from the heretics' spell (vss. 22–23). They should avoid intimate contact with the heretics (vs. 23*c*).

Some recent scholars have questioned the 'Gnostic' identification of the opponents and suggested that the author's purpose was to warn the church that the last days had arrived and that it should prepare for the coming judgment. This he did by using stereotyped phrases about false prophets from Jewish and Christian literature. He showed by Old Testament examples how God deals with such persons. He 'addresses the phenomenon of heresy and not any one specific form of error' (Brevard Childs). While the heresy is indeed characterized in generalities, many scholars feel that it is unmistakably Gnostic in character (so Helmut Koester).

Author and Date

Several possibilities exist.

a. He was Jude (Judas), the brother of Jesus. He is identified in 1:1 as a 'brother of James,' possibly the well-known James the brother of Jesus, who was head of the Jerusalem church (Gal. 1:19; 2:9; Acts 15:13 ff.; 21:18). Jesus, James, and Jude are named together in Mark 6:3. Modesty may account for his identifying himself as 'brother of James,' rather than as 'brother of Jesus.'

b. He was an otherwise unknown Jude who had a brother named James, also otherwise unknown. Both names were common in those days. In this case we have no idea who Jude was.

c. He was a bishop Jude (Judas) of the Jerusalem church, early in the reign of the Emperor Trajan (AD 98–117).

d. The author wrote under the name of Jude, of whom he may have been a disciple or an admirer.

This book was widely accepted in the church of the second and third centuries, but in the fourth and fifth centuries it often was placed among the 'disputed' writings, especially in the Eastern church. The author of 2 Peter, writing in perhaps the second quarter of the second century, reproduced in his work a large portion of the text of Jude (see pp. 344–6). The early church thought the author was Jude, the brother of the Lord.

Possibility b leaves unexplained how the book gained acceptance in New Testament scripture, if the author was some nondescript Jude. Possibility c leaves unexplained the phrase 'brother of James,' who obviously was some important, but now unknown, person. Some have assumed (without proof) that 'brother' was inserted into the text after the book was written.

Arguments in favor of d are impressive to many scholars. Jude 17–18 seems to refer to the apostles as great men of the past. And the type of heresy the author was combatting in the book fits best the Gnosticism of the early second century –

too late for Jude, the brother of Jesus.

However, it is possible that the book of Jude was written no later than AD 80–90. Gnostic trends had begun to appear at this time, and Jude, the Lord's brother, could have lived until AD 80 or a little later.

On balance, it seems best to hold that the brother of the Lord somehow stands behind the book, if not as its actual author, then as the teacher of the man who wrote it in his name.

The Use of Apocryphal Writings and the First Readers

There are two passages in Jude which directly depend on uncanonical books: vs. 9 and vss. 14–15. The first – the dispute of the archangel Michael with the devil over the body of Moses – according to early Christian writers comes from a first-century Jewish book, the Assumption of Moses. The second is a direct quotation from 1 Enoch 1:9. (See pp. 416–7).

The high esteem in which the author obviously holds these Jewish apocalyptic books and the readers' presumed familiarity with them may imply a Jewish-Christian background for the author and possibly for his readers.

A good guess for the place of origin is some Greek-speaking community of Palestine or Syria, possibly Antioch, in view of some similarity between the heretical teachers and those opposed in the Gospel of Matthew.

The Revelation to John

'Revelation' (from a Greek word translated in English 'apocalypse') means a disclosure of something hidden and unknown. In early Christianity it came to designate Jewish and Christian books which disclose what is happening in the heavens and what is to be the future of this world. They point out the implications of all this for life in the present earthly moment.

The Revelation to John is the second great apocalypse in our Bible. The first is the book of Daniel (see pp. 178–83). Many other books of this sort existed among the Jews between about the third century BC and the end of the second century AD (for example, 1 and 2 Enoch, the Sybilline Oracles, 2 Esdras [4 Ezra], 2 Baruch, the Apocalypse of Abraham, the Apocalypse of Elijah, and several of the Dead Sea Scrolls; for a discussion of some of these, see pp. 416–27).

Christians also developed this kind of literature – for example, our Revelation to John, the Shepherd of Hermas, the Christian edition of the Jewish book the Testaments of the Twelve Patriarchs, the Ascension of Isaiah, and the Apocalypse of Peter.

The Nature and Characteristics of Apocalyptic Literature

'Apocalyptic' is a general term that includes a literary form or genre ('apocalypse'), a theological way of thinking about the future ('apocalyptic eschatology'), and a social-political-religious movement ('apocalypticism') (P.D. Hanson). Apocalypticism arose in times of deep social-political-religious crisis, when a particular minority religious group had become oppressed and alienated from the dominant system under which it lived. This alienation led it to interpret its situation through a certain understanding of God and his purposes for the future (apocalyptic eschatology), and to a literary form (apocalypse) expressive of its outlook.

Apocalyptic eschatology had its roots in Old Testament prophecy (from Amos down) and even behind that to Israel's covenant faith in Yahweh as the creator and Lord of history, who was believed to be leading the chosen people toward a future of unimaginable glory. The plant of apocalyptic eschatology may have been watered by ancient Semitic myth through the royal cult in Jerusalem, by Persian (Zoroastrian) beliefs concerning the future, by Israel's wisdom teachers, and by various currents in Hellenism, and the like, but its major source of nourishment was the prophets of the Old Testament and Israel's covenant faith.

Apocalypticism arose first in the bitter time of the Babylonian captivity and in the depressed period under Persian domination following the return from exile. It found literary expression in the prophecies of Ezekiel, 2 Isaiah, and Zechariah (chaps. 1–8).

Another period of apocalypticism occured about 167 BC, when Antiochus IV Epiphanes attempted to stamp out Judaism and establish the worship of himself as the visible manifestation of Zeus. In this crisis the apocalyptic eschatology of the loyal and oppressed Jews crystallized in the apocalypse of Daniel.

Under Hasmonean (Maccabean) dominance (middle second century BC) alienated Jews (Hasidim) fled to the wilderness of Judea, interpreted their situation from the perspective of apocalyptic eschatology, and recorded it in apocalypses now among the Dead Sea Scrolls (see p. 420 ff).

The destruction of Jerusalem in AD 70 brought from the depressed Jewish community the apocalypse known as 2 Esdras (4 Ezra).

Christians, persecuted by Jews, abused by Roman magistrates, alienated from their social environment, and threatened by Roman emperors (Nero, Domitian), also interpreted their situation by the same theology and communicated their faith in such apocalyptic materials as 2 Thessalonians (chap. 2), Mark 13 (Matt. 24–25), the book of Jude, the Shepherd of Hermas, and, above all, in the Revelation to John. Apocalypses have appropriately been called 'tracts for bad times.'

Some characteristics are *more or less* common to the apocalypses.

a. *Characteristics of form:* divinely given visions to a holy seer; an angelic interpreter of the visions; psychological reaction of the seer; exhortations by the seer to the reader in view of what he has learned; the attributing of the visions and the writing that reports them to some ancient man of God (pseudepigraphy); the use of symbols drawn from nature (lions, bears, rams, locusts, trees, rushing water, etc.) to represent human and supernatural realities; and loose organization of materials.

b. *Characteristics of thought:* dualistic and deterministic theology (God, the angels, and the righteous locked in struggle with Satan, the demons, and the wicked; and two orders of reality – heavenly and earthly – with happenings on earth determined by heavenly decisions and events); sharp division between the elect and the wicked; division of all history into time periods preordained by God; belief in the nearness of the end of this age, the destruction of this evil world, and the inauguration of the age to come; the New Age as a transcendent (non-earthly) order to be introduced by God's direct act or through a Messiah; the New Age as a return to paradise (the end will be like the beginning); and the anticipatory experience of the New Age in the communal life of those who wait for it.

Theme and Outline

Theme: The triumph of Jesus Christ and his church

Introduction (1:1–11)
Superscription: The source, content, and importance of the revelation (1:1–3)
The greeting, doxology, and announcement of Christ's coming (1:4–8)
The occasion of the visions (1:9–11)

The visions (1:12—22:5)
The heavenly Christ's message to the churches through his servant John (1:12—3:22)
1. The description of the heavenly Christ (1:12–16)
2. John's reaction and his commission to write (1:17–20)
3. The letters to the seven churches (2:1—3:22)
God's plan for the church's final triumph (4:1—22:5)
1. The source of the church's triumph: God (chap. 4)
2. The agent of the church's triumph: Christ, the Lion-Lamb (chap. 5)
3. The grand strategy of the church's triumph (6:1—22:5)
a. The seal judgments (6:1—8:1)
b. The trumpet judgments (8:2—11:19)
c. The anti-church 'triple alliance': the certainty of its defeat and of the church's victory (12:1—15:4)
d. The bowl judgments (15:5—16:21)
e. The fall of Babylon (Rome) (17:1—19:5)
f. God's final victory through Christ over all the powers of evil (19:6—20:15)
g. The new heaven and the new earth (21:1—22:5)

The epilogue: Authentication of the message; warning not to alter the prophecy; the consequences of acceptance and rejection; benediction (22:6–21)

Apocalypses were meant to encourage the righteous to be faithful to God and their religious duties in times of persecution. The apocalypses said to the righteous: Trust in God, be loyal to God's requirements, and soon the dominion of evil authorities will come to an end; God will vindicate you and open to you the New Age of righteousness and glory.

Literary Form and Background

The book is both a letter and an apocalypse. It has a greeting like a letter (1:4–5*a*), messages of a practical and urgent nature to seven churches (chaps. 2–3), and the customary epistolary benediction (22:21). The heart of the book consists of visions bearing the characteristics of an apocalypse (see above).

The union of letter and apocalypse is to be seen in other Christian works of the period: 2 Thessalonians, Jude, 2 Peter. The proportion of apocalyptic matter is much greater in the Revelation to John than in other such combinations. This does not make the book principally a 'Jewish' work, as some have maintained, for Christianity early had appropriated apocalyptic eschatology and the literary type (genre) apocalypse (Mark 13; 2 Thess. 2; Matt. 24–25). The Revelation to John is, however, the apocalypse *par excellence* of the early church.

The visions (1:12—22:5) provide the content of the revelation given to the prophet John and the epistolary setting directs that content to the churches as warning and promise. The first vision (1:12—3:22), a Christophany (revelation of Christ), presents the authority for the book's message and its urgency; and the second (4:1—22:5), a Theophany, discloses God's plan for the future as worked out through his agent the Messiah, the Lion-Lamb.

The plan is presented in part in three series of judgments: in seven seals (6:1—8:1), in seven trumpets (8:2—11:19), and in seven bowls (15:1—16:21). The seal judgments appear to be introductory to the parallel trumpet and bowl judgments. All cover the same eschatological period and are not thought of as consecutive. The number seven suggests the totality of time and events.

Worked into these cycles of sevens are additional materials (interludes, forces behind the scenes, announcements of coming events) necessary for the forward movement of the plan. The reader has the feeling both of cyclical and progressive movement. The action mounts to a climax with the coming of Christ, the defeat of the powers of evil, and the inauguration of the (double) Kingdom (19:6—22:5).

The author skillfully weaves together traditional material from the Old Testament, Jewish apocalypses, pagan and Jewish mythology, and early Christian traditions. He does not quote earlier materials directly but absorbs them into his thought and message. The symbols suggest more than they say and set the imagination loose in a way that literal, logical patterns of composition cannot.

In theology the book is Judeo-Christian. The author joins the Old and the New Covenants and shows that God's purpose involves Moses and Jesus, Israel and the church. We hear both the Song of Moses and the Song of the Lamb (15:3). The God of this book is the God of beginnings (Alpha) and endings (Omega) (1:8; 21:6).

One scholar has suggested that the book was patterned after Greek drama, and that it has seven acts, with seven scenes in each act. Though the number seven is indeed prominent in the book, a systematic arrangement by sevens seems not to have been the author's intention as an organizing principle for the whole book. And it is unlikely that a Christian writer who warned the church so urgently against paganism would have couched his message in theatrical form.

Date and Circumstances

Irenaeus (*c*. AD 180) said that John 'saw the revelation ... at the close of Domitian's reign' (AD 81–96). Some scholars have argued for a date in the reigns of Vespasian (69–79) or Nero (54–68) for the writing of this book, but the evidence for its composition during the reign of Domitian is impressive.

Domitian, a moody, jealous, unpredictable tyrant, cut down all persons whom he regarded as a threat to his authority. He seems to have demanded worship of himself as Lord and God. He executed his niece's husband on a charge of atheism (perhaps the refusal to recognize his deity) and exiled the niece. Both may have been Christians. Many others were condemned for following a Jewish way of life – evidently for not supporting the religion of the state.

Domitian apparently was not an indiscriminate persecutor of the church, as Nero had been in Rome, but his selective terrorist tactics aroused fear in the church as well as in Roman society. The letter from Clement of Rome to the church at Corinth, known as 1 Clement (*c.* AD 95), refers to 'the sudden and repeated misfortunes and calamities which have befallen us.' The spread of emperor worship in the provinces (for example, a new temple for the cult of the emperor in Ephesus in the time of Domitian) certainly put pressure

The Seven Churches of Asia

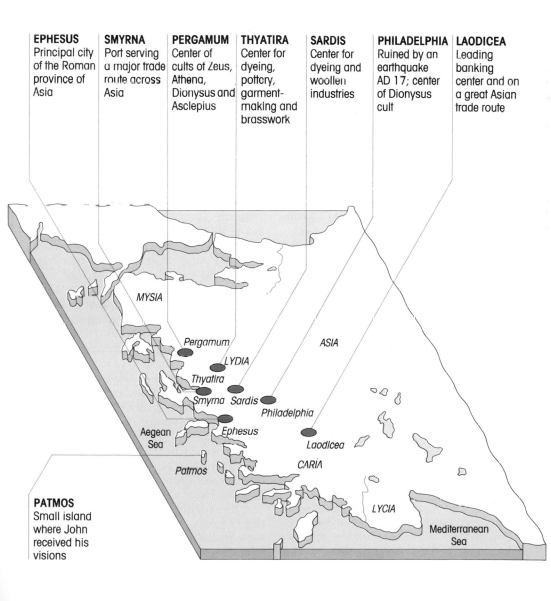

EPHESUS	SMYRNA	PERGAMUM	THYATIRA	SARDIS	PHILADELPHIA	LAODICEA
Principal city of the Roman province of Asia	Port serving a major trade route across Asia	Center of cults of Zeus, Athena, Dionysus and Asclepius	Center for dyeing, pottery, garment-making and brasswork	Center for dyeing and woollen industries	Ruined by an earthquake AD 17; center of Dionysus cult	Leading banking center and on a great Asian trade route

MYSIA

Pergamum

ASIA

LYDIA

Thyatira

Smyrna Sardis

Philadelphia

Aegean
Sea

Ephesus

Laodicea

Patmos

CARIA

LYCIA

Mediterranean
Sea

PATMOS
Small island where John received his visions

on the Christians of Asia Minor, where the seven churches of the Apocalypse were located.

It is evident that some Christians there had suffered persecution. The author of Revelation had been exiled to Patmos, a penal island for political offenders, because of his loyalty to Christianity (1:9). A Christian named Antipas, a member of the church at Pergamum, had been put to death for his fidelity to Jesus (2:13). The phrase 'where Satan's throne is' probably refers to Pergamum, which was the center of emperor worship. The author says that some Christians at Smyrna will face death (2:10). The souls under the altar are martyrs (6:9); others are to be killed as these have been (6:11). The harlot 'drunk with the blood of the saints and the blood of the martyrs of Jesus' (17:6; cf. 18:24; 19:2) suggests that fierce persecution lies ahead for the church, if it has not already begun. An hour of trial is coming to the whole world (3:10), that is, the awful days before the end, known in Judaism as the Messianic Woes. Through the suffering of those days the righteous will be purged for membership in God's kingdom and the wicked warned and called to repentance.

The hostility of the Jews (2:9; 3:9) made the Christian plight more bitter. They undoubtedly slandered the church before governmental authorities, seeking thus to dissociate Christianity from Judaism. The charge made by the Jews may have been that Christians, by preaching 'King Jesus,' were traitors to the emperor and the state (cf. Acts 17:7).

The outer pressure on the church from emperor worship and the Jews was matched by inner dangers: false teaching, false living, and false attitudes. Nicolaitans, possibly named after Nicolaus of Antioch (Acts 6:5), seem to have advocated Gnostic teaching (see pp. 318–9). Ephesus had succeeded in silencing these heretics, Pergamum tolerated them, but at Thyatira they dominated the church. The controversy they evoked split the church (2:2–4). In some of the churches spiritual apathy and self-satisfaction, due in part to material prosperity, threatened their future.

Both external and internal conditions point to the period AD 90–95 as the time of the writing of the Revelation to John.

Author and Place of Writing

The author's name appears several times as John (1:1, 4, 9; 22:8). No title identifies him, such as 'apostle.' He wishes to be known as a 'servant' of Christ, 'brother' and fellow-sufferer of the readers (1:1, 9). He bases his right to be heard on a direct commission from Christ through a vision (1:10–11). He apparently was well known to the readers.

Which John was he?
Possibilities are:

John, Son of Zebedee, the Apostle
Early church tradition (*e.g.,* Justin, Irenaeus, Clement of Alexandria, Origen) held to authorship by John the Apostle. Though there were some doubters in the second century, serious question about John the Apostle's authorship arose only in the third century, when Dionysius of Alexandria pointed out strong differences in style and thought between the Apocalypse and the Gospel of John. He credited the Apocalypse to some other John. From then on, the Eastern part of the church challenged the Apostle John's authorship.

Some scholars have cited evidence from the book itself in support of authorship by the Apostle, such as the high sense of authority and inspiration the writer possessed, and the similarities in language and thought to the Gospel of John (Christ as 'the Word,' 'the Lamb,' the Shepherd; the references to water and manna; the strong contrast between truth and falsehood, light and darkness, God and the devil; the love of the number seven).

Against authorship by John the Apostle, one may argue as follows: there are some grounds for believing that John the Apostle may have died at the same time as

The agora at Smyrna (modern Izmir).

his brother James (AD 44 – Acts 12:2); there is no claim to apostolic authorship in the Apocalypse and no mention of facts about the life of Jesus such as an apostle would know; the references honoring the apostles in Rev. 18:20; 21:14 would hardly have come from an apostle; the differences from the Gospel of John are as strong as the similarities; and in no case could similarities prove John the Apostle wrote the Apocalypse, since his authorship of the Gospel has not been indisputably established.

An Unknown Disciple of John the Apostle
Some scholars assume a circle of disciples, one of whom took the apocalyptic views and works of John, one of the 'sons of thunder' (Mark 3:17), and after his death wove them into our present Revelation to John (see p. 351). Thus the book appeared under the name of the Apostle, who therefore is meant in 1:1, 4, 9; 22:8.

John the Elder
Papias (c. AD 140) referred to an 'Elder John,' who passed on information about the Apostle John and the other apostles. 'Elder' here probably has a special meaning: it designates a member of a group who formed a link between the apostles and the next generation. They were especially venerated for their contact with the original apostles (see p. 352).

It may be that this Elder John wrote the book or made use of apocalyptic material which originally came from the Apostle John and that he was later confused with the Apostle John.

An Otherwise Unknown Prophet John
Though he is unknown to us, it is obvious that the author was well known to the readers. Like the Old Testament prophets, he spoke with great authority. John was his real name, not an assumed name. The Semitic flavor of his Greek and his thorough acquaintance with the Hebrew

Old Testament argue that he was a Jewish Christian.

The question of authorship cannot be settled yet.

The place of the visions was Patmos (1:9), but Patmos was not necessarily the place of writing. It is possible that after the author's release, he wrote in the city of Ephesus, where conditions were more favorable.

Interpretation of the Visions

Many ways of interpreting the visions have been proposed in the course of Christian history.

The Contemporary-Historical View
The supporters of this view regard the visions as wholly concerned with the circumstances of the author's time and with the future the author believed would soon issue out of those circumstances. They recognize as valid the author's picture of the struggle between good and evil and the certainty of God's and the church's ultimate triumph, but they do not believe any long-range predictions of future world events can be made from the visions.

The Continuous-Historical View
Some interpreters have seen the visions as containing predictions of events from the time of the author to the end of the world. They think that the letters to the seven churches predict successive periods in the life of the church – from the apostolic age to the second coming of Christ. A few have claimed to find references to the heresies of early Christian centuries, the spread of Islam, Charlemagne, the Crusades, the pope, etc. They have seen the book as a prophetic summary of the whole history of the church.

The Futurist View
According to this view, the visions refer entirely or principally to the final days before the end of the world. Futurists give little attention, if any, to the historical set-

ting of the book and to how the book would have served the needs of the church in the latter part of the first century. In fact, they hold that only Christians in the time of fulfillment (*i.e.*, at the end of time) could possibly understand the visions. According to this point of view, John wrote the book for the church at the end of history, not for the church of his own age.

The Mythic-Symbolic View
This approach holds that the author's purpose was to teach religious truths, not to predict the future. He accomplished this by the use of myths and symbols. To us they are at first grotesque and obscure, but behind them can be found meaningful theological concepts.

A symbolic interpretation appeared in the church of Alexandria around the end of the second century. According to this, the seven heads of the beast (chap. 13) are seven deadly sins; the ten horns of those heads are the serpent-like powers of sin; the stinging tails of the locusts (9:10) are the destructive power of immoral teachers in the church; the warrior on the white horse (19:11 ff.) is Christ, who opens heaven by giving the white light of truth to those who receive him; etc.

In our time some scholars have attempted to translate the myths and symbols into concepts of our time to show what they teach about human beings, their struggles in the world, their resources, and their future. They hold that the myths should not be taken literally and turned into predictions of future events but taken for what they really are: dramatic, poetic, mythic-symbolic representations of universal truth, whose meaning is not narrowly related to any set of historical circumstances.

Basic questions are before us today. Should we understand the book as primarily for ancient Christians and secondarily for us, or vice versa? And should we regard the book as a source of knowledge about world events of our time and of the future, or should we see it as a symbolic portrayal of religious truth about the

ultimate triumph of God and the righteous? In short, is the book dramatized
Christian theology, or is it predictive
prophecy? Or is it both?

A basic rule of modern biblical study is
that we must interpret all literature, including that in the Bible, in the light of the
historical situation out of which it arose
and to which it was addressed. When we
have determined as clearly as possible its
meaning for its first readers, then and only
then can we inquire about its meaning for
us (see pp. 70–72). This fundamental
principle eliminates the Continuous-Historical and Futurist views and leaves a
combination of the Contemporary-Historical and the Mythic-Symbolic views as
the soundest approach.

Message to the First Readers

The author strikes several important
notes:

a. *The church will come to its final inheritance only if it remains absolutely
faithful to God and Christ in the bitter
persecutions which have begun and which
will increase in fury.*

There can be no doubt that the writer
designed the book to meet the threat to the
church caused by state-enforced emperor
worship and by the hostility of the Jews.
The author was exiled because of his fidelity to Jesus Christ (1:9); Antipas the faithful witness was killed (2:13); Christians
were being slandered by Jews and some
were about to be imprisoned (2:9–10); a
group of martyrs under the heavenly altar
awaits yet other martyrs (6:9–11); Rome
will be 'drunk with the blood of the saints
and the blood of the martyrs of Jesus'
(17:6; cf. 18:24). The book is 'a call for the
endurance of the saints, those who keep
the commandments of God and the faith
of Jesus' (14:12).

If Christians die 'in the Lord,' they are
'blessed' (14:13). Christ and the author
make extravagant promises to faithful
Christians: the right 'to eat of the tree of
life, which is in the paradise of God' (2:7);
'the crown of life' (2:10); 'the hidden

manna,' miraculously preserved from the
wilderness days for consumption at the
banquet of the coming Messiah (2:17);
'power over the nations' (2:26); and face-
to-face fellowship with God in the glories
of the new heaven and earth (21:1—22:5).

b. *The church can meet its test only if it
becomes strong and pure within.* Wrong
teaching, wrong living, and wrong attitudes threaten the church from within.
The church must deal with immoral
Nicolaitans in a spirit of love, not in hostile criticism. Complacent, lukewarm
Christians must repent and be revived. Involvement in pagan practices must cease.
The church must be clothed in 'fine linen,
bright and pure,' that is, in righteous
deeds (19:8).

c. *The time of trouble which is coming
on the whole world is God's way of purg-
ing the righteous and calling the nations to
repentance.* That the church must pass
through 'the hour of trial' (*i.e.,* the period
of distress preceding the coming of the
Messiah with the New Age) and not be
rescued miraculously by a 'rapture' is
everywhere apparent in the book (7:14;
13:7, 10; 14:12; 17:6; 18:24).

But the hour of trial is a test for all the
people on earth (3:10). The test shows
both God's judgment on their sins and his
desire that they should repent (9:20;
11:13; 16:11). The judgments of the seals,
the trumpets, and the bowls are God's
warnings to the wicked in the hope of their
repentance. The God of the book of Revelation is a God who delights not in damn-
ing the wicked but in saving them.

d. *Those who trust in God and are loyal
to Christ are eternally secure, but those
who serve the devil and their own evil desires will perish.* Many members of the
church will experience the first death
(martyrdom) but will not be harmed by
the second death (the lake of fire – 2:11;
20:6, 14). True Christians will bear God's
seal upon them so that the judgments that
are coming on the earth will harm only the
wicked (7:1–8). The entire faithful church
(symbolized by the number 144,000),
though martyred (7:14; 13:7; 17:6;

The Roman Empire
at the Birth of Christ

The temple of Artemis, Sardis.

18:24), will dwell securely with the Lamb on Mount Zion (14:1–5). Though seemingly conquered by the two beasts (the Roman Empire with its self-deifying emperors, aided by the imperial priesthood), they are actually victors. They are the 'first fruits for God and the Lamb' from all mankind (14:4). These faithful martyrs will enjoy special sovereignty with Christ (20:4–6).

God will destroy wicked idolaters, the mighty men of the earth, the free and the slave, the rich and the poor – all who have been deceived by false gods and false worship, inspired by the devil (6:15–17; 13:11–17) – together with the corrupt civilization they have built (chaps. 17–18).

e. *The coming of Christ and his final victory over the forces of evil is at hand.* It is clear that the author was talking about events of the near, rather than the distant, future. He stated flatly that 'the time is near' (1:3), that the events 'must soon take place' (22:6), and that Christ said he was coming soon (22:7, 12, 20). Therefore his book should not be sealed up, as the book of Daniel was sealed in prospect of long delay in fulfillment (Dan. 12:4). The Revelation to John should rather be left unsealed for urgent reading, since 'the time is near' (22:10).

The whole early church believed that the second coming of Christ was near (Rom. 13:11–12; 1 Cor. 7:29–31; James 5:8; 1 Pet. 4:7; 1 John 2:18; and the above passages of the Revelation to John). The delay in the coming caused scoffers to doubt the validity of the hope; those who continued to believe had to defend their faith (2 Pet. 3:3–10).

Even Jesus seems to have expected the coming of the final kingdom during his own generation (Mark 9:1; 13:30), though he insisted the time was known only to the Father and under his authority (Mark 13:32; Acts 1:7). The disciples were to hope and to work meanwhile (Luke 19:12–27; Acts 1:8), making the most of the remaining time by living righteously and speaking the Word boldly (Col. 4:2–6; Eph. 5:3–16).

THE REVELATION TO JOHN

Since the author was talking about events in the near future, largely connected with the fall of Rome, we can hardly suppose that he had in mind specific events of twenty centuries later, as some interpreters of today claim.

The Value of This Book for Us

If the book does not predict specific historical events of our time, what, if anything, does it say to us? It ministers to our spirits; it does not satisfy curiosity about the future. Among its great teachings are:

a. This world was created by a God of wisdom, power, righteousness, and mercy. As Creator, God alone has the right to receive the worship of the creatures he made. The rulers of earth have no real authority over human souls. People should worship God only.

b. The power of evil in the world is great. It incarnates itself in Neros, Genghis Khans, Hitlers, and Stalins. The struggle with demonic power will be with us to the end. Only God can establish his kingdom by the defeat of evil; and this he will do through Christ at the last.

c. But in Jesus Christ's death on the cross Satan has already been defeated (12:7–11). Redemption is an accomplished fact (1:5–6; 5:5, 9–10). The kingdom of Christ is a reality in this human world (perhaps the meaning of 20:4–6). God rules over his universe. God's kingdom has come (7:10; 11:15; 19:6). Singing is the proper response of the church (5:9–10; 15:3–4). (Many scholars today see a strong element of 'inaugurated eschatology' in the Revelation to John, which sets it apart from Jewish apocalypses.)

d. The goal – the ultimate kingdom – toward which God's saving work is directed is an order free from sin and finite limitation in which God and the redeemed can live together in intimate fellowship. In the new Jerusalem there will be no need to separate God from a defiled people by temple walls. As children with their father, they shall see his face (21:22; 22:4).

e. While it awaits the End, the church must be on its guard against the seductive power of evil, whether incarnate in rulers who demand what belongs to God alone or in false teachers who lead the unwary into heresy and immorality (2:14–16, 20–23). The final kingdom is for those who 'conquer,' who are 'faithful unto death,' 'who wash their robes,' and who keep 'the words of the prophecy of this book.'

f. It is through suffering that Christians are to enter the kingdom of God. Though their enemies slay them and they experience the first death, they will not be hurt by 'the second death' (2:11; 20:6, 14), 'the lake of fire' (20:14). The whole church may be martyred (7:14; 13:7; 17:6) but God's seal is upon them. They are 'the first fruits for God and the Lamb' (14:4), who 'sing a new song before the throne.'

For further Reading on The Revelation to John
Barclay, W., *The Revelation of John*, two vols., 1959.
Beasley-Murray, G.R., *The Book of Revelation*, 1974.
Caird, G.B., *A Commentary on the Revelation of St. John the Divine*, 1966.
Morris, L. *The Revelation of St. John*, 1981.

For Further Reading on the Books of the New Testament
Childs, B.S., *The New Testament as Canon*, 1984.
Kee, H.C., *Understanding the New Testament*, 4th ed. 1983.
Koester, H., *Introduction to the New Testament*, two vols., 1982.
Martin, R.P., *New Testament Foundations*, two vols., 1975–78.
Perrin, N. and Duling, D.C., *The New Testament – An Introduction*, 1982.

The Manuscripts and the Search for the True Text

A 'manuscript' is a document which was 'written by hand.' Until the invention of printing with movable type in the fifteenth century, all written materials were produced by hand. Making copies of books of considerable length was a laborious and expensive process. And the copies were likely to be full of errors, because of the limitations of eye, ear, and hand (see p. 378).

Biblical Languages and Writing

As far as we know, writing began in picture form in Mesopotamia about 3500–3300 BC. Soon the pictures were modified into wedge-shaped ('cuneiform') impressions on clay. In Egypt another form of picture-writing, called hieroglyphics, appeared shortly before 3000 BC. About the seventeenth century BC the Canaanites invented an alphabet of some two dozen simple pictures, each representing one consonantal sound. The earliest example of alphabetic writing comes from about 1550 BC from graffiti scratched on stone in turquoise mines of the Sinai peninsula. The alphabet then passed from the Canaanites, or Phoenicians, to the Greeks and to modern languages.

We do not know how early the Hebrews began to write. Scholars have traced the Hebrew alphabet back to about 1000 BC. It is possible that Abraham could have written in some script or scripts, for writing had existed in Mesopotamia, from which he came, for more than a thousand years before his birth. It is virtually certain that Moses could write, in view of his education at the court in Egypt and the availablity of several scripts – Egyptian hieroglyphics, Akkadian cuneiform, and Canaanite scripts. Some five systems of writing were in use in Syria-Palestine in the Late Bronze Age (c. 1550–1200 BC).

It is unlikely, however, that Abraham wrote any materials now contained in our book of Genesis, and nothing that can be attributed with certainty to Moses is now present in the Pentateuch (see pp. 98–103). After the Exodus from Egypt, when the Israelites settled in Canaan, probably in the thirteenth century BC, they adopted the language of the Canaanites and their alphabetic writing.

After the Babylonian exile (sixth century BC) the Aramaic language and script came into common use among the Jews of Palestine. This language, closely related to Canaanite and Hebrew, originated in northern Syria in the late second millennium BC and spread widely as a language of international trade and diplomacy. It was used before the exile in Hebrew diplomatic circles (2 Kings 18:26) and was perhaps spoken in Samaria by Assyrian colonists who settled there after the destruction of the Northern Kingdom in 721 BC (2 Kings 17:24).

At the time of Jesus the popular language and script of the Jews was a dialect of Western Aramaic. The Old Hebrew language continued in use in learned circles (e.g., among the rabbis of Jerusalem and the priests of Qumran by the Dead Sea), and residents of Judea apparently still spoke it to some extent. Old Hebrew was emphasized in periods of religious and national revival, as during the Maccabean period of the second century BC and the Bar-Kochba revolt of AD 132–135. That Jesus knew Hebrew is evident from the fact that he read the lesson from the prophet Isaiah in the synagogue service at Nazareth (Luke 4:16–19). Some recent scholars have argued that Jesus also knew Greek and may have taught occasionally in it.

The language of the New Testament is Hellenistic Greek, which came mainly from the Attic dialect of the classical period (before c. 300 BC). The conquests of Alexander the Great (336–323 BC) and the resultant spread of the Greek language and culture through many lands brought about a simplification of the Attic dialect and produced a truly popular language for the empire. Though some literary people of the Hellenistic period imitated the Old Attic language, most of the Greek used was the popular sort – the language of the marketplace, the home, informal letters, and business documents.

Although some of the New Testament is written in a fairly cultivated Greek (such as parts of Luke-Acts, the Letter to the Hebrews, some sections in Paul's letters), most of the books use the common (*Koine*) Greek.

Three styles of Greek handwriting were in use from intertestamental times to the invention of printing in the fifteenth century: (1) a cursive, informal hand for rapid writing of receipts, letters, deeds, and accounts; (2) a formal 'book hand,' consisting of separated letters somewhat like our capital letters, for literary works (the letters are called 'uncials,' meaning 'a twelfth part' of a line of writing); (3) a flowing 'book hand,' with small connected letters, formal enough in style to be used for literary works (the letters are called 'minuscules,' meaning 'rather small').

It is likely that Paul and his amanuenses (secretaries) wrote to churches in the cursive script. When the letters were later copied as literature, the scribes put them in the uncial script until about the ninth century, when minuscule writing came into use. No early cursive manuscripts of the New Testament have been found. Some nine tenths of all New Testament manuscripts known today are minuscules. Many of the most important New Testament manuscripts are in uncial letters (see pp. 374–7).

A meadow of papyrus plants, papyrus of Ani, Egypt.

The Materials of Biblical Writings

In ancient times many materials were used for writing: clay (shaped into tablets), stone, skins of animals, bark, wood, bone, linen cloth, several metals, broken pieces of pottery (potsherds), and papyrus (a kind of paper made from the pith of the papyrus plant).

Skins (Leather)

In Egypt the use of skins for writing goes back to at least 2500 BC. How early skins were used for writing among the Hebrews is not known. Jeremiah's scroll, cut up with a scribe's knife and burned in 605 BC by Jehoiakim

(Jer. 36:23), was of leather or papyrus. Either could have been cut with such a knife.

The wide use of leather scrolls by the Qumran community for their sacred books (see pp. 420–27) points to a tradition about the use of leather for such writings. The Talmud later required all copies of the Law used in public worship to be written on skins of clean animals and to be in roll form – no doubt a requirement of long standing.

The earliest leather scroll fragments from Qumran date to the third century BC. Approximately one fourth of the manuscript finds at Qumran are copies on leather of the text of the Hebrew Scriptures. The manuscripts seem to have been prepared by scraping and rubbing, not by tanning. A superb example of a biblical scroll is the great Isaiah A manuscript, dating from about 100 BC. It is 24½ feet long and 10½ inches wide, with 54 columns of text on 17 sheets.

Refinements in the preparation of skins yielded material now known as parchment and vellum. The skins were soaked in limewater and the hair scraped off; then they were rubbed with pumice, treated with chalk, and stretched on a frame. A fine writing surface resulted. Vellum, made from calfskin, provided the best surface of all.

Roman writers credited Eumenes II, king of Pergamum (197–159 BC), with the invention of parchment. Actually it is more likely that he was the principal developer of its manufacture and use.

In the fourth century AD the best copies of the Scriptures, such as our present Codex Sinaiticus and Codex Vaticanus (see pp. 374–6), were on vellum, and in book, rather than roll, form.

Papyrus

The home of papyrus was Egypt, where from early times, possibly as early as 3000 BC, the tall plant from the marshes of the Nile delta furnished pith for the manufacture of a suitable writing material. The triangular-shaped stalk, about the thickness of a man's wrist and from 6 to 15 feet in height, was cut into sections about a foot long. The pith was then cut into thin strips. These were laid vertically side by side, with another layer placed horizontally on top, and possibly with some kind of glue bonding the two layers. Pressed until dry, cut to the size wanted, and smoothed with a piece of ivory, shell, or pumice these layers became a sheet of relatively smooth and durable writing material.

Sheets normally varied in size from about 6 by 9 inches to 12 by 15 inches. A roll of papyrus was made by overlapping the edges of individual sheets and gluing them together, until the desired length was achieved. The standard roll for literary works was about 30 to 35 feet long. Individual sheets were used for business accounts, brief letters, and the like. Writing was normally done on the side where the strips and fibers ran horizontally.

The original New Testament writers almost certainly used papyrus sheets and rolls. Such brief letters as Philemon and 2 and 3 John were written on single sheets. The Gospel of Matthew would fill a 30 to 35-foot roll. When the New Testament writings were collected toward the end of the first century and during the second (see pp. 32–5), they were copied not on rolls but in papyrus codices (books).

For several centuries tablets of wood, waxed and held together at one edge by cords or clasps in a kind of book, had been in use among the Romans for memoranda, accounts, school exercises, etc. Parchment was sometimes substituted for wood and a parchment notebook created for special texts.

It was natural that papyrus sheets should be used in this same way. The individual sheets were folded down the middle and several of them laid atop one another with their folds adjacent. When several such folded groups of sheets were brought together and sewed at the folds, a book was created. The sheets were arranged so that vertical strips of papyrus would face one another on opposite pages and horizontal strips likewise.

Scrolls were bulky and awkward to unroll. The book form was convenient to use and economical through its use of both sides of the papyrus. It was thus suitable for the large collections of writings contained in the Christian Bible. Strangely, the secular literature of the time continued to be written on rolls during early Christian centuries. And since the Jewish synagogues used rolls (scrolls) for their Scriptures, it is possible that Christians, particularly Gentile ones, wished to differentiate their Scriptures from those of Judaism, on the one hand, and from secular literature, on the other.

Writing on leather, parchment, vellum, and papyrus was done with a reed pen and ink. Some pens were split at the point to form a nib, and some were frayed like a small brush. One type of very black ink was made from lampblack (or smoke black) mixed with a solution of gum and water. The mixture was sometimes dried into small cakes and moistened when used. Another type came from nutgalls, green vitriol, and water. This ink turned in time into a rusty brown color.

The Manuscripts of the Bible

Old Testament Manuscripts

All original manuscripts of the Old and New Testament books have perished. When these books were first circulated, the original manuscripts were not thought particularly valuable. When they were later copied, the only concern of the copyists and their readers was for an accurate reproduction of their text.

The Jews retired their worn-out manuscripts to the Geniza – a chest or room in the synagogue for storage of holy, but no longer usable, books. Antiquity in a manuscript was no asset from their point of view. Fortunately for us, one such Geniza with its precious manuscripts, some dating as far back as the sixth century AD, was found in Cairo, Egypt, at the end of the nineteenth century. From it came a flood of information about the text of Old Testament books.

Until the discovery of the Dead Sea Scrolls in 1947, the most ancient Old Testament manuscript known (the Cairo Prophets) – other than the Nash Papyrus fragment (see below) – came from the end of the ninth century AD. The Dead Sea Scrolls have given us manuscripts that were made more than 1,000 years earlier; indeed, some fragments among the Dead Sea Scrolls go back to the third century BC (see below). It is possible now to trace the history of the transmission of the Old Testament text as never before.

New Testament Manuscripts
Greek manuscripts of the New Testament fall into four classes: papyri, uncials, minuscules, lectionaries. As of 1967 the following numbers of manuscripts had been catalogued in each group; papyri, 81; uncials, 266; minuscules, 2,754; lectionaries, 2,135 – making a total of 5,236. Since then a few have been added, bringing the total, according to a recent count, to 5,358.

Students of the New Testament are exceedingly fortunate to have so many Greek manuscripts from which to reconstruct the original text of the New Testament books. By contrast, students of the Greek classics are much more limited. We are told that Homer's Iliad is preserved in 457 papyri, 2 uncials, and 188 minuscules and that the writings of Euripides are preserved in 54 papyri and 276 parchment manuscripts (B.M. Metzger, *The Text of the New Testament*, 2nd ed., 1968, p. 34).

Some important Old Testament manuscripts are:

Fragments from Qumran cave 4
Pieces of Exodus, 1 Samuel, Jeremiah (*c.* 250–175 BC).

The Nash Papyrus (*c.* 150 BC)
The Ten Commandments and the *Shema* (Deut. 6:4)

Isaiah A Scroll (*c.* 100 BC)
A complete copy of the text of Isaiah on seventeen sheets of leather

Isaiah B Scroll (first century AD)
A fragmentary scroll of Isaiah, consisting mostly of chaps. 35–66 and some pieces of earlier chapters

The Dead Sea Psalms Scroll (second century BC)
41 canonical psalms and some non-psalm material

The Targum [Translation] **of Job** (*c.* 100 BC)
A fragmentary manuscript containing parts of Job 17:14—36:13 and 37:10—42:11 in Aramaic

The Cairo Prophets (AD 894)
The oldest dated Hebrew manuscript now known; contains both the former and the latter prophets of the Hebrew canon (see p. 18)

The Aleppo Codex (*c.* AD 930)
A complete Old Testament text

The Leningrad Codex (*c.* AD 1008)
A complete Old Testament text

The Papyrus Manuscripts

Almost all the papyrus manuscripts consist of, and clearly came from, manuscripts in book (codex) form. Only three or four are fragments from papyrus rolls. As noted above (p. 372), the church from the beginning of the second century found the papyrus codex cheaper and more convenient for its Scriptures.

The following are some of the important papyrus manuscripts and the symbols commonly used for them:

P[45] – *Chester Beatty Papyrus I*
30 leaves (mostly of the text of Mark, Luke, and the Acts) out of some 220 leaves originally devoted to the four Gospels and the Acts, dating to the third century

P[46] – *Chester Beatty Papyrus II*
86 leaves out of an original 104, containing Romans (some portions missing), Hebrews, 1 and 2 Corinthians, Ephesians, Galatians, Philippians, Colossians, 1 Thessalonians (portions missing), dating to about AD 200

P[47] – *Chester Beatty Papyrus III*
10 leaves out of an original 32, containing Rev. 9:10—17:2, dating to the late third century

P[52] – *Papyrus Rylands Gk. 457*
A tiny fragment (2½ by 3½ inches), containing John 18:31–33, 37–38 and dating to the first half of second century; the earliest of all manuscripts and fragments of any part of the New Testament

P[66] – *Bodmer Papyrus II*
104 pages and fragments of 46 other pages of the Gospel of John (1:1—6:11; 6:35—14:26; parts of 14:29—21:9), dating to about AD 200

P[75] – *Bodmer Papyrus XIV–XV*
102 pages out of an original 144 pages, containing most of the Gospels of Luke and John and dating to the early third century

The Uncial Manuscripts

‫א‬ – *Codex Sinaiticus* (the symbol is the Hebrew letter Aleph)

Discovered in the middle nineteenth century at the monastery of St. Catherine at Mt. Sinai by Constantin von Tischendorf. Remaining today are 390 leaves out of about 730 leaves, 242 of the Old Testament and 148 of the New, including in the latter category the Epistle of Barnabas and the Shepherd of Hermas. Now in the British Museum. Written in Egypt or Palestine about the middle of the fourth century and later corrected by several scribes. The only known complete copy of the Greek New Testament in uncial writing.

St Catherine's Monastery, Sinai, where the Codex
Sinaiticus was discovered in 1844.

A – Codex Alexandrinus

Apparently brought from Egypt to Constantinople by Cyril Lucar, patriarch of that city, and presented by him in 1627 to Charles I of England. Remaining today: 773 leaves out of about 820, 630 of the Old Testament and 143 of the New, with parts of Matthew, John, and 2 Corinthians missing. Now in the British Museum. Written in the fifth century and corrected by later scribes.

B – Codex Vaticanus

For many centuries the property of the Vatican Library in Rome, though largely unknown to the outside world until 1889–90, when photographs of it appeared. Remaining today: 759 leaves out of 820, 142 being of the New Testament. Missing: portions of Genesis, Psalms, and Hebrews; the entire books of 1 and 2 Timothy, Titus, Philemon, Revelation, and the books of Maccabees. Written in the fourth century, a tenth or eleventh century corrector having retraced the dim letters.

C – Codex Ephraemi Rescriptus

A palimpsest (re-scraped and reused) biblical manuscript of the fifth century, many of the pages rewritten in the twelfth or thirteenth century with a Greek translation of 38 discourses of St. Ephraem. Remaining today: 209 leaves, 64 of the Old Testament and 145 of the New. Missing: most of the Old Testament and the whole of 2 Thessalonians and 2 John. Underlying biblical text deciphered by Constantin von Tischendorf in 1841–42 and improved on by later scholars with the help of ultraviolet rays.

D(05) – Codex Bezae Cantabrigiensis

Presented in 1581 by Theodore Beza of Geneva to the library at Cambridge University. Contains most of the four Gospels and the Acts and a fragment of 3 John, all in both Greek and Latin, with the order of the Gospels being Matthew, John, Luke, Mark. Written in the fifth or sixth century.

W – Codex Washingtonensis

Brought from Egypt in 1906 by C.L. Freer and now in the Smithsonian Institution. Contains the four Gospels in the order Matthew, John, Luke, Mark. Dates from the late fourth or early fifth century.

θ – Codex Koridethianus (the symbol is the Greek letter theta)

From Koridethi in the Caucasian Mountains and now at Tiflis, in the Soviet Socialist Republic of Georgia. Contains the four Gospels. Dates from the ninth century but reflects in part a third to fourth-century text type.

The Minuscule Manuscripts

All are from the ninth century and later. They are more than ten times as numerous as the uncials (see p. 374). Some of them are ornate, one in gold letters on purple vellum. Many are descended from early types of texts. Of particular importance are the following: Families 1 and 13; and MSS. 33, 81, 157, 565, 579, 700, 1424, 1739, 2053. (For details see bibliography on p. 379.)

The Lectionaries (Books of Scripture readings for worship services)
The church adopted the synagogue practice of reading designated passages of
Scripture in services of worship according to a set pattern throughout the
year. In the church, beginning with Easter, the texts were assembled in
proper sequence for reading on Sundays, Saturdays, and (in some manuscripts) on weekdays. The lectionaries often preserve old forms of the New
Testament texts. It is not feasible to cite any individual lectionary manuscripts here, since they exceed 2,000 in number and scholars have not yet
studied all of them in detail.

Families of Manuscripts

As ever more manuscripts were discovered and their texts studied, it became
apparent that they could be grouped into families on the basis of the errors
and deliberate changes they contain.

The families or types now recognized are:

(a) The Alexandrian (including Codex Vaticanus, Codex Sinaiticus, P[46],
    P[66], P[75]), probably the family preserving most nearly the original text
    of the New Testament
(b) The Western (including Codex Bezae and in part Codex
    Washingtonensis)
(c) The Caesarean (including Codex Koridethianus, minuscule families 1
    and 13, and many lectionaries)
(d) The Byzantine (including Codex Alexandrinus in part and many late
    uncials and minuscules)

The Search for the Original Text

The Hebrew and Greek texts used by the translators of the King James Version rested on only a few – and often rather unreliable – manuscripts of the
many now in the hands of biblical scholars. Today we know better than those
translators did what the original wording of the biblical books was (see
pp. 42–5).

Readers of the Bible in most contemporary versions can see from bracketed sections of the text and from footnotes that some words and passages
they are accustomed to in the King James Version were contributed by persons other than the original authors of the books.

In Isaiah in the Revised Standard Version one finds a number of footnotes
referring to 'one ancient MS' which offers a different word or phrase from the
one printed in the text. The reference is to the great Isaiah A scroll from
Qumran, which presents some significant differences from the traditional
Hebrew text. These footnotes point out also that the ancient versions offer
other words, phrases, and meanings.

Mark 16:9–20, John 5:3–4, and John 7:53—8:11 contain material not present in the best manuscripts. These passages are bracketed or printed in a footnote in most recent English translations.

What led to the differences that appear in ancient manuscripts? And what kinds of differences are there? Ancient copyists and editors are responsible for the differences. The changes they introduced were of two types: unintentional and deliberate. Often copyists saw incorrectly; they confused look-alike letters, skipped lines of text, wrote words twice, transposed letters, etc. In commercial establishments, where several copyists wrote from one person's dictation, careless pronunciation, lack of attention, weariness, and distractions led to frequent mistakes. Errors arose also from writing passages from memory and from inaccurately judging whether marginal notes were to be included or omitted.

Sometimes copyists and editors deliberately altered language they regarded as rough, harmonized parallel passages where differences should have been preserved, removed discrepancies, left out or changed statements which were contrary to their theology, and filled out manuscripts that were damaged or thought incomplete.

In the search for the original text of the books of the Bible two general kinds of evidence from the manuscripts are important. The first is *external* evidence. What manuscripts support a given reading (wording) and what is the date of those manuscripts or, more important, what is the type or family of text embodied in them? If a manuscript is of early date, its reading gains in importance. However, a relatively late manuscript may contain important readings, if it was copied from a significant early manuscript or manuscripts. Important also is the geographical distribution of the manuscripts. A reading supported by manuscripts from a wide geographical area has a certain strength.

The second kind of evidence is *internal*. What is the original author most likely to have written in a passage where the manuscripts differ? Did a copyist smoooth out a difficulty in the text? Is there an obvious blunder in copying? Was there a deliberate change in a passage for stylistic or doctrinal reasons? Which reading would most naturally explain the rise of the variants? In general, the more difficult reading is to be preferred, since a copyist would likely try to smooth out a difficulty. In view of the tendency of copyists to combine and preserve alternative readings of the manuscripts before them, the shorter reading is often to be chosen by us.

And which reading best fits the style, vocabulary, and theology of the original author? Which makes most sense in the immediate context? By attending to such considerations manuscript variants can be evaluated and the true original text be approximated. For all the differences among the manuscripts of the Bible, scholars generally agree that no central doctrines of the Judeo-Christian faith are undermined by these differences. As a whole, the copyists were remarkably faithful to the texts they reproduced.

For Further Reading

Hayes, J.H., *An Introduction to Old Testament Study*, 1979.

Metzger, B.M., *The Text of the New Testament*, 2nd ed. 1968; *The Early Versions of the New Testament*, 1977; *Manuscripts of the Greek Bible*, 1981.

Wuerthwein, E., *The Text of the Old Testament*, 1979.

Biblical Lands and Archaeology

The Lands

The bitter struggle between the Israelis and the Arabs during the last fifty years or so and the clamor of Western powers for the oil of the Middle East have led to new interest in the lands at the eastern end of the Mediterranean Sea. Iran, Iraq, Syria, Lebanon, Israel, Jordan, and Egypt are now household words.

We may not fully understand the complex geography of this area and the reasons for the intense competition for its largely arid lands; but there is a general feeling that the future of mankind on this planet is somehow tied in with the destiny of this part of the world.

The importance of the Middle East is not simply a modern phenomenon. Here were the cradles of civilization: the Tigris-Euphrates river valley (modern Iraq); the long, green gash in the desert called Egypt; and the in-between 'bridge' lands of Syria and Phoenicia (Canaan).

The land stretching from the Persian Gulf northwestward up the Tigris-Euphrates valley, through northern Syria, and down the Phoenician coast to the Sinai desert has been called 'the Fertile Crescent.' Here there was water enough – from the two great rivers in the east and the rainfall in the west – to sustain settled life and international trade and travel.

The structure of the lands along the eastern end of the Mediterranean is very complex. The mountains, valleys, gorges (rifts), and plateaus run mainly north-south, but also northeast to southwest, northwest to southeast, and in some cases east-west.

In southern Caanan ('Palestine,' so named from the Philistines who lived there after about 1200 BC), starting from the Mediterranean shore, one travels eastward across (1) the coastal plain, (2) the rolling hills and the central mountains, (3) the Jordan Valley (Rift), and (4) the eastern plateau, which merges into the Arabian desert. The north-south lines, particularly of the coastal strip, have provided access to upper Canaan and Syria (and thus to Mesopotamia) and to Egypt on the southwest.

The great diversity in the surface of the area has always made political, economic, religious, and social unification difficult. With elevations ranging from about 9,100 feet above sea level at the crest of Mt. Hermon to about 1,290 feet below sea level at the Dead Sea, climates and flora and fauna varied widely. Houses of mud or sun-dried brick with straw roofs were adequate in the warm climate of the Jordan Valley, whereas stone houses roofed with beams of wood overlaid with branches and clay mixed with small stones, and furnished with braziers for heating in winter, were needed in the hill country. Because of its great diversity of land, climate, peoples, and natural life, Palestine is the world in miniature.

The lands occupied by the tribes of Israel east and west of the Jordan River covered some 10,000 square miles – about the size of Vermont. From Dan to Beersheba, the traditional north-south limits of Israel (*e.g.*, Judges 20:1), was about 145 air miles. In times of expansion, as under King David, Israelite territory took in southern and central Syria, including Damascus, and reached to the Red Sea on the south, a north-south distance of some 350 air miles.

In latitude Palestine falls in a line with southern Spain and Georgia in the U.S.A. In general its climate has two seasons: a rainy winter, with snow in the Lebanon mountains and occasionally in Jerusalem; and a long, dry summer.

The average temperature in Jerusalem (elevation *c.* 2500 feet) in August is about 74° F and in January about 48° F. During the same periods other places have temperatures as follows: Gaza 79° and 56°; Jericho (*c.* 825 feet below sea level) 88° and 59°; Acre 79° and 56°; Safad (elevation *c.* 2800 ft.) 75° and 45°.

The early (or 'former') rains, which soften the ground for plowing, fall in October and November. The heavy rains come in December–February. And the late (or 'latter') rains, which ripen the crops, descend in March and April.

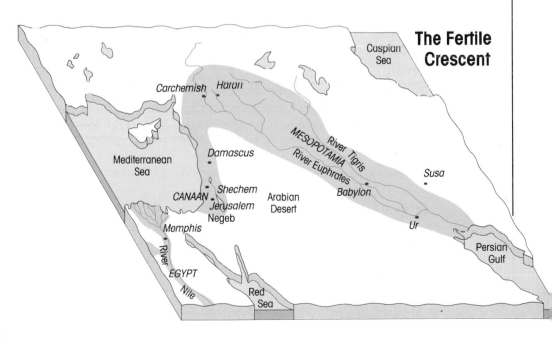

The Fertile Crescent

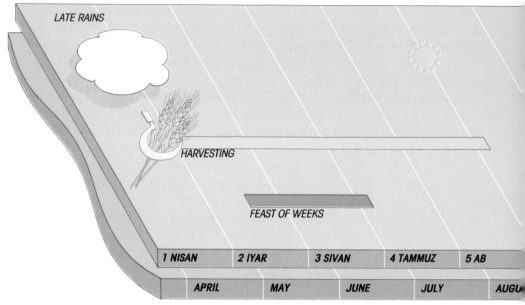

LATE RAINS

HARVESTING

FEAST OF WEEKS

1 NISAN	2 IYAR	3 SIVAN	4 TAMMUZ	5 AB
APRIL	MAY	JUNE	JULY	AUGU

Palestine: the Farming Year

The amount of rainfall varies widely according to elevation and location. The rain clouds come from the west. Where the mountains are highest (in Lebanon), annual rainfall reaches 60 inches. One high point in Galilee (Safad) has about 45 inches (New York City has some 40 inches), Jerusalem about 26 inches (London about 23 inches), the region south of Hebron to Beersheba about 10 to 15 inches, and Jericho about 5 inches. Northern Transjordan receives 20 to 30 inches because of the lower mountains of Samaria to the west, and southern Transjordan – opposite the higher Judean mountains – is dry (5 to 15 inches).

If the rains do not come at the right time in the right amounts, crops fail and famine may result. In Elijah's time a famine lasted more than two years (1 Kings 17:1; 18:1–2). Other famines are reported in the Old Testament (*e.g.*, Gen. 12:10; 43:1; 2 Sam. 21:1; 2 Kings 6:25) and in the New (Acts 11:28).

Prayers for rain (Zech. 10:1; *cf.* Joel 2:23) and rain-inducing ceremonies – such as occurred each day during the Feast of Tabernacles when water from the spring of Gihon was poured through a silver funnel into the ground below the altar of burnt offering of the temple in Jerusalem – were an important part of Israel's religious and economic life. The prophets of Israel strongly contended that Yahweh, not the Canaanite God Baal, controlled the rains and the crops the rains brought (Amos 4:7–8; Hos. 2:5, 8; Deut. 11:14; 28:12; Jer. 5:23–24; 14:22).

Palestine by our standards is a land poorly endowed, on the whole. The

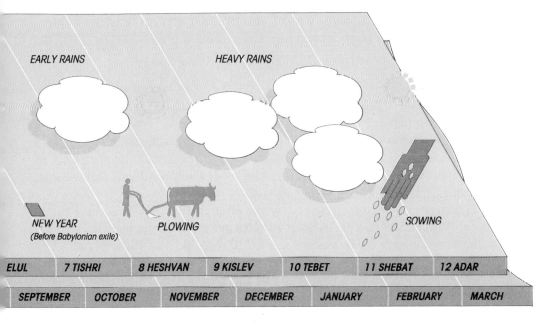

EARLY RAINS   HEAVY RAINS

NEW YEAR   PLOWING   SOWING
(Before Babylonian exile)

ELUL	7 TISHRI	8 HESHVAN	9 KISLEV	10 TEBET	11 SHEBAT	12 ADAR
SEPTEMBER	OCTOBER	NOVEMBER	DECEMBER	JANUARY	FEBRUARY	MARCH

central portion of the country consists of limestone hills and mountains without much depth of soil. Once covered with considerable forests, the mountains have been denuded through the centuries and the sparse soil has eroded as a result of the heavy winter rains. Small valleys among the hills are suitable for agriculture, but thousands of square miles are of little use. The maritime plain, the plain of Esdraelon (Megiddo), parts of the Jordan Valley, and the valleys of Galilee are relatively good, especially when irrigated.

The cut-up, rocky, and generally arid country doomed its inhabitants to hard work for a minimal level of existence. Modern Israelis have produced remarkable results through fertilization, reforestation, irrigation, swamp drainage, industrialization, and the like.

The shoreline of the country, in contrast to Phoenicia (modern Lebanon) to the north, is largely unsuited for sea-going commerce. The only natural harbor is at Acre-Haifa. Herod the Great constructed an artifical harbor at Caesarea (22–10 BC) by building a huge seawall into the Mediterranean. Solomon built a port on the Gulf of Aqaba (at Ezion-geber). Today Eilat, near that site, serves the Israelis for that purpose.

The ancient Hebrews looked on their land as 'a good land, a land of brooks of water, of fountains and springs, ... a land of wheat and barley, of vines and fig trees and pomegranates, a land of olive trees and honey' (Deut. 8:7–8). As compared to the desert areas in which Israel wandered for a generation in the time of Moses, the description is justified. But it is the poorest part of the Fertile Crescent, and life on this international bridge was difficult and insecure economically and militarily. The Promised Land was no Garden of Eden; hence, seers and prophets looked forward to the coming of that Garden in the latter days.

Archaeology in the Lands of the Bible

Its Origin and History

Modern archaeology began at the time of Napoleon's invasion of Egypt in 1798. Along with his troops Napoleon took 175 scholars, artists, and scientists to study and draw the antiquities of Egypt. Their results were published in seven volumes between 1809 and 1822.

The most important discovery by the French in Egypt was the Rosetta Stone. While constructing a fort at Rosetta in the Nile delta in 1799, soldiers came across a large black stone inscribed in three scripts: hieroglyphic, Demotic (a form of Egyptian script), and Greek. Working from the Greek, which turned out to be a translation of the Demotic and hieroglyphic text, scholars by 1822 unlocked the secret of hieroglyphics and henceforth were able to read the thousands of inscriptions on the monuments of ancient Egypt.

Archaeological digging in Mesopotamia was undertaken by the French and British in the middle of the nineteenth century. Paul Botta of France discovered the palace of the Assyrian king Sargon II (721–705 BC) at Khorsabad. Henry Layard of England uncovered at Nimrud (ancient Calah) the palace of Asshur-nasir-pal II (884–860 BC) and at Kuyunjik (ancient Nineveh) the palaces of Sennacherib (704–681 BC) and Asshurbanapal (668–627).

In the palace of Asshurbanapal the king's library of thousands of clay tablets was discovered by Rassam, Layard's associate. The tablets contained letters, contracts, dictionaries, grammars, receipts, tables of measures, lists of events, hymns, prayers, religious epics, medical reports, astronomical and astrological calculations, etc. They dealt with almost every field of learning known to scholars of that time. Among them were the Assyrian stories of the Creation and the Flood, which George Smith of the British Museum identified and interpreted (1872–76).

The deciphering of the wedge-shaped (cuneiform) writing was achieved mainly by an English army officer, Henry Rawlinson. At the risk of his life, between 1843 and 1847, he copied and finally interpreted Old Persian and Babylonian inscriptions placed by Darius I (522–486 BC) on a great rock cliff at Behistun, Persia.

Research in Palestine got under way near the beginning of the nineteenth century. The location of biblical towns was explored in 1838 by Americans Edward Robinson and Eli Smith. Their results were published in an important work entitled *Biblical Researches in Palestine, Mount Sinai, and Arabia Petraea* (1841).

The Rosetta Stone, now housed in the British Museum,
London, unlocked the secret of hieroglyphics.

French and British scholars carried on both surface and sub-surface explorations in the latter half of the nineteenth century. It was the British genius Flinders Petrie, who in 1890 at a mound in southwestern Palestine (Tell el-Hesi) set sub-surface exploration on a scientific basis. His careful methods of recording results, his recognition of mound stratification (see below), and, most of all, his discovery that levels of occuption in a mound can be dated from the type of pottery recovered from the different levels revolutionized archaeological method.

Refinements of Petrie's methods and the introduction of still other techniques have gone on in the twentieth century under Reisner and Fisher, W.F. Albright, G. Ernest Wright, Kathleen Kenyon, and others.

Today a new generation of Syro-Palestinian archaeologists has replaced the major founders of archaeology as a scientific discipline (the people just mentioned and others such as Glueck, de Vaux, Avi-Yonah, Aharoni, Yadin). The new archaeologists have launched an incredibly ambitious program throughout the Middle East under a new philosophy, new strategies of staffing and financing, and a refined and expanded technique (see below, pp. 390–91). The emerging 'greats' of our time are such people as Dever, Sauer, E. and C. Meyers, Rast, Seger, Stager, Geraty, Muhly, Shiloh, Kochavi, Kempinski, Ussishkin, Netzer, T. Dothan, Ben-Tor, A. Mazar, Hadidi, Barghouti, Ibrahim, and Matthiae.

National departments of antiquities are pushing forward on projects in Israel, Jordan, Syria, Lebanon, Cyprus, the Sinai Peninsula (Egypt), and the Arabian Peninsula (chiefly Yemen). Thousands of mounds remain to be examined for the light they can throw on the history and culture of the Middle East and on the literature that emerged from that part of the cradle of civilization.

Archaeological Method

1. *The first principle of modern, scientific archaeology is excavation by layers or strata.* It was in 1870 that Heinrich Schliemann learned at ancient Troy that ruined cities often had formed through the centuries into layered mounds, with the earliest layer at the bottom and successive cities atop each other, somewhat in layer-cake fashion. Flinders Petrie's expedition verified this at Tell el-Hesi in 1890, as has every scientifically conducted excavation of a mound since.

The Old Testament refers to a mound of this kind by the Hebrew word *tell*, a word whose meaning was not known when the King James Version was made in 1611. In that version Joshua 11:13 reads: 'But as for the cities that stood still in their strength, Israel burned none of them, save Hazor only.' The Revised Standard Version correctly renders the word *tell* by 'mound' as follows: 'But none of the cities that stood on mounds did Israel burn, except Hazor only.'

Cities were destroyed in many ways: by earthquake, flood, volcanic erup-
tion, fire, military conquest and pillaging, and abandonment due to the failure of the water supply. In many cases surviving inhabitants rebuilt the city,
or a portion of it, on account of its many advantages: its strategic location
(often on a prominent hill, at a good harbor, alongside a trade route, by a
good source of water); its peculiar sanctity for some tribe or nation, often as
a place of worship; its relative impregnability (its basically strong city walls,
defensive towers, and water tunnel). It was easier and wiser to level off the
destroyed buildings, patch up the walls, and rebuild inside the walls than
start from scratch at a new location.

The layers, of course, are not well defined over a whole mound. Pits for
storage and foundation trenches for buildings intrude into earlier levels.
Stone from previous buildings appear in a later level. The top of the mound
may be somewhat rounded, so that a stratum of occupation may not have the
same elevation everywhere. A rebuilding in some period may have extended
only over a portion of the mound. Confused layers are a headache for the archaeologist, but he must do his best to untangle them lest he confuse cultures
of different historical periods.

Archaeological
Methods

*Excavated
squares*

Stepped trench

*Successive
occupation
levels*

*Archaeologist's
sounding*

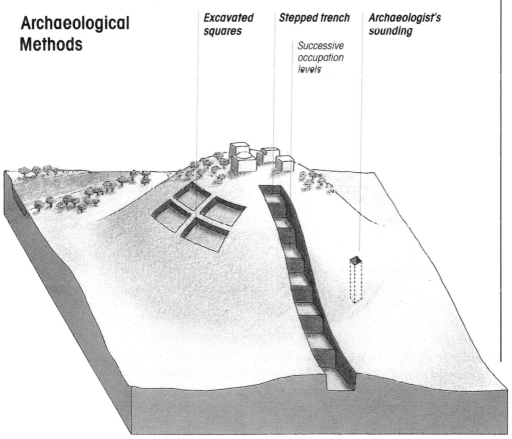

Today archaeologists do not excavate a stratum over its whole extent. To do so would remove forever all evidence of that layer and thus leave nothing for future excavators, who will certainly have better methods than ours. But, more importantly, the removal of an entire stratum leaves the excavator and other archaeologists no on-the-spot evidence of the sequence of layers to serve as a check on interpretation of the history of the mound. Thus archaeologists today excavate only selected areas of mounds and leave 'balks' (unexcavated strips, usually one meter wide, with carefully cut vertical sides) running across the area being excavated. Here the layers of occupation can be observed in the vertical face of the balks.

The mounds vary in size from an acre or two to two hundred acres (Hazor). In height the ruins vary from a few feet, representing one or two layers, to more than eighty feet and eighteen layers (Bethshan), and twenty-one levels at Hazor.

2. *The second principle of scientific archaeology is the classification and study of objects according to their form and style* – known technically as 'typology.' Ceramic (pottery) typology is the dominant form in excavations.

Flinders Petrie in 1890 discovered that pottery from the different layers of a mound varied considerably in form, decoration, type of materials used, and methods of making. He finally proved, against considerable opposition, that the different types of pottery came from different cultural periods, that the types can be dated approximately (by comparison with types known from datable contexts in Egypt and elsewhere), and that pottery can establish the chronology of the layers of a mound.

The use of pottery as a clue to dating is now far advanced. Not only are pieces and intact pottery objects dated from knowledge of types, but their age can be determined by heating the pottery and measuring the radiation. Most buried mineral substances absorb the natural radiation given off by uranium, potassium, and thorium in the earth. Absorbed radiation is released when the substance is heated. Since the rate of absorption is known and the amount absorbed can be measured when heated, the time of burial in the earth can be determined. The technique is known as 'thermoluminescence.'

All objects discovered are helpful in dating a level: the types of tools made (from stone, copper, iron); the tombs and burial objects; the shapes and materials of houses and public buildings; the jewelry; etc. When organic matter turns up in excavations, such as plants, wood, charcoal, shell, antler, burned bone, dung, and peat, the radiocarbon and other methods of dating can fix its approximate age.

All living things absorb carbon 14 from the atmosphere. At the death of the organism no further carbon 14 is absorbed. Through the process of decay, the carbon 14 begins to disintegrate at a rate known to scientists. By measuring the amount of carbon 14 remaining in the specimen and by knowing the rate of atomic disintegration, the time when that specimen was alive can be

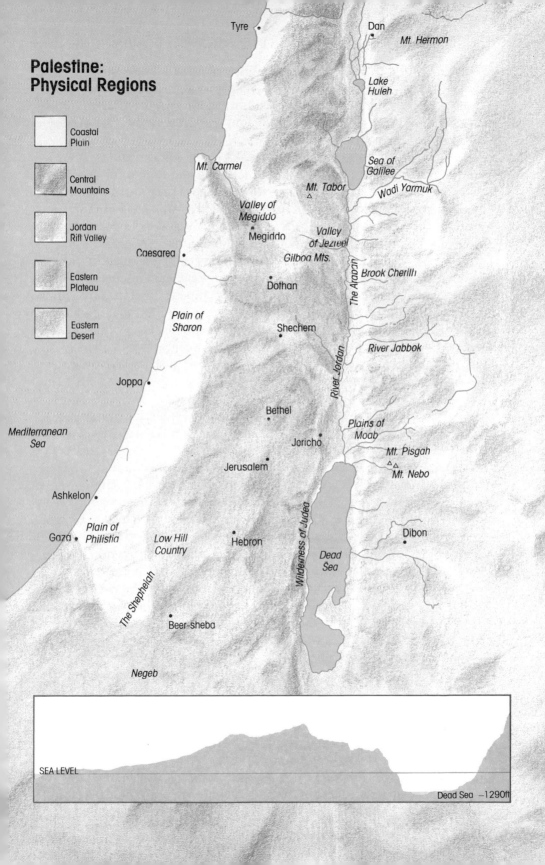

Palestine:
Physical Regions

Coastal Plain

Central Mountains

Jordan Rift Valley

Eastern Plateau

Eastern Desert

Tyre

Dan

Mt. Hermon

Lake Huleh

Mt. Carmel

Sea of Galilee

Mt. Tabor

Wadi Yarmuk

Valley of Megiddo

Megiddo

Valley of Jezreel

Gilboa Mts.

Caesarea

Brook Cherith

The Arabah

Dothan

Plain of Sharon

Shechem

River Jabbok

River Jordan

Joppa

Bethel

Plains of Moab

Jericho

Mt. Pisgah

Mediterranean Sea

Jerusalem

Mt. Nebo

Ashkelon

Dibon

Gaza

Plain of Philistia

Low Hill Country

Hebron

Wilderness of Judea

Dead Sea

The Shephelah

Beer-sheba

Negeb

SEA LEVEL

Dead Sea −1290ft

calculated (with a 5 to 10 percent possibility of error). The method is valid back to about 20,000 years. Fluorine, collagen, and potassium-argon dating is useful also. When dates have been established for a particular layer, all objects can be studied together and conclusions drawn about the kind of people who fashioned them.

3. *The third principle in scientific archaeology is systematic and accurate recording of data.* When a layer has been picked apart and most of the objects removed from their context, the excavator must have the kind of records that will allow him completely to visualize that layer exactly as he found it.

Full and accurate recording calls for aerial photographs of the mound; a contour map of it; the division of the mound into numbered areas (usually 5 × 5 meters) and numbered strata so that objects can be labeled to indicate their exact place of discovery; photographs and sketches of important objects in their context; detailed, scale drawings (by a competent architect) of important areas of a stratum; cataloging of distinctive pieces of pottery and of isolated objects (jewelry, seals, statues, coins, inscriptions, etc.) with sketches, descriptions, and photographs; drawings and photographs of balks. Laser-beam transits for quick and accurate mapping and, in special situations, resistivity surveying for discovering and plotting underground structures are employed.

Since about 1970 archaeology in Bible Lands has entered a new phase, almost a 'revolution,' so that scholars speak of 'the New Archaeology.' One of its features is a new multi-disciplinary approach to excavation. Interest has broadened from archaeology as a background for understanding the Bible and from a long-standing preoccupation with the history and religion of the Middle East to every aspect of the life of the peoples who lived there. Today excavation staffs include most of the following: geologists, geomorphologists, climatologists, zoologists, anthropologists, historians of technology, paleo-ethnobotanists, ethnographers, and computer programmers. The debris of the excavations is sifted for seeds, pollen, bone fragments, and all the tiny and bigger things that can yield information about the diet, diseases, longevity, environment, and domestic-social-economic life, as well as the political and religious life, of the former inhabitants. Religion, as a cultural factor, is still a center of attention, but it is no longer *the* center.

The second feature is readily apparent from all this: the secularization of the archaeology of 'the Holy Lands.' 'Biblical Archaeology' was long supported and conducted by people, scholars, and institutions with strong biblical and religious interests. Today even the term 'Biblical Archaeology' has become an embarrassment to archaeological scientists who wish to be known as 'Syro-Palestinian archaeologists.' The new anthropological, ecological, sociological interests have brought into Near Eastern archaeology university students looking for academic credit, the support of secular foundations and governmental agencies, and secular scientific groups from several parts of the world. Some indigenous Arab scientists and their governmental agencies are anxious to distance themselves from Christian and Jewish approaches to the archaeology of their lands.

Much of this is gain. The excavations are better planned, better staffed, better executed, better interpreted, better published, and much wider in their significance than formerly. Some of the advocates of the 'new archaeology' have pledged themselves to continuing interest in the relevance of their work for the understanding of the Bible. The more discerning realize that the archaeology of the region could hardly proceed without the historical data the Bible supplies. One of them has said, 'If it were not for the Bible the Israelites would be as little known as the Moabites, the Edomites, and the Philistines' (Philip J. King). Illumination of the Bible should proceed at an accelerated rate.

Archaeology and the Bible

Archaeological research in Palestine and the rest of the Middle East has thrown light on human life on this planet long before any parts of the Bible were written. So far as we can tell, the earliest parts of the Bible were composed after Israel settled in Canaan (c. thirteenth century BC), though the traditions on which they rest may go back far before that time (see pp. 108–9).

Archaeologists at work at a tell in north Syria.

How long humankind has been on the earth is uncertain. There is evidence from the Olduvai Gorge in East Africa that first tool-making activities began over two million years ago. In 1959 an Israeli team discovered at a site just south of the Sea of Galilee stone tools and bones (hominid, elephant, hippopotamus, crocodile, and various extinct animals) dating back more than 600,000 years. Caves in the side of Mt. Carmel have yielded skeletons and flint tools of 50,000 to 75,000 years ago.

People moved out of caves, settled in villages, and began cultivating wild grains and domesticating animals around the ninth millennium BC. Jericho, in the Jordan Valley, one of the oldest villages known, was in existence by about 8,500 BC.

It is evident that Abraham, Isaac, Jacob, and Joseph – long thought to have lived near the dawn of history, which Archbishop Ussher in the seventeenth century put at 4004 BC – were latecomers on the human scene. These patriarchs are now commonly dated between the twentieth and the seventeenth or early sixteenth centuries BC. And the writing of the Bible began several centuries later still. Though the Bible and the characters with which it deals seem very old to us, on the time chart of human life on this planet the Hebrews and their literature came into being only yesterday.

A discussion of how the Bible and archaeology are related is almost impossible in brief compass. All we can do here is indicate types of relationship and offer a few examples of each. You may explore the vast and fascinating field of archaeology through the books suggested at the end of this section (p. 410).

The Bible Guides the Work of Archaeologists
In many parts of the world there are no literary sources to assist archaeologists in interpreting what they find or even to give them some idea what to look for. The archaeological task is much easier when ancient literary sources, such as the writings of Herodotus and Strabo (Greece), Manetho (Egypt), Josephus (Palestine), and the Bible in both its Testaments, give help in forming the questions and in putting together the jigsaw puzzle of ancient data.

The Bible has played a major guiding role from the beginning of scientific exploration in Palestine. Edward Robinson's love of the Bible and masterful training in it in America and Germany led him and Eli Smith, an American missionary serving in the Near East, to explore the topography of Palestine in 1838 (see above, p. 384). With Hebrew and English Bibles, measuring tape, and a telescope in their hands, they identified over a hundred biblical places, thereby laying the foundations of biblical archaeology and geography. Robinson's biographers (H.B. Smith and R.D. Hitchcock) said of him: 'It was the supreme ambition of his life to explain and illustrate the Holy Bible. The one adjective in our language which he loved the most was *Biblical*. It was the watchword of all his studies.'

The restored post-Canaanite citadel at Arad, near the Dead Sea.

The Bible in one hand and a pick in the other would be an apt symbol for the work of the founders of archaeology in Palestine and many of their successors. From the Bible they learned in part where to dig, what to look for, how to interpret what they found, and a motive for disseminating their new knowledge.

Today's more secular archaeologists still cannot dispense with the Bible. One of them has written recently, 'The archaeologist working in ancient Syria-Palestine must turn to the biblical exegete and the historian for technical assistance.' And he goes on to remark that the archaeologist must 'be equipped with at least a working knowledge of Northwest Semitic languages and literatures as well as of biblical criticism' (W.G. Dever, in D.A. Knight and G.M. Tucker (eds.), *The Hebrew Bible and its Modern Interpreters*, 1985, p. 64). Without the Bible the mysteries of the lands of the Bible can hardly be unlocked.

Archaeology Illustrates Places and Objects Mentioned in the Bible.
Robert Koldewey, at the turn of the twentieth century, uncovered magnificent Babylon, the creation of Nebuchadnezzar II (605–562 BC). Nebuchadnezzar designed and constructed a great system of fortifications. It included the double Ishtar Gate in a double city wall. Rows of bulls and dragons in enameled brick covered the gate. He built a processional way, lined with

enameled lions, temples, and palaces. He rebuilt the Tower of Babel, which was already a thousand years old in his time. This Tower is visible today only in its ground plan. We can see what it looked like in the much better preserved ziggurat at Ur.

Hezekiah's water system (2 Kings 20:20; 2 Chron. 32:30), by which he ensured water for Jerusalem in case of siege by the Assyrians, is still visible in Jerusalem. His workmen dug a tunnel from the Spring of Gihon outside the city through about 1750 feet of limestone under the city to a reservoir inside the wall. An inscription in Hebrew on the tunnel wall described how the tunnel was cut through from both ends. This inscription is now in the Museum of the Ancient Orient in Istanbul.

We can stand today before the 'wonderful stones' which the disciples referred to as they left Herod's temple (Mark 13:1). Recent excavation outside the huge retaining wall of the temple area has exposed many finely chiseled stones belonging to that wall. Some of them are more than thirty feet long and are set together without mortar. To maneuver them into place, to say nothing about cutting them out, is a feat greatly to be admired.

One can walk up the original 200-foot wide stairway of 30 steps leading to the double gate on the south side of Herod's temple area, saunter along the paved street running east-west in front of the area, and peer into the ritual baths (for washing prior to entering the temple). All have been cleared by Israeli excavators in recent years. Here one is on pavement trod by Jesus and his disciples.

Archaeologists have uncovered many of the cities in which Paul preached. Notable is Corinth, where excavation has been going on since 1896. This fine city, the capital of Achaia and seat of the proconsul, was built on two terraces under the towering rock Acrocorinth (1886 feet high). At the city's center was the marketplace (agora) with its stately gate (propylaea), colonnades, shops, and basilicas (buildings for courts and public assembly). Towering over the marketplace on a hill just west was the Temple of Apollo. Seven of its original thirty-eight columns still stand.

At the center of the marketplace archaeologists found a large stone platform (bema) which served as a speakers' rostrum. Here the Roman proconsul and other officials heard petitions and addressed the public. The platform, originally covered with white and blue marble, had marble benches at the back and part way along the sides. Flanking the platform at ground level on either side were waiting rooms with marble benches, apparently for petitioners expecting audience with city officials. This platform is possibly the place where Paul was brought before the proconsul Gallio by his Jewish accusers (Acts 18:12–17).

'Robinson's arch', in the Herodian walls surrounding the Dome of the Rock. The arch originally carried steps from the temple to the city.

Steps leading to the double gate into Herod's Temple, Jerusalem.

We can now see and handle many of the coins mentioned in the New Testament. We can inspect the remains of synagogue buildings in Galilee from near the time of Jesus. Scrolls like he read from (Luke 4:17) came from a cave at Qumran by the Dead Sea. Lamps like the wise and foolish maidens carried (Matt. 25:1–12) fill our museums. Imagination has now given way to sight as a result of the work of archaeologists.

Archaeology Supplements and Explains Many Biblical Data.
The cherubim mentioned in the Old Testament as guarding the way to the tree of life (Gen. 3:24), as supporting the throne of God (Ps. 80:1), as overshadowing the ark of the covenant (Exod. 25:18–20), and as decorating the walls of the main room (the Holy Place) of the temple of Solomon (2 Chron. 3:7) turn out to be winged animals, often lions with human heads, such as supported and decorated the thrones of ancient kings. They were not rosy-faced little angels as imagined by famous modern painters.

The ivory house built by Ahab (1 Kings 22:39) was a house decorated with ivory ornaments (some inlaid in furniture and others hung on walls). The excavations of 1931–35 at Samaria uncovered many ivories of this type alongside the royal quarters in the debris of the Assyrian destruction of 721 BC. For Ahab to have built a house entirely of ivory would have been a feat that even an Egyptian pharaoh's wealth could hardly have achieved! Biblical references to weights and measures (the cubit, the span, the omer, the ephah,

Excavations at Tell Beer Sheva have greatly increased knowledge of its history.

the shekel, the talent, etc.), to utensils, to musical instruments, to weapons, to clothing, and the like are no longer mysterious, thanks to archaeology.

Especially valuable information has come from excavations in territories occupied by Israel's neighbors. The peoples who throng the pages of the Old Testament – the Amorites, the Horites, the Hittites, the Canaanites, the Arameans, the Philistines, the Egyptians, the Assyrians, the Moabites, the Ammonites, the Chaldeans, etc. – are now better known. Their cultures and their influence on Israel have come into clearer view.

Of some importance for our understanding of the background of the origins of Israel and of the nature of its language and culture – of how much importance is disputed – are the discoveries from Tell Mardikh (ancient Ebla) made by Italian archaeologists since 1964. The large mound (140 acres and 50 feet in height) lies about 35 miles south of Aleppo in Syria, on the ancient caravan route from Upper Mesopotamia to Canaan and Egypt.

During its most prosperous period (c. 2600–2250 BC) Ebla housed some 260,000 people. Its merchants carried on extensive commerce and cultural exchanges with cities of the Tigris-Euphrates region to the East and with those of the Syrian coastal area and Egypt to the Southwest.

The archaeologists dug up more than 17,000 tablets and fragments in a royal palace of this period. The tablets were written in cuneiform script in two languages: Sumerian and a hitherto unknown Semitic language, now called Eblaite. The texts contain economic records of the royal palace, lists of

various sorts (professions, animals, birds, fish, geographical names), scribal vocabularies (Sumerian words followed by Eblaite equivalents), a few historical accounts (a commercial treaty, a military campaign), and incantations (magical formulas) mentioning Eblaite deities.

In the early days of their decipherment and interpretation extravagant claims were made concerning their importance for understanding the Bible, such as: the Eblaite language is 'Old Canaanite,' a close relative of ancient Hebrew; cities mentioned in Genesis (Hazor, Jerusalem, Sodom, and Gomorrah) appear in these texts; biblical personal names (Eber, Abram, Israel, Esau, Ishmael, Saul, David) are present; and even the divine name 'Yahweh' (in the form 'Ya') occurs. Scholars now judge these claims extravagant and to some extent inaccurate.

Eblaite may be closer to Old Akkadian and Amorite than to Canaanite and Hebrew. Two personal names seem identical with biblical ones (Ebrum, Ishmael). The supposed names of Palestinian cities actually resulted from a misreading of the texts. And 'Ya' is apparently not 'Yahweh' at all but a short and familiar personal name-ending (hypocoristicon).

Only a small portion of the immense body of texts has been studied and published. Much of significance for the understanding of the Bible may yet appear. There are some values thus far: further knowledge of the economic and cultural life of a major Semitic civilization near Canaan and from which general area, according to biblical tradition, the Hebrew people came (Haran); information about the deities and syncretistic religion of Ebla – about the Semitic/Canaanite gods Dagan, Haddad, Resheph, Baal, about the standard Sumerian gods, about 'the god of my father' (cf. Gen. 43:23); and details about the Syrian/Mesopotamian city-state system, known to us from the Canaanites a millennium later.

The discoveries emphasize again that the forebears of Israel did not grow up in a cultural vacuum. Today we understand the stage on which Israel played out its life and destiny in a way undreamed of in the nineteenth century.

Archaeology Probes the Bible.

Archaeology raises important questions about information in the Bible and forces readers to look for adequate answers. The book of Genesis tells of Abraham and Isaac having dealings with Abimelech, 'king of the Philistines' (21:22–34; 26:1, 8, 14–15). However, Abimelech is a Canaanite, not a Philistine, name. Furthermore, archaeological evidence from Egypt shows clearly that the Philistines and other sea peoples invaded Egypt and Canaan early in the twelfth century, that they were repulsed by Ramesses III in several battles, and that they then settled down as vassals of the Pharaoh on the coastal

A volunteer excavates a cave used as a hideout during the Bar Kochba revolt AD 132.

Remains of the Israelite citadel, Hazor.

plain of southern Canaan. From the twelfth century on this coastal plain became known as 'the land of the Philistines.' There were actually no Philistines in Canaan in the early second millenium BC, the time of Abraham and
Isaac.

The explanation of the biblical references to the Philistines in the probable
time of Abraham and Isaac seems to be that the writer of Genesis used the
later name of the country in referring to events of earlier history. Abimelech
actually was king of Gerar in Canaan, a territory that later was known as 'the
land of the Philistines.' Hence he was called anachronistically 'king of the
Philistines,' much as we might in our time speak of 'the first governor of New
York' when we should more accurately speak of 'the first governor of New
Netherland' (the earlier name).

Archaeology also raises questions about the detailed biblical stories of the
capture of Jericho and Ai (Josh. 6–8). Some fifty years ago a British archaeologist reported that he had found the walls of Jericho (double wall) at

the time of Joshua and evidence of Jericho's destruction around 1400 BC by earthquake and fire. More recent excavations have shown that the double wall dates to a much earlier time (late third millennium BC) and cannot have been the one referred to in the biblical story. No walls certainly in use in the time of Joshua have come to light. In fact, only small traces of a town of the general period of Joshua (Late Bronze – c. 1550–1200) remain, and this town seems to have been destroyed and abandoned somewhere around 1325 BC – probably nearly a century before Joshua's time. Erosion of the mound has eliminated almost all trace of the fourteenth-century city. And there is no archaeological evidence for a city on this mound in the four centuries following Joshua.

These archaeological conclusions raise serious questions for students of the Bible. Was Jericho a small city in the fourteenth century, and was it perhaps captured by people related to the Hebrews, who had never been in Egypt, rather than by Joshua and the children of those Hebrews who had come out of Egypt? And was the capture less dramatic than that described in Joshua 6? Is the story a folktale, recorded long after the Hebrew invasion, perhaps with a historical nucleus but considerable embellishment as well?

Ai, the next city conquered by Joshua – according to the book of Joshua – is as much a puzzle as Jericho. Extensive archaeological investigations at et-Tell near Bethel have shown that there was a large (27.5 acre) walled city there between about 3000–2400 BC, but that the city was destroyed and lay in ruins until about 1220 BC, when a small (2.5 acre) unwalled village was built on the stumps of the old city. This village was abandoned about 1050 BC.

How does one fit the biblical account of Joshua's destruction of a large and formidable city (Josh. 8) into these archaeological data? If Joshua invaded the area prior to 1220 (the usual date suggested by scholars is about 1250), there was no city there at that time. If he invaded when the unwalled village was there (perhaps about 1125), the dramatic story of Joshua 8 is a gross exaggeration if not a falsification of the facts. Was Ai located somewhere else and not at et-Tell? No other suitable site appears in the vicinity. Is the story in Joshua 8 possibly the record of the capture of nearby Bethel, of which there is no account in Joshua but rather in Judges 1:22–25? Or was the ruin at Ai occupied by an advance contingent of defenders from Bethel to stave off Joshua's advance, so that there was a real confrontation there after all? Scholars are not yet in a position to offer conclusive answers to the puzzle of both Jericho and Ai, but the data from archaeology have forced them to examine the biblical material carefully for possible solutions.

Archaeology Corroborates the Bible.
The 'New Archaeology' has warned us against the use of archaeological data to 'prove the Bible.' Such use, the new archaeologists say, will distort our understanding of both archaeology and of the Bible. In their view, the whole

movement of 'Biblical Theology' at the middle of our present century led to distortions in both disciplines and happily has run its course.

The warning is timely and welcome. Presuppositions and predispositions *do* shape conclusions and should be constantly recognized and restrained. However, even the new archaeologists see that the two disciplines belong together and can inform one another.

It is evident to scholars in each discipline that Syro-Palestinian archaeology has offered both general and specific corroboration of biblical materials. As general corroboration, we may point to a definite compatibility between the picture of the ancient Near Eastern world we get from archaeology and that from the Bible. As an eminent biblical scholar and orientalist of an earlier generation (Millar Burrows) once put it: 'The picture fits the frame; the melody and the accompaniment are harmonious.'

The nations around Israel are distributed geographically and impinge on Israel historically in much the same way both in the Bible and in archaeology. There is general correspondence between the distribution of the nations, as indicated in the Table of the Nations of Genesis 10, and the historical facts as we know them from archaeology. One goes from 'Ur of the Chaldeans' into 'the land of Canaan' by way of 'Haran,' as indicated in Genesis 11:31. Assyria, with its capital of Nineveh, is located correctly near the land of Ararat (southeast Turkey) (2 Kings 19:37). The Philistines are properly placed in the lowlands of Palestine, with the Hebrews in the mountains above them (1 Sam. 13:20). People from Canaan go down to Egypt in time of famine, as both the Bible and archaeology indicate; and so on.

As for specific corroboration, the examples are legion. Jerusalem *was* in Canaanite hands until captured by David (2 Sam. 5:6–9), long after the time of Joshua. Omri *did* found the city of Samaria, as indicated in 1 Kings 16:23–24. Hazael of Syria *did* usurp the throne of Syria (2 Kings 8:7–15), as confirmed by a text from Shalmaneser III which refers to Hazael as 'a son of a nobody (who) seized the throne.' Nebuchadnezzar *did* destroy the fortified towns of Judah (Jer. 34:7); and we have the Lachish letters written shortly before he destroyed that city also. Jehoiachin *was* carried into Babylonian captivity (2 Kings 24:10–15), as attested by a tablet from Babylon listing a delivery of oil for the subsistence of 'Jehoiachin,' who is called 'the king of Judah.' Pontius Pilate *was* 'prefect of Judaea,' as a dedicatory inscription found at Caesarea indicates. According to an inscription found at Delphi in Greece, Gallio *was* proconsul of Achaia at a time when Paul could have had a hearing before him, as claimed in Acts 18:12–17. In general, the book of Acts and the letters of Paul represent the political situation of New Testament times as Josephus, Hellenistic-Roman writers, and archaeology know it.

But what has archaeology to say about the Bible's representation of the earliest periods of Israelite history and life, and even about the forebears, the

Patriarchs? Here present-day support from archaeology is not so clear as in the above examples.

The brilliant biblical scholar and archaeologist W.F. Albright, his students, and scholars influenced by them turned the tide for a while against Wellhausen, Alt, Noth, and others who held that the Patriarchal stories in Genesis contain little or no historical content. The Albrightians made a strong case for the Patriarchs as real historical persons and the events of their lives as conceivable in the socio-political and cultural context in which the Bible seems to place them. They saw the Patriarchs as one element in a general movement of Amorite people into Palestine from Upper Mesopotamia about the 20th–19th century BC and cited personal names, names of cities, and customs from Mesopotamian texts (Mari and Nuzi) of the 18th–15th centuries that seem to be reflected in the Patriarchal stories.

They pointed to such data as the following. It was the custom at Nuzi for childless couples to adopt a slave in order to have an heir; and, in the event of the birth of a true son, the adopted son would have to give way as principal heir (*cf.* Gen. 15:1–4). A childless wife was obliged to provide her husband with a concubine. The concubine and her offspring were protected legally against expulsion (*cf.* Gen. 16:1–4; 21:8–11). Rachel's theft of Laban's household gods (Gen. 31:30–35) is understandable in light of the information in the Nuzi texts that the position of head of the family and, accordingly, inheritance rights were associated with possession of the household gods.

Today the similarities are not wholly denied in the 'New Archaeology'; it is only argued that they cannot be used to establish the Patriarchs as historical persons and their date. Customs of this kind persisted for hundreds of years and even millennia. Folktales spun even in late times would naturally incorporate them.

Furthermore, such scholars say that it is not likely that complex historical details would be handed down without major distortion for more than a thousand years. And form-critical examination of the stories (see pp. 100–1) convinces many of them that the stories arose as independent units, were drawn together at various sanctuaries, shaped by their use in worship and teaching, supplemented with new stories, recorded in early written documents, and edited and reedited in accordance with the theological and literary tastes of the compilers of the Pentateuchal sources and the final redactors. A process like this, they say, is not apt to preserve much historical content. A considerable group of scholars today regards the stories as 'pious fiction'. (See p. 102.)

We cannot marshall here in detail the moderate-liberal (*e.g.*, John Bright) and conservative (*e.g.*, La Sor-Hubbard-Bush, Kitchen) arguments from archaeology and other disciplines for the essential historicity of the Patriarchal stories. The main lines of reasoning run about as follows.

1. In literary type (genre) the stories seem historiographical in nature and intent. The literature of the ancient Near East, as recovered by archaeology,

shows the Patriarchal narratives to be nearer to the autobiographical and biographical genres than to the historical legends and fictional tales of Egypt, Syro-Palestine, Anatolia, and Mesopotamia. The narratives are relatively sober and unembellished accounts of persons and families. Though they do serve a theological purpose in our present records, they seem not to be theological constructs without a historical basis.

2. The stories reflect the proper social, cultural, economic, and political conditions known to have existed in Syria and Canaan in the early second millennium BC.

The personal names of the Patriarchs and their families are similar to the names of Amorite (West Semitic) peoples of that period. The pastoral-nomadic lifestyle of the Patriarchs fits one element of the two-form (villager and pastoralist) society of the time. The social and legal customs of Upper Mesopotamia in the early second millennium BC explain many of the attitudes and actions of the persons and families described in the stories. The situation in Canaan at the time of Abraham's entrance into that country (the existence of Shechem, Bethel, Hebron, Dothan, Jerusalem, etc. as independent city-states and the largely open hill country allowing relatively free movement) agrees in the main with the data in the stories.

3. The character of the religion of the Patriarchs, as presented in the narratives, is appropriate for that period and stage in Israel's history and development. A family-god system was widely prevalent among ancient Amorite

Remains from the biblical period at Et Tell (Ai).

pastoral nomads of that time. The head of a clan chose the deity and entered into a personal, covenantal relationship with him. Loyalty to the patron deity continued through subsequent family generations. This is what we see in the Patriarchal stories. The deity is referred to as 'the God of Abraham' (Gen. 28:13), 'the Fear of Isaac' (Gen. 31:42), 'the Mighty One of Jacob' (Gen. 49:24) – the family God to which each Patriarch appeals and by which he swears.

The Patriarchs' name for their deity was 'El' (*e.g.*, El Shaddai – Ex. 6:3). The later name 'Yahweh,' revealed to Moses, is not used in the Patriarchal narratives. Israel's later cultic practices are not retrojected onto the Patriarchs. There is no officiating priesthood; the clan father alone acts as sacrificer and mediator with God. Israel's religion after Moses was markedly different from this.

4. Striking is the fact that the Patriarchs are portrayed as entering into relationships and performing actions strictly forbidden in later times under Mosaic law. Abraham married his half-sister (Gen. 20:12; see Lev. 18:9, 11; Deut. 27:22). Jacob had two sisters as wives at the same time (Gen. chap. 29; see Lev. 18:18). Abraham planted a sacred tree (Gen. 21:33; see Deut. 16:21). Jacob set up sacred pillars (Gen. 28:22; see Deut. 12:3). If these stories were fictional creations of later times, would their composers have represented the honored Patriarchs as indulging in these offenses against God?

Much can be said for the position that archaeology, along with critically established data from the stories themselves and related biblical materials, go a considerable distance in corroborating the essential historicity of the Patriarchal narratives.

Archaeology Reveals the Uniqueness of the Judeo-Christian Religion and Literature.
Since the latter decades of the nineteenth century archaeological discoveries have let us see striking similarities and differences between the life, thought, and literature of the Hebrews and other Near Eastern peoples, particularly the Canaanites and the inhabitants of Mesopotamia.

The stories of Genesis 1–11 are parallel at many points to tablets found in the library of Asshurbanapal (see p. 384) and elsewhere in Mesopotamia.

Three examples are:
1. The Creation Epic (*Enuma Elish*)
This is written on seven clay tablets of about one thousand lines. It concerns the origin of the gods from the union of the powers of chaos (Apsu and Tiamat) and the subsequent war between the gods and Tiamat in which Marduk destroys Tiamat and from her body forms heaven and earth. Marduk

King Asshurbanapal of Assyria, *c.* 668–627 BC.

establishes the sun, moon, and stars and creates man from the blood of a god (Kingu, Tiamat's general) in order that he may be the servant of the gods. The gods acclaim Marduk as their chief and exalt Babylon as his place of worship.

Both the Hebrew story (Gen. 1:1—2:3) and this Assyrian-Akkadian creation epic refer to a watery chaos at or near the beginning of all things (Tiamat equals *Tehom*, Hebrew for 'deep' in Gen. 1:2). The division of Tiamat into heaven and earth equals the dividing of the waters from the waters (Gen. 1:6–7). The order of creative acts is the same. The seven days of creation equal the seven tablets. And so on.

The differences, however, are far-reaching. In the Hebrew story God is the transcendent creator of matter. In the Assyrian-Akkadian myth god is male and female matter, and the many gods originate from sexual union. In the Hebrew story man is a creature, not essentially divine, who is made in God's likeness to be lord of the created order. In the other story man is essentially divine, since he was made from the blood of a god. He is to be the servant of the gods in order that the gods may be at ease. The Hebrew story is properly a creation story, whereas the other is a glorification of Marduk and his place of worship.

2. Enki and Ninhursag: A Paradise Myth

This myth comes from Nippur, in lower Mesopotamia. The six-column tablet on which it is written dates to the first half of the second millennium BC. It describes the land of Dilmun, the Sumerian 'Abode of the Blessed,' as a pure, clean, and bright land where there is no sickness, sorrow, old age, or death, and where fresh water from the earth rises to nourish plant and human life.

The god Enki successively impregnates the Sumerian mother goddess Ninhursag and their female offspring to the fourth generation. The last (the great granddaughter) yields to him only after a gift of cucumbers, apples (?) and grapes. Enki's semen is used to produce eight different plants, which, when eaten by Enki in order to know their nature, cause him to become sick in eight organs of his body, one being a rib. Ninhursag then curses Enki and subsequently heals him through the birth of eight deities, who in some way cure the sick members of his body.

Similarities to the Garden of Eden story in Genesis 2–3 are: the perfection of Dilmun; the fresh water from the earth (Gen. 2:6); the birth of the successive goddesses seemingly without pain or travail to the mother (cf. Gen. 3:16); the eating of the plants which resulted in a curse (Gen. 3:17–19); the reference to the rib (in Sumerian the word for rib means 'to make live'), thus perhaps explaining why Eve ('the mother of all living' – Gen. 3:20) was taken from Adam's rib. The differences, of course, are immense – notably, the crude, sexually-oriented polytheism and the lack of any ethical content in the story from Nippur.

3. The Gilgamesh Epic

Several versions of this epic from various periods and places of the Middle East have come to light. The best preserved came from the library of Asshurbanapal (668–627 BC) at Nineveh. George Smith of the British Museum in 1872 identified a portion of this epic as a flood story, calling it 'The Chaldean Account of the Deluge.' The epic was written on twelve tablets, the eleventh being the account of the flood, and was probably composed originally around 2000 BC.

The epic deals with the exploits of Gilgamesh, the youthful half-god and half-man ruler of Uruk, who, after many civic accomplishments and heroic acts, often in company with his close friend Enkidu, is brought to grief by Enkidu's death.

Haunted by the thought of his own coming death, he seeks out his ancestor Unapishtim, who has escaped death and become immortal. After a long and arduous journey to the west, through the mountains and over the Sea, he arrives at the land of the blessed, where Utnapishtim tells him how he has escaped the great flood and has been given immortal life by the gods. He advises Gilgamesh to secure a plant from the bottom of the sea and to eat it to gain immortality. Gilgamesh gets the plant, but a serpent snatches and devours it. In disappointment he returns to Uruk, seeking to be content with his mortality, and finding such joy in life as he can.

Tablet 11, Utnapishtim's account of the flood, parallels the biblical story in many details. The god Ea warns Utnapishtim in a dream about a coming deluge planned by the gods and advises him to build a ship in which he and 'the seed of all living things' might survive. According to Ea's instructions Utnapishtim builds the ship in the form of a cube, with six decks (*i.e.*, seven stories) and sixty-three compartments. He smears it with bitumen, provisions it, and loads it with gold and silver, family members, kin, boatmen, craftsmen, and beasts and wild creatures of the field – then battens down the ship's door and waits for the storm. For six days and nights the storm rages. On the seventh day it ceases. The ship comes to rest on Mt. Nizir, where it remains motionless for six days. On the seventh day Utnapishtim sends forth a dove, a swallow, and a raven. The first two return, but the raven does not. Utnapishtim and his companions disembark and offer sacrifices. The gods smell the sweet savor and 'crowd like flies about the sacrificer.' Ea reproaches Enlil for attempting the wholesale destruction of people. 'On the sinner impose his sin' he says, and then he offers suggestions of better ways than a flood to diminish mankind (by a lion, a wolf, a famine, a pestilence). Enlil thereupon blesses Utnapishtim and his wife and elevates them to a place among the gods in the land of the blessed.

So close are the parallels to the biblical story that we must suppose that some kind of relationship exists. Archaeology has not proved that a worldwide flood actually occured, but it has produced evidence of serious local floods. Thick layers of river mud have been found at several ancient sites in Mesopotamia (Ur, Kish, Fara, Nineveh). The dates of the layers do not coincide, and sometimes the layers did not even cover the whole site or nearby places. We probably must assume that the Hebrew and Babylonian flood stories go back to the memory of some destructive local flood in Mesopotamia. Claims from time to time that explorers have found the ark on Mt. Ararat or Mt. Judi have no scientific support.

The religious outlook of the Genesis story sets it apart from the Assyrian-Akkadian myth. Genesis declares that a purposeful and moral God, not capricious and feuding gods, caused the flood as a responsible judgment on evil people. The flood story thus became for Israelite writers the opportunity for illustrating the righteous mercy of God.

Parallels exist also between Hittite and Israelite covenants; Egyptian and Israelite proverbs; Canaanite and Israelite psalms, prophecy, and sacrifices; Persian (Zoroastrian) and Jewish views of the future; and Greek and Jewish concepts of the way God is related to the world (as Logos, Spirit, Wisdom).

The Hebrews did not live in a vacuum. They shared world views and traditions with the peoples among whom they lived. They used the thought forms and language of their day. The way to explain the similarities between the stories of Gen. 1–11 and Mesopotamian literature is probably to assume that Abraham, his family, and others brought Mesopotamian traditions with them when they migrated to Canaan. Israel's growing faith and experience transformed these traditions and made them the vehicle of its witness to God's activity in history and the world.

It is clear that the best minds and spirits of Israel adopted and adapted those elements of their cultural heritage and environment – myths, customs, laws, institutions, literary forms, and vocabulary – that were useful in expressing their view and experience of God. The great souls, like Amos, Isaiah, and Jeremiah, whose lives had been shaped by a righteous God, took the common clay in their hands and molded it into exquisite vessels for God's service. The clay was not unique; but the design, the workmanship, and the service to be rendered were.

For Further Reading
Aharoni, Y., *The Land of the Bible – A Historical Geography*, 1979; *The Archaeology of the Land of Israel*, 1982.
Avi-Yonah, M. and Stern, E. (eds.), *Encyclopaedia of Archaeological Excavations in the Holy Land*, 4 vols., 1975–78.
Cornfeld, G. and Freedman, D.N. *Archaeology of the Bible – Book by Book*, 1982.
Dever, W.G., 'Syro-Palestinian and Biblical Archaeology,' in Knight, D.A. and Tucker, G.M. (eds.), *The Hebrew Bible and Its Modern Interpreters*, 1985.
Finegan, J., *The Archaeology of the New Testament*, 1969.
Gardner, J.L. (ed.) with Frank, H.T., *Reader's Digest Atlas of the Bible: An Illustrated Guide to the Holy Land*, 1981.
Kenyon, K., *Archaeology in the Holy Land*, 3rd ed. 1970.
Pritchard, J.B. (ed.), *The Ancient Near East in Pictures Relating to the Old Testament*, 2nd ed., 1969; *Ancient Near Eastern Texts Relating to the Old Testament*, 3rd ed. 1969.
Snyder, G.F., *Ante Pacem: Archaeological Evidence of Church Life Before Constantine*, 1985.
Wright, G.E. et al. (the editors of the *Reader's Digest*), *Great People of the Bible and How They Lived*, 1974.
Yamauchi, E., *The Archaeology of New Testament Cities in Western Asia Minor*, 1980.

Between the Testaments

By the period between the Testaments we mean, strictly speaking, the time between the latest Old Testament book and the earliest New Testament book. There is no exact agreement about which books are to be thus identified; therefore we cannot define the exact limits of the period.

Scholars of a liberal outlook regard Daniel as the latest Old Testament book (c. 165 BC). Conservative scholars hold that no Old Testament book is later than the fifth/fourth centuries BC, when such works as 1–2 Chronicles, Ezra-Nehemiah, Malachi, and Esther appeared.

We are also not certain about the earliest New Testament book. Some conservative scholars believe that the Gospel of Matthew was written around AD 50, and some liberals and conservatives assign Paul's letter to the Galatians to about AD 48 or 49. Others, both conservatives and liberals, think 1 Thessalonians (AD 50 or 51) is the earliest. The time then *on outside dates* runs from around 400 BC to around AD 50.

Historical Events

The time between the Testaments divides into several periods:

The Jews under the Persians (539–332 BC)
Cyrus, the conqueror of Babylon (539 BC), and his successors (the most important being Darius I [522–486], Xerxes [486–465], Artaxerxes I [465–424], and Artaxerxes II [404–358]) allowed the Jews a large degree of self-determination. Restored to their homeland under Cyrus, Darius I, and others, they lived under the rule of a Persian governor and a Jewish high priest.

Economic conditions in the restored land were bleak, and religious life, centering in the renewed temple in Jerusalem, was perfunctory. Religious leaders made a strong effort to segregate the Jews from surrounding 'unclean' peoples, including the Samaritans.

Toward the end of the period, Persia's struggles with Egypt and Greece and internal conflicts weakened its authority and power. Alexander the Great (336–323 BC) brought about the fall of Persia at the battles of Issus (333 BC) and Gaugamela (331 BC).

Remains of the temple dedicated to Augustus by Herod, Samaria.

The Jews under Alexander the Great and the Ptolemies (332–198 BC)
The brief time of Alexander's conquests (334–323) was followed by a period
in which Alexander's generals shared authority over the conquered regions.
Ptolemy gained control first of Egypt (323) and then of Palestine (301).
Under Ptolemy and his successors the Jews apparently continued to have a
large degree of freedom, limited largely by the payment of taxes to Egypt.

A large Jewish community, with possibly a million people, flourished in
Egypt. The translation of the Old Testament into Greek for these and other
Greek-language readers began in the third century, according to tradition
under Ptolemy II Philadelphus (285–246 BC).

The Jews under the Seleucids (198–143 BC)
Seleucus, one of Alexander the Great's generals, made himself master of
Babylonia in 312 BC and of parts of Syria in 301. In 198 the Seleucid king Antiochus II defeated the Egyptian army at Panium near Mt. Hermon and
thereafter annexed Palestine.

The Jews were glad to be rid of Egyptian control but soon found the rule
of the Seleucids far worse. Though Antiochus III accorded his Jewish subjects many freedoms and privileges, Antiochus IV (Epiphanes, *i.e.*, 'the God
manifest' – 175–163 BC) tried to force his diverse territories and subjects into
a cultural and religious unity.

He promoted the worship of Greek gods, whom he identified with local deities, and demanded the veneration of himself as Zeus manifest in flesh. He confiscated money and valuables from various temples, including the temple of Yahweh in Jerusalem in 169 BC (1 Macc. 1:20–24; 2 Macc. 5: 15–21). He rewarded Jews who cooperated in his program of Hellenization (i.e., of promoting the acceptance of Greek culture and religion by Jews) and at last demanded that the Jews cease the practice of circumcision, Sabbath observance, and the food laws. He appointed the highest bidders to the post of high priest (2 Macc. 4:7–9, 23–27). One such appointee stole precious vessels from the temple and sold them to pay his obligation to Antiochus.

Antiochus' troops put down in blood Jewish resistance to the Hellenization of Judaism. They looted Jerusalem, butchered innocent people, and carried others into slavery. Antiochus built a citadel called the Acra near the temple and garrisoned it with foreign troops. It became the center for the Hellenizing activities of renegade Jews and their Gentile allies.

Copies of the Jewish Law were burned. Pagan altars were erected throughout the land. Jews were forced to eat the flesh of pigs. The worst offense of all to Jews was the erecting of an altar to Zeus in the temple itself and the offering of swine on it.

Jewish resistance was both literary and military. A writer loyal to the Law and the traditions of Judaism penned our book of Daniel apparently at the height of the crisis (pp. 178–83) to encourage the faithful to resist Antiochus' demands. He showed how God brought the faithful through their ordeal in a similar crisis of the past and how he would soon destroy the oppressing tyrant and give the long-promised kingdom (world sovereignty) to Israel.

A rural priest named Mattathias and his five sons began military resistance. This priest stoutly refused to offer sacrifice to a pagan god, slew the king's officer who demanded it, fled to the hills, and conducted guerrilla warfare from there. Those loyal to the Law (the *Hasidim*, 'pious ones') joined him. They destroyed pagan altars and forcibly circumcised Jewish children. Mattathias' son Judas Maccabeus (i.e., 'the hammer') carried on the struggle. He achieved smashing victories over the king's forces. He gained possession of the temple, tore down its pagan altar, erected a new one, installed faithful priests, and held a great ceremony of rededication (Hanukkah, i.e., 'Dedication') in December, 164 BC.

Under Judas' brothers Jonathan and Simon the resistance continued until political, as well as religious, independence was gained. Jonathan (160–143 BC) became the first Maccabean high priest, and Simon (143–134) became both high priest and ethnarch (i.e., 'ruler of the people').

The Independent Hasmonean Kingdom (143–63 BC)
According to the Jewish historian Josephus, the great-grandfather of Mattathias was Asamonaios (Hashmon). Hence the family was called

Hasmonean. These priests, turned political leaders as well, became more and more secular. They lost the support of the *Hasidim* ('pious ones'), formed alliances with the Romans, undertook foreign wars, and eventually adopted the title 'king.' Under John Hyrcanus (134–104 BC), Aristobulus I (104–103), and especially Alexander Janneus (103–76) zeal for conquest increased. Conquest was sometimes followed by the forcible conversion of conquered enemies to Judaism. Alexander Janneus oppressed the Pharisees, an opposition party within Judaism. Queen Alexandra (76–67), however, made friends of the Pharisees and brought peace and a degree of prosperity to the land.

A struggle between Hyrcanus II and Aristobulus II for the throne and the high priesthood (between *c.* 66 and 63) brought in the Romans to settle the dispute and ended the period of Jewish independence.

The Jews under the Romans (63 BC – AD 135 and later)
The Romans appointed Hyrcanus II as high priest and ethnarch but put him under the control of Syrian and Idumean governors. Before long Herod the Great (37–4 BC) was made king by Rome. His reign was marked by family conspiracies and murders. He carried out immense building operations, including a new temple in Jerusalem. On Herod's death a Jewish embassy to Rome asked for the abolition of kingly rule in Palestine.

Herod's territories were divided among his sons. Archelaus became ethnarch of Judea, Samaria, and Idumea (4 BC – AD 6). Herod Antipas became tetrarch ('ruler of a fourth of a kingdom') of Galilee and Perea (4 BC – AD 39). Herod Philip became tetrarch of Gaulanitis, Trachonitis, Batanea, and Auranitis (4 BC – AD 34).

Jesus spent his youth and public ministry in Galilee under 'that fox' Herod Antipas (Luke 13:32); and Jesus appeared before Herod after his arrest in Jerusalem (Luke 23:6–12).

Herod Agrippa I (AD 37–44), the grandson of Herod the Great, was appointed 'king' by the Romans, first over Herod Philip's territories, then also over those of Herod Antipas, and finally over Judea, Samaria, and Idumea. From AD 6 to 41 Judea, Samaria, and Idumea had been under Roman governors. Thus finally Herod Agrippa I ruled over all the territories held by his grandfather.

After Herod Agrippa I's death (AD 44), Rome placed all his realm under Roman procurators (governors).

Herod Agrippa II (AD 48 – *c.* 93), the son of Herod Agrippa I, before whom Paul appeared in Caesarea (Acts 25:13—26:32), was a puppet king for Rome in largely Gentile territories in the north and northeast of Palestine (Chalcis, Iturea).

The Jews rebelled several times against the Romans: AD 6 under Judas of

Herod built an aqueduct through Wadi Qilt, a river
bed in the Judean mountains.

Gamala ('Judas the Galilean,' Acts 5:37); around 44 under Theudas (Acts 5:36); 66–73 under Eleazar, Menahem, and the Zealots; 132–135 under Simon ben Kosibah (Bar Kochba) and Rabbi Aqiba.

In every revolt the Romans were victorious. Titus destroyed Jerusalem and the temple in AD 70, and Hadrian put down the rebellion of 132–135. He subsequently rebuilt Jerusalem as a pagan city, peopled it with Gentiles exclusively, and named it Aelia Capitolina.

The Literature

We can mention only Jewish literature here. (For Greek, Roman, and other literature of significance for an understanding of the New Testament, see the bibliography on p. 441.)

The Apocrypha

The books of the Apocrypha (called deuterocanonical books by Roman Catholics) are intertestamental writings. There are fifteen of these books; three, however, are not considered deuterocanonical by Roman Catholics (1 and 2 Esdras and the Prayer of Manasseh). The books of the Apocrypha are listed and described on pp. 210–25.

The Pseudepigrapha (called Apocrypha by Roman Catholics) are numerous and important.

During the three centuries before Jesus and the two immediately after him, Jews and Christians wrote some sixty-five books we know of that were not included in the Hebrew and the Greek (Septuagint) scriptures. We call them the 'Pseudepigrapha' because many of them claim to have been written by persons who clearly could not have authored them.

According to the director and editor of a major recent study and publication of these books (James H. Charlesworth), they may be divided into five literary types (genres). We shall look at one example of each type.

The first is, 'Apocalyptic Literature and Related Works.' 'Apocalyptic' books reveal God's hidden mysteries: what is going on in the heavenly realm and what the world's future is to be (see pp. 356–7). The Pseudepigrapha's most important example of this category is 1 Enoch (Ethiopic Enoch). It first came to modern scholars' attention in 1773 in an Ethiopic copy. Now we have more than forty manuscripts in that language and also copies (or portions) in Aramaic, Greek, and Latin. The original language seems to have been either Hebrew or Aramaic or possibly parts of it in each of these languages (as in Daniel; see p. 179). It is a great collection of materials by different authors dating from the third century BC to the first century AD. It apparently originated in Judea. Fragments of it in Aramaic were found among the Dead Sea Scrolls.

Herod the Great's citadel of Herodion south of Jerusalem.

The book contains the alleged visions of Enoch after he was taken up to heaven (Gen. 5:24). The visions pertain to the secrets of the heavenly world, particularly the hidden purposes of God for the consummation of world history and the inauguration of the kingdom of God. The consummator is to be the heavenly Messiah-Son of Man, who is hidden away and awaiting the moment of his coming to judge the world. The book warns people to prepare for this judgment and threatens the wrath of the Messiah-Son of Man on rich exploiters of the poor and on political oppressors.

The book contains much speculation about angels, including fallen ones, demons, astrology (astronomy), and the proper calendar (solar rather than lunar). Scholars consider 1 Enoch to be the most influential book of the Pseudepigrapha on the theology of New Testament writers. They find traces of the concepts of this book in the Gospels, Paul's letters, Hebrews, and Revelation. Jude 14–15 actually quotes 1 Enoch 1:9. Some have argued that even Jesus knew the book (or parts of it) and was influenced thereby to think of himself as the heavenly Messiah-Son of Man.

The second type is '*Testaments.*' Testaments employ the last-will-and-testament pattern found in Genesis 49. A parting leader gathers around him his children for dying instructions, blessings, warnings, and predictions about their future.

The best representative of this type is The Testaments of the Twelve Patriarchs. We have copies of this book in several languages (Greek, Armenian, Slavonic, and Hebrew and Aramaic fragments). Its original language seems to have been Greek and its author a Hellenistic Jew of Syria (H.C. Kee), who wrote it about the middle of the second century BC. There are ten or twelve Christian interpolations in the present text, made probably in the early second century AD.

The book contains a mixture of many elements: edifying expansions of Old Testament materials, a kind of philosophizing about human nature, about the cosmos, about angelology (good angels and bad ones), about the good life (uprightness, honesty, generosity, compassion, industriousness, self-control, piety, chastity, and brotherly love). There is also speculation about the future and a prediction of the coming of two Messiahs, one a high priest and the other a Davidic Messiah. Jewish ethics reaches its high point in the teachings of this book. It was this element that made the book so attractive to Christians.

The third type is '*Expansions of the Old Testament and Other Legends.*' This genre is well illustrated by the book of Jubilees. Jubilees offers a report of what God revealed to Moses during his forty days on Mt. Sinai (Ex. 24:18). An angel reviews for Moses the early history of mankind and of God's elect people prior to Moses' own time.

The review follows the course of Israel's history as outlined in Genesis 1 to Exodus 14. In the review the author condenses, omits, reshapes, explains, and supplements the biblical narratives. He divides the history from the creation to the covenant at Sinai into forty-nine periods of forty-nine years each. In this book forty-nine years is a 'jubilee' period. He perhaps wishes to indicate that a new world era began with the giving of the Law to Moses.

The author's purpose is to glorify the Jewish Law by showing that it originated in heaven, was practiced by the Patriarchs and other ancients, and has eternal validity. He wants his readers to obey it strictly in the testing times they are going through (the period of struggle with Hellenism). Stressed are Sabbath-keeping, the use of the solar, rather than the lunar, calendar, and the laws of purification, of circumcision, of tithes, and of separation from defiled and defiling Gentiles. There is minor emphasis on the promise that obedience to the Law will bring to the Jews a glorious future.

The fourth type, '*Wisdom and Philosophical Literature,*' may be described by comment on 3 and 4 Maccabees. 3 Maccabees (also called The Ptolemaica) is an historical romance about happenings after Ptolemy IV's defeat of Antiochus III of Syria in 217 BC.

The author tells us that Ptolemy's plan to enter the temple in Jerusalem was thwarted by God through a devastating stroke visited on that king. In revenge directed at both God and the Jews, Ptolemy deprived the Jews of their civil rights and attempted to force them all to be branded with the ivy leaf, the emblem of Dionysus. The Jews resisted. Ptolemy thereupon threatened to exterminate them by herding them together in a great amphitheatre and inciting five hundred crazed elephants to trample them. In answer to prayer two angels turned the elephants back on the king's forces.

The king, now convinced of the invincibility of the Jews and their God, ordered a seven-day festival of celebration, which became the beginning of an annual festival of commemoration. He commanded the protection of Jews everywhere and even looked the other way while loyal Jews slaughtered their apostate Jewish brethren.

In some respects the book is like the book of Esther, which also shows that the Jews are invincible. But here, in orthodox fashion, the credit is given to God, who is shown as rewarding the righteous and punishing the wicked. The author almost certainly was an Alexandrian Jew, who wrote in Greek, probably in the first part of the first century BC.

4 Maccabees is a philosophical treatise on the supremacy of reason over the passions and sufferings of the body and soul. It illustrates this supremacy by examples from the Old Testament (Joseph over sexual desire, Moses over anger, etc.) and from recent Jewish history (the triumph of Maccabean martyrs over their agonies). The sufferings of the martyrs are depicted in excruciating detail. Eleazar and the seven sons of one mother defied Antiochus IV Epiphanes out of loyalty to the Law and endured gladly the consequences. From their death came two results: personal immortality and vicarious atonement for their nation.

The passages about the atoning value of the death of righteous martyrs (6:28–29; 17:21–22) are among the most important passages in all the intertestamental literature. Such thinking was current in Judaism at the time of Jesus. It helps us understand the meaning he gave to his own death (see pp. 474–5).

The fifth type, '*Prayers, Psalms, and Odes,*' is perhaps best represented by The Psalms of Solomon. A collection of eighteen psalms, in many respects like those of the Old Testament, lament the seizure of power by foreign invaders and the corrupting of Jerusalem and the nation by a secularized, greedy religious leadership. The writers of these psalms look forward to the Messiah's destruction of the oppressors and to his establishment of the New Age. Meanwhile, they resign themselves – howbeit with expostulation! – to the present intolerable situation.

We have in Psalm 17 the most detailed characterization of the Son of David Messiah anywhere in the literature of the intertestamental period. His kingdom is to be an eternal, earthly order. He will rule wisely, with justice and

mercy, over the reassembled Jews and over the nations. Both he and his subjects will be free from sin.

The book was called 'The Psalms of Solomon' to gain importance and acceptance for it, since the Psalter of David (our book of Psalms) was a closed
collection by this time and Solomon was the next in fame as a songwriter
(1 Kings 4:32).

The Writings of Philo Judeus

Philo (c. 10 BC – c. AD 45), a distinguished Alexandrian Jew, learned in both
Judaism and Hellenism (especially Greek philosophy), left a large body of
writings. Their purpose was to show that Judaism and Hellenism occupy
common ground – that the best thought of the Greek world is also found in
the Jewish Scriptures and Jewish theology. He was thus a defender of
Judaism in an often hostile pagan environment. Some of his important works
are: The Life of Moses; The Exposition of the Laws of Moses; The Allegory
of the Jewish Law; Questions and Answers in Genesis and Exodus.

The Works of Flavius Josephus (c. AD 37 – c. 100)

Though not strictly a writer of the intertestamental period, Josephus is listed
here because of his importance. He was a priestly descendant of the Hasmo-
neans, a student of the various religious sects of Judaism, a commanding officer of Galilean Jewish forces in the war against Rome (AD 66–73), a captive
of the Romans, and then a sympathetic interpreter and mediator for them.
He at length settled in Rome on an imperial pension and gave himself to a
literary career. He tried to make Judaism understandable and acceptable to
Romans. As a Roman sympathizer, he was often criticized by Jews. His
works are: The Jewish War; The Antiquities of the Jews; The Life (of
Josephus); Against Apion.

The Dead Sea Scrolls (The Qumran Texts)

From the caves in the cliffs along the northwest side of the Dead Sea have
come the greatest manuscript discoveries of modern times. The manuscripts
belonged to a monastic Jewish community which settled by the Dead Sea, at
a place now called by Arabs Qumran, around the middle of the second century BC. The Romans destroyed the community in AD 68. It seems that the
members deposited their manuscripts in caves to protect them from possible
destruction at the hands of the Romans.

The founder or principal organizer of the community, called by the members 'The Teacher of Righteousness' or 'The Right Teacher,' whose name is
unknown, may have been a member of the Hasidim ('the pious ones'), who
opposed the efforts of Antiochus Epiphanes and his Jewish accomplices to introduce Greek culture and who resisted Jonathan and Simon Maccabeus' assuming the high priesthood (see p. 413). (Recently one of the pioneers of

Steps to a ritual immersion bath (miqveh) at Qumran.

Dead Sea Scrolls research, John C. Trever, has proposed that 'the Right Teacher' was the author of the book of Daniel. See p. 180.)

The *Hasidim* felt that the legitimate priestly line, the house of Zadok, had been unjustifiably ousted and worship in the temple at Jerusalem was being carried on by priests without divine authorization. Perhaps fearing for their lives and wishing to continue proper worship, a group of these *Hasidim* withdrew to the wilderness and established a community of their own. They probably were 'the Essenes,' referred to by several ancient writers as having lived by the Dead Sea.

About a dozen complete or fairly complete compositions have survived, most of them having come from Caves I and XI. Fragments run into the tens of thousands, varying from a column or two of text to tiny pieces containing a single letter of the alphabet. How many different texts altogether will finally be counted is anyone's guess. Identification and study of the thousands of fragments have been going on for some 35 years! Only a few of the manuscripts can be commented on here. For fuller information see the books on the Dead Sea Scrolls listed in the bibliography on p. 441.

1. Biblical Texts

Every book of the Hebrew Scriptures except Esther is represented among the biblical manuscripts and fragments found at Qumran. Many books appear in multiple copies (e.g., 25 copies of Deuteronomy, 30 of the Psalms, and 19 of Isaiah). Altogether some 70 texts of the Pentateuch have been found, more than for any other part of the Old Testament – clear evidence of the preoccupation of the community with the Law of Moses. Discovered also were Greek and Aramaic translations of parts of Scripture.

Four biblical manuscripts are more or less complete scrolls: two Isaiah scrolls, a Psalms scroll, and an Aramaic Job (see p. 373). These manuscripts and fragments show that several different Hebrew text types existed at Qumran. They enable us to get behind the standardized Hebrew text of about AD 100 to texts that were used to make the Samaritan recension and the Septuagint version of the fourth to second centuries BC. The discoveries are thus of immense value in recovering early forms of the Hebrew text (see p. 377–8).

2. The Rules

A well-preserved community rule book (now called 'The Manual of Discipline' or 'The Rule of the Community'), in a copy dating to the first half of the first century BC, covers the aims of the community, the requirements for entrance into it, the ritual of initiation, a brief summary of the community's beliefs, principles of community organization, rules of behavior in community life and in the meetings of the general assembly ('the Council of the Many'), conditions for progress to various stages of purity and recognition within the sect, a strict penal code (with punishments for various infractions) to be in force until the coming of the Prophet and the priestly and lay Messiahs, a description of the ideal community, and general counsels to the membership on doing the will of God in daily life. Twelve copies of parts of this work have been recovered.

Administrative buildings and storehouses at
Masada.

The community's regulations are preserved also in a second document called today 'the Damascus Document' (or 'the Damascus Covenant'), known from fragments found in the caves at Qumran and from medieval copies of the work. Here we learn that the community was raised up through 'the Teacher of Righteousness' (or 'Right Teacher') to be God's End-time, holy people. The strict rules, given by revelation to the Teacher, are to keep the community pure from the defilements of 'the children of the Pit' (*i.e.*, the outsiders, who are living in sin and error) and to prepare the community for its final destiny as the elect people of God.

Other manuscripts (the War Scroll and the Temple Scroll) also present rules of the community, but since they are strongly eschatological (dealing with last things), they will be discussed below.

3. Biblical Interpretation

Constant study of the Scriptures at Qumran resulted in several forms of biblical interpretation: commentaries on biblical books, for the most part on the prophets (Micah, Nahum, Zephaniah, Isaiah, Habakkuk); anthologies of biblical texts around special themes; paraphrases and expansions of bliblical texts to justify the sect's existence, teachings, and pattern of life. Their authors sought to show that the Scriptures, if interpreted aright (*i.e.*, according to the interpretation given by God to the 'Right Teacher'), predict the events of their own time and every detail of the founding, the life, and the glorious future of their community. In short, they read into the Scriptures what they wanted to find there.

4. Texts about the End-time

Books that unveil the future were very popular at Qumran, as indicated by the presence of a considerable number of fragments of the book of Daniel and of several nonbiblical apocalypses (on apocalyptic literature see pp. 356–7).

Noteworthy is the War Scroll (also called 'the War of the Sons of Light Against the Sons of Darkness'). This document is fairly well preserved and dates from the first century BC or the first half of the first century AD. Some half-dozen fragments in addition to the nearly complete scroll have been found.

The Scroll describes the forty-year war the Essene community ('the Sons of Light') will wage against the wicked nations around and allied apostate Jews ('the Sons of Darkness'). The war will be cosmic, with God and the archangel Michael, the other angels, and the righteous fighting against Belial (the devil), the evil spirits, the wicked nations, and the apostates. The chief and final enemy is 'the Kittim,' who are clearly the Romans.

The war will proceed in stages. Jerusalem will be captured from the enemy after six years and Temple worship restored. The remaining conquest will occupy thirty-three years, with release from warfare every seventh year and victory seesawing, until the Endtime when God will intervene to decide the war in favor of the Sons of Light. Then the community will come to rule in Jerusalem and over the world.

The purpose of the Scroll is to give the community members regulations for the proper conduct of the War. They must fight in accordance with the Law of Moses and observe all the laws of purity. They must be organized according to the procedures of Israel's warfare when the nation of old was in the wilderness.

Another document survived as an appendix to the Manual of Discipline (or Rule of the Community). It is now called 'the Rule of the Congregation' (or 'The Messianic Rule'). It describes the Endtime community and sets forth the duties of members of the future Congregation of Israel. These duties run from childhood education to adult participation in community life (as office holders, judges, and soldiers). Regulations regarding promotions in rank in the community are presented. And, finally, there is a description of a Messianic assembly and meal, participated in by the priestly Messiah (the Messiah of Aaron) and the lay Messiah (the Messiah of Israel).

In this category of writings we may mention fragments of a manuscript of around the middle of the first century BC which describes events to take place in the tenth Jubilee, when Melchizedek, a Priest-King (Gen. 14:18–19; Psa. 110:4), will expiate the sins of 'those of his inheritance' (the Sons of Light), carry out the Jubilee-year restoration of property, and judge and condemn Belial (the Prince of Darkness). Here Melchizedek seems to be identical with the archangel Michael and functions as a Savior and Judge – roles ascribed to Jesus, who is called in the New Testament book of Hebrews a priest 'after the order of Melchizedek' (Heb. 5:6; 7:1–3).

Then there is the great Temple Scroll – the longest scroll found at Qumran (66 columns and 27 feet long). According to its translator and interpreter (Y. Yadin), the work was first composed about 150–125 BC but comes to us in a copy of about the mid-first century AD. Yadin calls the work 'the basic *torah* or law of the Essenes' and thinks it was composed by 'the founder of the sect, the venerated Teacher of Righteousness.'

The Scroll is written in the first person, with God as the speaker. God is represented as giving to Moses detailed instructions concerning the building of the Temple, the laws to govern the Temple rites, and the life and arrangements in the city (Jerusalem) in which the Temple is to be located. The Temple complex is to have three square courts around the Temple building proper: inner, middle, and outer courts. A moat, to guard the Temple's sanctity, will surround the whole complex.

Great care to protect the purity and safety of Jerusalem is to be taken. There are to be no toilets there but a place of relief 3,000 cubits away; and no sexual relations are to be had within the city. People afflicted with impurity of any kind will be prohibited from entering. The Temple-city is to be like the camp of Israel in the wilderness; and the purity laws that applied to the camp and the Tabernacle there will apply here.

Special new festivals (New Barley, New Wine, New Oil, and New Wood) will be celebrated in the Temple under the leadership of the true Zadok priesthood, clad in holy garments. The festivals are to be reckoned according to the solar calendar.

A sizable section of the Temple Scroll deals with statutes that are to govern the life and activities of the King in that city: his marriage (no polygamy or divorce), his subordination to the High Priest in matters pertaining to making war, his rights in relation to war booty, his required use of an advisory council, etc.

The Essene community at Qumran and elsewhere was preoccupied with the coming Messianic Age and saw itself as the central actor in the Endtime events. The sect believed it was 'destined to be the shoot from which the new eschatological world will spring' (D. Dimant). It appears the members thought of this Age as a glorified earthly order, after the fashion of some of the Old Testament prophets. They saw the future to some degree as a return to an idealized past, as the coming of a new Garden of Eden.

5. Poetical and Liturgical Works

An important scroll, The Thanksgiving Psalms, from the first century AD and partly destroyed, apparently originally contained about forty hymns of thanksgiving. Some twenty-five are preserved. A number of them have an autobiographical flavor, reflecting the sufferings of a leader of the community (perhaps the 'Right Teacher') who so greatly shaped the community. The hymns thank God for salvation from pollution and transgression, for revealing his secrets to unworthy people, and for helping his creatures of clay toward perfection of way.

Another scroll, The Psalms Scroll, of the second century BC, contains forty-eight psalms, of which forty-one are in our book of Psalms. The extra seven (four of them previously known in various translations) glorify David, wisdom, and Zion, and praise the Creator of all. A prose supplement credits David with the composition of 4050 poetic pieces.

A large body of liturgical compositions has been recovered, giving evidence of the individual and corporate worship of the community. Shut off from Jerusalem temple worship and sacrifices, as the sect was, it conceived of prayer ('offering of lips') as a substitute acceptable to God. Thus there came into being prayers for the days of the week and for festival occasions; angelic blessings of the righteous; blessings of the community, its groups and individuals, by the overseers of the community, etc.

6. Miscellaneous Compositions

An oxidized copper scroll, found in two parts and opened by cutting into strips, contains a list of treasures of gold, silver, aromatics, and manuscripts hidden in various (now unidentifiable) locations. The sums are so immense that they stagger the imagination. Some have thought them to be the temple treasures, hidden by the Zealots from the Romans, or the holdings of the Essene community, or entirely fictional.

Two Horoscopes associate physical characteristics of various people with specific spiritual qualities. One seems to foretell the physical appearance and character of the coming royal Messiah: he will have red hair, a birthmark on his thigh, and will be extremely wise from his childhood. He is called 'the Elect of God.'

Documents from the Wilderness South of Qumran

In the 1950s and early 1960s caves in this area yielded pottery, coins, domestic objects, weapons, and manuscripts, mostly of the period of the Jewish rebellion against Rome of AD 132–35. The discoveries included a fairly extensive, but badly worn, roll of the Hebrew Minor Prophets and some Greek fragments of the same, a cache of thirty-five Aramaic, Greek, and Nabataean personal documents (owned by a woman named Babata) of the period AD 93–132, and some legal contracts of the first and early second centuries. From the personal documents and contracts we learn about loan, marriage, divorce, and tax proceedings of that time.

Some fifteen letters (fourteen on papyrus and one on a wooden board) written by scribes of the leader of the rebellion, Simeon ben Kosiba (called Bar Kokhba, 'Son of the Star'), were recovered. Most of them are addressed to his military commanders at En-gedi. They deal with matters of supply of grain, salt, and other substances and contain rebukes and threats of punishment for failure to fulfill his orders.

At the great fortress of Masada, built by Herod the Great, archaeologists found fragments of Genesis, Leviticus, Psalms, Ecclesiasticus (the Wisdom of Jesus the Son of Sirach), and a small piece of an Angelic Liturgy known from Qumran.

Religion

Some of the major characteristics of Jewish religion between the Testaments were:

A Firm Ethical Monotheism

This is the belief that there is *one* God, who is good and who requires goodness of all. After the return from Exile the Jews never again officially recognized foreign gods, as was done by certain preexilic Jewish kings (*e.g.,* Ahaz and Manasseh). There were periods when paganism pressed heavily on the Jews, especially under the Seleucid king Antiochus IV (see pp. 412–3).

Some Jews yielded to the pressures, as we have seen, but strong resistance destroyed the threat and led to a reaffirmation of ethical monotheism as the national faith.

The Jews had learned the lesson taught by the great prophets: Yahweh holds the nations in his hands; their gods are vanity; their idols are nothing (Isa. 41:21–24; 44:9–20). The postexilic Jews fully accepted the prophetic teaching that the disaster of the Exile was Yahweh's judgment for their idolatry (e.g., Ezek. 8–9). Individuals did indeed fall away, but never again the nation!

In fact, Judaism so honored and exalted Yahweh that his name became too sacred to utter, except in the ritual of the temple. People referred to Yahweh as God, Lord, God of heaven, King of heaven, Heaven, the Lord of Spirits, the Great Glory, the Head of Days, and the Most High God. They thought of Yahweh as living in the highest heaven, with archangels and myriads of angels at his command as his ministers in the world. Representing Yahweh in the world were also his Wisdom, his Word, his Spirit, his Presence. The elevation of God and the multiplication of intermediary beings in Judaism was both a strength and a weakness: it made God absolutely supreme but it tended to remove God from intimate relation to people and the world.

The Supremacy of the Law

It was Ezra (458 or 428 or 398 BC) who established the Law of Moses, apparently as found in the Pentateuch, squarely at the heart of Judaism (see p. 30). He reformed the nation on the basis of the demands of that Law. From this time on, God's will for the total life of humankind was thought to be found in the Law. All that was needed was to read, interpret, and apply it to every situation in life.

There soon grew up a body of interpretation of the Law that became as binding as the Law itself. Since the prescriptions of the ancient written Law did not apply directly to constantly changing cultural situations, it was necessary for experts, called scribes, to draw out the Law's general intent and apply it to those situations (as the Supreme Court of the United States must do with respect to another ancient document, the Constitution). The scribes claimed that their interpretations had come from Moses also, through a long chain of oral tradition.

The scribes worked sometimes as a body but often individually. Disciples of individual scribes passed along their teacher's interpretations. Thus 'schools' of interpretation arose which developed into parties or sects. The tradition of the Pharisees, for example, differed from that of the Essenes.

Since the Jews came to believe that the whole will of God for all time was written down in the Law of Moses, they saw no further need for prophets. Prophetic spirits, in order to be heard, had to write books under an ancient name (see the Pseudepigrapha, pp. 416–20). What the nation needed, rather

A fifth century AD synagogue under excavation at Katzrin, Golan.

than prophets, was scribes – to reconcile conflicting laws, to show what individual laws meant, and to indicate how to apply the Law in particular cases.

Synagogues – local places of worship – came into being in the postexilic period as places of instruction in the Law and the other scriptures. The Law was elevated, praised, and glorified; it was regarded as eternally existing. Jewish teachers said that it existed on heavenly tablets before the creation of the world; that angels practiced it in heaven; and that it would be practiced in the Age to Come.

Wisdom and the Law were practically equated. Wisdom writers claimed that Wisdom had descended from heaven and embodied itself in the Law. People were to meditate on the Law day and night, love it, and obey it in every detail. By obeying it they would find perfection before God and become worthy of God's rewards.

Such elevation of the Law inevitably introduced a strong element of legalism into Judaism. The individual did not always clearly see that strict obedience to the Law was his *response* to God's gracious forgiveness and help; often obedience to the Law became the means by which he sought to obtain grace. Thus one writer of the time remarks, 'Almsgiving delivers from death, and it will purge away every sin' (Tobit 12:9).

Mount Gerizim viewed from Mount Ebal.

This exaltation of the Law did not lead solely to a burdensome legalistic system. Many Jews loved the Law and sought to live by it as their response to God's merciful deeds in Israel's behalf. But in Judaism heart religion did tend to retreat behind a religion of outward conformity; this is clearly seen in Jesus' words about the legalism of the Pharisees and other contemporaries. Indeed, this has been a problem in Christianity through the centuries also.

Israel as a Holy People in Mission
The Jews never forgot that God had called them to a special relationship that involved both separation from the world and service to the world. The prophets had taught that Israel's election was not only to special privilege but also to special responsibility.

Since God was 'holy' (*i.e.*, separated from all that is common, profane, and unclean, and himself morally pure), Israel was to share God's holiness (Lev. 19:2: 'You shall be holy; for I the Lord your God am holy'). The separation of Israel from the uncleanness of pagan peoples, though frequently advocated by Jewish religious teachers before the Exile, was seriously undertaken first by the Jewish leaders Nehemiah and Ezra.

The most drastic accomplishment in Ezra's reform of the life of the nation under the Law brought from Babylonia was the divorce of foreign wives (Ezra 9–10). Ezra emphasized those demands of the Law which marked Jews as Jews (circumcision, rigid Sabbath observance, tithes for the support of the temple, etc.). Samaritans were especially to be avoided as unclean. Because of Jewish ostracism, the Samaritans founded a temple of their own on Mt. Gerizim in Samaria (John 4:20). The Jews, now sworn to uphold the Law in every respect (Neh. 9:38; 10:29), became an exclusive, separatist community, wholly committed to life in accordance with the Law and 'holiness' by the standards of that Law.

The *Hasidim* ('the pious ones') reaffirmed the separatist standard in the struggle against Greek defilement under Antiochus IV (175–163 BC). From the *Hasidim* appear to have come the separatist parties known as the Pharisees and the Essenes, which were so influential in Jesus' time.

Though it seems fundamentally contradictory to all that has been said, Israel's service to the nations was not entirely lost sight of in this period. The Second Isaiah and his disciples drew out the implications of Israel's monotheism for its understanding of its role under God. If there was no other God than Yahweh, Yahweh was implicitly Lord of all nations; and all peoples were someday to recognize this Lordship. Israel by its God-likeness was to draw all nations to Zion (Isa. 56:3–8; 66:18–21; Zech. 8:22–23; Mal. 1:11). The author of the book of Jonah was fully aware of Israel's mission under God to the nations (see p. 194).

Some of the books of the Apocrypha and Pseudepigrapha emphasize the inclusion of Gentiles as part of God's purpose for the End-time (Tobit 13:11; 14:6–7; 1 Enoch 10:21–22; Test. of Levi 4:4; 14:3–4; Test. of Naphtali 8:3). In the period between the Testaments some Gentiles became converts to Judaism (Judith 14:10; Acts 6:5; 13:43; Matt. 23:15). Paul encountered half-converts, known as 'God fearers,' in the Jewish synagogues almost everywhere (Acts 13:16, 26; 17:4, 17; 18:7).

A Glowing Hope for the Future

Israel's conviction that it was God's special possession among all peoples (Exod. 19:5) carried with it another conviction: God had planned a wonderful future for the chosen people (Gen. 12:2–3). A part of early covenant ceremonies between God and Israel was the utterance of blessings and curses. The blessings set forth God's rich rewards for obedience to the covenant (Deut. 27–28; Josh. 8:30–35).

The exact details of the future were differently conceived by various writers. At the heart of it was Yahweh's coming to an acknowledged supremacy over the whole earth, with Israel's temple as the place of contact between God and all people.

At the Day of Yahweh God will defeat all enemies in a mighty display of power and exalt Israel to prosperity, full righteousness, and perpetual security. God's temple in Jerusalem will be the center of worship and learning for all people and the seat of judgment for all disputes (Isa. 2:2–4).

The Old Testament prophets thought of God's kingdom as a glorified earthly order. Some of them saw this order as ruled by a descendant of David, who will be fully righteous, Spirit-endowed, God-fearing, and wise. Absolute justice in an order of peace, embracing even the animal kingdom, will prevail (Isa. 11:1–9).

Some writers held that two Messiahs would come: a political leader from the tribe of Judah and a priestly head from Levi or Aaron (Zech. 6:9–14 [see p. 206]; Test. of Simeon 7:2). The Essenes at Qumran expected first a prophet to come and then the Messiahs of Aaron and Israel (Manual of Discipline 9:10–11). Others saw no Messiah at all – only God as King.

The writers of apocalypses (see pp. 356–7) sometimes saw the coming of a new world after God's judgment of the earth, not a continuance, even in glorified form, of this earthly existence. One says that God's kingdom 'will appear throughout all his creation' (Assumption of Moses 10:1). Israel will be

Historical Outline and Chronology

BEFORE THE HEBREW PATRIARCHS
(Abraham, Isaac, Jacob)
(before the twentieth century BC)

Old Stone (Paleolithic) Age — ?600,000–10,000 BC
Life in caves; food collecting stage

Middle Stone (Mesolithic) Age — 10,000–8000
Cave-dwellers emerged from caves; food-producing stage
Jericho settled — 9000

New Stone (Neolithic) Age — 8000–4000
Pottery invented — 7000

Copper-Stone (Chalcolithic) Age — 4000–3200
Writing invented by Sumerians in Mesopotamia —
3500–3300

Early Bronze Age — 3200–2100
Egyptians and Mesopotamians (Sumerians, Akkadians)
developed advanced civilizations, with tools and weapons
of bronze

MIDDLE BRONZE AGE

exalted 'to the heaven of the stars' and will see its foes in Gehenna (10:9–10). And still other writers saw first a temporary earthly kingdom to be followed by an eternal heavenly kingdom (1 Enoch 91–104; 2 Baruch; 2 Esdras), the pattern adopted in the Revelation to John (chaps. 20–22) in the New Testament.

Usually, a period of war and tribulation was believed to precede the coming of the ultimate victory. The War Scroll of Qumran envisions a 40-year fight against the armies of darkness before the triumph of the Sons of Light (2:6). The elect will be led by the Prince of Light (Michael or Melchizedek) and the wicked Jews and Gentiles by the Angel of Darkness (Belial). (See pp. 424–5.)

For life in the new age the Essenes believed that God will build a new temple. The great Temple Scroll lays out in detail God's plans for that temple and sets forth the laws governing the temple rites. The temple will have three square courts around the temple building itself: inner, middle, and outer. A moat to guard the temple's sanctity will surround the whole complex. (See pp. 425–6.)

Between the Testaments the faithful looked not only back to Moses and

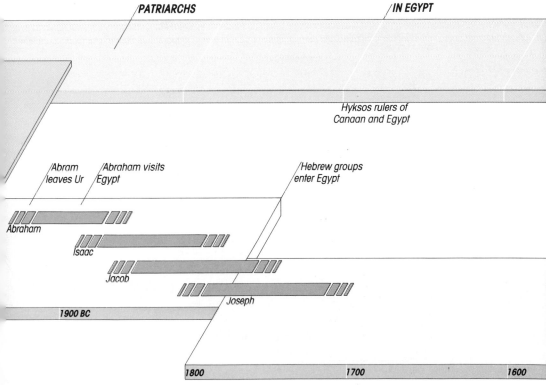

PATRIARCHS / **IN EGYPT**

Hyksos rulers of
Canaan and Egypt

Abram leaves Ur / Abraham visits Egypt / Hebrew groups enter Egypt

Abraham

Isaac

Jacob

Joseph

1900 BC

1800   1700   1600

The dates offered here are approximate only. The problems in constructing a chronology of the periods covered in this table are almost insurmountable. In general, I have followed the chronology offered in John Bright, *A History of Israel*, 3rd ed. 1981, pp. 465–73 and Floyd V. Filson, *A New Testament History*, 1964, pp. 395–400. For a comparison of the dates assigned to the kings of Israel and Judah by various scholars, see John H. Hayes and J. Maxwell Miller (eds.), *Israelite and Judaean History*, 1977, pp. 682–83. For an alternative set of New Testament dates, see Helmut Koester, *History and Literature of Early Christianity*, II, 1982, 103–04.

the Law for guidance but forward to the New Age for strength and courage to walk in the path Moses had marked out.

Religious Groups in Judaism

How many religious parties or sects there were in the period between the Testaments we do not know. Josephus (see p. 420) identified four groups, which he called 'philosophies'.

The Pharisees

The name probably means 'the separated (or separate) ones.' From what they were separated we do not know – probably from defilement and from those who were defiled (Gentiles and Jews who did not carefully obey the Law).

This group emerged around 140 BC from the *Hasidim* (see p. 413). Chiefly a lay group, it taught, developed, and passed on the oral interpretation of the Law. The aim of this interpretation was to bring the whole of life under the control of the Law. This oral tradition, now in the Mishnah (see bibliography at the end of this chapter), was often opposed by Jesus (*e.g.*, Mark 7:1–23).

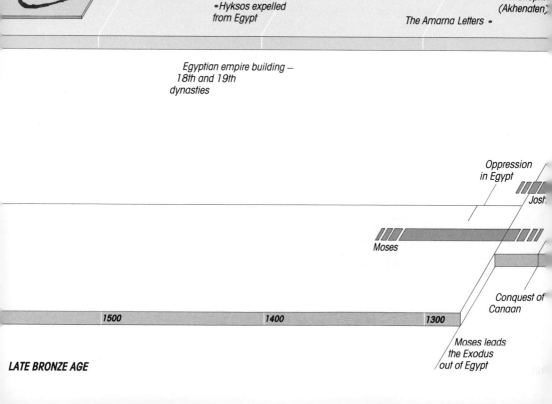

Invention of alphabet in Canaan or environs

•Hyksos expelled from Egypt

The Amarna Letters •

Amenophi (Akhenaten)

Egyptian empire building – 18th and 19th dynasties

Oppression in Egypt

Josh

Moses

Conquest of Canaan

1500   1400   1300

Moses leads the Exodus out of Egypt

LATE BRONZE AGE

The Pharisees emphasized ritual purity, tithing, Sabbath observance, fasting, almsgiving, prayers, synagogue attendance, and knowledge of the Law. They believed in human freedom under the divine sovereignty, in angels and demons, in the resurrection of the body, and in the coming of the Messiah and the kingdom of God. They held that the kingdom of God will come through God's power, not by force of human arms. Their numbers were not great (Josephus says some six thousand), but their influence with the people was weighty.

The Sadducees

Their name seems to derive from Zadok, the head of the old priestly family which long officiated in the temple in Jerusalem (1 Kings 1:26), or it may mean 'the righteous ones.'

As a definite party within Judaism, the Sadducees seem to have arisen in Maccabean times, probably in the time of Jonathan (160–143 BC) or Simon (143–134 BC). They appear to have been supporters of the Hasmonean high priests, who eventually also became kings; and they remained allied with these priest-kings most of the time until the coming of the Romans in 63 BC.

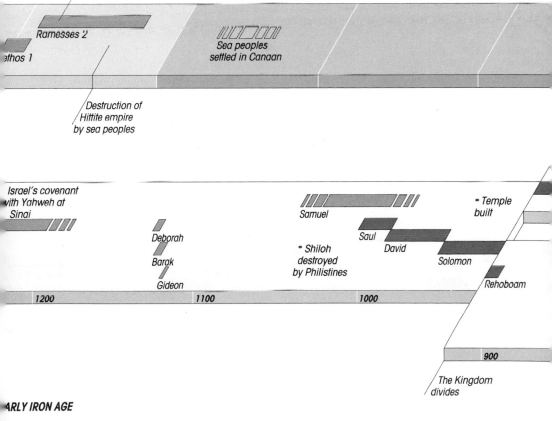

EXODUS AND
CONQUEST OF CANAAN   THE JUDGES

Ramesses 2

ethos 1

Sea peoples
settled in Canaan

Destruction of
Hittite empire
by sea peoples

Israel's covenant
with Yahweh at
Sinai

Samuel

• Temple
built

Deborah

Saul

Barak

• Shiloh
destroyed
by Philistines

David

Solomon

Gideon

Rehoboam

1200   1100   1000

900

The Kingdom
divides

EARLY IRON AGE

They continued in power under the Romans, whom they probably reluctantly served. They undoubtedly wished for the return of theocratic government in which they, as high priests, would head the state. They were an aristocratic, priestly party (possibly containing some wealthy lay Jerusalemites) concerned with Israel as a nation as well as with religion. They challenged the lay Pharisees' right to interpret the Law for the nation – their own priestly prerogative – and thus disputed the authority of Pharisaic oral tradition. They denied the Pharisees' doctrines of the resurrection of the body, rewards and punishment after death, and the existence of angels and spirits – probably since these teachings were not present in the Law. They attributed all human action to free will, rather than to fate or providence. They seem not to have had much favor with the Jewish people as a whole. With the fall of the temple in AD 70 they no longer played a significant role in Jewish life.

The Essenes
The name seems to come from the Aramaic equivalent of the Hebrew word *Hasidim*, meaning 'the pious ones.' Some scholars take it to mean 'healers.'
    As we noted above (p. 420), this group seems to have formed out of the

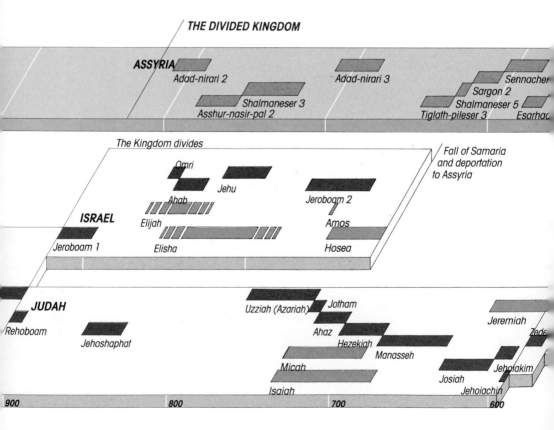

THE DIVIDED KINGDOM

Hasidim about 150 BC in protest against Jonathan Maccabeus' becoming high priest. They built their main center at Qumran by the Dead Sea. There were Essenes scattered in towns and villages of Palestine and in some large cities of the near East, like Damascus. Their total number was about four thousand, only about two hundred living at Qumran.

Their membership consisted of priests, Levites, and laity. At Qumran they were governed by a Council of the Community (consisting of representatives of the three groups) and by an overseer of the community's affairs.

Entrance to the community involved a two-year probationary period. Absolute obedience to the community's rules was enforced by penalties or expulsion. All property was held in common, and all worked at manual labor, chiefly in agriculture and handicrafts. They lived austerely, ate at a common table, cleansed themselves from all impurity by daily lustrations, and remained celibate (though some living outside Qumran seem to have been married).

The Essenes offered no sacrifices in the Jerusalem temple, or at Qumran, or in their places of residence elsewhere. They regarded the temple in Jerusalem as defiled by impure, unaccredited priests and the festivals

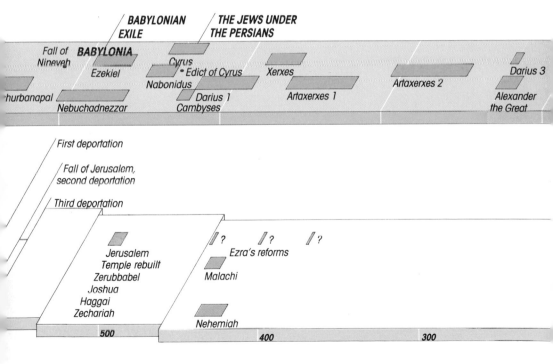

observed there as conducted according to an improper calendar. They lived by the solar, rather than the lunar, calendar. They regarded scripture study, prayers, and obedience to the Law (as they interpreted it) as a substitute for temple worship and saw the community itself as God's true temple. They separated themselves from the defilements of the world outside as much as possible. They were stricter in their interpretation of and obedience to the Law than the Pharisees.

Each year the total membership assembled at Qumran for observance of the Feast of the Renewal of the Covenant. At that time, new members were sworn in and old members were reviewed and ranked in proper status.

Their founder, 'the Teacher of Righteousness,' or perhaps more accurately translated, their 'Right Teacher' regarded the Essene community as the Elect of God, the people who would inherit the coming Kingdom. He interpreted the prophecies of the Old Testament as pointing in detail to events of his own day and the near future. He and they awaited the coming of a Prophet and two Messiahs and the transformation of the barren desert around the Dead Sea into a new Garden of Eden.

They all dreamed of the day when God would build the glorious temple of

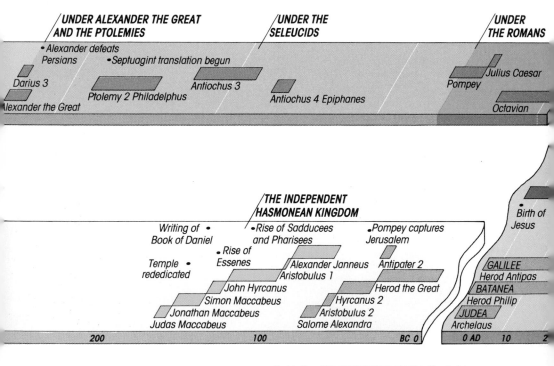

The date of Jesus' birth was put at least 4 years too late by Dionysius Exiguus, the head of a Roman monastery, in the early sixth century. He placed it 754 years after the founding of Rome. We know from data in Josephus' works that Herod the Great died 750 years after the founding of that city. That Jesus was born before Herod's death is clear from the Gospels (Luke 1:5; Matt. 2:1), but how much before is not known.

the New Age and restore the true line of priests (the Essenes) to its proper place and function in that temple and life would go forward under the leadership of the two Messiahs. Meanwhile, they lived by strict standards of purity in anticipation of the holy life of the coming Age. (See pp. 420–27 for a discussion of their manuscripts.)

The Zealots

Josephus assigns the origin of a fourth 'philosophy' among the Jews (the Zealots) to Judas of Galilee, who led a rebellion in AD 6 against a Roman census for the purpose of taxing the Jews. Luke characterizes one of Jesus' disciples as 'Simon who was called the Zealot' (Lk. 6:15; cf. Acts 1:13). These two writers thus assume that the Zealot party existed from near the beginning of the first century AD.

Many scholars today believe that the Zealots as an organized group came into being considerably later – about a decade before the beginning of the Jewish war against Rome (AD 66–73) – and that it is incorrect to refer to Judas of Galilee and Simon as 'Zealots.' They deny also that Jesus had to resist pressure to join a nationalistic movement spearheaded by 'Zealots.'

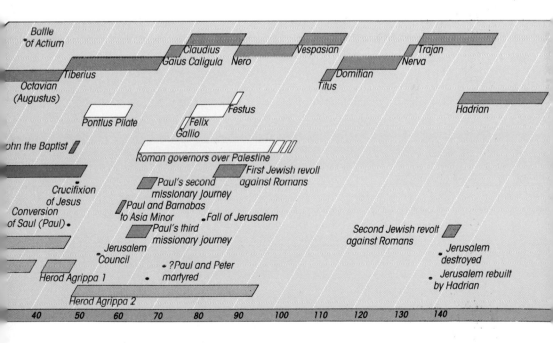

It may be true that the name is later than Judas and Simon. But that there was underground resistance to Rome that surfaced at various times between AD 6 and AD 73 (or 74), when the resistance movement collapsed at Masada, can hardly be denied. It was relatively quiescent from about AD 8–44 but gathered strength when Herod Agrippa I died and his territories became a Roman province (44). Before and during the war against Rome various resistance groups (Sicarii, followers of Eleazar, of John of Gischala, and of Simon bar Giora, and some Idumeans) vied for leadership of the resistance and were known as 'Zealots.'

Josephus is undoubtedly right that the roots of the resistance movement reached all the way back to Judas the Galilean – and actually beyond. Jesus certainly resisted whatever form of it existed in his time. It is possible that other disciples than Simon 'the Zealot' (Peter, James, John, and Judas Iscariot) were being enticed to active rebellion against Rome's claim to sovereignty over the Jews and the world.

All the Jewish resistance groups took their inspiration from Old Testament characters (Simeon, Levi, Phinehas, Elijah) who, in zeal for God's Law, slew those enemies of Israel – whether within or without – who attempted to subvert Israel's loyalty to God and his laws. Their heroes were also the Maccabees, who slew Antiochus IV's officers and soldiers, together with apostate Jews (see p. 413). To them, rebellion against Rome was a religious act, in the tradition of the fathers. They thought that such zeal, and particularly the martyrdom which resulted from it, would atone for the nation's sin (Num. 25:10–13; Sirach 45:23–24; 2 Macc. 7:30–38).

For Further Reading
Barrett C.K., *The New Testament Background – Selected Documents*, 1957.
Charlesworth, J.H. (ed.), *The Old Testament Pseudepigrapha*, 2 vols., 1983–85.
Danby, H.E., *The Mishnah*, 1933.
Leaney, A.R.C., *The Jewish and Christian World 200 BC to AD 200*, 1984.
Russell, D.S., *The Method and Message of Jewish Apocalyptic*, 1964.
Sparks, H.F.D. (ed.), *The Apocryphal Old Testament*, 1984.
Stone, M.E. (ed.), *Jewish Writings of the Second Temple Period*, 1984.
Vermes, G., *The Dead Sea Scrolls in English*, 1962; *The Dead Sea Scrolls – Qumran in Perspective*, 1978.

Colored plasterwork, Masada.

Measures of Length

Measures of Volume

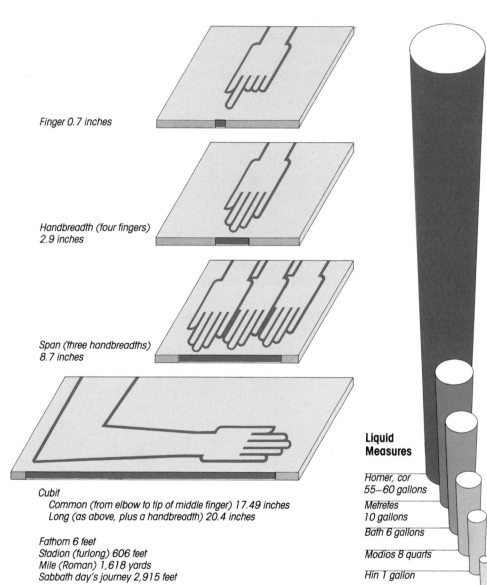

Finger 0.7 inches

Handbreadth (four fingers)
2.9 inches

Span (three handbreadths)
8.7 inches

Cubit
   Common (from elbow to tip of middle finger) 17.49 inches
   Long (as above, plus a handbreadth) 20.4 inches

Fathom 6 feet
Stadion (furlong) 606 feet
Mile (Roman) 1,618 yards
Sabbath day's journey 2,915 feet

Comments on Measures:
1. The equivalents in the table above are approximate.
2. There was no standard system of measures throughout Hebrew history. The Hebrews were influenced by Babylonian, Egyptian, Canaanite, and Greco-Roman systems, and within any one historical period there was no exact standardization. Thus there were frequent complaints about unjust measures and weights (Amos 8:5; Deut. 25:13–14).
3. Early people used the human body as a standard of measurement: the fingerbreadth, the handbreadth, the length of the forearm, the distance of the horizontal arm reach, the stride. In time they devised more sophisticated measures.

Liquid Measures

Homer, cor
55–60 gallons

Metretes
10 gallons

Bath 6 gallons

Modios 8 quarts

Hin 1 gallon

Sextarius 1 pint

Log 0.6 pint

Weights and Money

Hebrew Weights

Gerah	0.02 ounces
Bekah	0.2 ounces
Pim	0.26 ounces
Shekel	0.4 ounces
Litra	12 ounces
Mina	1.25 pounds
Talent	75.6 pounds

Old Testament Money

Shekel (11.4 grams)	
50 shekels	1 mina (500 grams)
60 minas	1 talent

New Testament Coins

4 quadrans (Roman, bronze)	1 as (Roman)
8 asses (Roman, bronze)	1 lepton (Jewish, bronze)
2 leptons	1 denarius (Roman, silver)
1 denarius	1 drachma (Greek, silver)
4 drachma	1 stater (Greek, silver)
1 stater	1 shekel (Jewish)
30 shekels	1 mina (Greek)
25 denarii	1 aureus (Roman, gold)

Dry Measures

Homer, cor 52 gallons
Lethech 26 gallons
Ephah 20.8 quarts
Seah 7 quarts
Omer 2 quarts
Kab 1.1 quarts

Comments on Weights and Money
1. Weights were usually of stone and sometimes inscribed. Often in Egypt and Babylonia they were in the shape of animals or fowl.
2. Before the minting of coins began, in the seventh century BC, precious metals, usually in the form of ingots, were weighed and used as a medium of exchange. The names of the weights were sometimes carried over as the names of the coins.
3. In New Testament times the rapid political changes in Judah and in the Greco-Roman world left in their wake a confusing number of monetary systems. Jews brought coins to Jerusalem of many kinds from all over the Middle East. Money changers therefore flourished in that city, especially since only silver coins of Tyre could be used in the temple.
4. 1 denarius was a day laborer's wage, 1 minah three months' wages, 1 talent more than fifteen years' wages.

The Jewish Calendar

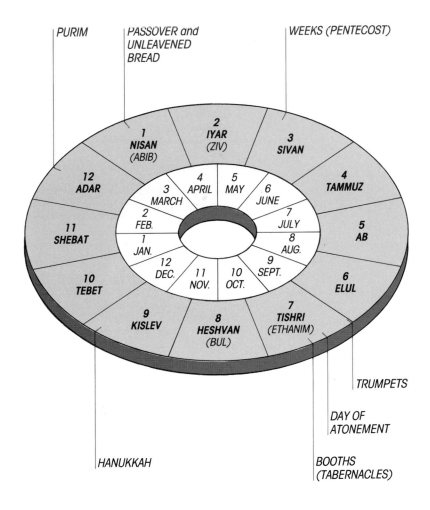

1. The beginning of the Hebrew year shown here falls at our March 21, the spring equinox. The Hebrews took this point of beginning from the Babylonians, probably after 605 BC, when the Babylonians gained control of Judah and the West. After the conquest of Canaan (late thirteenth century BC), and through the periods of the united and divided monarchies (roughly eleventh through the seventh centuries BC), the Hebrews followed the Canaanite calendar, which began the year at the fall equinox (September 21).

2. The names of the Hebrew months shown above are of Babylonian origin. The earlier names given for some are Canaanite.

3. The Hebrew calendar was solar-lunar. The year ran from one equinox to another. Months were calculated from new moon to new moon. Thus months were of about 30 days' length (one lunation actually lasts about 29½ days, and twelve lunations about 354¼ days). To make up the loss of 11 days per year (the solar year is 365¼ days) an extra month was inserted every two or three years. Usually Adar, the twelfth month, was duplicated.

4. The Essenes of Qumran by the Dead Sea seem to have followed a purely solar calendar of 364 days, divided into four seasons of 13 weeks each (91 days), each season having two months of 30 days and one of 31. This scheme caused festivals to fall always on the same day of the week. We do not know when this calendar first arose.

5. The Hebrew day began at sundown.

Special Days and Festivals in Israel

The Sabbath
From a root meaning 'to rest' or 'to cease'; the seventh day of the Hebrew week; origin of the Hebrew Sabbath unknown, though possibly from Moses; a day of rest for Israelites, animals, and slaves (Exod. 20:8–10; Amos 8:5; Neh. 13:15–22); in the postexilic period a day of religious assembly (Lev. 23:1–3); considered, along with circumcision, to be a distinguishing mark of Judaism; thirty-nine types of work on the Sabbath prohibited by Jewish rabbis.

Feast of Trumpets (New Year?)
A one-day celebration (first day of Tishri [September-October]) consisting of cessation from work, blast of trumpets, solemn assembly, special offerings in the temple, and singing (Lev. 23:24–25; Num. 29:1–6); perhaps the preexilic New Year, celebrated at that time in the fall (see p. 444).

Day of Atonement
Tenth of Tishri (September-October); a day of national fasting and repentance; sacrifices offered to cleanse the temple, the priests, and the people; the sins of Israel borne into the desert by a goat (Lev. 16:8–10, 20–22); only day of the year when the high priest entered the Holy of Holies in the temple.

Passover and the Feast of Unleavened Bread
Passover – probably originally a nomadic fertility (or lambing) festival, older than the Exodus from Egypt (Exod. 5:1; 10:9), which gained special meaning from the events of the Exodus (Exod. 12:1–28); became a family dinner around the eating of a roasted yearling lamb, with ceremonies that helped participants relive the Exodus from Egypt; a one-day celebration on the fourteenth of Nisan (March-April).

Unleavened Bread – originally an agricultural festival of thanksgiving at the beginning of barley harvest; featured the consecration of the first-born of man and beast to God and the redemption of first-born human males (Exod. 13:1–16); required abstinence from the use of leaven for seven days; Passover and Unleavened Bread observed together, Passover becoming the first day of an eight-day commemoration of the deliverance from Egypt (Exod. 12:1–20), Nisan 14–21.

Feast of Weeks (Pentecost)
A one-day, end-of-harvest, thanksgiving festival centering in the offering to God of a portion of the wheat harvest; occurred on the fiftieth day after the offering of the barley sheaf to God during the ceremonies of the Feast of Unleavened Bread (usually on sixth of Sivan [May-June]), roughly fifty days after Passover (Lev. 23:15–21); became in the postexilic period also a festival commemorating the gift of the Law (the Covenant) to Israel.

Feast of Tabernacles (Booths)
An eight-day (originally seven-day) autumnal festival of thanksgiving for all the harvests (grain, fruits, grapes, olives); also called 'the feast of ingathering' (Exod. 34:22) or 'the feast of the Lord' (Lev. 23:39); involved pilgrimage to the temple, elaborate animal sacrifices and cereal offerings (Num. 29:12–38), dwelling in leafy huts or booths (Neh. 8:14–18), and foliage (palm-branch) processions (2 Macc. 10:6–7); huts – originally booths for shelter in harvest time – reinterpreted later as symbols of Israel's wilderness wandering (Lev. 23:43); held Tishri 15–22 (September-October).

Feast of Dedication (Hanukkah)
Commemorated the rededication of the temple by Judas Maccabeus (Kislev 25 [November-December], 164 BC), after its defiling three years earlier by Antiochus Epiphanes (see pp. 412–3); an eight-day feast, with temple sacrifices, foliage processions, daily lighting of lamps and torches in front of houses and in the temple, and much singing and rejoicing.

Feast of Purim
A two-day festival (Adar 14–15[February-March]), celebrating the victory of Persian Jews over their persecutors (Esther 9:17–22); public reading of the book of Esther, cursing of Israel's enemies and blessing of Israel, exchanging of gifts and giving alms, and much drinking and hilarity.

Interior of Sepphardic synagogue in the Jewish Quarter of Jerusalem.

Part 3
THE BIBLE AND FAITH AND LIFE

God and Satan

God

The Bible is a book about God. It begins with a story about the creation of the heavens and the earth and ends with an account of a new creation in which God's purpose in the original creation is fulfilled. In the Bible God is said to be the Alpha and the Omega, the first and the last (Rev. 1:8; 22:13); and, to judge from the Bible's story as a whole, God is also all the letters in between.

Biblical writers did not hesitate to think and talk about God. Though biblical people were impressed with the mystery of God – Isaiah saw the Lord as 'high and lifted up' (Isa. 6:1) and Paul puzzled over God's mysterious ways (Rom. 11:33) – they also were powerfully aware that God to some degree had revealed himself to them and declared his purposes for their life and for all people.

What has God revealed to humankind, according to the Bible?

God Is to Be Known and Worshiped as 'Yahweh.'

In the ancient Near East a person's name was of great importance, for it represented the person's character and experiences (Gen. 17:5; 32:28; 1 Sam. 25:25). Similarly, a god's real person and character were concentrated in a name and that name was therefore powerful (Exod. 23:20–21; Jer. 10:6; Ps. 20:7).

God was worshiped by the patriarchs before Moses as 'El' (a general name meaning 'God' or 'deity'). Often characterizing words were added, as in the name El Shaddai (Exod. 6:3, where 'Shaddai' probably means 'the Mountain One,' though it is usually translated 'Almighty').

It was Moses who introduced the name 'Yahweh' to the Hebrew people (Exod. 6:2–3; here the RSV renders the Hebrew YHWH as 'the Lord'). The meaning of 'Yahweh' is not certain. Probably it means 'he causes to be' in the sense that he is the Creator. In Exod. 3:14 the translation 'I am who I am' probably should be rendered, 'I cause to be what comes into existence.'

'Jehovah' is not a Hebrew word but an artificial combination (perhaps made in the sixteenth century AD) of YHWH and the vowels of the Hebrew word 'Adonai,' meaning 'my Lord.' These vowels were placed beneath the consonants YHWH in the sixth-seventh centuries AD by Jewish editors of the Hebrew Scriptures (the Masoretes) to indicate that the sacred name Yahweh

Sunset over the Sea of Galilee.

out of reverence should not be pronounced but that 'Adonai' should be spoken instead. It was never intended by the Masoretes that the vowels should be combined with the consonants to create the word Jehovah. This word has thus been dropped in most of the recent English translations in favor of the term of long use among the Jews: 'the Lord.'

God Is Spirit.
1. God Is Both Far Away and Near at Hand.
Jesus declared, according to John 4:24, that, since God is Spirit, worship of God is not to be confined to any particular place. He is not a local deity. Israel had long believed that God was invisible, universal Spirit, whose tabernacle and temple in Israel were places of his earthly manifestation. Other nations around believed also that their deities were universal gods whose temples were places where they could be encountered by human beings.

While non-Israelite temples contained a statue of the god which was thought to house the god's person or essence, Israel forbade the making of statues or images of Yahweh and thought of Yahweh as invisibly enthroned above the two olive-wood cherubim (winged sphinxes) contained in the Holy of Holies of the temple.

2. God Is One Spirit.
Unlike the peoples around, Israel believed that God was One, not many: 'The Lord our God is one Lord' (Deut. 6:4). In the religions of other nations the forces of nature were personified, conceived of as male and female deities, organized into a structured relationship (a pantheon), and duly worshiped so that their benefits could be obtained. The worshiper's aim was to conform to the rhythms of nature so that the powers of nature would be good to them.

The Hebrews saw their God as Lord of nature. For them nature was the handiwork of God, but nature was not God (Ps. 8:3). Nature was the arena in which people encountered God as the Lord of their lives and their destiny. In the world of nature they are called to fellowship with God and to obedience to God's will. It is a quality of life that God wants, not simply indulgence in the bounties of nature.

3. Spirit Is Power
The basic meaning of the Hebrew word for 'spirit' is 'air,' which early people saw as 'wind' in nature and 'breath' in living beings. The concept of 'power' or 'energy' is fundamental to the word. God's Spirit is thus his active power: *creating* the physical universe (Gen. 1:2; Ps. 33:6); *enabling* people to accomplish heroic deeds (Judges 14:6; Acts 10:38) and to utter God's Word (Mic. 3:8; Luke 4:18); *transforming* the inner life of persons (Acts 15:9; Gal. 5:22–23); and *guaranteeing* the believers' participation in the life of the Age to Come (2 Cor. 1:22; Eph. 1:14).

God Is Light

1 John 1:5 says, 'God is light and in him is no darkness at all.' The context here shows clearly that by 'light' the writer means holiness, goodness, or righteousness, not natural light. Natural light is indeed said in the Bible to come from God (Gen. 1:3; Isa. 45:7). But it results from God's creative activity; it does not define what God is.

The symbolic use of 'light' is strong in the Bible. In the New Testament Jesus Christ, God's Son, is 'the light of the world,' who, if followed, will deliver from the darkness of sin (John 8:12–24). Christians are 'sons of God' and thus 'sons of light' (Luke 16:8; John 12:36; 1 Thess. 5:5). They, too, are 'the light of the world.' Others are to see their good deeds and praise the Father in heaven (Matt. 5:14–16).

When biblical writers said that God is 'holy' and that God's people must be 'holy' (Lev. 19:2; 1 Pet. 1:15–16), they meant that God and they belong together in a realm of mysterious power and moral purity altogether different from the weak, profane, and sinful order in which the sons of darkness dwell. 'Holiness' (1 Thess. 3:11—4:8; Heb. 12:14) is separation from the common and the unclean and is moral likeness to God (see pp. 488–90).

The understanding of light as a symbol of truth or knowledge (Ps. 43:3; 119:104–105) is in harmony with the understanding of light as moral goodness, for the truth God gives, according to the Bible, is knowledge of the true way of life, not of abstract truths.

God Is Love

This famous statement in 1 John 4:8 needs to be joined with the declaration that God has loved us (John 3:16; 1 John 4:10). To say only that 'God is love' might imply that God is impersonal, an abstract principle. To say only that God loved or loves might imply that loving is one of several activities, such as creating or judging. But to affirm both is to hold that God is fully personal and that 'all that he does is an expression of his nature, which is – to love' (C.H. Dodd).

We often hear that the God of the Old Testament is a God of wrath and that the God of the New Testament is a God of love. The contrast is not true to either Testament. Both emphasize both God's love and God's justice or wrath (see pp. 485–6). The writers of the Old Testament repeatedly declared God's love for Israel (Deut. 7:7–8; Hos. 11:1; Jer. 31:3; Ps. 103:17).

The concept of God as Father appears in the Old Testament as well as the New (Isa. 63:16; Ps. 103:13; Jer. 3:19; Mal. 2:10). The term Father implies authority and justice as well as tender affection. A father lays requirements on his children, if he truly loves them.

It is indeed true that the range and depth of God's love is more fully shown in the New Testament. Although the Old Testament occasionally declares God's concern for the salvation of the nations, which is to be accomplished through the life and witness of Israel (Gen. 12:3; Isa. 2:2–4; 45:22; 49:6; Zech. 8:23; the book of Jonah), the New Testament almost everywhere assumes the universality of salvation. In the church there are no distinctions of race, class, or sex (Gal. 3:28; Col. 3:11) and the final salvation of the kingdom of God embraces people of every nation and tongue (Rev. 7:9).

And the depth of God's love is greater in the New Testament. There is little evidence in the Old Testament that deliberate, individual sinners within Israel were to be offered mercy, forgiveness, and restoration. They were to be cut off from the people of God (Num. 15:22–36; Deut. 22:13–27). The God of infinite compassion, who loves enemies and bids his children do likewise (Matt. 5:43–48; Rom. 5:6–8), is the God Jesus exalted in his teaching and actions and thereby set the standard for the belief and activity of the Christian church (see p. 486).

God Is King.

The figure of the king in the ancient Near East offered an apt way of thinking and speaking about God. The king was sovereign, and God's subjects were servants. As king God was provider, shepherd, and judge of the people.

It is probable that the covenant sealed between God and Israel at Mt. Sinai (Exod. 20–24) and reaffirmed at Shechem by Joshua (Josh 8:30–35; chap. 24) followed the pattern of covenants made between ancient kings and vassal states to insure unswerving loyalty of the vassals and proper reward for loyal support. The covenants included a preamble in which the author of the covenant was named, with his titles, attributes, and genealogy; a prologue describing the previous acts of benevolence of the king in relation to his vassals; a statement of the obligations to be accepted by the vassal; blessings and curses as sanctions of the covenant; and some other elements (see pp. 113–5).

The kingship of God was taken so seriously that the establishment of a monarchy in Israel was resisted by Gideon (Judges 8:23) and Samuel (1 Sam. 8) as an affront to the kingship of Yahweh.

Israel's worship extolled the kingship of God (Ps. 24:7–10; 95:3; 97:1; 146:10). The prophets believed that someday God would extend his kingship over all the earth. At that day, either directly or through a chosen human representative, God would judge the nations and inaugurate a new order of peace, prosperity, and felicity (Isa. 9:2–7; 11:1–9; Hag. 2:6–9; Zech. 14:1–9). The New Testament makes much of the coming reign of God (the kingdom of God) and indicates clearly that early Christians believed it to be close at hand (Rom. 13:11–14; 1 Cor. 7:25–31; 1 Thess. 4:15–17; 1 Pet. 4:7; James 5:8). See pp. 502–7 on 'the second coming of Christ.'

Satan

Before the Babylonian Exile (sixth century BC) the Hebrews seem to have thought of God as the source of both good and evil. They viewed natural

disasters as divine punishment of wrongdoing (Deut. chap. 28; 31:17; 1 Kings 14:9–10). Because they believed God used the evil acts of people to advance his purposes (*e.g.*, Isa. 10:5–11, where the Assyrians are said to be sent by God to punish Israel), the Old Testament sometimes represents God as the author of evil (Job 2:10; Isa. 45:7; Amos 3:6).

Even moral evil was sometimes attributed to God, as when the Lord sent a lying spirit into the mouth of false prophets to deceive Ahab (1 Kings 22:19–23) and an evil spirit 'from the Lord' came to torment Saul (1 Sam. 16:14–15).

In the late Old Testament period and in the intertestamental period the increasing sense of God's holiness made his responsibility for evil, both moral and natural, seem difficult to accept. The problem is dealt with in part in the book of Job (see pp. 146–8). The influence of Zoroastrianism on Judaism during the Persian period (539–332 BC), with its strong emphasis on an evil being (Angra Mainyu) as the source of evil and the enemy of God, may have affected Jewish theology and helped to give rise to the concept of Satan developed in this period and contained in the New Testament.

The word Satan means 'adversary' or 'opposer.' It is used in the Bible principally in two senses:

The barren Judean wilderness.

As an angelic agent of God who opposes or tests people
1. An angelic being, who acted under the authority of God, put Job to the test (Job 1:6–12; 2:1–7); see also 1 Kings 22:19–23, where a heavenly spirit (here not called Satan) deceives Ahab through false prophets.
2. The adversary accused the high priest Joshua before the heavenly court because he was guilty of sin along with his people (Zech. 3:1–5).
3. The adversary told David to count the people of Israel (1 Chron. 21:1). The adversary here apparently acted as God's agent (see 2 Sam. 24:1).

As a being hostile to God and the originator and embodiment of all evil
1. He was referred to by names other than Satan in intertestamental writings and in the New Testament: Belial or Beliar, meaning 'the worthless one' (2 Cor. 6:15); Mastema, meaning 'hostility' (the Book of Jubilees); Beelzebul, meaning perhaps 'lord of dung' (Mark 3:22); the devil, meaning 'the slanderer' (John 8:44).
2. Some of his activities according to the New Testament are: ruling over this age (John 12:31; 2 Cor. 4:4); blinding the minds of unbelievers (2 Cor. 4:4); tempting believers to sin (1 Cor. 7:5); causing physical affliction (Luke 13:16); frustrating the activities of God's servants (1 Thess. 2:18); accusing believers before God (Rev. 12:10); causing persecution of Christians (1 Pet. 5:8); empowering the Antichrist for the final war against Christ and the righteous (2 Thess. 2:7–12).
3. Satan's origin is not indicated in the Bible, though some Bible students have claimed that Isa. 14:12 ff. and Ezek. 28:12–19 suggest that Satan was an ambitious angel who was cast out of heaven. But in both passages the reference is clearly to arrogant human beings – of Babylon and Tyre – and not to any ambitious angel.
4. What Satan is we shall never know, even as we cannot know what God is! Whether Satan is a personal antagonist of God who stands outside people as the inspirer of their evil thoughts and deeds, and who would exist whether people did or not, or whether Satan is humanity's personification of all the evil in individual people and in society has long been debated. The Bible is content to stress the reality of evil, whatever its source and exact nature, and to declare that God has acted in Jesus Christ to destroy its power.

People and Miracles

Humankind

We have seen that the Bible is a book about God and other supernatural powers (pp. 450–7). It is also a book about humankind. In fact, its interest in people is so strong that recently some scholars have said that its central concern is people – their place in the world, their problems as human beings, their resources, and their prospects for the future. From this point of view the Bible contains more 'anthropology' (statements about people) than 'theology' (statements about God).

Actually, both are in the center of the stage. The biblical drama involves three levels of existence: the supernatural (God, the angels, and the powers of evil); human beings; and animals and the world of nature.

The Bible's description of humankind is complex and varied. We cannot do justice to it in a few summary statements. But we can indicate some general emphases.

Human Beings Are God's Creatures.

In Hebrew-Christian thought humankind did not spring from the loins or from the blood of a god – as some ancient religions taught – but was *created* by God (Gen. 1). God formed human beings from the dust of the earth and gave them life by his own breath (Gen. 2). There is thus a fundamental distinction between God and humankind. God is above the world and humankind. The world and people are not a part of God but are the result of his creative activity. People are not divine and self-sufficient. They are dependent on God.

Human Beings Are Closely Related to Animals and Nature and, by the Creator's Will, Are Custodians of Both.

The dust from the ground, out of which the Creator formed people (Gen. 2:7), suggests the bond that unites them with nature. People are at home in the world of nature, derive their nourishment from it, and to some extent make the animals their friends and companions (Gen. 2:19–20).

But human beings are superior to the animals and maintain some distance from nature. They name the animals and use many of them for food. They are not absolute masters of the animals and nature, however. Animals and the land have rights too (Deut. 22:10; 27:21; Exod. 23:10–12).

Humankind Was Created in Two Sexes; and Persons Are Social in Nature.
Sex is a gift of God, and children are its fruit (Gen. 1:28). Woman was created to be man's companion and helper. God formed her from man's rib. She is from him and part of him and thus his equal – bone of his bone and flesh of his flesh (Gen. 2:23). The animals did not satisfy man's social needs, but the woman (and children) did. In union man and woman become 'one flesh' (Gen. 2:24; Mark 10:7–8).

A Person Is a Living Being, an Animated body, an Indivisible Unity of Flesh and Spirit.
When God breathed into Adam's nostrils the breath of life, he became 'a living being' (Gen. 2:7). The Hebrews thought of a person not as an incarnated soul, but as a living body. This body had many characteristics. The physical side was called 'flesh.' Then there was the 'aliveness,' the vitality they called *nephesh* (translated 'soul' in the King James Version). They termed the divinely given energies of the individual person 'spirit.' 'Heart' was the seat of feeling, will, and thought. In summary, we may say that the Hebrew-Christian view of a human being is that a person is *one* self in many aspects or functions – not a self composed of separate parts, body, soul, and spirit.

Human Beings Were Created to Live in Fellowship with God and in Obedience to God's Will.
They were created in the 'image' of God (Gen. 1:26–27; 9:6; Wisd. of Sol. 2:23; 1 Cor. 11:7; Col. 3:10). This means that people have a relationship to God not shared by animals. As people standing before a Person, they are not simply a part of nature. They reflect in their persons the qualities of God who created them. They are thus capable of a degree of sovereignty over nature.

Each person is of value to God (Gen. 3:9; Luke 12:6–7; 2 Pet. 3:9) and is individually responsible to God. Israel's early law codes made individual offenders responsible for their own actions (*e.g.*, Exod. chaps. 21–23). The prophets called for individual repentance and for personal obedience to God (Mic. 6:8), just as Jesus and New Testament writers did (Matt. 21:28–32; Rom. 12:1–3; Heb. 2:1–3). People are also collectively responsible to God (Num. chap. 16; Josh. chap. 7; Deut. 21:1–9).

Human Beings Are Frail and Sinful and, in Their Rebellion Against God, Often Become Utterly Corrupt in Their Thinking and Behavior.
Since they came from dust and return to dust, they are weak and mortal. 'All

flesh is grass ... the grass withers, the flower fades' (Isa. 40:6–8; 1 Pet. 1:24). Imperfection, ignorance, and suffering are their lot (Ps. 51:5; Eccles. 8:17; Job 5:7). By rebelling against God and following their own desires, they become corrupt – at odds with God and with one another.

Gen. 6:5 pictures human sinfulness before the flood in dark terms: 'The Lord saw that the wickedness of man was great in the earth, and that every imagination of the thoughts of his heart was only evil continually.'

Paul links the moral depravity of the world to people's refusal to give thanks for God's self-revelation in the created order. Their failure to honor and obey the God thus revealed led to idolatry, 'a base mind,' and frightful conduct (Rom. 1:18–32). Sin, a diabolical power, laid hold of their lives and brought them into slavery (Rom. 7:13–23). 'Death [*i.e.*, spiritual death, final death] spread to all men because all men sinned' (Rom. 5:12).

Paul did not say that all people sin and die because they are physically descended from Adam (*i.e.*, that sin is inherited by every descendant of Adam). He does say that Adam opened the door to sin and sinning and that sin is a monstrous reality in the world. But death comes by saying 'yes' to sin. Personal responsibility remains.

Sinful Human Beings Have the Potential for God-likeness.
The Bible tells the story of God's long pursuit of sinful humankind: through the righteous line from Seth and Enosh (Gen. 4:25–26), through Enoch (5:22–24), Noah (6:9), Shem (11:10 ff.), and Abram (Abraham); through the work of Moses and the giving of the covenant at Mt. Sinai; through the activity of the prophets; and through the mission of Jesus and the church.

The Bible promises that the tree of life, which God placed in the Garden at the beginning, will at last become fruit and medicine for the nations (Rev. 22:2). It is God's will that sin, death, ignorance, and suffering be vanquished forever (1 Cor. 15:54–55; 13:9–12, Rev. 21:4).

The God-likeness intended for humankind at the beginning (Gen. 1:26–27) becomes possible and actual through Jesus Christ, who is the likeness of God (Rom. 8:29; Col. 1:15–20; 3:9–10).

Miracles

The Bible holds that God, on the one hand, and the powers of evil, on the other, are active in the world and in the life of humankind and that both are capable of amazing deeds. These supernatural powers often operate through people. Pharaoh's magicians, agents of the Egyptian gods, were able to match some of the miracles of Moses and Aaron (Exod. 7:11, 22). We are told that false prophets and false messiahs will deceive many by signs and wonders, even endangering the elect (Matt. 24:24; 2 Thess. 2:9–12; Rev. 13:11–15).

Church commemorating the changing of water into wine, Cana.

The Pool of Siloam, with entrance to Hezekiah's tunnel.

Definition of Miracle
Most of the miracles in the Bible are deeds of Yahweh. The Bible sees a miracle of Yahweh as an act that shows his presence and purpose in the world – usually in an unexpected and intense way, and only to those who have eyes of faith.

Biblical writers did not conceive of nature as an ironclad system of law, in which every effect had a natural cause. They did not think of miracle as an act of God contrary to nature's laws. Since God created the world, it was absolutely dependent on God, who was continually active in it – in sustaining its ordained patterns and intervening from time to time in special ways to carry out divine purposes.

Purpose of Miracles
1. To Reveal God and Evoke Faith
Miracles are often called 'signs' in both Testaments. A sign is something which points beyond itself to an ultimate reality. It is a signpost or a finger pointing toward God. The miracles ('signs') Moses did – e.g., the rod turned into a serpent, and the leprous hand – were to point to the fact that God had appeared to Moses and that he was God's agent for the liberation of Israel (Exod. 4:1–8). Israel was to learn through the signs and wonders of the Exodus that Yahweh was God alone (Deut. 4:34–35). Jesus' miracle at Cana was a 'sign' pointing toward his 'glory' (*i.e.*, God's presence in him – John 2:11).

Biblical writers knew that miracles or signs do not automatically convince people. Pharaoh was not convinced (Exod. 7:8–13) and neither were Jesus' enemies: 'Though he had done so many signs before them, yet they did not believe in him' (John 12:37). Signs should call forth faith, but they do not compel it. Miracles were meant to evoke faith not only in Israel but also among the nations (Ps. 86:8–10; 105:1–6; Isa. 40:3–5; 52:10; John 20:30–31).

2. The Pledge of Future Fulfillment
God's marvelous deeds in the past are the pledge and guarantee of help in the future. The God who defeated the Egyptians by signs, wonders, mighty hand, and outstretched arm will drive out Israel's enemies from the Promised Land (Deut. 7:17–24). The God who fed Israel with manna in the wilderness will see that it eats to the full in that land (8:3–10).

Correspondingly, the miracles of the New Testament are the manifestation in the present of the power of the coming kingdom of God. Jesus claimed that his deeds were signs that the kingdom of God was present and active in his ministry (Luke 11:20; Matt. 12:28). By his deeds he was rescuing lives broken by the devil's power and destroying the power of the devil himself (Mark 3:22–27; Luke 10:18). The early church believed it had tasted of 'the powers of the age to come' (Heb. 6:5). It saw in the resurrection of Jesus 'the first fruits' of the resurrection of all Christians (1 Cor. 15:23).

Types of Miracles
1. Nature miracles: *e.g.*, the strong wind and the parting of the Red Sea at the Exodus (Exod. 14:21–22); the shadow that moved backward on the sundial (2 Kings 20:8–11); the floating axe head (2 Kings 6:5–7); Jesus' calming the tempest (Mark 4:35–41); the turning of water into wine (John 2:1–11).
2. Miracles of conception: *e.g.*, Sarah, Rachel, Hannah, and Elizabeth (Gen. 17:15–21; 30:22; 1 Sam. 1:19–20; Luke 1:8–25); the virgin Mary by the power of the Holy Spirit alone (Luke 1:26–38).
3. Miracles of national conquest and preservation: *e.g.*, the conquest of Jericho (Josh. 6), the victory by hailstones (Josh. 10:11), the destruction of the Assyrians and the preservation of Jerusalem in the time of Isaiah (2 Kings 19:35).
4. Miracles of personal preservation and healing: *e.g.*, Elijah fed by the ravens (1 Kings 17:4–6); the Hebrews preserved in the fiery furnace and Daniel in the lions' den (Dan. 3:19–27; 6:16–23); Jonah saved by the great fish (Jon. 1:17); Paul unharmed by the sting of a viper (Acts 28:3–6); Miriam and Naaman delivered from leprosy (Num. 12:9–15; 2 Kings 5:1–14); various sick people healed by Jesus (*e.g.*, Mark 2:3–12; 5:25–34; Luke 13:11–13), by Peter and the apostles (Acts 3:1–10; 5:12–16), by Paul (Acts 20:7–12; 28:8–9).

Mosaic of loaves and fish from Tabgha, Galilee.

5. Miracles of resurrection: Elisha and the Shunammite woman's son (2 Kings 4:32–37), Jesus and the widow's son at Nain (Luke 7:11–15), Jesus and Lazarus (John 11:17–44), Jewish saints at the time of Jesus' crucifixion (Matt. 27:52–53), the resurrection of Jesus (the four Gospels; 1 Cor. 15:4–8).

Workers of Miracles

The miracles recorded in the Bible are said to have occurred chiefly in four periods: (1) at the time of Moses, the Exodus, and the establishing of the nation in the Promised Land; (2) at the beginning of the age of the prophets (with Elijah and Elisha), a time of great pressure from Baal religion; (3) at the height of the Assyrian threat against the independence of Judah in the days of Isaiah; (4) in the period of the fulfillment of Old Testament prophecies concerning the end-time begun by Jesus and continued by the early church.

Miracles were part of the work of God's prophets. (Moses and in part Jesus [Luke 13:33–34] are to be included among the prophets.) The prophet acted for God and released the power of God in the crises of the nation's life.

The early church believed that Jesus did his mighty works by the power of the Holy Spirit (Matt. 12:28; Luke 4:14, 18; 5:17; Acts 10:38). It declared that this power was available to Christians to do the same works, and even greater works (John 14:12). Some Christians, under the power of the Holy Spirit, became workers of miracles and healers (1 Cor. 12:9–10, 28).

Evaluation of Miracles

The importance of a miracle depends on the extent to which it reveals God and his purpose. The resurrection of Jesus obviously tells us more about God and his purpose and activity than does a floating axe head (2 Kings 6:5–7) or a fish with a coin in its mouth for payment of the temple tax (Matt. 17:24–27).

We must look at miracles in their literary context. The 'miracle' of the sun's standing still (Josh. 10:13–14) resulted from the author's taking literally the poetic imagery in a source he used (vss. 12–13). The story cannot therefore be taken as a true miracle.

The book of Jonah is a short story which aims to teach a religious truth: God loves the Assyrians and desires their repentance and salvation. We are hardly justified in pressing the story about the fish into the category of genuine miracle (see pp. 192–4).

If the book of Daniel was written between 167 and 164 BC, as seems certain, then the stories of chaps. 1–6 are probably *haggadah*, popular stories designed to set forth religious and moral truths, not sober history (see p. 180).

As far as possible, we must look at miracle stories in the light of their oral and literary history. Scholars have found that many of the miracle stories of the Gospels have a stereotyped form like miracle stories in other literature (chiefly non-Jewish) of the period (*e.g.*, Mark 7:32–37; 8:22–26). In cases of healing such stories often run through several steps: the seriousness of the sickness and the attempted cures; the method used in the present healing; a demonstration of the reality of the cure; and the impression made on onlookers. Stories not told in this pattern (*e.g.*, Mark 10:46–52; Luke 14:1–6) seem to be older and nearer the original facts.

Parallel stories in the Gospels must be checked in order to find the more original version. For example, Mark 1:34 says, 'He [Jesus] healed many who were sick with various diseases,' whereas in the parallel passage in Matthew 8:16 we read, 'he ... healed all who were sick.' (See also Mark 6:5 and Matt. 13:58.) Matthew tended to heighten the miraculous element in Mark's account.

Such sifting of the miracle stories yet leaves a solid residue of mighty deeds. The heart of Israel's faith was that Yahweh is the living God, that nothing is too hard (wonderful) for him (Gen. 18:14), and that with God all things are possible (Mark 10:27). If the universe is not a closed, inflexible system – and many scientists today agree that it is not – and if God is the reality the Hebrews claimed him to be, God's activity in the world in unexpected and intense ways, as well as in familiar and undramatic ones, will not seem strange to people of faith. That God should work in the world chiefly through Spirit-empowered people is in line with his purpose to save the world by incarnating himself in the man Jesus.

Jesus Christ and the Way of Salvation

Jesus Christ

The flood of books in recent years about Jesus and, even more, his impact today on playwrights, athletes, and unchurched youth testify once again that Jesus is a man for all times.

What sort of person *was* he? Some theologians of a generation or so ago thought it unnecessary and unrewarding to ask. They said that what is important is not Jesus as he actually was, but only what the apostles believed him to be. It is the Christ of the apostles' faith and preaching who is the proper object of faith, not the historical Jesus. And, furthermore, they said, we can no longer recover the historical Jesus.

Today we think that it is both necessary and rewarding to inquire. We now see what ought to have been obvious all along: that Christianity's real roots are in Jesus himself; it was he who brought about the church's faith and message. If faith in him is to arise in our time, it will come about by *his* impact on us, not simply by the church's proclaimed and recorded faith.

If Jesus is God's example of what people ought to be, and if we are to grow into his likeness, as the New Testament holds (Rom. 8:29), then we must know what sort of man he was. In spite of the limited and sometimes conflicting information about the life of Jesus in the Gospels (see pp. 256–7), we now believe that we can recover a reasonably clear portrait of him. This portrait puts us in the crisis of decision – for Jesus or against him.

And what sort of person *is* he? If he is 'alive for evermore' (Rev. 1:18), if he can be with us 'to the close of the age' (Matt. 28:20), and if he has 'the keys of Death and Hades' (Rev. 1:18), it is imperative that we know him for what he is – for our destiny is in his hands and depends on our relation to him.

The Career of Jesus

Today scholars agree that it is not possible to write a life of Jesus (see p. 229). We cannot arrange the events of his career chronologically or identify with certainty its major turning points. Neither can we trace his psychological development and changes of strategy. Only the passion narrative offers anything like a connected account of his words and experiences.

Nevertheless, we do have considerable information about him. He was born in Bethlehem (some have argued for Galilee as his birth place) before the death of Herod the Great in 4 BC (see p. 439). A date between 6 and 4 BC is probable.

He attended the synagogue as a youth (Luke 4:16). As a boy he showed aptitude for learning and religious discussion (Luke 2:41–51). He worked as a carpenter before he began his ministry (Mark 6:3). He had no formal training for public teaching (John 7:15). He seems to have remained unmarried, though claims to the contrary have been made in recent years. Joseph may have died during Jesus' youth, and Jesus may have become the chief support of the family.

Probably between AD 26 and 28 (Luke 3:1–2) he responded to John the Baptist's appeal for repentance, an appeal based on John's conviction that the end of the age and the Messiah's fiery judgment were at hand (Luke 3:7–17). Along with multitudes of Jews, he was baptized by John in the Jordan river (Mark 1:4–11). At that baptism he was filled with the Holy Spirit, with the consciousness of a unique relationship with God, and with a sense of special mission (Mark 1:11).

He began to gather disciples, some of them from among the followers of John the Baptist (John 1:35 ff.; Mark 1:16–20). He taught and baptized for a time in Judea (John 3:22) and then, after the arrest of John the Baptist by Herod Antipas (Mark 1:14), he launched a preaching and teaching mission in the synagogues of Galilee (Luke 4:14–15). He taught also by the lakeside and in the open fields.

His Galilean mission, implemented by a mission carried out by twelve disciples (Mark 6:7–13), was acclaimed by multitudes who heard his teaching and witnessed his amazing deeds (Mark 3:7–10). But he soon aroused the hostility of influential Pharisees and the suspicions of Herod Antipas, the ruler of Galilee. The Pharisees objected to his liberal teaching and practice of the Law as they understood and observed it. They were offended most of all, apparently, by his claim of authority to declare what was binding in the Law and what was not (Mark 7:1–23; 10:2–9).

Herod Antipas feared the political consequences of Jesus' popularity with the multitudes and decided to take measures against him (Mark 6:14–16; Luke 13:31). Jesus withdrew for a time into territory to the north of Galilee. While there he seems to have decided on an appeal to the nation in its capital city.

He journeyed to Jerusalem with his disciples. It seems that he had been in Jerusalem at national festivals several times during his ministry. The Gospel of John refers to three Passovers there (2:13; 6:4; 11:55), thus implying at least a two-year ministry. Or the Synoptic Gospels may be accurate in assuming a ministry of a few months more than a year. His final visit to Jerusalem may have occurred at Passover time, AD 30.

His act of cleansing the temple caused the priestly authorities to arrest him by stealth because of his popularity (Mark 14:1–2). Following a grand-jury type hearing before a priestly body, he was turned over to the Roman procurator Pontius Pilate with the recommendation that he be sentenced to

Tiberias was founded by Herod Antipas c. AD 17.

death. After hearings before Pilate and Herod Antipas (Luke 23:6–12), he was executed by crucifixion. His disciples subsequently triumphantly claimed that God raised him from death and that he had appeared to them individually and collectively.

Jesus' Activities
Jesus' activity during his career assumed many forms:

1. Preaching and Teaching
He announced the coming of the kingdom of God (Mark 1:14–15; Luke 8:1) and instructed the disciples, in particular, concerning its nature and conditions for admission (Matt. 5:1 ff.). He had much to say about God and the will of God for those who believed in him and his message about the kingdom.

2. Exorcisms and Healing
The Gospels are full of accounts about Jesus' freeing people from demonic control and from afflictions of many kinds. He refused, however, to devote himself principally to a ministry of physical healing (Mark 1:35–39) and to authenticate his mission by miraculous acts (Mark 8:11–12).

3. Mission to Religious and Social Outcasts

Much of his time and energy was spent in the attempt to reach those outside the synagogue – the 'unchurched' people who made little or no attempt to observe traditional Jewish law.

Many of them were engaged in occupations which were thought to be immoral and dishonest, such as money-changing, money-lending, gambling, prostitution, thieving, and, above all, tax-collecting for Rome. These people are the 'sinners' or 'tax collectors and sinners' so often mentioned in the Gospels (Mark 2:15–17; Matt. 11:19; 21:32; Luke 7:37, 39; 15:1–2; 19:7).

Jesus repeatedly ate their 'unclean' and untithed food, and allowed them to touch him (Luke 7:39). He offered them forgiveness, membership in God's family, and a share in the blessings of the coming age (Mark 2:13–14; Luke 19:1–10; 7:36–50; 8:2). His meals with them were symbolic of their coming banquet together in the kingdom of God. In his culture eating with others was a sign of acceptance, reconciliation, mutual trust, and a sharing of life.

Jesus was attacked bitterly for his free association with such people (Mark 2:15–17; Matt. 11:16–19). He defended himself by comparing his mission to that of a physician (Mark 2:17). Much of his teaching was a defense of his conduct in calling 'sinners' to God's table (Luke 15; 18:9–14; Matt. 20:1–15; 21:28–32).

Church of the Primacy of Peter, Galilee, near the 'Place of the Coals' (John 21:9).

Roman bath at Hammat Gader, ancient Gadara.

4. Controversies with Religious Leaders
These controversies centered not only on his 'scandalous' association with 'sinners' but on his attitude toward the Jewish Law and his claim to authority. He challenged the validity of the food laws (Mark 7:14–23), broke Sabbath laws (2:23—3:5), set Genesis against Deuteronomy on the matter of divorce (Mark 10:2–9), and claimed the right to declare the true meaning of the Law (Matt. 5:21–48). He claimed authority to forgive sins (Mark 2:5) and to have God's power over Satan and the demons (Mark 3:22–27; Luke 11:20). He claimed the right to cleanse the temple of abuses (Mark 11:15–18). His controversy with religious leaders is recorded in both the Synoptic Gospels and the Gospel of John.

5. Personal Counseling
He dealt often with individuals: the rich man (Mark 10:17–22), Nicodemus (John 3:1 ff.), Zacchaeus (Luke 19:2–9), Mary (Luke 10:38–42), Simon the Pharisee (Luke 7:36 ff.). He made clear the cost of discipleship and brought about personal repentance and rebirth (Luke 19:2–10).

6. Formation of a Fellowship of Prayer, Obedience, and Suffering Service
He led his disciples in the practice of prayer (Luke 5:16; 6:12; 9:18; 11:1–4). He taught them by example and word the meaning of radical obedience to

God, whatever the personal cost (Luke 9:57–62; 13:31–33; Mark 8:31–35). He sent his disciples on a missionary journey (Mark 6:7–13) and led such journeys himself (Luke 4:14–15; 8:1; 9:51 ff.). He regarded his disciples as God's 'little flock' to whom God would give the coming kingdom (Luke 12:32).

His Statements About His Mission

Mark summarized the essence of Jesus' proclamation thus: 'The time is fulfilled, and the kingdom of God is at hand; repent, and believe in the gospel' (1:15).

John the Baptist announced the imminent judgment of God on the Jews and the nations. Jesus focused on the kingdom of God, or the rule of God, which would follow that judgment. Jesus seems to have expected the coming of God's kingdom during his generation (Mark 9:1; 13:30; Matt. 10:23), though he disclaimed knowledge of the exact date (Mark 13:32; *cf.* Acts 1:7).

He did not describe the kingdom but spoke of it in terms of a banquet (Mark 14:25; Matt. 8:11), 'life' (Mark 9:43; Matt. 7:14), and 'joy' (Matt. 25:21, 23). He clearly repudiated the political understanding of the kingdom advocated by the Zealots (see pp. 439–41) and refused to join their movement to establish it by force of arms (Mark 12:17; Luke 6:35; Matt. 5:41).

While the kingdom of God was for him principally future, he clearly believed that its power was at work in his deeds and his preaching and that the Scriptures concerning the last days (Isa. 35:5–6; 61:1) were being fulfilled in his ministry (Matt. 11:4–6).

Crucially important is Luke 11:20 (Matt. 12:28): 'If it is by the finger of God [Matthew has 'the Spirit of God'] that I cast out demons, then the kingdom of God has come upon you.' Here Jesus says that God's power is active in his present exorcisms and that the kingdom (rule) of God is actually being experienced *now* in the restoration to wholeness of disordered, enslaved people.

Furthermore, he goes on to say (Luke 17:20–21) that the coming of the kingdom of God cannot be predicted by the appearance of certain 'signs,' as visionaries of his time would have it, but the kingdom is present now in the lives of those who have been liberated and in the community of those who have faith and insight enough to recognize what is actually going on.

Gathered around Jesus were restored demoniacs, harlots, tax collectors, fishermen, and even a Zealot (Luke 6:15), who were eating together in celebration of the joy of their present experience of the kingdom of God (Mark 2:15–17) and in pledge of its consummation at the messianic banquet in the future kingdom (Matt. 8:11). Jesus and his disciples believed that the kingdom of God was present in foretaste and would be experienced soon in fullness. (See pp. 493–501.)

Did Jesus think that he was or was to be 'the Messiah,' the anointed king of the coming kingdom of God? There is strong evidence that he disliked the term and the role as his contemporaries conceived it. For them the Messiah was to be a descendant of David, who would destroy all the enemies of the Jews and rule in splendor over the reassembled, holy people of God (Psalms of Solomon, chap. 17). Or he would be the high priest of the New Age ('the Messiah of Aaron' mentioned in the Dead Sea Scrolls), who would serve in the Holy of Holies of the temple in the New Jerusalem, have fellowship with angels, be a light for the world, and have 'a branch of David' ('the Messiah of Israel') at his side. Jesus seems to have recognized that he was or would be neither of these.

The Gospel of Mark depicts Jesus as silencing those who accorded him exalted status (1:24–25, 34; 3:11–12; 8:29–30). Before the high priest he is represented as admitting that he regarded himself as the Messiah, but as quickly shifting to the term 'The Son of man' as more descriptive of his role (14:61–62). One scholar has said, 'Jesus imposed silence because of the nature of Messiahship as He conceived it to be. To Him it was not primarily a matter of status but of action' (Vincent Taylor, *The Gospel According to St. Mark*, p. 123). He was Messiah only in the breaking of Satan's power, in healing the sick, in forgiving sins, and in preparing a holy people for the coming kingdom of God.

The Jordan river below the Sea of Galilee.

Jesus was more concerned about his work than he was about titles. Many scholars of today believe that he employed none of the titles used by or about him in the Gospels (Messiah, Son or Son of God, Son of man, Son of David, Lord). They hold that these titles do not occur on his lips in what seem to be the earliest traditions about his teaching and ministry and moreover appear to reflect the post-resurrection beliefs of the first Christian community.

Other scholars are of the opinion that Jesus may have used 'Son' or 'Son of God' and 'Son of man' as descriptive of his self-estimate and mission, since these were freer of undesirable connotations and fairly expressive of his self-consciousness. And yet others think he also used 'Messiah' but radically reinterpreted its meaning in the light of the Suffering Servant concept of Isaiah 53. However this may be, it is widely agreed that he regarded himself as God's End-time representative and agent. He believed that he was speaking and acting for God.

Jesus was 'sent' as the Father's official delegate (Matt. 10:40; John 6:29; 13:20). He offered forgiveness, as if he stood in God's place (Mark 2:10). He interpreted the Law, even setting one part of it against another (Mark 10:2–9), as if he had sovereign authority. His 'I say to you,' over against the Law and human tradition, had the ring of divine right (Matt. 5:21–48). He offered salvation to tax collectors, harlots, and to the multitudes who did not observe traditional law as if he had the right to give it. He identified his finger with God's (Luke 11:20).

He seems to have followed to some degree in the footsteps of the Old Testament prophets (Mark 6:4; Luke 13:33). He taught much like the Wisdom teachers of his day. And he was an exorcist among other exorcists (Luke 11:19). But none of these roles – or all of them – reached high enough to embrace his sense of identity and destiny as End-time Deliverer.

Did he anticipate his death and speak of it as having redemptive significance? This is a difficult and much discussed question. Though it has often been denied that Jesus foresaw his death, the evidence supports the conclusion that he did. The course he pursued in his ministry was deliberately radical, and many of the charges laid against him had as their punishment death (practicing magic, blaspheming God, being a false prophet, deliberately breaking the Sabbath). He knew of the tradition of the martyrdom of the prophets and saw himself in part in the succession of the prophets (Luke 13:33–34). And almost before his eyes he had seen John the Baptist put to death.

Some scholars admit that he foresaw his death but deny that he gave it redemptive significance. He saw his death only as his personal 'transition to the divine glory' as coming King.

Some facts point to the opposite conclusion. Judaism at Jesus' time contained ideas about the atoning power of death, particularly the death of righteous martyrs (e.g., 2 Macc. 7:37–38; 4 Macc. 6:28–29; 17:21–22). Mark

10:45 ('For the Son of man also came not to be served but to serve, and to give his life as a ransom for many') echoes Isa. 53:10. Here 'ransom' corresponds to 'offering for sin.' Whether the statement came from Jesus or arose in the early church as the church's interpretation of the meaning of his death has long been debated. The words spoken over the bread and wine at the Last Supper (Mark 14:22–24; 1 Cor. 11:24–25) suggest that Jesus may have regarded himself as a Passover sacrifice for 'many' (Mark 14:24; Isa. 53:12), *i.e.,* 'the many,' everybody.

It would be strange indeed if Jesus, facing death, entertained no thoughts about the meaning of his death in relation to God's purpose for the salvation of humankind.

Scholars differ sharply on whether Jesus foresaw his resurrection (Mark 8:31; 9:31; 10:34) and whether he expected to return as the heavenly Son of man (Mark 8:38; 14:62; Matt. 10:23; Luke 17:24). A heavenly figure of this sort is known to us from 1 Enoch (46:1–4; 48:2–10; 61:5–8; 62:1–14, etc.), 2 Esdras (4 Ezra) (chap. 13), and possibly Daniel (7:13–14) and is viewed in some or all these books as conqueror and judge of evil nations at the last Day and as the eternal shepherd of the righteous.

Did Jesus think of himself as this coming Son of man? Or did the earliest church put sayings on his lips that he did not actually utter and a concept into his mind he did not hold? Strong arguments have been adduced for both

Ancient olive trees in the Garden of Gethsemane.

views. Some scholars believe that when he used the term, as he seems to have done, he was not using it in a futuristic (apocalyptic) sense but was referring to himself only as 'a man' (as in Psalm 8:4), or that he wished to characterize himself as a Spirit-filled prophet (as in some 90 occurences of the term in the book of Ezekiel), or that he had in mind not himself but the righteous people of God (as in Dan. 7:17–18, 22, 25, 27). Some allow that if he did use the term in the heavenly, futuristic sense (*e.g.,* Mark 8:38), he meant that someone other than himself would fulfill that conquering, judging role. And yet others think that 'Son of man' was Jesus' favorite self-designation and that he used it in multiple senses, including the futuristic one.

It is difficult, if not impossible, to separate the mind of Jesus from that of the early church, which clearly thought of him as the coming heavenly Son of man (Acts 7:56; 1 Cor. 15:47–49, where the idea but not the term 'Son of man' occurs; all four Gospels; Rev. 1:13?). At present, the question concerning Jesus' usage and meaning must be kept open.

The Source of His Power

The New Testament takes both the deity and the humanity of Jesus seriously. Mark represents Jesus as a divine being in human form, whose true identity and work are known to the demons but are hidden from people as a whole and even, for the most part, from the disciples (see pp. 242–3). Paul and John held that the eternal Word (Son) became flesh (Phil. 2:5–11; 2 Cor. 8:9; John 1:1–18).

Most readers of the New Testament do not realize how strongly its writers conceived the humanity of Jesus. Heretics in the early church denied that the Son of God, the heavenly Christ, had really come in the flesh (1 John 4:1–2; see pp. 348–9). Many passages show that Jesus was indeed authentically human.

Though Jesus had great perception and insight (John 2:25), he was limited in knowledge. He did not know when the Son of man would come (Mark 13:32). He asked questions for information, as ordinary people do (Mark 6:38). The disciples did not assume that he had all knowledge (Matt. 15:12). Luke says that he grew in wisdom (2:52).

Spiritual growth marked his relationship with God and his associates: he 'increased … in favor with God and man' (Luke 2:52); 'he learned obedience through what he suffered; and being made perfect he became the source of eternal salvation' (Heb. 5:8–9).

He prayed much during his ministry (Luke 3:21; 5:16; 6:12; 9:18; 11:1), and the power of the Holy Spirit came upon him (3:21–22; 4:14; 5:16–17; 6:19). He did his works by the power of the Spirit (Matt. 12:28; Luke 11:20; Acts 10:38). He promised the disciples that they would do the works he did, and greater works, because the Spirit would be given to them (John 7:39; 14:12; 20:22).

The tomb complex of the Bene Hezir in the Kidron Valley, undoubtedly seen by Jesus.

He pondered the Scriptures and found meaning in them for his life and ministry (Luke 4:16–20; Mark 2:25–27). The eternal Son became like us in every respect except our sinning (Heb. 2:14–17; 4:15). Therefore, he is our brother (2:11–13, 17).

The New Testament view is that in the days of Jesus' earthly life he did not draw on any hidden reservoir of deity, but found strength and did his work in the way open to all people.

We may conclude that he was uniquely endowed with intellectual and spiritual capacities, but his endowments fell within the boundaries of what we call human. His resurrection and exaltation removed him from the realm of the human (Matt. 28:18; Phil. 2:9–11). He is now universal Lord (Phil. 2:11; Rev. 1:5; 17:14).

Finally, we may note two general views of Jesus in the New Testament:
1. *He is God's official end-time delegate to humankind.* He is the point where God's graciousness and power contact people in their sin and bondage and give them a foretaste of the coming kingdom of God. And he will be God's agent in the inauguration of that coming kingdom.
2. *He is humankind's representative before God.* Jesus was fully human. He was tempted by Satan; he prayed; he read the Scriptures; he worked in the power of the Holy Spirit; and he suffered hostility, rejection, and death. Yet he overcame Satan and his enemies and called others to follow him. He seems

to have believed – certainly the church after him did – that his life, death, and resurrection would be redemptive for all humankind. He is thus the one in whom deity and humanity meet. He is both God's eternal Son and humankind's High Priest before God, as the author of the Letter to the Hebrews saw.

The Way of Salvation

When the early church called people to faith in Jesus as the promised Redeemer (Acts 2:22–40; 13:23–29; Rom. 1:1–4; 1 Cor. 15:3–4) and as the point of contact between heaven and earth (John 1:1–18; Phil. 2:6–11; Heb. 1:2–4; 2:9–18), it followed Jesus' own view of his God-appointed position and role.

What did the church mean when it promised 'salvation' through Jesus? Salvation is God's deliverance from all that threatens people, individually and collectively: sickness, poverty, personal and national enemies, Satan and the demons, sin, death, judgment, the lake of fire. Those whom God saves are restored to wholeness, health, well-being, and right relations with themselves and their fellows. Salvation, deliverance, restoration begins in this life and is completed in the coming kingdom of God.

What is the way of salvation, as presented in the New Testament?

Seeing and/or Hearing

Jesus believed that his deeds were signs of the kingdom's presence in his ministry (Luke 11:20), which, when seen, ought to lead to faith (Matt. 11:4–6). He congratulated the disciples for their opportunity to see and hear what prophets and kings had desired to witness (Luke 10:23–24). Sight should lead to insight (John 9). But he knew it did not always do so – for the disciples (Mark 8:18) or the multitudes (Matt. 11:20–24). He marveled that the people of Nazareth, who had seen or heard of his mighty works, still did not believe (Mark 6:2, 6).

Early Christian preaching often, if not always, told the story of Jesus' doings and bore witness to his resurrection (Acts 10:34–43; 13:23–31). Paul said that 'faith comes from what is heard, and what is heard comes by the preaching of Christ' (Rom. 10:17). Faith came to the Galatians by Paul's preaching of Christ crucified and by their hearing the message (Gal. 3:1–5). And, like Jesus, the church experienced the agony of seeing its message rejected (Acts 13:44–46; Rom. 10:18–21).

Faith (Trust)

Jesus called for faith in God (Mark 11:22) and faith in himself as the one in whom God's power was working and as God's spokesman (Matt. 11:2–6; Mark 1:15; Matt. 8:5–10). He declared, 'Everything is possible to one who has faith' (Mark 9:23 NEB).

En Karem, by tradition the birthplace of John the Baptist.

Faith for Jesus was trust in God's grace and power and in Jesus' own ability to help when human resources had failed (Mark 5:25–34; 9:17–29). Faith was absolute trust in a person and trust in that person's willingness and ability to supply what was needed.

Faith for Paul was complete reliance on Jesus Christ, God's Son, the one sent by God to deliver mankind from the power of sin and death (Rom. 7:21–25; 8:3–4; Gal. 1:4). Faith was openness to and acceptance of the power of God at work in the death and resurrection of Christ (Col. 2:12; Rom. 4:24–25).

In the New Testament, faith is a person's response to God's act in Jesus Christ when that act is declared (Rom. 10:17; 1 Cor. 1:21; 2:1–5). Faith is not an attitude one manages to stir up by one's own effort; it is response to God's initiative in Jesus Christ (John 6:37, 44).

Repentance (Conversion)

Repentance was preached by John the Baptist (Luke 3:3, 7–14), Jesus (Mark 1:15; Luke 13:3; 15:7, 10), Peter (Acts 2:38; 3:19), Paul (2 Cor. 7:10; 1 Thess. 1:9), and other New Testament writers.

Repentance in the New Tetament is not remorse, or even 'a change of mind.' It is a radical turning around in one's total life (Luke 3:8–14). It is absolute renunciation of false gods and a false way of life and the embracing of the true God and true life (Matt. 11:20–24). It is glad acceptance of the salvation God offers in Jesus (Matt. 12:41–42; 13:44–46; Luke 9:57–62).

Repentance is not the precondition of God's grace; it is a person's response to it. It both accompanies and follows the moment of faith or trust. It is putting one's house in order as the domicile for God.

Baptism is associated with repentance. It was so in the teaching and practice of John the Baptist (Mark 1:4–11). What baptism meant to John is not altogether clear. It probably was a rite of cleansing away of sins to prepare one who had 'turned around' to pass the test of the final judgment.

Jesus and his disciples baptized (John 3:22). It is likely that it was for them a sacrament of preparation for entrance into the coming kingdom of God.

The early church baptized (Acts. 2:41; 8:36–38), and Paul assumed that all Christians had been baptized (Rom. 6:3). For Christians, besides an act of preparation for the judgment and entering the coming kingdom, it was the act of incorporation into the death and resurrection of Jesus, the Messiah, and his resurrection-body, the church (Rom. 6:3–4; 1 Cor. 12:13). It was the occasion of the bestowal of the Holy Spirit (Acts 2:38; 1 Cor. 12:13), when one experienced in foretaste the power of the Age to Come (2 Cor. 1:22; Eph. 1:13–14; Heb. 6:4–5).

Obedience

For Jesus and the church, faith involved faithfulness or obedience. Jesus warned the disciples against those who called him 'Lord' but did not do the will of God (Matt. 7:21). Praise of Jesus' mother – and indirectly of Jesus himself – has little meaning, he said, if one does not 'hear the word of God and keep it' (Luke 11:27–28). One who *does* the words of Jesus is the wise person who builds on rock (Matt. 7:24–27).

So, for Paul, faith involves obedience to Jesus as Lord (Master). As Christ was obedient to God (Rom. 5:19; Phil. 2:8), so the Christian is to be obedient to God (Rom. 6:22) and to the Lord Jesus Christ, even in every thought (2 Cor. 10:5). One is to be obedient to the gospel (Rom. 10:16) and to the truth (Rom. 2:8). Paul can even speak of 'the obedience of faith' (Rom. 1:5).

What this means in practical terms is elaborately treated in the New Testament. It is having the mind of Christ, which means loving God and one's neighbor, and doing the works of love (Phil. 2:5 ff.; Rom. 12:3–21; 13:8–10; 1 Pet. 2:20–24; Heb. 13:1–6).

Obedience to Christ involves observing the Lord's Supper as the memorial of his sacrifice in our behalf and the pledge of future triumph and fellowship in the kingdom of God (1 Cor. 11:23–26; Mark 14:25).

And obedience means making disciples of people of all nations in the time before the coming of the kingdom (Matt. 28:19–20; Mark 14:9; Acts 1:8; Rom. 1:5).

The Old Community and the New

Someone has said, 'One man is *no* man.' The Bible expresses this truth in such statements as: 'It is not good that man should be alone; I will make him a helper fit for him' (Gen. 2:18); 'My dwelling place shall be with them; and I will be their God, and they shall be my people' (Ezek. 37:27); and 'I bow my knees before the Father, from whom every family in heaven and on earth is named' (Eph. 3:14). Even God is represented as surrounded by heavenly councilors (Ps. 82:1; 89:5–7; Rev. 4:4). According to the Bible, God and people are social beings.

It was at Mt. Sinai under Moses that the slaves from Egypt became an organized religious community. It was the second Moses, Jesus, who by his life, death, and resurrection brought into being the new community, the true Israel (Gal. 6:16; Mark 12:9; John 15:5; Phil. 3:3).

The new community, the Christian church, saw itself as fulfilling God's purpose when he formed the old community: the creation of a holy people, the members of which would live in loyal love with himself and one another, testify to his glory before the nations, and inherit, along with the converted nations, the wonderful future he was planning.

Several characteristics of both communities stand out in the Bible.

A Strong Self-Awareness as the People of God

We do not know how early the belief arose that Israel was God's called and chosen people. An early writer (see pp. 106–7) attributed this belief to Abraham (Gen. 12:1–3). It certainly flowered out in the time of Moses, when the covenant was sealed at Mt. Sinai between Yahweh and the liberated slaves. The great prophets Amos, Hosea, Isaiah, and Jeremiah repeatedly emphasized God's choice of Israel and Israel's obligations in view of that choice. The author of Deuteronomy discusses the reality and the mystery of Israel's·election (7:6–11; 9:4 ff.). The Second Isaiah, during the Exile, undertook to restore the nation's shattered confidence in its place in God's love and concern and to help it fulfill its proper role as God's Servant.

The prophets pointed out that election was not simply to special privilege but to special responsibility and special service. The responsibility and service consisted in receiving God's self-revelation, becoming like God in character, doing God's will, and sharing God's revelation with all people.

The prophets knew that Israel had failed to be loyal to the terms of its covenant with God and predicted the destruction of the nation. They said that God would preserve a remnant, to which would be given a victorious and righteous king, the Messiah. This remnant would carry out God's purpose in the world (e.g., Mic. 4:6–8; 5:2–9; Isa. 4:2–6; 10:20–22; Zeph. 2:7; Jer. 23:3–6; Joel 2:32).

Some scholars have argued that Jesus believed he was the Messiah of the remnant, that he symbolized this claim by appointing *twelve* disciples as 'the nuclear Israel,' and that he deliberately sought through these disciples to call out the remnant as his followers.

The argument founders on the fact that the Messiah of the remnant was a political-military figure who was to destroy the enemies of Israel (Mic. 5:2–9), a role Jesus clearly repudiated for himself (see pp. 472–3).

Jesus regarded his little company of followers as God's flock, which was to inherit the coming kingdom of God (Luke 12:32). But he does not seem to have used the idea of the remnant in connection with his disciples.

Paul made some use of that idea in stating his understanding of the church (Rom. 11:5). But he preferred to think of the church as the true children of Abraham (Gal. 3:6–9, 14, 16, 29; Rom. 4:11–12, 16–18), as those who were circumcized in heart not in the flesh (Rom. 2:28–29; Phil. 3:3). By this he meant people whose relationship with God rested on their faith, not on their meritorious works.

It was a constant source of wonder to Christians that they were privileged to be the people of God. This was especially true of Gentiles, who once had been 'separated from Christ, alienated from the commonwealth of Israel, and strangers to the covenants of promise' (Eph. 2:12). They were now 'a chosen race, a royal priesthood, a holy nation, God's own people,' whose purpose was to declare God's wonderful deeds (1 Pet. 2:9). They rhapsodized about God's choice of the church, which was made 'before the foundation of the world' (Eph. 1:4). 'We are God's children now,' they said (1 John 3:2). As children they knew they were heirs of the glories of the coming kingdom (Rom. 8:14–25; Gal. 4:1–7; Eph. 1:14).

The early Christians believed that the old Israel's relationship with God, based on Moses and the Mosaic covenant, had been superseded by a new relationship, based on the Messiah Jesus and a New Covenant (2 Cor. 3:5–18; Heb. 8:6–13). God's law, they said, is now written in the hearts of his true children, not on tables of stone, and they are God's true witnesses to the nations.

The conviction that they were God's chosen people, destined for entrance to the kingdom of God in the near future, and now were experiencing a foretaste of that future (see pp. 493–501) gave zest to their life and zeal to their witness.

Remembrance of the Past and Anticipation of the Future

The life of the old community was designed to call the past to remembrance. The feasts, the memorial objects (like the ark of the covenant), the literature, and the ceremonies of worship all pointed to God's gracious deeds in the past.

Israel's early creedal statements contained a review of God's redeeming acts (Deut. 6:20–25; 26:5–10; Josh. 24:2–13). The book of Psalms, the hymnbook of temple worship, celebrated his wonders of old. The sermons of Moses in Deuteronomy review in great detail God's marvelous works in Israel's history. The Passover ceremony made Israelite families participants forever in that holy occurrence when God rescued the chosen people from Egypt.

By remembering the marvelous deeds of God in ceremony and worship, the Israelites kept alive their national and religious consciousness. They were thus obligated to obey the terms of the covenant their God had given them at the founding of the nation.

The remembrance of the past also provided ground for their hope for the future. The God who had led them hitherto would lead them henceforth. By their fidelity to God's covenant demands, he would fulfill the covenant promises. The Lord would make Israel 'the head, and not the tail' (Deut. 28:13). The wealth of the nations would come to the temple (Hag. 2:7); the branch of David would rule in justice over Israel and the nations (Isa. 11:1–9; Jer. 23:5–6); and the earth would be full of the knowledge of the Lord (Isa. 11:9).

The Negev desert.

The call to remembrance was strong in early Christianity. The preaching dealt with God's gracious deeds in the history of Israel, culminating in the gift of the Savior Jesus Christ (Acts 13:16–41). In 2 Timothy readers are exhorted to 'remember Jesus Christ, risen from the dead, descended from David' (2:8). Paul asked the Ephesian elders to remember the words of the Lord Jesus (Acts 20:35). We owe the existence of the four Gospels to the church's remembering in its worship, teaching, preaching, disciplining of members, and controversy with opponents what Jesus had said and done (see p. 229).

The supreme act of remembrance, of course, was the Lord's Supper, at which Jesus' passion was recalled. Through the taking of the bread and wine the participants entered personally into the meaning of the original event.

Again, the remembering of the past offered ground for hope in the future. The Jesus who ate with his followers in the homes of Galilee (Mark 2:15; Matt. 11:18–19), on the green grass near the sea (Mark 6:30–44), and in an upper room in Jerusalem (Mark 14:15 ff.) would dine with them at the banquet in the kingdom of God (Mark 14:25). In fact, these meals were a foretaste of life in the kingdom (see pp. 493–501).

Loving Loyalty in Attitude and Deeds

Many people today believe that the New Testament is a book about God's love and the Old Testament is a book about God's wrath. Actually, in both Testaments God's love forms the basis of divine actions and divine requirements; and both have a place for God's wrath or judgment.

The old community saw God's love in the choice of Israel to be his people and in his gift of the covenant at Mt. Sinai. We can illustrate this from the book of Deuteronomy.

We read in this remarkable book that the God of the fathers brought the nation into being. God's holy will was revealed to it. God guided, protected, and disciplined it. He planned for it peace and prosperity in a good land. He showered unmerited love on it (Deut. 7:6–11). In view of his gracious attitudes and acts, his love should be reciprocated with love. This love should express itself in exclusive worship of God and in loving, just relationships with all members of the covenant community.

Deuteronomy defines in great detail the loving loyalty which members of the community were to express toward one another (see p. 120). God provides the motive for such attitudes and acts. God loved and showed mercy on a weak, afflicted people (5:15). His love for Israel can be explained by no characteristics or qualities of Israel itself (7:7; 9:4–5). Therefore, members of the community should show mercy to one another, even to foreigners in their midst (10:19).

In the church God's love was also the basis for Christians' loving attitudes and deeds. 'We love, because he first loved us' (1 John 4:19). He manifested his love above all in the gift of his Son, 'that we might live through him' (1 John 4:9; John 3:16).

Jesus built firmly on the Old Testament teaching about God. He enriched it, of course, by showing its depth and breadth. He addressed God in a way and with a meaning the Old Testament and Judaism had never known: *Abba*, that is 'Dear Father' or something close to 'Papa' or 'Daddy' in English (Mark 14:36; *cf.* Rom. 8:15). He taught his disciples to address God thus (Luke 11:2). He pictured God's love and concern as including the sparrows and the hairs of our head (Luke 12:6–7). He dramatized God's love for outcasts and thereby scandalized the Pharisees (see pp. 470–71). He showed God's love as embracing the hated Samaritans (Luke 10:30–37) and even national enemies (Matt. 5:41, 44) – at a time when some Jews were advocating bitter hatred of outsiders. Paul and other Christian writers followed Jesus in requiring love of enemies (Rom. 12:14, 20; 1 Pet. 2:20–23).

What love requires in practical terms was not spelled out in a code of law for the church as it was in Judaism. In principle, Christians were adult children, capable of determining what love demands (Gal. 3:23–29). However, there were guidelines for conduct.

Sometimes commands of the Old Testament were appealed to (Rom. 12:19–20; Gal. 5:14; Eph. 6:1–3). Church traditions and customs offered directions for behavior (1 Cor. 11:16). Codes of household responsibilities, based on Jewish and pagan codes, appeared in the church to guide the relationships between husbands and wives, parents and children, masters and slaves (Col. 3:18—4:1; Eph. 5:22—6:9; 1 Pet. 2:18—3:7). Lists of vices and virtues, more or less patterned after Jewish and Greek models, gave guidance (Rom. 1:29–31; Gal. 5:19–23; Phil. 4:8). Christian wisdom teachers, like the author of the book of James, worked out norms of conduct which expressed the essential character of Christianity.

Intimate concern for one another led to mutual prayers (Rom. 15:30; Col. 4:2–4; James 5:14), to confession of sins to one another (James 5:16), to the admonishing of fellow Chrsitians (1 Thess. 5:14), and to financial support of the needy (Acts 11:29–30; 2 Cor. 8–9). Christians addressed fellow church members as 'brothers.' Paul used the term eighteen times in the short letter 1 Thessalonians, apparently to convey to the Thessalonians his deep concern for them. The term was also used in Judaism in addressing fellow Jews (2 Macc. 1:1).

God's loving loyalty to people set the standard for social attitudes and acts in both the old and the new community.

The Roman theater, Caesarea, probably originally built by Herod the Great.

A Holy People in Mission

The purpose of God's choice of Israel, according to both Testaments, was that Israel should be a holy people in mission to all the world. This purpose finds expression in many passages of the Old Testament: 'You shall be holy to me; for I the Lord am holy, and have separated you from the peoples, that you should be mine' (Lev. 20:26; *cf.* 19:2; Deut 7:6; 14:2); 'you shall be to me a kingdom of priests and a holy nation' (Exod. 19:6; *cf.* Isa. 4:3; 6:1–8).

In the New Testament the concept of a holy people is strong also: 'as he who called you is holy, be holy yourselves in all your conduct; since it is written, "You shall be holy, for I am holy"' (1 Pet. 1:15–16); 'God's temple is holy, and that temple you [the church at Corinth] are' (1 Cor. 3:17; *cf.* Eph. 1:4; 2:21; Heb. 3:1); 'you are a chosen race, a royal priesthood, a holy nation, God's own people' (1 Pet. 2:9; *cf.* Rev. 1:5–6).

What did it mean to be a holy people? When Hebrew people said that God was 'holy,' they meant that God was above and beyond the universe (transcendent), different from humans and all their works, separated from the common and profane, and powerful, brilliant, and glorious beyond imagining. Under the influence of the teaching of the great prophets God's separation from human sin came to the fore (*e.g.*, Isa. 6:1–8), and his holiness came to mean also goodness or rightness. The basic ideas in God's 'holiness,' then,

The green hills of Samaria, seen from the ancient city.

consist of separation, glorious power, and rightness or goodness.

A holy people, accordingly, is a community set apart from the common and profane for God's possession and use. By virtue of its association with God, it shares in his power, and acts in accordance with his rightness or goodness by keeping the divine law.

From the standpoint of the great prophets Israel failed to become a holy people and to serve as God's light to the nations. Why did this happen?

Historical circumstances played their part. Israelites felt both the appeal and the pressure of the idolatrous religions in and around their land. Agricultural life in Canaan had long been tied to fertility deities, whose worship in sexual rites was thought important in bringing about fertility of lands, animals, and people. These practices were seductively attractive and economically important, it seemed, especially since Yahweh was thought to be a God of the desert.

The road to military security in that day (and today!) was alliance with a strong, friendly, outside power. The cost was the payment of tribute and recognition of the gods of that power (2 Kings 16:6–16). A fearful corruption of Israel's life and religion resulted from paying this price.

The religious establishments of the great powers around were impressive: ornate temples, many priests and priestesses, dramatic ceremonies, and elaborate sacrifices. Kings like Solomon and Ahab aped the architecture and worship practices of surrounding peoples. Hebrew religion turned in a ceremonial, rather than an ethical, direction – to the horror of the prophets (Amos 5:21–24; Mic. 6:6–8; Jer. 7:21–23).

The preoccupation with the Law, after the fall of Jerusalem and the destruction of the temple, and its exaltation over the life of the people led in the direction of legalism and salvation by works (see pp. 428–30).

There were great souls, of course, who kept alive the covenant faith and way of life and sought to fulfill Israel's responsiblity to the nations (the Old Testament prophets and the writers of the books of Jonah and Ruth), but the nation's record as a whole was dismal. John the Baptist, Jesus, and the church called the nation to turn away from ceremonial and legalistic religion to a religion of heart and life.

Jesus reaffirmed the emphases of the great prophets: exclusive loyalty to God and the rejection of all false gods ('You cannot serve God and Money' – Matt. 6:24 NEB); and the subordination of sacrifice to mercy (Matt. 9:13; 12:7; 23:3).

The church viewed all animal sacrifice as ineffective. Jesus' effective sacrifice of himself had replaced it (1 Cor. 5:7; Heb. 9:12–14). The church saw proper sacrifice as the offering of oneself to God in spiritual worship (Rom. 12:1; 1 Pet. 2:5).

Jesus and the church placed strong emphasis on personal, inner cleansing. God requires inner goodness and purity, not outward correctness (Mark

7:14–23; Matt. 5:21 ff.; Rom. 2:28–29; Col. 3:5–17). Holiness – that is, separation from all moral defilement – Spirit-empowerment, and godly character, were the hallmarks of early Christianity: 'Strive for peace with all men, and for the holiness without which no one will see the Lord' (Heb. 12:14); 'May God himself, the God of peace, make you holy in every part, and keep you sound in spirit, soul, and body, without fault when our Lord Jesus Christ comes' (1 Thess. 5:23 NEB).

Holiness of life was God's gift ('He who calls you is to be trusted; he will do it' – 1 Thess. 5:24 NEB) and resulted from the presence of the Holy Spirit, or Christ, or God in the Christian (Rom. 8:9–11).

The author of 1 Peter wrote that the Christians' task, as the holy people of God, was to 'declare the wonderful deeds of him who called you out of darkness into his marvelous light' (2:9). Under Paul and other Christian preachers the new community reached out to the Gentile world to fulfill Israel's mission to the nations. Paul regarded himself as God's apostle (special envoy) to the whole Gentile world (Rom. 11:13; 15:16). With incredible zeal he sought to complete his God-given mission in the brief period – as he viewed God's time clock – before the end of the age (Rom. 13:11–14; 1 Cor. 7:29–31). (See pp. 502–7.)

The church became God's 'holy temple in the Lord' (Eph. 2:21) in which a new humanity, without distinctions of race, class, or sex (Gal. 3:28; Col. 3:11), worshiped God in spirit and truth (John 4:24) and pressed on toward perfection of life (Phil. 3:12–15).

While the old and the new communities had much in common, there were strong differences as well. As we noted above, the two communities shared in remembrance and anticipation. A third word must be added to characterize the church properly: realization.

The church believed that it was the community for which righteous people long had hoped (1 Cor. 10:11; 1 Pet. 1:10–12). God had sent the Messiah in the person of Jesus of Nazareth (Acts 2:36). Through his ministry, death, and resurrection God had broken the power of Satan (Col. 2:15; Heb. 2:14–15). God had made the resurrected Christ reigning Lord. Christ awaited only the Father's time for introducing the final kingdom of God (Phil. 2:9–11; Acts 3:19–21).

Through Jesus' coming and work, the Holy Spirit, long expected as God's gift for the Messianic Age (Joel 2:28–32), had been poured out on the church (John 20:22; Acts 2:1 ff.). The church, because of the Spirit's presence in it, was the outpost of the coming kingdom of God, the kingdom in foretaste (see pp. 493–501).

In view of all this, radiant joy marked the church's life, and miraculous powers attended its ministry (see p. 465). There was a keener sense of the reality of personal and corporate redemption in the church and a brighter hope for the immediate future than in Judaism.

Remains of the Roman baths, Corinth.

Finally, Judaism was less missionary in spirit than early Christianity. Though there were attempts to reach Gentiles through the synagogues of the Dispersion, the Old Testament expectation that Yahweh's temple and obedient, glorified Israel would draw the nations to Jerusalem in the Messianic Age (see p. 431) did not provide a strong motive for active evangelization of the nations.

Christians, in the belief that the Messiah had come, that the life of the kingdom of God could be tasted in anticipation in the church, and that the establishment of the kingdom was very near, sought converts among the Gentiles with an enthusiasm never before witnessed by Jews.

The Christian in the World

What precisely is the relation of Christians to the kingdom of God, on the one hand, and to the world in which they live on the other? Answering this question will require careful attention to the meaning of the kingdom of God, the characteristics that mark the life of a Christian, and the nature of the world.

The Kingdom of God

In general, four views of what Jesus meant by the kingdom of God have been advanced in the last hundred years or so.

a. A new order of society here on the earth in which humanity will be organized through action inspired by love. It will come as people obey the will of God as taught by Jesus. We might call this *a religious-sociological conception*.

b. A new community (the church) raised up by Jesus and given authority over the lives of people – *an ecclesiastical conception*.

c. The rule of God in the individual human heart, that is, the inner acceptance of God's authority over one's life – *a spiritual conception*.

d. An order to be introduced by God at the end of history – *an eschatological* (having to do with 'last things') *conception*.

The last view is the one most New Testament scholars today believe Jesus held. He may have held it in one of four forms. There have been scholarly advocates for each form.

1. *The kingdom future.* Jesus expected the end of the world very soon, to be followed by the final judgment and the inauguration of a new heavenly order. He called people to repent so that they might enter this New Age. This kingdom was, for him, in no real sense present. He regarded it as near – in fact, there were signs of its coming – but it was still future. Its nearness placed people in an intense crisis and made extraordinary ethical demands on them. It forced them to a crucial decision for or against him and his announcement.

2. *The kingdom present.* Jesus believed the eschatological kingdom had actually arrived in his appearance, his works of power, his defeat of the forces of evil in personal and corporate life, and his formation of the church. The kingdom of God is really the rule of God over a redeemed people, and *that* is

possible within history. Though he talked about the coming of the kingdom in symbolic language (which makes it sound other-worldly), in actuality he expected life to continue on this earth and the gospel to spread to the ends of it. Christians are, then, in the kingdom as members of God's community, the church. This view has strong points of contact with *a*, *b*, and *c* above.

3. *The kingdom both present and future.* For Jesus the kingdom was chiefly future, but he believed it was so near it had driven a wedge into history in such a way that it could be said to have begun. In his works he saw the power of evil being broken, a new community being formed which would soon enter the coming kingdom, and life in this community anticipating life in the coming age. He taught that in response to God's gracious redemption, members were expected to live now by the standards of the New Age. Failure to do so would bring exclusion from the final kingdom soon to arrive.

4. *The kingdom interpreted existentially.* Jesus, using the dramatic language and thought forms of his age, announced the coming end of all things and urged people to repent and believe in him as the bringer of God's good news of final salvation. He was not really concerned with the end of the world and the inauguration of an objective new world order in its place. He was rather concerned with the end of history for the person in either life or death. He was offering people God's authentic existence (life) and calling them to be open to God's future, whatever that might involve. He also warned them of the tragic consequences of refusal (death or inadequate existence). People are called to do God's will with all their might while they continue in authentic living.

The third form above is probably faithful to more of the evidence concerning Jesus' view of the kingdom of God than any other. We may represent it as follows:

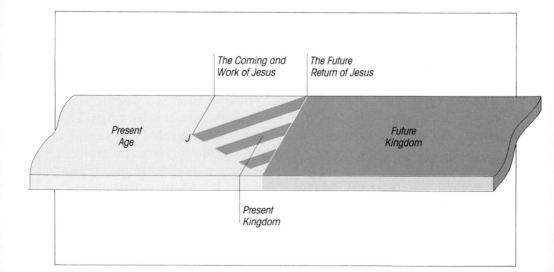

The yellow area at the left indicates the limits of the present age. Jesus, who is represented here by J, felt he was living in the last days of the present age. He saw the future kingdom of God (red area at right), which was to end the present age, as near. Its powers had overlapped the present age (striped area) and were at work in his preaching, teaching, healings, and expulsion of demons. His redeemed followers were already living in the manner of the future kingdom of God while they awaited the final kingdom.

If such was Jesus' view of the kingdom of God, the church after him was faithful to it, on the whole. The Christian community in Jerusalem believed that the Holy Spirit, the power of the age to come (Joel 2:28–32; Heb. 6:4–5), had been given to it (Acts 2:16 ff.). It seems to have patterned its worship after its idea of the nature of worship in the kingdom of God. Its communal meals (Acts 2:42, 46), like those enjoyed with Jesus (Mark 2:15; Matt. 11:19; Mark 6:35–44; Luke 22:14 ff.), were anticipations of the great banquet in the coming kingdom of God (Mark 14:25; Matt. 8:11). Its spirit of sharing, in which economic and social distinctions had largely disappeared (Acts 2:44–45; 4:32–35; 6:1 ff.), anticipated the sharing of the coming kingdom.

Paul emphasized the present aspect of the kingdom when he wrote to the Romans: 'the kingdom of God is not eating and drinking, but justice, peace, and joy, inspired by the Holy Spirit' (14:17 NEB). He said to the Colossians, 'He [God] has delivered us from the dominion of darkness and transferred us to the kingdom of his beloved Son, in whom we have redemption, the forgiveness of sins' (1:13–14; cf. 2 Cor. 5:17).

This sense of present membership in the kingdom of God must have been very strong in the church at Corinth. False teachers there persuaded many in the church to give up entirely belief in resurrection to life in a future kingdom and to concentrate on *present* redemption (see p. 286). Paul had to call that church back to the view that present experience was an anticipation, not a complete fulfillment, of the hope of Jesus and the church concerning the coming of the kingdom of God. The day of the Lord had not already come, as some had claimed (2 Thess. 2:2 ff.).

The church's view of itself seems to have been that it was 'a colony of heaven' (Phil. 3:20 Moffatt), an outpost of the final kingdom of God. It enjoyed in advance the powers and privileges of that kingdom, and it lived by its standards now. It expected the glorious coming of the kingdom of God in the near future (Rom. 13:11–12; 1 Cor. 7:29–31; James 5:8).

The Marks of a Christian

Nowhere in the New Testament are the marks of a Christian so completely presented as in the Sermon on the Mount (Matt. chaps. 5–7). The church preserved Jesus' teaching about the nature of Christian discipleship, and the author of the Gospel of Matthew gathered it together in a great sermon.

The sermon was put together for church members – for those who already had made the decision of faith in Jesus. It was not intended to be a pattern of discipline to qualify those who followed it for admission to the kingdom of heaven. According to the New Testament, we do not act our way into salvation; we act *in* salvation. This means increasingly acting out our response to the gracious deed of God in the gift of Jesus Christ and coming to maturity in him (Eph. 4:13). The Sermon on the Mount offers us a guide to this kind of growth.

From the Sermon on the Mount and the Gospel of Matthew as a whole, we may draw up Matthew's portrait of Christians. Christians have accepted the Father's revelation of Jesus as the End-time Deliverer (Messiah, Son of God, Son of man, 'God with us'). They have trusted implicitly in him, received forgiveness of sins, and become inwardly good (sincere, humble, loving) rather than only outwardly correct. They have dedicated themselves to imitating Jesus in acts of loving service in behalf of all people. They have faithfully carried out their mission of spreading the good news to all nations concerning the salvation available in Jesus. They are like the Father in character and activity (children of the Father – Matt. 5:45). (See the discussion of the Gospel of Matthew, pp. 234–40). By faithfully obeying and imitating Jesus

The top of the Mount of Olives, from the Bethphage chapel.

Characteristics of a Disciple of Jesus
in the Sermon on the Mount

Inner Life	Relation to God	Relation to Others	Relation to Things
Feels spiritual need (5:3)		Merciful (5:7)	
Repentant (5:4)		Reconciled (5:21–26)	
Humble (5:5)		Chaste (5:27–30)	
Desires right's triumph (or to do God's will) (5:6)		Faithful in marriage (5:31–32)	
Single-minded (5:8)		Truthful (5:33–37)	
Peace-making (5:9)		Actively benevolent (5:38–42)	
Joyful in persecution (5:10–12)		Loves enemies (5:43–48)	
Inner sincerity (6:1–18)	Seeks God's favor (6:1–18)	Unostentatious in giving (6:2–4)	
	Prays privately and simply (6:5–8)		
	Submits to God's will (6:10)		
	Depends on God for bread, forgiveness, and deliverance from evil (6:11–13)	Forgives trespassers (6:12, 14)	
	Penitent before God (6:16–18)		
Serenity (6:25–33)	Worships God alone and trusts completely in him (6:19–34)		Needs them but is not mastered by them (6:24–34)
	Eager in prayer (7:7–11)	Generous in judgment (7:1–5)	
	Radical in commitment (7:13–14)	Discriminating in approach (7:6)	
	Obedient to God's will as spoken through Christ (7:21–27)	Large-hearted (7:12)	
		Devoted to good works (7:15–20)	
Summary Inner goodness and integrity	**Summary** An obedient child of the Father	**Summary** Actively all-loving	**Summary** Needs them but is not mastered by them

Such character, relationship to God, and actions toward one's fellows make the disciple salt and light in the world (5:13–16).

they will be light and salt in the world and will be admitted to the kingdom of God (kingdom of heaven) at its coming.

Paul also saw Christians as children of God (Gal. 3:26; Rom. 8:15–16), who have trusted completely in Jesus as the End-time Deliverer sent from God (Rom. 3:22–25). Christians have been freed from sin (Rom. 6:6–7) and bondage to evil powers (Gal. 4:8–9). They have received the Holy Spirit as God's gift and pledge of final salvation (Rom. 5:5; 2 Cor. 1:22). They have the mind of Christ (1 Cor. 2:16) and thus seek to benefit others rather than themselves (Phil. 2:3 ff.). They live and serve in the church in the spirit of love, using their gifts for the benefit of all (Rom. 12:3–21; 1 Cor. 12:27—13:13). They fulfill the law of God by loving their neighbors as themselves (Rom. 13:8–10). Though they are free in Christ, they restrict their liberty if they find that their conduct is injuring fellow Christians (1 Cor. 8:7–13).

They are loyal citizens of the state, honoring established authority and paying their taxes (Rom. 13:1–7).

They press on toward moral perfection through imitating Christ and Christian leaders (1 Cor. 11:1; 1 Thess. 1:6; Phil. 3:12–17). They are spiritually and morally alert while they await the coming of Christ and the kingdom of God (Rom. 13:11–14; 1 Thess. 5:1–11). They actively preach the gospel or support those who do (2 Cor. 5:11–20; 1 Cor. 16:10–11; Gal. 6:6; Eph. 6:18–20).

The World

It is in the Gospel and epistles of John that we hear most about 'the world.' The term is used in these writings in several senses: the physical universe (John 1:10; 11:9; 17:5); the earth, as distinct from heaven (John 8:23; 18:36); humankind (John 3:16; 12:19); and evil people and their way of thinking and living (John 7:7; 17:14; 1 John 2:15–16). The last meaning is the dominant one in these books.

Characteristics of these evil people are: ignorance (John 12:35); unbelief (John 5:38); hatred of fellows (1 John 2:11); falsehood (1 John 2:22); and bondage to sin (John 8:34), death (1 John 3:14), and the devil (John 8:44).

For this author the world in the sense of the physical universe is good. It was created through the Word (John 1:3, 10). Human existence is not in itself evil, for the Word 'became flesh' (John 1:14). Although life on the earth is a lower form of existence than life in heaven – from which Jesus came, to which he returns, and in which he prepares a place for us (John 14:2) – it is a suitable meeting place for God incarnate and humankind and for human decision.

Both God and the devil are operating on the earth, and people must decide between them. Those who decide for Christ have life here and now (John 5:24). Those who decide against him remain under the devil's power (1 John 5:19) – in sin and in death (John 8:24).

A characteristic street in the old city of Jerusalem.

The earth, then, is a battleground where human destiny is decided. Evil people, who love the world and the things of the world (1 John 2:15–16) – that is, who find their satisfactions in the earthly and the created – attract people to their way of thinking and living. But other people are drawn by the Father to Jesus Christ and a higher life here and hereafter (John 6:37, 44).

The writer of the Gospel and the epistles of John was not an ascetic who renounced the created order as evil (see p. 318); rather he affirmed it as God's and as suited for God's purpose. He saw that the devil ('the ruler of this world' – 12:31) gets people in his power and makes their way of living appealing, even to those who have chosen Christ (1 John 2:15–16). But Christ's power is greater than the devil's (1 John 3:8; 4:4), and Christians need not fall victim to him.

Christians must live in the evil world (John 17:11, 15). They have a mission to the world, as Jesus had a mission to the world. They are to represent Jesus, even as Jesus represented God (John 17:18; 13:20). Like Jesus, they are to gather out of the world those whom the Father draws to Jesus (John 17:6, 9, 20).

But while they are 'in the world,' they are not to be 'of the world' (John 17:14–16). They are not to love the world but to love the Father (1 John 2:15). Sensuality, covetousness, and empty boasting, characteristic of people of the world, are not to capture them (1 John 2:16). They are to be set apart from the world's spirit and protected from the devil by God's powerful name (John 17:11; cf. Prov. 18:10) and by the Spirit (John 14:16–17; 1 John 4:4). They are separated from the world (John 17:16, 19) in order that they may have a mission to it (vs. 18).

Paul also stressed the Christians' separation from the world ('holiness' – see p. 312), but he also had something to say about their involvement with the world. As long as Christians are in the present age in an outpost of the coming kingdom of God, they have obligations toward this age as well as toward the coming kingdom. Christians are to honor the governing authorities and to pay their taxes (Rom. 13:1–7; cf. 1 Pet. 2:13–17). Paul may have known that Jesus said, 'Render to Caesar the things that are Caesar's, and to God the things that are God's' (Mark 12:17). But when the emperor and the state usurped the place belonging to God, Christian teachers counseled moral and spiritual resistance (see on the Revelation to John, pp. 363–7).

The writer of the second- or third-century Letter to Diognetus stressed the dual obligation of Christians:

> Christians cannot be distinguished from the rest of the human race by country or language or customs. They do not live in cities of their own; they do not use a peculiar form of speech; they do not follow an eccentric manner of life. ... Yet, although they live in Greek and barbarian cities alike, as each man's lot has been cast, and follow the customs of the country in clothing and food and other matters of daily living, at the same time they give proof of the remarkable and admittedly extraordinary constitution of their own commonwealth. They live in their own countries, but only as aliens. They have a share in everything as citizens, and endure everything as foreigners. Every foreign land is their fatherland, and yet for them every fatherland is a foreign land. They marry, like everyone else, and they beget children, but they do not cast out their offspring. They share their board with each other, but not their marriage bed. It is true that they are 'in the flesh,' but they do not live 'according to the flesh.' They busy themselves on earth, but their citizenship is in heaven. They obey the established laws, but in their own lives they go far beyond what the laws require. They love all men, and by all men are persecuted. ... They are reviled, and yet they bless. ... What the soul is in the body, that Christians are in the world. (Letter to Diognetus 5:1—6:1, Eugene R. Fairweather's translation)

Because Christians live only in the outpost of the kingdom of God they pray, 'Thy kingdom come'; and because they live in the present, evil age, they cry out, 'Lead us not into temptation, but deliver us from evil [the evil one]' (Matt. 6:13).

The Second Coming of Christ

The whole New Testament looks forward to the final triumph of Jesus Christ and his establishment of the glorious kingdom of God. New Testament writers believed that Jesus, who appeared in the world in humility and suffering, unheralded and unrecognized, would soon be revealed for what he really was: the mighty, long-promised Messiah, the God-appointed inaugurator of the end-time kingdom of God. The tiny mustard seed Jesus had planted during his earthly career (the present kingdom), valued in faith by his disciples but ignored or despised by 'the wise' (Matt. 11:25), would become a great tree (the future kingdom) for the nesting of the birds of the earth (the nations) (Matt. 13:31–34). The writers believed that at that time every knee would bow and every tongue confess his sovereign authority (Phil. 2:10–11).

The material in the New Testament concerning the future triumph of Christ is so abundant, so complex, and so difficult to interpret that it almost defies brief discussion. But we may take note of a few major points.

Terms Characterizing Christ's Triumph

Some passages speak of 'the revealing' of Jesus Christ (1 Cor. 1:7; 1 Pet. 1:7). Others refer to his 'appearing' (2 Thess. 2:8; 1 Tim. 6:14) or his 'coming' (Mark 13:26; Matt. 25:31) or to 'the day' of the Lord Jesus or Christ or Son of man (1 Cor. 1:8; Phil. 2:16; Luke 17:22).

Most striking of all the terms is the Greek word *parousia* (translated 'coming' in RSV) (Matt. 24:3; 1 Cor. 15:23; James 5:7). In a secular, everyday sense this word meant 'arrival' or 'presence' (1 Cor. 16:17; 2 Cor. 10:10). It was used in New Testament times as a special term to refer to the presence of a hidden deity or the visit to a province of a king, an emperor, or some other official. People were asked to get ready for the 'presence' of the king. The word therefore was especially appropriate for Jesus' future manifestation as King.

The New Testament does not speak of Jesus' 'second coming,' though Heb. 9:28 comes close to it. 'Second coming' goes back at least to the second century (to Justin Martyr).

The Purposes of Christ's 'Coming' or 'Presence'

Judgment of sinners (Matt. 24:48–51; 25:31–46; 2 Thess. 1:6–10)
The reward of the righteous by the gift of the kingdom (2 Thess. 1:5–10; 2 Cor. 5:10; Matt. 25:31–46)
The destruction of evil powers (1 Cor. 15:24–26; 2 Thess. 2:8; Rev. 19:11–21), thus the preparation for Christ's thousand-year reign (Rev. 20:4–6) and/or the absolute reign of God (1 Cor. 15:28; Rev. 21:5)

The Time of Christ's Coming

The whole New Testament represents it as near. Jesus apparently expected it during the generation of those living when he was speaking (Mark 9:1; 13:28–30; Matt. 10:23). Paul was convinced that it was near (Rom. 13:11–12; 1 Cor. 7:29–31; 1 Thess. 4:15–17; 5:1–10; Phil. 4:5). Other New Testament writers expected it soon (1 Pet. 4:7; James 5:8; 1 John 2:18; Rev. 1:1; 22:6–7, 10, 12).

How soon they thought of it as coming is uncertain. Jesus seems to have expected an interim between his death and the end during which the gospel would be preached inside and outside Israel by his disciples (Mark 13:10; 14:9). In that endeavor they would suffer persecution and sorrow (Mark 2:19–20; Luke 6:22; Matt. 10:28; Mark 8:34–35). Jesus' open attitude toward Gentiles during his ministry (Matt. 8:5–13; Mark 7:24–30) offers ground for believing that he intended the disciples to carry out a mission to them, which he himself could not do.

Paul clearly thought God had raised him up to preach to the Gentiles in the time before the end (1 Cor. 1:1, 7; Rom. 1:5; 11:13; 15:15–16; 2 Thess. 2:14). Some scholars have suggested that Paul believed the end would not come until his ministry was completed. But the evidence is inconclusive.

Luke expected some time yet before the end (19:11–27). He saw spreading the gospel to the nations as the church's ordained task in this period (Acts 1:6–8).

Neither Jesus nor the church set dates. Jesus denied knowledge of the time of the end (Mark 13:32) and counseled the disciples not to speculate. He told them to leave the time to God and to concentrate on their mission (Acts 1:7–8).

Jesus predicted the destruction of Jerusalem by the Romans (Mark 13:1–2; Luke 13:3–5, 34–35; 21:20–24). But how it was related in his mind to the end of the age is not clear.

There are no real clues in either Testament for setting the time of the second coming of Christ. (On the 'signs of the times' see below.) We are told to leave the date to God, to be about our Master's work in the meantime, and to be ready for the coming whenever it occurs (Mark 13:33–37; Luke 12:35–37).

The Manner of Christ's Coming

The coming of Christ is set forth in the New Testament in symbolic or picture language. Christ (the Son of man) will come veiled in clouds, surrounded by angels, in supernatural glory (Mark 13:26). There will be an archangel's call, a blast of a trumpet, a cry of command, and Christ's fiery descent from heaven (1 Thess. 4:16; 2 Thess. 1:7). Or he will come on a white horse at the head of the armies of heaven (Rev. 19:11–16). His coming will be sudden and unpredictable (Mark 13:33–37; Luke 17:20–37; 1 Thess. 5:2–4).

Usually the coming is represented as a descent from heaven to earth (1 Thess. 4:16; Acts 1:11; Rev. 1:7). But in some passages the manifestation of Christ's triumph seems to consist in his elevation from earth – that is, a movement from below upward (Luke 22:69, in contrast to Mark 14:62; Acts 7:56; Luke 24:26; John 12:23). Some scholars therefore think that Jesus' concept of his coming was a coming upward into his sovereignty – an exaltation – and that the church understood it as a coming back to earth. Whatever Jesus' concept, the church clearly believed in both Jesus' exaltation and his return (Acts 1:11).

The Interpretation of Christ's Coming

The Literalist View

Some interpreters attempt to fit together all passages in the Bible concerning Christ's (or God's) coming at the end of time and to construct from them a total picture of its nature and the exact sequence of events related to it. No consistent understanding results from such an attempt, as the many contradictory systems of the past and present show. Such interpreters simply tear passages from their historical and literary contexts and deny to biblical writers their individuality (see p. 73).

How does one fit Paul's view of the catching up of living Christians at the time of Christ's coming (1 Thess. 4:16–17) with the scheme in the Revelation to John where no such experience is mentioned? Will Christians go through the awful times that are coming on the earth, as predicted in Rev. 6:11; 13:7, 10, 15; or will they be rescued before these times come?

How can one fit together the many 'signs' of the end suggested in the Old and New Testaments? They simply defy logical or chronological arrangement. And many of them are frequently occuring natural phenomena with no significant value as definite signs of the end (Matt. 24:6–8). Their purpose seems to be to call believers to preparedness, watchfulness, and steadfastness – to keep them examining their own life and situation in the light of trends in the world in which they live – not to tell them when the end will arrive.

How does one reconcile Christ's coming 'in the same way as you saw him go into heaven' (Acts 1:11) with his coming on a white horse at the head of

The Dome of the Rock from
the Mount of Olives.

the armies of heaven (Rev. 19:11–16)? Are there two different comings, one to rescue living Christians and the other to destroy the forces of evil, or is there to be only one? Does the coming (or do the comings) precede the millennium (Rev. 20:4–6) – thus 'premillennialism' – or does it follow the millennium ('postmillennialism')?

And what is the religious significance of this speculation anyhow, especially when Jesus forbade such preoccupation (Acts 1:6–7? If it is God's business, God will see to it, and we should see to ours (Acts 1:8)! The problems are legion in this literalist approach.

The Conservative View
Other interpreters seek to take the coming of Christ seriously without taking it literally. They admit the pictorial and often inconsistent character of the New Testament descriptions of Christ's coming. They do not hunt out unmistakable signs of the end and arrange them in a sequence designed to determine its time. They do not seek to identify the Antichrist with some contemporary person or group. They do not place the millennium before or after the *parousia* (presence).

But they do insist on a real return of Christ to be with his people and to complete what he began. Though he is present with us now as the living Christ, his presence is veiled. We do not fully know him as he is and will be to us in the kingdom of God. Though his power is at work in us and in the world now, his mighty arm is restrained. At his coming his sovereignty will be manifested in all the earth. The kingdom he began in weakness, suffering, and death will be consummated in power. He will bring an end to the forces of chaos, sin, and death, and transform the created order into the Garden of Eden it was meant to be.

As one such scholar puts it, 'the importance of the *parousia* hope is not its representation of Jesus as moving from one point to another in the firmament, but its insistence that then he performs his awaited work of fulfilment' (G.R. Beasley-Murray).

Supporters of this view believe with biblical writers that human existence and the world itself are impermanent – 'here we have no lasting city, but we seek the city which is to come' (Heb. 13:14; *cf.* 1 Cor. 7:29–31; 2 Pet. 3:10) – and that God will complete in another order of existence what he began in this. In short, they hold to the heart of the New Testament hope, while allowing for the inconsistent and ancient forms in which it is expressed.

The Liberal Position
There are those who think that the New Testament teaching about the second coming of Christ does not rest on Jesus' belief about his future role. Jesus spoke not about a return in glory to the earth (a visitation) but only about a future vindication. He had nothing to say about the end of the world. He

looked forward to the spread of the kingdom of God through the world and to the universal acceptance of his teaching and work. That would be his vindication. He did, however, predict the fall of Jerusalem.

The early church took Jesus' words about his vindication and reshaped them in the light of Old Testament views concerning the day of the Lord and of apocalyptic materials from such books as 1 Enoch (see pp. 416–7).

We should recognize the church's apocalyptic reinterpretation of Jesus for what it is and free Jesus from it. There will be no second coming as the New Testament pictures it.

The Existentialist View

This position assumes that the whole New Testament view of the second coming of Christ is shaped by Jewish apocalyptic myths and by myths that circulated in the Greek world. Its advocates say that modern people cannot accept the myth of the descent of Christ with his angels to destroy the powers of evil and rescue the saints, whom he takes to heaven with him or into a transformed earthly order. The world view in this myth is an ancient one: heaven above; the earth below, under the power of the devil and demons; war between supernatural powers; etc. Though we cannot accept this myth, we can ask what the myth is trying to say to us.

It does not tell us anything about the course of events in the future. Such knowledge is not given to humankind. We live in faith. We can only be open to God's future, whatever the future may be. However, mythology of this kind can tell us what meaning Jesus has for our existence *in this world*.

It says to us that by our faith Jesus can be master of our inner life, that his spirit can dwell within us. The second coming of Christ and the coming of the Spirit to the believer are the same. There will be no future coming as an external event. As the Gospel of John tells us, both eternal life and judgment are present experiences. Jesus' victory is a victory inside the believer, not outside him.

The world will run its course. If there is an end, it will come about by natural causes, not by the mythical event the New Testament expects.

These positions cannot be evaluated properly here. Probably the second stands nearest to the faith of the writers of the New Testament. It holds that 'God will bring to perfect completion the work begun through Christ, and that the same Christ who stands at the center of Christian faith will also stand at the final boundary of human experience in time, in space, and in eternity' (Harvey K. McArthur).

The Bible's Inspiration and Authority

We come, finally, to the most difficult questions about the Bible. What, if anything, did God have to do with its origin? In what sense may we speak of the Bible as the Word of God? And how do we determine what in the Bible is binding on us as Christians?

It is true that many intellectuals of our time regard the Bible not as the Word of God but as a noble collection of ancient books which contain valuable teachings concerning human relationships and many human interest stories. Since it is part of our cultural heritage, they agree that an educated person probably ought to know something about it. But the church's claim that it came from God is mysterious to them and difficult to swallow. And that this ancient book has any right to dictate the shape of contemporary life – and particularly their own lives – is a questionable, if not an offensive, concept.

Even committed Christians are troubled by many things in the Bible that appear inconsistent with its alleged divine origin. The Bible seems too human and fallible to be the Word of God for humankind. To some Christians the ancient book is an embarrassment. They are quite content to leave it on the shelf to gather dust. Others feel that they ought to appreciate it and read it more, but its dated character turns them off. If anyone could speak up for the book, they would be glad to listen. Can anyone say for sure just what kind of book this is?

Frankly, the answer is no. But students of the Bible through the centuries have made a valiant attempt at an answer – and they are still trying. What the church means when it says that the Bible is a God-inspired book is a central question in contemporary theological discussion.

The Meaning and Purpose of 'Inspiration'

Behind this noun is the Latin verb *inspirare*, meaning 'to breathe into.' When we describe the Scriptures as God-inspired writings, we mean that God has somehow breathed into them. This claim is made in an important passage in 2 Timothy: 'from childhood you have been acquainted with the sacred writings which are able to instruct you for salvation through faith in

Christ Jesus. All scripture is inspired by God and [or, Every scripture inspired by God is also] profitable for teaching, for reproof, for correction, and for training in righteousness, that the man of God may be complete, equipped for every good work' (3:15–17).

In the Greek text 'inspired by God' is one word: *theopneustos*, meaning 'God-breathed.' Thus one recent translation (NIV) has: 'All Scripture is God-breathed...' The Old Testament concept of God's breath-spirit, particularly as the breath of life which God breathed into human nostrils (Gen. 2:7), comes to mind at once. God's breath is the divine vitality which makes people and the animals (Ps. 104:29–30) 'live.' The statement in 2 Timothy thus means that God's vitality, or life, is in the Scriptures so that they are able to achieve God's purposes.

What these purposes are is stated in 2 Timothy: to lead to salvation through faith in Christ Jesus, and to educate Christians (Christian leaders, especially) intellectually and morally so that they will be equipped for their service for God. The passage claims that the Scriptures are the instrument through which God works, that they are functionally powerful, that they can achieve in people who are instructed by them the life and service God desires.

The purpose of inspiration, according to the Bible as a whole, is not to satisfy people's curiosity about God, the world, or the inner life of people. Neither is it to instruct them in magic, in the arts, or in sciences so that they may control evil spirits and wrest from nature its benefits. It is not primarily the communication of knowledge. The purpose of inspiration is rather the establishing of a relationship with God in which people become like God in character, share in God's strength, and do God's will in daily life. While inspiration involves the communication of knowledge, this knowledge is always the basis for becoming and doing.

Some theologians have distinguished between inspiration and revelation. They have said that revelation is that process by which God showed chosen people what otherwise they could not have known, and that inspiration was the way God kept them from error when they communicated to others, verbally or in writing, what God had shown them.

It is doubtful that the distinction is valid. It supports the position that the Bible is inerrant – a view very difficult to defend, as the following discussion will show. The terms refer to the same reality, namely, God's self-disclosure to and conversation with chosen and responsive people and the continuing effects of this disclosure.

The Nature of Inspiration

How did God's vitality get into the Scriptures? Obviously he did not write the Scriptures with his finger, as we are told he did the tables of stone he gave to Moses (Exod. 31:18).

In the church there have been those who have believed that God dictated to human writers both the ideas and the words they were to write down. Others have conjectured that the human authors were free to write what they wished and that the Holy Spirit and the church subsequently approved what was written. Some have held that the Holy Spirit only guarded the human authors from making any errors. Still others have said that God inspired the thoughts of the human writers but left them free to choose their own words, style, and literary forms.

In our time it has become increasingly clear that the inspiration of the Scriptures is the result or by-product of God's inspiration of people whom he called to receive his self-revelation. These people were transformed and commissioned for service by God's self-disclosure. They then bore witness to the mighty deeds and words they had seen and heard – first in oral testimony and then directly or indirectly (i.e., through their disciples) in writing. God's revelation came *through* people into the Scriptures. Ordinarily God did not suspend their personalities (see below) but worked in and through them in their individuality. God was limited by their abilities, eccentricities, and faltering response. Accordingly, certain biblical writers' understanding of God's character and purposes was partial and distorted.

Recently, many scholars have been stressing the social character of inspiration. They see inspiration as God's gift to the community of Israel and to the Christian church, rather than to individual persons only. These scholars contend that the Holy Spirit inspired the whole Judeo-Christian movement out of which the Scriptures came – its leaders and doers, as well as its writers. 'Men [were] chosen by God to act and to live the biblical "deed" before it was recounted or written' (P. Benoit). They say that only thus can literature such as the Pentateuch or the Gospels, to which many people contributed over a long period of time (see pp. 98–103; 226–233), be regarded as inspired. Those who wrote were representatives of the community, and the community is therefore the real author of the literature.

Probably the truth lies in a combination of the last two positions. Israel and the church lived their literature before individuals wrote it down, but certainly those individuals had special gifts as writers and editors and have left on the literature marks of their own personalities.

Exactly how inspiration came to the old and the new communities and to their leaders and writers is a difficult question. God's self-disclosure and its accompanying message came to people in many ways, according to the Bible: in personal appearances, such as God made to Moses (Exod. 33:12–23); through an angel (Gen. 16:7–14; Luke 1:11 ff., 26 ff.); dreams (Gen. 28:10–17; Matt. 2:22); visions (Isa. chap. 6; Acts 10:3, 9–16); a direct voice (1 Kings 19:9–18; Mark 9:7); observation of nature (Jer. 1:11–14); and personal domestic experiences (Hosea).

The exact nature of the divine appearances, visions, and auditory experiences escapes us. In late Old Testament and intertestamental times visions became the standard means of revelation and in some of the literature the use of visions is to be regarded as a literary device (as in Dan. chaps 7–12). Ecstatic inspiration, highly esteemed in Greek life and culture, was valued in the church at Corinth (1 Cor. chap. 14).

Today many think that inspiration came to biblical people principally as the heightening of the total personality through personal relationship with God, even in some cases where the biblical record attributes it to visions and ecstatic states. God came to people through the events of their lives and times and through the interpretation of those events by sensitive, insightful people. Without interpretation the events would have been meaningless. The great prophets saw themselves as God's interpreters (Amos 3:7).

Jeremiah, for example, was a keen observer of national and international affairs. Through the events of his time he saw that in the game of power politics Israel's attempt to gain security by foreign alliances would lead to its destruction. The conclusion troubled him deeply. If Israel was to be destroyed, how then could God fulfill his purpose for the world through the mission of Israel? He came one day into the house of a potter, and there, through observing the potter's treatment of the clay, he received his answer: God could rework the clay into another vessel (Jer. 18:1–6).

A chariot race, pictured on a Roman lamp.

Hosea's tragic marriage was God's means of leading him to a profound understanding of God's love for Israel.

Jesus saw the tragic situation of his time and became convinced that Roman armies would destroy Jerusalem (Mark 13:1–2; Luke 21:20–24).

Although Paul did not rule out inspiration by way of ecstatic experience, he rated it low on his list of gifts of the Spirit (1 Cor. 12:10, 28–30) and glorified the place of the mind in religious expression (1 Cor. 14:6–19).

The conclusion is justified that 'inspiration came, not by the suspension of personality, but through the organ of personality' (H.H. Rowley) and through all its facets – mind, will, and emotions.

The Scope of Inspiration

We have seen that God breathed life and with it understanding of his purposes into both individuals and the community of which they were a part. To what extent did inspiration affect the Scriptures in their various aspects?

Some Jews of the intertestamental period believed that the Septuagint (the Greek Old Testament) was verbally inspired. God guaranteed the accuracy of the translation by causing all the translators, working independently, to agree word for word in their renditions.

Relief from the Arch of Titus, Rome.

The rabbis of the New Testament period held that every syllable, every letter, and even pecularities of spelling were the work of God's Spirit. Verbal inspiration, and thus verbal inerrancy, was long a dogma in Judaism and Christianity. It has present-day advocates: 'What Scripture says, God says' and 'God so inspired the biblical writers that their word is also His Word' (J.I. Packer).

Such absolute equating of God's Word with the words of Scripture certainly was not done by Jesus and the New Testament writers. Though they spoke of the Scriptures in the highest terms (John 10:35; 2 Pet. 1:20–21), they clearly did not equate God's will with the exact words of Scripture.

Jesus quoted Genesis with the intent of setting aside Moses' provision concerning divorce (Mark 10:2–9), and he nullified the Mosaic commandments concerning unclean foods (Mark 7:14–23).

The church regarded the whole sacrificial system of Israel as ended by Christ's sacrifice of himself and by the 'living sacrifice' of oneself to God (Heb. 10:1–10; Rom. 12:1). Christians regarded themselves as God's true children and therefore free from the letter of Jewish law and under the control of God's Spirit and the power of love within them (Gal. 5:13–18). Their assumed freedom with respect to the Law was scandalous in Jewish eyes. Christians saw the Old Testament as pointing toward and authenticating what had come to pass in Jesus and the church.

Both Old and New Testament writers used previous literary material with a freedom that argues against verbal literalism on their part. Early sources of the Pentateuch were interpreted and edited by later writers to suit new purposes (see pp. 98–103). The author of 1 and 2 Chronicles freely adapted material from 1 and 2 Samuel and 1 and 2 Kings (see pp. 137–8). Matthew abbreviated Mark's narratives, improved Mark's style, and in places altered his theology (see pp. 239). It is evident from the fact that the church approved *four* Gospels, often differing widely from one another, that it did not regard verbal and factual agreement as of any particular importance. All presented Jesus Christ as Savior and Lord and called for faith in and obedience to him – and that was sufficient.

Furthermore, the Bible's historical statements are not always accurate and consistent. A few examples must suffice. Was Jesus' last supper before his crucifixion the Passover supper (Mark 14:12–16), or was it held on the evening prior to the Passover (John 18:28; 19:14)? Did Jesus cleanse the temple at the beginning of his ministry (John 2:13–22) or at the end (Mark 11:15–18)? Did Jesus say to the rich man, 'Why do you call me good?' (Mark 10:18) or 'Why do you ask me about what is good?' (Matt. 19:17) – a considerable difference in meaning. Did the Lord tell David to number Israel and Judah (2 Sam. 24:1), or was Satan responsible for this (1 Chron. 21:1)? Did Abraham leave Haran after his father Terah's death (Acts 7:4) or sixty years before he died (Gen. 11:26, 32; 12:4)? Such problems and inconsistencies are to be found scattered throughout the Scriptures.

For early Christians the fountain of life, revelation, and inspiration was not the Scriptures but Jesus Christ, the one to whom the Scriptures bore witness. In John 5:39–40 we read, 'You [the Jews] search the scriptures, because you think that in them you have eternal life; and it is they that bear witness to me; yet you refuse to come to me that you may have life.' The church read the Scriptures for signs pointing toward Jesus and wrote books, like the Gospel of Matthew, to show how Jesus had fulfilled the hopes expressed in the sacred writings. The church sought life not in the Scriptures but in him to whom the Scriptures pointed.

For guidance in everyday life, Christians turned chiefly to the deeds and words of Jesus (1 Cor. 7:10), to Spirit-filled teachers and prophets in the church (1 Cor. 7:25), to church tradition (1 Cor. 11:16), to the guidance of the Spirit within themselves (Gal. 5:18), and to the Scriptures. Paul held that the records of the past were written down for the church's instruction. They were a mirror in which the church should be able to recognize itself and be warned and helped on its way to the promised future by what it saw there (1 Cor. 10:11). Anything in the Scriptures that did not point to Jesus and the church, shed light on the significance of Jesus' redemptive work – past, present, or future – or give direction to the church's life and mission in the world was largely bypassed.

Whether the Scriptures in all parts contained an infallible record of Israel's history or presented a sound world view or even a proper picture of God apparently was of little concern to them. Luke, for example, was impressed chiefly, and perhaps only, with the way Jesus was mirrored in Moses, the prophets, and all the Scriptures (24:27, 44–47) and how he fulfilled in his birth, personal life, ministry, death, and resurrection the deepest hopes of the Scriptures for the full redemption of humankind.

The New Testament church's approach to the Holy Scriptures was a Christ-centered approach. The Christians measured everything they found there by the revelation that had come in and through their Lord.

The Authority of the Bible

It has been said that there were two incarnations of the Word of God: one in human flesh (in Jesus of Nazareth) and one in human language (in the Bible). While the comparison is attractive and partially true, it is to some extent misleading, for only the first was an 'enfleshment' of the Word of God. The second is the written record of that enfleshment – the testimony to its reality, the explanation of its necessity, the description of the form of its manifestation, and the disclosure of its consequences for human life.

The belief that the Bible is an incarnation of the Word of God parallel to and on the same level as the incarnation in Jesus has misled many in the church. For them the Bible has been an object of worship, a fetish, an idol, which has wrongly received the reverence that belongs to God alone.

The Bible points to the absolute authority that stands over human beings: God. From the moment of Creation both people and animals have been subject to God's commandments. God's will was revealed for humankind in covenants given to the Patriarchs and especially in the Mosaic covenant. God punished disobedience to the terms of the latter covenant in the disaster of the Exile. God established a new covenant through the sending of Jesus, whose covenant law was the law of love. Through Jesus and by that law he will judge mankind at the last Day (Matt. 25:31–46). God is Creator and Ruler and as such has absolute authority over creatures.

The Bible is indispensable for us in that it tells us about the activity of God in the life of humankind and how people whom God called experienced and interpreted that activity. We learn about God's activity and purpose chiefly in the Bible.

We cannot prove that God was active in the experience of Israel and the Christian church. There are no unmistakable marks of divinity on the literature that arose in those communities. Even as it was not obvious to Jesus' contemporaries that God had sent his Son into the world as the End-time Deliverer, so it is not obvious that the Bible is a God-inspired book. In both cases certainty comes only through the venture of faith. But there are signs or signposts pointing toward God's activity.

First, there is a remarkable unity in Israel's historical experience. A sense of election, mission, and destiny dominated the whole of Israel's history. Moses, the nation's founder, structured Israel's position and function before God in a covenant. The prophets strove to hold the nation to its God-ordained course and predicted the fulfillment of the nation's service and destiny in the future. The church declared that this service and destiny were being accomplished through the appearance of Jesus and the establishment of a new community based on a new covenant, as predicted in Old Testament prophecy. There is a unity, a coherence, in all this historical experience that is amazing, to say the least.

Second, even as Jesus' mighty works were signposts pointing to his identity and mission (see p. 478), so there were signs of God's activity in Israel: in the wonderful events connected with the Exodus from Egypt, in the remarkable experience in the wilderness, and in the establishment of the nation in the Promised Land, for example. The Christian church saw evidences of God's activity in its works of power (Gal. 3:5; Rom. 15:18–19).

Third, the character of the people and the kind of society created under the old and the new covenants point to God's working. Majestic spirits like Moses, Amos, Jeremiah, the Second Isaiah, Jesus, and Paul, and their impact for good in human society, evidence a divine purpose at work in Israel's history.

Fourth, the Bible's explanation of our nature, situation in the world, and final destiny gives meaning and direction to our life and agrees with our knowledge as derived from other sources.

Since *people* wrote about their experiences with God, we ought not to expect inerrant fact and perfect understanding from their writings. When light shines through a glass, there is inevitably some distortion of the light. God took the risk of human distortion in order to communicate with us in our language and forms of thought. The clearest revelation, of course, came through those persons in whom there was the least opaqueness and imperfection.

We should therefore expect different levels of truth and some error in the Bible. The standard which we apply to all parts is the truth that came through Jesus Christ. We do not take vengeance on people who wrong us by hacking them to pieces in holy war, as Samuel ordered Saul to do in the name of the Lord and finally did himself (1 Sam. 15). We instead follow Jesus, who told us to love our enemies and who practiced what he counseled others to do.

We recognize that biblical standards were conditioned by the times and the situations in which they were set. In one situation readers were exhorted to obey governmental authorities (Rom. 13:1–7) and in another to resist them (see the discussion of the books of Daniel and Revelation).

There is no rule of thumb by which one can decide what biblical counsels are binding on us. There are, however, aids to decision-making.

First, we should examine any biblical command in the light of its literary and historical context. Only thus can its precise meaning be discovered. It may have been shaped for a particular situation and be valid in no other set of circumstances.

Second, we must judge it by the mind of Christ. If it does not agree with his spirit and deeds, it cannot be binding on us.

Third, we should pray for the guidance of the Holy Spirit. Christians are promised the help of the Spirit in knowing and doing the truth (John 14:26; 16:13).

Fourth, we ought to interpret the Scriptures and scriptural demands through studying with other Christians in groups. Christian comrades who struggle together with the Scriptures will often see the truth or error in a passage more clearly than individuals reading alone. And they will throw light on one another's problems by their individual perceptions and experiences.

Fifth, if possible, we should check our interpretation against the conclusions of the great minds of the church, past and present, and evaluate it against truth from other fields of learning (psychology, sociology, etc.).

Sixth, when truth commends itself to us after we have taken these steps, we must act on it in faith. Deep certainty and further truth come only by obeying the truth we have found, not by praising it or toying with it.

It has been the experience of multitudes through the centuries that when they approached the Scriptures thoughtfully and prayerfully a wonderful thing happened to them. The veil of doubt, unbelief, and cynicism fell from their eyes. They began to see the glory of the Lord Jesus and to be changed into his likeness (2 Cor. 3:12–18). Then they recognized the 'limitations' of the Bible for what they really are – the marks of God's condescension to reach us in our humanness and fallibility.

Further Reading on pp. 450–507
Bornkamm, G., *Jesus of Nazareth*, 1960; *Paul*. 1971.
Earle, R., *Behold, I Come*, 1973.
Furnish, V.P., *Theology and Ethics in Paul*, 1978; *The Love Command in the New Testament*, 1972.
Hanson, P.D., *The People Called – The Growth of Community in the Bible*, 1985.
Kümmel, W.G., *The Theology of the New Testament*, 1973.
Minear, P.S., *Christian Hope and the Second Coming*, 1954.
Neill, S., *Jesus Through Many Eyes – Introduction to the Theology of the New Testament*, 1976.
Saunders, E.W., *Jesus in the Gospels*, 1967.
Westermann, C., *Elements of Old Testament Theology*, 1982.
Zimmerli, W., *Old Testament Theology in Outline*, 1978.

Further Reading on pp. 508–517
Achtemeier, P.J., *The Inspiration of Scripture*, 1980.
Boice, J.M. (ed.), *The Foundation of Biblical Authority*, 1978.
McKim, D.M., *The Authoritative Word*, 1983.
Youngblood, R. (ed.), *Evangelicals and Inerrancy*, 1984.

519

INDEX

Photograph acknowledgments

The Bible Society 38, 57
British Library 35, 43, 73
British Museum 36, 71, 77, 104, 137,
140, 142, 147, 161, 168, 170, 172, 197,
202, 214, 219, 222, 273, 276, 300, 332,
335, 370, 385, 407, 511
Tim Dowley 2, 16, 20, 86, 123, 132, 139,
151, 158, 162, 186, 192, 204, 209, 211,
218, 229, 241, 249, 251, 252, 266, 274,
283, 289, 301, 319, 321, 330, 331, 337,
347, 354, 395, 396, 401, 412, 415, 421,
440, 456, 461, 469, 473, 475, 479, 496,
512
*John Rylands University Library,
Manchester* 37
Scripture Union 24, 33, 103, 269, 296,
315, 317, 328, 361, 366, 375, 405, 430,
484, 491
Jamie Simson 105, 122, 126, 179, 181,
261, 279, 281, 287, 298, 303, 305, 311,
341, 391, 429
Peter Wyart 27, 31, 51, 107, 127, 129,
154, 165, 167, 175, 188, 190, 205, 207,
213, 220, 225, 227, 235, 236, 245, 247,
250, 258, 263, 268, 284, 324, 338, 345,
349, 393, 397, 417, 422, 451, 455, 462,
464, 470, 471, 477, 487, 488, 499, 505